Lecture Notes in Computer Science 12204

More information about this series at http://www.springer.com/series/7409

Fiona Fui-Hoon Nah · Keng Siau (Eds.)

HCI in Business, Government and Organizations

7th International Conference, HCIBGO 2020
Held as Part of the 22nd HCI International Conference, HCII 2020
Copenhagen, Denmark, July 19–24, 2020
Proceedings

 Springer

Editors
Fiona Fui-Hoon Nah
Missouri University of Science
and Technology
Rolla, MO, USA

Keng Siau
Missouri University of Science
and Technology
Rolla, MO, USA

ISSN 0302-9743   ISSN 1611-3349 (electronic)
Lecture Notes in Computer Science
ISBN 978-3-030-50340-6   ISBN 978-3-030-50341-3 (eBook)
https://doi.org/10.1007/978-3-030-50341-3

LNCS Sublibrary: SL3 – Information Systems and Applications, incl. Internet/Web, and HCI

This Springer imprint is published by the registered company Springer Nature Switzerland AG
The registered company address is: Gewerbestrasse 11, 6330 Cham, Switzerland

Foreword

The 22nd International Conference on Human-Computer Interaction, HCI International 2020 (HCII 2020), was planned to be held at the AC Bella Sky Hotel and Bella Center, Copenhagen, Denmark, during July 19–24, 2020. Due to the COVID-19 coronavirus pandemic and the resolution of the Danish government not to allow events larger than 500 people to be hosted until September 1, 2020, HCII 2020 had to be held virtually. It incorporated the 21 thematic areas and affiliated conferences listed on the following page.

A total of 6,326 individuals from academia, research institutes, industry, and governmental agencies from 97 countries submitted contributions, and 1,439 papers and 238 posters were included in the conference proceedings. These contributions address the latest research and development efforts and highlight the human aspects of design and use of computing systems. The contributions thoroughly cover the entire field of human-computer interaction, addressing major advances in knowledge and effective use of computers in a variety of application areas. The volumes constituting the full set of the conference proceedings are listed in the following pages.

The HCI International (HCII) conference also offers the option of "late-breaking work" which applies both for papers and posters and the corresponding volume(s) of the proceedings will be published just after the conference. Full papers will be included in the "HCII 2020 - Late Breaking Papers" volume of the proceedings to be published in the Springer LNCS series, while poster extended abstracts will be included as short papers in the "HCII 2020 - Late Breaking Posters" volume to be published in the Springer CCIS series.

I would like to thank the program board chairs and the members of the program boards of all thematic areas and affiliated conferences for their contribution to the highest scientific quality and the overall success of the HCI International 2020 conference.

This conference would not have been possible without the continuous and unwavering support and advice of the founder, Conference General Chair Emeritus and Conference Scientific Advisor Prof. Gavriel Salvendy. For his outstanding efforts, I would like to express my appreciation to the communications chair and editor of HCI International News, Dr. Abbas Moallem.

July 2020   Constantine Stephanidis

HCI International 2020 Thematic Areas and Affiliated Conferences

Thematic areas:

- HCI 2020: Human-Computer Interaction
- HIMI 2020: Human Interface and the Management of Information

Affiliated conferences:

- EPCE: 17th International Conference on Engineering Psychology and Cognitive Ergonomics
- UAHCI: 14th International Conference on Universal Access in Human-Computer Interaction
- VAMR: 12th International Conference on Virtual, Augmented and Mixed Reality
- CCD: 12th International Conference on Cross-Cultural Design
- SCSM: 12th International Conference on Social Computing and Social Media
- AC: 14th International Conference on Augmented Cognition
- DHM: 11th International Conference on Digital Human Modeling and Applications in Health, Safety, Ergonomics and Risk Management
- DUXU: 9th International Conference on Design, User Experience and Usability
- DAPI: 8th International Conference on Distributed, Ambient and Pervasive Interactions
- HCIBGO: 7th International Conference on HCI in Business, Government and Organizations
- LCT: 7th International Conference on Learning and Collaboration Technologies
- ITAP: 6th International Conference on Human Aspects of IT for the Aged Population
- HCI-CPT: Second International Conference on HCI for Cybersecurity, Privacy and Trust
- HCI-Games: Second International Conference on HCI in Games
- MobiTAS: Second International Conference on HCI in Mobility, Transport and Automotive Systems
- AIS: Second International Conference on Adaptive Instructional Systems
- C&C: 8th International Conference on Culture and Computing
- MOBILE: First International Conference on Design, Operation and Evaluation of Mobile Communications
- AI-HCI: First International Conference on Artificial Intelligence in HCI

Conference Proceedings Volumes Full List

http://2020.hci.international/proceedings

7th International Conference on HCI in Business, Government and Organizations (HCIBGO 2020)

Program Board Chairs: **Fiona Fui-Hoon Nah, Missouri University of Science and Technology, USA, and Keng Siau, Missouri University of Science and Technology, USA**

- Kaveh Abhari, USA
- Michel Avital, Denmark
- Denise Baker, USA
- Valerie Bartelt, USA
- Kaveh Bazargan, Iran
- Langtao Chen, USA
- Constantinos Coursaris, Canada
- Brenda Eschenbrenner, USA
- Ann Fruhling, USA
- JM Goh, Canada
- Netta Iivari, Finland
- Qiqi Jiang, Denmark
- Yi-Cheng Ku, Taiwan
- Murad Moqbel, USA
- Eran Rubin, USA
- Hamed Sarbazhosseini, Australia
- Norman Shaw, Canada
- Austin Silva, USA
- Martin Stabauer, Austria
- Chee-Wee Tan, Denmark
- Deliang Wang, Singapore
- Werner Wetzlinger, Austria
- Dezhi Wu, USA
- I-Chin Wu, Taiwan
- Cheng Yi, China
- Dezhi Yin, USA
- Jie Yu, China

The full list with the Program Board Chairs and the members of the Program Boards of all thematic areas and affiliated conferences is available online at:

http://www.hci.international/board-members-2020.php

HCI International 2021

The 23rd International Conference on Human-Computer Interaction, HCI International 2021 (HCII 2021), will be held jointly with the affiliated conferences in Washington DC, USA, at the Washington Hilton Hotel, July 24–29, 2021. It will cover a broad spectrum of themes related to Human-Computer Interaction (HCI), including theoretical issues, methods, tools, processes, and case studies in HCI design, as well as novel interaction techniques, interfaces, and applications. The proceedings will be published by Springer. More information will be available on the conference website: http://2021.hci.international/.

General Chair
Prof. Constantine Stephanidis
University of Crete and ICS-FORTH
Heraklion, Crete, Greece
Email: general_chair@hcii2021.org

http://2021.hci.international/

Contents

Social Media, Digital Commerce and Marketing

Digital Transformation and Intelligent
Data Analysis

Towards Conversational E-Government

An Experts' Perspective on Requirements and Opportunities of Voice-Based Citizen Services

Matthias Baldauf(✉) and Hans-Dieter Zimmermann

FHS St. Gallen University of Applied Sciences,
Rosenbergstrasse 59, 9001 St. Gallen, Switzerland
{matthias.baldauf,hans-dieter.zimmermann}@fhsg.ch

Abstract. While chatbots are an increasingly applied new channel for government services, voice-based citizen services and corresponding scientific knowledge on their requirements and design are still scarce. In order to pave the way for prospective conversational e-government services for voice assistants, we conducted five semi-structured expert interviews with government representatives experienced with e-government issues as well as engineering and design experts familiar with voice interfaces. We analyzed their responses on relevant topics such as accessibility, authentication, data protection and open government data and APIs, as well as collected their rich application ideas for a first generation of voice-based citizen services. Based on these results, we derived a set of implications and considerations for both providing the fundamentals as well as designing and implementing conversational e-government services.

Keywords: Conversational interface · Conversational government · Chatbot · Voice assistant

1 Introduction

In the last few years, so-called *conversational interfaces* have reached the mass-market. They enable users to interact with their smartphones and other ubiquitous devices such as connected loudspeakers in a natural way to obtain information, access Web services, and issue commands (cf. [11]). They appear in form of chatbots (chatting robot) supporting written requests and voice assistants understanding voice commands, both utilizing the potential of artificial intelligence. Accordingly, conversational interfaces provide intuitive natural language-based human-computer interfaces. Although the technology and respective applications are still in their infancy, there are numerous applications being implemented, especially in the business world, where the term "conversational commerce" already was coined [17]. For example, users can apply chatbots to book and check in for flights or to get product recommendations.

In the case of voice assistants, numerous custom extensions are available for either Amazon's Alexa or Google Assistant, usable either on dedicated devices

© Springer Nature Switzerland AG 2020
F. F.-H. Nah and K. Siau (Eds.): HCII 2020, LNCS 12204, pp. 3–14, 2020.
https://doi.org/10.1007/978-3-030-50341-3_1

or just regular smartphones. Recently, it was reported that merely in Q3 2019 more than 28 million so-called "smartspeakers" have been sold globally [4].

As conversational interfaces use natural language to interact with applications, it can be hypothesized that interaction barriers will be lowered, with great potential also for citizen services. The Open Government movement aims, among others, at improving engagement of citizens in public sector activities and, thus, to focus on more citizen-centric service offerings. Key issues of Open Government are transparency, participation, collaboration, to generate participatory and collaborative dialogue [18]. Therefore, conversational interfaces for e-government services can be understood as part of corresponding multichannel strategies (see [9,10]). Only recently, the UK government has launched a voice-based service for Alexa and Google Assistant to make information access easier for citizens [6] – one of the first appearances of publicly available "conversational government" services.

In this paper we focus on voice-based conversational interfaces and aim to identify and to analyze the requirements for designing and implementing useful and user-accepted voice-based citizen services. Following a short summary on existing related findings from literature, we present the results of five semi-structured expert interviews with government representatives experienced with e-government issues as well as engineering and design experts familiar with voice interfaces. Based on the corresponding results, the contribution of this paper includes a first set of implications for enabling voice-based e-government services as well as several ideas for suitable first applications, both from an experts' perspective.

2 Related Work

Whereas so-called chatbots offering e-government services can be found in practice in the meantime, voice-based services are not yet deployed broadly, if at all. We hardly have scholarly knowledge about experiences or requirements of voice based governmental services, especially from a non-technical perspective. There is some literature available addressing conversational interfaces in the e-government context from the perspective of deploying artificial intelligence (e.g., [2,12]. Furthermore, technical, design, as well as linguistic challenges have been addressed in prior research (e.g., [1,3]). Issues such as the citizen's or public authority's perspective including multi- or cross-channel or process integration issues or legal/regulatory issues have hardly been addressed so far. In a comprehensive literature study, Madsen and Hofmann investigated the literature of multichannel management in the public sector [9], but aspects of requirements for any channel have not been subject to any of the identified papers at all.

As one of a few papers Lindgren and Jansson [8] take a more broad, interdisciplinary perspective and propose a conceptual framework for public e-services. Three dimensions of public e-services have been defined, which are "Public", "e-", and "Services". Several characteristics for each of the dimensions have been identified; they could be interpreted as success factors or requirements for respective services. These are, among others: need to ensure comprehensive legal framework with different degrees of discretion (dimension public), a technical artifact, constituted of Internet-based technology, some degree of interaction, connections to other information systems, e.g., back-office systems (e-dimension), or service as a process must be perceived as a process in which value is co-created by consumer and supplier (services dimension). Hence, studying the dimensions including their identified characteristics and adopting them might be a starting point to derive more concrete requirement for conversational e-government services.

Beyond the public sector, conversational interfaces are being used more widely in the business domain where the term "conversational commerce" has been established already. But although there are several systems implemented facilitating consumers' interaction with suppliers, e.g., such as product search or flight check in, there is not a rich body of research literature available either. In a rather recent study, the authors present an exploratory study on customers' perception of conversational commerce [17]. Applying a broad perspective, the study reveals opportunities, challenges, as well as process implications of conversational commerce and provides a comprehensive framework. Therefore, also the knowledge about conversational commerce might provide a further starting point for developing criteria for a successful development of conversational government services.

In summary, there is hardly any scholarly literature available addressing voice-based citizen services, their requirements beyond technical aspects nor challenges and opportunities. Issues such as the citizen's or government authority's perspective including cross- or multi-channel or process integrations or legal/regulatory issues are missing in the literature so far.

3 Method

To learn more about potential requirements, challenges and opportunities of voice-based citizen services, we conducted a set of expert interviews in Switzerland. We deliberately focused this early investigation on government representatives with knowledge on (e-)government services and processes as well as senior staff of technology companies experienced in realizing voice interfaces and services. We outline our plans for studying and integrating requirements from a citizen perspective in the final section of this work.

Table 1 gives an overview about the interviewed participants: P1, P2, and P3 were government representatives on different governmental levels (city, province, state), each one with several years of experience in public service and responsible for e-government matters. P4 and P5 were experts with engineering and design backgrounds. Both have been holding leading positions in several projects involving voice interfaces.

Each interview with the participants was conducted by two researchers. They kicked-off the conversation with a short introduction on the recent state-of-the-art of voice assistants and asked for the interviewee's knowledge level to consider it during the interview. The actual interviews were semi-structured following a guideline with central questions. These addressed opportunities for facilitating access to e-government services as well as requirements and challenges, e.g. from a technical, legal, or organizational perspective. Furthermore, we asked them for potential application fields and concrete ideas for voice-based citizen services.

The interviews took between 60 and 90 min and were conducted between April and June 2019. Both researchers took notes on the interviewees' comments. Additionally, the interviews were audio-recorded on a smartphone for later analysis. During post-study analysis, we identified common themes in the interviewees' responses and clustered related statements into requirement groups.

Table 1. Participants of the expert interviews.

Id	Job	Institution
P1	Chief digital officer	City government
P2	Group leader service development	Federal chancellery
P3	Head E-government	Province government
P4	Software project manager	Digital agency
P5	Innovation manager	Software company

4   Results

In the following, we report on the results of the expert interviews. First, we report on collected requirements of voice-based government services, then we outline application ideas generated by the participants.

4.1   Requirements

This section summarizes and groups participants' statements regarding overall requirements.

Design of (Governmental) Voice Interfaces. The interviewees with experience in implementing voice-based services, P4 and P5, advised to consider humans' cognitive limitations when designing a voice interface. Both emphasized the importance of short, precise answers of a respective voice assistant for governmental purposes. P4 mentioned a certain fatigue of users of voice assistants, when dialogues are lengthy and require more than three consequent user requests.

P5 recommended designing a voice assistance service for integration in a user's routines. An example is a weather forecast for the day, often used in the morning during having breakfast. He noted that many governmental services, in contrast, address non-routine, irregular tasks. For example, reporting a change of residence to the local registration office is a relatively rare event. Several simpler tasks such as accessing information on governmental services (e.g., opening hours of a governmental office) can be solved by popular voice assistants without any custom extension, since this information is available on the authorities' official Web pages and can be found through a Web search.

P3 emphasized that a voice assistant for governmental services should provide functionality beyond information access. As examples he mentioned pro-active notifications by a respective assistant, such as suitable context-aware reminders for dates of the carbage collection. Additionally, he considered hedonistic aspects very important: "Such a voice assistant must provide added value for the citizens, yet, at the same time, should be fun to use".

Accessibility. Based on experiences from prior e-government projects, P4 mentioned an important requirement of respective digital citizen services: Accessibility. In contrast to other applications, such services must be usable by as many user groups as possible to not exclude citizen minorities.

Authentication. The need for an authentication of the user became evident for several advanced e-government services involving privacy-critical information. P5 elaborated on recent technical possibilities to realize user authentication for voice-based services: One factor authentication methods include speaker recognition (solely relying on voice characteristics) as well as a password-style method involving a private pin. For example, purchases via Amazon Alexa can be confirmed by saying a self-defined four-digit pin code.

Alternative two-factor authentication techniques make use of the user's personal device. When an authentication is required, the voice assistant notifies the user's smartphone. Using a typical push notification, a custom authentication app then shows a respective prompt for the user to confirm the authentication request. This may either be realized by a push notification or, according to P5, by audible or non-audible sound signals sent by the voice assistant and detected by the smartphone app to ensure the physical proximity of the device (and its owner, respectively).

P1 related to the authentication mechanism implemented in a chatbot for governmental services. Therein, a user may identify herself using her personal tax reference number. P1 considered this solution sufficient for several governmental services, since "the potential for abuse is very limited". He notes, that several additional security measures can be implemented which do not make authentication harder for the user. For example, ordering official documents such as a tax report may only be allowed once per month. In addition, "automated misuse of these services must be prevented", P1 emphasized.

P2 confirmed this approach and claims "a simple, low-threshold solution for the user" too. Potential errors should be rather corrected later by withdrawal, for example.

As authentication proofs the real identity of a user, here the citizen, the described technologies can be used as well for a weaker identification. Here, a certain identity can be proofed which not necessarily has to be the true identity of the citizen.

User-Perceived Security. Furthermore, P2 argued for a user-centered investigation of security measures for voice-based citizen services. Since there are currently no such services offered in Switzerland, there is no validated knowledge on how strong respective identification and security measures need and are expected to be. "Maybe citizens do not consider their government data that sensible?", he added.

P5 mentioned a related user-oriented security aspect of future voice-based services: "How can a voice assistant communicate that its user is authenticated, or a secure connection has been established?" The acceptance of advanced voice-based services may depend on the citizen's trust in a respective voice assistant, he added.

P1 reported on related requirements regarding a recently launched chatbot offering governmental services. To protect personal data, user sessions are reset after 30 min. All entered data are then cleared and the user informed, respectively. He concluded that also a voice assistant must provide such functionality and clearly communicate its behavior.

Processing Privacy-Relevant Information. The handling and protection of privacy-relevant information was a central topic in several interviews. After having detected a wake-up word ("Ok, Google!", e.g.) locally, today' popular voice assistants such as Alexa and Google Assistant send the users' utterances to remote data centers for analyzing and understanding the content. For example, P2 considered data protection "a major challenge".

While P5 noted that Google and Microsoft are about to build local data centers (especially for cloud-provided office software), P4 emphasized that these companies do not guarantee any specific location for processing collected voice data. He further noted that users need to consent that their voice data can be used for training purposes before they are able to use Alexa, for example. In a similar vein, users of a conversational government service on a mass-market voice assistant must be made aware again, that their voice data may be analyzed in global data centers and be used for other purposes—out of scope of the authority providing the service. P5 mentioned the availability of alternative voice assistants that can be installed on own hardware and process data only locally. Yet, he considered such assistants currently not suitable to reach citizens on a large scale.

Robustness of Speech Recognition. To ensure best recognition rates and successful voice-based services, P4 recommended implementing highly structured use cases. He mentioned the example of a mobile app for national public transport: When planning a route, the starting point and destination can be spoken, instead of cumbersomely typed in. Due to the limited vocabulary, the stops can even be spoken in vernacular language (due to a tailored speech recognition engine).

While talking about the quality of today's speech recognition, we asked the interviewees on how important they estimated the support of vernacular language for the acceptance of voice-based citizen services. While P4 considered understanding vernacular language as a crucial requirement for the citizens' acceptance, the remaining interviewees held another opinion. P5 attributed a minor relevance, since "speaking standard language can be expected for bank and governmental services". He added, that, based on his experience with voice services, "about 70% of vernacular utterances are correctly recognized by the big players", anyway. P1 and P3 agreed that, in a first step, offering conversational services supporting vernacular language is not relevant. P1 emphasized that not vernacular but standard language is the administrative language. Additionally, P4 pointed out, that e-government services in many cases might involve several special terms, mass-market voice assistants might have trouble understanding. As consequence, respective services should be designed to not rely on the recognition of such rare terms.

Governmental Processes and Culture. All interviewees agreed that the digitalization of governmental processes poses special requirements. P4 mentioned the complexity of several core processes, partly resulting from rigid authority structures having evolved over long periods of time. Based on own experiences, P4 recommended reconsidering a governmental process before offering a related voice-based service.

P2 noted that advanced digital citizen services such as voice-based services provide a major paradigm shift for governments and their processes: Instead of citizens visiting a governmental office, sophisticated digital services approach the citizens.

P3 also addressed the governmental culture and mentioned potential reservations of civil servants. Especially the topic of "big data" and publishing governmental data sets in form of "open government data" are seen critical due to data protection concerns, according to P3.

Technical Implementation and Integration. Regarding the technical implementation of voice-based citizen services, P3 held the view that governments should not take the lead. Instead, third parties should be motivated to create respective citizen-oriented services based on open government data.

To realize more sophisticated interactive services beyond information access and to initiate governmental processes through third party applications, respective APIs (Application Programming Interface) are required. However, such "Open Government APIs" (in analogy to recently emerging Open Banking APIs, e.g.) are still a vision. None of the authorities of the interviewed governmental employees P1, P2, and P3 currently offers such publicly accessible service interfaces.

4.2   Application Ideas

During our interviews, the participants generated various ideas for voice-based governmental services. In the following, we shortly outline application ideas mentioned by several interviewees including some thoughts regarding their implementation.

Requesting Official Documents. From time to time citizens need to provide official documents such as a statement from the debt collection register, criminal records, parking permit, or residence certificates to apply for a visa or a job, e.g. Requesting such a document could be implemented through a rather simple dialogue. But as most of the documents contain very personal information the core requirement is an authentication of the user as a precondition to provide the service. Furthermore, it can be assumed that some municipalities will not allow to leave these data the country which has an implication of which voice platforms can be utilized. In addition, these documents are subject to charges which constitute another challenge.

Reporting Damages. Many cities offer Websites and apps to report damages to public infrastructures such as potholes and broken street lights ("Fix my Street", e.g.), etc., but also to report general complaints or even to collect citizens' ideas. A low-threshold voice-enabled interface could motivate citizens to report incidences even more. Although an authentication is not needed some kind of identification (maybe optional) would be helpful to prevent false reports but also to enable further communication and follow up with the user, e.g., to ask for more details or to give feedback to the user. A challenge would be the issue of exact localization of the incident to be reported. Whereas voice-enabled services used on smartphones may make use of the device's localization capabilities, using a smart speaker, which is located usually at home, would need some further functionalities to capture the location of a reported damage, in case it is needed.

Information Retrieval and Calculator. Another area of potential applications could be the retrieval of information and, in addition, a calculator. Relevant information for citizens is any information offered by a community which is relevant to citizens, e.g., tax related information, responsibilities for certain issues within an administration, poll and election related information, etc. A further area of application to think about could be to use voice-enabled services to access open government data repositories.

In case a citizen wants to or has to determine whether he or she is eligible for a certain service, such as reduction of health insurance rates, a calculator could be offered. Such a calculator, known from related Websites, could guide a user through the application and ask for the respective information and finally present the result to the user via voice output.

Similar services have been implemented as a chatbot already. Authentication or identification might not be needed for these kinds of services, nevertheless, it might be helpful to store data and/or results to follow up on a case online or in direct interaction with people from administration which would require some kind of identification or even authentication. A challenge might be the limitations of speech recognition as users articulate their concerns in many different forms of verbalization.

Reminders. One possible field of application identified is a city's calendar for garbage and waste paper collection. In this specific case of a city, the collection plan has a certain structure and is defined per year but contains irregularities because of holidays and other circumstances. Thus, citizens need to consult a source of information to find out the respective date. Today, this is solved via paper-based information sheets as well through an online e-government application which is also available as a mobile app. As these data are (rather) static and publicly available anyway and as there is no need for integrating the process into existing administration applications and also further functionalities such as authentication or payment is not necessary, but on the other hand this information are needed by citizens throughout the year, this case is a candidate for first conversational e-government service. Related generic reminder applications are available for Amazon's Alexa assistant, e.g., yet require the user to import calendar data assuming certain technical skills.

Relocation Assistant. In case citizens plan to relocate within or between cities, several public services have to be involved. For citizens it may be a challenge to identify all services and to contact them in time. Therefore, a relocation assistant could guide a citizen through the relocation process. The service not only could provide necessary information about what, when, and who, but also could remind people of tasks and deadlines. Of course, this service is rather complex and needs several functionalities already discussed, such as authentication of the citizen, in case the service should support issues such as registering a change of address, payment, full integration into administration's services, and others. Furthermore, it has to be defined as one channel of a multi-channel strategy; here, the voice assisted service can be understood as a further touchpoint to support the citizen along the so-called citizen journey [14]. This kind of voice-supported assistant could also be applicable to other domains of governmental services, e.g., in the areas of unemployment benefits or building applications.

5   Discussion and Implications

In our discussion, we derive implications for paving the way for and designing and implementing voice-based citizen services.

Providing Government Data and APIs. All three involved government representatives expected to see the development of voice-based citizen services by third parties, not by public institutions. Given the required special skills and the efforts for providing respective services for several different voice platforms, such an open innovation approach seems reasonable. Lots of municipalities started Open Data initiatives and published remarkable amounts of data sets (mainly resulting in mobile apps). Open Government Data also provide the base for prospective voice-based citizen services facilitating information access (cf. [15]). However, to enable the development of advanced interactive services, third parties need to be allowed triggering and initiating government processes. Corresponding Open Government APIs seem a crucial building block to boost the creation of more future powerful voice-based citizen services.

Selecting Suitable Citizen Services. The design of convenient user-accepted voice interfaces involves several challenges (cf. [7]). Since audio feedback is non-persistent and it is harder to communicate the state of a current process than in a graphical user interface, the length of a conversation with a voice assistant should be limited. Regarding the use case, voice-based services work well when they can be integrated into people's daily routines (typically while performing another primary activity). Many government services seem to have an opposite character. E.g., filling in a complex tax form is time-consuming, needs the person's entire attention and is done rarely (and in long periods).

We conclude that, first, citizen services for voice assistants need to be carefully selected regarding their complexity and periodical usage to provide true sustainable value. Second, several government services might need to be rethought on the path to truly citizen-oriented e-government services. Similar as traditional government processes were optimized for today's e-government Web portals, a related step seems necessary for offering advanced complex government services via voice assistants.

Ensuring Accessibility. While voice-based services provide great potential for blind people, government services provided via a voice assistant obviously exclude deaf and dumb citizens. In order to ensure overall accessibility, voice-based citizen services should not cover fundamental or critical government processes or rather complete alternative channels such as a Web platform.

Convenience over Strong Authentication. Advanced personalized citizen services will require authenticating the current user, obviously. Providing a simple, yet strong authentication for shared voice assistants is still a challenge. Recent approaches (e.g. [5]) rely on multi-factor authentication involving a mobile device. However, the requirement of installing an additional custom authentication app on the smartphone may hamper the acceptance of respective voice-based services. The government representatives agreed that there might not be the need for technically strong authentication, since either the consequences of a misuse are limited or government processes provide corrective means, such as the later withdrawal of an illegitimately obtained document, for example. They all recommended to focus on the convenience and good usability of respective services during design.

Considering Privacy-Relevant Data. Currently, it cannot be expected that mass-market voice assistants will ensure a certain location for remotely processing speech samples. Therefore, the respective privacy and data protection regulations cannot be confirmed during the deployment and installation of the actual voice service – what should be considered for citizen services involving privacy-relevant data. While Google announced offline support for their voice assistant only recently [16], the impact on custom extensions is not clear yet.

6 Conclusion and Outlook

In this paper, we investigated requirements and opportunities of voice-based citizen services in order to pave the way for a next generation of digital government services: conversational e-government. We reported on the results of five expert interviews with government representatives experienced with digital citizen services as well as senior staff of technology companies familiar with realizing voice interfaces and services. We found that the foundations to develop and implement voice-based citizen services are still rather undecided in many respects. For example, authentication for conversational e-government as well as the investigation of related privacy concerns require further investigation (extending existing trust models for conversational interfaces, e.g. [13]). Based on the interviewees' responses and assessments, we derived several implications as first requirements and considerations from an expert perspective.

The above presented results have been derived from interviews as well as from literature. Based on the findings, we will pursue future activities: First, the citizen perspective shall be investigated following a mixed methods approach. We plan to study citizens' perception, acceptance, as well as requirements in focus groups and an online survey. Second, prototypes of voice-based citizen services shall be developed to demonstrate possible functionalities, study their acceptance and derive concrete design guidelines for the conversational e-government.

References

1. Al-Sarayreh, K., Al-Qutaish, R., Al-Majali, M.: Incorporating the biometric voice technology into the e-government systems to enhance the user verification. WSEAS Trans. Comput. **7**, 435–452 (2008)
2. Androutsopoulou, A., Karacapilidis, N., Loukis, E., Charalabidis, Y.: Transforming the communication between citizens and government through AI-guided chatbots. Gov. Inf. Q. **36**(2), 358–367 (2019). https://doi.org/10.1016/j.giq.2018.10.001. http://www.sciencedirect.com/science/article/pii/S0740624X17304008

3. Cabrera Paraiso, E., Barthès, J.-P.A.: A voice-enabled assistant in a multi-agent system for e-government services. In: Ramos, F.F., Larios Rosillo, V., Unger, H. (eds.) ISSADS 2005. LNCS, vol. 3563, pp. 495–503. Springer, Heidelberg (2005). https://doi.org/10.1007/11533962_45
4. Canalys: Amazon smart speaker shipments crossed 10 million mark in Q3 2019 (2019). https://www.canalys.com/newsroom/worldwide-smartspeaker-Q3-2019. Accessed 27 Jan 2020
5. Futurae: Smart Assistant Authentication (2019). https://futurae.com/platform/smart-assistant/. Accessed 03 Oct 2019
6. Government Digital Service: Government uses Alexa and Google Home to make services easier to access. https://www.gov.uk/government/news/government-uses-alexa-and-google-home-to-make-services-easier-to-access. Accessed 03 Oct 2019
7. Klein, L.: Design for Voice Interfaces. O'Reilly Media, Inc., Sebastopol (2015)
8. Lindgren, I., Jansson, G.: Electronic services in the public sector: a conceptual framework. Gov. Inf. Q. **30**(2), 163–172 (2013). https://doi.org/10.1016/j.giq.2012.10.005. http://www.sciencedirect.com/science/article/pii/S0740624X13000026
9. Madsen, C., Hofmann, S.: Multichannel management in the public sector-a literature review. Electron. J. e-Gov. **17**, 20–35 (2019)
10. Madsen, C.Ø., Kræmmergaard, P.: Channel choice: a literature review. In: Tambouris, E., et al. (eds.) EGOV 2015. LNCS, vol. 9248, pp. 3–18. Springer, Cham (2015). https://doi.org/10.1007/978-3-319-22479-4_1
11. McTear, M., Callejas, Z., Griol, D.: Introducing the conversational interface. The Conversational Interface, pp. 1–7. Springer, Cham (2016). https://doi.org/10.1007/978-3-319-32967-3_1
12. Mehr, H.: Baidu replaces Google to become number two in smart speaker market in Q2 2019. Artificial Intelligence for Citizen Services and Government (2017). Accessed 03 Oct 2019
13. Nasirian, F., Ahmadian, M., Lee, O.K.: AI-based voice assistant systems: evaluating from the interaction and trust perspectives. In: AMCIS 2017 (2017)
14. Ng, J., Dudley, E., Lin, D.Y., Mancini, M.: Implementing a citizen-centric approach to delivering government services (2015). http://www.mckinsey.com/industries/public-sector/our-insights/implementing-a-citizen-centric-approach-to-delivering-government-services. Accessed 03 Oct 2019
15. Porreca, S., Leotta, F., Mecella, M., Vassos, S., Catarci, T.: Accessing government open data through chatbots. In: Garrigós, I., Wimmer, M. (eds.) ICWE 2017. LNCS, vol. 10544, pp. 156–165. Springer, Cham (2018). https://doi.org/10.1007/978-3-319-74433-9_14
16. Schalkwyk, J.: An All-Neural On-Device Speech Recognizer. https://ai.googleblog.com/2019/03/an-all-neural-on-device-speech.html. Accessed 03 Oct 2019
17. Tuzovic, S., Paluch, S.: Conversational commerce – a new era for service business development? In: Bruhn, M., Hadwich, K. (eds.) Service Business Development, pp. 81–100. Springer, Wiesbaden (2018). https://doi.org/10.1007/978-3-658-22426-4_4
18. Wirtz, B.W., Birkmeyer, S.: Open government: origin, development, and conceptual perspectives. Int. J. Public Adm. **38**(5), 381–396 (2015). https://doi.org/10.1080/01900692.2014.942735

Designing Community-Based Open Innovation Platforms Based on Actual User Behavior

Claas Digmayer(✉) and Eva-Maria Jakobs

Department of Textlinguistics and Technical Communication, Human-Computer Interaction Center, RWTH Aachen University, Campus-Boulevard 57, 52074 Aachen, Germany
`claas.digmayer@rwth-aachen.de`

Abstract. Community-based open innovation platforms offer a promising approach to use the collective intelligence of target groups as a knowledge resource in product development processes. Their success depends on how such platforms can be designed in a user-centric way. This requires the consideration of factors such as communicative usability and sociability.

In a study, the interaction between users when submitting ideas and commenting on ideas on an innovation platform was investigated. The analysis provides indications of usage strategies that encourage or discourage collaboration between users to further develop ideas. Guidelines for user interaction (code of conduct) and for the usable design of community-based innovation platforms are derived from the findings.

Keywords: Community-based open innovation platforms · Usability · Sociability

1 Introduction

Today's information society is characterized by a multitude of technological advances that enable innovative products and services for end users. Many innovation projects, however, do not take actual customer needs sufficiently into account: In the innovation process, customers often play a purely recipient role without co-determination rights – products are developed for the target group, not in cooperation with it, which causes product launches on the market to fail [1]. However, innovations are essential for the competitiveness of companies, especially in a dynamic competitive environment [2]. Knowledge is the central prerequisite for the development of innovations [3]. The knowledge of customers allows conclusions to be drawn as to whether a product idea offers added value for a target group. However, such knowledge of customer needs can only be gained through dialogue with the target group [4].

The open innovation approach makes such knowledge of target groups usable for the development of products and services: the collective intelligence of (potential) customers serves as a knowledge resource in product development processes. Open innovation methods such as community-based innovation platforms motivate customers to submit, comment, rate and collaboratively develop innovative proposals online in Web

F. F.-H. Nah and K. Siau (Eds.): HCII 2020, LNCS 12204, pp. 15–33, 2020.
https://doi.org/10.1007/978-3-030-50341-3_2

2.0 environments within a limited time frame [5]. In view of the Grand HCI Challenge "Learning and Creativity" [6], community-based innovation platforms represent a promising opportunity for users to gain knowledge and develop new or unusual ideas with others.

From a business point of view, these innovation methods have a high potential for obtaining target group-specific knowledge in high quality and quantity: From user-generated contributions, information on needs and corresponding solutions as well as trends in terms of design preferences can be derived. The successful application of the method depends significantly on how it is possible to design the platforms in a customer-centered way: The more users submit ideas and improve existing ideas according to the principle of co-creation, the higher the output of generated need and solution information. The successful implementation of open innovation platforms therefore requires a high level of platform usability on the one hand and high-quality social interaction (sociability) on the other. Research on open innovation, which is predominantly economic in nature, hardly deals with these questions.

In a study on one community-based innovation platform user interaction via commenting was analyzed. The analysis of the commentary sequences makes it possible to obtain indications of interaction problems and corresponding requirements for the usability and sociability of open innovation platforms.

The study focuses on three research questions:

1. Quantitatively: At which points in time during the life of an innovation platform do users participate with contributions (idea submissions, comments, ratings)? How extensive are discussions between users (length of chains of related comments)?
2. Qualitatively: For what purposes are idea comments used? Which types of comments promote co-creation and sociability, which ones hinder both aspects?
3. Quantitatively and qualitatively: Which challenges of platform and community design can be identified from the contributions on the platforms?

The results are discussed in terms of requirements for the design quality of community-based innovation platforms – both from the perspective of (communicative) usability and sociability.

2 Theoretical Background

2.1 Co-creation Online

Co-creation is defined as "[…] any act of collective creativity, i.e. creativity that is shared by two or more people." [8]. According to this approach, users jointly develop existing products incrementally: Each participant contributes to a common pool of knowledge that would not arise as a public good under a market institutionalization [9] and initiates further improvements by other participants. Co-creation thus enables a multi-perspective view of the subject matter [10] and continuous optimization of content in iterative cycles [11].

Participation in co-creation processes requires extensive domain knowledge, dedication and motivation [8]. Users invest such a high level of effort due to various incentives, which Füller [12] divides into four categories: Rewards (e.g.: material prizes), needs (e.g.: prospect of implementing an idea), curiosity (e.g.: pleasure in new challenges) and intrinsic motives (e.g.: participation in the product development process).

Collaboration between customers according to the principle of co-creation is mainly written and internet-based using web-based writing technologies [13]. Rowley et al. [14] describe how users of online product forums use web-based writing technologies to collaboratively generate content: Users publish suggestions for improvement in the form of comments on existing products. Other users, in turn, continuously publish comments in which they take up and develop the initial suggestion for improvement. Rapid feedback from users on published contributions is the basis for this type of co-creation [13]. For companies, such user-generated improvements of idea descriptions submitted by other users represent a high added value: On the one hand, idea proposals are more elaborated in this way and their marketability is increased, on the other hand, companies can forecast market acceptance based on user feedback.

2.2 The Design of Community-Based Open Innovation Platforms

Open innovation refers to the targeted use of incoming and outflowing knowledge to promote internal innovation and to expand markets for the external exploitation of innovation [15]. Open innovation platforms are one method of achieving this goal. On such platforms, companies ask customers for structured input of topic-related suggestions for improvement and ideas [9]. Community-based open innovation platforms aim at establishing a predominantly hedonically oriented innovation community. Such communities consist of groups of end consumers who voluntarily develop improvements to existing or completely innovative products [16].

The collaborative development of innovations is enabled by community functions (comment function, news function, tagging, integration of social media such as Twitter feeds). Some of the community-based competitions offer co-development functions that allow co-authoring in the production of content [5]. In innovation communities, both need information and solution information can be collected at various stages of development, from brief descriptions to fully implemented prototypes [17].

The literature on methods of open innovation, which is mainly based on economic science, only occasionally mentions design requirements for community-based open innovation platforms. The requirements are directed towards the evaluation of ideas, the retention of users and the development of a community.

Evaluation of Ideas: Open innovation platforms should offer conventional evaluation functions (e.g. voting or ranking) which users can use without explanations or help [18].

User Loyalty: Users should be motivated to visit open innovation platforms frequently and to stay on the platform for a longer period of time per visit - corresponding incentives are created by functions such as ranking lists, announcements of new ideas in competition via app or the connection of social media such as Facebook or Twitter [19].

Community Development: Requirements for the design of community-based open innovation platforms aim to give users the impression of being part of a community of innovators with expertise in a common field. Such an innovation community can be established in particular through the use of community functions, such as chat functions, user profiles or discussion forums. Submitted ideas should be able to be recommended and evaluated using community functions [19].

The requirements described are mostly limited to the naming of functions that are to be implemented in innovation platforms. With regard to the design of functions, it is assumed that users adapt their actions to the characteristics of the platforms [20]: Users are assumed to familiarize themselves with open innovation platforms if they have sufficient interest in the task to be solved and the subject area and thus qualify for participation in innovation activities (self-selection). Users are expected to use strategies such as trial and error to learn applications. According to von Hippel [20], the usability of open innovation platforms is guaranteed if users can participate even with little domain-related knowledge. Such approaches lack design requirements that consider the actual needs of users.

2.3 Communicative Usability

Usability is an essential criterion in the design, implementation and optimization of electronic applications. The field of usability research is significantly influenced by disciplines such as psychology, technical subjects and ergonomics. The definition of what is meant by usability varies in part depending on the subject. Shackel [21], for example, defines usability as the interaction of efficiency, effectiveness and user satisfaction. Nielsen [22] names six design criteria for usable websites: Hypertexts should be easy to learn, memorable, error-free as well as pleasant and efficient to use. However, such definitions often do not consider linguistic-communicative aspects of system design [23, 24]. Jakobs combines both aspects in her approach to communicative usability. Communicative usability focuses on the question how linguistic and semiotic means can contribute to making the dialogue between humans and technical artefact transparent, trouble-free and enjoyable. The approach is based on action theory and focuses on communicative modes (as the most important modality for the exchange between user and machine), superordinate action contexts (e.g., how the communicative design supports goal hierarchies of users), action contexts (e.g., does the design consider domain-specific or socio-cultural conditions) as well as the interplay of content, interface and aids.

2.4 Sociability

Sociability is a concept developed by Preece [25, 26] to evaluate the success of online communities. It records the quality of interaction between users in online communities in relation to the components purpose, users and guidelines. The purpose of a community is described as the common focus of all members on a topic, a need, information, offer or support; it embodies for each member the reason for participating in the community. Users are considered in terms of their role in the interaction, examples of roles are Leader, protagonist, entertainer or moderator. Regarding community guidelines, two types of guidelines are considered according to their implicitness: Informal rules based on a common language and common standards that guide social interaction and formal rules that are laid down in registration guidelines or codes of conduct.

According to Preece [27], sociability can be evaluated and promoted. It distinguishes between purpose and user-related criteria. Purpose-related criteria include the number of messages sent, interactivity, reciprocity and the quality of user-generated contributions. Preece describes the criteria as follows:

- The number of messages sent reflects the commitment of the members and is an indication of the extent to which the community fulfils its purpose.
- Interactivity is measured by the number of comments posted by users in response to a topic.
- Reciprocity refers to the ratio in which users accept support from the community and make contributions themselves. An example of reciprocity is the number of questions a user asks in a community in relation to the answers he or she publishes to questions from other users.
- The quality of contributions is measured by the length and the style of wording of the contributions. The quality of contributions can be made visible by providing community members with a function for rating comments.

The number of community members is perceived as user-related success criterion for sociability. The success of policies within a community can be determined by the extent of rude and offensive comments. The trustworthiness of members is measured by the number of exclusions from the community due to inappropriate behavior.

An essential statement of the sociability approach is that the way the interactors behave is influenced by the design of the interaction environment. Sociability therefore requires the careful design of the functions and framework conditions through which users can interact with each other. Initial design decisions - especially regarding guidelines for community use - must be continuously checked for suitability and adapted to the needs of the users [27].

3 Methodology

3.1 Data Collection

A community-based innovation platform focusing on the topic of mobile communication was selected for the study. The platform offers users the opportunity to enter ideas in a limited time frame (platform lifetime: originally 64 days, after an extension at the end of the first period 96 days in total) and comment on them using a simple web forms, rate ideas by awarding them stars. The platform provides brief descriptions of the task, but no rules of conduct. The ideas, idea comments and idea ratings were collected - the entire corpus comprises 269 idea descriptions, 655 comments and 742 ratings.

3.2 Data Preparation

The database was enriched by the publication dates of the idea descriptions, the relationships between ideas and comments, and the relationships between ideas and ratings. In addition, interrelated comments (based on direct references to the content or authors of previous comments) were grouped into comment sequences. For each comment, the position within the corresponding comment sequence was determined (depth of comment). The lengths of the comment sequences were added to the database.

3.3 Data Analysis

The data analysis examined the chronological distribution of submissions, types of comments and types of comment sequences.

Time Course of the Submissions: The ideas were sorted chronologically. The platform duration was determined based on the start and end of the submission period and divided into 20 segments (five percent steps). For each segment, the number of ideas published during this period was determined as well as the number of associated comments and ratings.

Types of Comments: Comment categories were inductively formed from the material in a qualitative content analysis. The comments of the database were assigned to the categories by two annotators. Differing annotations and difficulties in assigning comments were discussed and resolved. Problems that arise when using certain comment types were annotated.

Types of Comment Sequences: Commentary sequences were qualitatively examined in terms of their composition of comment types. The annotation was carried out in the same way as the determination of the comment types. The comment sequence types were qualitatively examined regarding their potential for promoting and reducing co-creation and sociability.

4 Results

4.1 Frequency of Submissions

The results of the analysis show a discontinuous publication behavior of users. Many ideas were submitted on a few individual days, and on the majority of all days no or few ideas were submitted. Figure 1 shows the distribution of publications over time: Significantly more ideas were submitted at the beginning, middle and especially towards the end of the platform lifetime.

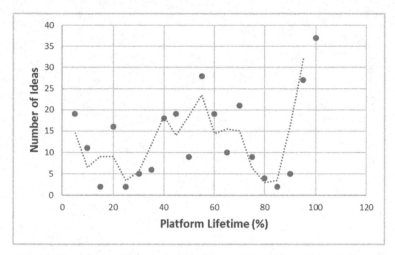

Fig. 1. Distribution of ideas submitted during the lifetime of the platform.

The distribution of comments (see Fig. 2) and ratings (see Fig. 3) according to submitted ideas shows that peaks of highly commented and rated ideas are located at the beginning, the middle and the end of the platform lifetime.

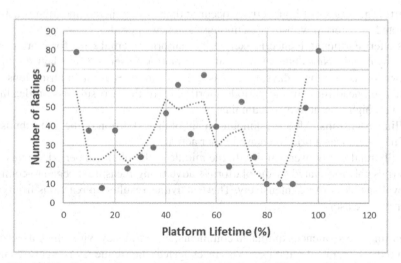

Fig. 2. Distribution of comments submitted during the lifetime of the platform.

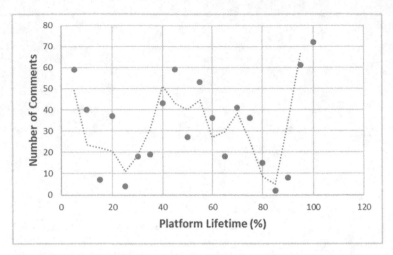

Fig. 3. Distribution of ratings submitted during the lifetime of the platform.

An increased number of idea submissions leads to an immediate increase in comments and ratings. Five measures appear to have a direct impact on user activity (submission of ideas, comments and ratings):

- Advertising: Periods of high activity occur at times when the competition is actively promoted on external websites (technology and news portals).
- Newsletter: Further influence is exerted by platform-internal calls for more participation by e-mail: Newsletters were sent to all platform users on two days during the platform period. On both days, there was a significant increase in contributions.
- Submission deadlines: In the periods shortly before the two submission deadlines, days with high user activity accumulate.
- Deadline extensions: After the announcement of the extension of the first submission deadline, there was a brief increase in user activity.
- Mutually reinforcing user activity: In the middle of the platform period, 5 individual users (possibly motivated by the platform's advertising measures) began to comment and evaluate ideas more intensively. These activities resulted in reactions from other rather passive users.

Regarding the sequences of related comments, the frequency with which users comment on the comments of other users was investigated (the frequency is measured in the length of the comment sequences). The data analysis identified 118 comment sequences consisting of 324 comments. The majority of all sequences consist of two to three comments (see Table 1).

Table 1. Distribution of comment sequences according to their length

Sequence length	Amount (Percentage)
2 comments	74 (62,71%)
3 comments	27 (22,88%)
4 comments	8 (6,78%)
5 comments	3 (2,54%)
6 comments	3 (2,54%)
7 comments	1 (0,85%)
9 comments	1 (0,85%)
14 comments	1 (0,85%)

4.2 Contents of Comments

Users of the platform use comments to clarify difficulties in understanding ideas, to negotiate the innovative content of ideas and to develop ideas further. Five main types of comments were identified in the content analysis: Questions about ideas, endorsement of ideas, criticism of ideas, suggestions for improvement of ideas, and author reactions. The distribution of the comment types is shown in Table 2, the individual types are described below.

Table 2. Distribution of comment types

Comment type	Amount (Percentage)
Questions	74 (11,3%)
Endorsement	183 (27,94%)
Criticism	126 (19,24%)
Improvements	121 (18,47%)
Reactions to comments	151 (23,05%)

Questions about ideas: Users of the innovation platform address questions to the authors of idea descriptions in order to obtain additional information for a better understanding of the described idea. Questions refer to the target group (10.81% of all questions), the functionality (71.62% of all questions) or design aspects (17.57% of all questions) of an idea.

The question about the target group of an idea aims at two difficulties of understanding: It is either unclear whether the idea is suitable for the target group as a whole. Other questions relate to the usability of the idea for a subset of the target group with special restrictions such as wearers of pacemakers.

Questions about the functionality of an idea result from inaccurate or incomplete idea descriptions and aim at increasing the elaboration of an idea.

Questions about the design implementation are asked in order to be able to understand design decisions directed at the size, material, arrangement, color or shape of design elements of an idea.

Endorsement: This category records positive comments on the ideas of others. One third of all endorsements (31.15%) consist of a short praise ("Great idea!") to which no justification is added. The rest (68.85% of all ideas) are justified by

- listing advantages of the idea (19.13% of all endorsements),
- emphasizing individual aspects of the idea (15.3% of all endorsements),
- applying the idea to a practical situation (14.75% of all endorsements),
- positively highlighting the elaboration of the idea (13.66% of all endorsements) and by
- comparing the idea with existing products (6% of all endorsements).

Justified endorsements highlight the innovative potential of an idea and provide other users with arguments why an idea should be positively evaluated.

Listing of advantages: Some ideas are evaluated by simply listing advantages such as ease of use, proximity to the target group or protection of the user's health.

Highlighting of aspects: The commentator cites a single aspect or object from the idea description as the reason for his or her positive perception.

Application to a practical situation: The commentator describes a recurring everyday problem that could be solved by the idea and thus emphasizes its value.

Highlighting the elaboration: In several cases, the positive perception of ideas refers to the idea description and added files such as images.

Comparison with existing products: The idea is compared to existing solutions and thus exemplified as solution to issues of such products.

Criticism: Rejections are used to criticize ideas posted on the platform. A small minority of rejections are not justified (2.14% of all rejections). The majority of rejections (97.86% of all rejections) are justified by

- questioning the feasibility of the idea (2.53% of all criticisms),
- criticizing the quality of the drafting of the idea description (5.06% of all criticisms)
- criticizing the idea as being too complex (5.39% of all criticisms),
- questioning the usefulness of the idea for the target group (8.23% of all criticisms),
- criticizing the usability of the idea (10.78% of all criticisms)
- pointing out that the idea already exists (65.87% of all criticisms)

Reasoned refusals reduce the perceived innovation potential of submitted ideas. In the case of references to already existing ideas, the criticized idea submission is denied any innovative potential - and thus the right to participate in the competition. Reasoned rejections are explained below.

Lack of feasibility of ideas: Commentators doubt whether the idea can be implemented as a product.

Poor quality of drafting: Commentators criticize the quality of idea descriptions.

Lack of usefulness of ideas: Comments in this subcategory question whether an idea is suitable for the target group.

Lack of usability of idea implementations: With comments in this subcategory users criticize weaknesses in the usability of an idea implemented as a product.

Idea theft: The most frequent criticism of ideas is the accusation of adopting ideas on the platform of already submitted ideas (59.42%) or existing products (40.58%). The majority of the accusations (56.52%) are substantiated by stating a hyperlink leading to similar ideas on the innovation platform or to articles of existing products.

Improvement suggestions for ideas: Suggestions for improvement help users discover the potential for optimization of submitted ideas and support idea authors in improving their submissions. Suggestions for improvement refer to

- the design of an idea (3.88% of all suggestions for improvement),
- alternative areas of application for an idea (4.3% of all suggestions for improvement),
- improving the elaboration of an idea (12.3% of all suggestions for improvement),
- the technical implementation of an idea (32.79% of all improvement suggestions) and
- the extension of an idea (46.72% of all improvement suggestions).

Suggestions for improvement are explained below.

Design suggestions: Design Suggestions focus on the visual appearance of the idea implemented as a product - users use this sub-category of suggestions for improvement to show possibilities for optimizing design aspects.

Suggestions for alternative areas of application: This subcategory of suggestions for improvement indicates areas of application in which the idea could be used beneficially.

Elaboration suggestions: Comments in this subcategory show possibilities for optimizing an idea. They refer to the scope of the idea description, the creation of visualizations, structuring as well as formulation hints. Notes on scope recommend a more detailed and precise description of the entire idea or individual aspects. Recommendations for the creation of visualizations guide authors as to the form (e.g. as a sketch) and tools (e.g. image editing software) in which an idea can be visualized.

Proposals for technical implementation: Proposals for technical implementation refer to the question of which technologies or mobile phone components can be used to implement an idea as a product.

Extension suggestions: Users state possibilities how the benefit of ideas can be increased by additional content, features or functions. Users often suggest combining the commented idea with an idea they have submitted themselves.

Reactions: Some of the comments are written by authors who explicitly address the content of comments on their ideas. The majority of reactions can be assigned to one of the four comment types described above (87.41%) - reactions mainly refer to rejection of ideas (36.42% of all reactions) and questions (23.18% of all reactions), less frequently to suggestions for improvement (15.89% of all reactions) and endorsements (11.92% of all reactions). In addition, there is a sub-category of reactions criticizing the behavior of users of the platform (12.58% of all reactions). Behavioral criticism refers to both ratings of ideas and commentary content. Criticism of ratings is published when low ratings are not justified with a comment or when rating and justification in the comment do not match. Criticism of comment content refers to comments that are perceived as inappropriate.

4.3   Comment Sequences

The distribution of the 118 commentary sequences among the four categories mentioned can be seen in Table 3. There is a clear majority of commentary episodes that have a positive impact on user interaction (77.97% of all episodes). A minority of the consequences have a negative impact (22.03% of all consequences). The categories are explained below.

Table 3. Distribution of comment types

Comment sequence types	Related to sociablity	Related to co-creation
Promoting	56 (47.46%)	36 (30.51%)
Hindering	7 (5.93%)	19 (16.1%)

Sociability-promoting comment sequences: Sociability-enhancing discussions are discussions in which users express and negotiate positions on an idea. Such an exchange of views enables the formation of a community on the innovation platform. There are three reasons for this exchange of views: To clarify questions about an idea, to negotiate criticism of an idea and to praise an idea. The majority of these commentary sequences consist of only two comments (76.79% of the sociability-promoting commentary sequences), which are usually published on the platform at short intervals one after the other. Three-part chains supplement the above-mentioned two-part chains by thanking for the reaction to the first comment (63.64%), by a specification of the question asked at the beginning (42.86%) or by an objection to the rejection of criticism of an idea (14.29%). The only sequence comprising four comments begins with a question that is answered by the author of the idea. The questioner finds the answer insufficient and specifies his question, whereupon he receives a more precise answer from the author of the idea.

Sociability-hindering comment sequences: Sequences in which users accuse each other of misconduct are an obstacle to the development of sociability. There are two consequences: First, sociability-reducing consequences inhibit the perceived quality of social interaction and second, they distract users from activities that generate profit for the platform operator (evaluation and further development of ideas). Comment sequences in which users accuse each other of misconduct result from criticism of ideas as well as from the accusation that the idea has been adopted. Such sequences are among the longer consequences on the platform: 42.86% consist of three comments, 14.29% of four comments, 42.86% of six comments. The accusation of misconduct represents a serious damage to the reputation of the commentator – the need for clarification of the accusation causes longer consequences of comments which, in contrast to other commentary sequences, have an aggressive to offensive style of wording. Sociability-reducing commentary sequences make it difficult to build trust between users.

Co-creation-promoting comment sequences: Comment sequences foster co-creation on the innovation platform if users further develop collaboratively submitted ideas via comments. The results show that improvements in ideas can result from endorsements (5.56% of co-creation-supporting comment sequences), questions (8.33% of co-creation-supporting comment sequences) or the accusation of idea theft (22.22% of co-creation-supporting comment sequences). In the third case, the original idea is expanded in response to the accusation of idea theft in order to distinguish it from the existing idea or product. In the majority of all cases, an improvement proposal is submitted directly without prior discussion (63.89% co-creation-promoting commentary sequences). Direct suggestions for improvement lead to two different types of commentary sequences: either one or more endorsements of the improvement suggestion (27.78% of co-creation-promoting comment sequences), or iterating suggestions for improvement (36.11% of co-creation-promoting comment sequences).

Co-creation-related are among the longest commentary sequences on the innovation platform: 50% of the episodes contain between three and fourteen comments. Especially relevant for co-creation on the innovation platform are iterative suggestions for improvement: Optimizations of an idea are mutually improved by different users. In this way, ideas are further developed by the community instead of by individual representatives of the community. However, suggestions for improvement are seldom added to the idea descriptions: Only in 5.2% of all idea descriptions text passages were identified which indicate revisions based on suggestions for improvement (usually starting with a note ("To clarify:", "Update:", "Explained in more detail:").

Co-creation-hindering comment sequences: Comment sequences impede or prevent co-creation if suggestions for improvement of ideas are rejected by the author, if it is pointed out to users that suggestions for improvement have already been submitted as ideas or if accusations of adopting ideas are rejected. In the first two cases, no further suggestions for improvement were submitted after the rejection of a suggestion for improvement – the rejection of suggestions for improvement ends all interaction abruptly. Desired effects such as iterating suggestions for improvement are thus prevented.

In the third case, the focus of user interaction shifts: Users no longer work together on the further development of ideas, but act against each other to clarify the accusation of idea theft. Discussions about the similarity of ideas or ideas and existing products are not made usable for co-creation, e.g. by proposing extensions of the discussed idea that would result in a significant difference to the objects of comparison. Instead of promoting co-creation, discussions end in accusations of idea adoption.

The discussion-interrupting effect of the three cases also indicates that commentary sequences in this category are very short: 73.64% consist of only two comments, 10.53% of three comments and 15.8% of four comments. Co-creation-reducing commentary sequences make it difficult to build trust between users.

5 Discussion

5.1 Implications for the Design of Innovation Platforms Regarding Communicative Usability

Platforms represent a hypertext genre for the acquisition of need and solution information from target groups. The main goal for users to offer such information is the prospect of winning a prize by submitting an idea. Achieving this goal is impeded on the one hand by competing users (and their strategies for gaining an advantage, see Sect. 5.2), and on the other hand by the platform design. The results indicate several problems for users to screen, submit, comment on and rate ideas. These problems are related to the quality of the communicative platform design regarding (the interplay of) content, interface and help features (see Sect. 2.3).

Screening ideas: Users interested in submitting an idea are confronted with the high volume of user-generated information, which poses two major challenges:

- Users cannot invest the necessary time to check whether an idea to be submitted already exists as a contribution on the platform – there are multiple submissions of similar idea descriptions which lead to discussions about idea theft.
- Users who wish to participate in the development of solutions to specific topics or questions can only identify suitable contributions with high efforts.

For the challenges described, approaches are needed that automatically check contributions for topic affiliation and arguments contained in them. A promising approach could be to offer search and proposal functions which apply text mining methods. Such interface elements allow to access the platform contents using topic tracking and argumentation mining on the basis of automated part of speech annotation. Categorization of contributions offers users the possibility to check short descriptions of their ideas for similarity to existing contributions before publication or identify ideas in their own field of expertise for co-development activities.

Creation of ideas: Ideas submitted to the innovation platform show fluctuating quality, especially regarding the linguistic implementation: Contributions contain many orthographic errors and deficiencies in coherent text structure. Such issues should be addressed with platform functions: Authors should be offered powerful writing technologies (instead of simple web forms) that support idea structuring and formulation as well as the creation of supplementary files such as visualizations. Help features should guide the user in every step of the process, e.g. by suggesting technical terminology. The most important feature to support users in creating ideas is content provided by the platform operators: Such content needs to state clearly what the operators expect from the users, how submissions will be used by the operators and which criteria submissions need to meet in order to be considered as adequate to win a prize.

Commenting: Idea comments are often brief and can lead to difficulties of understanding or undesired reactions on the part of the authors, if they are not carefully formulated (see Sects. 4.2, 4.3). Since comments are submitted in the same way as idea submissions via web forms, it is likely that commentators face the same problems as idea authors. Such problems can be solved with writing technologies as described above. Another problem is the use of comments to link ideas: This strategy is used by users to promote their own ideas (see Sect. 4.3). From the point of view of platform operators, such proposals are particularly promising as they show synergies between submissions. From the users' point of view, such suggestions for combining ideas can only be indicated via comments, where they remain largely invisible. Desirable would be platform functions that allow different ideas to be linked and emphasize the added value.

Rating: The sociability of a community-based innovation platform is decreased if users rate ideas with a low score and do not justify the evaluation via comment. Authors suspect that other users try to gain competitive advantages in this way. To prevent such strategies, the platform design should connect commenting and rating in a way that only justified ratings are allowed. The examined platform allows to rate ideas with a score between one and five stars – in such cases explanations are needed as to what the individual scores mean from the point of view of the platform operator. It should be explained in which cases which score is suitable for an idea of which level of elaboration.

5.2 Implications for the Design of Innovation Platforms Regarding Sociability

The results indicate that user interaction on the examined innovation platform takes place only sporadically during the runtime as well as purposefully in short commentary sequences (see Sect. 4.1). However, findings like mutually reinforcing user activity (see Sect. 4.1) and co-creation-promoting comment sequences (see Sect. 4.3) show the potential of user interaction for innovation platforms. Such positive interaction can, however, be disturbed by negative interaction, which is manifests, for example, in the accusation of idea theft (see Sect. 4.2). According to the measures of sociability (see Sect. 2.4), the examined platform shows a relatively low quality of social interaction. Interaction problems arise from particular comment types and types of commentary sequences. Identified problems are described below. For each problem, rules are proposed which are intended to promote confidence building, sociability and co-creation as a code of conduct on community-based innovation platforms. The rules should be monitored by moderators, multiple violations should be punished by blocking user accounts or withdrawing access to the comment function. To encourage community interaction and co-creation, the reward and incentive system should be expanded: *Community awards* should be awarded for frequent constructive comments and *co-developer awards* for improvements.

The results indicate that some of the interaction problems are caused by a lack of quality in the submission of ideas: Qualitatively inferior idea descriptions and appendices are criticized, inferior idea descriptions result in inferior comments. A first step is to encourage users to submit ideas in the best possible quality.

Rule 1: Make sure to submit ideas in the best possible quality.
General interaction problems arise from unobjective and insulting formulations in comments. Users should be obliged to follow the rules of netiquette. The netiquette should be made available on the platform additionally.

Rule 2: Please comply with the netiquette. Violations will be punished by blocking user accounts or the comment function.
It is often the case that users only comment on descriptions of ideas, but do not take up comments from other users. Reactive comments neither promote confidence building nor co-creation. Users should be encouraged to comment discursively.

Rule 3: In your comments, always consider the comments that were previously published on the idea in question.
Interaction problems arise from all comment types, they are described below per type. Questions are often formulated in a less concrete way so that it not obvious which aspect of the idea is referenced. A corresponding guideline should encourage users to formulate questions concisely.

Rule 4: If you have a question about an idea, always indicate to which point of the idea description and which aspect mentioned there you refer to. Add all necessary information to your question so that other users of the platform can understand your question.
A common problem is unfounded endorsement and criticism – the author of the idea cannot understand which aspect of the idea is evaluated; other users cannot use such comments as basis for a discussion. Commentators should be required to provide mandatory justifications for idea evaluations.

Rule 5: When evaluating an idea, always give a reason so that other users can participate in the discussion.
Endorsement and criticism that are given by applying an idea to a practical situation from the everyday life of the commentator offer advantages for users and for the platform operator: From the user's point of view, praise can be better understood; from the platform operator's point of view, such descriptions provide need information that can be used for product development.

Rule 6: When evaluating an idea, please always address situations in everyday life where the implementation of the idea would have an impact.
Criticism of ideas is often the starting point for unobjective, insulting reactions. Furthermore, the results indicate that rejections are used to reduce the chances of ideas submitted by other users. Abuse of the commentary function must be prevented. For this reason, each rejection should be accompanied by a precise description of what the comment refers to. Unsubstantiated criticism does not enable authors to improve their ideas. Justifications should be mandatory in the context of rejections.

Rule 7: When you criticize an idea, always indicate to which point of the idea description and which aspect mentioned there you refer to. Criticism of ideas must always be justified with arguments and contain constructive suggestions for improvement.
The most frequently discussed topic is the accusation of idea theft. Such comments reduce the quality of social interaction, building trust and co-creation. In addition, the accusation of idea theft ends other discussions abruptly. For this reason, accusations of adoption should not be discussed publicly between users. Instead, users should report

suspected idea theft to the platform operator, who will investigate the case and take action. In addition, users should be informed about how the competition jury assesses ideas that have been submitted several times.

Rule 8: If you find that an idea has been submitted to the platform before or exists as a product, please report this to the platform operator. Such matters should not be discussed between users of the platform. If a similar idea is submitted by several users, the jury will evaluate the version that was submitted first.

As the high amount comments that are not part of comment sequences as well as the low amount of the comment type 'reaction' indicate, reactions to comments by authors of ideas are often omitted, thus preventing continuous interaction on the platform. Authors should be required to respond to each comment. Violations of the guidelines should be taken into account in the evaluation by the competition jury.

Rule 9: If one of your ideas is commented on, always write a comment in which you react to the corresponding contribution. Missing reactions to comments from the community will result in a devaluation of the idea by the jury.

The results indicate that authors often do not take up criticism or suggestions for improvement to revise their idea descriptions. They should be motivated to improve their own ideas by means of appropriate guidelines.

Rule 10: If suggestions for improvement are made or weaknesses of your idea are revealed in the comments, please revise your idea accordingly.

Authors often respond to criticism by merely denying counterarguments. To encourage interaction and co-creation, authors should always be required to justify such statements with pro-arguments.

Rule 11: If you want to refute criticism of your ideas, this is always done objectively and by providing arguments.

6 Conclusion

User comments offer promising opportunities to improve ideas on innovation platforms. From the user's point of view, suggestions for improvement promote the quality of social interaction and confidence building between users. From the operator's point of view, they increase the quality of solution information and increase the market potential of product developments. Ideally, users apply collaboration-oriented usage strategies such as iterative co-creation in order to continuously optimize ideas from each other.

If the platform operator does not communicate desired and undesired behavior in the interaction between users in a concise and comprehensible way, the quality-increasing potential of user comments is reversed: platform participants apply informal competition-oriented rules in order to gain competitive advantages for themselves and corresponding disadvantages for competitors. Clear formal behavioral guidelines as well as their monitoring and enforcement by moderators are an essential requirement for the design of community-based innovation platforms: Only with such measures can continuous, constructive, collaboration-oriented community interaction and the successful application of the open innovation method be guaranteed. Such measures must be supported by high usability as well as functions that enable users to focus on the collaborative development of ideas.

References

1. Ogawa, S., Piller, F.T.: Reducing the risks of new product development. Sloan Manage. Rev. **47**, 65–72 (2006)
2. Von Hippel, E.: The sources of innovation. In: Boersch, C., Elschen, R. (eds.) Das Summa Summarum des Management, pp. 111–120. Gabler, Wiesbaden (2007). https://doi.org/10. 1007/978-3-8349-9320-5_10
3. Jakobs, E.-M., Spinuzzi, C.: Professional domains: writing as creation of economic value. In: Jakobs, E.-M., Perrin, D. (eds.) Handbook of Writing and Text Production, pp. 359–384. De Gruyter/Mouton, Berlin/Boston (2014)
4. Spinuzzi, C., et al.: Making the pitch: examining dialogue and revisions in entrepreneurs' pitch decks. IEEE Trans. Prof. Commun. **57**(3), 158–181 (2014)
5. Hallerstede, S. H., Bullinger, A. C.: Do you know where you go? A taxonomy of online innovation contests. In: Proceedings of the 21st Professional Innovation Management Conference (2010)
6. Stephanidis, C., et al.: Seven HCI grand challenges. Int. J. Hum. Comput. Interact. **35**(14), 1229–1269 (2019)
7. Sanders, E.B.-N., Stappers, P.J.: Co-creation and the new landscapes of design. CoDesign **4**(1), 5–18 (2008)
8. Reichwald, R., Piller, F.T.: Interaktive Wertschöpfung: Open Innovation, Individualisierung und neue Formen der Arbeitsteilung. Gabler, Wiesbaden (2009). https://doi.org/10.1007/978-3-8349-9440-0
9. Ruth, A., Houghton, L.: The Wiki way of learning. Australas. J. Educ. Technol. **25**(2), 135–152 (2009)
10. Lakhani, K.R., Panetta, J.A.: The principles of distributed innovation. Innov. Technol. Gov. Glob. **2**(3), 97–112 (2007)
11. Füller, J.: Refining virtual co-creation from a consumer perspective. Calif. Manage. Rev. **52**(2), 98–122 (2010)
12. Nambisan, S., Baron, R.A.: Virtual customer environments: testing a model of voluntary participation in value co-creation activities. J. Prod. Innov. Manag. **26**(4), 388–406 (2009)
13. Rowley, J., Kupiec-Teahan, B., Leeming, E.: Customer community and co-creation: a case study. Mark. Intell. Plann. **25**(2), 136–146 (2007)
14. Chesbrough, H.W.: Open Innovation: The New Imperative for Creating and Profiting From Technology. Harvard Business School Press, Boston (2010)
15. Franke, N., Shah, S.: How communities support innovative activities: an exploration of assistance and sharing among end-users. Res. Policy **32**(1), 157–178 (2003)
16. Piller, F.T., Ihl, C., Vossen, A.: A typology of customer co-creation in the innovation process (2010). https://papers.ssrn.com/sol3/papers.cfm?abstract_id=1732127. Accessed 29 Jan 2020
17. Haller, J.: Open Evaluation: Integrating Users into the Selection of New Product Ideas. Springer, Wiesbaden (2013). https://doi.org/10.1007/978-3-8349-4487-0
18. Nakatsu, R., Grossman, E.: Designing effective user interfaces for crowdsourcing: an exploratory study. In: Yamamoto, S. (ed.) HIMI 2013. LNCS, vol. 8016, pp. 221–229. Springer, Heidelberg (2013). https://doi.org/10.1007/978-3-642-39209-2_26
19. Von Hippel, E.: User toolkits for innovation. J. Prod. Innov. Manage. **18**(4), 247–257 (2001)
20. Shackel, B.: Human factors and usability. In: Preece, J. (ed.) Human-Computer Interaction, pp. 27–41. Prentice Hall, Hemel Hempstead (1994)
21. Nielsen, J.: Hypertext and Hypermedia. Academic Press, Boston (1990)
22. Jakobs, E.-M.: Kommunikative usability. In: Marx, K., Schwarz-Friesel, M. (eds.) Sprache und Kommunikation im technischen Zeitalter: Wieviel Internet (v)erträgt unsere Gesellschaft?, pp. 119–142. De Gruyter, Berlin (2012)

23. Ziefle, M., Jakobs, E.-M.: New challenges in human computer interaction: strategic directions and interdisciplinary trends. In: Proceedings of the 4th International Conference on Competitive Manufacturing Technologies, pp. 389–398. University of Stellenbosch, South Africa (2010)
24. Preece, J.: Online Communities: Designing Usability, Supporting Sociability. Wiley, Chichester (2000)
25. Preece, J., Rogers, Y., Sharp, H.: Interaction Design: Beyond Human-Computer Interaction. Wiley, Chichester (2007)
26. Preece, J.: Sociability and usability: twenty years of chatting online. Behav. Inf. Technol. J. **20**(5), 347–356 (2001)
27. Matzat, U.: Reducing problems of sociability in online communities: integrating online communication with offline interaction. Am. Behav. Sci. **53**(8), 1170–1193 (2010)

Investigating Patients' Visits to Emergency Departments: A Behavior-Based ICD-9-CM Codes Decision Tree Induction Approach

Yen-Yi Feng[2], I-Chin Wu[1(✉)], and Yu-Ping Ho[3]

[1] Graduate Institute of Library and Information Studies, School of Learning Informatics,
National Taiwan Normal University, Taipei, Taiwan
icwu@ntnu.edu.tw
[2] Emergency Medicine, Mackay Memorial Hospital, Taipei, Taiwan
[3] Department of Information Management, Fu-Jen Catholic University, Taipei, Taiwan

Abstract. Increasing healthcare costs have motivated researchers to seek ways to more efficiently use medical resources. The aim of our study was to adopt the explanatory data-mining approach to identify characteristics of emergency department (ED) visits for ED management. To that end, we adopted a behavior-based decision tree (DT) induction method that considers medical diagnoses and individual patients' information, i.e., 11 input variables, in order to analyze characteristics of patients' visits to EDs and predict the length of the stays. We interpreted the results based on the communicability and consistency of the DT, represented as a behavior-based DT profile in order to increase its explanatory power. Among the major preliminary findings, the DT with International Classification of Diseases diagnosis codes achieved better clinical values for explaining the characteristics of patients' visits. Our results can serve as a reference for ED personnel to examine overcrowding conditions as part of medical management.

Keywords: Behavior-based profile · Decision tree · Emergency department · International Classification of Diseases diagnosis codes

1 Introduction

The emergency department has become the most important and busiest unit in most hospitals. Since the initiation of National Health Insurance (NHI) in Taiwan in 1995, outpatient numbers and medical expenses have grown quickly. According to Taiwan's Ministry of Health and Welfare, from 2012 to 2017 the cost of emergency cases in Taiwan rose from 18,283,211,000 to 21,645,524,000 points. It is noted that one-fourth of costs are centered in Taipei and New Taipei City. Interestingly, the number of ED visits and distinct patient visits decreased from 2012 to 2017 (12,614,216/4,261,052 to 11,730,241/4,198,223). This shows that the average cost for each ED visit is increasing. Uscher-Pines et al. [1] show that a large proportion of all ED visits in the United States are for nonurgent conditions. In fact, studies have revealed that the percentage of nonurgent ED visits in the U.S. comes to at least 30% of all ED visits [2, 3]. Nonurgent ED visits

© Springer Nature Switzerland AG 2020
F. F.-H. Nah and K. Siau (Eds.): HCII 2020, LNCS 12204, pp. 34–45, 2020.
https://doi.org/10.1007/978-3-030-50341-3_3

are typically defined as visits for conditions for which a delay of several hours would not increase the likelihood of an adverse outcome. Use of the ED for nonurgent conditions may lead to excessive health care costs, unnecessary testing and treatment, and weaker patient–primary care provider relationships. Interestingly, in our cooperating hospital approximately 87% of patients remain in the ED for less than two hours and they could be Nonurgent ED visits.

Healthcare data mining provides outstanding possibilities for the discovery of patterns, rules and knowledge hidden in medical data. Healthcare institutions can adopt data-mining techniques and applications to predict trends in patients' conditions and behaviors, as well as their future requests, needs and conditions. In turn, physicians can refer to the results to determine diagnoses, prognoses and treatments for patients and reduce subjectivity in decisions about their treatments [4]. Pendharkar and Khurana [5] compared the use of a classification and regression tree, chi-square automatic interaction detection and support vector regression with data from 88 federal and specialty hospitals in Pennsylvania to build length-of-stay (LOS) prediction models. Their results showed no significant difference in performance in terms of the root mean square errors of the three models. However, among the three models, the classification and regression tree provided a decision tree (DT) that is easy to understand, interpret and express as decision-making rules. Graham et al. [6] used three algorithms, i.e., logistic regression, decision tree, and gradient boosted machine (GBM), to build the prediction model for patient admissions to two major hospitals' EDs in Northern Ireland. The research identified factors related to hospital admissions including hospital site, patient age, arrival mode, triage, care group, previous admissions in the past months and years. The results show that the GBM algorithm achieved the best prediction capability, but decision tree and logistic regression also performed well. The research suggests that practical implementation of the models can help advance resource planning and the avoidance of bottlenecks in patient flow.

Our early research first proposed a multi-objective stochastic optimization model that minimizes patient LOS and Medical Wasted Costs (MWCs) simultaneously to solve the problems of the medical resource allocation in the ED of Taiwan [7]. That is, a multi-objective simulation optimization algorithm that combine NSGA II with MOCBA algorithms was developed to search the Pareto set of non-dominated medical resource allocation solutions by allocating simulation replications/budgets effectively. Finally, the hybrid method, i.e., NSGA II_MOCBA algorithm, generates more accurate and more suitable allocation solutions for ED decision-makers than the current solution implemented in EDs does. However, this research did not select the proper feature automatically in the first step. Accordingly, we adopt a DT induction method to construct a prediction model with explanatory capability that can identify key features to detect ED overcrowding in the early stage by using explanatory data-mining techniques. We also incorporate the International Classification of Diseases, Ninth Revision, Clinical Modification (i.e. ICD-9-CM) diagnosis codes to construct a behavior-based DT model for understanding the characteristics of the visits and their types of diseases. In this paper, we further adopt and modify the communicability and consistency indicators proposed by Karhade et al. [8] to examine the profiles of the behavior-based DTs. Overall, we sought to evaluate the explanatory power of behavior-based DTs and profiles to generalize patients' visits in the ED.

2 Research Objectives and the Approach

2.1 The Explanatory Data Mining: Behavior-Based Decision Tree Generation

We collect 44,151 of 45,080 valid medical records of patients' visits to the ED from July 1, 2010, to December 31, 2010, from the health information system of Mackay Memorial Hospital in Taipei, Taiwan. Figure 1 shows our explanatory data-mining and analytical process. In this work, we focus on explaining the behavior-based DTs instead of data mining techniques.

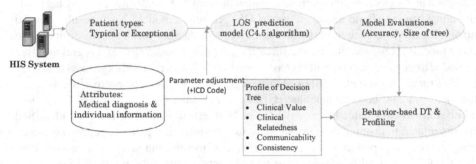

Fig. 1. Explanatory data mining

- We adopt a DT method involving a C4.5 algorithm to analyse patients' behaviors in the ED during visits with various LOSs. We analyse the visits based on patients' individual information and doctors' medical diagnoses, and incorporate ICD-9-CM diagnosis codes to refine the behavior-based DT induction method for the ED. With those strategies, we ultimately sought to know the effect of including diagnostic codes in investigating characteristics of patients' visits to EDs.
- We adopt a DT induction methodology to codify tacit interconnections of attributes and relate important decision-making rules to the outcomes of actions taken based on the decisions made. Ultimately, using the methodology enabled us to open up the so-called black box of decision making. In this paper, we explain the results based on the communicability, consistency and clinical values, as interrelated measures, of each DT profile. Overall, we aim to evaluate the extent of behavior-based DTs and the explanatory power of associated profiles.

We propose a novel way to divide an unbalanced dataset by using rules that are extracted from the Apriori algorithm. There are 11 attributes for the algorithm included types of patients' individual information (IAs) and medical diagnosis (DAs), as shown in Table 1. Then, we use the Apriori Algorithm to partition the dataset into frequent and infrequent ED patient behavior. Then two types of patient behavior (PB) – typical and exceptional patient behavior – are identified based on the support and confidence behavior; others are represented as exceptional behavior. These rules are termed patient behavior rules. Three are 1311 rules and 1001 rules are generated for the first and second half year of 2010 respectively. That is, we can partition the data into two types of ED visits by the rules. We adopt rule-based classification methods to construct the model and extracted the rules for future predictions [9]. Next, we add the ICD-9-CM diagnosis codes to increase the explanatory power of the DT from the perspective of diseases. We adopt C4.5 algorithm as the method for each experiment and tenfold cross-validation to evaluate the accuracy of the results of predictions. The target attribute is LOS, in values of short, medium and long, as shown in Table 2. In short, we predict the patients' LOS based on the input variables. Accordingly, six DTs are constructed with and without the diagnosis codes based on various LOSs.

Table 1. Attributes for generating association rules

Types	Attributes
Individual attributes (IAs)	Arrival Day, Mode of Arrival, Arrival Time, Age
Diagnostic attributes (DAs)	X-Ray, CT, Lab, Pattern, Temperature, Triage, Disposition, ICD codes

Table 2. Average LOS of each cluster of two sets of data in the first half year of 2010 (Unit: hour (hr.))

Sets	Cluster 0 (short)	Cluster 1 (medium)	Cluster 2 (long)
2010-H1	2 h	15 h	49 h
2010-H2	2 h	16 h	52 h

2.2 Measurement of Complexity and Consistency Indicators

The communicability of the DT relates to the complexity of the DT, which is determined the number of decision-making attributes in the DT. The number of decision-related attributes included in the DT serves as a determinant of the complexity of the DT. The greater prevalence of a decision-making rule in the DT denotes that the rule was consistently applied to make more decisions regarding a large number of distinct initiatives. In turn, the frequency with which decision-making rules are applied represents the consistency with which the tacit decision rational is applied for the subset of visits [8]. We use communicability, which includes complexity, and consistency, the two indicators of evaluation criteria, to access the characteristics in each DT.

3   Evaluation Design and Results

3.1   Parameter Testing of the Prediction Model

We have listed the input variables included for all DAs and IAs in Table 1. The target attribute is LOS in values of short, medium and long. We adopt rule-based classification methods to construct the model and extracted the rules for future predictions. For the C4.5 algorithm of the DT, we need to decide the minimum number of instances per node (minNumObj) and the confidence factor (CF) for pruning, which in the C4.5 algorithm is error-based pruning to evaluate errors in decision making at each node of the tree. We set the minNumObj in the DT at 10. The greatest and least CF values in Weka needed to appear as, for example, (0, 0.5), in which a small value corresponds to heavy pruning and a large one to too little pruning.

We used tenfold cross-validation to evaluate the accuracy of the prediction results and extended the concept of confusion table to evaluate the capacity of each method to predict the actual label (i.e. short LOS, medium LOS or long LOS). Our evaluation results show no difference between the accuracy of two DTs with and without the diagnosis codes under various CF settings. Accordingly, we focused on the size of the DT to determine the CF value, as shown in Table 3. Based on the size of the trees, we set CF at 0.35 for DTs with and without the diagnosis codes. Altogether, 73 and 86 nodes emerged between the DTs.

Table 3.   Results of parameter testing

	Parameter		Accuracy			
	CF	Tree size in DT	All	Cluster0 (short)	Cluster1 (medium)	Cluster2 (long)
Without ICD	0.25	5	91.58%	92.25%	92.06%	98.84%
	0.30	5	91.57%	92.23%	92.06%	98.84%
	0.35	86	91.53%	92.16%	92.07%	98.82%
With ICD	0.25	5	91.59%	92.27%	92.07%	98.85%
	0.30	5	91.51%	92.21%	92.02%	98.80%
	0.35	73	91.45%	92.11%	92.00%	98.78%

Note. CF = confidence factor

3.2   Results of Behavior-Based DT Profiles

We have listed the input variables included for all DAs and IAs in the fourth row of Table 4, which also includes the attribute of ICD-9-CM diagnosis codes. The target attribute was LOS in values of short, medium and long. The results of behavior-based DT profiles as shown in Table 4.

Table 4. Profiles of behavior-based decision trees (DT)

DTs	DT without ICD		DT with ICD	
Illustrated DTs	■ =DAs ;□=IAs		■ =DAs ;□=IAs	
Notations in the DT	➤ = The thicker the line, the more decisions that were consistently made with the decision-making rules			
Attributes	DAs: lab, X-ray, temperature, triage IAs: Arrival day, mode of arrival, arrival Time, age		DAs: lab, ICD, temperature, triage IAs: Arrival day, mode of arrival, arrival time, age	
	Repetitive	Non-repetitive	Repetitive	Non-repetitive
% of Diagnostic (DAs)	7 (26.92%)	4 (50%)	6 (40%)	4 (50%)
% of Patient (IAs)	19 (73.08%)	4 (50%)	9 (60%)	4 (50%)
Measure of Complexity	26/10 260%	8/10 80%	15/10 136.36%	8/10 72.73%
Measure of Consistency	Rules with the first and second greatest percentages = {50.96%, 45.26%}		Rules with the first and second greatest percentages = {50.90%, 45.21%}	
Medical Implications	• Patients' behavior can be inferred by numerous attributes with more rules. • Predicting patients' behaviors with DTs could be problematic since behaviors in the ED were inconsistent. • The attending physician concluded that there is a lower clinical value for reference.		• Patients' behavior can be inferred by a few attributes with fewer rules. • Predicting patients' behaviors with DTs could be relatively easy since behaviors in the ED were similar. • The attending physician concluded that there is a higher clinical value for reference.	

Behavior-Based Profile (Attributes): The numbers of non-repetitive DAs and IAs are identical for the two DTs. Regarding attributes within the sets of DAs and IAs, the DT without diagnosis codes include the X-ray attribute, whereas the DT with the codes dose not. After consultation with the attending physician, we learned that X-rays is not an important attribute for explaining the results of patients' behavior for predicting LOSs. In addition, diagnosis codes, patient age, frequency of laboratory testing and patient arrival times are important for analysing the behaviors of patients that cause overcrowding in EDs, as shown in Fig. 2. Thus, the behavior-based DTs with ICD codes can select better features for predicting and explaining the ED visits behaviors.

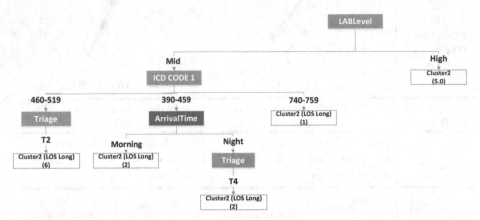

Fig. 2. DT with ICD codes for longest LOS

Behavior-Based Profile (Complexity): The results reveal that adding diagnosis codes reduced the complexity of the DT, which correlated negatively with communicability. In other words, the lower the complexity, the greater the communicability. The complexity of the DT without the codes was 260.0%, whereas that of the DT with the codes was 136.36%.

Behavior-Based Profile (Consistency): Both DTs achieve similar consistency for the rules with the first and second greatest percentages. The top two rules show the frequency of laboratory test is an important attribute to predict patients' LOSs. We do not list the ranking of the third rule because its percentage was less than 1%.

3.3   Results of DTs for Various LOSs

Due to the large size of short and medium LOSs of DTs, we only show the DTs with ICD codes for long LOSs in Fig. 2. However, we list the DTs' profiles for patients with short, medium and long LOSs in Appendix A. Apparently, the more LAB tests patients take, the more LOS they will have. In addition, patients with different LOSs will have different kinds of ICD codes, especially patients with the longest LOSs, as shown in Table 5.

Types of ICD Codes: Table 5 shows that different types and numbers of ICD codes will appear in the DTs with various LOSs. The longest one had ICD codes that appear most for patients with serious diseases, i.e., ICD codes 390–459, 460–519, and 740–759. Appendix B shows the full list of ICD-9-CM codes with categories of diseases. Furthermore, most of the patients who belong to the longest LOSs have diseases of

Table 5. ICD codes for DTs with different LOSs

Short	Medium				Long
140–239	001–139	390–459	780–779	390–459
240–279	140–239	460–519	800–999	460–519
320–359	240–279	520–579	E&V	740–759
460–519	280–289	580–629		
580–629	290–319	630–679		
780–779	320–359	680–709		
E&V	360–389	710–739		

the respiratory system (ICD codes 460–519) and were distributed into triage level 2. Therefore, they stayed in the hospital for a longer time. In addition, some of the ICD codes only appear in the DT with medium LOS. The information can assist in finding other attributes to discover why patients belong to different LOSs.

EDs as a Shortcut for the Public: Most of the patients who belong to the shortest LOSs had neoplasms (ICD codes 140–239) and endocrine, nutritional, and metabolic diseases, as well as immunity disorders (ICD codes 240–279) and were admitted to the hospital on weekends. On the contrary, patients who belong to the medium LOSs with the same ICD codes were admitted to the hospital on weekdays. This may result from their urgent conditions. We can infer that patients who come to the hospital on weekdays require more treatment for the same ICD codes; thus, they have longer LOSs. Moreover, among patients with diseases of the genitourinary system (ICD codes 580–629) with medium LOSs, most were admitted to the ED on weekdays, as shown in Fig. 3(a). However, some patients admitted to the ED on weekends had non-urgent conditions, e.g., did not have a fever, as shown in Fig. 3(b). We would advise that patients with minor signs or illnesses utilize self-diagnostic platforms to confirm the necessity of going to an ED or instead looking for a suitable clinic. In addition, patients can check the ED's patient load using an app offered by the hospital to decide if they should go to the ED immediately or register online before going to the hospital to avoid ED overcrowding.

In sum, profiles of DTs can help clinical staff gain a comprehensive view of patients' behaviors in the ED and make comparisons among profiles. In the longer version of our paper, we will explain the three DTs related to visits with short, medium, and long stays to examine in detail patient behaviors in the ED.

3.4 Clinic Scores of the DTs

We then evaluate the two DTs in terms of CV and CR by consulting with the cooperated attending physicians. The clinical score of 3 indicates that the rule has a high clinical value. The clinical score of 2 means the rule has a general clinical value. However, the clinical score of 1 shows the rule cannot be inferred and it is not valuable. If the rule does not have clinical reference value, the clinical status condition should be checked based on risk factors like smoking, age, heart rate, and so on. The score of 3 means

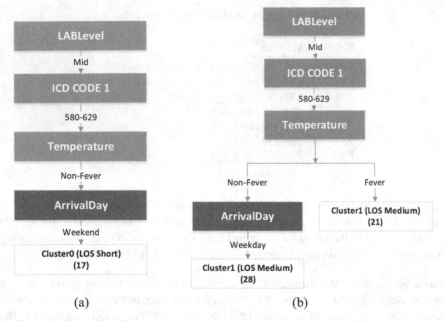

(a)   (b)

Fig. 3. (a). Patients with diseases of the genitourinary system with short LOSs (b). Patients with diseases of the genitourinary system with medium LOSs

inference is the same as clinical inference. The score of 2 shows it closes to clinical inference. However, the score of 1 indicates that the rule cannot be inferred and need more evidence but does not mean the rule is incorrect.

Although results showed that DTs with or without ICD codes achieve similar LOS prediction results in terms of accuracy as shown in Table 3, the attending physician who evaluated Table 6 points out that the clinical value of DTs with ICD codes is better than that of DTs without ICD codes, as shown in Table 6. Apparently, the DTs without ICD codes have low clinical value and normal relatedness, whereas the DTs with ICD codes have high clinical value and relatedness. This is primarily because the DTs with ICD codes included more diagnosis-oriented attributes (e.g., ICD-9-CM codes), which increased the explanatory value of the decision tree. That is, DTs with ICD codes include more relevant and fewer irrelevant attributes. For example, "X-rays" is not an important attribute for explaining the results of patients' behavior exclusive of the DTs with ICD codes

Table 6. Clinical Sores of DTs

	Without ICD Code		With ICD code	
	CV	CR	CV	CR
Short	1	2	3	3
Medium	1	2	3	3
Long	1	2	3	3

4 Conclusion

The chief contribution of our work is the proposed behavior-based DT induction method that considers medical diagnoses and individual patients' information in analysing the characteristics of patients' visits to EDs in terms of their behaviors. The DTs with diagnosis codes were better than the DTs without the codes from the perspective of clinical score, complexity, and explanatory power, although the profile of each DT can offer ED staff an overview of patients' behaviors in EDs. Furthermore, diagnosis codes, patient age, frequency of laboratory testing, and patient arrival times are important for analyzing the behaviors of patients that cause overcrowding in EDs. Although the ICD code attribute can increase the explanatory power of the DT, the number of instances of each rule is not significant. Accordingly, we may focus on specific diseases to increase the robustness of the model in a future study. Altogether, our results can serve as a reference for ED personnel to understand overcrowding in terms of LOSs and ICD diagnosis codes as part of efforts to provide higher-quality care in the ED.

Acknowledgments. This research was supported by the Ministry of Science and Technology of Taiwan under Grant MOST 108-2410-H-003-132-MY2.

Appendix A: Various DTs' Profiles Based on Decision Tree Analysis Results

See Table A.1

Table A.1. DT profiles for patients' with short, medium, and long LOSs

Experimental Group	Cluster0 (Short LOS)		Cluster1 (Medium LOS)		Cluster2 (Long LOS)	
Repetitive attribute	Repetitive	Non-repetitive	Repetitive	Non-repetitive	Repetitive	Non-repetitive
Diagnostic attribute	5	4	6	4	4	3
Individual attribute	8	4	9	4	1	1
Communicability	Inversely related to complexity of the DT: One key measure of complexity of a DT is the number of decision attributes included in the DT.					
Complexity of DT	13	8	15	8	5	4
Measure of Complexity	{The number of decision attribute, The maximum number of decision rule attributes in the leaf, Total number of leaves}					
	{13, 6, 18}	{8, 6, 18}	{15, 6, 35}	{8, 6, 35}	{5, 4, 5}	{4, 4, 5}
% of decision attributes	{The number of decision attributes/The number of input attributes}					
	118.18% (13/11)	72.73% (8/11)	136.36% (15/11)	72.73% (8/11)	45.45% (5/11)	36.36% (4/11)

(continued)

Table A.1. (*continued*)

Experimental Group		Cluster0 (Short LOS)		Cluster1 (Medium LOS)		Cluster2 (Long LOS)	
% of decision attributes		(Diagnostic attribute or Patient attribute)/The number of decision attributes					
	IA	38.46% (5/13)	50% (4/8)	40% (6/15)	50% (4/8)	80% (4/5)	75% (3/4)
	PA	61.54% (8.13)	50% (4/8)	60% (9/15)	50% (4/8)	20% (1/5)	25% (1/4)
Consistency		Number of decision made consistently using the same decision rule: Thicker					
{Single rule/Total rules}		5.56% (1/18)		2.86% (1/35)		20% (1/5)	

Appendix B: List of ICD-9-CM Codes

See Table B.1

Table B.1. ICD-9 codes with name of the associated disease

ICD codes	Diseases
ICD-9 codes 001–139	Infectious and parasitic diseases
ICD-9 codes 140–239	Neoplasms
ICD-9 codes 240–279	Endocrine, nutritional and metabolic diseases, and immunity disorders
ICD-9 codes 280–289	Diseases of the blood and blood-forming organs
ICD-9 codes 290–319	Mental disorders
ICD-9 codes 320–389	Diseases of the nervous system and sense organs
ICD-9 codes 390–459	Diseases of the circulatory system
ICD-9 codes 460–519	Diseases of the respiratory system
ICD-9 codes 520–579	Diseases of the digestive system
ICD-9 codes 580–629	Diseases of the genitourinary system
ICD-9 codes 630–679	Complications of pregnancy, childbirth, and the puerperium
ICD-9 codes 680–709	Diseases of the skin and subcutaneous tissue
ICD-9 codes 710–739	Diseases of the musculoskeletal system and connective tissue
ICD-9 codes 740–759	Congenital anomalies
ICD-9 codes 760–779	Certain conditions originating in the perinatal period
ICD-9 codes 780–799	Symptoms, signs, and ill-defined conditions
ICD-9 codes 800–999	Injury and poisoning
ICD-9 codes E and V codes	External causes of injury and supplemental classification

Source: https://en.wikipedia.org/wiki/List_of_ICD-9_codes

References

1. Uscher-Pines, L., Pines, J., Kellermann, A., Gillen, E., Mehrotra, A.: Deciding to visit the emergency department for non-urgent conditions: a systematic review of the literature. Am. J. Managed Care **19**(1), 47–59 (2013)
2. Young, G.P., Wagner, M.B., Kellermann, A.L., Ellis, J., Bouley, D.: Ambulatory visits to hospital emergency departments: patterns and reasons for use. JAMA **276**(6), 460–465 (1996)
3. Niska, R., Bhuiya, F., Xu, J.: National hospital ambulatory medical care survey: 2007 emergency department summary. Natl. Health Stat. Report **26**, 1–31 (2010)
4. Milovic, B., Milovic, M.: Prediction and decision making in health care using data mining. Kuwait Chapter Arab. J. Bus. Manage. Rev. **1**(12), 126 (2012)
5. Pendharkar, P.C., Khurana, H.: Machine learning techniques for predicting hospital length of stay in Pennsylvania federal and specialty hospitals. Int. J. Comput. Sci. Appl. **11**(3), 45–56 (2014)
6. Graham, B., Bond, R., Quinn, M., Mulvenna, M.: Using data mining to predict hospital admissions from the emergency department. IEEE Access **6**, 10458–10469 (2018)
7. Feng, Y.Y., Wu, I.C., Chen, T.L.: Stochastic resource allocation in emergency departments with a multi-objective simulation optimization algorithm. Health Care Manage. Sci. **20**(1), 55–75 (2017). https://doi.org/10.1007/s10729-015-9335-1
8. Karhade, P.P., Shaw, M.J., Subramanyam, R.: Patterns in information systems portfolio prioritization: evidence from decision tree induction. MIS Q. **39**(2), 413–433 (2015)
9. Feng, Y.-Y., Wu, I.-C., Chen, T.-L., Chang, W.-H.: A hybrid data mining approach for generalizing characteristics of emergency department visits causing overcrowding. J. Libr. Inf. Stud. **17**(1), 1–35 (2019). https://doi.org/10.6182/jlis.201906_17(1).001

Massive Semantic Video Annotation in High-End Customer Service
Example in Airline Service Value Assessment

Ken Fukuda(✉) ⃝iD, Julio Vizcarra, and Satoshi Nishimura⃝iD

National Institute of Advanced Industrial Science and Technology (AIST),
Tokyo 1350064, Japan
ken.fukuda@aist.go.jp

Abstract. In high-end hospitality industries such as airline lounges, high star hotels, and high-class restaurants, employee service skills play an important role as an element of the brand identity. However, it is very difficult to train an intermediate employee into an expert employee who can provide higher value services which exceed customers' expectations. To hire and develop employees who embody the value of the brand, it is necessary to clearly communicate the value of the brand to their employees. In the video analysis domain, especially analyzing human behaviors, an important task is the understanding and representation of human activities such as conversation, physical actions and their connections on the time. This paper addresses the problem of massively annotating video contents such as multimedia training materials, which then can be processed by human-interaction training support systems (such as VR training systems) as resources for content generation. In this paper, we propose a POC (proof of concept) system of a service skill assessing platform, which is a knowledge graph (KG) of high-end service provision videos massively annotated with human interaction semantics.

Keywords: Video annotation · Knowledge graph · Behavior analysis · Video retrieval · Training support system · Service excellence

1 Introduction

In high-end hospitality industries such as airline lounges, high star hotels, and high-class restaurants, employee service skills play an important role as an element of the brand identity. However, it is very difficult to train an intermediate employee who can provide the basic core value proposition specified in the manual into an expert employee who can provide higher value services which exceed customers' expectations (Service excellence "Level 4 Surprising Service" [3]). To hire and develop people who embody the value of the brand, it is necessary to clearly communicate the value of the brand to employees. Companies are using scenario-based role-play and other customer service contests for training. However, the skills evaluated in role-play are conventionally accessible only by playing and viewing the movie selected from a huge video archive. Also, the skills evaluated depend on the context, and it is not easy to convey the evaluated points clearly

F. F.-H. Nah and K. Siau (Eds.): HCII 2020, LNCS 12204, pp. 46–58, 2020.
https://doi.org/10.1007/978-3-030-50341-3_4

to the trainees. This is a major problem for global companies when educating human resources at overseas branches and when providing education to its alliance companies where cultural background is not shared.

Recently, the video annotations have gained popularity in the area of video analysis, among the academic community as well industry for commercial applications that handles computer's vision systems [15]. An increasing interest for understanding the actions that occur in the video clips for a wide number of applications have motivated the research in this area [18].

In the video analysis, specially analyzing human behaviors, an important task is the understanding and representation of human activities such as conversation, physical actions (pose, angle vision, spatial position in the scene, etc.). The discovery of skills, behaviors patterns or training learning base models might be computed easier by analyzing formal representations of human actions as knowledge graphs. Usually the video annotations are written manually which is a time-consuming task and requires special attention in fine details within small periods of time (scenes per second).

In this paper, we propose a POC (proof of concept) system of a service skill assessing platform, which is a knowledge graph (KG) [16] of high-end service provision videos massively annotated with human interaction semantics. The approach takes into account the conversation, physical actions, activities and skills presented in the scene. The main objective is to represent large amount of human information from a high number of video frames for further analysis and reasoning. The process of knowledge graph exploitation can be computed by ontology inferences, graph theory algorithms or machine learning (ML) techniques.

2 Related Work

Recently, a significant number of approaches addressed the problem of human activity recognition and its representation through several annotation techniques have been proposed. However, most of researches implemented machine learning (ML) techniques that in general require a large number of tagged data for their training. Acquiring large amount of labeled data has been an obstacle which these models depend their efficiency. Respect to automatic annotation on videos the work of Duchenne et al. [6] used movie scripts as a training data set but it was limited to annotated content using solely the video's conversation. The work associated the text to the script discovering the action on the scene. One important issue was the lack of a proper video analysis of physical actions. Moreover, Kaiqiang Huang et al. [8] developed an empirical study of annotation models using machine learning and transfer model. This research presented an alternative that avoided the manual annotations in the training dataset. The works presented good performance for general and common actions. For specific cases of study many gaps could not been address though. Similarly, Fuhl et al. [7] proposed a transfer learning model for video annotation with the advantage of including a self training method that addressed the limitation of labeled image data. The algorithm achieved accurate point annotation focused mostly in eye gestures.

Regarding action recognition, the work of Das Srijan et al. [5] proposed a hybrid model with handcrafted approach (video's frame descriptors) and machine learning.

They focused primarily in action recognition instead of only objects identification, i.e., motion, pose and subject performing. The work included similar actions discrimination but the spatial-temporal processing was suggested to be explored. Additionally, Yang Xiao et al. [17] proposed a CNN model for human-human and human-object interaction on dynamic image in depth videos. Whereas the works included spatial-temporal action handling. The researched mentioned the necessity of relaxing the strong requirement on training sample size.

Tackling the task of video summarization, the work of Zhang Ke et al. [19] implemented video long short-term memory for selecting automatically key frames. They introduced a technique that addressed the necessity of large amount of training data by reusing auxiliary annotated video summarization data sets.

Processing video annotation using natural language processing (NLP) and linguistic characteristics, the work of Hendricks Lisa et al. [1] localized moments (temporal segments) in the videos from natural language text descriptors. The work included temporal processing. The work integrates local and global features. The scope of the work was limited to the text descriptions.

Creation annotations as input to machine learning models, the method of Jingkuan Song et al. [13] proposed a semi-supervised annotation approach for graph-based learning algorithms using partial tags (tagged and not tagged data). The work aimed to construct graphs that embed the relationships among data points in order to create image and video annotation. These annotations define concepts in the scene.

2.1 Discussion of the Related Work

Although many significant improvements have been achieved recently in video annotations and presentation, most of the research projects were focused on machine learning techniques for human action annotation missing temporal processing, representation in the semantic level and the interactions among physical behaviors and events. Nevertheless, the main disadvantage of these proposals is that they need an immense amount of tagged data for training to obtain a robust and reliable result. Moreover, many works were limited to annotated videos for specific purposes not considering external events, conversations and their connection to physical actions. In contrast, we processed and represented the video's content for a wider range of characteristics described in a knowledge base (physical actions, skills and events). The novelty of the presented work is the conceptual-semantic representation of the human actions and skills, events occurred in the scene and their relation with other users or objects on the time. One advantage is that our approach does not need large training data set. The relation between annotations to physical behavior is straightforward captured and described through a knowledge bases and used to created video graphs.

Comparing our contribution with the related work, we processed the physical actions, comments and annotations such as skills and actions separately in the end connected as a final graph. The methodology generated relations among all the video's components for a final representation as excerpt of knowledge. We took into account the spatial-temporal processing into the knowledge graphs.

3 Methodology

The system consists from DNN detectors and a set of service process annotation ontologies and a KG converter. The input video is splitted into image frames by the DNN detector and annotated with bounding boxes, 3D person poses information, face orientation axes, body orientation axes, and then annotated with the ontologies for what human interaction is occurring in the frame. The combined information is converted into a KG to store in a triple store for computation.

The generation of Knowledge Graph is composed from three stages. First, the video is processed in order to construct automatically its conceptual representation as knowledge graph that captures the video's content, actions, conversations and user's behavior of each scene. Secondly, once the knowledge graphs were created the staff's behavior is measured and his/her customer service performance is calculated by consulting the knowledge graph. This step scores users and creates their profile. Finally, the performance of the staff members can be visualized and profiled via a skill assessing platform (Fig. 1).

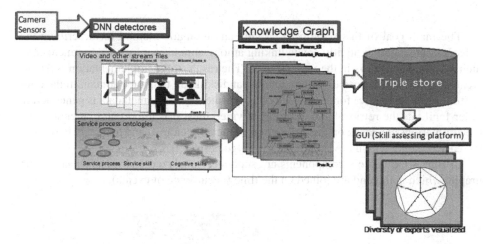

Fig. 1. System overview.

3.1 Knowledge Graph Construction

In order to generate the knowledge graph, the system processes two different sources: 1) the human skills and actions manually annotated on video files using the software ELAN [2]. For the skills and actions annotation, an ontology for skills and services in the domain of airline industry was developed [10]. 2) The physical behavior presented in the video is analyzed by machine learning techniques using Python [11] packages such as YOLO [4] and 3DMPPE multi-person 3D pose estimation [9]. After obtaining the video's content from the previous sources the representation as knowledge graph is computed by graph theory algorithms (expansion and edges creation). As complementary, process their metadata information is also generated. For each frame a representation (knowledge graph) is created. In the end, all the sub graphs are interconnected on time lapses and stored in a graph database that provide efficient mechanism of the inclusion and extraction (see Fig. 2).

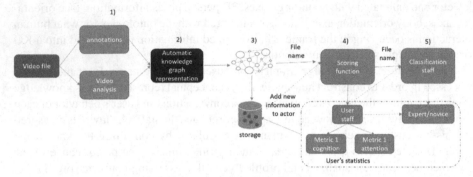

Fig. 2. General methodology.

The main goal of this stage is to provide an automatic method for describing the video's content and explicitly create linking among annotations, actor's comments and their physical behaviors in the video frames. The result of the implementation (system) creates graphs that describe frames, actions, and skills on temporal domain in the conceptual level (semantic) for each video clips. Furthermore, the metadata is generated in order facilitate the retrieval and indexing of video files. It is important to mention that the annotations are based on the description of the all scenarios and human behaviors in the case of study which are stored as knowledge base (KB).

In Fig. 3 the video's components are separately analyzed and transformed as sub graphs which in the end are joined on the time (occurrence of events).

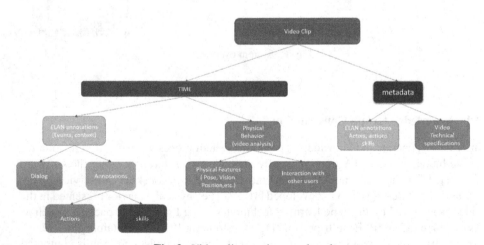

Fig. 3. Video clips sections analyzed.

Regarding the processing of human dialog, the comments are represented as graphs by means of lexical dependencies produced by natural language processing (NLP). Each concept that composes the comment can provide information such of context, domain or type of entity.

The general diagram that contains all the elements described in the knowledge graph are presented at the Fig. 4. The elements are grouped as: 1) video file's general information obtained from ELAN annotation, 2) the conversations transformed to graph also generates a corpus, 3) the catalogue of actions and skills that occur in the video and 4) the video analysis of human physical activity.

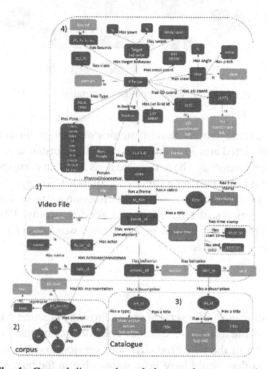

Fig. 4. General diagram knowledge graph representation.

After conducting the automatic knowledge graph creation, the methodology is able to create metadata as a graph as well. Figure 5 represents the elements considered (video's technical information, scene's content and summary) auto-generated for the moment only from 1) ELAN files.

3.2   Analysis on the Knowledge Graphs

After processing the 1) video's sources and generating their 2) formal representations, the next step is to 3) inspect the knowledge graphs stored by SPARQL queries [12]. In order to accomplish this task, the staffs' skills, conversation and actions are analyzed using metrics that measure the level of expertise.

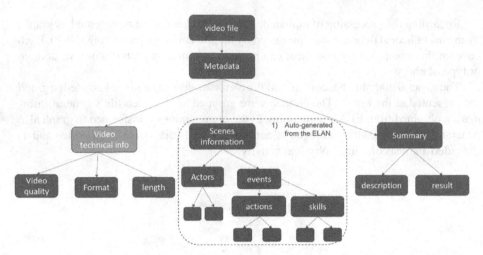

Fig. 5. Video metadata generated.

In order to assign a score to users, several metrics were taken into account. In our case study the metrics considered are: 1) in the conversation for instance; if the staff member mentions the customer's name. 2) The action and activities that correspond to the correct service (understanding in requesting a flight cancellation). 3) Physical behaviors such as bowing (Japanese polite manners) and talk in direction to the customer.

As result of this process, the excellence of service deployed by the employees (namely, company representatives) can be explicitly assessed and profiled to support training the skills that are required.

4 Example

By massively annotating customer service video clips and creating a knowledge graph, it is now not only possible to retrieve specific "episodes" of human interaction but also to calculate the content of the delivered customer service, and it has become possible to evaluate the context that would have been impossible in the past when a human had to perform a very time-consuming task of repeatedly and finely replaying the video to check the content. In this section an example of the massive semantic video annotation is presented.

4.1 Experiment

Four grand staffs of an air-line company (two experts and two intermediates) were asked to go through the same training scenario in the company's training facility and were video recorded. The scenario was as follows: a customer arrived late to the check-in counter and the boarding time had already passed. The grand staff had to tell the customer that he/she cannot board the booked flight and had to offer alternative options, which are all not ideal for the customer (i.e. have to pay extra money to be on time at the destination or be late for 2 or 3 h). The challenge was a kind of "service recovery" [14] process, i.e., how to manage the customers anger, deliver memorable experience and gain customer loyalty at the same time.

4.2 Observations

The following three features differentiated expert and intermediate ground staffs. All four grand staffs suggested the same 4 alternatives (however, the order of the offerings and the order of presenting accompanying information were different).

1) The experts not only listen to the customer's requests, but also recites back to the customer, while the intermediate recites less. One expert (Exp_1) recited four requests of the customer and the other expert (Exp_2) recited eight times, while one intermediate staff (Int_1) repeated zero times and the other (Int_2) recited only one time during a five minutes discourse.
2) Experts always provide follow-up information when they had to present information unfavorable to the customer. Exp_1 provided optional information to help the customer's decision immediately after the negative information. The ratio for Exp_1 was 100% and Exp_2 provided 60%. On the contrary, intermediates tended to wait for the customers response to the negative offering without any follow-up. The ratio of no follow-up for Int_1 was 63% and for Int_2, it was 67%. As a result, the customer understandably felt uncomfortable with unfavorable information.
3) All experts leaned a little forward toward customers, while intermediates generally leaned away from customers or stood straight.

4.3 Querying the Knowledge Graph

1) Calling the customer's name:
   The following query (Fig. 6) show the difference in how often an expert and intermediate call the customer's name. staff01from the video file E1S4a191115called 6 times 梅村(Umemura) while the rest of the staff members that call once or zero times.
2) Empathy by humble words:
   Similarly, the number of times that the expert staff says humble words was higher compared to the novice (Fig. 7). The cases considered were: "申しわけございません。, 申しわけない, 申し訳ありません, 申し訳ございません(I'm sorry)", " 大変申しわけございません(I'm terribly sorry)" and "申します(I will tell you)".
3) Confirm read-back (times):
   In this example the query counts the number of times that a staff read-back the customer's request in the dialogue (Fig. 8).

5 Knowledge Graph Exploitation

In this section a set of users (airline staff members) were profiled after analyzing and representing their behavior on several video clips. The staffs' statistics are displayed via

Fig. 6. Calling the customer's name.

Fig. 7. Empathy by humble words.

a web system (skill assessment platform). This tool has the goal of capturing the staffs' expertise in customer service from multiple measures.

The underlining assumption is that service excellence is an art orchestrated from multiple skills and the same level of excellence is conducted by different sets of skills by different experts. Thus, if a training support system can profile the combination of skills deployed by each expert, then the system aids the human resource department to provide

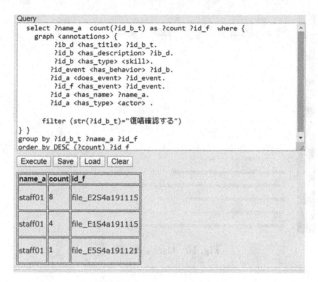

```
Query
   select ?name_a  count(?id_b_t) as ?count ?id_f  where {
      graph <annotations> {
            ?ib_d <has_title> ?id_b_t.
            ?id_b <has_description> ?ib_d.
            ?id_b <has_type> <skill>.
            ?id_event <has_behavior> ?id_b.
            ?id_a <does_event> ?id_event.
            ?id_f <has_event> ?id_event.
            ?id_a <has_name> ?name_a.
            ?id_a <has_type> <actor> .

         filter (str(?id_b_t)="復唱確認する")
} }
group by ?id_b_t ?name_a ?id_f
order by DESC (?count) ?id_f
```

Execute Save Load Clear

name_a	count	id_f
staff01	8	file_E2S4a191115
staff01	4	file_E1S4a191115
staff01	1	file_E5S4a191121

Fig. 8. Confirm read-back.

an evidence based, and more precise and effective training calcium to the intermediates of different personalities.

5.1 Web System for User Analysis

The visualization system displays staff members' information regarding to their customer service. Based on this analysis the company might create strategies in order to improve interaction between customer and company's representatives. The Fig. 9 presents the dashboard that summarizes the number of users as "expert" or "intermediate".

Fig. 9. Dashboard for statistics (type and number of users)

In addition, the Fig. 10 displays charts of the user's profile pointing the main metrics (skills and actions) performed in the video clip.

Fig. 10. User's profile

Fig. 12. Table metadata

Complementing the previous charts, Fig. 11 and Fig. 12 list the staffs and the metadata respectively produced after processing the video clip.

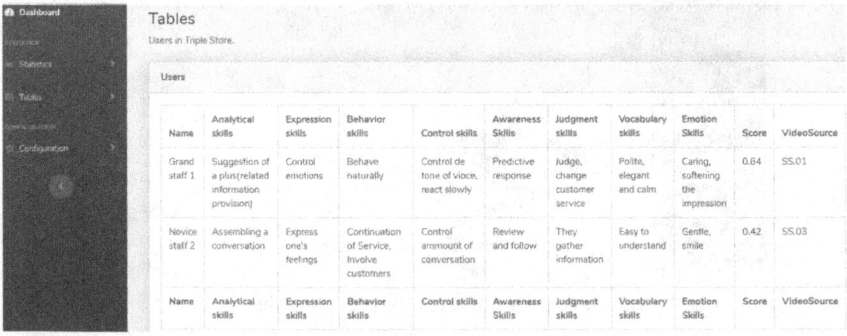

Name	Analytical skills	Expression skills	Behavior skills	Control skills	Awareness Skills	Judgment skills	Vocabulary skills	Emotion Skills	Score	VideoSource
Grand staff 1	Suggestion of a plus(related information provision)	Control emotions	Behave naturally	Control de tone of vioce, react slowly	Predictive response	Judge, change customer service	Polite, elegant and calm	Caring, softening the impression	0.64	SS.01
Novice staff 2	Assembling a conversation	Express one's feelings	Continuation of Service, Involve customers	Control ammount of conversation	Review and follow	They gather information	Easy to understand	Gentle, smile	0.42	SS.03
Name	Analytical skills	Expression skills	Behavior skills	Control skills	Awareness Skills	Judgment skills	Vocabulary skills	Emotion Skills	Score	VideoSource

Fig. 11. Table users

6 Conclusions

In this paper, we proposed a methodology that aims automatic representation of human behaviors presented in video clips via knowledge graphs. Our approach combined video analysis (physical actions), descriptions (annotations) such as actions, skills and events and conversation analysis. The goal was to create knowledge graphs based on the video's content. The graph created can be analyzed by several methods such as machine learning, graph-based reasoning, etc. As an introductory method of exploitation, the graphs were retrieved and analyzed by SPARQL queries.

The methodology can be applied to any kind of scenarios presented in the video and different languages. And for our case of study, the video analysis (human behavior and interactions) was focused in airline's customer service (interaction between staff members and customers) and the language processed was Japanese.

The results obtained after implementing the methodology were: the 1) fast and automatic representation of human behaviors as well the explicit description of interactions among events, users, actions and conversation in video scenes. 2) The optimization in representing a massive number of graphs that describe the entire video clip (one graph for each scene).

An additional knowledge graph exploitation tool was proposed for analyzing staff members in the area of customer service and in consequence classify them as experts or intermediates.

Our long-term goal is to make the values derived from human interaction computable. To this end, we developed a POC system that assesses the value of airline ground operation experts. Experiencing the service provided by the experts ("value in use") is a medium to convey the value of the company and representing the context as a knowledge graph enables the computation of those values. The annotation procedure includes manual annotations, but the platform helps to identify new challenges for DNN detection and is designed to incorporate new achievement in DNN as modules.

Future efforts can be focused on optimization the graph's storage with techniques such as graph embedding.

Acknowledgments. Part of this work was supported by Council for Science, Technology and Innovation, "Cross-ministerial Strategic Innovation Promotion Program (SIP), Big-data and AI-enabled Cyberspace Technologies" (funding agency: NEDO).

References

1. Anne Hendricks, L., et al.: Localizing moments in video with natural language. In: Proceedings of the IEEE International Conference on Computer Vision, pp. 5803–5812 (2017)
2. Brugman, H., Russel, A., Nijmegen, X.: Annotating multi-media/multi-modal resources with ELAN. In: LREC (2004)
3. CEN/TS 16880:2015 Service Excellence
4. Chandan, G., Jain, A., Jain, H., et al.: Real time object detection and tracking using deep learning and OpenCV. In: 2018 International Conference on Inventive Research in Computing Applications (ICIRCA), pp. 1305–1308. IEEE (2018)

5. Das, S., et al.: A new hybrid architecture for human activity recognition from RGB-D videos. In: Kompatsiaris, I., Huet, B., Mezaris, V., Gurrin, C., Cheng, W.-H., Vrochidis, S. (eds.) MMM 2019. LNCS, vol. 11296, pp. 493–505. Springer, Cham (2019). https://doi.org/10.1007/978-3-030-05716-9_40

6. Duchenne, O., Laptev, I., Sivic, J., Bach, F., Ponce, J.: Automatic annotation of human actions in video. In: 2009 IEEE 12th International Conference on Computer Vision, pp. 1491–1498. IEEE (2009)

7. Fuhl, W., et al.: MAM: transfer learning for fully automatic video annotation and specialized detector creation. In: Leal-Taixé, L., Roth, S. (eds.) ECCV 2018. LNCS, vol. 11133, pp. 375–388. Springer, Cham (2019). https://doi.org/10.1007/978-3-030-11021-5_23

8. Huang, K., Delany, S.J., McKeever, S.: Human action recognition in videos using transfer learning. In: IMVIP 2019: Irish Machine Vision & Image Processing, Technological University Dublin, Dublin, Ireland, 28–30 August 2019. https://doi.org/10.21427/mfrv-ah30

9. Moon, G., Chang, J.Y., Lee, K.M.: Camera distance-aware top-down approach for 3D multi-person pose estimation from a single RGB image. In: Proceedings of the IEEE International Conference on Computer Vision, pp. 10133–10142 (2019)

10. Nishimura, S., Oota, Y., Fukuda, K.: Ontology construction for annotating skill and situation of airline services to multi-modal data. In: Proceedings of International Conference on Human-Computer Interaction (2020, in press)

11. Oliphant, T.E.: Python for scientific computing. Comput. Sci. Eng. 9(3), 10–20 (2007)

12. Quilitz, B., Leser, U.: Querying distributed RDF data sources with SPARQL. In: Bechhofer, S., Hauswirth, M., Hoffmann, J., Koubarakis, M. (eds.) ESWC 2008. LNCS, vol. 5021, pp. 524–538. Springer, Heidelberg (2008). https://doi.org/10.1007/978-3-540-68234-9_39

13. Song, J., et al.: Optimized graph learning using partial tags and multiple features for image and video annotation. IEEE Trans. Image Process. 25(11), 4999–5011 (2016)

14. Stuart, F.I., Tax, S.: Toward an integrative approach to designing service experiences lessons learned from the theatre. J. Oper. Manage. 22, 609–627 (2004)

15. Thomas, A.O., Antonenko, P.D., Davis, R.: Understanding metacomprehension accuracy within video annotation systems. Comput. Hum. Behav. 58, 269–277 (2016)

16. Villazon-Terrazas, B., et al.: Knowledge graph foundations. Exploiting Linked Data and Knowledge Graphs in Large Organisations, pp. 17–55. Springer, Cham (2017). https://doi.org/10.1007/978-3-319-45654-6_2

17. Xiao, Y., Chen, J., Wang, Y., Cao, Z., Zhou, J.T., Bai, X.: Action recognition for depth video using multi-view dynamic images. Inf. Sci. 480, 287–304 (2019)

18. Xu, Y., Dong, J., Zhang, B., Xu, D.: Background modeling methods in video analysis: a review and comparative evaluation. CAAI Trans. Intell. Technol. 1(1), 43–60 (2016)

19. Zhang, K., Chao, W.-L., Sha, F., Grauman, K.: Video summarization with long short-term memory. In: Leibe, B., Matas, J., Sebe, N., Welling, M. (eds.) ECCV 2016. LNCS, vol. 9911, pp. 766–782. Springer, Cham (2016). https://doi.org/10.1007/978-3-319-46478-7_47

Exploring Students' Search Behavior and the Effect of Epistemological Beliefs on Contradictory Issues

Yuan-Ho Huang[✉] [iD]

Department of Library and Information Science, Fu Jen Catholic University, New Taipei, Taiwan
yuanho@lins.fju.edu.tw

Abstract. The internet is awash with misinformation and disinformation. It is challenging to educate students in critical thinking and proper searching strategies. This study explored the relationship among epistemological beliefs, cognitive style, media multitasking, and information searching behaviors when students encounter contradictory scientific information. Pre-experimental design, interviews, questionnaires, observation, and search log analysis were adopted in this study. A total of 94 students were recruited to participant this study. The result has shown that science and technology (S&T) students did hold higher scientific literacy; however, there was no significant difference between S&T and non-S&T students regarding epistemological beliefs, cognitive style, and media multitasking. Nonetheless, this study found that there is significant relationship between media multitasking and cognitive style and between media multitasking and web navigation style. All students' epistemological beliefs changed significantly from their pretest to posttest, indicating that students possess higher-order knowledge and thinking disposition.

Keywords: Epistemological beliefs · Cognitive style · Search strategies · Media multitasking

1 Introduction

Plenty of misinformation and disinformation are on the web. People might be unaware of paradoxical information. It is important to equip students with knowledge that can improve their critical literacy skills for the digital age [1]. In addition to the subject expertise knowledge, what key factors influence the evaluation of information?

Previous research has shown that people with more sophisticated epistemological beliefs are more likely to consider multiple aspects comprehensively [2]. Another research study indicated that students with changeable epistemological beliefs could affect information search technique and be able to deal with complex issues [3, 4]. The relationship between information search behavior and cognitive style has been investigated to some degrees of correlation [5]. People often apply several kinds of media at the same time, and previous research on media multitasking has shown that it has an impact on the process of information filtering [6].

© Springer Nature Switzerland AG 2020
F. F.-H. Nah and K. Siau (Eds.): HCII 2020, LNCS 12204, pp. 59–68, 2020.
https://doi.org/10.1007/978-3-030-50341-3_5

Thus, we proposed the following research questions. First, are there any differences between science and engineering (S&T), social science, and liberal arts students regarding media multitasking, epistemological beliefs, cognitive style, information search strategies and behaviors? Second, are there any differences in search behaviors between S&T, social science, and liberal arts students when they deal with conflicting scientific information? Third, what are the relationships between undergraduates' media multitasking, epistemological beliefs, cognitive style, and their information searching behaviors? Fourth, will undergraduate students change their minds after searching on the web to investigate conflicting scientific information and present higher-order knowledge and thinking disposition?

2 Literature Review

2.1 Epistemological Beliefs and Critical Thinking

Epistemological beliefs are the beliefs about the nature of knowledge and knowing. Previous research has explored students' thinking and beliefs about how knowledge is constructed and evaluated from different perspectives [7]. Schommer [8] investigated students' beliefs about knowledge and how these beliefs affect comprehension, and proposed a scale to measure the degrees of beliefs in innate ability, simple knowledge, quick learning and certain knowledge. Her subsequent studies have shown that the less students believe in simple knowledge (to seek single answers and avoid integration), the more precise their assessment of comprehension [9, 10]. Moreover, Schommer-Aikins and Hutter [2] indicated that individuals who hold sophisticated epistemological beliefs are willing to modify their thinking with multiple perspectives and recognize the complex nature of everyday issues.

2.2 Epistemological Beliefs, Information Search and Credibility Evaluation

There is a relationship between epistemological beliefs and information search. Whitmore [3] found that epistemological beliefs affect not only search technique, the evaluation of information, and the ability to recognize authority, but they also affect information search process (ISP) which includes topic selection, focus formulation, and collection. Her subsequent research also indicated that undergraduates with transitional epistemological beliefs exhibited the capability to handle conflicting information sources and acknowledge authoritative information sources [4].

Kienhues, Stadtler, and Bromme [11] explored German university students' different levels of epistemic beliefs and decision making when they deal with conflicting versus consistent medical information. The study was conducted using experimental design, composed of two intervention groups that conducted web searching in conflicting versus consistent information and one control group that did not perform a web search. The results have shown that the epistemic beliefs of the intervention group were more advanced after the web search. The intervention group that encountered conflicting information had less certainty in the ability of experts and made a specific decision after the web search.

Most people rely on search engines to search information on the web; therefore, the search engine results affect the users' choice of information. It is also challenging if the users have little prior knowledge about science when they search conflicting scientific information. Novin and Meyers [12] explored the types of bias from the search engine results page (SERP) and identified four cognitive biases: priming, anchoring, framing, and the availability heuristic. The priming effect occurs at the initial stage of searching. Users usually catch the image before reading information. Anchoring is when students access information in a top-down manner and trust the top result in a hierarchical list, leading students to ignore various perspectives or conflicting information. Framing is when people usually try to minimize cognitive work and narrow the multiple perspectives. Availability heuristic is a cognitive bias about the usefulness and ease of use, it is challenging for non-experts to decide the right information when confronting popular but questionable information.

2.3 Media Use, Cognitive Style and Information Search Behavior

It is common that people concurrently use multiple media at the same time, such as reading a newspaper while listening to music or watching TV while using the Internet. Ophir, Nass, and Wagner [6] proposed a Media Multitasking Index (MMI) to measure the level of media multitasking and explored the difference in information processing styles between heavy and light media multitaskers. The result showed that heavy media multitaskers are more sensitive to bring obstructed with irrelevant information, and they have less capability for the transition to another task due to lack of the ability to screen the unrelated information.

Kinley, Tjondronegoro, Partridge, and Edward [5] investigated the relationship between cognitive style and search behavior. They found four key aspects of web search behavior: information searching strategies, query reformulation behavior, web navigation styles, and information processing approaches. The cognitive styles were classified as wholist (wholes), analytic (parts), verbaliser (words) and imager (pictures) according to Riding's CSA test [13]. Information searching strategies were classified as top-down, bottom-up, and mixed ways. The result indicated that users with verbaliser and wholist cognitive styles adopt the top-down approach for search strategies while users with analytic and imager cognitive styles choose the bottom-up approach. Web navigation styles were categorized into sporadic and structured; the former refers to an unstructured navigation, while the latter is using a systematic approach during web searching. Users with verbaliser cognitive style adopt the sporadic navigation style while users with analytic, wholist, and imager cognitive styles adopt the structured navigation style. Information-processing approaches were categorized into scanning, reading, and mixed approaches. Users with verbaliser and analytic cognitive styles adopt scanning approaches, while users with wholist and imager cognitive styles adopt reading approaches.

3 Methodology

Pre-experimental design, interviews, questionnaires, observation, and search log analysis were adopted in this study.

3.1 Sample, Search Task and Research Design

The message of calling for participants were announced via the social media of Fu Jen Catholic University campus. We provided registration system for students and the goal is to recruit 30 students respectively from three major disciplines, science and engineering (S&T), social science, and literal arts. In the end, from S&T, social science, and liberal arts, the author recruited 27, 38, and 29 students, respectively.

The author discussed with a professor in physics to design one search task with two contradictory opinions on climate change. We provided six reasons for two sides of information: "climate change is caused by nature" versus "climate change is caused by human", and asked questions about whether there is consensus regarding climate change and their personal position to the reason caused by nature or human. Participants were assigned the search task and were asked to complete various questionnaires at different stages—pre-search, during the search, and after the search task. They were asked to complete the search task (read the one page information, and freely search on the web), write short answers and think aloud within 30 min. PowerCam software was employed to video record student search behavior.

3.2 Measures

Six types of scales were adopted to examine media multitasking behavior, scientific literacy, epistemological beliefs, and cognitive style. Those scales measured media multitasking index [6], scientific literacy [14], epistemological beliefs [8], and cognitive style [15]. Furthermore, the topic-specific epistemic beliefs proposed by Kienhues, Stadtler, and Bromme [11] were applied to conduct the posttest of epistemological beliefs.

$$\text{MMI} = \sum_{i=1}^{10} \frac{m_i \times h_i}{h_{total}} \tag{1}$$
$$(m: \text{types of media};\quad h: \text{hours in one week})$$

The students' searching behavior were classified based on the categorization of search strategies by Kinley, Tjondronegoro, Partridge, and Edward [5] and Thatcher [16, 17].

4 Results and Discussions

4.1 Scientific Literacy, Epistemological Beliefs, Cognitive Style, and Media Multitasking Index

In terms of scientific literacy (scored by a professor in physics, ranging from 0 to 100), S&T students gained a significantly higher score than non-S&T students. However, there was no difference among different groups regarding the measurement of epistemological beliefs and cognitive style (score from 1 to 6). The overview of different scales is shown in Table 1.

The Media Multitasking Index (MMI) developed by Ophir, Nass, & Wagner (2009) was adopted to measure the level of multitasking behavior. The mean of MMI was 3.03, which indicated most undergraduate students used three kinds of media at the same time. There was no difference among S&T, social science, and liberal arts students. Students spent the most time in web surfing (mean = 15.06), listening to music (mean = 12.16), reading print media (mean = 10.51), and text messaging (mean = 9.95) in one week.

Table 1. The overview of scientific literacy, epistemological beliefs, cognitive style and MMI of S&T, social science and liberal arts students

Items	S&T		Social science		Liberal arts	
	Mean	Std.	Mean	Std.	Mean	Std.
Scientific literacy	78.3	11.2	68.4	12.4	69.5	10.5
Epistemological beliefs-simple knowledge	3.4	0.8	3.6	0.9	3.3	0.9
Epistemological beliefs-certain knowledge	3.6	0.7	3.5	0.7	3.1	0.5
Epistemological beliefs-quick learning	3.3	0.5	3.4	0.5	3.1	0.8
Epistemological beliefs-innate ability	2.9	0.8	3.1	0.8	2.8	0.6
Cognitive style-creating style	4.5	0.7	4.4	0.7	4.4	0.7
Cognitive style-planning style	4.7	0.6	4.7	0.8	4.9	0.5
Cognitive style-knowing style	4.4	0.5	4.1	0.8	4.1	0.7
MMI	2.9	1.2	3.0	1.2	3.3	1.0

4.2 Web Search Behaviors

Students' searching behavior in this study coincided with Novin and Meyers's four cognitive biases from the search engine results page (SERP) [18].

This study used Kinley, Tjondronegoro, Partridge, and Edward [5] 's proposed four aspects of web search behavior: information searching strategies, query reformulation behavior, web navigation styles, and information processing approaches. The overview of web search behaviors is shown in Table 2. In this study, regarding information search strategies, most students chose top-down instead of bottom-up strategies, which indicated that most students searched for a general topic rather than specific information at the beginning; however, social science and liberal art students adopted mix methods more so than S&T students. In terms of web navigation style, social science and liberal art students adopted a more structured navigation style than sporadic navigation style (unstructured navigation), while S&T students adopted these two navigation styles equally. Moreover, in terms of information-processing approaches, S&T students spent more time on reading, while social science and liberal art students spent more time on the combination of scanning and reading.

The typologies of search strategies proposed by Thatcher [16, 17] were applied. Most students adopted a parallel hub-and-spoke strategy (see Fig. 1), following a path in a new browser window and then returning to the marker page while keeping the other result open. The second most common strategy that students adopted was the broad first strategy, through which the students searched for a general topic first. These two search strategies of students showed main characteristics of multitasking, speed and broad-scale browsing instead of in-depth reading. In addition, social science students tended to try more multiple search strategies than other groups.

Table 2. The overview of web search behaviors of S&T, social science and liberal arts students

Items	S&T		Social science		Liberal arts	
	N	%	N	%	N	%
Information searching strategies-[top down]	18	67%	21	55%	14	48%
Information searching strategies-[bottom up]	0	0%	3	8%	2	7%
Information searching strategies-[mixed]	7	26%	13	34%	12	41%
Information searching strategies-[others]	2	7%	1	3%	1	3%
Web navigation-[sporadic]	13	48%	12	32%	11	38%
Web navigation-[structured]	14	52%	26	68%	18	62%
Information-processing approaches-[scanning]	6	22%	6	16%	7	24%
Information-processing approaches-[reading]	14	52%	12	32%	10	34%
Information-processing approaches-[mixed]	7	26%	20	53%	12	41%

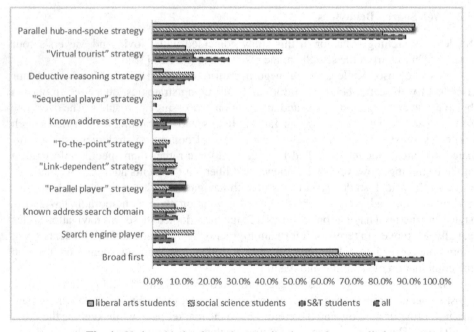

Fig. 1. Various kinds of search strategies that students applied.

4.3 Relationships Among Epistemological Beliefs, Cognitive Style, Media Multitasking, and Web Search Behaviors

In order to explore the relationship among epistemological beliefs, cognitive style, media multitasking, and web search behaviors, all students were categorized as high versus low score groups for epistemological beliefs, cognitive style, media multitasking based on the mean value of each construct. The high/low MMI group did significantly affect the web navigation style with chi-square analysis at $p < 0.05$ level, and high/low of the innate ability in epistemological beliefs is related to the web navigation style at $p < 0.1$ level (Table 3). High MMI group and High epistemological belief about innate ability tended to apply more structured approach than sporadic approach in web navigation style.

Table 3. Chi-square comparison of web navigation style versus MMI, epistemological beliefs-innate ability

Web navigation style	MMI		Epistemological beliefs-innate ability	
	Low	High	Low	High
Sporadic	23	13	20	16
Structured	24	34	21	37
Chi-square	4.502**		3.381*	

*$p < 0.1$, **$p < 0.05$

In terms of the mean difference analysis of low/high MMI groups in four constructs of epistemological beliefs and three constructs of cognitive style, only creating and planning from cognitive style have shown the difference significantly (Table 4). This indicated that the high MMI group showed more creating and planning cognitive styles than the low MMI group. Compared to previous research about heavy media multitaskers [6], this study's result has shown a more positive effect when heavy media multitaskers searched contradictory information on the web.

Table 4. The mean difference of low/high MMI groups in cognitive style

Cognitive style	Creating			Planning		
	n	Mean	t	n	Mean	T
Low MMI	47	4.25	2.91**	47	4.55	2.548*
High MMI	47	4.64		47	4.95	

*$p < 0.05$, **$p < 0.01$

4.4 The Change of Epistemological Beliefs Toward Conflicting Scientific Information

All students' epistemological beliefs changed significantly from their pretest to posttest with t-test analysis at the $p < 0.01$ level, indicating that students possess higher-order knowledge and thinking disposition.

The climate change question about whether there exists consensus or not changed significantly from their pretest to posttest with chi-square analysis at the $p < 0.05$ level. Some students changed their response from a Yes/No to one of uncertainty after they searched on the Internet (Table 5).

Table 5. The pretest and posttest of the climate change question about whether there exists consensus or not

Pretest	Posttest			
	No consensus	Consensus	Not sure	Total
No consensus	30	14	10	54
Consensus	10	26	3	39
Not sure	1	0	0	1
Total	41	40	13	94

The climate change question about its cause- human, nature, and both - changed significantly from their pretest to posttest with chi-square analysis at the $p < 0.05$ level. The ratio of choosing "both" as the cause for climate change decreased after they searched on the Internet. Some students changed their answer from the cause of both to the cause by nature or by human, showing that they changed their viewpoints from a neutral position to these two opposite sides (see Table 6).

Table 6. The pretest and posttest of the climate change question about its cause

Pretest	Posttest			
	Nature	Human	Both	Total
Human	5	4	0	9
Nature	3	36	11	50
Both	4	15	16	35
Total	12	55	27	94

5 Conclusions

This study explored the relationship between epistemological beliefs, cognitive style, media multitasking, and search behaviors when undergraduates deal with contradictory information. Undergraduate students usually used three kinds of media concurrently. There were no differences between S&T students, social science students, and liberal arts students in terms of epistemological beliefs and cognitive style.

There were some different web search behaviors among the different groups. S&T students tended to adopt mix navigation styles and non-S&T students were more apt to use a structured navigation style. S&T students spent time on the reading information-processing approach, while non-S&T students spent time on both scanning and reading.

Students with high MMI used more structured than sporadic in terms of web navigation style and showed more creating and planning in cognitive style. Those students' epistemological beliefs in innate ability have shown more structured web navigation style.

All students' epistemological beliefs changed after searching information on the web, indicating students might have the ability for reflective thinking and deal with the misinformation and disinformation on the web.

This was an exploratory research of undergraduates' epistemological beliefs and information search modifications when facing conflicting information. Further research on the investigation of students' thinking process would help to clarify the cause of the relations among different constructs in this study.

References

1. Zakharov, W., Li, H., Fosmire, M.: Undergraduates' news consumption and perceptions of fake news in science. Portal Libr. Acad. **19**(4), 653–665 (2019)
2. Schommer-Aikins, M., Hutter, R.: Epistemological beliefs and thinking about everyday controversial issues. J. Psychol. **136**(1), 5–20 (2002)
3. Whitmore, E.: Epistemological beliefs and the information-seeking behavior of undergraduates. Libr. Inf. Sci. Res. **25**, 127–142 (2003)
4. Whitmore, E.: The relationship between undergraduates' epistemological beliefs, reflective judgement, and their information-seeking behavior. Inf. Process. Manage. **40**, 97–111 (2004)
5. Kinley, K., Tjondronegoro, D., Partridge, H., Edward, S.: Modeling users' web search behavior and their cognitive styles. J. Assoc. Inf. Sci. Technol. **65**(6), 1107–1123 (2014)
6. Ophir, E., Nass, C., Wagner, A.D.: Cognitive control in media multi-taskers. PNAS **106**(37), 15583–15587 (2009)
7. Hofer, B.K., Pintrich, R.R.: The development of epistemological theories: beliefs about knowledge and knowing and their relation to learning. Rev. Educ. Res. **67**, 88–140 (1997)
8. Schommer, M.: Effects of beliefs about the nature of knowledge on comprehension. J. Educ. Psychol. **82**(3), 498–504 (1990)
9. Schommer, M., Crouse, A., Rhodes, N.: Epistemological belief and mathematical text comprehension: believing it's simple doesn't make it so. J. Educ. Psychol. **85**(3), 406–411 (1992)
10. Schommer, M.: Epistemological development and academic performance among secondary students. J. Educ. Psychol. **85**(3), 406–411 (1993)

11. Kienhues, D., Stadtler, M., Bromme, R.: Dealing with conflicting or consistent medical information on the web: when expert information breed lay-persons' doubts about experts. Learn. Instr. **21**(2), 193–204 (2011)
12. Novin, A., Meyers, E.: Making sense of conflicting science information: exploring bias in the search engine result page. In: Proceedings of the 2017 Conference on Conference Human Information Interaction and Retrieval, pp. 175–184. ACM. (2017)
13. Riding, R.: Cognitive Styles Analysis. Learning and Training Technology. Birmingham, UK (1991)
14. Brossard, D., Shanahan, J.: Do they know what they read? Building a scientific literacy measurement instrument based on science media coverage. Sci. Commun. **28**(1), 47–63 (2006)
15. Cools, E., Van den Broeck, H.: Development and validation of the cognitive style indicator. J. Psychol. Interdisc. Appl. **141**(4), 359–387 (2007)
16. Thatcher, A.: Information-seeking behaviours and cognitive search strategies in different search tasks on the WWW. Int. J. Ind. Ergon. **36**(12), 1055–1068 (2006)
17. Thatcher, A.: Web search strategies: the influence of web experience and task type. Inf. Process. Manage. **44**(3), 1308–1329 (2008)
18. Novin, A., Meyers, E.: Making sense of conflicting science information: exploring bias in the search engine result page. In: Proceedings of the 2017 Conference on Conference Human Information Interaction and Retrieval, pp. 175-184. ACM (2017)

Exposing Undergraduate Students to the Challenges of Integrating Technology in Healthcare Delivery

Laura Ikuma[1]([✉]), Isabelina Nahmens[1], Craig M. Harvey[1], Dan Godbee[2], and Tonya Jagneaux[3]

[1] Louisiana State University, Baton Rouge, LA 70803, USA
likuma@lsu.edu
[2] East Baton Rouge Parish Emergency Medical Services, Baton Rouge, LA 70807, USA
[3] Our Lady of the Lake Regional Medical Center, Baton Rouge, LA 70808, USA

Abstract. Healthcare is increasingly incorporating industrial engineering tools into process improvement initiatives. This includes integrating technology into healthcare delivery, which is an appealing solution to "fix" problems. However, inserting technology without the proper systems integration can limit utility and success. Exposing industrial engineering students to these challenges is critical in training future healthcare leaders. This paper highlights the senior design capstone project for industrial engineering undergraduate students, which is a two-course sequence in the last year of their curriculum. Several of these projects focused on using technology to improve healthcare processes, providing hands-on experience with the challenges of integrating technology in real healthcare systems. These projects can be evaluated in terms of sociotechnical systems components, which considers the system dimensions of the person, task, technology, environment, and organization. Students found that patient-facing technology had more challenges from the other aspects of sociotechnical systems, which influenced the potential sustainability and success of the efforts. They gained an appreciation of the complexity of systems and how technology alone is insufficient to produce lasting, meaningful change. This experience served to prepare industrial engineering students for careers in healthcare and other highly complex industries.

Keywords: Healthcare · Technology integration · Undergraduate education

1 Introduction

Challenges in healthcare delivery systems is an ever-present and growing concern that is being addressed from multiple directions including implementation of technology solutions. Previous research has documented the difficulties in incorporating technology in healthcare, such as organizational barriers [1, 2], challenges in pilot testing technology prior to full-scale implementation [3], and inappropriate technology adoption [4, 5]. Many of these challenges are the result of not fully understanding all aspects of the complex healthcare systems.

© Springer Nature Switzerland AG 2020
F. F.-H. Nah and K. Siau (Eds.): HCII 2020, LNCS 12204, pp. 69–79, 2020.
https://doi.org/10.1007/978-3-030-50341-3_6

Industrial and systems engineers are well-positioned to tackle these complex health-care problems as their education and training incorporates technological, management, economic, and personnel aspects of improving systems. Indeed, many industrial and systems engineers are entering the healthcare field for this reason, and therefore university curriculum needs to evolve to prepare graduates for these careers.

The purpose of this study is to evaluate how undergraduate student projects in an industrial engineering program that focus on technology integration in healthcare expose students to larger challenges impacting project success. The evaluation frames the projects within a sociotechnical systems perspective, considering the person, task, technology, environment, and organization dimensions of each system. By exposing undergraduate students to these challenges, they will be better prepared for careers in healthcare as process improvement leaders, having experienced the need for a systems approach to technology integration for healthcare solutions.

2 Methods

2.1 Project Setting

The projects took place in either a local hospital or the public emergency medical service (EMS) in Baton Rouge, Louisiana, USA. Project champions at either the hospital or EMS provided project descriptions to the course instructor, who then distributed the descriptions to students. Students ranked projects by interest, which the instructor used to assign teams of three to four students. Students were required to undergo any necessary training and testing, such as completing patient privacy training and verifying vaccinations, background checks, etc. Students then worked with the project champions to determine access to data, on-site visits, and interactions with other pertinent staff.

2.2 Education Setting

Each project reported here was completed by industrial engineering undergraduate students as part of their required coursework in their final year of studies. The projects took place over two courses, taken sequentially and lasting approximately nine months. Students spent 10–15 h per week on project work, including report and presentation preparation. The first half of the project documents the current processes, identifies problems, and develops solutions. In the second half of the project, the student teams implement at least one of their solutions, either through small pilot studies, full-scale implementation in limited areas, or simulations. Their final deliverable includes an evaluation of success in terms of efficacy, cost, and other metrics of interest to the project sponsor. Teams receive continuous advice and feedback from the healthcare providers and from a mentoring faculty member. Through this process, students apply concepts from coursework to a real problem in a real-time environment.

2.3 Evaluation of Project Success

The use of technology in healthcare necessitates a larger sociotechnical systems perspective to evaluate success. Cresswell and colleagues [6] argue that the effective implementation of healthcare information technology depends not only on technical aspects but also on social, organizational, and wider socio-political factors. The Systems Engineering Initiative for Patient Safety (SEIPS) promotes evaluation of five components that will influence success of patient safety and other process improvement initiatives within healthcare: person, task, technology, environment, and organization [7]. Both of these approaches are based in sociotechnical systems theory, which posits that the success of systems depends on multiple components, taking a systems perspective, rather than parts in isolation. This study uses the five components of sociotechnical systems to evaluate the success of each project and which components may have been neglected.

3   Results

The following four projects were selected to highlight healthcare projects in the two settings (hospital and EMS) that integrated technology as a solution. The projects include reducing patient falls in inpatient hospital units, improving food delivery to inpatients, using telemedicine in EMS, and using data analytics for decision-making in unit-hour utilization of ambulances. Each project is described, and solutions are categorized into one of the dimensions of sociotechnical systems (person, task, technology, environment, and organization).

3.1   Project 1: Fall Management

The goal of the fall management project was to reduce patient falls on inpatient units of a hospital. The project took a systems approach by making recommendations that incorporated technology, changes to patient room layout, nursing workflows, and management strategies. At the start of the project, students observed an integrated bed alarm system that was intended to prevent patient falls. The system provided remote monitoring, whereby nurses could monitor activity from the nursing station and be alerted when a patient tripped the alarm. However, the systems were often either unplugged or turned off, and there was no consistent policy enforced as to when a patient's bed alarm should be used nor how the alarm should be checked for proper use.

A second problem initially noted was that call buttons, which serve as a communication tool between patients and nurses and as a television remote control, were often out of reach of patients while in bed. This creates a fall risk when patients attempt to retrieve the call button.

The students worked with the nurses to conduct a quick process improvement event to address some of these issues. The team ultimately recommended the following:

- Use clips to secure the call buttons to the bed
- Check the bed alarms and cable plugs when nurses perform rounding
- Use software already integrated with the bed alarm system to monitor patients remotely at the nurses' station
- Add an additional check by transporters on the bed alarm cable plug when a patient returns to the room after a procedure

While the project did not last long enough to track if patient falls decreased as a result of these changes, the team did find the addition of clips increased the call buttons within reach of the patient in one unit, but had no effect on the second unit studied. The percentage of call buttons within reach increased from 91% to 100% in one unit and from 40% to 81% in the second unit after the process improvement event. The percentage of bed alarm cables plugged in slightly decreased for one unit (89% to 85%) but increased in the second unit (67% to 97%). The changes realized in this project can be categorized into the five sociotechnical systems components (Table 1).

Table 1. Fall management project sociotechnical systems components

Sociotechnical systems component	Project elements
Person	No explicit changes
Task	Change workflow of nurse rounding to include purposeful alarm monitor check Change workflow of patient transporters to check alarm monitor plug when returning patient to room
Technology and tools	Bed alarm system Software to monitor bed alarms and patients remotely
Environment	Use clips to secure call buttons within reach of patients
Organization	No explicit changes

3.2   Project 2: Food Delivery

A food delivery project sought to decrease the overall delivery time of meals to inpatients. One piece of technology in use was an automated ordering system that allowed patients to order their meals. The meal tickets could be displayed on a screen ("C-Board", Fig. 1) in the preparation area for ease of assembly. While this system afforded patients autonomy in selecting food and helped ensure the right food went to the right patient, the overall delivery time did not necessarily improve. In fact, after extensive observations by the students, the root cause of delivery time problems appeared to be an imbalance in staffing between tray assemblers and tray delivery staff. A second potential problem was the capacity limitations of the carts used to deliver trays to patient floors. A third problem was the high turnover rate of employees in this department.

Even though the causes of delays touched on several areas of sociotechnical systems, the hospital focused on balancing staffing and possibly improving the C-Board system (Table 2). Given that the main problem was the personnel imbalance or shortage, the team used simulation tools to find the optimal balance of personnel and tray cart size to reduce delivery times to under one hour. Some improvements were suggested to the C-Board system to further highlight allergies and other dietary restrictions. Although mistakes in tray preparation were not prevalent, these improvements would help reduce errors in the tray orders. Another suggestion was to change the order of the resulting meal

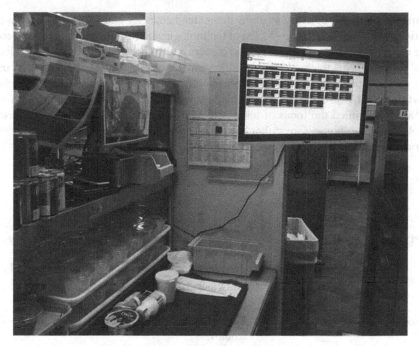

Fig. 1. Food tray automated ordering system

ticket to match the flow of food and drink items in the preparation area, which would serve to further error-proof against missing items and reduce time spent navigating the ticket and the preparation layout.

Table 2. Food delivery project sociotechnical systems components

Sociotechnical systems component	Project elements
Person	No explicit changes made
Task	Adjust number of personnel to optimize workflows
Technology and tools	Modify C-Board to highlight allergies and dietary restrictions Change ticket order to match layout of preparation area
Environment	No explicit changes made
Organization	No explicit changes made

3.3 Project 3: Telemedicine in EMS

The local EMS asked students to investigate the use of telemedicine (or telehealth) to link paramedics and patients in the field with a medical professional on duty (physicians, nurse practitioners, etc.) Telehealth is defined as technology-enabled health and care management and delivery systems that extend capacity and access [8]. Given this definition, the students developed a list of technological requirements (tablet-style computing devices, speaker, microphone, and camera capabilities, etc.) and sought feedback from all users on what telehealth might achieve in the EMS setting. The students focused on the technological and environment requirements including peripheral equipment to support the tablet, noise and lighting levels, and bags to transport the equipment on-site. The team also limited the focus of telemedicine use to patients with chronic disease in need of routine, in-home care rather than acute emergencies. Table 3 summarizes the components of the project by sociotechnical system component.

Table 3. Telemedicine project sociotechnical systems components

Sociotechnical systems component	Project elements
Person	Limited to patients with chronic disease requiring in-home care
	Training manual for using the technology created
Task	Workflow to use equipment specified in training manual
Technology and tools	Defined communications technology and peripherals required
Environment	Defined proper noise, lighting, and power requirements for use
Organization	No explicit changes defined

3.4   Project 4: Ambulance Unit-Hour Utilization (UHU)

A second project at the local EMS focused on using analytics of ambulance response times, location of calls, transport times, etc. to create a visualization and decision tool. Using database and GIS (geospatial information systems) software, the student team created heat maps (Fig. 2) showing highest use areas compared to the location of ambulances, crews, EMS stations, and emergency departments. This tool was extremely useful, providing data to present to the local funding government as evidence to request additional resources. The data also helped EMS make allocation decisions for ambulance and crew placement to meet expected demands. Last, the data illustrated how recent changes in healthcare access as a result of emergency room closures impact the community. The project directly affected only the technology and organization components of the sociotechnical system (Table 4).

4   Discussion

4.1   Project Barriers and Enablers for Success

Due to the nature of the course, students are able to implement their suggested improvements either through small pilot studies or simulations, but they are rarely able to fully

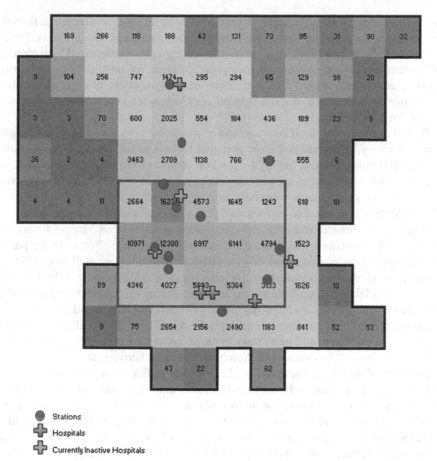

Fig. 2. Example heat map generated from ambulance UHU project tool showing number of incidents by location

Table 4. Ambulance unit-hour utilization project sociotechnical systems components

Sociotechnical systems component	Project elements
Person	No explicit changes
Task	No explicit changes
Technology and tools	Software tool to combine location and number of calls
Environment	No explicit changes
Organization	Tool used to make business case for funding and resource allocation requests

implement their suggestions in the time period of the class. Other studies point to the difficulties in technology pilot implementations as they often leave more questions than answers [3]. Despite pilot-scale implementation, student analysis and feedback from the sponsors during the project gives insight into potential success and sustainability. Table 5 summarizes barriers and enablers of success for each project, categorized by sociotechnical system component. Across all four projects, there are only two major barriers directly related to technology. However, there are ten barriers from other dimensions, highlighting the importance of a full systems approach when conducting improvement initiatives in healthcare.

The fall management, food delivery, and telemedicine projects all involved patient-facing technology, which created more potential barriers to successful implementation than the UHU project, which largely focused on decision tools used by EMS management. In the fall management project, the students learned that the technology "fixes" such as plugging in the alarm were easy in comparison to coordinating with nursing staff to determine a reasonable, enforceable policy on bed alarm monitoring. Although the initial results showed improvements, the students realized that barriers from other sociotechnical dimensions may limit the sustainability of their efforts. At the person level, the students witnessed a lack of motivation from the nursing staff to use the bed monitoring software, and actions from patients and their families to actively defeat the bed alarms they felt were cumbersome rather than ensuring safety. From a task perspective, students realized they were asking already overworked nurses and transporters to add another step to their routines of checking the bed alarms. The students recognized this barrier and worked to add these tasks in the simplest forms possible, understanding that the steps may still be overlooked. Some of the largest barriers came from the organization dimension. The hospital did not have a clear policy on which patients should use the bed alarm systems and how to enforce use, and there was little time available during the project to train nurses on the bed alarm and software use. This resulted in a lack of buy-in overall and also contributed to the lack of motivation from the individual nurses. Despite all of these barriers, some enablers included adding the clips to the call buttons, which reduced the opportunities for falls by keeping the call buttons within reach of patients. Another enabler is the strong motivation from all levels of hospital management to reduce patient falls. With the analysis, it becomes clear that management could use this motivation to make changes to policy and training resources devoted to fall management.

The food delivery project originally started with a request to evaluate the C-Board system of managing patient food orders to reduce delivery time, but students quickly realized that this technology was not the root cause of delays. After performing observations of the system, it was apparent shortcomings in the task and person components of the system were the problem. Despite the ease of "fixing" with technology, simply changing the C-Board technology was not going to decrease food tray delivery times. Barriers existed in other sociotechnical system components: the department experienced high employee turnover, and the physical environment placed constraints on how many trips were necessary to deliver trays to patient floors given the capacity of the current tray cart. To address this last barrier, one of the suggestions from the students was to invest in a combination of additional personnel to deliver trays and one larger capacity cart to reduce trips back to the food preparation area.

Table 5. Enablers (+) and barriers (X) to project success, by sociotechnical factor

	Fall management	Food delivery	Telemedicine	Ambulance UHU
Person	X: Lack of motivation from nurses to use software X: Patients/families using workarounds to defeat the bed alarm	X: High employee turnover	X: Patient trust in decisions made remotely X: Providers uncomfortable making remote decisions	
Task	X: Adding tasks to rounding and patient transport to already high levels of workload			+: Use of tool requires no change to tasks
Technology & tools	X: Bed alarms not plugged in		+: Technology is modern X: potential data security issues with patient-sensitive data	+: Data required is already collected and available
Environment	+: Clips added to call buttons reduces fall opportunities	X: Layout of hospital floors versus cart capacity dictates number of trips		
Organizational/Social	+: Strong motivation to reduce number of falls X: Lack of consistent policies for use of bed alarms X: Lack of time devoted to training on bed alarm systems		X: Cost of purchasing the technology (publicly funded entity)	+: Any request for government funding requires objective justification, which the tool provides

The telemedicine project was perhaps the most exciting in terms of considering the latest technology for healthcare. However, students learned they had to balance the desire to use the latest technology with the constraints of a real system. While the majority of their project time was spent defining the technology and equipment needs against environmental constraints in terms of lighting, noise, power availability, and size, the team learned that the bigger barriers were going to fall into the person and organization components of the system. In general the response from providers was positive, given the potential to care for patients real-time without the stress and time of transport. While the healthcare providers liked the idea of using technology to provide assistance remotely, they were wary of making medical decisions without seeing a patient in person. The cost and return on investment was also a concern. Given EMS is a publicly funded entity, the EMS agency had to make a case for investing in cutting-edge technology using tax funds. As a result, EMS personnel do consult with other healthcare providers while in the field but do so through phone calls instead of higher-tech solutions.

The ambulance UHU project was an easier sell and has higher potential for sustainability because it didn't involve patients directly and thus avoided some of the more challenging aspects of sociotechnical systems integration. It simply manipulated already available data to make decisions. It also did not require the modification of any current processes, meaning providers (EMS in this case) did not have to change their ways. The project made changes to technology by providing a new tool and at the organization level by strengthening the ability of EMS to advocate for resources. Students experienced how complex data sets could be analyzed and communicated successfully to make decisions that directly affect the well-being of a community.

4.2   Implications for Preparing Engineering Students for Careers in Healthcare

These projects were extremely useful in preparing undergraduate engineering students for the larger challenges they might face in the healthcare industry and in their careers in general. While the stereotype of engineers focusing on technology may have driven some of the initial excitement for these projects, both the students and project sponsors quickly learned that technology would be a minor part of project success. This emphasizes the need for engineering students, particularly in industrial engineering, to be well-rounded in managing all aspects of systems, going beyond technology to include people, tasks, environment, and organizational components of each system. Curriculum development therefore should include opportunities to apply systems engineering principles and experience first-hand the challenges and consequences of considering (or failing to consider) all aspects of the sociotechnical system. This is especially true in healthcare, which is a growing field for industrial engineers, as healthcare systems are particularly complex.

5   Conclusions

Overall, projects using technology to analyze performance and resource needs seemed to be more successful than technology directed at patient interactions. Much of this appeared to be due to larger sociotechnical systems issues, such as lack of consideration of human factors in organizations, as opposed to problems with the actual technology.

In all, students learned how technology in isolation cannot solve healthcare delivery problems, but that using technology as one tool in a larger systems perspective can be powerful.

References

1. Lluch, M.: Healthcare professionals' organisational barriers to health information technologies—a literature review. Int. J. Med. Informatics **80**, 849–862 (2011)
2. Waterson, P.: Health information technology and sociotechnical systems: aprogress report on recent developments within the UK National Health Service (NHS). Appl. Ergon. **45**, 150–161 (2014)
3. Hertzum, M., le Manikas, M., á Torkilsheyggi, A.: Grappling with the future: the messiness of pilot implementation in information systems design. Health Inf. J. **25**(2), 372–388 (2017)
4. Coye, M.J., Kell, J.: How hospitals confront new technology. Health Aff. **25**(1), 163–173 (2006)
5. Adaba, G.B., Kebebew, Y.: Improving a health information system for real-time data entries: an action research project using socio-technical systems theory. Inf. Health **43**(2), 159–171 (2018)
6. Cresswell, K.M., Bates, D.W., Sheikh, A.: Ten key considerations for the successful implementation and adoption of large-scale health information technology. J. Am. Med. Inform. Assoc. **20**, e9–e13 (2013)
7. Carayon, P., et al.: Work system design for patient safety: the SEIPS model. BMJ Qual. Saf. **15**, i50–i58 (2006)
8. American Telemedicine Association: Telehealth basics. https://www.americantelemed.org/res ource/why-telemedicine/. Accessed 29 Jan 2020

Detecting Deceptive Language in Crime Interrogation

Yi-Ying Kao, Po-Han Chen$^{(\boxtimes)}$, Chun-Chiao Tzeng, Zi-Yuan Chen,
Boaz Shmueli, and Lun-Wei Ku

Institute of Information Science, Academia Sinica, Taipei, Taiwan
a3721a3721@yahoo.com.tw, {bhchen,zychen,lwku}@iis.sinica.edu.tw,
archery@cc.tpa.edu.tw, boaziko@gmail.com

Abstract. Deception detection is a vital research problem studied by
fields as diverse as psychology, forensic science, sociology. With cooperation with National Investigation Bureau, we have 496 transcript files,
each of which contains a conversation of an interrogator and a subject
of a real-world polygraph test during interrogation. Researchers have
explored the possibility of natural language process techniques in gaming, news articles, interviews, and criminal narratives. In this paper, we
explore the effect of the frontier natural language process technique to
detect deceptiveness in these conversations. We regard this task as a
binary classification problem. We utilize four different methods, inclusive of part-of-speech extraction, one-hot-encoding, means of embedding
vectors, and BERT pre-trained model, to capture hidden information of
transcript files into vectors. After that, we take these vectors as training samples of a hierarchy neural network, which is constructed by a
fully-connected layer and/or an LSTM layer. After training, our system
can take a transcript file as its input and classify whether the subject is
deceptive or not. An F1 score 0.733 is achieved from our system.

Keywords: Voice and conversational interaction · Deception
detection · Interrogation · Text analysis · Deep learning application

1 Introduction

Deception detection is a vital research problem studied by fields involving human
interaction. The discrimination between truth and lies has drawn significant
attention from fields as diverse as psychology, forensic science, sociology.

In this paper, we target the detection of deception in the interviews of real-
world crime interrogation. With cooperation with National Investigation Bureau,
we explore the effect of the frontier natural language process technique for deceptive language detection. Specifically, we utilize the transcript files of the polygraph test during interrogation. The polygraph test procedure has three phases:

© Springer Nature Switzerland AG 2020
F. F.-H. Nah and K. Siau (Eds.): HCII 2020, LNCS 12204, pp. 80–90, 2020.
https://doi.org/10.1007/978-3-030-50341-3_7

1. **Pre-test phase**

   In the pre-test phase, the polygraph is not used. The pre-test starts with the interrogator having an interview with the subject. Here, the interrogator will ask the subject questions that are directly related to the case ("related questions") and questions that are not directly related to the case ("control questions"). Examples of a related question and a control question are "這件案件是不是你先攻擊被告？" (In this case, did you attack the defendant first?) and "在你的經驗裡有沒有犯錯但說謊不認錯的經驗？" (In your experience, have you ever made any mistake but lied and did not admit it?). These questions may be open-ended or close-ended. With the conversation, the interrogator examines the behavior, body language, and speech of the subject. During the phase, the interrogator also decides what questions should be asked when the polygraph is connected. This phase can take from 30 min to 90 min.

2. **Test phase**

   The pre-test phase leads to the test phase, during which the actual polygraph participates. The interrogator first explains to the subject that how the test will be conducted, introducing how the polygraph works and the closed-end questions to which the subject will be questioned later. The subject is then moved to the polygraph room and connected to the polygraph machine. The polygraph machine measures the subject's respiration, heartbeat rate, blood pressure, and perspiration. Following the hook-up, the interrogator asks the subject a series of close-ended (i.e., yes/no) questions, for example, "Did you steal the money?". The subject is expected to answer with either a "yes" or a "no". The polygraph records the physiological responses during this phase. Once the questioning is over, the subject is disconnected from the polygraph machine.

3. **Post-test phase**

   The last phase is the post-test phase. During this phase, the results of the pre-test and test phases are analyzed by the interrogator, and he/she makes a decision regarding the truthfulness of the subject.

For methodology, we define our task as a binary classification problem to predict whether a subject is deceptive or innocent based on his/her interviewing transcript with the interrogator. With the aid of CKIP parser [1], fastText pre-trained word vectors[1] and BERT pre-trained model [2], we propose four different modeling system with fully-connected and/or LSTM [3] neural networks to perform prediction based on the encoded transcript data.

CKIP is an open-source library that is capable of performing natural language process tasks on Chinese sentences, such as word segmentation, part-of-speech tagging. fastText is a lightweight library for text representation. Its pre-trained model, trained on Common Crawl and Wikipedia corpus, has the ability to capture hidden information about a language such as word analogies or semantic. As for BERT, which stands for Bidirectional Encoder Representations from

---

[1] https://fasttext.cc/docs/en/crawl-vectors.html.

Transforms, is the state-of-the-art contextual embedding model that can turn a sentence into its corresponding vector representation. LSTM (Long Short Term Memory) is a special kind of recurrent neural network (RNN) structure that is capable of learning long-term dependencies. It is very suitable for processing sequence data such as conversations since the meaning of a word in a sentence usually depends on previous words.

We apply four different methods including (1) part-of-speech extraction, (2) one-hot-encoding, (3) mean of word embedding vectors and (4) BERT model to each utterance of interrogator and subjects. After that, we use a hierarchical method to aggregate the hidden representations of them, and then generate a single prediction label which indicates the deceptiveness or honesty.

2 Background

Even though the literature indicates that many types of deception can be identified because the liar's verbal and non-verbal behavior varies considerably from that of the truth teller's [4], the reported performance of human lie detectors rarely achieves at a level above chance [5]. The challenge for people to distinguish lies from truths leads to the design that the annotators are the people who express instead of the people who receive, which causes the lack of real data.

Recent advances in natural language processing motivate the attempt to recognize the deceptive language automatically. Researchers have explored its possibility in gaming [6,7], news articles [8], interviews [9], and criminal narratives [10]. However, some of the previous works conducted experiments in pseudo experiments or were required hand-craft features, which might include human bias. This issue may make the developed models unable to be applied to real situations.

In this paper, we use the data from real-world crime interrogation as well as modern natural language process techniques to address the task of predicting deceptiveness and honesty in transcript files during interrogation.

3 Dataset

With cooperation with the National Investigation Bureau, we have 496 transcript files of polygraph tests during interrogation. Each of the transcript files consists of a field indicating the case is judged as lying or not and 220 conversation entries on average. For each conversation entry, in addition to the utterance of the interrogator and the subject, it contains two additional numbers. One of them indicates whether the entry is a question or an answer while the other denotes whether the entry belongs to the related question or control question. Table 1 illustrates two sample conversation entries in a transcript file.

Note that when we say a "transcript file," it stands for a file that contains "sentences," each of which consists of "words." A transcript file corresponds to an interrogation case. The dataset contains 496 transcript files comprising 226 deceptive cases and 270 honest cases. In total, there are about two million

Table 1. Two sample conversation entries of a transcript file. It's originally written in Chinese. We translate it into English for demonstration purpose.

Text	These three people often cheat on exam?	Not often
Question/answer	Question	Answer
Related/control question	Control	Control

characters. To parse the Chinese content, we utilize CKIP parser to extract the part-of-speech information and segment each sentence into word-level tokens. There are 24853 unique Chinese and English words, numbers, and punctuation in our dataset.

The part-of-speech information can be put into a neural network classifier (detailed in the following "Part-of-speech Extraction" section). As for sentence segmentation, we can convert each token-formatted sentence into a vector representation. These representation vectors can then be put into our LSTM model to encode the transcript file. We also utilize BERT pre-trained embedding model to encode transcript files directly. Finally, we use the encoding of each transcript file to predict whether a subject is deceptive or not. Details of how we convert sentences into vectors are elaborated in the next section.

4 System Overview

4.1 Part-of-Speech Extraction

In this method, we make a hypothesis that if a person lies in a conversation, he/she will use more words to express contrast, e.g. "however," "but," "nevertheless." Furthermore, people who are deceptive will have more chances describing an event in third-person point to keep themselves away from it. In short, we believe that if a person lies, there may exist some patterns in the words he/she uses. We extract part-of-speech with CKIP parser from each transcript file and count the number of each part-of-speech tag. Then we take them as entities of input features and feed them into a fully-connected linear binary classifier. Table 2 shows a sample result of part-of-speech extraction.

Table 2. A sample result of part-of-speech extraction. It shows pairs of a Chinese word and its corresponding part-of-speech tag. The Chinese sentence means: "In this case, did you attack the defendant first?"

這(Nep) 件(Nf) 案件(Na) 是(SHI) 不(D) 是(SHI) 你(Nh) 先(D) 攻擊(VC) 被告(Na)

Except for the "Part-of-speech Extraction" method mentioned above, in general, we take the following steps on each of the structures we propose to address the task:

1. Embed each sentence in transcript files into a vector representation,
2. Encode each transcript file into vector format based on the sentence-level encoded vector obtained from the previous step, and
3. Train the binary classifier by leveraging vectors obtained from step two.

For step one mentioned above, we utilize three different methods (detailed in the following sections) to embed hidden information into representation vectors:

- One-hot-encoding
- Mean of embedding vectors
- BERT model

Despite the difference between these methods to encode a transcript file, we use the same hierarchical neural-network structure, as depicted in Fig. 1, to perform classification and prediction. Additionally, we take the same steps to train neural networks. The followings are details about embedding sentences.

4.2 One-Hot-Encoding

We apply one-hot-encoding process, to encode each sentence of a transcript file into a one-hot vector as described below:

1. Extract all the words that appear in transcript files, inclusive of questions from interrogator and answers from the subject, into a vocabulary set.
2. For each transcript file, prepare a vector which has elements as many as the number of words in the vocabulary set. Each of the elements corresponds to a word in the vocabulary set and is assigned to 0 initially.
3. Assign the element to 1 if its corresponding word appears in the sentence.
4. Finally, we take the vector containing zeros and ones as the representation vector of a sentence.

For example, assume we have a vocabulary set containing words: this, is, an, apple, a, pen, and assume each word corresponds to index 0 to 5 of a vector. Then we can encode a sentence "this is an apple" to a vector containing $\{1, 1, 1, 1, 0, 0\}$ while the sentence "this is a pen" will be encoded to a vector with the value $\{1, 1, 0, 0, 1, 1\}$.

After converting all the sentences in transcript files with the process mentioned above, we feed these result vectors into an LSTM network sequentially, taking the last hidden state as the encoding of a transcript file. As for the binary classifier, we use a fully-connected linear neural network, followed by a sigmoid activation function. We input the last hidden state of the LSTM network to the classifier and take the output to be the prediction of the system. Figure 1 depicts the process.

4.3 Mean of Embedding Vectors

For each sentence in a transcript, we collect all the words appearing in it, using the fastText pre-trained model to encode these words into vectors. Next, we

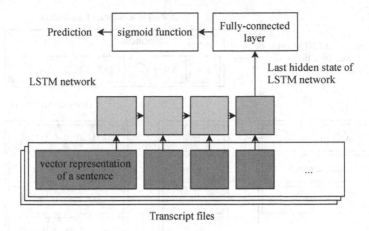

Fig. 1. This figure describes that how we process data after obtaining vector representation of sentences. Vector representation of each sentence is fed into a LSTM network. The last hidden state of LSTM network is then forwarded into the binary classifier which is made up of a fully-connected neural network with sigmoid activation function.

calculate the mean of these vectors element-wisely, then concatenating the result with two other numbers, which respectively indicate whether the entry is a question or answer and whether it belongs to relation question or control question. We assign 1.0 to the first number if the entry is an answer or 0.0 if it's a question. Likewise, we assign 1.0 to the second number if the entry is a related question or 0.0 if it's a control question. Figure 2 illustrates the concept. After converting each sentence to a vector, we input them into the neural network described in Fig. 1.

4.4 BERT Model

BERT is a contextual embedding model. It captures both meanings of the word and the information of its surrounding context. Unlike the fastText pre-trained model, which addresses the embedding task in word-level, the BERT model can process sentence-level embedding. Therefore, we can use the BERT pre-trained model to encode each sentence of a transcript directly.

Next, we take the same methods as the previous structure to concatenate two additional numbers, get the encoding of transcripts, and train the linear classifier. Figure 3 illustrates how we obtain a sentence vector, which is the input of the LSTM network.

5   Experiments

We use pairs of transcript representation vector and the corresponding label as the ground truth to train this classifier. There are 496 cases consisting of 226 deceptive cases and 270 honest cases in our dataset.

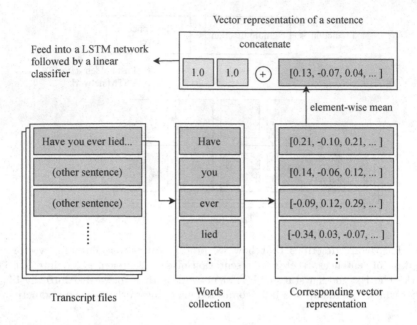

Fig. 2. This figure illustrates how we convert a sentence in a transcript file into vector format, which can be the input of the following LSTM network with the "Mean of Embedding Vectors" method. Though sentences here are in English, we can take the same step on any language to get the sentence vector as long as the sentence is parsed into words.

We split our dataset into a training set, a validation set, and a testing set. To make our experiment more reliable, we use cross-validation with stratification based on class labels (deceptive and honest). We split our dataset into ten splits, taking one of them to be the validation set, another to be the testing set, while the splits left out are aggregated to be the training set. With stratified sampling, training and validation sets contain approximately the same percentage of deceptive/honesty cases.

Besides, we train our models with transcripts that contain (1) control questions only (2) related questions only (3) both control and related questions to compare the impact of various types of conversation entries. What's more, we randomly generate embedding vectors as a baseline to perform sanity checks assuring our embedding vectors actually extract hidden information from conversations of our dataset.

To train the classifier, we use one of following optimizers: Adadelta [11], Adam [12], RMSprop [13], SGD with momentum [14], with binary cross-entropy loss and apply dropout [15]. We perform grid search based on the validation error to pick the best hyper-parameters and optimizer. The test result is tested on the testing set.

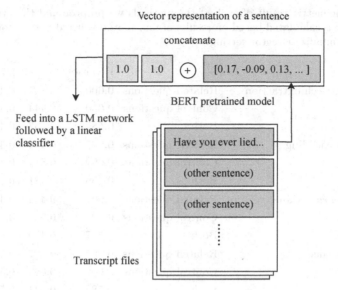

Fig. 3. The figure illustrates the way to encode each sentence in a transcript with the aid of BERT pre-trained model.

6 Results

We measure each of the settings described in the experiments section with metrics including precision, recall, and F1 score. The result is showed in Table 3. According to the result, we have findings listed below.

1. All of the methods we propose in this paper have a higher F1 score than the randomly initialized vectors setting. It indicates that these methods indeed extract some hidden information from our data, and the classifier has learned some underlying pattern of deceptive language.
2. **One-hot-encoding has a higher F1 score**
   Much to our surprise, the "One-hot-encoding" method has a better F1 score than any other method. In the setting of using both related and control questions, it is about 33% higher than the average F1 score. We don't expect the result because we think that the BERT pre-trained model, which can extract not only the meaning of words but contextual information of a sentence, should be more powerful and have a better performance. On the other hand, the one-hot-encoding process can only annotate whether the word exists in a transcript file.
3. **Using control questions only gets a higher F1 score**
   From Table 3, we can see that all methods except "Part-of-speech Extraction" have a higher F1 score in the scenario of using control questions only. On average, the F1 score of using control questions only is about 6% higher than using both questions, 23% higher than using related questions only.

Table 3. The metric result of each of the methods we propose and the average. The average value is calculated based on results of four methods listed above, not including the random initialized vector setting.

		Precision	Recall	F1 score
Part-of-speech extraction	Related questions	0.600	0.467	0.476
	Control questions	0.650	0.444	0.466
	Both	0.587	0.467	0.452
One-hot-encoding	Related questions	0.805	0.454	0.402
	Control questions	0.690	0.811	0.733
	Both	0.559	0.981	0.712
Means of embedding vectors	Related questions	0.607	0.404	0.462
	Control questions	0.595	0.560	0.543
	Both	0.557	0.469	0.471
BERT model	Related questions	0.605	0.527	0.500
	Control questions	0.600	0.552	0.523
	Both	0.584	0.541	0.506
Average	Related questions	0.654	0.463	0.460
	Control questions	0.634	0.592	0.566
	Both	0.572	0.615	0.535
Randomly initialized vectors	N/A	0.668	0.333	0.311

7 Discussion

We are curious about why the one-hot-encoding method has a better F1 score. To further investigate what our model learns in the one-hot-encoding setting, we generate vectors whose elements all assigned to 0 except one element to be 1 to be inputs of the model. These vectors can be thought of as a sentence with only one word. The followings are some one-hot-encoding-format words that are generated with the method mentioned above. Our model considered these words to have more possibility being deceptive: 台北 (Taipei, a location name), 台中 (Taichung, a location name), 手機 (mobile phone), 提到 (mention), 四月 (April). Most of them are related to locations. On the contrary, these words are considered to have more possibility being honest: 監視器 (monitor), 女朋友 (girlfriend), 回家 (come back home), 例如 (for example), 摸 (touch). However, we can't say the sentence containing words above has more possibility to be deceptive/honest due to the complexity of the deep learning model. Computation in a neural network is not linear. Minor change to the input may lead to a significant change to the output. It just gives us a direction to a more in-depth investigation.

As for the reason why using control question only has a higher F1 score, we guess it's because that sentences belonging to control questions have more words while one belonging to related questions, in which the subject just responses either yes or no, has less. The representation vectors of sentences belong to control questions hold more hidden information than that belong to related questions. As for the reason why the setting of using both related and control questions has a lower f1 score than using control questions only, we guess that related questions might be noise due to the short answers, which often only have one word from subjects.

8 Conclusion

In this paper, we utilize four different methods, including part-of-speech extraction, one-hot-encoding, means of embedding vectors, and BERT model, to capture the hidden information of real-world transcript files which contain conversations from interrogators and subjects. Besides, we use a hierarchical neural network to detect whether the conversation is deceptive or not. Finally, we compare the metric of each method and have a discussion.

After training, our system can classify the deceptive case and honest. However, we still can make our system more robust and reliable by collecting more training samples and combining some deep learning techniques such as transfer learning and multitask learning. Although improvements can be made, we believe that our methods can be the basis of more complicated neural network structures, which may be additional aids in the fields such as psychology, forensic science, and sociology someday. Moreover, the methods and structures mentioned in the paper are not restricted to Chinese transcripts. They can be applied to any other language and even other scenarios.

References

1. Ma, W.-Y., Chen, K.-J.: Introduction to CKIP Chinese word segmentation system for the first international Chinese word segmentation bakeoff, pp. 168–171. Association for Computational Linguistics (2003)
2. Devlin, J., Chang, M.-W., Lee, K., Toutanova, K.: BERT: pre-training of deep bidirectional transformers for language understanding. arXiv preprint arXiv:1810.04805 (2018)
3. Hochreiter, S., Schmidhuber, J.: Long short-term memory. Neural Comput. 9(8), 1735–1780 (1997)
4. DePaulo, B.M., Lindsay, J.J., Malone, B.E., Muhlenbruck, L., Charlton, K., Cooper, H.: Cues to deception. Psychol. Bull. 129(1), 74 (2003)
5. Vrij, A.: Detecting Lies and Deceit: The Psychology of Lying and Implications for Professional Practice. Wiley Series on the Psychology of Crime, Policing and Law (2000)
6. Azaria, A., Richardson, A., Kraus, S.: An agent for deception detection in discussion based environments. In: Proceedings of the 18th ACM Conference on Computer Supported Cooperative Work and Social Computing, pp. 218–227 (2015)
7. de Ruiter, B., Kachergis, G.: The mafiascum dataset: a large text corpus for deception detection. arXiv preprint arXiv:1811.07851 (2018)
8. Pisarevskaya, D.: Deception detection in news reports in the Russian language: Lexics and discourse. In: Proceedings of the 2017 EMNLP Workshop: Natural Language Processing Meets Journalism, pp. 74–79 (2017)

9. Levitan, S.I., Maredia, A., Hirschberg, J.: Linguistic cues to deception and perceived deception in interview dialogues. In: Proceedings of the 2018 Conference of the North American Chapter of the Association for Computational Linguistics: Human Language Technologies, Volume 1 (Long Papers), pp. 1941–1950 (2018)
10. Bachenko, J., Fitzpatrick, E., Schonwetter, M.: Verification and implementation of language-based deception indicators in civil and criminal narratives. In: Proceedings of the 22nd International Conference on Computational Linguistics, vol. 1, pp. 41–48. Association for Computational Linguistics (2008)
11. Zeiler, M.D.: ADADELTA: an adaptive learning rate method. CoRRabs/1212.5701 (2012). http://arxiv.org/abs/1212.5701
12. Kingma, D.P., Ba, J.: Adam: a method for stochastic optimization. CoRR abs/1412.6980 (2014). http://arxiv.org/abs/1412.6980
13. Hinton, G.: Neural Networks for Machine Learning - Lecture 6a - Overview of Mini-Batch Gradient Descent (2012)
14. Qian, N.: On the momentum term in gradient descent learning algorithms. Neural Netw. **12**(1), 145–151 (1999)
15. Srivastava, N., Hinton, G., Krizhevsky, A., Sutskever, I., Salakhutdinov, R.: Dropout: a simple way to prevent neural networks from overfitting. J. Mach. Learn. Res. **15**, 1929–1958 (2014)

Transformation Action Cycle

Suggestions for Employee Centered Transformation to Digital Work in SMEs

Johanna Kluge[1]([email]), Martina Ziefle[1], Achim Buschmeyer[2], and Cornelia Hahn[2]

[1] Chair of Communication Science/Human Computer Interaction Center, RWTH Aachen, Campus-Boulevard 57, 52074 Aachen, Germany
kluge@comm.rwth-aachen.de

[2] Derichs u Konertz GmbH u Co. KG, Oranienstraße 27-31, 52066 Aachen, Germany

Abstract. The transformation to innovative and digital work environments is one major task for the working world. Actively shaping change processes in such a way that employees find the best possible working conditions offers many opportunities and potentials. On the one hand, it improves the working climate and employee loyalty. On the other hand, it creates optimal conditions for employees to optimally develop their potential. Requirements for employees and employers arise from changes due to the digital transformation of work. Both perspectives were considered in this paper. Focus is on the employees perspective and transformation in SMEs.

On the basis of quantitative and qualitative surveys, fields of action in organizations were identified in this paper that are particularly relevant for the transformation process. An action transformation cycle has been developed, including fields of action in organizations from which specific measures for a transformation strategy can be inferred. An evaluation in an SME in the construction industry showed the transformation action cycle as useful tool for the support in planning transformation measures.

Keywords: Digital transformation · SME · Transformation strategy

1 Introduction

At this moment, the world of work is drastically changing. Business models, forms of organizations, and working processes are being altered, digital working environments are more and more implemented. This refers on the one hand to digital production solutions (industry 4.0) but also to the application of digital systems for Information and communication (e.g. digital tools for knowledge management or other processes) [1]. To be ready for the future, organizations must face this change [3]. There are different views on the nature of the change, its final objective and the ways to achieve it [4]. The resulting open questions often concern the most important resource of a company: its employees. Especially in times of "war of talents", the integration of an employee-centered transformation strategy is important. On the other hand, there are clear requirement profiles from the employer side for the employees of the future. Altogether, management approaches

© Springer Nature Switzerland AG 2020
F. F.-H. Nah and K. Siau (Eds.): HCII 2020, LNCS 12204, pp. 91–109, 2020.
https://doi.org/10.1007/978-3-030-50341-3_8

for industry 4.0 and human resources 4.0 are on the rise [1, 2, 5]. The current literature introduces requirement profiles for employees which take the changed requirements and working conditions into account. Employees should be flexible, willing to learn, innovative, and able to think entrepreneurially [3]. These requirements stem from the changing working conditions, the change of classical job descriptions, the changing work- and learning environments, and the changed management structures, which are increasingly moving away from a traditional hierarchical work organization. This is associated with a stronger focus on self-organization, knowledge management and teamwork [1].

Small- and medium-sized enterprises (SMEs) have a special role in this change towards digital work in contrast to large companies or startups [6]. While Large companies often have more resources available making a digital transition but are, due to their size and structure, slow to change. In contrast, to that startups have high levels of motivation and change flexibly, but often have low limited available resources. SMEs in contrast to that, are dependent on a cautious, resource-saving change. For SMEs it is particularly important to integrate the workers to achieve a change they perceive as smooth and satisfactory, thereby preventing staff turnover, psychological burdens, and major disruptions of the daily business. Integrating workers and achieving smooth and satisfactory change for them is particularly important for SMEs to prevent Staff turnover, psychological burden and major disruption of daily business [7]. A holistic base for transformation strategies for SMEs is thus, on the one hand, built by the company's perspective on necessary, sustainable, innovative, and digital corporate strategies, and on the other hand by the perspective of the employees and their needs, requirements, and worries. In this paper, these two perspectives, their common ground, and their differences are considered. The paper focusses on quantitative and qualitative empirical studies on the employees' perspective on the digitization of the workplace in general, and for the specific use case of a SME in the construction industry. The employees' perspective is examined based on literature. Both perspectives are combined in a *transformation action cycle* which is evaluated for the construction industry.

The aim is to unite the perspectives of the employees and the employer, thus enabling SMEs to identify employee-centered measures for the planning of transformation strategies and to involve the employees as a key driver for success.

2 Perspectives on the Requirements for Employees in a Changing Work Environment

The changes a digital work environment introduces affect different aspects of the working conditions (e.g., flexibility in processes and products), environments (e.g., machine collaboration), and methods (e.g., the frequent use of information and communication technologies) [4]. All of these, in turn, affect the employee. In the short term, employees are confronted with massive changes in their working environment, daily tasks, and routines, which might lead to stress [3]. In the medium to long term, changing perspectives alter competence profiles, job descriptions and working structures. To successfully implement these changes, the demands on employees from an organizational perspective must first be understood.

To be able to appropriate support employees and derive information and communication measures, it is also essential to understand the needs and concerns of the workforce. For that reason, employer and employee perspectives are considered in the following section. Additionally, the perspective of a SME from the construction industry is provided as an example.

2.1 Organizational Perspective

Companies face several aspects that especially shape the working life and thus the company's future. Four main aspects that impact the future of work, and therefore shape the organizational perspective on transformation, can be identified: *fast knowledge growth, digitization, globalization, and demographic change* [8].

Fast Knowledge Growth. Changes caused by the development of production and industrial work in western Europe address the strengthening of services on the one hand, and the development and production of increasingly complex and high-quality products on the other [9]. This results in the growing importance of knowledge work, knowledge exchange and knowledge building. The resulting requirements do not only concern the technical infrastructure and working tools of a company, but the employees' ability to learn and adapt and their speed of learning as well [10, 11].

Digitization. Additionally, the rapid technological development of production, information, and communication technologies, demands a certain speed of development, regarding the selection, equipment and introduction of new technologies, from the companies [12, 13]. This results in new challenges for employees and managers, which affect all areas of the company, from occupational health and safety to corporate culture [14]. One example is the change of the boundary between the private and professional life of employees due to home office possibilities. The resulting requirements for employees address their competence in dealing with changing workflows, their ability to adapt to new technical tools and equipment, and whether they responsibly handle changes in working methods, such as working independent of the location, constant availability and flexible working hours [15].

Globalization. The increase in the networking between people and businesses causes the national borders for trade and development, business locations, and teams to fade. Internationally operating companies and intercultural teams require different and more social skills to enable cooperation independent of location and mother tongue. Organizations thus rely on employees with social and cultural skills [16, 17].

Demographic Change. Demographic change will lead to a shift in the population structure. Consequently, more people of advanced age, and fewer younger people, will be in gainful employment. This will lead to several necessary changes in the organization of the working environment. Additionally, this causes a "war of talents", which means that qualified employees will be a scarce and sought-after resource on the labor market of the future [18]. As a result, companies will need to attract good employees, retain them for as long as possible, and offer them optimal conditions to fully realize their potential. The expectations of the employees will thus be more strongly oriented towards making full use of their potential, which means their willingness to get involved, self-awareness and reflection regarding prevention (in terms of occupational safety and health protection) to ensure their own health.

2.2 Employee Perspective

When investigating the employee's perspective on the future of work, a differentiation by age is useful, because several studies have shown generational differences regarding motivational drivers and competences [19, 20].

Since the future of work will be characterized by older employees due to demographic change, the requirements of an older workforce are relevant [21]. However, a new generation of employees, whose attitude and competence are different from that of previous generations, will enter the labor market as well.

Studies could show that there are generational differences in job-related motivations [22]. While younger workers aspire to career development and growth, older workers attach more value to a good working atmosphere and maintaining the status quo [23, 24]. A drastic change of working conditions might thus be perceived as negative by this group of employees, especially when facing new and complex technological equipment. While several studies could show a negative relation between technology adaption and age, the overall perceived stress related to technologies at work decreases with increasing age [25, 26]. This might be because they compensate less technical skills with a more general job experience.

Regarding job tasks, older employees desire job enrichment, e.g., in terms of being a mentor [23, 27]. In contrast, younger generations—e.g., the millennials (born 1980–1990)—were characterized by aspiring to have self-realization and independence. Working conditions thus need to be flexible with a high potential for personal development to be attractive for potential employees of that generation [20]. Additionally, studies have shown that the working profile should integrate responsibility and challenging tasks [28]. This illustrates, that there are generational differences in the requirements for job-related aspects. An integration of those perspectives is thus important for an employee-centered transformation strategy.

In the future, employees will thus be confronted with expectations and requirements arising from the changing work conditions digitization causes, but they will also have their own demands. Because of the changing labor market and the "war of talents" arising from demographic change, it is important to integrate the employee's perspective in future strategies. This should include a combination of *change* and *consistency*. Change thereby refers to innovative and modern workflows, that provide the opportunity for self-realization, especially for younger workers. Consistency refers to the preservation of the values and culture of a company, which leads to a good working climate that supports a changeover that enables all employees with their different potentials and needs to participate in that change.

2.3 Perspective of a Classic Industry: Construction Industry

The challenges of a successful digital transformation are particularly tangible in the construction industry. To develop, plan and construct a complex building, an interdisciplinary team with all kinds of different skills and educational backgrounds is required. High quality standards and an increasing number of licensing requirements cause even more challenges. On top of these complex structures and processes, SMEs do usually not have the financial opportunities and resources to invest in new and still undeveloped digital technologies. This causes them to act cautiously when it comes to change. Due to already existing company-structures, SMEs are less flexible than start-up companies. Because SMEs rely on existing processes and a certain level of customer satisfaction to keep up their daily business, they depend on a long-term, sustainable development. On the other hand, decisions can be put to practice faster in SMEs than in large companies. There is therefore always a difficult balancing act between changing and preserving the existing. Because of this, it comes as it is no surprise that the productivity of the construction sector, compared to other economical branches, has been stagnating over the last couple of years in comparison to other economical branches. Over the last 10 years, the construction industry has only seen a productivity growth of around about three percent, whereas the growth in other industries was significantly higher. Digitally supported work processes are thus of great importance for the future of the construction sector. Construction-specific digital approaches (e.g., Building Information Modeling (BIM)[1]) are currently only used by 4% of the all companies in the entire construction industry [29]. The potential of this these digital approaches for the construction industry lies in the reduced complexity of information flows, the centralisation of information, and the decentralisation of the access to information. This is both an enormous opportunity and a massive challenge, because the introduction and use of such systems must be suitable for the highly heterogeneous group of employees involved in the process (e.g., different educational backgrounds). Due to the highly heterogeneous nature of the process participants, this is both an enormous potential and the greatest challenge. Because both the introduction and use of the system must be suitable for the different employees (e.g. diversity in educational background or profession) involved in the process. For that reason, the digitization process of the workflows in the construction sector is very complex. Especially for SMEs, it is of great importance to be able to take part in the competition for new employees on the one hand, and to keep experienced employees on the other [6]. Thereby, the well-being, satisfaction and health of the employees play a decisive role. Not in the least because of this, a planned digitization strategy is of great importance. One the one hand it should involve the employees and prevent excessive demands and a bad working environment caused by the change. On the other, it should meet the demands and desires the employees have with supporting measures. The existing high potential the construction industry has, can be realized by a structured digital transformation approach which involves the individual employees and promotes acceptance.

---

[1] BIM enables the digital mapping of all construction processes and thus creates the interface for cooperation with lower information losses in processes of construction companies.

3   Empirical Surveys of the Employees' Perspective: Fact Sheets

To investigate the employees' perspective on the digitization of work, empirical studies were used. First, focus groups were carried out. Subsequently, a quantitative online survey was conducted. To integrate the construction industry as a specific use case, an employer survey was conducted in a construction company. In the following section we present the fact sheets of the three studies and their main results.

3.1   Focus Groups

To identify people's worries and needs regarding the future of work, two focus groups were conducted. The advantage of focus groups compared to pre-structured interviews is that it has the potential to capture unfiltered free associations and thoughts. Each focus group was split into two semi-structured discussions. First the participants reflected on the status quo of digitization in their working environment and their experience with the transformation to digital processes. Afterwards the challenges and "dos and don'ts" of digital transformation were discussed. In the second part, the topic of the discussion were the stakeholders responsible for the digital transformation and participation opportunities for employees. Additionally, wishes for the design of transformation processes were queried.

Participants of the focus group were selected based on work experience whilst ensuring a diverse field of expertise (paramedics, research assistant, safety engineer, consultant, librarian). The seven selected participants had ages ranging from 24 to 58 (M = 38.14, SD = 15.5). Five of them were male und two were female.

To ensure a good setting for the conversation, the participants were randomly split in two discussion groups. The focus groups were carried out in German in September 2018.

The execution of the focus groups was based on an interview guideline. To provide everyone with the same picture of the topic that would be discussed, the participants were first shown a short introductory video on the digitalization of the working world.

The conversations were recorded, transcribed in accordance with the GAT 2 standard and analyzed using a consensual approach of thematic qualitative content analysis [30].

Main Results. First, two main categories were identified: Organization and Qualification.

Organization. This category includes several requirements and general conditions regarding digital transformation that organizations should consider.

The category has several subcategories based on the group discussion: leadership, error management, and participation (Table 1).

Qualification. This main category includes aspects of education and training in the context of work regarding the changing conditions caused by digitization. It has three subcategories: handling of data, lifelong learning, and superordinate competences (Table 2).

Table 1. Identified subcategories of *Organization*

Subcategories of *Organization*	
Leadership	In this subcategory requirements for sustainable management have been formulated. In detail, the insecurity of the workforce should be reduced, support should be given, and a common mindset should be established
Error management	This subcategory regards the organization's culture in dealing with mistakes. A constructive error culture is seen as a prerequisite for a successful digital transformation, especially during the transition phase
Participation	This category consists of ideas to increase the acceptance of, and commitment to, both the organization and the transformation process. This can be achieved by the employee's participation in organizational processes- and structures

Table 2. Identified subcategories for *Qualification*

Subcategories to *Qualification*	
Handling of data	This subcategory describes the competence in the handling of date. This includes large data volumes and data security
Lifelong learning	In this subcategory includes all aspects of one's professional qualification are supplemented. The focus is here on the changing learning conditions due to caused by digitization, including changing job profiles, working materials- and systems, and business models
Superordinate competences	This subcategory supplements describes the additional competences necessary competences to be able to be successful in the digitalized working world. Besides the classic job profiles. This includes social and technical skills

Summary. The results of the focus groups show two main topics of discussion: Organization and Qualification. Within these categories, the need for strong leadership, which takes responsibility and provides guidance and support, is expressed. Constructive error management was seen as another aspect required for a successful transformation to digital working models. Additionally, the participants expressed a desire for their participation in the change process. Regarding professional qualification, the awareness of the need for lifelong learning became apparent. The skills, independent of occupational profiles, that must be mastered to be successful in the digital working world were also discussed.

3.2 Quantitative Employee Survey

To gain deeper insights on the employees' perspective on the transformation of work, a quantitative online survey was conducted.

On the basis of existing literature and the conducted focus groups, various factors were identified as relevant target variables. In this context, the participants were asked to evaluate motivational aspects (e.g., the flexibility of working hours, the increase in the quality of work, improved communication) and potentially burdensome aspects (e.g., tighter schedules, increasingly complex work processes, more work). Overall, 18 items regarding the attitude towards motivational aspects and 15 items considered the burdensome aspects. For the analysis the items were combined to the variable *motivational aspects* (Cronbach's α = .94) and *burdensome aspects* (Cronbach's α = .95).

Empowerment was recorded using an instrument by Spreitzer which included the dimensions meaning, competence, self-detection, and impact [31]. Self-efficacy towards technology (SET) was measured using an instrument by Beier [32].

All items were evaluated on a six-point Likert scale, ranging from $1 = I$ *totally disagree* to $6 = I$ *totally agree*.

Sample. 507 participants aged between 19 and 66 (M = 46.18 years of age, SD = 11.82) participated in the survey. The sample approximately consisted of an equal number of men (n = 253) and women (n = 254). All respondents live in Germany. Participants varied with regard to the industrial sector in which they are working and level of education. The data was collected in June 2018.

To analyze the connection between the examined variables (Empowerment; KUT; Age) and the perception of motivational and burdensome aspects, a correlation analysis was conducted. The level of significance (p) was set to .05.

Main Results
Figure 1 illustrates the results of the correlation analysis. Only the significant correlations are included. The results of the correlation analysis show that there is a negative relation between age and motivational aspects ($r = -.25$; n = 507; $p < .01$) and burdensome aspects ($r = -.12$; n = 505; $p < .01$). Thus, older participants agree less with the burdensome aspects of workplace digitization, but also less with motivational aspects, than younger participants do.

In addition, a weak correlation between all dimensions of empowerment and the motivational aspects was found. Only competence ($r = -.24$; n = 507; $p < .01$) and self-detection ($r = -.13$; n = 507; $p < .01$) have a negative correlation with the burdensome aspects. Thus, the less the participants believe they are able to master the necessary skills of their profession (competence), the more they perceive barriers regarding digitization. The same applies to participants who experience a low self-determination in their working environment (self-determination), like the choice of work equipment, methods, or work processes.

A medium-strong correlation was found between self-efficacy towards technology and motivational aspects. Participants who show a higher self-efficacy in dealing with technology (SET) also show a more positive attitude towards the positive aspects of the digitization of the workplace ($r = .30$; n = 507; $p < .01$).

Additionally, the evaluation of motivational and burdensome aspects shows a positive correlation ($r = .12$; n = 507; $p < .01$). Thus, a more positive attitude towards motivational aspects also results in a higher evaluation of the negative aspects.

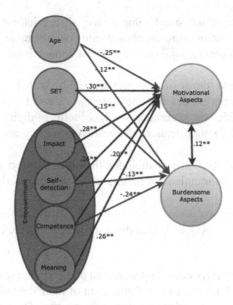

Fig. 1. Correlation analysis

Summary. Overall the results show, that personal factors, such as age, or self- confidence with regard to regarding the use of technology, and psychological empowerment, are connected to the attitude towards motivational and burdensome aspects of workplace digitization.

3.3 Employee Survey in a Construction Company

To uncover the specific demands in the construction industry, an employee survey was conducted based on the results of the quantitative and qualitative analyses described above. The aim was to supplement the results with the specific perspective of the employees of a construction company.

The questionnaire included demographic data including age, gender, work experience, and work area. In the second section, the participants were asked for their attitude towards the digital transformation of the workplace in general. In addition, they evaluated various fears regarding the digitization of their own workplace. Finally, the participants ranked a set of seven potentially negative aspects. All answers were provided on a six-point Likert-scale ranging from 1 = *totally agree* to 6 = *totally disagree*.

Overall, N = 85 participants completed the survey. Their ages ranged from 20 to 64 (M = 41; SD = 13) and their work experience ranged from 1 to 48 years of experience (M = 19.84; SD = 15.60). N = 44 participants work in the company's technical sector, n = 26 in the commercial, administrative and planning sector, and n = 11 were craftsmen. With n = 60 the sample is predominantly male (n = 24 female).

Main Results. Because of the small sample size, all results were analyzed descriptively. For the analysis, items were combined into four thematic variables (data handling, knowledge and learning, communication and connectivity, and improvement of work and processes).

Data handling includes the positive aspects of dealing with data and the connectivity of data. Such as the opportunities for one's own work and for the company. *Knowledge and learning* includes the statements on the benefits of digitization for knowledge and learning, such as the simplification of knowledge sharing and increased available knowledge.

Communication and connectivity includes the positive effect of the use of digital systems, such as better communication flows and a better connection between working areas.

Improvement of work and processes includes the positive aspects of digitization for one's own ability to solve work task, and the improvement of the company's processes as well.

Predominantly Positive Attitude. In general, all participants expressed a positive attitude towards the several aspects of the digitization of their workplace. Figure 1 shows the sample's evaluation of the several aspects of digitization. Overall, a medium level of agreement with the different aspects was found. The improvement of work and processes received the highest level of agreement (M = 4.46; SD = .66). The positive aspects of data handling were the least positively evaluated aspect (M = 4.02; SD = .67).

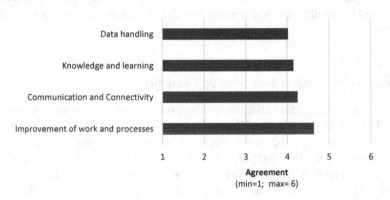

Fig. 2. Attitude towards the digitization of the workplace in a construction company

To get a better understanding of the employees' opinion, we considered the perception of digitization of the workplace for the different departments separately (Fig. 2).

The separated analysis of the attitude towards digitization shows that there is a difference in the attitude prevalent in different departments of the company. The participants from the craftmanship department perceive less benefits compared to the other two questioned departments (Fig. 3). For them motivational aspects like data handling and knowledge and learning are less convincing arguments in favor of workplace digitization,

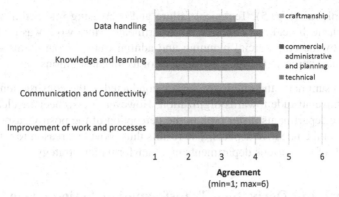

Fig. 3. Attitude towards digitization of workplace in the construction company according to department

than they are to the other departments. Also, the benefit of work and process improvement is less beneficial for the craftmanship department than for the other departments of the company.

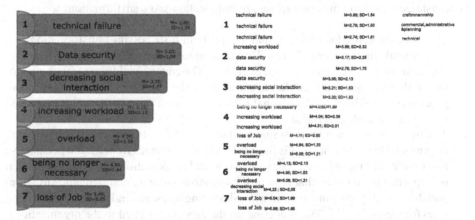

Fig. 4. Worries regarding digitization   **Fig. 5.** Worries regarding digitization in departments

Overall, the ranking of the possible disadvantages of the digitization of work show little concern regarding the risk of losing their job and being no longer necessary (Fig. 4). The highest priority was given to worries regarding technical aspects: firstly, technical failure and secondly, data security. Worries concerning process- and task-related problems like overload, increasing workload, and decreasing social interaction, were ranked in the middle. In general, the answers show little existing worry or fear of overload.

The participants tended to be more concerned about the smooth operation of new technical solutions.

The separate analysis of the ranking within the departments showed a dissimilar picture. Differences were found regarding the excessive demands and the concern to become superfluous (Fig. 5). Technical failure and decreasing interaction were fears felt more by the technical and commercial departments. More work was ranked as the smallest risk by the commercial planning and administrative departments - probably because they also perceive the most advantages of technical solutions.

Summary. In summary, the employee survey conducted in the construction company showed a positive attitude towards digitization. However, it also became clear that the attitudes of the departments differ both in the perception of the positive aspects and in the weighting of the negative aspects. The results thus provide a reason to integrate the different needs of the various departments in a transformation strategy.

4   Summary and Derivates - Transformation Action Cycle

The previously presented results show several main aspects that should be included in the development of an employee-centered transformation strategy. Using the empirical results and the literature-based factors we identified, a short and compact model was designed to provide a first structured point of reference to integrate important aspects in a transformation process for digital change that considers the requirements for the employers and employees regarding the digital transformation process. Four main aspects can be translated into recommendations for communication and transformation:

1. Qualification and education are major aspects in a successful transformation to a digital work environment [2, 15]. This is common sense in literature but was also emphasized by the employees (see Sect. 3.1). The educational frame is thus a major task field that organizations should integrate in the transformation to digital work processes. Especially for SMEs that have to deal with limited resources compared to, e.g., large-scale enterprises.
2. The literature and the empirical studies showed that the organizational frame is very important. On the one hand, it is important to guide changes from a meta perspective and control and include aspects as education and participation. On the other hand, it is important to keep the character of the organization (e.g., demographic structure) and different departments in mind when designing measures and strategies for digital transformation [5, 12]. The reflection on the aspects assigned to the organizational frame is thus indispensable when thinking about transformation strategies.
3. Personal and individual aspects influence the digital change of an organization. These can be personal factors like the attitude towards technology, psychological empowerment, or job-related preferences which may differ in different generations of employees [2,7,20]. But they also include personal goals and qualification needs. For that reason, this task field should not be underestimated when designing user-centered strategies for digital change and development.
4. Employees desire a good error management, forms of participation, and a culture of leadership that includes support and the establishment of common mindsets, stability, and reliability of corporate values, as well as modernity and progressiveness. Organizational value structures, that include corporate values (both internal and external), leadership guidelines, and participation possibilities for employees, are thus another factor for a successful transformation strategy [18, 27].

From the identified task areas for transformation, an overview of the fields of action for the transformation to digital work environments was derived. This can be used to derive more detailed aspects.

Transformation Action Cycle
Figure 6 shows the transformation action cycle for an employee-centered transformation strategy for digital change, that was developed based on the aspects identified in this paper. The main focus is on the employee-centered approach. On this basis, four fields of action were developed. These were based on literature and the empirical results, as described above (qualification, educational frame, organizational value structure, and personal task field). The subdivisions (outer ring) also offer a useful tool for the structuring and orientation of the fields of action. While the fields of action describe the superordinate fields, the outer ring describes the thematic fields that can be used to derive concrete measures. The latter are each located at the intersection of the two inner fields of action to which their content belongs. The distinction is made to structure the measures and should not be regarded as strictly selective. All aspects influence each other and each functions as a gear wheel in the digitization process. At the interface of the organizational and educational framework *participation, trainings* and *prevention of overload* have been arranged. These aspects were placed in the field of *organizational frame* because they need an organizational framework to be able to provide measures

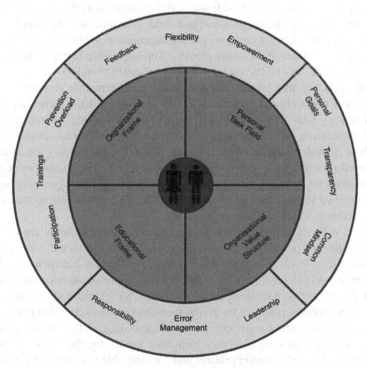

Fig. 6. Transformation action cycle

derived from these aspects (e.g., regarding the provision of necessary resources). Especially *participation* is an aspect that needs to be embedded, accompanied and supported by the organization, e.g., regarding the necessary instructions for leaders and employees. The aspects also belong to the educational field, because participation processes and their designs need to be learned, both by the employers and the employees. Moreover, the prevention of work overload, and trainings, belong to the organizational frame as well, since this provides the necessary frame for courses and measures against an overload of work (which is closely linked to trainings). Finally, since its content is a form of education, both aspects belong to the educational field as well.

At the intersection of the educational and the organizational value structure field, the aspects *responsibility, error management* and *leadership* were placed. *Responsibility* thereby refers to the educational task field, because taking more responsibility, and thus relieving the employer of responsibility, is a learning process. It is also associated with the field of organizational value structure, because transferring and taking responsibility is part of an organizational value structure that includes aspects like the trust in employees and is thus a necessary condition for the empowerment of employees. Moreover, leadership is on the one hand closely connected to the organizational value structure because, for a great part, values are communicated, reproduced and shaped at this level. A common mindset is thereby shaped by the organizational values. On the other hand, it is also connected to the personal task field because the more individuals comply with the corporate values, the higher the meaning component of psychological empowerment and the intrinsic work motivation is [31]. Additionally, transparency is a relevant aspect between the organizational values and the personal task field. *Transparency* includes transparent communication about changes and transparent information policies to give employees a comprehensive overview of the entire process. This supports a better understanding of decisions and workflows and encourages solution-oriented thinking [2].

Personal goals are also a factor for a possible transformation strategy, associated with the personal task field and organizational value structure. Considering the personal goals of employees in the transformation strategy to digital working environments can be achieved by addressing job related goals (such as a higher level of education) or private goals (such as flexible working hours because of family obligations) which are more easily achieved after the digital conversion of the workplace. The guiding principle here should be to adapt the working conditions to the needs of the employee by using digital means and not vice versa. Thus, a higher motivation and commitment to the employer, as well as a better working climate, arises [5, 8].

Associated with the organizational frame and personal task fields are the aspects *empowerment, flexibility* and *feedback*. To discover negative evolvement (on a process-, technical- and social-level) at an early point in time, *Feedback* is indispensable, both for the management and the staff. *Flexibility* refers to the opportunities organizations offer regarding the distribution of working time, models and locations, to allow their employees to reach their optimal potential by giving them the option to combine personal (e.g., taking on the care for family members) and work goals (e.g., a fulltime job, additional qualifications). *Empowerment* is a very important aspect for the future of work, an employee-centered transformation process and a sustainable workforce. Empowerment should on the one hand belong to the organizational task field, because it is a holistic organizational task [8, 33]. On the other hand, it should belong to the personal task field, because it requires an intensive dialogue at the personal level.

Overall, the transformation action cycle has to be read as an integrative summary of the employees' and employers' needs for the transformation to digital working environments on an empirical and literature supported base.

5   Evaluation of the Transformation Action Cycle During Operation in Construction Industry

As an example, the transformation action cycle was tested and evaluated in a SME of the construction industry that was in the middle of a digital transformation process. All four fields of action turned out to be important for the successful implementation of digitalization or change management in an existing culture or organisational structure in general. But when tested in a medium-sized construction company, it turned out that when planning a transformation process which includes all fields of action and task fields, the complexity increases rapidly due to the high diversity of the employees and the many external participants involved in the work of a construction company. Thus, the role of the construction manager was of particular interest for the evaluation since all relevant and critical aspects come together (cost- quality-, and time-related topics, operational-safety requirements) there. For that reason, it makes sense to choose this area as an example for the evaluation. As a process, the introduction of a new system for internal communication and knowledge management was used, which offers location-independent access to all relevant data and communication processes, as well as multimedia support for documentation and administration. Therefore, as a first point of evaluation, a tool for the selection of the specific process or role for applying the transformation action cycle would increase usability.

In the analysed field of business, the personal task- and organizational frame field were the most important. For the observed group of employees, it was critical to have benefits like less administrative work and more flexibility, which would give them more time to concentrate on their key responsibilities and could lead to an overall stress reduction on the long term. As a consequence, employee satisfaction increases, and stress-related dissatisfaction and overwork decreases. This would, in turn, lead to a better stability in the execution and quality of the processes. The communication of the long-term goal of that change process was found to be crucial for acceptance, because during the transformation process the overlapping use of the old and new system could turn out to increase the workload. Thus, feedback on, and transparency of, the long-term goal were relevant aspects for the transformation process according to the transformation action cycle. Ways to cope with an increase in the time used for tasks because of the use of digital systems, is on the one hand clarity that overwork should be prevented and on the other hand how it should be prevented. Therefore, it is more important than ever that employees have a clear understanding of the overall process, which can only be achieved through transparency.

For this reason, and in general, it proved to be important to have the employees participate in the change process as early as possible. Participation proofed to be the best way to spot ambiguities, errors or deficiencies early on.

As digitalization is new to most employees, especially to those of a higher age or corporate affiliation, the educational task area proved to be particularly useful. In the here described use case, personal trainings in smaller groups or one-on-one sessions, in which the employees get to test the new system hands-on, were the basis for a successful transformation. The aspect of *responsibilities* was also very important. For the considered process, having a responsible contact person, who can easily be reached at any time in case of questions or uncertainties, showed to be a driver for the implementation in the daily work. For a SME, not disrupting daily business and going easy on resources usually have the highest priority during a change process. It is therefore essential to have additional trained staff to support the employees during the transformation process. For the considered company, it thus seemed to be helpful to have a certain number of key users, who received a more intensive training, and could later share their knowledge with the different areas and locations/constructions sites.

The organizational value structure can only be influenced indirectly by taking concrete measures. The experience of the transformation process in the here described use case showed that leadership has a particularly important role. Leaders should serve as examples and should thus exemplify and reproduce corporate values. In the considered process, e.g., the decision of the management to move the company to another city. Employers gave negative feedback on that decision. A retroactive evaluation of this decision found that aspects such as transparency and considering personal goals were not taken into account here. The decision of the management was subsequently classified as a wrong decision and corrected. In this way, the management tried to set a good example regarding the maintenance of the company's value structure by establishing a good error management, taking into account the personal circumstances of the employees, and supporting the common mindset that includes feedback. In general, constant user feedback regarding the implementation process remains as crucial at any time. Additionally, the experience that giving feedback leads to change is important to support empowerment in the workforce. Especially in times of change, a common mindset, affects all fields of action of the here presented action cycle, facilitates the implementation of change and provides a secure framework for employees and managers in times of change.

In conclusion the here presented transformation action cycle proofed to be a helpful visualization and structuring aid. The task areas could all be confirmed as being relevant. In practice, the appointing of the aspects to the fields of action was rather unstable and influenced each other in an iterative way. After the application in the practical example, it can be concluded that the arrangement of the individual aspects should rather be criss-cross than separated into individual sections.

Especially for SMEs and resource-saving approaches, each transformation process must be planned individually and depending on the chosen approach, it must be decided to which extent each field of action has to be integrated in the planning strategy. The transformation action cycle can be a good tool for the support of that decision process.

6   Outlook

The transformation action cycle is a basic overview of the relevant aspects for the digital transformation in SMEs. The evaluation in the construction industry showed that all fields of action include aspects that should be integrated in an employee-centered planning process. However, it also showed, that the arrangement of the aspects in the outer ring was rather unstable. Additionally, the evaluation process clearly showed, that, due to a fast-growing complexity, not every aspect might have to be considered for the planning and implementation of the digitization of a process in a SME. As a next step, support for prioritization should thus be developed.

Moreover, a third part which provides possible concrete measures for the transformation to a digital process should be added. An example is the use of key-users for the implementation of new digital processes.

Additionally, an employee-centered transformation strategy should integrate a user-centered evaluation of the success of the digital transformation process. This also has to be developed and integrated in the future work. The aim is to develop a more concrete model for the digital transformation of SMEs based on empirical results. This can then be used to derive concrete measures and task areas and will continue to be evaluated and developed through practical application.

Acknowledgements. This research was funded by the Project SiTra 4.0 (German Ministry for research and education, reference no. 02L15A000-02L15A004). We thank all participants for taking part in the studies and sharing their opinion with us.

References

1. Frazzon, E.M., Hartmann, J., Makuschewitz, T., Scholz-Reiter, B.: Towards socio-cyber-physical systems in production networks. Procedia CIRP **7**(2013), 49–54 (2013)
2. Hecklau, F., Galeitzke, M., Flachs, S., Kohl, H.: Holistic approach for human resource management in industry 4.0. Procedia CIRP **54**(1), 1–6 (2016)
3. Romero, D., et al.: Towards an operator 4.0 typology: a human-centric perspective on the fourth industrial revolution technologies. In: Proceedings of the International Conference on Computers and Industrial Engineering (CIE46), Tianjin, China, pp. 29–31, October 2016
4. Buschmeyer, A., Schuh, G., Wentzel, D.: Organizational transformation towards product-service systems—empirical evidence in managing the behavioral transformation process. Procedia CIRP **47**(1), 264–269 (2016)
5. Shamim, S., Cang, S., Yu, H., Li, Y.: Management approaches for Industry 4.0: a human resource management perspective. In: IEEE Congress on Evolutionary Computation (CEC), pp. 5309–5316. IEEE, July 2016
6. Lindner, D., Ludwig, T., Amberg, M.: Work 4.0–concepts for smart working SMEs. HMD Praxis der Wirtschaftsinformatik **55**(5), 1–21 (2018)
7. Meyer, J.: Workforce age and technology adoption in small and medium-sized service firms. Small Bus. Econ. **37**(3), 305–324 (2011). https://doi.org/10.1007/s11187-009-9246-y
8. Schermuly, C.C.: New Work-Gute Arbeit gestalten: Psychologisches Empowerment von Mitarbeitern, vol. 10167. Haufe-Lexware, Freiburg im Breisgau (2019)
9. Boes, A.: *Informatisierung, Wissen und der Wandel der Arbeitswelt*. na (2005)
10. Dombrowski, U., Riechel, C., Evers, M.: Industrie 4.0–Die Rolle des Menschen in der vierten industriellen Revolution. Industrie **4**, 129–153 (2014)
11. Loebbecke, C., Picot, A.: Reflections on societal and business model transformation arising from digitization and big data analytics: a research agenda. J. Strateg. Inf. Syst. **24**(3), 149–157 (2015)

12. Schneider, M.: Digitalization of production, human capital, and organizational capital. In: Harteis, C. (ed.) The Impact of Digitalization in the Workplace. PPL, vol. 21, pp. 39–52. Springer, Cham (2018). https://doi.org/10.1007/978-3-319-63257-5_4
13. Gudergan, G., Buschmeyer, A., Krechting, D., Feige, B.: Evaluating the readiness to transform towards a product-service system provider by a capability maturity modelling approach. Procedia CIRP **30**, 384–389 (2015)
14. Bauer, W., Hämmerle, M., Schlund, S., Vocke, C.: Transforming to a hyper-connected society and economy – towards an "Industry 4.0". Procedia Manuf. **3**, 417–424 (2015)
15. Lehner, F., Sundby, M.W.: ICT skills and competencies for SMEs: results from a structured literature analysis on the individual level. In: Harteis, C. (ed.) The Impact of Digitalization in the Workplace. PPL, vol. 21, pp. 55–69. Springer, Cham (2018). https://doi.org/10.1007/978-3-319-63257-5_5
16. Wiersema, M.F., Bowen, H.P.: Corporate diversification: the impact of foreign competition, industry globalization, and product diversification. Strateg. Manag. J. **29**(2), 115–132 (2008)
17. Gubán, M., Kovács, G.: Industry 4.0 Conception. Acta Technica Corvininesis-Bull. Eng. **10**(1), 111 (2017)
18. Sommer, L.P., Heidenreich, S., Handrich, M.: War for talents—how perceived organizational innovativeness affects employer attractiveness. R&D Manage. **47**(2), 299–310 (2017)
19. Czaja, S.J., et al.: Factors predicting the use of technology: findings from the center for research and education on aging and technology enhancement (CREATE). Psychol. Aging **21**(2), 333–352 (2006)
20. Cennamo, L., Gardner, D.L.: Generational differences in work values, outcomes and person-organisation values fit. IEEE Eng. Manage. Rev. **39**, 24–36 (2008)
21. Hertel, G., Zacher, H.: Managing the aging workforce. In: The SAGE Handbook of Industrial, Work, & Organizational Psychology, vol. 3, pp. 1–93 (2015)
22. Ng, T.W.H., Feldman, D.C.: The relationships of age with job attitudes: a meta-analysis. Pers. Psychol. **63**(3), 677–718 (2010)
23. Kooij, D.T., Jansen, P.G., Dikkers, J.S., De Lange, A.H.: The influence of age on the associations between HR practices and both affective commitment and job satisfaction: a meta-analysis. J. Organ. Behav. **31**(8), 1111–1136 (2010)
24. Kogovsek, M., Kogovsek, M.: Retaining mature knowledge workers: the quest for human capital investments. Procedia – Soc. Behav. Sci. **106**, 2280–2288 (2013)
25. Kluge, J., Hildebrandt, J., Ziefle, M.: The golden age of silver workers? In: Zhou, J., Salvendy, G. (eds.) HCII 2019. LNCS, vol. 11593, pp. 520–532. Springer, Cham (2019). https://doi.org/10.1007/978-3-030-22015-0_40
26. Tarafdar, M., Tu, Q., Ragu-Nathan, T.S., Ragu-Nathan, B.S.: Crossing to the dark side: examining creators, outcomes, and inhibitors of technostress. Commun. ACM **54**(9), 113 (2011)
27. Kooij, D.T., Guest, D.E., Clinton, M., Knight, T., Jansen, P.G., Dikkers, J.S.: How the impact of HR practices on employee well-being and performance changes with age. Hum. Resour. Manage. J. **23**(1), 18–35 (2013)
28. Schaar, A.K., Calero Valdez, A., Hamann, T., Ziefle, M.: Industry 4.0 and its future staff. Matching millennials perceptions of a perfect job with the requirements of digitalization. In: Paper presented at the 7th International Conference on Competitive Manufacturing (COMA 2019), Stellenbosch, South Africa, pp. 246–252 (2019)
29. Tauchert, J., Thiessen, T.: Digitalisierung der mittelständischen Bauwirtschaft in Deutschland. Statusevaluation und Handlungsempfehlungen (2018). https://kommunikation-mittelstand.digital/content/uploads/2018/10/Status-Quo_Digitalisierung_Bauwirtschaft.pdf
30. Selting, M., Auer, P., Barth-Weingarten, D.: A system for transcribing talk-in-interaction: GAT 2. Gesprächsforschung - Online-Zeitschrift zur verbalen Interaktion 12, 1–51 (2011). ISSN 1617-1837. https://www.gespraechsforschung-ozs.de

31. Spreitzer, G.M.: Psychological empowerment in the workplace: dimensions, measurement, and validation. Acad. Manag. J. **38**(5), 1442–1465 (1995)
32. Beier, G.: Kontrollüberzeugungen im Umgang mit Technik. Report Psychologie **9**, 684–693 (1999)
33. Liden, R.C., Wayne, S.J., Sparrowe, R.T.: An examination of the mediating role of psychological empowerment on the relations between the job, interpersonal relationships, and work outcomes. J. Appl. Psychol. **85**(3), 407 (2000)

It's About the Documents
Re-engineering Business Processes in Public Administrations

Christopher Lentzsch[(✉)] and Thomas Herrmann

Ruhr-University of Bochum, 44780 Bochum, Germany
{christopher.lentzsch,thomas.herrmann}@ruhr-uni-bochum.de

Abstract. Business processes in public administration heavily rely on the exchange and transformation of information. The potential improvements through the introduction of supporting ICT are enormous. In this paper we report on several problems we found during the redesign of a business process for electronic invoices in a public administration and show how improving document handling as a part of proper information exchange could improve the whole process and highlight why it is a key challenge for such processes.

Keywords: Business process management · Socio-technical design · Information systems

1 Introduction

Business process management is focused on activities. In public administrations, these activities are to a large extent a transformation of information. Such processes can enormously profit from the use of ICT [1]. Therefore, the current and ongoing transformation from paper-based documents towards electronic workflows offers a great chance to exploit these benefits. Considering the used documents and their handling as central parts of the process re-engineering allows exploiting this potential.

The main motivation for putting the used documents into focus was that a consultancy agency presented an e-invoicing process and ICT solution which included only one document: the (e-)invoice. The present paper-based process relied on and produced many different documents. Handling such documents and their information is important to leverage the improvement potentials of ICT — though, it is often not considered [2]. Therefore, we decided to focus on it.

In this case study, the business processes are captured with documents and information transformation in its center using ethnographic techniques. Additionally, found artifacts, used documents, and file storages are captured, analyzed, and represented in a document model. The model is used to guide the process discovery phase and identify issues during the process analysis phase. To ensure the resulting processes and technological support fits the organizational needs and provides a sufficient process experience, socio-technical heuristics, and design goals are employed and used to spot further issues, understand the underlying causes and guide decisions during the redesign. The

© Springer Nature Switzerland AG 2020
F. F.-H. Nah and K. Siau (Eds.): HCII 2020, LNCS 12204, pp. 110–118, 2020.
https://doi.org/10.1007/978-3-030-50341-3_9

final designs have been discussed with the process participants in workshop sessions following the socio-technical walkthrough method [3, 4].

The case study was performed in the accounting department of a large public administration and accompanied the introduction of a process to handle electronic invoices (e-invoices). The handling of invoices was mainly paper based and supporting ICT was only partially present. The motivation to 'digitize' — beside fulfilling EU and federal requirements — was to improve transparency, error handling and reduce the processing time. The change was initiated by an EU regulation, requiring the organization to process e-invoice by the end of 2019.

We identified many problems during the process analysis phase which would be easy to resolve through the use of unified and cross-cutting ICT and ease the introduction of new electronic workflows. A key element to do so was the introduction of a central document management system which would provide the required information for every process step and thus increase the availability of information and therefore the overall transparency.

2 Background and Related Work

The implementation of the EU directive 2014/55/EU in Germany requires all bodies of public administration to accept e-invoices since the end of 2019. The format of an e-invoice is defined in EN 16931. Increasingly, companies are obliged to issue their invoices as e-invoices. The reference implementation of this norm is the XML-based 'XRechnung' (transl. XInvoice) format. The older ZUGFeRD format has been updated in version 2.0 to conform to the standard. The submission of electronic invoices is done through central submission platforms. For small businesses, it is possible to upload an invoice to this platform via the web or use the platform to create the invoice completely. Such electronic invoices can easily be processed using ICT and thus enable an enhanced technical support.

Currently, the most popular way of visualizing and modeling processes is BPMN 2.0 [5] which serves as a general purpose notation suitable for most domains [6, 7]. For the use in public administrations specialized notations and methods are available like PICTURE [8] which provide a very limited set of elements and – in the case of PICTURE – even activities; while this simplification can beneficial – especially when the process is discussed verbally – it can also be a burden when complex activities need to be reflected in the model. SeeMe [9] is another general purpose notation and method to model process with a focus on communication and socio-technical aspects. The set of needed symbols is small and the number of relations connecting elements is reduced through embedding elements. Another interesting aspect of SeeMe is the option to express 'uncertainty' — parts of the model can be marked as incomplete or unknown. Having this explicitly expressed can help during the analysis and re-engineering to identify problematic areas and helps to understand the model. SeeMe is designed to be used in collaborative modeling workshops where the process model serves as a boundary object [3]. These workshops are called socio-technical walkthroughs. By reviewing the process step by step and the involvement of all stakeholders a common understanding of the process is achieved. Every participant can propose changes and discuss them with the relevant stakeholders immediately to understand its impact.

Public administrations are a special environment for process redesign projects as they pose some challenges to the project with their large number of processes and process variants, organic structures with many interfaces and layers of hierarchy and wide margins of discretion to decide [10, 11]. In this setting, not all process variants can be considered and optimized. However, the problems found are often present in many processes and their variants. Therefore, overarching solutions promise relevant benefits [11]. One Area where such potentials are often present is the support of ICT and the digitization of paper-based assets [2]. Although the interplay of business processes and information management is of particular importance to leverage these potentials, it is not reflected in many approaches for such projects [2].

3   Case Study

This case study has been performed in the accounting department of a public administration during the switch from a paper-based invoice handling to an E-invoicing workflow. Due to changes in EU regulations the administration was forced to accept and process e-invoices. This obligation triggered a general project to digitize all procedures of the department. Up to this point, the handling of orders and invoices had been completely paper-based. Besides, the department's own internal processes the process departments which rely on the central accounting department (its clients) also needed to reflect the new requirements. In the most common case, the clients handled the order process themselves and forwarded the invoices to central accounting for payment and archiving – less common (but in some cases required) is the involvement of central accounting already at the time of ordering or even before that.

3.1   Approach for the Case Study and Goals

Process capturing was performed in all units of the accounting department and three external client departments that rely on the central invoice handling processes. This ensured that the designed process would also address the needs of clients and the required interfaces are present and fit together. Involving this set of stakeholders enabled us to design the process with respect to the socio-technical dimension and provide the means for communication and feedback.

The main functional goal of the redesign project was to fulfill the requirements set forth by the EU regulation and accept e-invoices. However, also non-functional dimensions, such as transparency, error handling and reduction of processing time, were included as transparency has already been identified as a major problem.

The transparency problem is particularly evident in relation to payment reminders: The accounting department was not able to retrace unpaid invoices. It was unclear whether the original invoice was lost, never received, or still being processed. The same is true for corrections: if an invoice was corrected by a supplier the correction could only be reflected with manual effort as the status of the original invoice was unclear and its current location. Only if it was already fully processed it was present in the ERP-System otherwise it was not possible to find it without asking each individual clerk in the different units of the accounting department.

To fulfill both sets of requirements the approach of the re-engineering project followed the business process management life cycle [12]: After identification of the relevant and most important processes for invoice handling inside the central department and in the client department. The processes were captured using ethnographic techniques. The ethnographic phase was guided by the flow of actual documents in the department and their processing. Actual documents served as a boundary object between the ethnographer and the process participants.

The processes were modeled using the SeeMe notation [9] to allow for discussing the to-be process with the participants during the redesign and in workshops easily. Also, because the technical basis for the new process has not been decided and requirements were unclear. Therefore, expressing 'vagueness' explicitly was important. Documents were represented in an additional UML class model [13] which is suitable and common for modeling documents [14]. Although, most notations for process models (including SeeMe) include elements to represent documents, resources or entities. We needed a deeper understanding of the employed documents and their respective information types. We needed to understand what they represented and when they were real duplicates.

The resulting models were annotated with issues the process participants uttered during the ethnographic phase to identify the pain point for them and potential weaknesses of the executed process. Additionally, the process models were inspected using a heuristic evaluation method for socio-technical processes [15, 16] to identify systematic flaws and reflect the participants, e.g. considering job fit or monotony.

Based on this analysis and the formal requirement of e-invoicing processes the new to-be processes were created. Design alternatives were considered with regard to the non-functional modeling goals and their compatibility with the socio-technical heuristics. To ensure the resulting processes are useful for the organization they have been inspected together with process participants and other relevant stakeholders using the socio-technical walkthrough (STWT) method in the accounting department itself. A separate session was conducted with the client departments of the main organization to reflect both perspectives and ensure the interfaces match. The to-be process was designed with the principle of data minimization and privacy in mind and additionally reviewed by an additional external privacy expert to pay respect to the GDPR's requirement of privacy by design [17].

3.2 Identified Processes

The payment process and related processes were present in the department in many different variants and forms and for a large variety of purposes — from renting and leasing contracts to invoices for construction projects and large scale production facilities. This is common for public administrations and working with all of them is hardly possible but the found issues are often present across the multiple instances and variants and therefore profit from similar measures [11]. For this case study, only the handling of regular invoices and the corresponding procedure of ordering from the client departments have been in the center of attention – however, existing related processes have also been studied and partially reflected in the process models but were not re-designed. These regular processes should serve as a blueprint for other more complex cases, but because they were by a magnitude more common they promised the most potential. Also, the processing of traveling costs or payroll related processes have been omitted from the analysis and redesign for this project.

Generally, three different ways — from the perspective of the client departments — are common for the procurement. Low value orders: The client department itself is required to fulfill the legal requirements. Guidelines on how to fulfill them are available as well as forms that can be used to include the relevant legal clauses. For high value orders, the relying department has to ask the central department to handle the ordering and payment. The legal requirements are more complex and several checks of the manufacturer or supplier have to be performed. Additionally, more complete reasoning about the choice of the product and its supplier have to be given. To initiate such procurements a special standardized form is available. The third case are exceptions: the range from projects which require international invitations for tender, simple online orders which include non-EU states or orders which are based on framework contracts.

3.3   Identified Issues

While the actual order and invoice handling process is specific to the case study the observed problems and their underlying cause may be present in one form or another in other processes and other bodies of public administrations.

In the following, we report problems that serve as examples for the 79 issues found during the ethnographic phase and the heuristic evaluation - if issues were already known from the ethnographic phase, they have been omitted during the heuristic evaluation. We further generalized the issues and removed exceptions to reduce the risk of identification for individual clerks and ensure to address structural challenges. The finalized issue register contained 45 entries. The majority of the problems had an impact on the processing time (16 cases). Matching those issues with the socio-technical heuristics, they all matched the "proper information exchange and access".

During the ethnographic phase in the client departments and the analysis of used and produced artifacts, it became clear that special practices have emerged to cope with this issue. Several departments shared an Excel-sheet, which replicated the original form (which is provided by the central department). This replicated form offered common default values through drop-down menus. But some of the actually required fields were missing or were consistently ignored and not filled in, which has been accepted for years by the central department. The central department's clerks also created specialized notices to address common flaws in the received documents and ask the original sender to correct these. Although, each unit of the central accounting department had a common template for such notices. Each clerk maintained her own version of the notice and added handwritten annotations to the documents to give further information. Despite these specialized documents incomplete information, errors and missing attachments were common within the process and hindered its smooth operation.

The employed documents (official and unofficial forms) have been present in many different versions. The use of old and outdated versions was common. Two main reasons for that are that changes of official forms are not announced (if only minor adjustments are made) and that many departments created templates or created new documents through editing copies of previous ones. This kept the old forms and templates in the loop instead of the new updated version of the form. These old documents were on the hand missing information which was important to handle the cases quickly but in some cases also asked for information that was no longer required and difficult to acquire. Thus, increasing the processing time of the whole case.

The client departments all expressed that handling the orders and invoices is only a small part of their daily work and that they have a hard time to distinguish the regular from the exceptional cases and that it is hard to keep all the criteria in mind. They have to check to correctly initiate the right process. For the examined departments all cases apart from the default case were so rare that they had to rely on documentation or ask for help to fulfill such tasks.

The clerks in the central department on the other side could all distinguish the different cases easily and knew how to handle the legal requirements and what guidelines to follow. For them, interruptions posed a major problem: These were on the one hand telephone calls were they needed to advise the client departments on how to handle a case; or colleges coming into the office and asking for a missing invoice or how a specific invoice has been handled. Both happen frequently because of the lack of practice in many client departments and because there is no central register of the invoices and orders nor any way to get the current status of an invoice or who is currently working on it.

How these cases are handled once the missing invoice or order is found, depends on the clerk. The handling of errors and missing information is handled differently depending on the clerk. Some send all documents back to the client department with a short note about the flaw and the request to fix it; others call the department and ask for the missing information and add a handwritten note to the document. Clear criteria of how these two cases are distinguished do not exist. While there is only one original case file, all units of the central department store their own copy with their corrections and updates. This ensures that they can find the case without retrieving the original case file and their changes are documented. But, the changes are not back-propagated to units that were previously involved in handling the case. This can introduce new problems, e.g. if you ask unit two they won't know about corrections in unit five and therefore answers regarding the same case will differ depending on the unit contacted. There were no rules for the replacement of employees in the case of absence.

Several clerks had to check information that is present only on paper sheets and had to manually enter it into the ERP-System. Some entries are duplicated on the paper forms and need to be filled in several times manually. In case of missing information, the clerks often had to "google" to find a person they could try contact. Another issue was the post service which often caused delays between the department because it either took long or letters and messages got lost.

The main problem was the lack of transparency which made it hard and costly to resolve problems because the search for information was tedious and required information often not available. Other problems related to the breaks of media which are caused by the only marginally technical support for paper-based processing, the lack of a central and up-to-date repository of current information, forms, and guidelines, the bad usability of the employed software and the duplication of effort that stemmed from the missing reuse of already present information.

3.4 Improved Process Design

For the new to-be process, a focus had been set on an integrated technical solution which does not only support the users in fulfilling the task at hand but also provides help and required information to its users. It is set up as a web service to handle invoices but also to already place orders easily in the correct way and review the archive of orders and invoices later. Apart from the technical means attention has been paid to mark the responsibilities clearly and include contact persons in case of errors or if help is needed. To ease communication identifiers have been designed to be pronounceable with little ambiguity and already carry relevant information, such as the current year or similar. Inside the central accounting department, the files can be easily shared to review them together with a college but are otherwise protected by a role-based access model.

A special focus is on the storage of documents and their versions, which build as the central system which provides the relevant information to all steps of the processes. To ensure all invoices and orders are known and all different formats can be handled; we propose a semi-central collection through a central gateway. Every department gets an individual email address to process all orders and invoices. Automatically e-invoices are extracted and represented in the new web platform as well as other common and processable formats. Once the invoice is accepted as correct by the client department, it is forwarded to central accounting. This also serves as an entry point for digitizing paper invoices. Apart from this is enabled central accounting to notice stale invoices and help to clear them or find unhandled invoices once a manufacturer or supplier sends a payment reminder and check its legitimacy. To ensure further development of the platform ways to engage in a continuous improvement process has been included, such as feedback forms and user questionnaires.

To ensure the to-be process not only fixes problems of the old flawed process but also improves the overall process for its participants. We held two STWT-Workshops one with the central accounting department which was attended by members of all the involved units. The second workshop took place with two different client departments. Overall both workshops considered the proposed to-be process usable and wanted it to replace the current process. Several improvements to provide further help during the handling of invoices and orders have been proposed as well as update notifications if the status of a case changes in the central accounting department. However, the general flow of the process and the general technical support infrastructure did not need to change.

With regard to the privacy evaluation no major flaws cloud be identified as only required information was handled and the access was restricted through a role-based access model. Further, the central document handling made deletion and handling of possible requests to the right of access easy. However, with only the process and document model, the risk assessment was limited from an external point of view.

4 Discussion

Overall, the followed approach was successful in identifying the pain points for the users and potential flaws in the process execution. The re-engineered to-be processes were accepted by the process participants and other relevant stakeholders in the final STWT-Session. The document-centric approach resulted in process models with enough depth to understand the current issues found during the ethnographic phase and heuristic inspection. This was particularly helpful when decisions had to be made during the re-engineering phase. It allowed for concrete planning of supporting ICT and the design of the relevant interfaces between different units and departments.

Using the heuristics helped to inspect the processes in a systematic manner and ensured to pay respect to all relevant areas. It automatically provided a structure to organize the identified problems – the ones spotted during heuristic evaluation as well as the issues captured during the ethnographic phase. Many problems have already been identified during the ethnographic observation and were uttered by the process participants as common pitfalls and annoyances. Additional problems have been found during the heuristic evaluation of the captured processes. Through clustering, the different problems and further inspection overarching problems could be identified. Using ethnographic techniques and following the paper trail allowed us to capture the 'real' process and how it is executed as opposed to how it should be executed. It helped to open up conversations with the process participants as the followed document served as a boundary object and the participants did not get the feeling of being under surveillance.

However, the document-centric approach was helpful for considering design alternatives and getting the details of the process right for the public administration at hand. But the overarching problems of missing transparency were already known and obvious in the organization. Also, the benefits of replacing paper trails with digital workflows are well known. Besides that, it helped to observe the back and forth between the central accounting department and its clients to understand what support is needed to enable the clients to provide the information needed and follow the required guidelines. Otherwise, including the ordering process for all possible types of orders and resulting invoices would not have been considered, which resulted in creating a one-stop-shop. The order and invoice handling process is augmented with the supporting documentation and means to contact experts to support the clients and provide them the required help.

5 Conclusion

The potentials found for digital solutions and ICT support in public administrations are enormous. We found – in this case study – that the management of information is a key challenge to solve for a successful process. But has to be implemented as an overarching solution. The digital storage of case files which was handled individually in each unit of the central accounting department created isolated islands and the result can be considered harmful as the information regarding the same case is different in each of the units and does not reflect the final outcome. Identifying such structures can be hard as they make perfectly sense from the individual unit's point of view.

References

1. Krcmar, H.: Informationsmanagement. Springer, Heidelberg (2015). https://doi.org/10.1007/978-3-662-45863-1
2. Krcmar, H.: Einführung in das Informationsmanagement. S. Springer, Heidelberg (2015). https://doi.org/10.1007/978-3-662-44329-3

3. Herrmann, T., Kunau, G., Loser, K.U., Menold, N.: Socio-technical walkthrough: designing technology along work processes. In: Proceedings of the Eighth Conference on Participatory Design: Artful integration: Interweaving Media, Materials and Practices, vol 1, pp. 132–141 (2004)
4. Herrmann, T.: Systems design with the socio-technical walkthrough. In: Whitworth, B., de Moor, A. (eds.) Handbook of Research on Socio-Technical Design and Social Networking Systems. Information Science Reference (2009)
5. Object Management Group: Business Process Model and Notation, v2.0. Object Management Group (2011)
6. Meyer, A., Smirnov, S., Weske, M.: Data in business processes. Universitätsverlag Potsdam (2011)
7. Muehlen, M., Recker, J.: How much language is enough? Theoretical and practical use of the business process modeling notation. Seminal Contributions to Information Systems Engineering, pp. 429–443. Springer, Heidelberg (2013). https://doi.org/10.1007/978-3-642-36926-1_35
8. Algermissen, L.: Prozessorientierte Verwaltungsmodernisierung: Gestaltung der Prozesslandschaft in öffentlichen Verwaltungen mit der PICTURE-Methode. L. Algermissen (2006)
9. Herrmann, T.: SeeMe in a nutshell–the semi-structured, socio-technical Modeling method. http://www.imtm-iaw.ruhr-uni-bochum.de/wp-content/uploads/sites/5/2011/09/Seeme-in-a-nutshell.pdf. Accessed 29 July 2015
10. Lück-Schneider, D.: Geschäftsprozessmanagement in der öffentlichen Verwaltung. Forschungsstelle für Betriebsführung und Personalmanagement (2012)
11. Becker, J., Algermissen, L., Falk, T.: Prozessorientierte Verwaltungsmodernisierung: Prozessmanagement im Zeitalter von E-Government und New Public Management. Springer, Heidelberg (2009)
12. Dumas, M., Rosa, M.L., Mendling, J., Reijers, H.: Fundamentals of Business Process Management. Springer, Heidelberg (2013). https://doi.org/10.1007/978-3-642-33143-5
13. Object Management Group: UML 2.0 Superstructure - Final Adopted Specification. Object Management Group (2003)
14. Glushko, R.J., McGrath, T.: Document Engineering: Analyzing and Designing Documents for Business Informatics & Web Services. MIT Press, Cambridge (2008)
15. Schafler, M., Lacueva-Pérez, F.J., Hannola, L., Damalas, S., Nierhoff, J., Herrmann, T.: Insights into the introduction of digital interventions at the shop floor (2018)
16. Herrmann, T., Jahnke, I., Nolte, A.: Evaluating socio-technical systems with heuristics - a feasible approach? In: Proceedings of the 2nd International Workshop on Socio-Technical Perspective in IS Development Co-located with 28th International Conference on Advanced Information Systems Engineering (CAiSE 2016), Ljubljana, Slovenia, 14 June 2016, pp. 91–97 (2016)
17. Lentzsch, C., Loser, K.-U., Degeling, M., Nolte, A.: Integrating a practice perspective to privacy by design. In: Tryfonas, T. (ed.) HAS 2017. LNCS, vol. 10292, pp. 691–702. Springer, Cham (2017). https://doi.org/10.1007/978-3-319-58460-7_47

Teamwork in Virtual World - Impact of "Virtual Team" on Team Dynamic

Bin Mai[1]([✉]), Brittany Garcia[1], Lei Xie[2], OP McCubbins[1], and Jinsil Seo[1]

[1] Texas A&M University, College Station, TX 77843, USA
{binmai,brinni,opmcc,hwaryoung}@tamu.edu
[2] Texas State University, San Marcos, TX 78666, USA
l_x6@txstate.edu

Abstract. Teamwork has long been recognized of its fundamental importance to the operations and success of professional organizations. With the recent development in information and communication technology, the organization structure and operation frameworks for teamwork also evolve. The resultant emergence of "virtual team" has become a significant adaptation of teamwork in today's digital global society. In this paper, we describe our research design for one of the first studies in the impacts of "virtual team" on several important factors of team dynamics and team leaderships, compared to those in traditional teamwork in physical proximity. We also present our preliminary results about the impacts of "virtual team" on team creativity and team member psychological safety.

Keywords: Teamwork · Virtual team · Team dynamic · Team leadership · Psychological safety · Team creativity

1 Introduction

Teamwork, usually defined as multiple people interacting with each other over a period of time to achieve a common goal (Carlos et al. 2015), is of fundamental importance to the operations and success of organizations and permeates almost all facets of today's professional organization landscape (O'Neill and Salas 2018). Traditionally, teamwork has been studied within the context of human communication in a physical environment within close proximity (Goldense 2017). However, the rapid development of information and communication technology (ICT) and the resultant increasing globalization have necessitated the evolution of organization structure and operation frameworks for teamwork. As a result, all aspects of teamwork need to adapt to the emerging digitization of the global society (Han et al. 2017), and the deployment of virtual teams "is recognized by organizations and researchers to meet many of these facets of societal and technological evolutions" (Großer and Baumöl 2017).

In this research we adopt the definition of "Virtual Teams" by Schweitzer and Duxbury (2010) as "teams whose members do not share a common workspace all of the time, and must therefore collaborate using information and communication technology (ICT) tools". We investigate how a collaborative virtual environment can affect

The original version of this chapter was revised: The first name of the fourth author was corrected. The correction to this chapter is available at https://doi.org/10.1007/978-3-030-50341-3_43

F. F.-H. Nah and K. Siau (Eds.): HCII 2020, LNCS 12204, pp. 119–127, 2020.
https://doi.org/10.1007/978-3-030-50341-3_10

the factors that determine team dynamics. We propose comparative studies between physical teamwork and virtual teamwork. In this study, our virtual team environment is represented by audio and visual signal communications (e.g., video conferencing).

The interests in leadership in teams are growing in scholarship and practitioners alike (Carson et al. 2007; Mehra et al. 2006; Morgeson et al. 2010). While abundant research has covered the various aspects of virtual teams and their performance, we notice that there is scant amount of investigation into the comparison and contrast of teamwork in physical teams versus teamwork in virtual teams. There are fundamental differences between these two types of teamwork format milieu. For example, in the physical environment teams are better at reading each other's emotional display, which is a good indicator of team conflict (Mallen et al. 2003). However, in the virtual environment the virtual distance between individuals generates chasm in understandings (Berry 2011). Physical distance creates psychological distance too.

More specifically, two factors in team collaboration are of specific interests in our study: team psychological safety and team creativity. Team psychological safety is defined as a shared belief that the team is safe for interpersonal risk taking (Edmondson 1999). According to Edmondson (1999), this factor "is meant to suggest ... a sense of confidence that the team will not embarrass, reject, or punish someone for speaking up. This confidence stems from mutual respect and trust among team members"; and "team psychological safety involves but goes beyond interpersonal trust; it describes a team climate characterized by interpersonal trust and mutual respect in which people are comfortable being themselves". Team creativity, based on Amabile's (1983) conceptualization of creativity, refer to the degree to which the team's output is judged to be "(a) it is both a novel and appropriate, useful, correct, or valuable response to the task at hand and (b) the task is heuristic rather than algorithmic".

Teams operate differently in face-to-face environment and virtual environment. Literature shows that when people collaborate in a virtual environment, they are less likely to form a trust or mutual beneficial bond among team members. Statistical analyses indicate that psychological safety is an integral indicator of building trust, creating a climate for effective team learning, which leads to team creativity in both collaborative environments (face-to-face and virtual). For example, Kessel et al. (2012) found the connection between psychological safety within the team and creative team performance when sharing information and know-how from 73 teams (face-to-face). Recent scholars have explored the possible mediating role of psychological safety on the effect of organizational factors on team creativity. Examining the relationship between subordinates and supervisors in a team environment, Javed et al. (2017) found that when a psychological safety climate was created and protected by the team, inclusive leadership is positively related with creativity. Many other studies also corroborated the link between psychology safety and team creativity in various kinds of teams, including health care teams, engineering teams, multi-cultural teams, and industrial teams (Hu et al. 2018; Lenberg and Feldt 2018; Kennel et al. 2017; Paulus et al. 2016). However, no study has been done to investigate how the relationships between team psychological safety and team creativity would be affected by the mode of the meeting.

Another aspect of team dynamics that could be significantly affected by the mode of meeting is team member interaction. Since the purpose of a team is to work together to achieve a common goal, the team members' roles and functionalities become highly correlated and interdependent, and thus necessitate effective interactions (Hambley et al. 2007). Laura et al. (2006) also pointed out that team members' interactions would best be studies "in terms of the communication patterns used to deal with task conflicts and maintenance of team member relationships". Again, there are scant studies to address the impact of meeting mode on the team members' interactions.

These are the gaps in the current literature that this study intends to fill. More specifically, in this study, we want to address the following research questions:

1. What are the impacts of mode of meeting (i.e., physical meeting vs. virtual meeting) on the relationship between team psychological safety and team creativity?
2. What are the impacts of mode meeting on team member interactions?

The rest of the paper is organized as follows: we present our research model in Sect. 2; we describe our study design in Sect. 3, followed by data analysis and discussion in Sect. 4. We conclude in Sect. 5.

2 Research Model

Summarizing our explanation in Sect. 1, we now illustrate our research model as in Fig. 1.

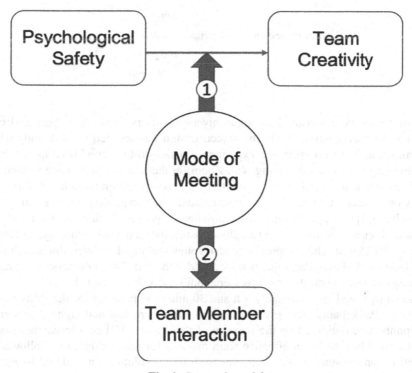

Fig. 1. Research model

Our research question 1 is represented by arrow 1, and research question 2 is represented by arrow 2.

3 Study Description

The study involved 27 participants (male = 17 and female = 10). Some descriptive statistics for the participants are summarized in Table 1.

Table 1. Participant descriptive statistics.

Factors	Variable	#
Gender	Male	17
	Female	10
Age	<20	9
	20–30	14
	31–40	4
Highest degree	High School	10
	Undergraduate	7
	Masters	9
	PhD	1
	None	7
Year of professional experience	<1 year	1
	1–5 years	13
	6–10 years	6

Participants were recruited through university listservs and were scheduled on a first come first serve basis. A within-subjects design was adopted for this study where all participants were grouped and experienced a face-to-face condition and a virtual condition (e.g., video conferencing with Zoom) in the same session. Face-to-face and virtual environment conditions were counterbalanced to determine which condition each group would experience first. Groups were created based on participant availability with the least being 3 people per group and the most being 4 people. Participants were assigned the task of discussing a solution for two global issues, the global water shortage and global warming, for 25 min. These topics were also counterbalanced to determine which topic would be discussed first. Participants were asked at the end of their discussion to present their idea to a researcher. All sessions were audio and video recorded.

The study lasted approximately 1 h and 30 min. The protocol for the study was as follows: i.) Participants were given a consent form to review and sign, after signing participants were debriefed on the purpose of the study; ii.) Then a researcher played a short clip of how to be an effective team member for participants; iii.) Followed by instructions on the study task, which was to discuss a solution for a global issue (i.e., water shortage in the world or climate change); iv.) After instructions were given if the first condition was a face-to-face interaction the researcher would turn on all recording devices, remind participants the allotted time and exit the room. If the first condition was the virtual environment interaction a researcher would divide the group into separate rooms with a laptop prepared for the participant to log into Zoom for a video conference, remind participants the allotted time and begin recording the Zoom session; v.) After the 25 min was up a researcher would reenter the room, or Zoom room, for the group's final solution presentation; vi.) Participants were then given a post survey, debriefed and able to leave.

4   Data Analyses and Discussions

4.1   For Research Question 1

Results from CLPM. Since we are studying two variables (i.e., team psychological safety and team creativity) that are measured at two occasions (i.e., face-to-face meeting and virtual meeting). We thus constructed a cross-lagged panel model (CLPM) to study the association of the two variables with each other over the two occasions. The CLPM results are presented in the following Fig. 2.

This cross-lagged panel shows correlations between the two factors, psychological safety and team creativity in two different times (i.e. face-to-face and virtual environments). Our study found that team creativity in face-to-face environment influenced team psychological safety in virtual environment (B = -0.157, p = 0.003). This result indicates that the higher the team creativity the team members perceived from face-to-face meeting, the lower the psychological safety they perceive in the virtual environment. This result is in alignment with the traditional findings in literature that trust, of which psychological safety is a critical indicator, in the virtual environment is harder to establish than in the physical environment. With all the technological advancement, people seem to be still learning to feel comfortable in virtual environment.

It is also found that psychological safety and team creativity at virtual environment are significantly and positively correlated to these two factors during the face-to-face meeting. This result can be interpreted as that, the higher the psychological safety (team creativity) perceived by the team members during face-to-face meeting, the higher the psychological safety (team creativity) will be perceived during virtual meetings (B = 1.087, p < 0.001, and B = 1.015, p < 0.001, respectively). Since these factors in face-to-face environment are positively correlated to them in virtual environment, it implies that the measures we can take to improve team psychological safety and team creativity in the face-to-face environment may also be taken in the virtual environment to improve virtual teams' team psychological safety and team creativity.

Other correlations studied using CLPM did not yield any additional significant results. We believe one of the reason is the sample size (a total of 27 participants in 8 teams).

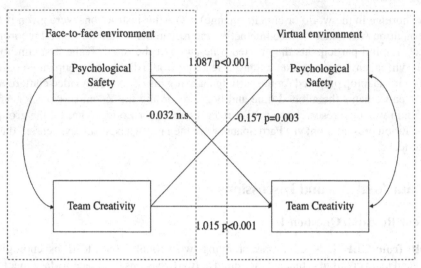

Fig. 2. Results of multi-group CLPM. (Note: Values are standardized path coefficients. Model fit for the full sample (N = 27))

Results from T-test. We also ran t-test to compare the values of measurement of team psychological safety, as well as those of team creativity, in face-to-face environment vs in virtual environment.

For team psychological safety, the result is shown in the following Table 2.

Table 2. Comparison of team psychological safety in two environment.

Paired samples t-test						
			t	df	p	Cohen's d
p_t1	–	p_t2	−1.009	26	0.322	−0.194

Note: t1 – face-to-face environment, t2 – virtual environment.

For team creativity, the results is shown in the following Table 3.

Table 3. Comparison of team creativity in two environment.

Paired samples t-test						
			t	df	p	Cohen's d
t_t1	–	t_t2	4.438	26	<.001	0.854

Note: t1 – face-to-face environment, t2 – virtual environment

From these results, we notice that our data indicate in general, team creativity as perceived by the team members is lower in virtual environment than that in face-to-face environment. This result conform with our results from the CLPM that people are still getting used to collaborating in virtual environment, and virtual meeting service providers have much potential and opportunities in helping people to achieve more effective virtual collaborations. The lack of significance in the comparison of team psychological safety, may stem from, among others, the limited sample size of our experiment.

4.2 For Research Question 2

One suitable tool to use in studying our research question 2 would be Social Network Analysis (SNA). SNA allows researchers to examine and visualize relational information (Han et al. 2016). SNA is particularly useful when exploring large networks (McCubbins 2016), it may provide useful insight into smaller networks as well. Networks that are visualized through SNA software can provide a deeper qualitative understanding that could be more challenging to obtain quantitatively (Borgatti et al. 2013).

As part of our study, we sought to collect social interaction data through a sociometric questionnaire. Participants were asked to rate their level of interaction with other members on their team. This data was then used to create an adjacency matrix to run SNA statistical procedures within UCINET, a SNA software (Borgatti et al. 2002). While the analysis of the networks did not provide use with a deeper qualitative understanding of the networks, Table 4 summarizes the descriptive statistics of the Face-to-Face and Virtual Meeting networks. The small size of the teams in the study design, and the resulting networks created, prevented a more robust analysis of the resulting Face-to-Face and Virtual Meeting networks.

Our SNA on our data did not yield any significant results regarding the possible difference between the team interactions in the two environments. We believe this is again due to the limited sample size. The results of the SNA is shown in Table 4.

Table 4. Descriptive network statistics for face-to-face and virtual meeting teams.

Measure	Face-to-face	Virtual meeting
# of Nodes	27	27
# of Ties	66	62
Density	0.09	0.08
Average degree	2.44	2.30

5 Conclusions

Teamwork has been long recognized as a fundamentally important factors in the organizations. As the fast advancement of information and communication technology, the organization structure and thus the operation frameworks for teamwork also evolve quickly. We recognize the emerging significance trends of the "virtual team" in today's increasingly interconnected digital global society. While abundant research had been done to study teamwork within the context of traditional teamwork in close physical proximity environment, the studies in the teamwork dynamics in virtual environment is severely lacking.

In this study, we contribute to the study of teamwork dynamics in virtual environment by investigating the impacts of physical meeting vs. virtual meeting on the relationship between two critical factors in teamwork dynamics: team psychological safety and team creativity. In addition, we also attempt to study the impacts of mode of meeting on team member interactions.

Our initial findings showed a correlation between face-to-face interactions and virtual interactions. Positive team creativity during face-to-face interactions was correlated with lower psychological safety in the virtual environment which can be explained by individual's lack of experience in such environments. Team creativity went down as well in the virtual environment as opposed to face-to-face. These findings highlight the discrepancy individuals feel when moving and interacting between different environments. This provides opportunities for virtual meeting service providers to develop technologies individuals can experience and become accustomed to.

We also found that when participants reported high on any factor (team creativity or psychological safety) there was a positive correlation in the virtual environment with respective factors. This provides direction for future research to investigate methods that support team creativity and psychological safety in face-to-face interactions and then apply those methods to a virtual environment. By doing so, such methods will provide a virtual environment more conducive to team work.

The main limitation of this study is the sample size. The amount of participants gathered provided enough individuals to create small groups but not large ones. Many of the analyses we conducted on our data did not yield significant results, and thus limiting the insights from this study. There is a possibility that greater interactions can occur in these environments with a larger number of members in each group.

The authors plan on conducting further investigations into team member interactions in these environments. We are currently in the process of transcribing and coding the video data. We will then proceed to conducting data analysis compare and contrast the team dynamics and team leaderships in physical team versus in virtual team environment.

References

Amabile, T.M.: The social psychology of creativity: a componential conceptualization. J. Pers. Soc. Psychol. **45**(2), 357–376 (1983)

Balthazard, P., Waldman, D. A., Howell, J., Atwater, L.E.: Modeling performance in teams: the effects of media type, shared leadership, interaction style, and cohesion. In: Paper Presented at the Meeting of the Academy of Management, Denver, Colorado (2002)

Bell, B., Kozlowski, S.: A typology of virtual teams: Implications for effective leadership. Group Org. Manage. **27**(1), 14–49 (2002)

Berry, G.: Enhancing effectiveness on virtual teams: understanding why traditional team skills are insufficient. J. Bus. Commun. **48**(2), 186–206 (2011)

Borgatti, S.P., Everett, M.G., Freeman, L.C.: UCINET 6 for Windows: Software for Social Network Analysis. Analytic Technologies, Harvard (2002)

Borgatti, S.P., Everett, M.G., Johnson, J.C.: Analyzing Social Networks. SAGE Publications, London (2013)

Carson, J., Tesluk, P., Marrone, J.: Shared leadership in teams: an investigation of antecedent conditions and performance. Acad. Manag. J. **50**(5), 1217–1234 (2007)

Edmondson, A.: Psychological safety and learning behavior in work teams. Adm. Sci. Q. **44**, 350–383 (1999)

Goldense, B.: The changing nature of collocation: physical vs. virtual teams. Mach. Design **89**(12) (2017)

Großer, B., Baumöl, U.: Virtual teamwork in the context of technological and cultural transformation. Int. J. Inf. Syst. Project Manage. **04**, 21–35 (2017)

Hambley, L.A., O'Neill, T.A., Kline, T.J.: Virtual team leadership: the effects of leadership style and communication medium on team interaction styles and outcomes. Organ. Behav. Hum. Decis. Process. **103**, 1–20 (2007)

Han, G., McCubbins, O.P., Paulsen, T.H.: Utilizing social network analysis to measure student collaboration in an undergraduate capstone course. NACTA J. **60**(2), 176–182 (2016)

Han, S., Chae, C., Macko, P., Park, W., Beyerlein, M.: How virtual team leaders cope with creativity challenges. Eur. J. Train. Dev. **41**(3), 261–276 (2017)

Hu, J., Erdogan, B., Jiang, K., Bauer, T.N., Liu, S.: Leader humility and team creativity: the role of team information sharing, psychological safety, and power distance. J. Appl. Psychol. **103**(3), 313 (2018)

Javed, B., Naqvi, S.M.M.R., Khan, A.K., Arjoon, S., Tayyeb, H.H.: Impact of inclusive leadership on innovative work behavior: the role of psychological safety. J. Manage. Organ. **25**(1), 117–136 (2019)

Kennel, V., Jones, K., Reiter-Palmon, R.: Team innovation in healthcare. In: Team Creativity and Innovation, p. 307 (2017)

Kessel, M., Kratzer, J., Schultz, C.: Psychological safety, knowledge sharing, and creative performance in healthcare teams. Creativity Innov. Manag. **21**(2), 147–157 (2012)

Lenberg, P., Feldt, R.: Psychological safety and norm clarity in software engineering teams. In: Proceedings of the 11th International Workshop on Cooperative and Human Aspects of Software Engineering, pp. 79–86. ACM, May 2018

Mallen, M., Day, S., Green, M.: Online versus face-to-face conversation: an examination of relational and discourse variables. Psychother. Theor. Res. Pract. Train. **40**(1–2), 155 (2003)

Mehra, A., Smith, B., Dixon, A., Robertson, B.: Distributed leadership in teams: the network of leadership perceptions and team performance. Leadersh. Quart. **17**(3), 232–245 (2006)

Morgeson, F., DeRue, D., Karam, E.: Leadership in teams: a functional approach to understanding leadership structures and processes. J. Manag. **36**(1), 5–39 (2010)

O'Neill, T., Salas, E.: Creating high performance teamwork in organizations. Hum. Resour. Manag. Rev. **28**(4), 325–331 (2018)

Peralta, C., Lopes, P.N., Gilson, L., Lourenco, P., Pais, L.: Innovation processes and team effectiveness: the role of goal clarity and commitment, and team affective tone. J. Occup. Organ. Psychol. **88**, 80–107 (2015)

Paulus, P.B., van der Zee, K.I., Kenworthy, J.: Cultural diversity and team creativity. In: The Palgrave Handbook of Creativity and Culture Research, pp. 57–76. Palgrave Macmillan, London (2016)

Schweitzer, L., Duxbury, L.: Conceptualizing and measuring the virtuality of teams. Inf. Syst. J. **20**(3), 267–295 (2010)

Townsend, A., DeMarie, S., Hendrickson, A.: Virtual teams: technology and the workplace of the future. Acad. Manag. Exec. **12**(3), 17–29 (1998)

Zaccaro, S., Rittman, A., Marks, M.: Team leadership. Leadersh. Quart. **12**(4), 451–483 (2001)

Insights from the Apple *Human Interface Guidelines* on Intuitive Interaction

Dan McAran[1]([⊠]) and Norman Shaw[2]([⊠])

[1] Toronto, Canada
[2] Ryerson University, Toronto, Canada
norman.shaw@ryerson.ca

Abstract. Research on intuitive interaction in the academic community developed early in the millennium with the pioneering research of groups in Australia and Germany. Apple has produced a wide array of products and technologies which are widely proclaimed as "intuitive" leading to great commercial success. As far as can be determined Apple has never produced a white paper or any other document detailing the process or components of intuitive interaction. Apple, however, does provide *Human Interface Guidelines* (Guidelines) which frequently mention the "intuitive" as a desirable goal. This paper analyses the references to the "intuitive" and related key words in the Guidelines seeking to understand the context in which these references appear, and thereby identify elements that comprise "intuitive" interaction as outlined in the Guidelines. The results show broad correspondence to the aspects of intuitive interaction that has been developed by academic researchers triangulating the academic research performed. The analysis provides additional insights concerning the nature of intuitive interaction laying the basis for further research.

Keywords: Apple · Intuitive interaction · Familiar · Metaphor · Hints

1 Introduction

The success of Apple and, in particular the apple smartphone, is attributed to the intuitiveness of these products. In the academic Information Systems (IS) literature little has been published on the nature on intuitive interaction. However, an intuitive interaction research stream has emerged from the academic design discipline starting with the pioneering work of Blackler [1] in Australia and Hurtienne [2] in Germany. As documented in the recent work *Intuitive Interaction: Research and Application* [3], much progress has been made in identifying the processes behind intuitive interaction and the methods by which it can be studied.

There has been little connection between the academic research and the commercial providers of technology. Palmer, Ogunyoka, and Hammond [4] offered perspectives concerning intuitive interaction during the introduction by IBM of a health kiosk into the Kenya market highlighting the importance of culture and context to intuitive interaction.

D. McAran—Chartered Professional Accountant

© Springer Nature Switzerland AG 2020
F. F.-H. Nah and K. Siau (Eds.): HCII 2020, LNCS 12204, pp. 128–140, 2020.
https://doi.org/10.1007/978-3-030-50341-3_11

Hespanhol [5] investigated intuitive interaction in the urban environment. Cave, Blackler, Popovic, and Kraal [6] researched intuitive interaction in an airport.

This paper attempts to bridge the gap between the academic research and commercial practice. The focus of the paper is Apple products. In the Apple *Human Interface Guidelines* (Guidelines) there are frequent references to "intuitive". The text in which the references appear is analyzed as to context with related words and phrases. This provides an ability to correlate "intuitive" references in the Guidelines with other characteristics appearing in the text, and then developing a set of terms related to intuitive interaction. This result is then compared to the definitional and functional aspects of intuitive interaction found in intuitive interaction academic research.

The remainder of this paper is organized as follows. Section 2 presents a brief review of the literature; Sect. 3 presents the method used; Sect. 4 is the results; Sect. 5 is the discussion; Sect. 6 discusses limitations of and future research; Sect. 7 is the conclusion.

2 Literature

Academic research on intuitive interaction with technology was commenced separately by Alethea Blackler in Australia and Jörn Hurtienne in Germany in the early years of the millennium. Blackler, Mahar, and Popovic [7] used experiments to measure the degree of "intuitive" use of technology. A technology familiarity questionnaire was developed and used in a series of experiments to relate observed intuitive use directly to technology familiarity. During the analysis of experiments, the main factors used to identify "intuitive" use were time to complete tasks, latency, subjective certainty and the degree to which there was verbalization in the use of the technology.

Hurtienne [2] focused his research on the relation of image schemas, from the work of Lakoff and Johnson [8], to intuitive use. An easy to identify image schema used in the design of intuitive interfaces is the "container" image schema which differentiates between "interior versus exterior" or "in and out". Image schemas are used to make interface designs more familiar and thereby more intuitive [2].

Several different definitions of intuitive interaction have emerged. Intuitive interaction is defined by Blackler as "applying existing knowledge in order to use an interface or product easily and quickly, often without consciously realizing exactly where that knowledge came from" [3, p. ix]. The German researchers defined intuitive interaction as "A technical system is intuitively usable if the users' unconscious application of prior knowledge leads to effective interaction" (Mohs, Hurtienne, Israel, Naumann, Kindsmüller, Meyer and Pohlmeyer [9, p. 130] as cited in Blackler and Hurtienne [10, p. 8].

Researchers at the University of Georgia provided a more multifaceted definition: "interactions between humans and high technology in lenient learning environments that allow the human to use a combination of prior experience and feedforward methods to achieve their functional and abstract goals" [11, p. 107].

Continua of intuitive use have been developed both from the German and Australian research. Recently, Blackler, Desai, McEwan, Popovic, and Diefenbach [12] have updated the previously created continua into the Enhanced Framework for Intuitive Interaction (EFII), which seeks to explain how the conceptual frameworks inter-relate, and to provide guidance for designers. See Fig. 1.

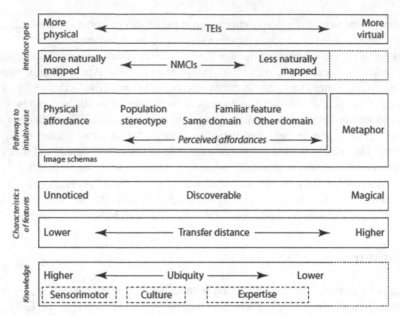

Fig. 1. Enhanced framework for intuitive interaction (EFFI). Source: Blackler et al. [12].

A further theoretical model, the Intuitive Interaction Hierarchy (IIH), focusing on the cognitive aspects of intuitive interaction was developed by Still and Still [13].

Gradually an alternative subjective approach has emerged from the intuitive interaction research stream. Naumann and Hurtienne [14] created the Questionnaire for the Subjective Consequences of Intuitive Use (QUESI) which identifies the following factors as comprising intuitive interaction: Subjective Mental Workload, Perceived Achievement of Goals, Perceived Effort of Learning, Familiarity, and Perceived Error Rate. Similarly, the INTUI questionnaire of Ullrich, and Diefenbach [15] identifies the following factors: Effortlessness, Verbalizability, Gut Feeling, and Magical Experience. McAran [16] use a different approach by developing a novel perceived intuitiveness construct and integrating the construct into the Technology Acceptance Model (TAM) [17].

The scope of intuitive interaction research continues to expand. A particular focus on intuitive interaction has been on aging and intuitive interaction [7, 18, 19]. Interestingly, Fischer [20] describes how intuitive interaction can be applied to the agile development process. Hurtienne, Klöckner, Diefenbach, Nass, and Maier [21] have shown that design using image schemas can be effectively used to create innovative interface designs. Overall, the importance of intuitive technology can be seen in the increasingly pervasive and experiential nature of technology [22].

3 Method

The Apple Human Interface Guidelines [23] were accessed online. These guidelines cover all Apple technologies, primarily iOS, macIOS, watchOS, tvOS, but also thirteen additional Apple technologies such as Apple Pay, SiriKit, and Wallet. Each of the guidelines associated with these technologies was reviewed three times and notes were created in regards to the significance of the text. Where there was reference to "intuitive", extraction was made of related associated text to identify text that would provide insight into the nature of intuitive interaction.

Terms that have appeared in the intuitive interaction literature as related to intuitive interaction were also highlighted and the related text extracted. An example of such a term would be "feedback". Further, terms were identified, such as "hints", that could be potentially related to intuitive interaction, but have not yet been explored in the literature. After this analysis was completed, a comparison was made of the characteristics of intuitive interaction found in the existing intuitive interaction literature.

The methodology used has resemblance to the grounded theory of Corbin and Strauss [24] which advocates creation of detailed memos and the use of constant comparison until theoretical saturation is complete. In this research, detailed notations were made for selected sections of text selected from the Apple Guidelines. The selected text, however, revealed many potential theoretical relations which, because of the length limitation of this paper, could not be fully developed. An example of a potential theoretical relation not developed would be the relation of color in interface design to intuitive interaction. Color can be seen as a type of image schema [2]. It would not be possible to suggest that theoretical saturation as prescribed by Corbin and Strauss [24] has been achieved. However, it is asserted that the review of the text of the Apple Guidelines has been reflective in the sense developed by Schön [25], potentially mitigating the failure to reach theoretical saturation.

In order to quantify the degree of agreement between the academic research on intuitive interaction and the salient factors identified in the Apple Guidelines, a simple measure of agreement is calculated.

4   Results

Most significantly in the Apple Guidelines (iOS App Architecture, Onboarding) advice is provided to "First and foremost, make your app intuitive" [23]. There are forty-five uses of the term "intuitive" or "intuitively" in the text of the Apple Guidelines. The textual analysis of the Apple Guidelines is presented as follows:

- Direct confirmation of characteristics of intuitive interaction.
- Indirect confirmation of characteristics of intuitive interaction.
- Additional insights that can be found in the Apple Guidelines that can be contextually related to intuitive interaction.

Because of space limitations only salient results are reported. Direct confirmation of characteristics of intuitive interaction was found in the Apple Guidelines for the following prominent themes in intuitive interaction research: the familiar and image schemas. There are twenty-five uses of the word familiar in the text extracted for review. Two extracts in which "familiar" appears in the same context as "intuitive" are detailed in Table 1 below.

Table 1. Extracted text relating familiar to intuitive.

Section of Apple guidelines	Relevant text	Comments
Technologies Carplay Introduction	Well-known iOS paradigms, including interface elements, icons, text appearance, and terminology provide a familiar, intuitive experience	Because of the juxtaposition in the text of the words familiar and intuitive this indicates a close relationship between the concepts
Technologies Carplay Architecture Navigation	When possible, use standard navigation components like tab bars and table views. Users are already familiar with these controls, and will intuitively know how to get around your app	This text indicates a close direct relationship between familiar and intuitive interaction

Image Schemas are also a prominent area of intuitive interaction research. The following two extracts from the Apple Guidelines indicate support for use of image schemas in interface and application design (Table 2).

Table 2. Extracted text relating image schemas to intuitive.

Section of Apple guidelines	Relevant text	Comments
Apple Design Guidelines iOS Views alerts	Place buttons where people expect them. In general, buttons people are most likely to tap should be on the right. Cancel buttons should always be on the left	The placement of the Cancel button can be interpreted as an image schema
Apple Design Guidelines macOS Selectors Sliders	Users expect the minimum and maximum sides of sliders to be consistent in all apps. For example, the user should always move a vertical volume slider upward for greater volume and downward for lower volume	This is an example of an image schema: up is more; down is less [10]

Indirect confirmation of characteristics of intuitive interaction found in the intuitive interaction research stream: these are consistency, feedback, simplicity and metaphor. There were fifteen references to consistent or consistency within the text selected for review. The two most relevant references are below (Table 3):

There were 16 mentions of feedback in the text selected for review (Table 4).

Table 3. Extracted text relating consistency to intuitive.

Section of Apple guidelines	Relevant text	Comments
Apple Design Guidelines iOS Themes Design Principles	A consistent app implements familiar standards and paradigms by using system-provided interface elements, well-known icons, standard text styles, and uniform terminology	The concept of consistency can be related to "familiarity" which is prominent in research of Blackler [1]. In this particular section consistency is seen as implementing the familiar
Apple Design Guidelines iOS Extensions Sharing and Actions	Craft a familiar interface. For share extensions, the system-provided composition view is familiar and provides a consistent sharing experience throughout the system	Apple emphasizes familiar and consistent in interface design; this can be related to the "intuitiveness" of Apple technology. This text links familiar to consistent; indirectly linking consistent to intuitive

Table 4. Extracted text relating feedback to intuitive.

Section of Apple guidelines	Relevant text	Comments
Apple Design Guidelines iOS Themes Design Principles	Feedback acknowledges actions and shows results to keep people informed. The built-in iOS apps provide perceptible feedback in response to every user action	In Hespanhol [5] there is an emphasis on the importance of feedback in intuitive interaction
Apple Design Guidelines macOS User Interaction Providing User Feedback	Feedback tells people what an app is doing and helps them understand the results of actions and what they can do next	This relates feedback to feedforward. Both these functions can be related to intuitive interaction. This can be seen as confirmation of feedforward [11] and feedback [5]

The following additional factors identified in existing intuitive interaction research and can be related to text extracts from the Apple Guidelines (Table 5).

Intuitive interaction can be also linked to additional sets of factors that can be identified in the text of the Apple Guidelines. Some of these additional factors are identified in Table 6. Because of space limitations only a limited number of factors are identified (Table 7).

Table 5. Extracted text relating simplicity and metaphor to intuitive interaction.

Section of Apple guidelines	Relevant text	Comments
Apple Design Guidelines macOS Accessibility Best Practices	Simplicity—Enabling familiar, consistent interactions that make complex tasks simple and straightforward to perform	This text links familiar and consistent to simplicity and thus indirectly to intuitive
Apple Design Guidelines iOS Themes Design Principles	People learn more quickly when an app's virtual objects and actions are metaphors for familiar experiences…Metaphors work well in iOS because people physically interact with the screen	This is almost the same as the use of metaphor for intuitive interaction that has been prominently discussed by Blackler [3]

Table 6. Extracted text relating tangible user interfaces (TEIs) and adaptable to intuitive interaction.

Section of Apple guidelines	Relevant text	Comments
Apple Design Guidelines iOS Themes Design Principles	The direct manipulation of onscreen content engages people and facilitates understanding. Users experience direct manipulation when they rotate the device or use gestures to affect onscreen content. Through direct manipulation, they can see the immediate, visible results of their actions	Direct manipulation would be a component of a touch interface. This is confirmation of factor related to intuitive interaction found in the Tangible User Interfaces (TEIs) component of EFII model
Apple Design Guidelines iOS Interface Essentials	Most iOS apps are built using components from UIKit … This framework lets apps achieve a consistent appearance across the system, while at the same time offering a high level of customization. UIKit elements are flexible and familiar. They're adaptable…	This relates "familiar" to "consistent", "flexible" and "adaptable". Familiar is directly related to "intuitive" [3]. "Adaptable" was identified as a component of intuitive interaction by McAran [16]. There is a potential new factor to be investigated "flexible" in regards to intuitive interaction

Table 7. Salient codes assigned to extracted text from the Apple guidelines with comparison to the EFFI model and intuitive interaction research (As Represented in Blackler [3])

Apple guideline	Count (>n = 3)	Component of EFFI Model	Found in intuitive interaction research (Yes/No)	Notations
Image schemas	8	Yes	Yes	Discussed in Hurtienne [2]
Consistent	5	No	Yes	Mentioned in Hurtienne and Blackler [10]
Cues	5	No	Yes	Discussed in Blackler [3]
Familiar	5	Yes	Yes	Discussed in Blackler [1]
Hints	5	No	No	No substantive discussion in Blacker [3]
Navigation	5	No	Yes	Mentioned in Palmer [4]
Predictable	5	No	No	No substantive discussion in Blackler [3]
Simple	5	No	Yes	Mentioned in McAran [16]
Easy to use	4	No	Yes	Mentioned in Palmer [4]
Feedback	4	No	Yes	Mentioned by Hespanol [5]
Clear	3	No	Yes	Mentioned in McAran [16]
Efficient	3	No	No	No substantive discussion in Blacker [3]
Flexible	3	No	No	No substantive discussion in Blacker [3]
Lenient learning environment	3	No	Yes	Discussed in O'Brien et al. [11]
Visual	3	No	Yes	Discussed as part of feedback Hespanol [5]

The above table represents the number of respective codes assigned to the extracted text. Simple agreement of salient factors found both in Apple Guidelines and EFII model is: $2/15 = .133$. This would be low agreement. Simple agreement of salient factors found both in Apple Guidelines and intuitive interaction research with technology as characterized by the Blackler [3] chapter book is: $11/15 = .733$. This would be moderate agreement.

5 Discussion

This discussion is limited to highlighting the most significant observations that can be made from the textual analysis.

Again, intuitive interaction is defined by Blackler as "applying existing knowledge in order to use an interface or product easily and quickly, often without consciously realizing exactly where that knowledge came from" [3] (p. ix). The German researchers defined intuitive interaction as "A technical system is intuitively usable if the users' unconscious application of prior knowledge leads to effective interaction" (Mohs et al. [9], (p. 130) as cited in Blackler and Hurtienne [10] (p. 8). The base concept found in both these definitions is "applying existing knowledge" and "prior knowledge": the research has broadly confirmed the prime factor of both these definitions through the numerous and salient references to the importance of the "familiar" in the Apple Guidelines.

There is additional substantive agreement with the definition created by O'Brien [11]. The concept of feedforward does appear in the definition of intuitive interaction created by O'Brien and her colleagues: "interactions between humans and high technology in lenient learning environments that allow the human to use a combination of prior experience and feedforward methods to achieve their functional and abstract goals" [11] (p. 107). Feedback has been related to intuitive interaction by Hespanhol [5]. Notably Feedback and the related concept of feedforward do not appear at present in the EFII model. In addition, the Apple Guidelines provide a significant focus of the quality of the user experience: an example is found in iOS App Architecture Onboarding "Anticipate the need for help. Proactively look for times when people might be stuck". This extract can be related to the "lenient learning environments" found in the O'Brien et al. [11] definition.

Beyond confirming base agreement to the definitions of intuitive interaction, there are other significant findings. Of particular interest is the relation of learning speed to the use of metaphor and familiar features "People learn more quickly when an app's virtual objects and actions are metaphors for familiar experiences" (IOS Themes – Design Principles). The use of metaphor and familiar features fit directly into the EFII theoretical framework. The speed of learning can be logically related to the amount training required which has been identified as a key aspect of intuitive interaction [16].

The Apple Human Interactions on User Control contains subtler aspects of intuitive interaction that are not directly represented in the EFII model. In the IOS Interface Essentials the following text appears "This framework lets apps achieve a consistent appearance across the system, while at the same time offering a high level of customization. UIKit elements are flexible and familiar. They're adaptable". The structure of the paragraph relates familiar to consistent, flexible, and adaptable. McAran [16] found adaptability as key to the creation of a novel Perceived Intuitiveness (PI) construct. Because of the strong correlation of familiar to intuitive interaction, consistent, flexible, and adaptable should also be considered for further intuitive interaction research.

Naumann and Hurtienne [14] created the Questionnaire for the Subjective Consequences of Intuitive Use (QUESI). Ullrich and Diefenbach [15] developed the INTUI questionnaire. These questionnaires use a subjective factor approach to the assessment of intuitive interaction. The factors identified are (1) From the QUESI questionnaire: Subjective Mental Workload, Perceived Achievement of Goals, Perceived Effort of Learning, Familiarity, and Perceived Error Rate; and (2) From the INTUI questionnaire: Effortlessness, Verbalizability, Gut Feeling, and Magical Experience.

Some of these factors were identified in the Apple Guidelines as supporting intuitive interactions. As an example, the importance of the cognitive workload is stressed in Apple Guidelines (QUESI questionnaire: Subjective Mental Workload). Additionally, iOS App Architecture Navigation advises "Always provide a clear path. People should always know where they are in your app and how to get to their next destination. Regardless of navigation style, it's essential that the path through content is logical, predictable, and easy to follow." This can be seen as generally consistent with the factors of Perceived Achievement of Goals, Perceived Effort of Learning, and Perceived Error Rate from the QUESI questionnaire.

In the Apple Guidelines there are seventeen references to "easy/easy to use" and five to "efficiency" which can be conceptually related to the INTU factor of Effortlessless. In regards to the INTU factors "magical experience" and "gut feeling", the use of "visual cues to identify potential destinations and preview the effect of dropping content" (iOS User Interaction Drag and Drop) and the Apple Guideline references to "natural" interfaces are conceptually related. In iOS Themes – Design Themes the comment is made "Touch and discoverability heighten delight and enable access to functionality and additional content without losing context" (IOs Themes, Design Themes): "Delight" can be seen as affectively related to "magical experience".

There are other connections that can be made to intuitive interaction research. Still and Still (2018) focus on the cognitive aspects of intuitive interaction: The Apple Guidelines refer to the need to "reduce cognitive load" (Technologies, Accessibility, Introduction). Macaranas, Antle, and Riecke [26] note the importance of discoverability in intuitive interaction with a technology. In the iOS, App Architecture, Onboarding the injunction is made "Make learning fun and discoverable" (iOS, App Architecture Onboarding). Discoverable is one of the dimensions appearing in the EFII model with an assigned range from Unnoticed to Magical.

One of the notable observations from the review of the text was the occurrence of the words: cue (6 times), clues (1 time), and hints (12 times). The close relation of clues to intuitive interaction can be seen in the excerpt from macOS, Icons and Images, Custom Icons section of the Apple Guidelines "The best icons use familiar visual metaphors that are directly related to the actions they initiate….When an icon depicts an identifiable, real-world object or recognizable app task, it gives first-time users a clue to its function and helps experienced users remember it". This text relates "familiar" to "visual metaphors" and "clues". This relates "clues" by inference to "intuitive". Blackler

[3] identified clues and hints as related to the process of intuition but these concepts were not explored in her research.

In the Guidelines they are references to "fluid motion" (iOS, Themes, Design Themes) and "flow": "A familiar, flowing experience keeps users engaged" (iOS, Visual Design, Animation) and "Use the system-provided setup flow to give users a familiar experience" (Technologies, HomeKit, Setup). Consequently, it would be an area of future research to relate the intuitive interaction experience with technology to flow theory as developed by Csikszentmihályi [27].

Notably the research found low simple agreement of the salient factors found in Apple Guidelines to the EFII model. In contrast, there was moderate simple agreement of the salient factors found in Apple Guidelines to topics found in intuitive interaction research (as represented in [3]), this may indicate that there may be significantly more factors that influence intuitive interaction than are included in the EFII model.

6 Limitations and Future Work

The main limitation is that the selection of results to report was highly dependent on the judgement of the researchers. This limitation was amplified by the decision to report only the most salient results because of the space limitations of this paper. The quantification of the level of agreement used only simple agreement. Furthermore, this paper is limited to Apple technology which may not be representative of computer technology in general.

In the Apple Guidelines, a common theme is that of "hints". The concept of "hints" has been developed in relation to intuition itself. Specific research could be performed to develop the relationship between the concept of "hints", "clues" and "cues" and intuitive interaction. Similar research could be performed in relation to "flow" and intuitive interaction.

Finally, it may be possible to associate the various concepts that have been developed in this paper and from the extant literature on intuitive interaction into a structural equation model. As no research has been identified where this has been done, the use of Partial Least Squares Structural Equation Modelling (PLS-SEM) may be indicated as it has been identified as appropriate for exploratory research (Hair, Hult, Ringle, and Sarstedt [28].

7 Conclusion

This research has found broad correspondence between the characteristics that have been identified for intuitive interaction in the academic research stream and the characteristics identified in the Apple Guidelines. Academic researchers should further explore the role of intuitive interaction in technology acceptance theory. Practitioners should consider intuitive interaction in the design of new technology. While a number of the known factors that contribute to intuitive interaction have been triangulated from this research, some additional factors such as "hints" and "flow" were also identified which could be the basis of further research. In addition, given the numerous factors that have been identified to date related to intuitive interaction, the creation of a statistical model using methods such as PLS-SEM may be indicated to allow for the quantification of the contribution of the factors identified to a novel intuitive interaction dependent variable.

References

1. Blackler, A.: Intuitive interaction with complex artefacts. Ph.D. dissertation. Queensland University of Technology, Brisbane, Australia (2006). https://eprints.qut.edu.au/16219
2. Hurtienne, J.: Image schemas and design for intuitive use: Exploring new guidance for user interface design. Ph.D. dissertation. Technische Universitat Berlin, Germany (2009). https://depositonce.tu-berlin.de/handle/11303/3050pdf. Accessed 30 Dec 2019
3. Blackler, A. (ed.): Intuitive Interaction: Research and Application. CRC Press, Boca Raton (2018)
4. Palmer, J., Ogunyoka, T., Hammond, C.: Intuitive interaction in industry user research: context is everything. In: Blackler, A. (ed.) Intuitive Interaction: Research and Application, pp. 213–226. CRC Press, Boca Raton (2018)
5. Hespanhol, L.: City context, digital content and the design of intuitive urban interfaces. In: Blackler, A. (ed.) Intuitive Interaction: Research and Application, pp. 173–194. CRC Press, Boca Raton (2018)
6. Cave, A., Blackler, A. L., Popovic, V., Kraal, B. J.: Examining intuitive navigation in airports. In: Design Big Debates: Pushing the Boundaries of Design Research, DRS 2014, Umea, Sweden (2014)
7. Blackler, A., Mahar, D., Popovic, V.: Older adults, interface experience and cognitive decline. In: Design—Interaction—Participation, 22nd Annual Conference on the Australian Computer–Human Interaction Special Interest Group, OZCHI 2010, Brisbane, Australia (2010)
8. Lakoff, G., Johnson, M.: Metaphors We Live By. Chicago Press, Chicago (1980)
9. Mohs, C., et al.: IUUI: intuitive use of user interfaces. In: Bosenick, T., Hassenzahl, M., Muller-Prove, M., Peissner, M. (eds.) Usability Professionals, pp. 130–133. Usability Professionals' Association, Stuttgart (2006)
10. Blackler, A.L., Hurtienne, J.: Towards a unified view of intuitive interaction: definitions, models and tools across the world. MMIInteraktiv **13**, 36–54 (2007)
11. O'Brien, M.A., Rogers, W.A., Fisk, A.D.: Developing a framework for intuitive human–computer interaction. In: 52nd Annual Meeting of the Human Factors and Ergonomics Society, New York (2008)
12. Blackler, A., Desai, S., McEwan, M., Popovic, V., Diefenbach, S.: Perspectives on the nature of intuitive interaction. In: Blackler, A. (ed.) Intuitive Interaction: Research and Application, pp. 19–40. CRC Press, Boca Raton (2018)
13. Still, J.D., Still, M.L.: Cognitively describing intuitive interactions. In: Blackler, A. (ed.) Intuitive Interaction: Research and Application, pp. 41–62. CRC Press, Boca Raton, FL. (2018)
14. Naumann, A., Hurtienne, J.: Benchmarks for intuitive interaction with mobile devices. In: 12th International Conference on Human–Computer Interaction with Mobile Devices and Services (MobileHCI 2010), 7–10 September, Lisboa, Portugal, pp. 401–402 (2010)
15. Ullrich, D., Diefenbach, S.: INTUI: exploring the facets of intuitive interaction. In: Ziegler, J., Schmidt, A. (eds.) Mensch und Computer 2010, pp. 251–260. Oldenburg, Munich (2010)
16. McAran, D.: Development of the technology acceptance intuitive interaction model. In: Blackler, A. (ed.) Intuitive Interaction: Research and Application, pp. 129–150. CRC Press, Boca Raton (2018)
17. Davis, F.D.: Perceived usefulness, perceived ease of use, and user acceptance of information technology. MIS Q. **13**(3), 319–340 (1989)
18. O'Brien, M.: Lessons on intuitive usage from everyday technology interactions among younger and older people. In: Blackler, A. (ed.) Intuitive Interaction: Research and Application, pp. 89–112. CRC Press, Boca Raton (2018)

19. Reddy, R.G., Blackler, A., Popovic, V.: Adaptable interface framework for intuitively learnable product interfaces for people with diverse capabilities. In: Blackler, A. (ed.) Intuitive Interaction: Research and Application, pp. 113–127. CRC Press, Boca Raton (2018)
20. Fischer, S.: Designing intuitive products in an agile world. In: Blackler, A. (ed.) Intuitive Interaction: Research and Application, pp. 195–212. CRC Press, Boca Raton (2018)
21. Hurtienne, J., Klöckner, K., Diefenbach, S., Nass, C., Maier, A.: Designing with image schemas: resolving the tension between innovation, inclusion and intuitive use. Interac. Comput. **27**, 235–255 (2015)
22. Yoo, Y.: Computing for everyday life: a call for research on experiential computing. MIS Q. **34**(3), 213–231 (2010)
23. Apple: Human Interface Guidelines. https://developer.apple.com/design/human-interface-guidelines/. Accessed 30 Dec 2010
24. Corbin, J., Strauss, A.: Basics of Qualitative Research. Sage, Los Angeles (2008)
25. Schön, D.A.: The Reflective Practitioner: How Professionals Think in Action. Basic Books, New York (1983)
26. Macaranas, A., Antle, A.N., Riecke, B.E.: Intuitive interaction: balancing users' performance and satisfaction with natural user interfaces. Interac. Comput. **27**(3), 357–370 (2015)
27. Csikszentmihályi, M.: Flow: The Psychology of Optimal Experience. Harper & Row, New York (1990)
28. Hair, J.F., Hult, G.T.M., Ringle, C.M., Sarstedt, M.: A Primer on Partial Least Squares Structural Equation Modeling (PLS-SEM). Sage, Thousand Oaks (2014)

The Effect of Queuing Technology on Customer Experience in Physical Retail Environments

Gabriele Obermeier[(✉)], Robert Zimmermann, and Andreas Auinger

University of Applied Sciences Upper Austria, Steyr, Austria
{gabriele.obermeier,robert.zimmermann,
andreas.auinger}@fh-steyr.at

Abstract. Queuing systems manage the order of customers waiting for their service encounter fairly and equitably and influence the perception of their experience in a physical retail store. In this field study, we investigate a self-service and a human-operated queuing system, both offering additional features, designed to offer a higher level of personalization and convenience for the customer's waiting time. Our study shows that advanced queuing technologies in stores, with generally low customer frequency and short waiting times, show no statistically significant effect on a customer's perception of the overall customer experience, satisfaction or intention to repurchase. However, customers were satisfied with the technologies and evaluated their queuing experience as effortless, easy and quick, which shows general support for those technologies. Beyond the statistical analysis, our mixed-method approach contributes to a broad understanding of advanced queuing technology for practitioners, retailers and developers of such systems.

Keywords: Customer experience · Queuing · Self-service technology · Field study · Digital retail

1 Introduction

Waiting for service is one of the most unpleasant but unavoidable events in everyday life [1]. When we encounter a queue at medical facilities, hairdressers, banks or retail stores, our perception of the service delivery is directly affected [1]. Waiting was mentioned among the main reasons that encourage customers to buy online instead of visiting a physical store [2]. In the 1980s, scientists started to recognize the importance of queue management [3] and the impact of waiting time on customer experience [4]. In 1985, Maister [5] and Haynes [6] found that the feeling of equitability has a positive effect on the customer's perception of waiting time. Sasser et al. [7] observed that customers feel very angry if somebody successfully sneaks into the line ahead. In order to treat customers equitably and fairly, we often encounter queuing systems in stores, especially where products or services require customer-specific and intensive consultation. Queuing systems such as First-In, First-Out (FIFO) enable fair processing of lines, described as "social justice" by Larson [3]. One well-known example of a FIFO system is a ticket queue, in which customers receive a consecutive number by which customers are

© The Author(s) 2020
F. F.-H. Nah and K. Siau (Eds.): HCII 2020, LNCS 12204, pp. 141–157, 2020.
https://doi.org/10.1007/978-3-030-50341-3_12

called out or which is displayed on a centrally placed monitor [8]. Those systems apply to so-called "invisible" queues, in which people are not standing in line one behind another [8]. A more recent study has shown that customers prefer invisible ticket queues above physical queues [9]. The development of information systems (IS) entails that firms increasingly provide technologies, such as self-service technology (SST), which have been introduced widely in retail environments [10]. Almost 30 years ago, the topic of SST in retail gained a lot of attention, when researchers of service literature began to examine relevant factors that are of great importance for customer participation with SSTs at servicescapes [11, 12]. SSTs enable customers to take over control of the situation or transactions in waiting and queuing situations [11]. Convenience and the quick and accurate ability to perform the task, are necessary attributes [13, 14] in order to encourage customers to use SSTs. From the retailer's perspective, SSTs have mainly been introduced to save labour costs as machines are able to take over tasks from human beings [11].

We conducted face-to-face interviews with a qualitative and quantitative questionnaire after customers visited a telecommunications store in an Austrian shopping mall. Our study investigates the human-computer interaction between customers and a queuing technology based on the concept of ticketing and offered as both a self-service and human-operated system. In order to make the waiting time more pleasant for customers, the retailer's intentions by providing an advanced queuing system were, first of all, to offer customers the possibility to move freely around the closer area of the store or to use the time productively carrying out errands. Second, by being called upon by name, the telecommunication provider expects to provide a more personal entry into the service consultation between employee and customer. Finally, the goal was to improve the whole experience and to ensure the customer's intention to repurchase. Therefore, our work contributes to the understanding of the influence of in-store retail technology on customer experience, demonstrated by the usage of a queuing technology in a telecommunications store. Consequently, we pose the following research questions for this work: How does a queuing technology affect the customers' perception of the experience in a service-oriented retail store? Are there differences in interacting with human- or self-service-based queuing technologies?

The paper is organized in the following way. Section 2 provides the theoretical background on customer experience and SSTs in retail. Section 3 presents the queuing technology and its functionalities. Section 4 outlines the research methodology concerning participants and the questionnaire used in this work. The results are presented in Sect. 5 and structured based on the four different approaches of our study: First, we observed customers of a telecommunication store to evaluate their approach and avoidance behaviour when using SST. Second, we focused on measuring the cognitive, affective and physical first-order constructs in line with Bustamante et al.'s [15]. In-Store Customer Experience (ISCX) scale. Third, we investigated the customer's willingness to use additional functions of the SST, such as taking a picture to enable employees a faster recognition of the customer. Fourth, we outline the qualitative feedback of customers' overall satisfaction. Section 6 shows the findings of this study and gives recommendations for retailers. Further, the limitations of our study are discussed in this section. Concluding, Sect. 7, provides a summary of our findings.

2 Theoretical Background and Related Work

Our study is based on two topics: First, we will define the construct of customer experience and discuss the term in association with the importance of queuing. Second, we will present related work in IS research on self-service technologies in retail environments.

2.1 In-store Customer Experience

Queuing theory is a formal concept applied in service-oriented industries and studied in the field of operations management improving the flow of queues, such as in hospital pharmacy [16]. Maister [5], who analysed queuing from the psychological and behavioural perspective, claims that the customer's entire perception of service quality is significantly influenced by the experience in the queue. Service and customer experience are often used interchangeably in service research [17]. As stated by Meyer et al. [18], customer experience can be defined as "[...] the internal and subjective response customers have to any direct or indirect contact with a company. Direct contact generally occurs in the course of purchase, use, and service and is usually initiated by the customer" (p. 1). To Lemon et al. [19] customer experience is "[...] holistic in nature and involves the customer's cognitive, affective, emotional, social and physical responses to the retailer" (p. 70). Bustamante et al. [15] designed the ISCX-scale, a third-order formative model, to measure cognitive, affective, social and physical experiences in physical retail environments. ISCX stands for In-Store Customer Experience and is based on the Strategic Experiential Modules (SEMs) as proposed by Schmitt [20]. SEM proposes to strategically create customer experience with elements that influence the human's state of mind and behaviour, such as affective and cognitive experiences [20], which can be explained as follows: Affective customer experiences such as being in a good mood or feeling contented or surprised [15] are human emotions that influence customer experience and behavioural outcomes [21]. Dahm et al. [22] reported that the affective state of mind in queues at supermarket checkouts shows a strong negative effect as the number of people increases in the line behind the focal customer. The emotional elements related to the shopping experience are excluded if shopping trips are assessed mainly for utilitarian reasons [23] or if customers are exposed to an unknown situation at the service encounter [11]. In this case, the psychological concept of cognitive experience is more active. The cognitive state of mind is defined as a person's conscious thinking, allowing people to create opinions, receive, and process information, and evaluate their environment [24]. Cognitive states of mind occur when the shopping environment awakens curiosity, inspiration, or interest [15]. The physical element of customer experience refers to the retailer's environment, the products in the store, as well as its personnel, and practices [15]. According to Schmitt [20], the physical experience relates to the active verb "act", as well as to motivational and inspirational feelings. The use of in-store technology has an impact on consumers' perception of the atmosphere in physical retail stores [25]. Retailers can use this knowledge to introduce triggers in the retail environment, such as SSTs, through which the customer's thinking engages [15]. De Keyser et al. [26] emphasize that in-store technology plays an important role in customer experience. Consequently, behavioural outcomes, such as customer satisfaction [19, 27–30] and intention to repurchase (IR) [29, 31, 32] (as part of customer loyalty) are both factors used by researchers and practitioners to evaluate how customers perceived their shopping experience.

2.2 Self-service Technologies in Retail Environments

Few field studies about SSTs in physical retail environments have been conducted in the past decade [33]. Numerous researchers use the well-known TAM as the theoretical basis on technology acceptance of decision support technologies [13, 34]. Moreover, many studies focus on decision support technologies, such as Djelassi et al.'s [10] work on the experience with self-checkout and self-scanning devices and perceived waiting time. The authors proved that the satisfaction with the technology increases the more interactively the SST has been designed (e.g., self-scanning). Even though the authors showed a link to overall satisfaction with the store, this connection is more difficult to establish as customers might attribute the experience with SSTs to themselves rather than to the store. Dabholkar [11] was one of the first who studied the influence of SST usage on perceived service quality and the effect of cognitive and affective perception of waiting. In any waiting situation, control has been found to be a strong determinant of service quality, as well as enjoyment for long waiting times. Roy et al. [32] performed an online questionnaire on multiple smart retail technologies, such as smart checkouts, personal shopping assistance, and point of sale smart displays. All of these technologies promoted a positive influence of the SST on the customer's satisfaction. Various studies on queuing systems and waiting emotions can also be found in the literature on hospitality [35], transportation [36], and operations management [37].

The objective of our study is to investigate whether queuing technology affects the perceived customer experience of the queuing process in retail environments. For this purpose, we used an SST and a human-operated queuing system, both of which were evaluated by customers. The goal is to draw conclusions that support practitioners in developing in-store technologies as well as to make retailers aware of important factors when implementing in-store technology.

3 The Functionality of the Queuing Technology

This study discusses queuing technologies, which are implemented at stores of several telecommunication providers. Those stores are typically consultancy-intensive as the majority of customers demand an individual consultation by a service employee. Depending on the frequency in the store, customers need to wait for a personal service encounter. The advanced queuing technology presented in this study aims to create an enhanced customer experience and to offer a pleasant perception of the unavoidable waiting time. The system has been developed by an Austrian retail-software and consulting company specialised on in-store technologies. The hardware supplier, an international IT-systems company, provides devices with touch-screen monitors for all kinds of self-service encounters. The web application is developed in responsive design, enabling an automatic adjustment of the content on any device and screen size [38]. Therefore, the application can be used as SST on a touch-screen monitor, as well as from a 'Human Greeter' (HG), in order to arrange the next possible service encounter with another employee. The HG refers to an employee who welcomes customers at the entrance of the store and queues them by using a portable tablet computer with the same software. If the HG is not present or busy queuing others, customers are offered the possibility of using the SST at the entrance of the telecommunications store. See Fig. 1.

Fig. 1. Self-service technology in a telecommunication retail store. *Note: Photo has been adjusted for reasons of secrecy*

During the process of queuing, customers decide on how they would like to be notified about the upcoming service encounter. Customers can either be called using their name as given to the HG/SST or informed by a text message five minutes prior to the appointment. Both options require the input from the customer at a keyboard on the touch screen or waiting for the HG to enter the information. It is also possible for users of the SST to skip those options by clicking on the "Continue" button several times. In this case, the system creates a consecutive ticket number by default. Both queuing possibilities (SST/HG) provide an estimated waiting time, which is automatically calculated by the number of employees logged in to the system and the number of customers in consultancy or waiting ahead. In case of low frequency in the store, customers tend to directly approach the counter of a free employee instead of queuing. Figure 2 gives an overview of the possibilities of approaching a service encounter at the retail store.

The main purpose of the queuing technology, as described by the developer, is to provide a convenient and fair FIFO-queuing-process in which customers are not forced to stay in the store during the waiting time and leave the store perceiving a great customer experience.

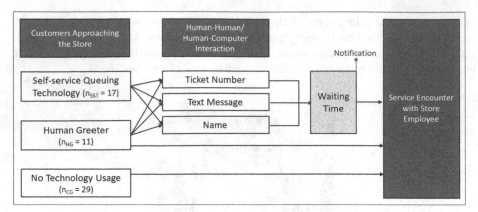

Fig. 2. Queuing process at the telecommunication store

4 Research Design and Methodology

In order to investigate the customer's perception of the queuing technology, a mixed-methods field study has been carried out in one of the telecommunication provider's stores located in a shopping mall in Vienna, Austria. We did not interfere in the daily business for our study. Firstly, we observed how customers approached the retail store and their behaviour with the SST or the service employee as HG. Secondly, we investigated the impact of queuing technology on customer experience and consequently on satisfaction and intention to repurchase. In this case, data has been collected by a quantitative approach. Thirdly, we got deeper insights from a quantitative evaluation of the customer's technology usage. In the last step, customers expressed the overall satisfaction in their own words. The following subsections will provide the segmentation of participants, as well as the data collection procedure.

4.1 Participants

In total, 60 interviews were completed on four days in June and July 2019 at the entrance of a telecommunications store in a well-established shopping mall in Vienna. While considering the gender balance, customers were chosen at random to participate in a structured face-to-face interview using quantitative and qualitative questions after their store visit and were not aware of the questionnaire in advance. Each day, there were between 60 and 70 people visiting the store. Because of the relatively low customer traffic on the days of observation, the majority of customers were able to approach an employee directly or did not have to wait for more than one minute before their appointment came up. Overall, the survey was conducted with approximately 20% of the total amount of people having a service consultation with one of the store's employees on each of the four survey days. To reduce a negative emotional bias in the statistical analysis, we excluded three people whose problems could not be solved by the company and subsequently rated their overall experience as "(very) bad". Consequently, the resulting sample included 57 persons between the age of 17 and 75 (mean age = 37.89, SD = 13.968), of which

29 were men (50.9%) and 28 were women (49.1%). We split the participants into two experimental groups who either used the SST to get a queuing ticket ($n_{SST} = 17$) or were queued by the HG ($n_{HG} = 11$). The control group consists of 29 participants ($n_{CG} = 29$) who did not have contact with either the SST or the HG. These customers directly approached free service employees or were offered help without queuing. In total, 85% of participants had been regular customers of the telecommunications provider before they entered the store on the respective day of the investigation. More than three quarters had already encountered self-service queuing technology before of which 20% knew the system from this retail store and 27% from another location.

4.2 Questionnaire

To measure customer experience in a retail store we adapted a questionnaire design proposed by Bustamante et al. [15]. The scale measures participant's cognitive (3 items), affective (3 items) and physical experience (3 items). Contrary to Bustamante et al. [15], we did not include questions about the social construct to focus on the evaluation of the store and the use of the technology, independent of the employees' consultancy and service abilities. All items were measured with a Likert scale ranging from 1 ('highly disagree') to 5 ('highly agree'). The questionnaire was conducted with survey software Questback [39] running on a tablet device. According to the automatic logging, the completion of the questionnaire took an average of 8.5 min. Additionally, our questionnaire addressed participants' overall satisfaction with the store (1 item) and intention to repurchase (1 item) both derived from Turner and Schockley [29]. We also included sample selection questions (2 items), asked for participants' previous SST experience (1 item [10]), trust in the SST (4 items [40]), satisfaction with the queuing system (1 item [29]) and participant's demographics (3 items). For the open question on overall experience [29], customers' answers were written down by the researcher in an open text field on the tablet device. Furthermore, we collected the customers' self-evaluation on technology readiness (2 items [41]) and need for interaction (2 items [42]).

5 Results

The evaluation of the results is divided into four categories: First, we present the observations from the field. Second, we conducted a statistical analysis in which Bustamante et al.'s [15] ISCX scale is used. Third, we present the findings from the customer's evaluation of the interaction with the SST. Finally, we evaluate customers' qualitative feedback on the overall experience.

5.1 Situational Observation of Customers Entering the Store

An initial concern was whether shoppers entering the store would notice the SST and start the queueing procedure. We observed that some shoppers who stopped and looked at the monitor did not instantly interact with it. In this case, the customers were either able to directly approach a service employee because of low frequency in the store or were directed to the SST by an employee. The purpose of the SST was not obviously clear to users, who had not been in contact with the system before. Those customers were able to use it after reading the text on the screen, being informed by an employee or watching other people using the SST. Still, they were looking for a monitor where they could check their waiting number and how many people were ahead in the queue. Experienced customers, who obviously knew the system already, immediately approached the SST. The majority of customers were busy checking whether the company was calling up customers in the right order and that no other customers were jumping the queue. Two customers who had been welcomed by the HG directly asked if he could take care of their problem directly instead of providing a queuing number.

5.2　Statistical Analysis of Customer Experience

In the following subsections, we present the findings from our statistical analyses on customer experience, satisfaction and intention to repurchase. Respective group differences and effect sizes are provided as well.

Descriptive Statistics. After the store visit, customers were asked questions about their cognitive, affective and physical experience in the store. Skewness and kurtosis values suggest all items deviate from a normal distribution. This is further confirmed by the very significant p values of the Kolmogorov-Smirnov test and Shapiro-Wilk test, which in total suggest the validity of non-parametric testing. Due to their non-parametric nature, a Kruskal-Wallis test was used to check whether the customer experience of people using SST, HG and control group differs significantly from each other. Furthermore, a Mann-Whitney U test with Bonferroni corrected significance level was conducted to pinpoint the differences between SST, HG and control group. Finally, we tested the effect size of the discovered differences by using Cohen's d. The software SPSS (v. 26) [43] was used to analyse the data of our questionnaire. The results of the descriptive statistics on customer experience, satisfaction, and intention to repurchase are presented in Table 1.

Group Differences and Effect Sizes. We conducted a Kruskal-Wallis test for non-parametric statistics and small samples to analyse differences in customer experience between participants who did not queue by using technology (control group) and the ones who either used the SST or were queued by the HG. We observed no significant differences in customer experience perception between HG, SST and control group except for the cognitive item "Interest". Consequently, the item was analysed with a Mann-Whitney U test for each group combination to discover which groups significantly differ from each other. The results are outlined in Table 2.

As Table 3 shows, the Mann-Whitney U test (U = 143.5) shows a significant difference (p = 0.0155), even at the Bonferroni adjusted significance level (p = 0.016), of the cognitive item "Interest" between the control group (Median = 4) and SST (Median = 3). The effect size according to Cohen [44] is d = 0.737 which represents a medium to large effect.

5.3　Quantitative Analysis of Interaction with SST

We evaluated customers' perceived convenience using the SST by the questionnaire items effort, easiness, and quickness adapted from Colwell et al. [10]. The analysis shows that

Table 1. Descriptive statistics

Item	M	SD	Skew.	Kurt.	K-S/p[a]	S-W/p
Cognitive						
The environment of this retail store, the display of its products, services, etc.:						
C1. Awaken my curiosity	3	1.088	− 0.325	− 0.271	0.193/<0.001	0.906/<0.001
C2. Inspire me	3	1.093	0.118	− 0.258	0.221/<0.001	0.903/<0.001
C3. Interest me	3	1.217	− 0.323	− 0.712	0.185/<0.001	0.905/<0.001
Affective						
The environment of this retail store, the display of its products, services, etc., make me feel:						
A1. In a good mood	4	0.934	− 0.551	0.205	0.231/<0.001	0.872/<0.001
A2. Contented	4	0.844	− 0.437	− 0.599	0.22/<0.001	0.843/<0.001
A3. Surprised	3	1.187	0.038	− 0.817	0.156/0.001	0.918/0.001
Physical						
The environment of this retail store, the display of its products, services, etc., make me feel:						
P1. Comfort	4	0.964	− 0.387	0.738	0.243/<0.001	0.866/<0.001
P2. Energy	4	0.772	− 0.780	2.185	0.291/<0.001	0.811/<0.001
P3. Well-being	4	0.789	− 0.484	− 0.551	0.23/<0.001	0.824/<0.001
Overall satisfaction	5	0.331	− 2.361	3.703	0.522/<0.001	0.385/<0.001
Intention to repurchase	5	1.101	− 1.747	1.704	0.437/<0.001	0.582/<0.001

[a]Lilliefors Significance Correction

Note: Median (M), Standard Deviation (SD), Skewness (Skew.), Kurtosis (Kurt.), Kolmogorov-Smirnov test (K-S), Shapiro-Wilk (S-W) test and their significance (p)

customers (n = 28), independently of the self-service or human-operated technology, rated the three convenience items with the maximum value. Only one person chose the second-best possible answer for the quickness with the HG.

Furthermore, the survey contained questions about using the additional functions of the SST as presented in the aforementioned Sect. 3. In this section, customers evaluated their willingness to expose their real name and phone number (only available for SST users) for an intentionally more personalized customer experience. In total, nine of 17 SST users and two of eleven HG users were willing to reveal their name. Regardless of SST or HG, customers were, except for one person (Likert-rating: 4), very satisfied with the queuing process (Likert-rating: 5).

Overall, it can be stated that trust towards the company itself (median = 4.5) was rated slightly higher than trust with regard to the deletion of the data after the store visit (median = 4.0). It needs to be stated that there is no clear evidence for the items "trust"

Table 2. Group differences SST, HG and control group

Item	Kruskal-Wallis H	df	Asymp. Sig.
Cognitive			
C1. Awaken my curiosity	1.533	2	0.465
C2. Inspire me	1.451	2	0.484
C3. Interest me	6.228	2	**0.044**
Affective			
A1. In a good mood	1.275	2	0.529
A2. Contented	0.654	2	0.721
A3. Surprised	0.253	2	0.881
Physical			
P1. Comfort	2.653	2	0.265
P2. Energy	1.910	2	0.385
P3. Well-being	2.603	2	0.272
Overall satisfaction	3.574	2	0.167
Intention to repurchase	4.750	2	0.093

Table 3. Mann-Whitney-U tests and effect sizes

Cognitive Item "Interest"	Median comparison	Mann-Whitney U	Z	Exact. Sig. (2-tailed)*	(η^2)	d_{Cohen}
Control group-SST	4–3	143.5	−2.435	0.0155	0.119	0.737
Control group-HG	4–3	113	−1.443	0.151	0.049	0.452
SST-HG	3–3	87	−0.314	0.767	0.003	0.116

*Bonferroni corrected significance level = 0.016

and the self-evaluation on "technology readiness" and "need for human interaction" in our small sample (n = 28). Notably, it needs to be stated that the five participants who had no trust in data deletion, indicated maximum rating on the need for human interaction and lower indication for technology readiness. Finally, the evaluation shows that the two customers who were queued by the HG and exposed their name to the employee showed full trust in data deletion and the company, but would still not consider being notified by a text message sent to their private phones. The vast majority (n = 22) of customers queuing with technology (n = 28) indicated a general preference towards interacting with the person who provides the service as an indicator for the construct "need for human touch" [42]. However, none of these results could be proven at a statistically significant level due to the small sample size.

5.4 Qualitative Analysis of the Overall Customer Satisfaction

In order to get a deeper insight into the evaluation of the overall experience, we used one item of customer satisfaction adapted from Turner and Shockley [29]. The answers have been coded by repetitive patterns given in the answers during the interviews. Table 4 provides the five most frequently mentioned answers and direct statements.

Table 4. Customer satisfaction statements

#	Code	No. of times mentioned	Example statement (translated from German to English)
1	Friendly employees	28	*"The service was perfect. The employee was very friendly and helpful"*
2	Competent employees	23	*"I have experienced very courteous consultancy by the service employee. She showed me a lot of different options and how to improve cost-effectiveness"* *"The employee knows a lot about Apple. I'm impressed"*
3	Employees fulfilling customer's needs	17	*"The employee was very motivated to answer all of my questions. Also, I had the feeling to get a very individual consultation. It was a very positive experience"*
4	Satisfied feeling	16	*"I always leave this shop satisfied"* *"I'm very satisfied with the performance in this store. Actually, I came here today, to terminate my contract. But now I got a really good offer, which I took"*
5	Helpful employees	15	*"My visit today was very informative. Everything was done satisfactorily. I only had a little problem, but they helped me with it"*

6 Discussion and Future Research

In this study, we investigated the influence of human- and technology-based queuing technology on customers' evaluation of their experience and willingness to repurchase in a real-life retail setting. It is important for retailers to introduce some kind of queuing management in their stores where products or services require intensive consultation to be given by a service employee. For situations where several people request a service encounter at the same time, we strongly believe that having no queuing technology at all would result in an unfair and chaotic queuing situation, as Haynes [6] and Katz [4] claimed in their studies.

The intention of the retailer was to provide a relaxed and fair queueing process in the store. However, based on the observations we made when customers approached the store in the first section of our analysis, we point out that there are several issues to consider. We have noticed that customers are obviously used to screens that display the order of numbers in the queue and how many people are ahead of themselves. When this information was not provided, we got the impression that customers experienced stress observing the fair handling of the queue. Moreover, it is highly likely that customers would like to base their initial decision as to whether to join the queue or pass the store this time, on the total number of people in the queue. Furthermore, retailers must assume the fact that not all customers are aware of the purpose and function of the SST. Therefore, the purpose for which the SST exists should be clearly visible and easily understandable as should the information concerning how it can be used. In addition, we believe that the system would profit from a short demonstration video playing on the SST screen to show how the queuing process works and why name and number can be volunteered. Moreover, we believe that a service employee assisting customers to queue at the SST would help to better deal with the process.

Considering the statistical results from the adapted ISCX-measurement [15], we come to the conclusion that there are no pertinent differences concerning the cognitive, affective, and physical customer experience perception among customers using the queuing technology (SST, HG) or no technology at all. The item *Interest,* related to the cognitive construct, showed a significant difference between the SST and the HG in favour of the HG. However, we suggest not interpreting this single significant item as a strong result. Additionally, we measured no statistically significant difference in customers' overall satisfaction and intention to repurchase. Therefore, our study was not able to prove that the implementation of the queuing technologies (SST, HG) presented in this paper has a direct impact on the evaluation of the overall customer experience, measured by cognitive, affective and physical constructs. However, from a financial perspective, the SSTs might help retailers to save labour costs as these systems are able to take over human tasks during the queuing process [11] while the HG would require an additional employee to greet and queue customers. Moreover, we believe that in stores, where the customer frequency, and therefore waiting times, are generally higher, the presented advanced functions of the queuing technology (e.g. leaving the store to carry out errands) can be very helpful to reduce the unpleasant feeling of wasting time in the queue of a retail store. We argue that retailers with consultancy-intensive products should introduce some kind of queuing technology to provide an easy and fair management of customers.

As assessed in the third part of our analysis, the evaluation of satisfaction for both queuing systems (SST and HG) demonstrates that customers were pleased with the necessary effort, ease, and speed. The three different notification options (i.e., ticket number, name, and text message by entering one's phone number) revealed that the willingness to expose one's name is much higher than the willingness to give the personal phone number. The fact that most of the participants who entered their name are male (10) would support Weijters et al.'s [34] TAM-based results which show that the influence of perceived usefulness on attitude towards using the SST is stronger for men than for women. Literature in brain research [45] has proven that the intention of calling customers by their names helps to personalize the experience as researchers detected greater brain activation when hearing one's own name. We assume that the decision to not expose the phone number during the queuing process is based on the lack of necessity at this stage. The impression that the phone number would be at everyone's disposal at the SST might evoke the feeling of discomfort and is likely to create involvement costs, which are too high for too little expected value. Another reason probably lies in the customer's general reluctance towards the exposure of personal data arising from repeated stories of data breaches recently reported in the media [46]. We strongly relate these results to the so-called "privacy paradox" which describes the contradiction between the customer's concerns about lack of privacy and carefree behaviour at the same time [47].

Finally, the answers to the qualitative question on the customer's whole experience of the store visit proved that the service provided by employees makes up the most important element of the whole experience. The queuing procedure and also the retail environment play a significant role in the impression of the brand and the store, but still, service capabilities remain in the mind of the customers after leaving the retailer's store rather than the whole experience. In contrast, we strongly believe that the queuing technology and its advanced features in stores, which have generally high customer frequency and consequently higher waiting times, can provide a major advantage for customers.

Some limitations of the study need to be mentioned as follows: First, we are aware that the small sample size distorted the results of the statistical analysis of customer experience, especially in terms of identifying differences between technology users (n_{HG} = 11. n_{SST} = 17). Bigger samples, by surveying the same store for a longer period of time or by replicating the study in a more frequented store, would increase the statistical significance and decrease limitations in terms of the study's generalizability. Second, the factors influencing the participant's evaluation in field studies in a retail environment are countless. Future research may be applied in a laboratory environment to reduce the number of influencing factors. Third, the evaluation of the queuing process might be better scheduled directly after the actual transaction whereby researchers can be sure that the given answers are independent of the quality of products or the service encounter. Finally, future studies could investigate the experience of queuing technology in conjunction with cultural differences in the perception of waiting time, for example by adding Hofstede's [48] dimensions of culture. The implications of these points indicate further possibilities for future research in the domain of in-store technologies and customer experience.

7 Conclusion

Our work contributes to the understanding of the impact of in-store retail technology on customer experience and intention to repurchase as demonstrated by the usage of SST and human-operated queuing technology in a retail environment. Even though we were not able to confirm strong evidence for differences between using queuing technology and directly approaching a service employee on customer experience factors in our adapted model, our findings show insights for retailers and practitioners related to introducing queuing management systems into their store as well as for developers designing such systems. In all cases, the focus of consultancy-intensive retail shops, such as telecommunication stores, lies on the capabilities of the service personnel. Queuing is one part of the whole experience, which could add good impressions and create the foundation for a good start into an individual's service encounter. Moreover, the absence of a convenient and fair queue management could cause anger and dissatisfaction for store visitors. However, customer satisfaction after the store visit depends on the degree of expectation fulfilment, the competence and friendliness of employees, and on whether customers are persuaded that they made a good deal or their problem has been solved. Therefore, in situations involving a short waiting time, as in our field study, we recommend introducing a FIFO queuing management system, which offers a convenient and fair experience for waiting customers. For highly frequented stores or especially busy phases, we strongly encourage retailers to introduce queuing technologies. We also believe that additional services, such as notifying the customer via text message, provide a great benefit for big stores, where customers expect longer waiting times. Additionally, we would recommend installing monitors that show the number of tickets ahead to provide visible evidence for the fairness of the queuing system. Being aware of important factors influencing the evaluation of queuing technology helps retailers and developers to understand the process and set the right management actions in terms of personnel planning and developing system features accordingly.

Acknowledgements. The present work was conducted within the Innovative Training Network project PERFORM funded by the European Union's Horizon 2020 research and innovation program under the Marie Skłodowska-Curie grant agreement No. 765395. This study reflects only the authors' view, the EU Research Executive Agency is not responsible for any use that may be made of the information it contains.

References

1. Voorhees, C.M., Baker, J., Bourdeau, B.L., Brocato, E.D., Cronin Jr., J.J.: It depends: moderating the relationships among perceived waiting time, anger, and regret. J. Serv. Res. **12**, 138–155 (2009)
2. KPMG: Anteil der Befragten, die aus folgenden Gründe lieber in Online-Shops anstatt in Ladengeschäften einkaufen, weltweit im Jahr 2016 [Chart]. https://de.statista.com/statistik/daten/studie/786111/umfrage/gruende-fuer-das-online-shopping-weltweit/
3. Larson, R.C.: OR forum—perspectives on queues: social justice and the psychology of queueing. Oper. Res. **35**, 895–905 (1987)

4. Katz, K., Larson, B., Larson, R.: Prescription for the waiting-in-line blues: entertain, enlighten, and engage. Sloan Manag. Rev. **4**, 44–53 (1991)
5. Maister, D.H.: The Psychology of Waiting Lines. Harvard Business School, Boston (1984)
6. Haynes, P.J.: Hating to wait: managing the final service encounter. J. Serv. Mark. **4**, 20–26 (1990)
7. Sasser, W.E., Olsen, R.P., Wyckoff, D.D.: Management of Service Operations: Text, Cases, and Readings. Allyn & Bacon, Boston (1978)
8. Xu, S.H., Gao, L., Ou, J.: Service performance analysis and improvement for a ticket queue with balking customers. Manag. Sci. **53**, 971–990 (2007)
9. Kuzu, K.: Comparisons of perceptions and behavior in ticket queues and physical queues. Serv. Sci. **7**, 294–314 (2015)
10. Djelassi, S., Diallo, M.F., Zielke, S.: How self-service technology experience evaluation affects waiting time and customer satisfaction? A moderated mediation model. Decis. Support Syst. **111**, 38–47 (2018)
11. Dabholkar, P.A.: Consumer evaluations of new technology-based self-service options: an investigation of alternative models of service quality. Int. J. Res. Mark. **13**, 29–51 (1996)
12. Bitner, M.J.: Servicescapes: the impact of physical surroundings on customers and employees. J. Mark. **56**, 57–71 (1992)
13. Kallweit, K., Spreer, P., Toporowski, W.: Why do customers use self-service information technologies in retail? The mediating effect of perceived service quality. J. Retail. Consum. Serv. **21**, 268–276 (2014)
14. Colwell, S.R., Aung, M., Kanetkar, V., Holden, A.L.: Toward a measure of service convenience: multiple-item scale development and empirical test. J. Serv. Mark. **22**, 160–169 (2008)
15. Bustamante, J.C., Rubio, N.: Measuring customer experience in physical retail environments. J. Serv. Manag. **28**, 884–913 (2017)
16. Nosek, R.A., Wilson, J.P.: Queuing theory and customer satisfaction: a review of terminology, trends, and applications to pharmacy practice. Hosp. Pharm. **36**(3), 275–279 (2001)
17. Klaus, P., Maklan, S.: EXQ: a multiple-item scale for assessing service experience. J. Serv. Manag. **23**, 5–33 (2012)
18. Meyer, C., Schwager, A.: Understanding customer experience. Harvard Bus. Rev. **85**, 116 (2007)
19. Lemon, K.N., Verhoef, P.C.: Understanding customer experience throughout the customer journey. J. Mark. **80**, 69–96 (2016)
20. Schmitt, B.: Experiential marketing. J. Mark. Manag. **15**, 53–67 (1999)
21. Lucia-Palacios, L., Pérez-López, R., Polo-Redondo, Y.: Cognitive, affective and behavioural responses in mall experience: a qualitative approach. Int. J. Retail Distrib. Manag. **44**, 4–21 (2016)
22. Dahm, M., Wentzel, D., Herzog, W., Wiecek, A.: Breathing down your neck!: The impact of queues on customers using a retail service. J. Retail. **94**, 217–230 (2018)
23. Babin, B.J., Darden, W.R., Griffin, M.: Work and/or fun: measuring hedonic and utilitarian shopping value. J. Consum. Res. **20**, 644–656 (1994)
24. David, D., Miclea, M., Opre, A.: The information-processing approach to the human mind: basics and beyond. J. Clin. Psychol. **60**, 353–368 (2004)
25. Poncin, I., Mimoun, M.S.B.: The impact of "e-atmospherics" on physical stores. J. Retail. Consum. Serv. **21**, 851–859 (2014)
26. De Keyser, A., Köcher, S., Alkire, L., Verbeeck, C., Kandampully, J.: Frontline Service Technology infusion: conceptual archetypes and future research directions. J. Serv. Manag. **30**, 156–183 (2019)

27. Puccinelli, N.M., Goodstein, R.C., Grewal, D., Price, R., Raghubir, P., Stewart, D.: Customer experience management in retailing: understanding the buying process. J. Retail. **85**, 15–30 (2009)
28. Verhoef, P.C., Lemon, K.N., Parasuraman, A., Roggeveen, A., Tsiros, M., Schlesinger, L.A.: Customer experience creation: determinants, dynamics and management strategies. J. Retail. **85**, 31–41 (2009)
29. Turner, T., Shockley, J.: Creating shopper value: co-creation roles, in-store self-service technology use, and value differentiation. J. Promot. Manag. **20**, 311–327 (2014)
30. Brakus, J.J., Schmitt, B.H., Zarantonello, L.: Brand experience: what is it? How is it measured? Does it affect loyalty? J. Mark. **73**, 52–68 (2009)
31. Alexander, M., MacLaren, A., O'Gorman, K., White, C.: Priority queues: where social justice and equity collide. Tour. Manag. **33**, 875–884 (2012)
32. Roy, S.K., Shekhar, V., Lassar, W.M., Chen, T.: Customer engagement behaviors: the role of service convenience, fairness and quality. J. Retail. Consum. Serv. **44**, 293–304 (2018)
33. Obermeier, G., Auinger, A.: Human-computer interaction in physical retail environments and the impact on customer experience: systematic literature review and research agenda. In: Nah, F.F.-H., Siau, K. (eds.) HCII 2019. LNCS, vol. 11588, pp. 51–66. Springer, Cham (2019). https://doi.org/10.1007/978-3-030-22335-9_4
34. Weijters, B., Rangarajan, D., Falk, T., Schillewaert, N.: Determinants and outcomes of customers' use of self-service technology in a retail setting. J. Serv. Res. **10**, 3–21 (2007)
35. Kembe, M.M., Onah, E.S., Iorkegh, S.: A study of waiting and service costs of a multi-server queuing model in a specialist hospital. Int. J. Sci. Technol. Res. **1**, 19–23 (2012)
36. Psarros, I., Kepaptsoglou, K., Karlaftis, M.G.: An empirical investigation of passenger wait time perceptions using hazard-based duration models. J. Public Transp. **14**, 6 (2011)
37. Bielen, F., Demoulin, N.: Waiting time influence on the satisfaction-loyalty relationship in services. Manag. Serv. Qual. **17**, 174–193 (2007)
38. Google Developers: Responsive Web Design. https://developers.google.com/search/mobile-sites/mobile-seo/responsive-design?hl=en
39. Questback GmbH: EFS Survey (2018)
40. Morgan, R.M., Hunt, S.D.: The commitment-trust theory of relationship marketing. J. Mark. **58**, 20–38 (1994)
41. Parasuraman, A., Colby, C.L.: An updated and streamlined technology readiness index: TRI 2.0. J. Serv. Res. **18**, 59–74 (2015)
42. Lee, H.-J., Yang, K.: Interpersonal service quality, self-service technology (SST) service quality, and retail patronage. J. Retail. Consum. Serv. **20**, 51–57 (2013)
43. Corp, I.B.M.: Released. IBM SPSS Statistics for Windows, Armonk (2017)
44. Cohen, J.: Statistical Power Analysis for the Behavioral Sciences. Routledge, Abingdon (2013)
45. Carmody, D.P., Lewis, M.: Brain activation when hearing one's own and others' names. Brain Res. **1116**, 153–158 (2006)
46. Chakraborty, R., Lee, J., Bagchi-Sen, S., Upadhyaya, S., Rao, H.R.: Online shopping intention in the context of data breach in online retail stores: an examination of older and younger adults. Decis. Support Syst. **83**, 47–56 (2016)
47. Norberg, P.A., Horne, D.R., Horne, D.A.: The privacy paradox: personal information disclosure intentions versus behaviors. J. Consum. Affairs **41**, 100–126 (2007)
48. Hofstede, G., Bond, M.H.: Hofstede's culture dimensions: an independent validation using Rokeach's value survey. J. Cross Cult. Psychol. **15**, 417–433 (1984)

Protect Our Health with Cleaner Cars – How to Gain Customer Acceptance for Air Pollution Decreasing Retrofit Purchase

Joachim Reiter[1(✉)], Uwe Hartmann[2], Larissa Greschuchna[1], Jaline Westrich[1], Aliyah Moertl[1], Laura Cherkaoui[1], Maike Breier[1], Malgorzata Olbrich[1], Carolin Hoffmann[1], Andreas Franz[2], Johannes Wenserit[2], and Andrea Mueller[1]

[1] Offenburg University of Applied Sciences, Badstrasse 24, 77652 Offenburg, Germany
joachim.reiter@hs-offenburg.de
[2] MANN+HUMMEL GmbH, Schwieberdinger Strasse 126, 71636 Ludwigsburg, Germany

Abstract. Automotive service suppliers are keen to invent products that help to reduce particulate matter pollution substantial, but governance worldwide are not yet ready to introduce this retrofitting of helpful devices statutory. To develop a strategy how to introduce these devices to the market based on user needs is the objective of our research. The contribution of this paper is three-fold: we will provide an overview of the current options of particulate matter pollution solutions (I). This corpus is used to come to a more precise description of the specific needs and wishes of target groups (II). Finally, a representative empirical study via social media channels with German car owners will help to develop a strategy to introduce retrofit devices into the German market (III).

Keywords: Particulate matter pollution · Brake dust filter · Retrofit · Automotive after market · Millennials · Social media · Customer acceptance

1 Particulate Matter Pollution Retrofit Market

In Europe about 324 million cars create a 127 billion Euro after market with two categories of service providers for car repair: about 84,000 Original Equipment Service (OES) and 378,000 Independent After Market (IAM) share this market turnover nearly half-and-half [1]. Air pollution and attempts to defraud by several big car brands unsettle the automotive industry and especially the customers in the last years. Also, alternative drive systems like e-cars enter the market.

But, not only motors are a source of health hazards: even more braking causes an enormous part of particulate matter pollution worldwide. What could be a clue for this challenging situation? Brake filter technology could be an excellent solution, because emerging fine dust is directly absorbed by a filter in the brake system. The filter production company Mann+Hummel, Ludwigsburg, Germany, and Offenburg University conduct a unique research project: The objective is to identify the willingness of young health-sensitive customers to invest in a brake filter device in a representative survey in Germany.

© Springer Nature Switzerland AG 2020
F. F.-H. Nah and K. Siau (Eds.): HCII 2020, LNCS 12204, pp. 158–173, 2020.
https://doi.org/10.1007/978-3-030-50341-3_13

We try to find out, where customers would expect this innovative retrofit, how much they would spent and what additional services they would like to get offered by service and product providers. Retrofit providers can use this information to fulfill customer needs on less air polluting cars and facilitate the decision to buy and use a car nowadays.

2 Related Work

The individual generations of the German population are currently undergoing a major structural change in terms of prioritizing people´s health and environmental protection. In this chapter we describe the specific characteristics of the addressed target groups.

2.1 Target Group: Millennials

According to a study on environmental awareness from 2018 [2] there are two social milieus, which are especially environmentally aware and therefore willing to spend more money for health promoting and ecologic alternatives of consumer goods – the Critical Creatives and the Young Idealists. Both of which share the opinion that, in accordance to the future development of traffic and transport, the environment should be polluted as little as possible [3].

Critical Creatives include mainly highly-educated females in a broad age range from 30 to 70 years who are looking for self-fulfillment and independence. Further, they are tolerant, cosmopolitan and interested in social, as well as cultural topics, while considering the government's current commitment to environmental and health protection as inadequate. On average, two to three cars are owned per critical creative household. However, the median usage amounts to under 10,000 km per car and year. They highly support the utility of bicycles and public transport, but the terms of use in Germany are still considered unappealing today. Critical Creatives make up about 13% of Germany's total population [3].

Young Idealists on the other hand are willing to fully live and act actively sustainable while supporting and engaging in social and ecological projects, campaigns and lifestyles. Additionally, diversity, tolerance and respect depict important values of young idealists. They are represented by mainly females, their age ranging from 14 to 30 years who enjoy a rather high level of formal education. Furthermore, they believe that environmental and health protection portrays one of the major challenges in German society, which therefore should be prioritized in all political fields of action. In terms of transport, the Young Idealists prefer to ride their bicycles or to take public transportation.

However, over 70% of their households own one or more cars, which is most likely due to the fact that one third of the Young Idealists still live with their parents and/or are able to use their cars. Travelling and getting to know the world is a very important aspect in this group's life, so they tend to fly often. Nonetheless, they are aware of the according ecologic effects and make rather more compensation payments than others. In terms of consumer behavior, Young Idealists try to buy as many environmentally friendly products as far as possible with their current rather low income. However, they still prefer to use modern technology and tend to shop online. Overall, only 5% of the total German population are represented by Young Idealists [3].

On the contrary, more than half of the precarious milieu assumes that economical and health protection is not a basic requirement to ensure future prosperity. This group considers the contribution of citizens concerning this issue to be sufficient, but government engagement is also examined as critical. The Precarious mainly consist of people with low levels of formal education and wages, who are rather pessimistic and see themselves as losers of current social developments. In general, they are less mobile and rarely use public transport, due to the rather high costs. The majority still has at least one car per household, but averagely does not drive more than 10,000 km per year. As well as Critical Creatives, the Precarious milieu consists of 13% of the total population in Germany [3].

2.2   Challenge: Reduction of Air Pollution in Europe

As one of the first countries to adopt environmental practices and policies in the European Union, Germany constantly implements air quality and action plans, such as low emission zones in cities to reduce air pollution and the accompanied fine particle dust emissions [4, 5]. The introduction of these policies led to many Germans having to retrofit specific filters to their cars to reduce Diesel soot in order to still be able to drive in certain city areas with low emission zones [5, 6]. By 2018, over 50 of these low emission zones were in operation, reducing up to about 10% of PM_{10}-fine particles after these mass concentrations exceeded European standards and regulations in the first place [6, 7]. These zones also highly benefit human health, as they reduce the exposure to particulate matter from emission sources, which is a cause of elevated mortality rates through lung-deposited diseases [8, 9].

Besides Germany and its citizens prioritizing environmental and health protection, the European Union is taking major steps in the same direction [10]. Considering these implications and developments about the German and European society regarding their environmental awareness, the topic of retrofitting brake dust filters to reduce particulate matter could become increasingly interesting.

2.3   Quantitative Approach

In order to fully identify the target groups' requirements, their desires, needs and willingness to invest in the retrofit of a brake filter device, a survey was conducted. As the focus lied on the comprehensive quantification of human actions, behavior, and decisions of the target group, the empirical study has a quantitative approach.

Besides, this method can be used to obtain a large sample to be able to make representative statements about possible targets. Standardized, mostly written, but nowadays also electronic surveys are particularly suitable for this purpose. For these reasons, a questionnaire-based online survey was conducted.

The typical research process of an empirical study can be roughly divided into four process phases. These include the theoretical phase, the empirical phase, the evaluation phase and last but not least the practical phase. Initially, the research problem is phrased in order to be able to deduce hypotheses deductively and then evaluate them in the research process. Then the research design is used to determine the procedure for the data collection of the survey, possible variables and measurement operations. Subsequently, the data is collected. The evaluation of the data is carried out using statistical methods. Finally, the findings are interpreted in relation to the theoretical model [11].

The research question and therefore the key findings of this empirical study lie in identifying the unknown target group. To determine the intended audience a two-step methodical approach was used. First of all, expert interviews were conducted with car repair shops to be able to narrow down a potential target group.

A total of five garage owners and employees were interviewed. These interviews revealed that rather younger people show a great interest in the topic of health protection, environment and retrofitting.

Furthermore, the experts estimated that the costs for the installation of four filters including the filter price would approximately lie around 250 €. According to the experts' experience, consumers would also be more willing to retrofit car parts if they were supported by monetary incentives. Subsequently, hypotheses were developed to investigate the central research question. The following six hypotheses were decisive:

- H1: Millennials are more willing to retrofit a brake filter.
- H2: If retrofitting is subsidized by the state, 75% of car owners are in favor of the brake filter.
- H3: If there is no legal filter obligation, potential customers would not retrofit it.
- H4: The potential target group is interested in a visible brake filter with an individually selectable design.
- H5: If the brake filter is mounted by the customer himself, he will buy it online.
- H6: Potential customers are willing to pay more than 200 € for the brake dust filter.

From these hypotheses, questions for the questionnaire could now be derived to determine the opinion of the potential target groups. All in all, the questionnaire consisted of 27 questions that not every respondent received. Depending on which answer was chosen, the survey was continued or ended earlier.

The interview included 17 closed questions with a single selection, one closed question with multiple selections, eight questions that the respondents were able to answer with a 6-point Likert scale and one open question.

The study was conducted online and disseminated through social networks to generate the highest possible reach. The advantages of using social platforms are e.g. the accessibility of different age groups and the use of paid advertisements to reach potential respondents using specific filters.

To select the appropriate social network, a channel analysis was first carried out. As a result, the platform Facebook was selected for the distribution of the survey, as it was possible to reach different age groups, while focusing environmentally-interested car lovers in bigger German cities through ad filters.

To reach as many people as possible, suitable Facebook groups and Internet forums that deal with topics such as sustainability, particulate matter or the automobile were also included. Finally, the survey was shared as a post via the author's private accounts and as a paid advertisement via the Offenburg University page.

Interested parties had time to participate in the survey from December 6th to December 15th 2019. It was conducted anonymously and without a time limit for answering the questions.

In the last step, the survey was evaluated using quantitative analyses. For this purpose, the program SPSS was used for and after preparing and filtering the data set. This enabled the following evaluation to only use data sets that were complete, including the question about retrofitting such a brake filter technology.

In order to gain further insights into the potential target group, univariate analysis methods (frequency distribution) and multivariate analysis methods (cross tables, cluster analysis) were performed.

3   Customer Acceptance Study: Evaluating the Wishes and Needs on Retrofit Services in Germany

In this survey in cooperation with MANN+HUMMEL among German car owners with a return of n = 248 completely filled and relevant questionnaires, the research was focused on the acceptance potential of retrofitting a brake filter device and the identification of the target group as well as the development of a strategy to introduce such devices into the German market.

In the following chapter an overview of the people who would retrofit, would not or are not sure about this yet will be given and the reasons for those decisions will be further described and interpreted. Afterwards, a strategy on how to bring those devices into the German market will be discussed. Finally, some more advice and ideas will conclude this paper.

3.1   Demographic Details

As shown in Table 1, 36.3% out of the 248 people who completed the questionnaire are interested in installing a brake dust filter, while 26.6% do not want to retrofit and 37.1% are not yet sure. However, comparing the proponents to the opponents suggests that there is a basic acceptance for this kind of device. We asked the participants of the survey: Would you have such a break dust filter, regardless of the cost, on your car retrofit?

Table 1. Willingness to retrofit

	Frequency	Percentage	Valid percentage	Cumulated percentage
Yes	90	36.3%	36.3%	36.3%
No	66	26.6%	26.6%	62.9%
I am not sure yet	92	37.1%	37.1%	100.0%
Total	248	100.0%	100.0%	

When describing the demographic and socioeconomic values of the target group more precisely, it is interesting to see, that 46.4% of the responding women are confident about retrofitting. Only 36.7% of men count to the proponents of a brake dust filter. If the opponents are also compared by gender, it is observable that a small part of women is against the filter, since only 5.4% of them say no. The number of male opponents on the other hand amounts to 29.2% and is therefore way higher than that of women. Consequently, women are more likely in the target group than men.

The age of potential customers does not seem to influence their decision to retrofit a brake filter device. When looking at those who would not like to retrofit on the other hand, 64.1% of the 30 to 59 year olds are sure about their decision. The 18 to 29 year olds, as well as the 60 year olds and older, are the ones who are most likely to retrofit a brake dust filter. Only 12.6% of the 18 to 29 year olds would directly say that they are not interested in upgrading their car with devices reducing emissions.

With this result, it is possible to partly approve H1 that states that Millennials are more willing to retrofit a brake filter, as previously described in chapter two. Nevertheless, almost half of the young people (45.3%) are unsure whether they would buy a filter or not.

This age category includes students, trainees, self-employed entrepreneurs and employees. When having a closer look at those who would retrofit this filter in general out of the respondents, the 52.6% of the self-employed and 50% of trainees are the most certain about retrofitting. Those are followed by the pensioners and then the students.

However 48.8% of all participating students and 40% of trainees are quite unsure as well, which comes in hand with the description of the 18 to 29 year olds where exactly this effect occurred. The analysis of the results also shows that 44.9% of people who live in cities and 42.2% of suburb residents are the most confident about retrofitting a brake dust filter. Only of those living in the countryside, more inhabitants are still unsure about the retrofit (41.7%) than confident with it (33.3%).

3.2 Customer Characteristics

In the following, the psychographic characteristics are described. Among other things, the willingness to retrofit depends on the age of the car. The older a car the less willing people are to retrofit such a device. That means that 38.1% of the people with a car older than 20 years would not retrofit whereas only 22.5% of the ones having a car between 0 and 5 years would also not retrofit.

From the other side, cumulated 69.8% of the proponents have a car between 0 and 10 years. Looking at the different types of car drivers, it is obvious that people who say 'economical driving is important to me' are most certain concerning this retrofit device. 56.1% out of this category would say that they are willing to upgrade and only 14.6% directly oppose. Those economical drivers, as well as the ones who just use their car to get from one place to another, are the ones with the best potential, since most of them would retrofit and just a few of them are not interested.

Nonetheless, those who pay more attention to the appearance of their car would not retrofit such a brake dust filter. These are the ones who chose 'I tune my car' (with 50% who would not retrofit) or 'I like driving a nice car' (with 40.5% who would not retrofit). The results also show that owners of premium cars like Audi, Mercedes and BMW tend to not wanting the filter retrofitted, while owners of mid-range cars like Seat, Opel and Ford are more inclined.

When it comes to retrofitting a particulate matter filter, environmental awareness is a key factor. It is clear to see that with 88.9%, the great majority of people who are not environmentally conscious, would not retrofit such a device, whereas the majority of people who would like to retrofit a filter would certainly describe themselves as at least more environmentally conscious (83.7%). Due to the presented survey, it becomes clear that environmental protection is one of the strongest motives for retrofitting a brake dust device. Accordingly, the main target group contains people who care about the environmental protection.

3.3 Customer Motivations

To find out more about our target group further motives were queried from people keen to retrofit a filter. At the same time, reasons against retrofitting were collected from those who are not yet sure about the retrofit, as well as from those who clearly have no interest in retrofitting such a device.

The following results are derive from a basis of 87 persons interested in the retrofit. Different statements on a scale from 1 (no motivation at all) to 6 (very strong motivation) were evaluated. The outcome is summarized in Table 2.

Table 2. Evaluated motives for retrofitting a brake dust filter device

Aspects for retrofitting	Percentage in categories ≥ 4	Mean values (aspects)[a]
Reduced health risk	91.9%	5.2
Environmental protection	87.3%	5.2
State subsidies	58.5%	3.9
Cleanliness of rims	49.4%	3.6
Noticeable design	15.0%	1.9

[a]Among all proponents of the filter

Based on this study two aspects stand out particularly as motives - reduced health risk and environmental protection. 56.3% of interested people state that environmental protection is a very strong reason for retrofitting such a device. If the positive answers of the range (4 to 6) are cumulated, it becomes clear that 87.3% of those who would retrofit a device on their car values this aspect as a big motivation for doing so. Furthermore, 55.2% evaluate the reduced health risk as a very strong motivation for buying this filter. Cumulated with the positive answers of the range, a percentage of 91.9% is received, which shows the importance of this reason overall.

Looking at the mean of these answers, there are the two highest means of 5.2 for environmental protection and 5.2 for reduced health risk. These results show that people would especially buy such a technology for health and environmental reasons, which further explains the high environmental consciousness of the proponents of the filter. As previously described in chapter two, the respondents are concerned about the environment and their health, but they are also prepared to take countermeasures.

Another reason for retrofitting the filter would be the possible state subsidy for emission-reducing devices. A narrow majority of those who would have the filter retrofitted see precisely this as a reason for retrofitting. Even though a high percentage of respondents are more likely to retrofit a brake dust filter with state subventions, hypothesis H2, as seen in chapter two, is rejected as a percentage of 75% is not quite reached.

In the study, respondents assessed if the cleanliness of their rims while using the device would be a reason to retrofit or if it is rather not a motive. This aspect has a mean of 3.6, which shows the indifference of this topic concerning the filter. Half of the people say the cleanliness of their rims would be at least rather a motive for retrofitting a brake dust filter, while also half the people find it rather no reason. This answer also has a scope, where respondents were able to choose from 1 (no motivation at all) and 6 (very strong motivation).

So, there is no clear answer which represents the majority but two answers that lead to the recognition that there is no significant connection between the cleanliness and the purchase. Eventually, another aspect was analyzed. The question was whether the noticeable design is a reason for retrofitting.

More than 84% of the people interested in the purchase evaluate this aspect in the scope between 1 (no motivation at all) to 3 (rather no motive). Out of these 84% even 58.7% say that it is clearly no reason for a purchase. Only 15% find the filter's striking design to be a reason for buying this device with the lowest mean of 1.9.

In order to identify the reasons of the respondents, who are not sure about the purchase yet, or those, who are not interested in it at all, propositions were also made at this point. These were evaluated according to 'motive against buying' or 'not a reason against buying'.

Due to this evaluation it was assessed, which aspects keep people from buying the filter and where Mann+Hummel could invest to convince potential buyers of retrofitting a brake dust filter. The following results base on 60 people who would not retrofit at all and 87 people, who are not sure about it yet.

Those statements were assessed on a scale from 1 (I don't agree at all) to 6 (I fully agree). 1 means that people don't see an aspect as a reason for not buying the device. 6 instead means that one aspect strongly prevents them from retrofitting.

Table 3 shows these evaluated aspects by opponents and doubters with their equivalent cumulated percentages and mean values.

By far the strongest reason against retrofitting this new technology represents the additional cost for installation and maintenance. Almost 70% of those who are not interested in this filter at all and even 75.8% of those who are not sure yet, say that it is at least rather a reason for not buying the brake dust device. This outcome is further supported by the mean value of 4.3 and 4.4 which shows the clear tendency that it is a stronger reason against such a retrofit. This recognition leads to the result that costs

Table 3. Evaluated aspects preventing people from retrofitting a brake dust filter device

Aspects against retrofitting	Percentage in categories ≥ 4		Mean values (aspects)[a]	
	Opponents	Note sure yet		
Noticeable design	31.7%	25.2%	2.4	2.3
Complexity of the retrofit process	35.0%	39.0%	2.7	3.0
No obligation for this filter	36.7%	37.8%	3.0	2.9
No State subsidies	46.6%	51.6%	3.3	3.5
Effort for going to the workshop	51.7%	37.8%	3.5	3.2
Costs for installation and maintenance	69.9%	75.8%	4.3	4.4

[a] Among all opponents and waverers of the filter.

besides the acquisition costs should be held minimal and communicated clearly before purchase.

Moreover Mann+Hummel should display that the installation and the change of the filter is executed with a regular brake change. This goes hand in hand with the next aspect about the effort of a garage visit. People aren't interested in such extra effort, so Mann+Hummel needs to indicate how this is not needed in the first place. Therefore, around 40% of those who are not sure about the filter yet could still be convinced to retrofit after all.

Furthermore, the lack of state laws seems to be a reason to not retrofit the filter for about half the mentioned participants. We find a half and half distribution about aspects concerning the laws. Less than 40% of both groups state that the absence of laws concerning the filter oppose them from buying a filter. Thus, hypothesis H3 from chapter two can be rejected, because as there is no legal obligation, people will not retrofit a brake particle filter. The aspect of lack of subsidies is very equally evaluated, so that there is no clear outcome if people rather see this as a reason against retrofitting a filter. The complexity of the retrofit process does not deter 60–65% of people from buying the filter either.

The least important reason against the purchase is the eye-catching design. It's mean of 2.4 shows that people would not say no to the filter because of the design. Respondents who are not convinced yet have an even lower mean of 2.3 for the aspect design which means that for them it represents an even lower motive against the technology.

3.4 Marketing Mix: Lessons Learned

Following the previous identification of the acceptance potential and the target groups, selected insights of the empirical study are assigned to the four elements of the marketing mix, in order to derive a successful strategy for the market launch of the brake filter device. This serves the purpose of developing a detailed marketing structure, which provides information about the characteristics, which the product must have in order to convince the potential target group to retrofit the brake filter. It also displays the maximum cost of the filter, the distribution channel by which the target group wishes to purchase the product, and how the communication policy must be created to attract potential buyers.

In order to filter out characteristics of the product, the respondents were questioned about their acceptance of an individual painting for the brake filter. More than 38% of the respondents, who said yes to the filter, are very interested in an individual painting for their brake filter. If the percentages of the more interested to extremely interested persons are cumulated, a percentage of over 65% is achieved. As a result, individual painting is an attractive product design for those willing to buy, which they are happy to use. A very similar distribution can be seen for those who are not sure yet if they will retrofit the filter. Here, the cumulative percentage of the more interested to extremely interested respondents is nearly 66%.

Based on the motives for the retrofit, it could already be concluded that the noticeable, eye-catching design of the filter is no reason for retrofitting. Therefore, it can be said that the individual painting is not a decisive characteristic of the filter, but the individual design can make the product more attractive for the target group after the decision for retrofitting. Consequently, the own color choice should be offered as an option for the buyers in any case. As seen in chapter two, hypothesis H4 can partly be verified for this particular study.

Furthermore, the desire for having such a brake particle filter already integrated into the basic equipment of cars was surveyed. With 71.7%, the clear majority would like such an opportunity, while 15.5% are not interested.

Another aim of the survey was to find out if the target group is interested in having the filter professionally retrofitted in a garage or if they prefer to retrofit it by themselves. The best distribution channel for the brake filter can subsequent be chosen from the survey. While looking at the evaluation, it is clear that 67.4% of the supporters of the filter would like it to be professionally installed in a car repair shop. The remaining 32.6%, or almost a third, would like to assemble the filter on their own. A very similar distribution can be seen for those who are still uncertain to retrofit the filter. Here, almost 70% would have the filter retrofitted in the workshop, while about 30% would mount it by themselves.

Among those who are not sure whether they want to retrofit the filter yet, the high number of retrofits in garages can be explained by the fact that almost 40% had previously reported that they have reservations that the retrofitting process is very complex. It is therefore likely that many doubters do not dare to retrofit the filter themselves and prefer to visit a garage. Based on the fact that about two thirds of the supporters and still uncertain respondents would retrofit the filter in the garage, an indirect distribution should be chosen, namely via car repair shops.

However, the retrofitting process is not as complex as expected by potential buyers and could be communicated to the target group very clearly via video material. As a result, some doubters, and consequently potential customers, decide to install the filter themselves, and the main reason against retrofitting – the costs of installation and maintenance – is eliminated.

Among others, the respondents who install the filter themselves were also analyzed with regard to their preferred place of acquisition. It is clearly seen that almost everyone who installs the filter themselves is ordering it online. Among the supporters, almost

27% and among the insecure ones, exactly 25% are online buyers. Thus, hypothesis H5 from chapter two can be verified ceteris paribus. Moreover, almost 5% of the supporters and 3.6% of the insecure ones want to buy the filter in a garage. A negligible quantity < 4% will buy the filter from a car or tire dealership. In order to serve the whole target group, an additional distribution channel, namely online trade, must be opened up for the filter.

With regard to the costs of the filter including installation, it can be said that there is a very low acceptance of high costs. Approximately 59% of the supporters and those who are still uncertain have said that they do not want to spend more than 200 € for the filter including installation. About 30% accept a price between 200 € and 250 €. Only 9% find a compensation between 250 € and 350 € acceptable. The curve of cost-readiness approaches the x-axis exponentially and shows clearly that the higher the price for the filter including installation, the fewer people are willing to buy the filter. Finally, at over 450 € only one person is willing to retrofit the filter.

Overall, the cost acceptance level and willingness to purchase a brake particle filter is rather low and under 200 €, so hypotheses H6 from chapter two is rejected. It can be said that if a successful product launch of retrofit devices should be achieved on the German after-sales market, the price of the product and installation must be kept as low as possible, possibly under 200 €. A solution for this challenge could be to offer governmental support in the form of subventions for retrofit devices that are used for environmental protection, human health and the decline of air pollutions through transport and traffic.

In order to reach the right target group, a fitting communication strategy must be developed. As it is clear from the motives for retrofitting, the focus of communication needs to be on reducing health risks and protecting the environment. If a campaign is created for the filter, everything should revolve around these key points.

3.5 Multivariate Analysis: Specific Customer Segmentation

Our results from univariate and bivariate analysis mentioned so far were confirmed and further substantiated by a multivariate cluster analysis. For the proponents, we used the aspects for retrofitting as cluster variables and obtained three homogeneous and communication relevant clusters, again resulting in the central aspect of reducing health risks, that was rated as 'strong' to 'very strong motivation' in each cluster. In the first and largest cluster (51 elements) 'protecting the environment' was similarly high rated and we additionally found an overrepresentation for 'State subsidies'.

The latter was not the case for cluster 2 (13 elements). 'Cleanliness of rims' and 'Noticeable design' were clearly underrepresented in both clusters. A rather small, but interesting group, that showed overrepresented ratings for 'Cleanliness of rims' and 'Noticeable design', was found in a third cluster (13 elements).

So, we have to focus on reducing health risks and protecting the environment for each cluster, but we should also pay attention to the design aspect, in order to address persons from Cluster 3. This is not conflicting with the attitudes of the other two clusters, because these persons showed not to be disturbed by the brake filter's visibility.

In order to find more hints for an adequate communication towards the clusters, we analyzed the clusters' matching with the types of car drivers, mentioned above.

Describing economical drivers, as well as the ones who just use their car to get from one place to another, or who are simply dependent on their car, as 'pragmatists', we have a high correspondence to clusters 1 and 2.

On the other hand, we find those who pay more attention to the appearance of their car (I tune my car, I like driving a nice car, I keep my car well maintained) clearly overrepresented in cluster 3, describing them as 'car lovers'.

Consequently, communication should focus on pragmatists. Assumed car (owner's) properties as solidity and reliability should be projected on the reduced influence on health and environment. Additionally, an attractive design could be propagated to gain the segment of car lovers – with the option of individual break filter coloring. A wish, that was overrepresented especially in this segment.

Analogously, a cluster analysis was conducted for the filter's opponents – with the aspects against retrofitting as cluster variables. The first cluster is characterized by 'Costs for installation and maintenance' as the central reason for denial, whereby all other reasons are rated not very high (≤ 3.22 in mean values). The second cluster consists of 'fundamental sceptics'. All reasons for denial are rated high (≥ 4.23 in mean values). In cluster 3, we have notorious opponents, as all reasons for denial are rated very low (≤ 1.85 in mean values).

Following a pragmatic approach, communication should focus on cluster 1 and 3. The highest potential influence we should have on cluster 1, where pragmatics are over-represented again. The goal should be to keep costs as low as possible, ideally combined with State subsidies. As the environmental consciousness is high among all respondents in the study, there seems to be a clear potential to convince this group. Car lovers are overrepresented in cluster 3. It seems to be very hard to gain this segment. But even here, we found a tendency towards more environmental consciousness.

This could be a starting point to reduce the denying attitude, potentially supported by design aspects, if we further assume, that this group's low rating of that aspect was induced by the general refusal.

4   Conclusion

Mann+Hummel is able to develop a strategy to increase the acceptance of retrofit purchases in accordance with customer requirements based on the explained survey results from Offenburg University.

The right target group is essential for the company for a successful sale. The empirical study shows which reasons induce the defined target group to retrofit and thus to purchase the filter in Germany. It should be noted, that the intrinsic motivation such as health risk minimization and environmental protection is extended by the extrinsic motivation in form of monetary compensation.

4.1   Recommendations

After all, five recommendations are the most important for the introduction and future development of the brake dust filter:

– Recommendation 1: Keep costs low for the target groups
Since here the ideal of an extrinsic motivation prevails and the filter reaches acceptance, it is recommended that the costs of the product including retrofitting in workshops should not exceed the limit value: According to the research results, the limit is 200 € including workshop services for the end customer. Furthermore, attention should be paid to the General Operating Permit in accordance with the German Road Traffic Licensing Regulations, which is helpful in the event of retrofitting by a garage or customer. It is important to point out that this should not result in any additional costs for the end consumer.
– Recommendation 2: Filter as basic equipment for new cars and competitive advantage for car producers
Starting from the retrofit business field, Mann+Hummel should arrange co-operations with the automotive suppliers in order to deliver future basic equipment devices for rake dust filters in all new cars. Then the filter would be already integrated in the product and would facilitate market entry at the outset.

This way the innovative product would achieve a wide range of popularity and reputation in the beginning of the launch. Also car producers could communicate this new health-promotion device in their cars and use this fact to find higher acceptance by the addressed target groups: the brake dust filter would attract new customers to buy this specific car brand. This recommendation of a basic equipment is based on assessments of potential customers and therefore respondents of the underlying survey.

– Recommendation 3: Legal equipment obligation for fast and powerful market entrance
The chance of a future governmental filter obligation could offer Mann+Hummel a fast market entry and growth of success in the brake dust filter market: a legal equipment obligation would speed up the distribution in the market. The brake dust filter is an easy to install and economic technology, which is combined with the brake change routine and can to filter fine dust particles that emerge while braking until the next service interval for the car brakes comes up.
– Recommendation 4: Economies of scale and garage owners' acceptance
High volume production could not only reduce production costs but would also generate additional public range for this innovative product, as well as an acceptable purchase price for final customers. Garage owners could be invited for trainings on the installation of the product, which is important because they are the direct contact to the customers – the car owners. If the mechanics in the workshop can show the advantages of the brake dust filter, customers will listen to them and accept the higher costs probably more easily. As output increases, the costs of the individual product are lower for the final customer.

This innovative product represents an opportunity for Mann+Hummel in order to generate acceptance of retrofitting by end customers in cooperation with the garage owners and workshop mechanics. It is important that the ministry of health also provides support in the form of monetary funding and communication of benefits. With this intention, the extrinsic motivation is further encouraged.

- Recommendation 5: Segment-oriented communication to address additional target groups

The results from cluster analysis show, that there should be a concentration on Pragmatists with communication focus on health and environment. Additionally, an attractive design should be propagated to gain the segment of Car Lovers – with the option of individual break filter coloring. This is not conflicting with the Pragmatists' attitudes, as the showed not to be disturbed by the brake filter's visibility.

Another insight was surprising but also very interesting, because it is an absolute new target group for retrofitting: we found in our survey a very high acceptance potential by young female car owners. This is not a classic target group for car retrofitting, but these women are highly sensitive for health-promotion and environmental-friendly products.

Addressing this new target group with e.g. an emotional appealing social media campaign in YouTube or Instagram, there is a high potential for selling the innovative brake dust filter system. Even for older cars the retrofit at a reasonable price would be interesting for the female car owners. Also new cars with the brake dust filter system could be used by a car manufacturer brand as a unique selling proposition e.g. a brake dust filter supported BMW Mini as a women-preferred car model.

The results of this underlying study show that retrofitting the filter will be accepted and the motives are clearly based on intrinsic and extrinsic motivation. Important aspects are monetary incentives as well as a legal regulation, which should thus be taken into account when introducing the filter to the after-sales market.

4.2 Limitations and Future Work

The initial hypotheses regarding the potential target group could mostly be fully, or at least partly confirmed by the study carried out. Provided, that a brake dust filter is desired and retrofitted, the results show a strong interest especially by a young and female target group. The previous results of the survey also show how powerful external incentives as governmental subsidies are to potential consumers.

Extrinsic motivation might show very attractive for Mann+Hummel market entry with the brake dust filter system – alongside motives such as minimizing health risks and environmental protection are also very important. [12, 13] For this reason, it is important to tweak and tune all relevant aspects of the levers for external motivation additionally. However, motivating and convincing the target group not only extrinsic will be a great challenge for the company.

For this reason, it is advisable to put the customer benefit of a cleaner environment and the reduction of health risks at the center of the communication strategy, while still proposing potential reasons to buy the filter as well, such as being able to customize the design of the brake dust filter to fit the appearance of the vehicle. Overall, it can be said that an optimal interplay of extrinsic and intrinsic motivation should be focused as a strategy of Mann+Hummel.

From the many comments made in the survey, one factor can be identified that needs to be illustrated in the context of communication. Many respondents are unsure how to dispose of the filter. Some people fear a complicated disposal. For this reason, information about disposal should be provided. A video could also be helpful, which illustrates the disposal process in detail and clarifies all open questions.

Another marketing tool to increase awareness of the filter and establish it in society after introducing it to the German market can be the sponsoring of car sharing companies, such as "car2go". On the one hand, this serves the advertising purpose, but the filter can also increasingly be seen as a health protecting product by inhabitants of German cities on the other hand.

The filter introduction to the after-sales market is a future horizontal product expansion. Which enables a transfer of the technology to other means of transport such as buses, trucks, trains and motorcycles or airplanes and thus a future corporate strategy.

New value streams are created by opening up new markets, winning new customers and reducing production costs. As a young, female and health-sensitive target group has been identified, the initiative can be taken to implement fitting communication instruments such as social media channels.

Finally, the research results show that there is high potential for a brake dust filter in the future especially for the young target group of 'Young Idealists' with environmental and health-promotion reasons. Car manufacturers could also make their contribution to the well-being of people by equipping their own company vehicles with this filter. Therefore, they can act as a role model for all economic players.

References

1. Wolk, A., Nikolic, Z., Aboltin, D.: The Car After Market in Europe, Bergisch Gladbach (2017)
2. Federal Ministry for the Environment, Nature Conservation and Nuclear Safety: Environmental Awareness in Germany 2018 (10033), Berlin (2018). https://www.bmu.de/en/public ation/umweltbewusstsein-in-deutschland-2018/. Accessed 18 Jan 2020
3. Federal Ministry for the Environment, Nature Conservation and Nuclear Safety: Environmental Awareness in Germany 2018, Berlin, pp. 14–15, 25, 64, 73–82 (2018)
4. do Paço, A., Alves, H., Shiel, C., Filho, W.L.: A multi-country level analysis of the environmental attitudes and behaviours among young consumers. J. Environ. Plann. Manag. **56**(10), 1532–1548 (2012)
5. Gollata, J.A., Newig, J.: Policy implementation through multi-level governance: analysing practical implementation of EU air quality directives in Germany. J. Eur. Public Policy **24**(9), 1308–1327 (2017)
6. Cyrys, J., Peters, A., Soentgen, J., Wichmann, H.E.: Low emission zones reduce PM10 mass concentrations and diesel soot in German cities. J. Air Waste Manag. Assoc. **64**(4), 481–487 (2014)
7. Cyrys, J.: Low emission zones in Germany: a reliable measure for keeping current air quality standards? In: Bundesgesundheitsblatt – Gesundheitsforschung – Gesundheits-schutz, Heidelberg, no. 61, pp. 645–655 (2018)
8. Georgy, S.: Assessment of health risks due to heat and fine particles in Germany: an epidemiological study approach. In: Bundesgesundheitsblatt – Gesundheitsforschung – Gesundheitsschutz, Heidelberg, no 62, pp. 782–791 (2019)
9. Hennig, F.: Ultrafine and fine particle number and surface area concentrations and daily cause-specific mortality in the Ruhr area, Germany, 2009–2014, Bethesda (2018)
10. European Commission: Leading the way to a climate-neutral EU by 2050, Brussels (2019). https://ec.europa.eu/environment/efe/news/leading-way-climate-neutral-eu-205 0–2019-08-26_en. Accessed 18 Jan 2020

11. Stein, P.: Forschungsdesigns für die quantitative Sozialforschung. In: Baur, N., Blasius, J. (eds.) Handbuch Methoden der empirischen Sozialforschung, pp. 135–140, Springer, Heidelberg (2014). https://doi.org/10.1007/978-3-658-21308-4_8
12. Grigoratos, T., Martini, G.: Brake wear particle emissions: a review. Environ. Sci. Pollut. Res. **22**(4), 2491–2504 (2015). https://doi.org/10.1007/s11356-014-3696-8
13. Lelieveld, J., et al.: Cardiovascular disease burden from ambient air pollution in Europe reassessed using novel hazard ratio functions. Eur. Heart J. **40**(20), 1590–1596 (2019)

POS Product Presentation Concepts - Analysis of Affective, Conative and Cognitive Components in Decision Making

Vanessa Schwahn[1], Achim Burkhardt[2], Andrea Mueller[2], and Christina Miclau[2(✉)]

[1] Bertrandt AG, Riedwiesenstrasse 13-17, 71229 Leonberg, Germany
[2] Hochschule Offenburg – University of Applied Sciences, Badstrasse 24, 77652 Offenburg, Germany
christina.miclau@hs-offenburg.de

Abstract. This paper is based on a study, which was conducted in the Multi-Channel Management Laboratory of Offenburg University in June 2019 using a convenience sample. The potential participants were recruited via the e-mail distribution list of the University as well as postings on the notice board. A total of 38 people took part in the study. The present study examines the effect of shelf placement of a wine rack with regard to block formation and vertical or horizontal structuring of these blocks. The results show that a wine rack that is arranged by product blocks according to wine type is perceived as significantly more orientation-friendly than a wine rack that is characterized by a manufacturer-oriented block formation. The perceived orientation friendliness influences the customers' emotions experienced during the shopping process. Furthermore, the influence of these emotions on the satisfaction of the orientation friendliness was confirmed. It can be recommended to the stationary retail trade to structure wine shelves by placing products according to wine types within product blocks.

Keywords: Point of sale · Product arrangement · User experience · In-store orientation friendliness · Customer emotion

1 Research Issue

The revenue ratio between stationary and online trade in Germany illustrates the superiority of stationary trade despite the strong growth of online trade in recent years. In 2017, stationary trade had a market share of more than 86% [1]. These figures intensify the relevance of stationary trade and justify further efforts of optimization in this field.

In this article, the consumers' in-store orientation as well as their emotions are of particular interest. The orientation and the associated unproblematic and quick finding of products is of great importance for a retail company. If consumers can't find desired products or the required search time takes too long, there is a risk the customer giving up and leaving the shop without buying [2, 3]. In addition to direct sales losses, the lack of orientation friendliness of shop environments can, under certain circumstances, lead

© Springer Nature Switzerland AG 2020
F. F.-H. Nah and K. Siau (Eds.): HCII 2020, LNCS 12204, pp. 174–187, 2020.
https://doi.org/10.1007/978-3-030-50341-3_14

to negative emotions such as insecurity, stress or anger and ultimately impair consumer satisfaction.

The focus of this paper is on the investigation of different measures of placement policy as well as on the investigation of cause-effect relationships of non-observable variables of consumer behavior with the aim of making recommendations to the stationary retail trade. Accordingly, the primary research question is: "What influence does shelf placement have on consumer behavior?" The results of the conducted laboratory study should provide information about the advantage of certain placement decisions and their influence on consumer behavior and the correlation between the consumer's inner processes during a store visit. The investigation of the emotions is a specificity of this contribution. At the current state, just the influence of perceived orientation friendliness on the emotions of consumers during online shopping has been investigated. However, previous studies on block formation and shelf structuring in the context of shelf placement neglect the emotions of customers during their store visit.

2 Related Work

Block formation is about the formation of product groups and their arrangement within the shelf [4]. There are various ways of grouping and arranging the articles on the shelf. In block formation, a distinction can be made between the variants of product block, manufacturer block, theme-oriented block formation and value-oriented block formation [5].

Product Block: When forming product blocks, articles with the same or similar properties are placed next to each other. A shelf for hair care serves as an example: shampoos, conditioners and hair treatments are placed here in groups [5]. In the case of a product block, the customer has a good overview and the possibility of comparing individual products, e.g. with regard to price, which is the reason for many retailers to implement this arrangement type [6].

Manufacturer/Brand Block: In this case of block formation, articles from one manufacturer are grouped together and placed next to each other [5]. The manufacturer or brand block is usually preferred by the manufacturer for presentation purposes [6]. If different products of a brand or manufacturer are presented together, the probability of a substitution or composite purchase of products of the same brand or manufacturer increases [5]. The advantages of a manufacturer block are the easy integration of new product variants, the unproblematic refilling of articles and optical aspects. It is assumed that this arrangement is best for brand-conscious consumers [2]. A disadvantage is that it is more difficult for consumers to compare different article characteristics [6].

Theme-Oriented Block Formation: Articles are grouped according to "usage context, consumers or experience complexes". This type of article arrangement is most reasonable if a special target group is to be addressed [5]. An example could be the joint placement of articles on a barbecue shelf: various barbecue sauces, charcoal, barbecue lighter, paper plates, napkins, decorative items, etc. are placed together.

Value-Oriented Block Formation: In value-based block formation, items are sorted by price and placed in descending order in a vertical sequence from top to bottom. This type of merchandise arrangement has been used in practice all along, but is always combined with the other types of block formation mentioned above [5].

Besides, the mentioned types can be structured horizontally, vertically or as cross blocks within the shelf. The cross block is a mixture of vertical and horizontal structuring. Here, for example, a shelf is sorted vertically according to manufacturer (manufacturer block) and horizontally according to a specific article characteristic (product block) [5].

3   The Model Used for the Given Study

The partial model developed in the present study is based on the so-called Environmental-Psychological Consumer Behavior Model of Esch and Thelen [7], which is based on the work of Titus and Everett [18] and considers both emotional and cognitive reactions as decisive for consumer behavior. [18] According to this model, the information rate resulting from the environment influences the perception of the environment, which in turn influences the search behavior of consumers. This in turn influences the search success, which determines the search satisfaction of the consumer [7]. The present partial model assumes an influence of shelf placement and the shopping experience of consumers on their perception of the orientation friendliness of shelves in stores. This has an impact on the emotions felt during the visit, which in turn are related to the consumers' satisfaction assessment of the shelf (Fig. 1).

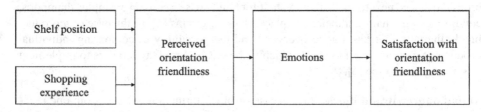

Fig. 1. Partial model of the effect of shelf placement

Both external information from the outside world and internal information are used for orientation. The shop design represents the external information, which is obtained from the environment [8]. With regard to the implementation of shelf placement, this article focuses on the formation of placement groups (block formation) and the determination of the shelf structure, i.e. the vertical or horizontal arrangement of these blocks. In particular, the manufacturer-oriented block formation is compared with the product-oriented variant and the vertical arrangement with the horizontal arrangement of the placement groups. The influence on the perceived orientation friendliness of the shelf is to be investigated.

The following hypotheses were formulated (Table 1):

Table 1. Hypotheses of the given study

H 1a	The orientation-friendliness of a shelf in which the articles are arranged according to the principle of product block formation is perceived significantly better than a shelf in which the articles are arranged according to the principle of manufacturer block formation
H 1b	The orientation friendliness of a vertically arranged shelf is perceived significantly better than the orientation friendliness of a horizontally arranged shelf
H 2	The greater the shopping experience, the better the perceived orientation friendliness of the shelf
H 3	The higher (lower) the orientation friendliness of the shelf is assessed, the more intense positive and less intense negative (intense negative and less intense positive) emotions are experienced during the store visit
H 4	The more intense positive (negative) emotions are felt during the store visit, the higher (lower) is the satisfaction with the orientation friendliness of the shelf

4 Operationalization of the Variables

In the following chapter, the operationalization of the variables is discussed in detail.

4.1 Operationalization of Block Formation and Shelf Structure

The wine rack set up for the experiment contained a total of 42 facings distributed over three shelf elements. The facings were not changed in the course of changing the structure to ensure comparability. In the arrangement, it was ensured that there were a minimum of two and a maximum of eight facings of an article. A minimum of two facings was observed in retail and represents the minimum to ensure that an article is not overlooked on the shelf. A maximum of eight was set, as a shelf width comprises eight facings and thus represents one third of the total width of the shelf. Prices were neglected in the arrangement. The three variants of shelf placement examined in this study are presented below.

Shelf Arrangement 1: Manufacturer's Block Vertical
In this type the wine bottles were sorted vertically by manufacturer (see Fig. 2).

Shelf Unit 1	Shelf Unit 2	Shelf Unit 3
Manufacturer 1	Manufacturer 2	Manufacturer 3
Manufacturer 1	Manufacturer 2	Manufacturer 3
Manufacturer 1	Manufacturer 2	Manufacturer 3

Fig. 2. Scetch of shelf arrangement no.1

It was ensured that within the producer blocks the wine types, i.e. rosé, red and white wines, were placed together, but that across blocks the wine types of the producers were not placed on the same shelves (e.g. all white wines of the respective producers were placed on the upper shelf, all rosé wines on the middle shelf and all red wines on the lower shelf). This would correspond or at least be very similar to the horizontal product block formation by wine type. It also allows the participants to orient themselves horizontally according to product types instead of manufacturers, that should be avoided.

Shelf Arrangement 2: Product Block by Wine Type (Horizontal)
In this case, the blocks were formed horizontally and according to the article characteristics of the type of wine (red, rosé or white). Thus, on the upper level of the shelves there was rosé wine over the entire width of the shelves, red wine on the middle level and white wine on the lower level (see Fig. 3). Care was taken to ensure that the producers were next to each other within the vertical product block. However, for the same reasons as with shelf arrangement 1, the respective manufacturers were not placed vertically one below the other, so that a match with a manufacturer block is ruled out. This means that test persons could not orient themselves by the manufacturers, but only by the horizontal structure of the product blocks.

Shelf Unit 1	Shelf Unit 2	Shelf Unit 3
Rosé wine	Rosé wine	Rosé wine
Red wine	Red wine	Red wine
White wine	White wine	White wine

Fig. 3. Scetch of shelf arrangement no.2

Shelf Arrangement 3: Product Block by Wine Type (Vertical)
In the third case of shelf placement the article characteristics of the wine type (red, rosé or white) were used as a criterion for block formation. Whereas the arrangement was done in a vertical direction (see Fig. 4). The first shelf element thus consisted of red wine across all three shelf levels, the middle one of rosé wine and the third, far right, of white wine. Within the product blocks, an attempt was made to place articles from the same manufacturer next to each other. However, it was also avoided to place articles from the same manufacturer next to each other across the product blocks, so that an orientation of the test persons primarily towards the manufacturers was excluded. The orientation should be on the product blocks according to wine types in vertical direction.

Shelf Unit 1	Shelf Unit 2	Shelf Unit 3
Red wine	Rosé wine	White wine
Red wine	Rosé wine	White wine
Red wine	Rosé wine	White wine

Fig. 4. Scetch of shelf arrangement no.3

4.2   Operationalization of the Shopping Experience

The shopping experience is composed of the customers' knowledge on the placement of goods in certain shopping locations (specific knowledge) and of the knowledge on the placement of goods in certain product groups in general (general knowledge). Therefore, it is determined by how often a consumer visits a particular store and how often certain products of a product group are purchased by (these) consumers, regardless of the location [9, 10]. Since the experiment took place in the Multi-Channel Management Laboratory at the Offenburg University, it is impossible that the test persons had already been able to gain shopping experience in the store. However, it is possible that they already had experience in purchasing wine, i.e. general knowledge in the form of, for example, schemes and associated expectations about product placement. Because of this aspect the participants were asked: "How often do you buy wine?" [10].

It can be assumed that the more often test persons buy a product of a particular category of goods, the greater their shopping experience is [11]. The possible answers range from "once or more than once a week", "once or more than once a month", "several times a year" and "once a year" to "less often [than once a year]".

4.3   Operationalization of the Perceived Orientation Friendliness

To measure the perceived orientation friendliness of the shelf, a multi-item scale by Wang was used (see Table 2, [10]).

Table 2. Operationalization of the perceived orientation friendliness according to Wang [10]

Items of orientation friendliness	Scale for measurement
1. How do you rate the overview in this store?	1 = "Very confusing"to
2. How do you rate the overview on the shelves?	6 = "Very clear"
3. In this store, you can find what you are looking for immediately	1 = "Strongly disagree" to
4. In this store, you have to ask the sales staff to help you find your way around	6 = "Totally agree"
5. The arrangement of the products in this store makes shopping easier	
6. You never feel lost while shopping	
7. Shopping can be done comfortably and quickly	
8. The products are placed within the store in such a way that you can easily find them	

The first item is not used because it is not about assessing the orientation friendliness of the entire store, but only that of the shelf. For the same reason, "shop" is replaced by "shelf" for items 3, 5 and 8. Items 4 and 6 are also not used because they relate on a second and third factor and therefore have no direct influence on the assessment of the ease of orientation. This results in the multi-item scale for the measurement of perceived orientation friendliness, which is to be assessed on the basis of the values 1 ("Do not agree at all") to 5 ("Totally agree").

Since the scale was changed, the internal consistency was recalculated with Cronbach's Alpha. With a value for Cronbach's Alpha of $\alpha = 0.937$, the reliability of the scale can be assumed. The values of the selectivity of the individual items are also in a high range with values between 0.796 and 0.884.

4.4 Operationalization of the Emotions

Mau developed a German-language scale to measure emotions during virtual and non-virtual shop visits [12]. The so-called D-IKE scale contains 37 adjectives that are assigned to a total of 13 emotions. Among them are six positive and seven negative ones. The emotion "surprise" is assigned to the negative ones here, although it can also be perceived as a positive emotion by consumers depending on the context [see 12]. The emotion experienced during the test is to be evaluated using the adjectives on a scale from 1 ("not at all") to 5 ("very intense"). The order of the individual adjectives was shown in the questionnaire in a mixed and random order in order to avoid sequence effects. Figure 5 shows the 37 adjectives of the six positive and seven negative emotions.

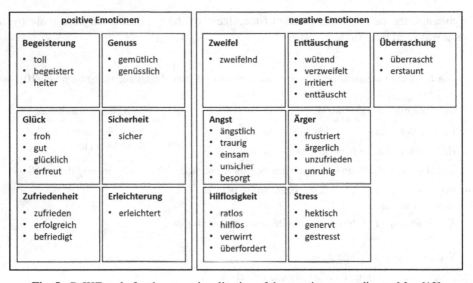

Fig. 5. D-IKE scale for the operationalization of the emotions according to Mau [12]

4.5 Operationalization of the Satisfaction with the Orientation Friendliness

A single-item scale was chosen to measure the respondents' general satisfaction with the orientation friendliness of the shelf to measure satisfaction with single-item scales, see Table 3, e.g. [10].

Table 3. Scale for the operationalization of the satisfaction with the orientation friendliness

	1 strongly disagree	2	3	4	5 totally agree
I am satisfied with the orientation friendliness of the shelf					

5   Qualitative User Experience Study

The experiment was carried out in the Multi-Channel Management Laboratory at the Offenburg University in June 2019. The laboratory simulates a retail store with two rows of shelves facing each other. One of the two shelves consists of five shelf sections, each about one meter wide, and contains "snacks" on four shelf levels. The other shelf consists of six shelf sections, i.e. it is about six metres long in total and has only three shelves. This shelf is a wine shelf, which contains various wine bottles, mostly from the Ortenau region in Germany. The wine rack was used exclusively for the experiment.

The potential test persons were recruited via the e-mail distribution list of the Offenburg University and postings on the notice board at the Gengenbach campus. A total of 38 people took part in the study. Four of them solved the search task incorrectly by putting a different wine in the shopping basket than the one on the shop-ping list. In order to solve the task correctly, they would have had to continue the search and this would probably have led to a different result of their evaluation. Therefore, the sample was adjusted for the number of these participants and their results were excluded from further investigation. Lastly the adjusted sample contains 34 persons. Eleven of the subjects were presented with shelf arrangement 1, eleven others with shelf arrangement 2 and twelve with shelf arrangement 3 (see Sect. 4). There were 18 female and 16 male persons among the participants with the age range of 18 to 60 years, whereas the majority of the test persons (more than 70%) being between 20 and 25 years old. One person is in the age range of 18–25 years, five persons are in the range of 25–30 years and two persons each are 30 and older.

At the beginning of each testing session a quick greeting and the explanation of the task took place. At this time there was no view of the wine rack so that the participant could not have been biased. The test persons received a shopping list with three different wines to search for. They were also asked to speak out their thoughts during the search task (Think Aloud-method). The shopping list contained the names of three wines. For this purpose, a white, a red and a rosé wine of three different producers were selected, so that different blocks had to be searched for both in the product block formation and in the manufacturer block formation. The following wines were specified: "Family Winery Renner; Rosé Kabinett, dry", "Winery Schloss Ortenberg; Rivaner, dry" and "Winery Simon Huber Spätburgunder". The prices were neglected in the shelf arrangement. Thus, it was avoided that the participants could orient themselves by the prices on the shelves. After the search for the three different wines on the shelf was completed, the questionnaire was handed out. It contained demographic information such as gender and age, as well as questions on the perceived ease of orientation, on the emotions felt while shopping and on their satisfaction with the orientation friendliness of the shelf. Subsequently, it was asked whether anything was particularly positive or negative. The results of the Think Aloud-method and the final open question should support the findings of the questionnaire.

6 Findings

The following section describes the results achieved within the study.

6.1 Influence of Shelf Placement on the Perceived Ease of Orientation

To test hypotheses 1a and 1b, two of the shelf arrangements are compared. To test whether the influence of the product-oriented block formation has a favorable effect on the orientation friendliness compared to the manufacturer-oriented block formation, the results of the perceived orientation friendliness of shelf arrangement 3 and shelf arrangement 1 are compared. They differ only in the variant of block formation, but not in their vertical or horizontal arrangement. In order to verify the advantage of a vertical arrangement over a horizontal arrangement with regard to the perceived ease of orientation, the results of shelf arrangement 3 and shelf arrangement 2 are compared. They differ in the direction of arrangement but not in the variant of block formation.

In order to examine the influence of the shelf arrangement (Hypotheses 1a and 1b) on the perceived ease of orientation in pairs, a T-test for independent samples is conducted. An assumption is the normal distribution of the perceived orientation friendliness of the respective sample [13]. According to the Shapiro-Wilk test this is given for all three samples ($p > .05$).

Hypothesis 1a: The average orientation friendliness of the vertically arranged product blocks in shelf arrangement 3 (M = 3,550, SD = 0.919, n = 12) is perceived significantly better than that of the vertically arranged manufacturer blocks (M = 2,436, SD = 1,046, n = 11), $t(21) = -2,718$, $p = .007$. The effect strength is $r = 0.51$ and thus corresponds to a strong effect.

Hypothesis H1a is therefore confirmed.

Hypothesis 1b: Although the average perception of the orientation friendliness of the vertically arranged product blocks (M = 3.550, SD = 0.919, n = 12) is rated better than that of the horizontally arranged product blocks (MD = 3.382, SD = 0.772, n = 11), the result is not significant, $t(21) = -0.473$, $p = .321$.

Hypothesis 1b must be rejected as a result.

Hypothesis 2: The influence of the shopping experience on the perceived orientation friendliness was tested using Spearman's rank correlation. It was found that the shopping experience did not correlate significantly with the perceived orientation friendliness (rs = -0.102, $p > .05$, n = 34). This means that the shopping experience has no influence on how the orientation friendliness of the shelf is perceived.

Hypothesis 2 is rejected accordingly.

6.2 Influence of the Shopping Experience on the Perceived Ease of Orientation

When asked about their shopping experience, almost 10% of the participants state that they have a great shopping experience with wine by buying wine once or several times a week. Half of the test persons, and thus the majority, state that they have a great shopping experience with one or more wine purchases per month. Nearly 30% of the participants say that they buy wine several times a year, while about 6% of the them buy wine only once a year or even less frequently and therefore have little shopping experience.

6.3 Influence of the Perceived Orientation Friendliness on the Emotions

According to hypothesis 3, an influence of the perceived orientation friendliness on the two emotional dimensions is expected: The higher or lower the perceived orientation friendliness of the shelf structure, the more intense positive and less intense negative or more intense negative and less intense positive emotions are experienced during the store visit. To test the influence of orientation friendliness on the two dimensions of emotions, a simple linear regression analysis was carried out. The condition of normal distribution is given for the variables of the emotion dimensions according to the Shapiro-Wilk test ($p > .05$).

Hypothesis 3: The results of the regression analyses show that the general regression model becomes significant in each case. The perceived orientation friendliness has an influence, as assumed, on both positive emotions ($R^2 = 0.483$) and negative emotions ($R^2 = 0.555$). This means that 46.7% of the positive and even 54.1% of the negative emotions can be explained by the perceived orientation friendliness. The negative emotions can therefore tend to explain the perceived orientation friendliness to an even greater extent than the positive emotions.

The results support hypothesis 3, since an effect of perceived orientation friendliness on both dimensions of the emotions in the expected direction is proven.

6.4 Influence of Emotions on the Satisfaction with Orientation Friendliness

According to hypothesis 4, a connection is assumed between the emotions experienced, i.e. their two dimensions, and the consumers' satisfaction judgement regarding the orientation friendliness of the shelf. This connection is checked by means of a multiple regression analysis. The two dimensions of emotion (positive and negative emotions) are the predicators.

Hypothesis 4: When running the multiple regression analysis, the general regression model of the emotion dimensions ($R^2 = 0.499$, $F(2,31) = 17.425$, $p < .001$) be-came significant. The coefficient of determination shows that the emotions experienced by the test person during the store visit have a significant influence on his/her satisfaction with the orientation friendliness of the shelf. 50% of the variance can be explained by the two dimensions of emotions. Regarding the dimensions of the emotions, both a significant positive correlation between the experienced positive emotions and the satisfaction rating ($ß = .329$, $p < .05$) and a significant negative correlation between the experienced negative emotions and satisfaction ($ß = -0.486$, $p < .01$) can be found.

Hypothesis 4 can be accepted accordingly.

Figure 6 illustrates that the average satisfaction with the vertical arrangement of product blocks by wine type in shelf arrangement 3 is highest (M = 3,667), followed by the horizontal arrangement of product blocks by wine type in shelf arrangement 2 (M = 3,273). On average, participants are least satisfied with the vertical arrangement of manufacturer blocks in shelf arrangement 1 (M = 2,818).

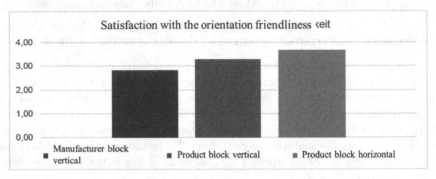

Fig. 6. Mean of satisfaction with the orientation friendliness of the three shelf arrangements

7   Final Evaluation and Recommendation

According to **Hypothesis 1a**, the orientation friendliness of product-oriented block formation by wine type is determined to be significantly better than that of manufacturer oriented block formation. Right at the beginning of the testing, most of the test persons who were faced with shelf arrangement 3 identify the middle vertical shelf block as a rosé wine block. In this block the wine bottle was stated which is listed first on the shopping list: "I need a rosé and it is in the middle here." This way, the majority of the test persons recognize the structuring criteria by wine type and in the second step search for the producer "Familienweingut Renner" quickly. Some test persons even try to search for the wine type first when searching in shelf arrangement 1. This shows that the wine type is the primary grouping criterion for these consumers. "I first look for the colors. This isn't working, so I'll just read the names."

The quick recognition of the shelf arrangement by product block formation according to wine type can be explained by the law of similarity. Elements that are perceived as similar are grouped together. The criterion of similarity of elements is often the color [14]. Since the different types of wine differ in color, it is easy to identify the three blocks as a group based on their color. The manufacturer blocks, on the other hand, do not have conspicuous color differentiating features. It can be assumed that the name of the producer or the logo is not as striking as the color characteristic and can therefore be identified less quickly and used as a grouping criterion in perception. The result confirms the results of a study by Mollà, Múgica and Yagüe [15], who also identify the wine type as the most important grouping criterion, hence recommend the formation of product blocks by wine type when placing the wine on the shelf [15]. A further reason for the significantly worse orientation friendliness by brand blocks in the present study could be the brand strength, which is generally not particularly pronounced for wine brands. This circumstance may explain the quite different results on the advantageousness of block forms ac-cording to product or manufacturer blocks. In order to clarify this question, empirical studies on the influence of brand strength on the effectiveness of the block formation are useful.

Hypothesis 1b: The difference between the perceived orientation friendliness of shelf arrangement 2 and shelf arrangement 3 turns out to be not significant. This means that there is no difference in the perceived ease of orientation between a vertical and a horizontal arrangement of the products on the shelf. However, in all the studies described above, the advantage of vertical structures has always been shown due to the vertical search structures of customers [9].

The superiority of the vertical structuring of the shelf, which contrary to expectations is not significant, can be explained by the Law of Proximity [14]. Since there are only three levels of shelving in a shelf, they are unusually far apart from each other. The individual shelf levels are each perceived as a group that belongs together. If the arrangement of products also corresponds to this perceived structure, as is the case with a horizontal structure, perception could be particularly easy. Besides the perception of a vertical structuring of the product blocks could be complicated by widely spaced shelf levels.

Hypothesis 2, which assumes a positive correlation between the shopping experience and the perceived orientation friendliness, was rejected. Certain patterns in memory, which were formed by the experience of previous visits to stores, were assumed to make it easier to find one's way around. Esch and Thelen [7] provide a possible reason that could counteract the direction of the relationship. According to these findings, the more experience a person has with other shops, the higher the consumer's demands on the shop's atmosphere and the orientation friendliness of a shop's environment are. Above all, if the shop design and its atmospheric effect differs greatly from the previously experienced store environment, this is judged particularly critically [7]. Since the atmospheric effect in the laboratory differs greatly from real shop environments, it can therefore be assumed that the orientation friendliness, especially of consumers with a certain amount of shopping experience, is judged very critically and the assumed positive effect on the perceived orientation friendliness is thus cancelled.

Hypothesis 3: A significant influence of the perceived orientation friendliness of the shelf on the dimensions of emotions could be demonstrated. It can be explained by considering the appraisal theories that the perception of orientation friendliness as the result of a cognitive process has an influence on the experience of positive or negative emotions [16]. The orientation friendliness of the shelf obviously plays an essential role in the evaluation of the situation by customers. For example, it can be either a support in achieving the objective or an obstruction in the pursuit of objectives, i.e. finding products. The perceived orientation friendliness explains even more negative emotions than the positive emotions. This is an indication that especially the lack of orientation friendliness in the context of the inner evaluation process is classified as a relevant variable during the search of products and is perceived as an obstacle to the achievement of an objective.

186   V. Schwahn et al.

The results support Bost's statement. Lack of orientation can be described "as a feeling of lack of safety and environmental control. This feeling of insecurity leads [...] to negative mood changes (stress and anger reactions)" [17].

Hypothesis 4: The results of the study confirm that the satisfaction with the orientation friendliness of the shelf depends on the emotions that the test persons feel during the search task. Satisfaction with the orientation friendliness can be explained by the dimensions of the emotions. Positive emotions have a significant positive influence, just as negative emotions have a significant negative influence on the satisfaction rating. However, it can be seen that the influence of negative emotions on the satisfaction rating is stronger and has a higher significance value than the influence of positive emotions. This can be understood as an indication that positive emotions are partly a basic requirement when consumers form their satisfaction judgement according to the Kano model [19]. Accordingly, negative emotions have a disproportionate influence on satisfaction compared to positive emotions.

8   Limitations and Future Work

In summary, it can be stated that product-oriented block formation according to the criterion of the wine type leads to a significantly better perception of the orientation friendliness of a wine rack than manufacturer oriented block formation. No significant results could be obtained regarding the advantage of vertical or horizontal block structuring. It can be assumed that this is due, among other things, to the large distance between the three shelf levels, which could lead to a more difficult perception of vertical structures.

Furthermore, a positive influence of the shopping experience on the perceived orientation friendliness of the shelf could not be confirmed. The results of the study support the assumed connection between the perceived orientation friendliness of the shelf and the emotions experienced. The satisfaction rating can also be explained to a large extent by the two dimensions of the emotions.

Based on these results, when placing and arranging wine bottles on the shelf with a relatively small range of wines, it can be recommended to the stationary retailer to arrange the wine bottles in product blocks, sorted by wine type. By confirming the influence of the perceived orientation friendliness on the emotions experienced during the store visit and its influence on the satisfaction rating of the orientation friendliness, the following conclusions can be drawn: A product-oriented block formation has a positive effect not only on the perception of orientation friendliness, but also on the emotions and the consumers' satisfaction judgement.

References

1. N.N. E-Commerce in Deutschland, Statista Dossie, p. 13 (2019). https://de.statista.com/statistik/studie/id/6387/dokument/e-commerce-statista-dossier/
2. Wittmann, N., Lischke, F.G.: Marken-Blöcke steigern den Umsatz. Studie zur Bedeutung des Regalaufbaus fruchthaltiger Getränke. Lebensmittel Zeitung **50**(16), 62 (1998)

3. Kroeber-Riel, W.; Weinberg, P.; Gröppel-Klein, A.: Konsumentenverhalten, 9. Auflage. Muenchen, p. 463 (2008)
4. Zielke, S.: Kundenorientierte Warenplatzierung. Modelle und Methoden für das Category Management, p. 12. Zugl.: Koeln, Univ., Diss., 2001, Stuttgart (2002)
5. Haller, S.: Handelsmarketing, 4. Auflage, Herne, p. 179f (2018)
6. Geister, S.: Kreuzblock versus Produktblock. Dynamik im Handel (11), 50–55 (1996)
7. Esch, F.-R., Thelen, E.: Zum Suchverhalten von Kunden in Läden - theoretische Grundlagen und empirische Ergebnisse. Journal fuer Marketing 36(3–4), 112–125 (1997)
8. Esch, F.-R., Billen, P.: Förderung der Mental Convenience beim Einkauf durch Cognitive Maps und kundenorientierte Produktgruppierungen. In: Trommsdorff, V. (ed.) Handelsforschung 1996/97. VerlagPositionierung des Handels, pp. 317–337. Gabler, Wiesbaden (1996). https://doi.org/10.1007/978-3-663-05654-6_17
9. Berghaus, N.: Eye-Tracking im stationären Einzelhandel. Eine empirische Analyse der Wahrnehmung von Kunden am Point of Purchase, pp. 65–251. Zugl.: Duisburg, Essen, Univ., Diss., 2005, Lohmar (2005)
10. Wang, H.-H.: Orientierung in bekannten und unbekannten Ladenumwelten. Theorie, Befunde und Implikationen, pp. 52–129. Springer Gabler, Wiesbaden (2013)
11. Russo, J.E., Leclerc, F.: An eye-fixation analysis of choice processes for consumer nondurables. J. Consum. Res. 21(2), 274–290 (1994)
12. Mau, G.: Die Bedeutung der Emotionen beim Besuch von Online-Shops. Messung, Determinanten und Wirkungen. Zugl.: Göttingen, Univ., Diss., (2009) Wiesbaden, pp. 89–118 (2009)
13. Raab, G.; Unger, A.; Unger, F.: Marktpsychologie. Wiesbaden: Springer Fachmedien Raab et al. 2016, p. 2019 (2016)
14. Behrens, G.: Das Wahrnehmungsverhalten der Konsumenten, Thun, Frankfurt a.M.; pp. 252 f (1982)
15. Mollà, A., Múgica, J.M., Yagüe, M.J.: Category management and consumer choice. Int. Rev. Retail Distrib. Consum. Res. 8(2), 225–241 (1998)
16. Brosch, T., Scherer, K.R.: Plädoyer für das Komponenten-Prozess-Modell als theoretische Grundlage der experimentellen Emotionsforschung, p. 200 (2008)
17. Bost, E.: Ladenatmosphäre und Konsumentenverhalten. Springer, Heidelberg (1987). https://doi.org/10.1007/978-3-642-51471-5
18. Titus, P.A., Everett, P.B.: The consumer retail search process: a conceptual model and research agenda. J. Acad. Mark. Sci. 23(2), 106–119 (1995)
19. Kano, N., et al.: Attractive quality and must-be quality. J. Jpn. Soc. Qual. Control (Jpn.) 14(2), 39–48 (1984)

A Review on Quality of Service and SERVQUAL Model

Zhengyu Shi and Huifang Shang[(✉)]

School of Art Design and Media, East China University of Science and Technology,
Shanghai 200237, China
945308090@qq.com, hfshang@ecust.edu.cn

Abstract. In field of service design, the research and application of service quality plays an important role in the development and competition of enterprises
by establishing brand image and generating market effect. Therefore, experts in
management and marketing have studied it and found that the quality of service
in the industry has a great impact on consumer satisfaction, consumer experience and brand loyalty. Based on the research and development of the concept
of service quality, PZB, a famous American marketing expert team, established
SERVQUAL (SQ) model through the test of retail cases, and constantly revised
and improved it, which was applied to multiple service industries. Through literature review, this paper analyzes the application of SERVQUAL model in China
and abroad, mainly involving retail industry, medical service industry, e-commerce
industry, tourism service industry and other service fields. The study found that
SERVQUAL model plays a guiding role in evaluating the management of emerging enterprises, consumers' preference for services, and resource allocation of
service industries in developing countries. In addition, this paper compares the
application of SERVQUAL (SQ) model and its derivative SERVPERF (SP) model
in the service field, and finds that SP model is mainly a result-oriented quality of
service study, while SERVQUAL model is mainly a result-oriented quality of service study based on process dynamic change. In the multi-field studies, it is found
that SERVQUAL model, as a common basic model, combines the Fuzzy theory,
Functional quality deployment and Kano model to comprehensively evaluate the
service quality in the application field and provide decision support for enterprise
development. Finally, this article discusses and summarizes the study of service
quality, revises and improves the research model, and looks forward and proposes
future service quality studies to provide more market and social value to service
industry.

Keywords: Service quality · SERVQUAL model · Quality evaluation

1 Introduction

In the early 1970s, as the economic recovery in western countries gradually emerged,
the service industry also developed and inspired many research teams to explore. In the
development process, researchers in economics mainly focused on the nature of services,

© Springer Nature Switzerland AG 2020
F. F.-H. Nah and K. Siau (Eds.): HCII 2020, LNCS 12204, pp. 188–204, 2020.
https://doi.org/10.1007/978-3-030-50341-3_15

while those in management paid more attention to the application of theories, during which the concept of quality was introduced into field of services.

Professor Gronroos (1982) first proposed the concept of Customer Perceived Service Quality [1]. Gronroos held that quality of service was a subjective category, which depends on the comparison between consumers' expectation of quality of service and the actual perceived level of service. Subsequently, more scholars carried out researches on service quality. Lehtinen (1982) et al. identified service quality as three components: interaction quality, entity quality and company quality [2]. Lewis and Booms (1983) believed that service quality was a tool which measured whether enterprise service level meet consumers' expectations [3]. Gronroos (1984) divided quality of service into two parts, then defined them as technical quality and functional quality [1]. Parasuraman (1988) holds that quality of service is the difference between the level of quality of service actually perceived by consumers and the level of quality of service expected [4]. Leblanc and Nguyen (1988) listed service quality as five components, namely corporate image, internal organization, physical support of service production system, employee/customer interaction and customer satisfaction [5]. Hedval and Paltschik (1989) defined the quality of service as two dimensions, namely the willingness and ability to serve, the physical and psychological accessibility [6].

International Standardization Organization (ISO) defined service quality and formed the concept of service quality [7]: In the process that price competition in the market gradually changes to service quality competition, service quality becomes more and more important in the consumption process and becomes the first production factor of service enterprises. Service quality should meet the needs of consumers and the interests of other beneficiaries, so service providers need to consider more from the perspective of consumers and other beneficiaries. Service enterprises need to improve service quality and generate more added value through scientific management, development and utilization of new technologies.

Based on literature review and research, this paper concludes that service quality is generated by the actual contact between service providers and consumers, expressing consumers' subjective feelings on the process of service experience. Service providers improve the quality of services through internal management and support systems.

This paper takes SERVQUAL model as the entry point to research service quality. It finds that the impact of service quality on consumers is mainly reflected in psychology, behavior, satisfaction, loyalty and other aspects, while the impact on service providers is mainly reflected in service equipment, technical support, employee behavior, corporate culture, product functional quality and after-sales service. According to the development of service industry in China and abroad, service enterprises are facing the problems and opportunities of service quality management. In this paper, through the modification of the service quality model by domestic and foreign scholars, combined with the theoretical method of engineering system, the structure of the service quality model is optimized, and the research and development of service quality are discussed and prospected.

2 SERVQUAL Model

2.1 Introduction to SERVQUAL Model

SERVQUAL (SQ) is the abbreviation of "Service Quality". The model is an evaluation system that reflect consumers' perceptions and expectations of the received services, and is applied to the measurement and marketing management of service quality. SERVQUAL model theory was formally proposed by Parasuraman, Zeithaml and Berry (PZB), three American marketing experts, in 1988, to measure consumers' service perception. Its core theory is "service quality gap model". Specifically, it's the gap that between consumers' actual perception of service quality and their expectation of service quality. SERVQUAL model is mainly composed of five dimensions and 22 items, namely, tangibility, reliability, responsiveness, assurance and empathy.

2.2 Development of SERVQUAL Model

SERVQUAL model theory was founded by Parasuraman, Zeithaml and Berry (PZB) in 1985, mainly used in the field of marketing. PZB research team established 10 measurement dimensions of service quality gap model to study consumers' evaluation on the quality of services provided by service providers [8]. The 10 dimensions are reliability, sensitivity, convenience, competence, politeness, communication, trustworthiness, security, danger and empathy.

PZB (1988) three researchers conducted a comprehensive qualitative study on the meaning of service quality, and determined that service quality is the gap between consumers' perception of service and service expectation [4] (as shown in Fig. 1), namely SQ (Service Quality) = P (Perception of Service) − e (Expectation of Service).

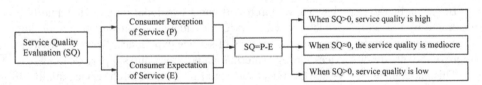

Fig. 1. Service quality assessment process

For further research and development of SERVQUAL model, PZB research team has found through many experiments that in the marketing service industry, the improvement of consumers' service perception mainly includes the following five aspects:

- Tangible: The physical structure of the equipment provided by the service, the associated service facilities and the appearance of the service personnel.
- Reliability: Service providers provide consumers with the reliability and consistency of quality services and the ability to accurately fulfill service commitments.
- Responsiveness: Service providers can provide services and responses to consumers in a timely manner.

- Assurance: Service providers build rapport with consumers and consumer trust in the services provided.
- Empathy: The extent to which service providers provide emotional care and extended emotional support to consumers.

Since consumers' expectation of service quality will change over time, SERVQUAL model is used to track the dynamic change of service quality on a regular basis to reflect the trend of service value. PZB (1991) obtained that the five dimensions of SERVQUAL had a certain correlation through factor analysis, further optimized the SQ model, and then put the model into five independent customer samples for testing [9, 10]. The results show that SERVQUAL model is universal. Therefore, PZB established SQ as the core and standard of service quality measurement.

In the following researches, scholars repeated used SERVQUAL model and verified the applicability. Carman (1990) conducted scale tests in four scenarios: dental school patient clinic, business school placement center, tire shop and emergency hospital, and found that reliability, tangible and safety accounted for a high proportion of consumers' service perception [11]. Cronin and Taylor (1994) conducted a survey on people using hospital services within 45 days, and used SERVQUAL scale to determine the relationship between customer satisfaction and service quality [12]. Finally, five dimensions and 22 variables were confirmed.

2.3 Use of SERVQUAL Model

SERVQUAL model typically contains five dimensions and 22 items. The distribution of the 22 project problems is as follows: Tangibility contains 4 project problems, Reliability contains 5 project problems, Assurance contains 4 project problems, Responsiveness contains 4 project problems, and Empathy contains 5 project problems. Each item contains an item question and item options on a Likert scale of order 7 or 5.

After the SERVQUAL test model passed the reliability and validity tests, questionnaires were distributed to the subjects. After the end of the test, the questionnaire was collected to study the collected effective data and carried out statistical calculation. The formula is as follows:

$$SQ = \sum_{k=1}^{n} W_k \sum_{i=1}^{m} (\overline{P_i} - \overline{E_i}) \tag{1}$$

In the formula above, k represents the kth service element, n represents a total of n service elements, W_k represents the weight of the kth service element, i represents the ith problem, m represents a total of m problems, $\overline{P_i}$ represents the average sensory index value of the ith problem, $\overline{E_i}$ represents the expected mean value of the ith problem, and SQ represents the final evaluation of service quality.

3 Application of SERVQUAL Model

3.1 Application Status

With development of the service industry, consumers pay more and more attention to service quality. Therefore, more and more scholars study service quality through the application of SERVQUAL model in service industry.

Through the research in ISI Web of Science (WOS) database, Taiwanese scholars Ya Lan WANG, Tainyi LUOR, Pin LUARN and Hsi Penglu (2015) discussed and analyzed 367 SCI and SSCI journal articles of SERVQUAL model in the past 15 years (1998–2013). The results showed that the research on application of SERVQUAL model was on the rise, and under influence of economic growth and government policies, applications in business management and corporate decision-making accounted for the largest proportion, followed by information systems and data management, then leisure and entertainment services, and finally health care services [13].

3.2 International Application of SERVQUAL Model

While applying SERVQUAL model, international researchers modified SERVQUAL model with the change of application field, and sorted out, extended and expanded the research results. The application of the model gradually expanded from business management to banking, library information management, medical care and other fields.

By using SERVQUAL model, the research team explored the development status of the industry, understood consumers' preferences and behavioral intentions, and predicted future development trends. Baker and Crompton (2000) established hypotheses through a structural equation model and analyzed experimental data, and concluded that the perceived performance quality of the tourism industry had a greater impact on consumers' behavioral intention than satisfaction [14]. Dabholkar, Shepherd and Thorpe (2000) used SERVQUAL model to conduct a longitudinal study of service design, and to understand and predict the dynamic change of service quality in the retail industry by establishing a chronological framework [15]. In the e-commerce industry, Devaraj, Ming and Kohli (2002) studied consumer satisfaction and preference in B2C e-commerce channels by establishing technology acceptance model, transaction cost analysis model and service quality model [16].

In addition, research team used SERVQUAL model to test consumers' perception of service quality, and the results provided guidance for service providers in terms of service quality and service decision-making. Neha (2013) conducted a service evaluation test on consumers with the help of SERVQUAL model, and verified whether retail stores could improve service quality according to the gap between consumers' expectations and perceptions [17]. Mobarakeh and Ghahnavieh (2015) used SERVQUAL model to study the customer service quality of a travel agency and proposed relevant service strategies to narrow the gap between service expectation and perception [18]. Palese and Usai (2018) used SERVQUAL model to collect social data to measure the service quality of community shopkeepers and help them to provide service strategies [19].

Research teams tested SERVQUAL model's universality in service quality testing by using it in different industry domains. Arpita, Ceeba and Reena (2010) used SERVQUAL model to study the applicability of service quality evaluation of retail stores in northern India [20]. Vassiliadis, Fotiadis and Tavlaridou (2014) used SERVQUAL model to classify medical services provided by a public hospital in Greece, proving the universality and effectiveness of SERVQUAL model in measuring the quality of medical services [21]. Three scholars, Bansal, Gaur and Chauhan (2016), based on SERVQUAL model, researched the tourism items provided by e-commerce services and verified the universality of SERVQUAL model in evaluating the service quality of e-commerce providers [22].

In terms of resource allocation, research teams used SERVQUAL model to evaluate the service quality in the industry field, so as to reasonably and effectively invested and used resources for small and medium businesses and developing countries. Chakravarty (2011) conducted a service study on outpatient hospitals in India. Considering that the service operation of hospitals is limited by resources, SERVQUAL model was adopted to measure the service perception of consumers and provide targeted decisions for hospital service management [23]. Meesala and Paul (2016) used SERVQUAL model to evaluate the service quality of patients in 40 different private hospitals in Hyderabad, India, to provide service management strategies and guidelines for the better survival and development of their medical service enterprises [24].

3.3 Application of SERVQUAL Model in China

In this paper, the application of SERVQUAL model in China is summarized through the retrieval of Cnki database. 1651 articles collected in the past 20 years (1998–2019) were retrieved in the database, as shown in Fig. 2:

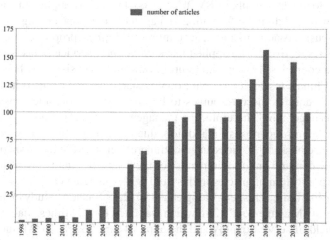

Fig. 2. SERVQUAL model application paper publishing data graph

According to the data graph, the application of SERVQUAL model increases gradually and tends to be flat. Its research fields are mainly business economy, business administration, quantitative economy and library information management. By searching the database of Cnki, this paper divides the applied articles into industry fields. The specific data are shown in Fig. 3:

Research Field		Number of Articles	%
01.	Commercial economy	264	17
02.	Industrial and commercial management	252	16
03.	Quantitative Economics	163	10
04.	Library information files	117	7
05.	Education	94	6
06.	Logistics economy	87	6
07.	Tourism economy	86	6
08.	financial	85	5
09.	Public health and preventive medicine	73	5
10.	Industrial economy	71	5
11.	Transportation economy	70	4
12.	Communication economy	60	4
13.	Public management	52	3
14.	Nursing	50	3
15.	Social	42	3

Fig. 3. SERVQUAL model applies the paper category data graph

According to the data graph, SERVQUAL model is mainly applied in business economy management and digital information management in China, among which business economy and business administration account for the highest proportion, accounting for 17% and 16% respectively. The applied research in other service fields is not as extensive as in other countries. Through literature review and analysis, study believes that the reason is that China's research on service quality starts late and China is in a developing country, which requires more resources to be invested in economic construction and information management. Therefore, the management of service quality in those area take relatively large proportions. In addition, due to the rise of the knowledge age and the Internet age, education services and e-commerce services are increasingly valued by people, and the demand and requirements for their service quality are also higher and higher, so the proportion of articles in this field is also increasing.

In Chinese literature, Zhisheng Hong et al. (2012) published "Study on the Research of Service Quality Management" [25], which was cited for 224 times, mainly introduced the research field of service quality and the application of SERVQUAL model, as well as the prospect of future dynamic changes of service quality and service management in the market.

Through the cited data in this paper, the study indicates that SERVQUAL model applies to different service fields in China. Li Cui (2010) et al. used SERVQUAL model to conduct data investigation and analysis on Chinese commercial Banks, discussed service quality issues, and put forward suggestions for improvement [26]. Meihong Zhu (2011) et al. adopted the modified SERVQUAL model to study the service quality of Chinese express delivery enterprises, and improved competitiveness of enterprises by improving service quality and strengthening service management [27]. Based on the background of sharing economy, Wenming Zuo (2018) et al. adopted the modified SERVQUAL model to study the service quality of online ride-hailing, and finally proposed management suggestions [28].

According to the literature data, SERVQUAL model also has been applied in other fields, and it has a large space for application. This model can provide service improvement directions for service providers with limited resources and help enterprises make management decisions and improve service quality.

4 SERVPERF Model

4.1 Introduction of SERVPERF Model

With the increasing number of researches on the SERVQUAL model, SERVQUAL model is modified and optimized constantly, but the model still has some shortcomings: For example, measuring consumers' expectation and perception of quality of service over the same time period lacks comparability, using the gap model to measure service perception results in the double calculation of quality of service expectations, SERVQUAL model needs to measure the perceived value and expected value of consumers, and the operation process is complicated.

Based on the shortcomings of SERVQUAL model, professor Cronin and Taylor (1992) further proposed SERVPERF (SP) model based on SERVQUAL model by testing and studying the four service industries including bank service, Agricultural pest control, dry cleaning service and fast food service [29]. In their study, the two professors showed that SERVPERF model was superior to SERVQUAL model in reliability and validity, and believed that the theoretical basis of SERVQUAL model was confused with the concept of customer service satisfaction, so service expectation in SERVQUAL model should be abandoned and service perception should be directly used to measure service quality.

Subsequently, many scholars also studied the service quality model and came to the conclusion that service expectation is weakened and service perception of consumers is used to represent service quality. Boulding (1993) et al. developed a behavior model of perceived quality of service through the Yebess framework, and found that different expectations had a negative effect on quality of service through the results of two tests, and service perception had a positive effect on its quality [30]. Hartline and Ferrell (1996) developed and tested the service employee management model, and the results showed that consumers' perception of employee service was a direct factor affecting service quality [31]. The above scholars have shown that service perception can measure the support of service quality through researches.

SERVPERF model mainly measures quality of service through service performance, while SERVQUAL model mainly measures quality of service by the gap between consumers' perception of service and their expectation of service. On basis of projects, SERVPERF model still maintains the five dimensions of SERVQUAL model and the system of 22 projects, but directly uses perception of consumers receiving services in practice as evaluation criteria.

4.2 Application of SERVPERF Model

Validated by many research, SERVPERF model has been proved to be practical and reliable in the service field. Compared with SERVQUAL model, SERVPERF model does not need to measure service expectations and is more convenient to use. Marshall and Smith (2000) discussed the application of SERVPERF model in community public services, and measured the experience and evaluation of community consumers on purchasing services through the scale coefficient of SERVPERF model [32]. Hossain and Islam (2013) studied the service performance of four private university libraries in Bangladesh through SERVPERF model [33]. Tan Le and Fitzgerald (2014) studied the service quality of two public hospitals in Vietnam through SERVPERF model, and concluded that assurance and empathy were the key factors for the service quality of hospitals [34]. Mahmoud (2015) used SERVPERF model to discuss the quality of service in Syrian universities [35].

The above studies show that SERVPERF model is widely used in many fields, has high validity and reliability, and can quickly and effectively analyze the factors of service quality.

4.3 Conclusion of Model Application

As for the evaluation of SERVQUAL model, PZB (1994) pointed out that SERVQUAL model measures consumers' perceptions and expectations [36], and contains more information about service quality in the measurement process, which is more abundant than the SERVPERF model in terms of content and predicts the service trend. In addition, with the change of time, enterprise managers can understand the reasons for the change of consumers' preference for services through the experimental data of SERVQUAL.

According to the corresponding research purposes, SERVPERF model can be selected for the current purposeful service quality test (results-oriented). SERVQUAL model can be used to study the dynamic change of quality of service (process-oriented).

5   Comprehensive Evaluation of Service Quality

5.1   Service Quality Evaluation Based on Fuzzy Theory

Fuzzy theory was first put forward in 1965 [37], which is used to satisfy people's thinking process, provide relatively stable description, and define multiple, complex and ambiguous phenomena, mainly aiming at a number of management problems involving uncertainty in various industrial fields.

In SERVQUAL model, research tests usually adopt multi-order Likert scale, which uses clear and definite values to represent the feelings of subjects. However, in the process of actual service quality evaluation, consumers are based on fuzzy memory of service perception, combining subjective information with intangible feelings, and cannot flexibly and accurately provide certain values [38, 39]. So a more realistic approach to language assessment is used instead of clear Numbers.

The combination of SERVQUAL model and fuzzy theory conforms to the fuzziness of evaluators' subjective judgment and can better provide improvement strategies for enterprise management. Wu wanyi (2004) et al. used fuzzy language framework and SERVQUAL measurement scale to effectively link the market position and service quality strategies of five large hospitals in Tainan [40]. Aydin and Pakdil (2008), through the combined application of fuzzy theory and SERVQUAL model, measured and summarized the expectation and perception of international airline passengers for service quality, and provided enterprise decision makers with improvement projects and suggestions for service [41]. Braendle, Sepasi and Rahdari (2014) established an improved 7-order fuzzy SERVQUAL scale to measure the service quality of Banks by issuing questionnaires to their bank customers, measuring the weight of the bank's service items, perceived performance and expected performance [42].

According to most literature studies, the combination of SERVQUAL model scale and Fuzzy theory is applicable in many service industries, and can describe consumers' perceptions and expectations of service quality more accurately, which is conducive to improving the effectiveness of enterprise management.

5.2 Service Quality Evaluation Based on QFD

Quality function deployment (QFD) is mainly through listening for the voice and opinions of consumers, taking consumer demand as the main factor of service organization, and expanding service quality into products, processes and production systems, so as to realize the full deployment of quality functions for services [43]. This functional system converts consumer demand information into actions and designs to maximize consumer satisfaction [44]. The main feature of QFD is that it can reduce the design cost and time. Through a multi-level process transformation, the voice of consumers can be transformed into specific service contents [45].

Through SERVQUAL model, researchers obtain the service demand of consumers and establish the basis for QFD model. QFD model summarizes the service characteristics of consumers through consumer demand, lists the service requirements and service characteristics into a relational matrix, and discusses the strength of the relationship between consumer demand and service characteristics. Yildirim, Ozcan (2019) et al. conducted a study on the quality of public service in Ardahan [46], evaluating the quality of service and providing improvement strategies through the gap between local citizens' actual experience perception and expectation of service area.

QFD model takes the weight ratio of competing companies to consumer demand as a reference to further obtain important service characteristics. By using SERVQUAL model and fuzzy quality function deployment, scholars Zai Zai, Youzhen Jin and Zhongguo Quan (2016) studied the consumer services of Samsung and LG's electronics companies and proposed improvements [47].

Through research of most literatures, the combination of SERVQUAL model and QFD method can provide a deeper understanding of the service demand characteristics of consumers. Research uses SERVQUAL model to obtain the service demand of consumers and converts it into service characteristics through QFD, which improves the efficiency of service design and improvement.

5.3 Service Quality Evaluation Based on Kano Model

Professor Noriaki Kano (1984), from Tokyo institute of technology, formally proposed Kano model [48], which classified and prioritized service demands according to the objective functions of product service and the subjective experience of consumers. Through the influence of product quality attributes of different categories on consumer satisfaction, professor Noriaki Kano divided the product service quality characteristics into five categories: basic demand, expectation demand, charm demand, indifference demand and reverse demand.

Research through the five dimensions of SERVQUAL model and 22 project measures of consumer demand, again after induction of Kano model, through the perspective of service quality for service requirements in terms of classification, draws service priority arrangement and the weight ratio of the project, the last modification design for the high priority services.

Vassiliadis, Tavlaridou and Fotiadis (2014) surveyed the service quality evaluation of Greek public secondary hospitals by patients [49], obtained the key attributes of patient satisfaction and behavioral intention and reasonably allocated limited resources for the service quality of hospitals.

Tingyi Jiang and Hongpeng Yang (2018) established a hybrid model, mainly combines SERVQUAL model, Kano model and Refined Kano model [50]. The team proposed differentiated service strategies by studying the owner services of property companies. This strategy can effectively solve the problem of communication and cognition of property disputes and maintain the competitiveness of property companies to a certain extent.

In the above studies, SERVQUAL model and Kano model were combined to conduct questionnaire experiments, and the service types and quality attributes of consumers were classified to obtain the most influential service items. Based on this, strategy improvement and resource allocation of enterprise services were carried out.

6   Summary and Discussion

6.1 Service Quality Research Model

Through literature review and practical case studies, this paper improves and modifies the previous research model of service quality, as shown in Fig. 4:

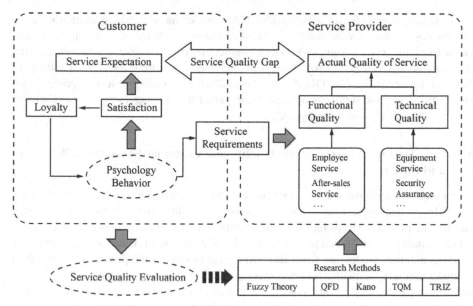

Fig. 4. Service quality research model

First of all, according to the psychology and behavior of consumers, the research obtains the service requirement of consumers, which determines the content of relevant services, and service mechanism emerges accordingly. In the process of interaction between services and consumers, actual quality of services is reflected by quality of functions and technologies, and affects psychological and behavioral characteristics of consumers. Secondly, after receiving the service, consumers have a psychological evaluation of their service, generate satisfaction and define the quality of the service, and set expectations for receiving similar services. Its satisfaction will affect consumers' loyalty to the service and affect to consumers' behavior and characteristics. In the end, this paper studies the gap between consumers' service expectation and actual service perception to obtain the service quality evaluation, and then applies the research method of engineering system to obtain the key factors in the service, so as to improve the service items in the functional quality and technical quality.

6.2 Study Quality of Service from the Angle of Science and Service Content

SERVQUAL model is developed based on the marketing domain and then applied to various service domains. This model mainly uses psychological experiment method to carry on the empirical surveys, uses structural equation, multi-level linear regression equation and so on mathematical model to carry on the statistics. In the process of service design and system optimization, SERVQUAL model is integrated with fuzzy mathematics, system simulation, DEA and other system engineering methods, providing reference for improving service quality.

In database search statistics, SERVQUAL model has developed from traditional enterprises to new service industries. Most of the research focus on e-commerce services, tourism services, logistics services, medical services, education services, catering services, hotel services and government management, and are gradually expanding. In different service fields, SERQUAL model is evaluated according to service content, service requirement and service quality, providing enterprise managers with comprehensive consideration of resource management.

6.3 Relationship Between Service Quality and Customer Satisfaction, Behavior and Loyalty

Service quality and customer satisfaction have different structural concepts, but they are interrelated. Because consumer satisfaction is formed through the perception of service quality and provides a basis for the improvement of service quality. However, in contrast, service quality is considered to be a relatively high content of actual service cognition, while consumer satisfaction tends to be more emotional. In the process of research, it is found that service quality is one of driving factors influencing consumer satisfaction, and different levels of service quality have different influences on satisfaction, while consumer satisfaction will lead to changes in attitude and purchase intention.

Consumers' loyalty is caused by the synergy of perceived service quality, personal willingness and social influence. Therefore, the improvement of customer loyalty should be considered from various aspects. Research find that improving service quality and increasing consumption interaction can promote consumer behavior, indicating that consumer behavior is positively correlated with service quality.

There is a certain correlation between service quality and customer satisfaction, behavior and loyalty. In different research fields and service contents, discussion and research can be conducted according to cultural differences, education level, age, income level and other factors of consumers. In order to further deepen the relationship between the four, it is necessary to explore dynamic change of new and old consumers on service quality, influence between service quality and other factors, and change of perceived difference of service quality.

6.4 Comprehensive Evaluation of Extended Service Scale

In service quality evaluation, many researchers use total quality management system (TQM), system simulation, critical incident technique (CIT), quality function deployment (QFD) and other methods to evaluate quality. Although SERVQUAL model is still the main method in study of service quality. But in China, the comprehensive development and expansion are few, so study of service quality model needs further innovation. In future exploration, quality of service model and engineering system model are developed universally, the structure of quality of service model can be unified, and the key factors of quality of service research can be studied by using conventional enterprise indicators.

According to different regions and national conditions, research on service quality has potential value. In regions with limited resources, research can guide small and medium-sized enterprises to make effective investment in service quality and provide decision planning for enterprise leaders. In developing countries, the study provides recommendations for improving service quality in different service sectors, provides policy guidelines for governments, and provides more value for market and society.

6.5 Conclusion

According to the development of service quality research, this paper takes SERVQUAL model as the entry point to expand its application in service field. Based on relevant literature on service quality, this study finds that relevant factors affecting service quality mainly include the psychology, behavior and satisfaction of consumers, as well as the functional and technical services of service providers. Through collecting literature data from domestic and foreign databases, it indicates that SERVQUAL model is widely used in the field of business management and digital information. By comparing the applications of SERVQUAL and SERVPERF models, it finds that SERVQUAL model is more informative and can influence the development trend of service field. Through the research of SERVQUAL model combined with engineering system model, it is found that the integrated model can effectively evaluate service quality, guide service enterprises to make reasonable management decisions and resource investment.

This paper summarizes the research of SERVQUAL model on service quality, and finds that SERVQUAL model is universal, scientific and instructive in application. SERVQUAL model can intuitively evaluate the service perception of consumers and reflect the key factors influencing service quality. Through data observation, the test reliability and validity of SERVQUAL comprehensive model are very high, and scientific theories are used to conduct data statistics and analysis to help service enterprises accurately find service demand points. In applied research in different regions and countries, SERVQUAL model can guide small and medium-sized enterprises to make effective investment, provide reasonable resource allocation strategies and service management policies for national governments.

Above all, service quality and SERVQUAL model has application value for service companies and government agencies, has a guiding value for the development of economy and social management. In the future research development, comprehensive research on service quality can give full play to greater potential and value in various service industries.

References

1. Gronroos, C.: Marketing in Service Companies. Liber, Malmo (1983)
2. Lehtinen, J.R., Lehtinen, U.: Service quality: a study of quality dimensions. Unpublished working paper, Service Management Institute, Helsinki (1982)
3. Lewis, R.C., Booms, B.H.: The marketing aspects of service quality in emerging perspectives on service marketing. In: Berry, L., Shostack, G., Upah, G. (ed.) American Marketing, Chicago, pp. 99–107 (1983)
4. Parasuraman, A., Zeithaml, V.A., Berry, L.L.: SERVQUAL: a multiple-item scale for measuring consumer perceptions of service quality. J. Retail. **64**(1), 12–40 (1988). https://doi.org/10.1016/0737-6782(88)90045-8

5. Leblanc, G., Nguyen, N.: Customers' perceptions of service quality in financial institutions. Int. J. Bank Mark. **6**(4), 7–18 (1988). https://doi.org/10.1108/eb010834
6. Hedvall, M.-B., Paltschik, M.: An investigation in, and generation of, service quality concepts. In: Avlonitis, G.J., et al. (eds.) Marketing Thought and Practice in the 1990s, European Marketing Academy, Athens, pp. 473–83 (1989)
7. Liu, W., Liu, G.: Quality Management, p. 220. Yanshi Press, Beijing (2004)
8. Parasuraman, A., Zeithaml, V.A., Berry, L.L.: A conceptual model of service quality and its implications for future research. J. Mark. **49**(4), 41–50 (1985). https://doi.org/10.1177/002224298504900403
9. Parasuraman, A., Berry, L.L., Zeithaml, V.A.: Perceived service quality as a customer-based performance measure: an empirical examination of organizational barriers using an extended service quality model. **30**(3), 335–364 (1991). https://doi.org/10.1002/hrm.3930300304
10. Parasuraman, A., Berry, L.L., Zeithaml, V.A.: Refinement and reassessment of the SERVQUAL scale. J. Retail. **67**(8), 1463–1467 (1991). https://doi.org/10.1021/nl0492436
11. Carman, J.M.: Consumer perceptions of service quality: an assessment of the SERVQUAL dimensions. J. Retail. **66**(2), 33–55 (1990). https://doi.org/10.1016/0737-6782(90)90032-A
12. Taylor, S.A., Cronin, J.J.: Modelling patient satisfaction and service quality. J. Health Care Mark. **14**(1), 34–44 (1994)
13. Wang, Y.L., Luor, T., Luarn, P., Lu, H.S.: Contribution and trend to quality research–a literature review of SERVQUAL model from 1998 to 2013. Informatica Economica **19**(1), 34–45 (2015). https://doi.org/10.12948/issn14531305/19.1.2015.03
14. Baker, D.A., Crompton, J.L.: Quality, satisfaction and behavioral intentions. Ann. Tour. Res. **27**(3), 785–804 (2000). https://doi.org/10.1016/S0160-7383(99)00108-5
15. Dabholkar, P.A., Shepherd, C.D., Thorpe, D.I.: A comprehensive framework for service quality: an investigation of critical conceptual and measurement issues through a longitudinal study. J. Retail. **76**(2), 139 (2000). https://doi.org/10.1016/S0022-4359(00)00029-4
16. Devaraj, S., Ming, F., Kohli, R.: Antecedents of B2C channel satisfaction and preference: validating e-commerce metrics. Inf. Syst. Res. **13**(3), 316–333 (2002). https://doi.org/10.1287/isre.13.3.316.77
17. Chhabra, N.: Measurement of consumer's perception of service quality in organized retail using SERVQUAL instrument. Manage. Dyn. **13**(1), 70–82 (2013)
18. Mobarakeh, S.K., Ghahnavieh, F.R.: A survey on the performance of Siahat Gasht tour and travel agency from the viewpoint of customers using SERVQUAL model. Int. J. Sci. Manage. Dev. **3**(6), 394–402 (2015)
19. Palese, B., Usai, A.: The relative importance of service quality dimensions in e-commerce experiences. Int. J. Inf. Manage. **40**, 132–140 (2018). https://doi.org/10.1016/j.ijinfomgt.2018.02.001
20. Khare, A., Parveen, C., Rai, R.: Retailer behavior as determinant of service quality in Indian retailing. J. Retail Leisure Prop. **9**(4), 303–317 (2010). https://doi.org/10.1057/rlp.2010.14
21. Vassiliadis, C.A., Fotiadis, A.K., Tavlaridou, E.: The effect of creating new secondary health services on patients' perceptions: a Kano service quality analysis approach. Total Qual. Manage. Bus. Excell. **25**(7–8), 897–907 (2014). https://doi.org/10.1080/14783363.2014.904564
22. Bansal, A., Gaur, G., Chauhan, V.: Analysis of service quality provided by goibibo.com in tourism industry. Glob. J. Enterpr. Inf. Syst. **8**(2), 40–47 (2016)
23. Chakravarty, A.: Evaluation of service quality of hospital outpatient department services. Med. J. Armed Forces India **67**(3), 224 (2011). https://doi.org/10.1016/s0377-1237(11)60045-2
24. Meesala, A., Paul, J.: Service quality, consumer satisfaction and loyalty in hospitals: thinking for the future. J. Retail. Consum. Serv. (2016). https://doi.org/10.1016/j.jretconser.2016.10.011

25. Hong, Z., Su, Q., Huo, J.: Study on the research of service quality management. Manage. Rev. **24**(7), 154–165 (2012). https://doi.org/10.14120/j.cnki.cn11-5057/f.2012.07.016

26. Cui, L., Chen, S.: Research on service quality evaluation and improvement countermeasures of commercial Banks in China – based on improved SERVQUAL model. Res. Dev. **149**(04), 92–95 (2010). https://doi.org/10.13483/j.cnki.kfyj.2010.04.039

27. Zhu, M., Miao, S., Zhuo, J.: An empirical study on chinese express industry with SERVQUAL. Sci. Technol. Manage Res. **31**(08), 45–52 (2011)

28. Zuo, W., Zhu, W.: Research on service quality management of online car-hailing based on SERVQUAL in sharing economy: case study of Didichuxing and Uber. J. Manage. Case Stud. **11**(4), 349–367 (2018)

29. Cronin Jr., J.J., Taylor, S.A.: Measuring service quality: a reexamination and extension. J. Mark. **56**(3), 55–68 (1992). https://doi.org/10.1177/002224299205600304

30. Boulding, W., Kalra, A., Staelin, R., Zeithaml, V.A.: A dynamic process model of service quality: from expectations to behavioral intentions. J. Mark. Res. (JMR) **30**(1), 7–27 (1993). https://doi.org/10.1177/002224379303000102

31. Hartline, M.D., Ferrell, O.C.: The management of customer-contact service employees: an empirical investigation. J. Mark. **60**(4), 52–70 (1996). https://doi.org/10.1177/002224299606000406

32. Marshall, K.P., Smith, J.R.: SERVPERF utility for predicting neighborhood shopping behavior. J. Nonprofit Public Sect. Mark. **7**(4), 45 (2000). https://doi.org/10.1300/J054v07n04_05

33. Hossain, M.J., Islam, M.A., Saadi, M.S.: Evaluating users' experience of service performance using SERVPERF scale: a case study of some private university libraries in Bangladesh. Ann. Libr. Inform. Stud. **60**(4), 249–259 (2013)

34. Le Tan, P., Fitzgerald, G.: Applying the SERVPERF scale to evaluate quality of care in two public hospitals at Khanh Hoa Province, Vietnam. Asia Pac. J. Health Manage. **9**(2), 66–76 (2014)

35. Mahmoud, A.B., Khalifa, B.: A confirmatory factor analysis for SERVPERF instrument based on a sample of students from syrian universities. Educ. Train. **57**(3), 343–359 (2015)

36. Parasuraman, A., Zeithaml, V.A., Berry, L.L.: Reassessment of expectations as a comparison standard in measuring service quality: implications for further research. J. Mark. **58**(1), 111–124 (1994). https://doi.org/10.1177/002224299405800109

37. Zadeh, L.A.: Fuzzy sets. Inf. Control **8**(3), 338–353 (1965)

38. Hu, H.-Y., Lee, Y.-C., Yen, T.-M.: Service quality gaps analysis based on Fuzzy linguistic SERVQUAL with a case study in hospital out-patient services. TQM J. **22**(5), 499–515 (2010). https://doi.org/10.1108/17542731011072847

39. Lin, C.J., Wu, W.W.: A causal analytical method for group decision-making under fuzzy environment. Expert Syst. Appl. **34**(1), 205–213 (2008). https://doi.org/10.1016/j.eswa.2006.08.012

40. Wu, W.Y., Hsiao, S.W., Kuo, H.P.: Fuzzy set theory based decision model for determining market position and developing strategy for hospital service quality. Total Qual. Manage. Bus. Excell. **15**(4), 439–456 (2004). https://doi.org/10.1080/1478336042000183587

41. Aydin, O., Pakdil, F.: Fuzzy SERVQUAL analysis in airline services. Organizacija **41**(3), 108–115 (2008)

42. Braendle, U., Sepasi, S., Rahdari, A.H.: Fuzzy evaluation of service quality in the banking sector: a decision support system. Fuzzy Econ. Rev. **19**(2), 47–79 (2014)

43. Mazur, G.: QFD for service industries. In Proceedings of the Fifth Symposium on Quality Function (1993)

44. Lampa, S., Mazur, G.: Bagel sales double at host marriott: Using quality function deployment. Japan Business Consultants (1996)

45. Dube, L., Johnson, M.D., Renaghan, L.M.: Adapting the QFD approach to extended service transactions. Prod. Oper. Manage. **8**(3), 301–317 (1999). https://doi.org/10.1111/j.1937-5956. 1999.tb00310.x
46. Yildirim, K.E., Yildirim, A., Ozcan, S.: Integrated usage of the SERVQUAL and quality function deployment techniques in the assessment of public service quality: the case of Ardahan Municipality. Bus. Econ. Res. J. **10**(4), 885–901 (2019)
47. Cho, I.J., Kim, Y.J., Kwak, C.: Application of SERVQUAL and fuzzy quality function deployment to service improvement in service centres of electronics companies. Total Qual. Manage. Bus. Excell. **27**(3/4), 368–381 (2016). https://doi.org/10.1080/14783363.2014.997111
48. Kano, N., et al.: Attractive quality and must-be quality. J. Jpn. Soc. Qual. Control **41**(2), 39–48 (1984)
49. Vassiliadis, C.A., Fotiadis, A.K., Tavlaridou, E.: The effect of creating new secondary health services on patients' perceptions: a Kano service quality analysis approach. Total Qual. Manage. Bus. Excell. **25**(7/8), 897–907 (2014). https://doi.org/10.1080/14783363. 2014.904564
50. Chiang, T.-Y., Perng, Y.-H.: A new model to improve service quality in the property management industry. Int. J. Strateg. Prop. Manag. **22**(5), 436–446 (2018)

Evaluating Potential of Gamification to Facilitate Sustainable Fashion Consumption

Marta Waydel-Bendyk(✉)

iKLEID, Zurich 8044, Switzerland
mwaydel@gmail.com

Abstract. The world is faced with a growing problem of the overconsumption of fashion. The UK Parliament Environmental Audit Committee highlights that current model is untenable in the long term and that there is an urge for alternative fashion business models [1]. At the same time customers have vast ability to impact the fashion market. However, it is not an easy task to consume clothes in a sustainable way and it requires extra effort. This makes it crucial to recognize digital space and its potential to facilitate more Sustainable Fashion Consumption (SFC). Thus, with a growing usage of technology in people's everyday lives the idea of gamified social application (GSA) to influence consumer behaviour is researched in the context of SFC.

The literature review on sustainable fashion and gamification was undertaken to explore the subject and to develop appropriate research questions. Taking into consideration the complexity of SFC it was required to look into various academic areas such as psychology, sociology, macro marketing and economics, in order to discover ways to change fashion consumption through different game elements. The primary data is based on mixed research methods. It includes both qualitative and quantitative research. The prospective method for disclosing complexity of the subject was the comprehensive answers to qualitative interviews. The examination of the collected data suggests that well-designed GSA has the potential to foster SFC. In addition, gamification could be a useful tool in raising awareness through positive reinforcement about the consequences of fashion overconsumption.

Keywords: Sustainability · Fashion · Consumer Behaviour · Motivation · Gamification · Innovation · Technology

1 Introduction

The overconsumption of fashion is causing a significant increase in waste production. Thus, the aim of this study is to explore methods that could motivate people to reduce their consumption of fashion and lengthen the lifecycle of clothing, to encourage the buying of fewer but better quality garments and to inspire people to think more about the consequences of their shopping. Thus, it is essential to understand why, when and how consumers make conscious shopping decisions through the moral and personal beliefs that are involved in sustainable consumption in comparison to unconscious behaviour of fashion shopping. Virtual platforms have fundamentally changed consumers' behaviour.

© Springer Nature Switzerland AG 2020
F. F.-H. Nah and K. Siau (Eds.): HCII 2020, LNCS 12204, pp. 205–215, 2020.
https://doi.org/10.1007/978-3-030-50341-3_16

Consumers are no longer merely passive recipients of information. With the introduction of the web 2.0 they have become active producers of content. As a result, in the last decade, social networks with user-generated content (UGC) have become a powerful tool for communication and for influencing people's behaviour.

It is crucial to understand how to engage an audience, especially when the subject may not necessarily be a priority for them, and how to motivate people to change their behaviour towards sustainable fashion consumption (SFC). There is a trend for using gamification, which is the use of game mechanics in non-game contexts in order to engage audiences and direct participants into action [2]. However, it is important to implement the right game mechanics in an appropriate way in order to get desirable effects [3]. Zichermann writes, games can get people to take actions against their own self-interest, in a predictable way [4].

2 What Influences Consumer Behaviour Towards SFC?

The importance of sustainable fashion was established in order to highlight the urgency of the fashion overconsumption situation. It seems that even when people are aware of the issue and care about it they think it is so overwhelming that transformation in their behaviour will not make any difference. Therefore, for SFC to become a reality the whole fashion system would have to be reorganised. At the same time even small modifications in individuals' behaviour on a bigger scale could have a great impact and initiate further improvements. Thus, it is important to empower people to ameliorate their fashion consumption habits.

Fashion is a very important cultural construct, which influences many fields of humans' lives. It is a tool for communication that needs to be present [5]. Belk explains possession as an instrument to sustain self-image and connection to place [6]. However, there is currently a growing trend where the experience of buying is becoming more important than the possessions themselves. This could be due to globalisation and changes in people's lifestyles; they are often forced to relocate on account of jobs or studies. Bardhi, on the other hand, describes people with nomadic lifestyles who seem to rely more on access-based consumption and place more value on experiences than possessions [7]. Often the symbolic meaning of things is not transferable to other cultures, and those possessions become useless. Bardhi argues that nomads avoid nostalgia and have a flexible sense of self, which facilitates their mobile lifestyles. The associated phenomenon of temporary access to consumption is visible in the growth of access-based consumption, based on the 'experience value' of objects [8]. Examples of this tendency can be seen in the popularity of car- and flat-sharing platforms such as Zipcar.com and Airbnb. Morgan and Birtwistle point out that with volumes of clothes purchased and increasing donations, charity shops have reached the capacity they can process [9]. Ha-Brookshire and Hodges discovered that the main motivation for the donation of clothing to charity is not altruism but is rather self-oriented, such as making more space for new purchases. This points to a close relationship between the disposal and acquisition of clothes [10]. Regardless of those theories, fashion consumption is growing and is frequently treated as compensation for some other failure to improve mood [11].

People with low confidence tend to shop more and on impulse [12]. Low self-esteem may largely be the result of aggressive marketing campaigns presenting retouched, emaciated models, celebrities and avatars as ideals of beauty. Therefore, it is necessary to change consumers' values so that their priorities will concentrate less on physical appearance and the ownership of material things and more on gaining satisfaction from other achievements such as education or experiences. This could also make people generally happier, uplift their self-confidence and minimise impulsive shopping behaviour.

Consumers have different motivations when buying clothes. The difference between utilitarian and hedonic buying is that the former is perceived as work - it is a functional and rational duty, while hedonic buying is based on enjoyment and fun tasks [13]. Consumers who buy clothes for fun are more likely to buy SF, as they might want to experiment with new products [14]. Thus, hedonic fashion buying is positively related to SFC. This way of shopping seems to be more associated with females. People who enjoy buying clothes may also investigate further and be more open to new solutions [14]. Kollmuss and Agyeman proved, people less often respond to negative information [15]. Thus, the facts about SF should be presented in a fun and engaging way without focusing exclusively on the problems, which can influence negatively emotional engagement.

The survey participants indicated price to be one of the main obstacle to SFC. However, the secondary research showed that people were willing to pay more for better quality clothes [16]. The grounds for such an inconsistency may lie in a lack of information about SF. However, awareness is positively related to changing attitudes towards SFC.

Education about SF could also help to reshape people's perceptions [17]. However, merely raising awareness will not change people's behaviour. As mentioned before, changing behaviour is very difficult, especially to do something that may not be a priority for many.

3 Does Gamification Have the Potential to Change Behaviour?

Gamification is a strategy most commonly used to generate engagement with a subject that would not normally be attained. The basic idea is that by incorporating game mechanics into everyday activities, they can become more fun and therefore more engaging. It's like using natural hacks to get people to engage more [18].

With growing technology usage and a huge amount of participants on social networks, social media seems to be an ideal channel for discussion, collaboration and education about SFC. However, as noted earlier, raising awareness is one thing and changing people's behaviour is much more difficult. The volume of information with which people are bombarded daily is massive. Therefore, consumers are becoming more selective and tend to concentrate only on what is useful and meaningful for them. In order to reach a wider audience the sustainable message in GSA could be discreet initially and grow with the player's engagement.

There have been many attempts at gamification which have not been effective and have produced the opposite effect to that expected, where people felt manipulated and forced to do something. Therefore, even if advertised well GSA needs to be designed in a proper way in order to work. The simple application of a game mechanism is not enough; it needs to have the right structure and take into consideration the social and cultural context. If gamification neglects emotional engagement, it could work against efforts to encourage pro-SFC behaviour in the long term. In order to achieve emotional engagement GSA must be purposeful for participants; thus there is a need to understand precisely the target market first.

While implementing gamification it is useful to think of the participants as players. Players are at the centre of the game, and from their point of view it is about them. GSA should be designed in a fun way that will make them feel in control of their actions and enable them to make meaningful choices. The role of GSA should be to create an enjoyable experience that will engage users for an extended period of time [19].

The demographics of gamers, according to the Entertainment Software Association, shows the average age is 30 years old and 47% of game players are women. Women tend to play more social, casual games while men prefer first-person shooter types [20]. This information is important because there is a preconception that the gaming world is strongly dominated by males. Whereas the true picture is more positive for the application of GSA in the context of SFC, since women seem a more suitable target in being more interested in SF with a more hedonic approach towards clothes shopping.

In order to better understand the needs of the target audience it is worth looking at player types. Amy Jo Kim has proposed four types of players, as presented in Fig. 1 [21].

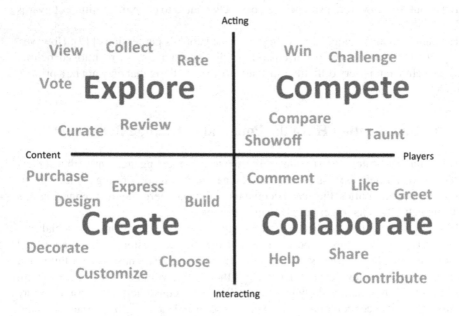

Fig. 1. Player types [21]

The survey results show that most participants enjoy creating while playing, which means expressing themselves, building and customising things. Competing was found to be very popular as well, which confirmed the need for challenges and the possibility for showing off. For the best results GSA should combine those and give users options to choose how they want to use the application.

While researching consumers' behaviour it is also worth to look at the behaviour change model. Fogg argues that it is important to leverage motivation since in the case of non-urgent behaviour, such as SFC is perceived by many; motivation tends to be lower [22]. He also states that people have temporary moments of being able to do hard things that help them achieve the most valuable behaviour, which is equivalent to their current motivation. In order to communicate behaviour change he merges 'motivation', 'triggers' and 'ability'. His model demonstrates that when individuals have both high motivation and high ability, when triggered to do something they do it (Fig. 2) [22].

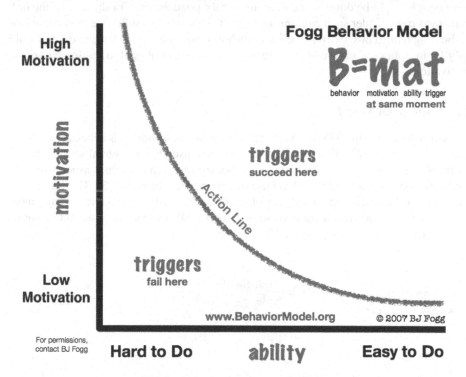

Fig. 2. Behaviour change model [22]

In Fogg's model, motivation is positively related to behaviour change and it is an essential ingredient in the process [22]. With motivation people can find a sense of self-direction. However, it is necessary to adopt the right motivation techniques with the correct amount and timing of triggers in order for GSA to work. It is important to remember that each individual can be motivated by very different things, these can depend on the situation or personal interest and to understand users' internal triggers for habitual behaviour [23]. At the same time users may not always behave in a rational way and therefore it is vital to observe their real actions and react accordingly.

GSA could give participants the opportunity to boost their self-acceptance through communicating positive messages. Instant feedback and a variety of reinforcement through tangible or nontangible rewards for positive actions could influence behaviour. If GSA is designed with priorities that are supportive of SFC, then narcissism and vanity could be used for a good cause.

The most desirable motivation within a gamified system is intrinsic motivation, where people are doing things because they find them interesting, are passionate about them and are not looking for other kinds of reward. In intrinsic motivation players have a sense of ability and accomplishment and the feeling that they are in control of their own actions. Yet this kind of motivation is very difficult to achieve. Therefore, a reward system could be helpful to mobilise people to activities too. Prizes need to be appropriately designed and suited to certain tasks, as problems could occur within the reward system. For example, if the reward is highly valuable, participants tend to cheat. Also people might be doing something just for the prize and not for the sake of the task in its own right. Under such circumstances the GSA might not influence their behaviour in the long term. Thus, extrinsic rewards such as points, badges or leader boards should only be indicators of progression towards a real, meaningful goal to reinforce intrinsic motivation.

3.1 Conceptual Model

In order to learn whether GSA can influence consumer behaviour it is necessary to investigate the variables affecting a person's intention to use an experiential service. Based on the theories outlined above, the framework for research combines aspects of both goal-directed behaviour [24] and the use of experiential services [25]. The framework aims to measure the importance of ease of use on attitudes, the significance of enjoyment both on attitudes and the intention to use GSA, and finally the weight of subjective norms regarding those intentions (Fig. 3).

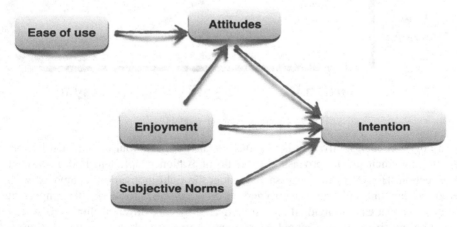

Fig. 3. Research model

In order for gamification to be successful it is also crucial that it is easy to use. Nonetheless, a GSA should be able to give a learning experience as well. Research confirmed that ease of use is positively related to attitudes towards the use of GSA. This is particularly true in the case of SF where early adopters of technology may not be necessarily early adopters of fashion.

Further, GSA should focus on providing useful tools that could urge participants to act in a sustainable way. Even when people are not very engaged with the subject, they may be more willing to try if the experience is fun. The tested hypothesis enjoyment is positively related to attitudes towards the use of GSA and Enjoyment is positively related to the intention to use GSA were accepted. It proved that enjoyment has a big impact on both attitudes and intentions. Therefore, GSA must be effortless, enjoyable and engaging in order to work.

It must be remembered that there are different categories of fun: easy, hard, serious and 'people factor' [26]. A combination of all of those could be implemented according to participants' preferences at different stages of the GSA to encourage more people and to engage them for a longer period of time. GSA should strive to evoke a 'state of flow' in players, which is an overwhelming and gratifying positive emotion [27].

The concept of flow is a highly desirable state in GSA, as described by Csikszentmihalyi [28]. It is a state where people are engaged and enjoy the activity to the point that they lose consciousness of time and other activities around them. According to McGonigal, flow is 'the single most overwhelming and gratifying positive emotion we can feel' [27]. She also states that there is nothing as engaging as working on the edge of skills. Flow can happen organically in a variety of different situations and activities. Some of the characteristics which help flow to appear are clear goals and a balance between perceived challenges and perceived skills, especially when movement through the channel is challenging and variable, as presented in Fig. 4 below.

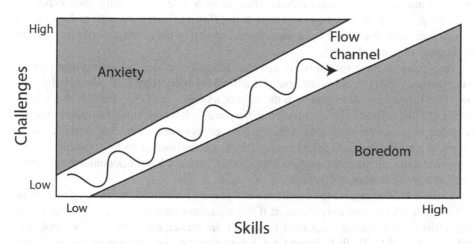

Fig. 4. Relationship of flow to skills and challenges [28]

Various secondary research demonstrated that in a technological environment attitudes towards the use of GSA are positively related to the intention to use it [25, 29]. This hypothesis was also confirmed by a research survey. The research model shows that attitudes are influenced by two variables: ease of use and enjoyment. Therefore, GSA should concentrate on these in order to encourage the intention to use it (Fig. 5).

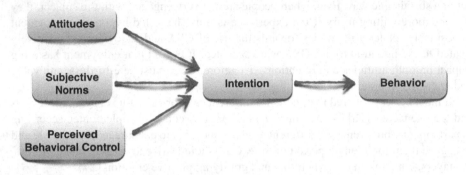

Fig. 5. Theory of planned behaviour model

Subjective norms are important predictors of player behaviour in online games [30]. Research confirmed that subjective norms are positively related to the intention to use GSA. The social aspect plays a significant role especially in small communities; GSA can create that by, using group formats [31]. External factors can provide reasons for action. Thus, GSA needs to take into consideration social and cultural factors in order to engage the audience. Adequate marketing strategies play also an important role.

The theory of reason, action and planned behaviour shows strong links between intention and behaviour, reality indicates that many people fail to change their behaviour in the long term despite the best intentions. It is difficult to alter behaviour as the adoption of new habits and social and cultural pressures, as well as many other barriers often stand in the way of planned change.

According to Fogg only three things can change behaviour in the long term: having an epiphany, changing one's environment and taking baby steps [22]. Those baby steps could be formed and activated with the help of an engaging GSA. Further, those small habits should be positively reinforced if they are to become sustained behaviour and in order to reinforce emotionally the player's engagement. A reward strategy, which supports cooperation and healthy competition, can motivate users by appealing to their desire for status and peer recognition. This kind of feedback has the potential to encourage SFC and create further action plans.

Even if GSA meets all the conditions and players have the best intention to perform SFC, some actions can only be taken if the necessary infrastructure is provided [15]. Therefore, it is important not only to spread the message but also deliver tools that will facilitate SFC. Well-designed GSA would seem to have the potential to overcome many barriers: it could provide the infrastructure needed for disposal channels and help consumers to find lower-priced products. It could also inspire people to wear SF products and present them as trendy and desirable.

4   Conclusions

Gamification seems to be a real opportunity to influence, engage and inspire people. It has the potential to make every day-life activities more fun and engaging, and therefore more willingly and more easily performed.

However, it is not easy to change behaviour, and GSA needs wider support to achieve desirable results. The problem of the overconsumption of fashion is so complex that in order for SF to become a reality ideally the whole economic system would change. Nevertheless, GSA has the potential to stimulate small actions, which on a bigger scale could have an impact and initiate further changes. GSA can be an inexpensive and enjoyable way to approach environmental problems. The introduction of game elements will not solve each and every issue, but it could affect the way consumers behave in a variety of situations.

GSA has the potential to boost self-acceptance through various game mechanics and by motivating people towards different actions, which could also affect a reduction in impulsive shopping behaviour. It would be most appropriate for GSA to target people who enjoy shopping, as hedonic fashion buying is positively related to SFC.

It is essential to realise that there is no one method to make a game fun and motivational for everyone. There are various kinds of fun, and the appropriate one should be implemented ideally where the player will reach a state of flow.

The research indicates that the spreading of awareness of SFC in a positive way is important in influencing attitudes. They can encourage citizens to think about the impact of their behaviour and to consider new actions they can take. Therefore, GSA should convey messages in fun and engaging ways in order to realise its potential to reshape people's values and their perceptions of their ability to make a difference.

As motivation is an inseparable element in the changing of behaviour, GSA must focus on finding suitable motivators, concentrating mainly on intrinsic ones. Extrinsic rewards, meanwhile, should only be a reference of development towards the real goal of strengthening intrinsic motivation.

If designed well, GSA has the potential to be a tool for the finding of new solutions, with aggregated ideas of participants and the help of various competitions. However, without purpose and emotional drivers GSA would be effective at best in the short term and the extrinsic rewards would have only a small impact or no lasting effect on behaviour.

As attitudes to GSA are closely related to the intention to use it, thus, strong emphasis should be put on enjoyment and ease of use as they have an impact on those attitudes. Furthermore, subjective norms play a significant role in decision-making. They determine not only the intention towards the use of GSA but also fashion consumption choices in everyday life.

The limitation of GSA is its need to overcome external factors. If barriers to action remain and the necessary infrastructure will not be provided, then the prospects for gamification to influence people's behaviour towards SFC will remain significantly restricted, regardless of its powers of motivation. Additionally, GSA needs to find the way to create a connection between physical and virtual realities. SFC exists in physical reality and is about material goods, while fashion consumption is embedded in social practices. GSA adds the virtual aspect and has the ability to link those two spheres and influence action in the real world.

References

1. UK Parliament: House of Commons Environmental Audit Committee. Fixing fashion: clothing consumption and sustainability: Fashion: it shouldn't cost the earth, HC1952, February 2019 (2019)
2. Patel, K.: All the World's a Game, and Brands Want to Play Along. Advertising Age (2010)
3. Werbach, K., Hunter, D.: For The Win. Wharton Digital Press, Philadelphia (2012)
4. Zichermann, G., Linder, J.: Game-Based Marketing. Wiley, Hoboken (2010)
5. Black, S.: The Handbook. Thames & Hudson, New York (2013)
6. Belk, R.W.: Possessions and the extended self. J. Consum. Res. **15**, 139–168 (1988)
7. Bardhi, F., Eckhardt, G.M.: Access-based consumption: the case of car sharing: table 1. J. Consum. Res. **39**(4), 881–898 (2012)
8. Chen, Y.: Possession and access: consumer desires and value perceptions regarding contemporary art collection and exhibit visits. J. Consum. Res. **35**, 925–940 (2009)
9. Morgan, L.R., Birtwistle, G.: An investigation of young fashion consumers 'Disposal Habbits'. Int. J. Consum. Stud. **33**(2), 190–198 (2009)
10. Ha-Brookshire, J.E., Hodges, N.: Socially responsible consumer behaviour? Exploring used clothing donation behaviour. Cloth. Text. Res. J. **27**(3), 179–196 (2008)
11. Giddens, A.: Modernity and Self-Identity. Stanford University Press, Stanford (1991)
12. Sheldon, K.M., Kasser, T.: Getting older, getting better: personal strivings and psychological maturity across the life span. Dev. Psychol. **37**, 491–501 (2001)
13. Babin, B.J., Darden, W.R., Griffin, M.: Work and/or fun: measuring hedonic and utilitarian shopping value. J. Consum. Res. **20**, 644–654 (1994)
14. Gam, J.H.: Are fashion! conscious consumers more likely to adopt eco! friendly clothing? J. Fash. Mark. Manag. Int. J. **15**(2), 178–193 (2011)
15. Kollmuss, A., Agyeman, J.: Mind The gap: why do people act environmentally and what are the barriers to pro-environmental behaviour? Env. Educ. Res. **8**(3), 239–260 (2002)
16. Academic.mintel.com. Fashion Online – UK (2014)
17. Cialdini, R.B.: Crafting normative messages to protect the environment. Curr. Dir. Psychol. Sci. **12**(4), 105–109 (2003)
18. Radoff, J.: Game On. Energize Your Business with Social Media Games. Wiley, New York (2011)
19. Werbach, K., Hunter, D.: The Gamification Toolkit: Dynamics, Mechanics, and Components for the Win. Wharton Digital Press, Philadelphia (2015)
20. The Entertainment Software Association. Industry Facts - The Entertainment Software Association (2015)
21. Kim, A.J.: Community Building on the Web. Peachpit Press, Berkeley (2000)
22. Fogg, B.J.: BJ Fogg's Behaviour Model (2014). http://behaviourmodel.org/
23. Eyal, N.: Hooked: How to Build Habit-Forming Products (2014)
24. Bagozzi, R.P., Dholakia, U.: Intentional social action in virtual communities. J. Interact. Mark. **16**(2), 2–21 (2002)
25. Nysveen, H., Pedersen, P.E., Thorbjrnsen, H.: Intentions to use mobile services: antecedents and cross-service comparisons. J. Acad. Mark. Sci. **33**(3), 330–346 (2005)
26. Lazzaro, N.: Why we play: affect and the fun of games. In: Sears, A., Jacko, J.A. (eds.) Human-Computer Interaction, pp. 155–176. CRC Press, Boca Raton (2009)
27. McGonigal, J.: Reality Is Broken. Penguin Press, New York (2011)
28. Csikszentmihalyi, M.: Flow. Harper & Row, New York (1990)
29. Moon, J.W., Kim, Y.G.: Extending the TAM for a world-wide-web context. Inf. Manag. **38**(4), 217–230 (2001)

30. Hsu, C.L., Lu, H.P.: Why do people play online games? An extended TAM with social influences and flow. Exp. Inf. Manag. **41**(7), 853–868 (2004)
31. Bagozzi, R.P., Dholakia, U.M.: Antecedents and purchase consequences of customer participation in small group brand communities. Int. J. Res. Mark. **23**(1), 45–61 (2006)
32. Ajzen, I.: The theory of planned behaviour. Organ. Behav. Hum. Decis. Process. **50**(2), 179–211 (1991)

Features of Smart City Services in the Local Government Context: A Case Study of San Francisco 311 System

Wei-Ning Wu(⊠)

National Sun Yat-sen University, Kaohsiung, Taiwan
weiningwu@mail.nsysu.edu.tw

Abstract. The 311 system, a type of smart city initiative, has been adopted by local governments in the United States and has been concluded to increase citizen-initiated contact, instigate service coproduction, and improve citizen relationship management. Despite the importance of the 311 system in the service delivery process, few studies have examined the development and main features of a 311 system case study. Public managers could learn from the experience of other cities, as reported in a 311 system case study. San Francisco has one of the most successful 311 systems in the United States, and its development experience would be a learning case for numerous local governments. Hence, this study provides a comprehensive understanding of San Francisco's 311 system, helping local public managers assess 311 system operation and providing evidence as to how these managers can develop an effective 311 system in their municipality.

Keywords: ICT · Citizen relationship management · Urban management

1 Introduction

At the local level, smart city initiatives are evident in urban development and in increased interaction between governments and the public. Smart city initiatives emphasize information delivery and communication tools to individuals collaborating with the governance process, change the means of contact employed, and increase the number of participants in the public service delivery process [1]. The advantages of smart city initiatives include the provision of a convenient approach through which participants can connect, different initial conditions for information delivery, data transparency, open participation for gaining feedback from external actors, open collaboration with common value-added services, and ubiquitous engagement with an integrated governance structure and process [2].

In some municipalities, local governments play various roles related to different citizens' issues through many smart city initiatives because they are facing a complex set of citizen problems. The 311 system, a centralized citizen service system or citizen relationship management (CRM) system, is considered a type of smart city initiative; in such systems, information and communication technologies (ICTs) are employed to

© Springer Nature Switzerland AG 2020
F. F.-H. Nah and K. Siau (Eds.): HCII 2020, LNCS 12204, pp. 216–227, 2020.
https://doi.org/10.1007/978-3-030-50341-3_17

link citizens with public agencies, having a beneficial influence on citizen–government relations [3, 4].

Since it was developed in the city of Baltimore in 1997, the 311 system has received increasing attention and been adopted in numerous municipalities [5]. Scholars and professional research institutes such as the International City/County Management Association and Government Finance Officers Association have advocated an expanded role for the 311 system in citizen–government interaction processes [6, 7]. Local governments with 311 service systems place emphasis on immediate response to citizens' demands; this public service delivery mechanism is an accountable and efficient method of increasing citizen satisfaction and has been adopted in several local governments in the United States [8].

The City and County of San Francisco began implementing the 311 system in 2007, and San Francisco is now one US example of city hall successfully applying the 311 system to manage citizen relationships and maintain the quality of its interaction with citizens [9, 10]. In addition, San Francisco is an example of a city that adopted a full CRM system through Web 2.0, and its experience can be an invaluable reference for other municipalities that are conducting 311 services through call-based and web-based approaches [11, 12]. The 311 system in San Francisco gained recognition as a Designated Citizen-Engaged Community in 2010–2012 and was the Lagan Innovation Award Winner in 2010 because of the high performance and positive reputation of its 311 operations. Hence, the San Francisco 311 system (SF311) can be considered an example of how a large city can successfully employ the system.

This study recognizes the importance of the 311 system in local government management and is particularly interested in use of the 311 system at the local level. More specifically, this study attempts to determine the features of SF311. This work provides an opportunity to learn more about the development of 311 system and explore the case of SF311, including its background and main characteristics.

2   Background on the 311 System in the United States

The new public management movement in the 1990s United States was a genuine CRM movement [13]. Since it was developed in Baltimore in 1997, the 311 system has received increasing attention and has been adopted by numerous municipalities. Initially, 311 was one of a series of abbreviated numbers (N11 codes) that the Federal Communication Commission (FCC) introduced in the 1990s to enable citizens to obtain immediate assistance from government by dialing a single three-digit number. Baltimore was the first US municipality to implement the 311 number to decrease the number of nonemergency calls to 911 [14].

One of the initial purposes of the 311 system was to support the 911 system. Because the 911 number receives many nonemergency calls, emergency services are sometimes delayed and urgent information is not acquired. Upon its adoption, SF311 alleviated congestion of the 911 emergency call services and enhanced the city's capacity to respond to citizens' demands [15].

Because of the 311 system's success in Baltimore, the FCC approved the use of the number nationwide. Adoption of the 311 system at the local level has continued to grow rapidly since the US Federal Chief Information Officer announced on March 3, 2010, the creation of a uniform Open 311 application programming interface, offering 311 comments and requests from citizens through Internet or smartphone interfaces [3].

3 Main Functions of the 311 System

The 311 system, a centralized citizen service system or CRM system, is considered a type of ICT in a smart city and links citizens to public agencies, benefitting the citizen–government relationship [16]. In addition, the 311 system is advocated as a managerial tool that uses citizen feedback to improve performance by facilitating communication between citizens and public officials, triggering competitiveness, and enhancing efficiency in government operations and interaction and the exchange of information between public officials and citizens toward the specific operational goal of resolving specific service deficiencies [17].

The main goal of the 311 service is to give citizens an active role rather than being passive service recipients in the service delivery process [16]. Mutual information delivery and communication as well as frequent interaction decrease the "gap" between citizens and city hall [5]. When citizens actively use the 311 system, their degree of satisfaction with city hall is higher because public officials can respond to and solve their problems [17].

The 311 system offers a platform on which a citizen can contact public officials inexpensively and easily (i.e., fewer obstacles) and have a high-quality service encounter. Governmental adoption of the 311 system, which has the advantage of being easier and more convenient than traditional contact modes, results in a change in citizen–government interaction, and the volume of citizen contact with public officials increases [5]. Crucially, governments that adopt the 311 system are stating that they will listen to citizens' requests and solve any service problems. By taking advantage of the 311 system, public managers can resolve feedback from citizens [15]. Because they have a convenient means of participating in government, citizens may feel a stronger connection with public officials. The 311 system can improve a strained citizen–government relationship by leading to open and easy access to public officials, information transparency, and improvement of inadequate service delivery [18, 19].

The 311 system has informing and consultation functions because it enables two-way communication between citizens and city hall and offers an alternative approach to information exchange within citizen–government interaction. Citizens can gain reliable information, and their requests are responded to efficiently. In addition, integrating an e-service into the 311 system is considered an alternative to increasing the response capacity of government toward citizens' requests [20].

4 Characteristics of SF311

San Francisco was the 41st municipality to adopt the 311 system in the United States, and the system was first adopted in March 2007. SF311 originated when Gavin Newsom was the mayor of San Francisco. Gavin Newsom proposed the 311 line service when he was a supervisor in 1999. When he was elected mayor, customer service remained his high priority. On March 29, 2007, Mayor Newsom announced the opening of a new citizen service system in San Francisco that offered residents, visitors, and businesses a 24-h nonemergency service and information assistance. Before the creation of the free 311 line, calls from citizens went to the Department of Public Works and the citizen call centers during daytime hours [21]. Through a learning process, SF311 system developed unique characteristics and advantages to serve people in the San Francisco area [10].

Crucially, 311 digital services were a vital case when the Federal Chief Information Officer (FCIO) of the United States considered the creation of a uniform Open 311 application programming interface. Before the FCIO officially announced the uniform Open 311 application programming interface on March 3, 2010, San Francisco had already developed (in 2008) an ICT-enabled service reporting website on which citizens could leave comments and requests. As time has passed and the needs of its citizens have increased, San Francisco has gradually adapted the 311 system to enable daily communication between citizens and public officials, resulting in solutions to service requests and even disaster assistance responses. This study identifies the main characteristics of SF311, which include collaboration in citizens' service requests, two call numbers for requesting information and services, multiple approaches to citizen-initiated contact through the 311 system, financial capacity to support 311 system development, seamless service-oriented culture in government, and service performance measurement.

4.1 Collaboration in Citizens' Service Requests

SF311 provides a one-contact interface with a choice of multiple accessible contact channels; the system decreases citizens' uncertainty and their time spent on making service requests and searching for service information [5]. The easy and convenient mode of contacting the government through the 311 system is more beneficial to citizens than more traditional contact modes. Citizen–government interaction has changed, and the amounts of citizen-initiated contact with public officials and citizen participation in public affairs have increased.

To develop a one-contact interface with multiple channels for residents, San Francisco's government has developed a collaborative style of public management in which 50 departments of the city and county are integrated; these departments work independently and compete for limited governmental resources [9, 21]. The customer service representatives (CSRs) in the SF311 were the catalyst in developing the collaborative public management style for internal governmental agencies and external stakeholders because these CSRs had professional training regarding various situations of citizen-initiated contact and knew how to search for and immediately forward information to other agencies [10].

4.2 Two Call Numbers for Requesting Information and Services

One of the initial purposes of adopting the 311 system was to support the 911 system. Because numerous calls to 911 are nonemergency calls, emergency services are delayed and urgent information is not delivered in some municipalities. Similar to in other cities, SF311 has been credited with alleviating congestion in the 911 emergency services and enhancing the capacity to respond to citizens' demands [15]. Since implementing the 311 hotline for nonemergency calls and city services, the City and County of San Francisco has educated citizens on the functions and benefits of SF311 and instructed residents that 311 should be dialed for everything except emergencies. Citizens within the limits of the City and County of San Francisco are now able to dial 311 to connect with any San Francisco governmental agency and even connect to the 211 calling service by transfer from SF311.

If the call is about an emergency, a citizen dials 911; otherwise, the citizen uses the 311 call service to ask about any city service, make a request, or submit a problem to the 311 officials. In some cases, 311 centers receive an emergency call, and the 311 system forwards the call or reports to the 911 center immediately. Also, when 911 centers receive calls about nonemergency issues, they forward the call to a 311 center. Prior to implementation of SF311, 50% of calls received by San Francisco 911 center were regarding nonemergency services; thus, SF311 is expected to prevent nonemergency calls from going through the 911 center.

4.3 Multiple Approaches to Citizen-Initiated Contact Through the 311 System

SF311 comprises a traditional offline phone system and a digital system for members of the public who would like to contact the city government. In the traditional approach, citizens dial the three numbers (311) using a phone or cell phone. In the digital approaches, citizens can use the SF311 Mobile App, the website, Twitter, or Facebook to report public service issues and obtain information [22].

Regarding the website, citizens can search for information independently by browsing the 311 website, which offers considerable information about general community services and transactions (e.g., noise complaints, potholes, lost pets, and volunteering opportunity information), businesses (e.g., permits, licenses, starting a business, and contracts with the city), building construction (e.g., inspection requests, building codes, building complaints, and new or existing permit services), and city environmental issues (e.g., graffiti and garbage). In most cases, citizens complete the online form when they are in need of a service or information.

In addition, as part of SF311, Facebook and Twitter pages have been established on which citizens can communicate with CSRs. Citizens can have request a service and report any city service issues through SF311 Facebook and SF311 Twitter. SF311 Facebook and SF311 Twitter also display the latest information about city events, news, and policy statements to quickly deliver information to various resident groups, especially those who are of Facebook or Twitter users [23]. Citizens can download and install the SF311 Mobile App on their mobile device. Within this app, citizens can send pictures and a brief description of the quality of any public service or city environmental issue to the government together with a map or address-based location. The SF311 Mobile App has a tracking function, and users of the app can track the status of their service-requested case and obtain a report of its completion [9, 12].

4.4 Financial Capacity to Support 311 System Development

Budget limitations have been considerable challenges in the adoption and long-term development of digital technologies in local governments [17]. In some cases, local governments have experienced organizational capacity problems and have had limited resources to develop and update their ICTs. San Francisco's government has high financial capacity in launching a 311 system and investing in the continuous development of this system. Table 1 shows that the per capita cost of SF311 in the 2009–2010 financial year (FY09-10) was $14.06, which was the highest among those of the 15 municipalities in a survey of 311 contact centers in selected cities and counties that was conducted by Pew Charitable Trusts' Philadelphia Research Initiative. The first year's operating budget and startup capital costs, which included construction and hardware and software purchases and excluded the first-year operating budget, were both third highest among those of the 15 wealthy municipalities. The cost per 311 call was $3.15, which is the additional financial burden of an increase in the number of 311 system users. Increasing the numbers of users has been the main service goal of San Francisco's government since the 311 system was adopted.

Table 1. Annual budget and startup capital costs of a 311 system

City or County	FY09-10 budget	FY09-10 cost per capita is based 2008 estimated population	FY08-09 budget	First year operating budget excludes startup year capital costs etc.	Startup capital costs include construction, hard/software purchase; exclude first-year operating budget	2009 cost per call is based on budget figures adjusted to match the period of the last available call volume
Baltimore, MD	$4,700,000	$8.24	$5,800,000	$4,000,000	n/a	$5.41
Charlotte-Mecklenburg, NC	$7,278,861	$8.08	$7,115,057	$2,304,343	$4,100,000	$4.37
Chicago	$4,965,897	$1.74	n/a	n/a	$4,000,000	$1.15
Columbus, OH	$1,583,158	$2.10	$1,510,239	$798,000	n/a	$5.49
Dallas	$3,700,000	$3.48	$4,458,000	n/a	n/a	$3.72
Denver	$1,500,000	$2.51	$1,500,000	$1,100,000	$3,313,000	$3.39
Detroit	$1,548,421	$2.03	$2,156,493	n/a	n/a	$7.78
Houston, TX	$5,000,000	$2.23	n/a	$4,358,505	$3,659,135	$2.22
Los Angeles	$3,128,980	$0.98	$4,423,317	$5,700,000	$4,000,000	$2.69
Miami-Dade, FL	$10,971,000	$4.76	$11,548,421	$9,000,000	n/a	$4.30
New York City	$46,000,000	$5.74	$50,000,000	$16,900,000	$25,000,000	$2.57
Philadelphia, PA	$2,830,914	$1.59	$2,059,272	$2,059,272	$4,000,000	$2.20
Pittsburgh, PA	$199,951	$0.64	$152,488	$112,075	n/a	$4.08
San Antonio, TX	$1,700,000	$1.33	$1,795,200	n/a	n/a	$1.39
San Francisco	$10,952,000	$14.06	$11,790,000	$6,500,000	$8,600,000	$3.15

Source: Survey of 311 contact centers in select cities and counties, Pew Charitable Trusts' Philadelphia Research Initiative. December 2014. Used by permission. www.pewtrusts.org/philaresearch.

4.5   Seamless Service-Oriented Culture in Government

The 311 system delivers seamless services around the clock and all year. These services enable citizens to conveniently participate in the public service delivery process, make immediate contact with public officials, and track the status of their requests, reducing their time costs and uncertainty [24]. When SF311 was first implemented, the city mayor told the residents that the whole governmental organization had created a service-oriented culture that would become apparent during public service encounters [10]. The local government in San Francisco marketed the 311 system with the slogan "Don't stand in line, get 311." Table 2 shows how the service-oriented culture has evolved in San Francisco.

The annual average number of calls per 100 residents in San Francisco was 446 in 2009, dramatically higher than in other municipalities (e.g., twice that in New York). In addition, the service-oriented culture continually reminds public officials of the need for managing the citizen–government relationship, and the 311 system is considered to develop service-oriented organizational culture within the government [23].

Table 2. Population and number of 311 calls

City or County	2008 estimated population (Census Bureau)	2008 total calls (calendar year unless otherwise noted)	2009 total calls (calendar year unless otherwise noted)	2008 monthly average call volume	2009 monthly average call volume	2009 annual average calls per 100 residents
Baltimore, MD	636,919	978,968	970,937	81,581	80,911	152
Charlotte-Mecklenburg, NC	890,515	1,768,907	1,648,087	147,409	137,341	185
Chicago	2,853,114	4,533,125	4,309,708	377,760	359,142	151
Columbus, OH	754,885	274,811	288,527	22,901	24,044	38
Dallas	1,279,910	1,298,929	1,196,957	108,244	99,746	94
Denver	598,707	495,948	443,061	41,329	36,922	74
Detroit	912,062	279,775	238,123	23,315	19,844	26
Houston, TX	2,242,193	n/a	2,256,511	n/a	188,043	101
Los Angeles	3,833,995	n/a	1,402,656	n/a	116,888	37
Miami-Dade, FL	2,398,245	2,411,000	2,650,000	200,917	220,833	110
New York City	8,363,710	16,099,505	18,707,436	1,341,625	1,558,953	224
Philadelphia, PA	1,540,351	n/a	1,113,159	n/a	92,763	72
Pittsburgh, PA	310,037	49,910	49,048	4,159	4,087	16
San Antonio, TX	1,351,305	n/a	1,293,372	n/a	107,781	96
San Francisco	808,976	3,972,924	3,608,824	331,077	300,735	446

Source: Survey of 311 contact centers in select cities and counties, Pew Charitable Trusts' Philadelphia Research Initiative. December 2014. Used by permission. www.pewtrusts.org/phi laresearch.

4.6 Service Performance Measurement

Adopting new CRM models or methods enhances citizens' ratings of governmental service performance [25]. The 311 system is the main and first step of city service centralization. Viewed as an innovative CRM system, the 311 system enhances citizens' satisfaction with governmental and public service performance [23]. When city agencies respond to citizen service requests, the 311 system collects performance data through the mechanism that tracks service requests. The performance data are useful for future policy considerations [18]. Service performance and citizen satisfaction are enhanced when public officials respond to citizen concerns and solve public service problems [3, 26].

Table 3 reveals that SF311 has performed at a high level when responding to citizens' requests. In 2008 and 2009, the annual average call-handling time (in seconds) in San Francisco was less than only that in the City of Chicago among the aforementioned 15 municipalities. However, based upon the evidence presented in Table 3, the 2009 annual average number of calls per 100 residents was 151 in Chicago, whereas that in San Francisco was 446. Therefore, San Francisco is clearly capable of receiving more calls and has a shorter average call-handling time.

The difference between the 2008 and 2009 annual average answer speed (call-waiting time) was 8 s (decreasing from 38 s in 2008 to 30 s in 2009), indicating that the response

Table 3. 311 system performance measurement

City or County	2009 annual average call-handling time (seconds)	2008 annual average call-handling time (seconds)	2009 annual average speed of answer, aka call-waiting time (seconds)	2008 annual average speed of answer, aka call-waiting time (seconds)	2009 annual average abandoned call rate	2008 annual average abandoned call rate	2009 annual average pct of calls transferred (transfer rate)
Baltimore, MD	120	120	5	5	3.0%	3.0%	6.0%
Charlotte-Mecklenburg, NC	166	151	17	63	2.6%	9.6%	33.0%
Chicago	70	69	61	81	19.0%	23.0%	35.0%
Columbus, OH	117	128	24	26	1.4%	1.9%	21.0%
Dallas	120	n/a	231	119	15.0%	12.0%	n/a
Denver	189	158	27	32	7.7%	9.5%	42.5%
Detroit	123	116	33	38	11.5%	n/a	12.0%
Houston, TX	129	n/a	32	n/a	3.9%	n/a	n/a
Los Angeles	90	n/a	60	24	12.7%	6.3%	40.0%
Miami-Dade, FL	268	249	83	73	16.5%	15.3%	6.7%
New York City	228	199	18	8	3.6%	1.3%	36.0%
Philadelphia, PA	372	n/a	105	n/a	26%	n/a	18.6%
Pittsburgh, PA	180	150	n/a	n/a	45.0%	21.6%	0.01%
San Antonio, TX	100	n/a	n/a	n/a	8.4%	n/a	13.0%
San Francisco	88	92	30	38	14.4%	17.8%	1.9%

Source: Survey of 311 contact centers in select cities and counties, Pew Charitable Trusts' Philadelphia Research Initiative. December 2014. Used by permission. www.pewtrusts.org/philaresearch

capacity of SF311 was enhanced, with government decreasing the time spent waiting by citizens contacting the city via the 311 line. In addition, the annual average abandoned call rate was 3.4% lower in 2009 (17.8% in 2008 vs. 14.4% in 2009). Notably, the 2009 annual average percentage of calls transferred (transfer rate) was low at 1.9%; this indicates that the 311 CSRs were able to appropriately handle the callers' various demands and requests, not needing to frequently transfer citizens' calls to other public agencies.

4.7 Discussion

Given previous experiences of adopting new digital technology in government, most scholars and practitioners would doubt the advantage of new technologies in smart city initiatives. In numerous cases, the information and technology infrastructures adopted by governments have not worked well or gained support at any appreciable level; adopting new digital technologies thus does not necessarily ensure that public sectors and the public will connect [6]. Hence, when governments advocate the advantages of an innovative system such as the 311 system, many people cast doubt on the performance of 311 system functions and the system's influence because of the limited citizen-initiated contact and failure of previous CRM government applications [16].

The present study examined the development and main characteristics of the 311 system implemented in the City and County of San Francisco. Currently, case studies of 311 systems have explored those of Boston, New York, and Chicago. However, the SF311 case offers considerable information about the lessons learnt by and effort made by the local government when planning and maintaining comprehensive CRM within the boundaries of the local government. The SF311 case shows that when developing a 311 system, the long view must be taken; such a system is not created overnight. Rather, a well-developed 311 system is constructed incrementally using various interrelated strategies and with continuous support from city leaders and sufficient financial capacity [10].

Understanding the possibilities and limitations of the use of social media in the governance process helps public managers devise strategies, innovate information technology, and minimize negative influences. Because of the widespread use of ICTs and social media within public organizations, the governance process is more complicated than previously. In numerous cases, adoption of innovative technology has created more uncertainty in public organizations, and such technology commonly has opposition. Resistance of new information technology and the limited range of use of such technology may prevent the public from understanding the advantages and functions of ICTs. Hence, the role of government is more critical, especially the role of city mayors and managers. The SF311 case shows that support from city leaders can lead to the successive development of a 311 system. Ex-Mayor Gavin Newsom strongly supported the new telephone hotline service when he was a member of the Board of Supervisors (Newsom and Dickey, 2013). Once the 311 call service had been implemented, subsequent mayors supported and updated the 311 system, which came to include a 311 offline call service and 311 online service [9].

Similar to the adoption of other technology in local government, the 311 service system was constructed on the assumption that governmental capacity could be employed to change certain outcomes. However, the issues of access inequality and the political influence of CRM adoption may limit further development of the 311 system. Businesses have used CRM systems to maintain or improve their relationship with purchasers of their products. Governments have followed a similar trajectory. However, unlike that in private businesses, CRM in governments is far more difficult and politically charged because of long-standing perceptions that government is not concerned about citizens' voices or dealing digitally with citizens' affairs [17]. In addition, public officials face more complex issues and limitations than business managers, such as budget constraints, re-election, and public policies. Hence, when governments advocate the advantages of an innovative system such as the 311 system, many people cast doubt on the success of 311 system functions and the system's influence because of the political characteristics of citizen participation in public affairs and previous CRM failures in government [16].

In addition, because ICTs are adopted to enable social inclusion and public partic-ipation, citizens have equal access to government regardless of age, gender, education, or disability. However, participation dilemmas may occur if ICTs do not work well; new e-government initiatives have risks because a digital divide can limit the access of more disadvantaged citizens to their government [20]. In practice, a digital divide causes an imbalance in participation among various citizen groups with different demographic backgrounds. Use of the 311 system may both enhance the participation of "connected" groups but further limit the access of "unconnected" groups to government, which, in turn, increases the digital divide. The role of information technology in government is primarily to enhance public participation and contact with public officials and to decrease social and economic divides [6, 24].

5 Conclusion

The 311 system is a communication platform, comprising a calling service and city online service, and a new participation mechanism through which citizens can access govern-mental websites, interact with public officials, and participate in community affairs. Compared with traditional participation methods such as public hearings and citizen advisory boards, the 311 system offers citizens a means of contacting public officials at lower cost and more easily (because of fewer obstacles) in a high-quality service encounter. Crucially, governments that adopt the 311 system state to citizens that they will listen to the citizens' requests and solve service problems highlighted by citizens. By taking advantage of the 311 system, public managers can resolve the dissatisfaction of citizens.

This study introduces an example of a 311 system for local governments to consider when they are planning to construct a 311 system and highlights lessons for local gov-ernments that have already implemented a 311 system. In addition to exploring the main functions and development of SF311, this study determines the main characteristics of SF311: (1) collaboration in citizens' service requests; (2) two call numbers for request-ing information and services; (3) multiple approaches to citizen-initiated contact through the 311 system; (4) financial capacity to support 311 system development; (5) seamless service-oriented culture of government; and (6) service performance measurement. The issues of access inequality and political influence on CRM adoption may limit further development of SF311, as explored in this study.

References

1. Nalchigar, S., Fox, M.: Achieving interoperability of smart city data: an analysis of 311 data. J. Smart Cities **3**(1), 1–13 (2019)
2. Stimmel, C.L.: Building Smart Cities: Analytics, ICT, and Design Thinking. Auerbach Publications, Boca Raton (2015)
3. Wiseman, J.: Innovations in public service delivery: Issue No 01: Can 311 call centers improve service delivery? Lessons from New York and Chicago. Inter-American Development Bank (2015)
4. Chatfield, A.T., Reddick, C.G.: Customer agility and responsiveness through big data analytics for public value creation: a case study of Houston 311 on-demand services. Gov. Inf. Q. **35**(2), 336–347 (2018)
5. Holzer, M., Schwester, R., McGuire, A., Kloby, K.: State-level 311 systems: leveraging service enhancement and performance measurement at the state level. Book States **38**, 409–413 (2006)
6. Clark, B.Y., Brudney, J.L., Jang, S.G.: Coproduction of government services and the new information technology: Investigating the distributional biases. Public Adm. Rev. **73**(5), 687–701 (2013)
7. Nam, T., Pardo, T.A.: Understanding municipal service integration: an exploratory study of 311 contact centers. J. Urban Technol. **21**(1), 57–78 (2014)
8. Minkoff, S.L.: NYC 311: a tract-level analysis of citizen–government contacting in New York City. Urban Aff. Rev. **52**(2), 211–246 (2016)
9. Lee, J.H., Hancock, M.G., Hu, M.C.: Towards an effective framework for building smart cities: lessons from Seoul and San Francisco. Technol. Forecast. Soc. Chang. **89**, 80–99 (2014)
10. Newsom, G., Dickey, L.: Citizenville: How to Take the Town Square Digital and Reinvent Government. Penguin Press, New York (2013)
11. Jung, K., Park, S.J., Wu, W.N., Park, H.W.: A webometric approach to policy analysis and management using exponential random graph models. Qual. Quant. **49**(2), 581–598 (2015)
12. Wu, W.N.: Citizen relationship management system users' contact channel choices: digital approach or call approach? Information **8**(1), 8 (2017). https://doi.org/10.3390/info8010008
13. Reddick, C.G.: The adoption of centralized customer service systems: a survey of local governments. Gov. Inf. Q. **26**(1), 219–226 (2009)
14. Schwester, R.W., Carrizales, T., Holzer, M.: An examination of the municipal 311 system. Int. J. Org. Theory Behav. **12**(2), 218–236 (2009)
15. Wheeler, A.P.: The effect of 311 calls for service on crime in DC at microplaces. Crime Delinquency **64**(14), 1882–1903 (2018)
16. Thomas, J.C.: Citizen, customer, partner: rethinking the place of the public in public management. Public Adm. Rev. **73**(6), 786–796 (2013)
17. Reddick, C.G.: Customer relationship management (CRM) technology and organizational change: evidence for the bureaucratic and e-government paradigms. Gov. Inf. Q. **28**(3), 346–353 (2011)
18. Eichenthal, D.R.: Using 311 data to measure performance and manage city finances. Gov. Financ. Rev. **24**(4), 70–76 (2008)
19. White, A., Trump, K.S.: The promises and pitfalls of 311 data. Urban Aff. Rev. **54**(4), 794–823 (2018)
20. Cavallo, S., Lynch, J., Scull, P.: The digital divide in citizen-initiated government contacts: a GIS approach. J. Urban Technol. **21**(4), 77–93 (2014)
21. Naff, K.C.: Nancy Alfaro as an exemplary collaborative public manager: how customer service was aligned with customer needs. Public Adm. Rev. **69**(3), 487–493 (2009)
22. Gao, X.: Networked co-production of 311 services: investigating the use of Twitter in five US cities. Int. J. Pub. Admin. **41**(9), 712–724 (2018)

23. Wu, W.N., Jung, K.: A missing link between citizen participation, satisfaction, and public performance: evidences from the city and county of San Francisco. Int. J. Pub. Sect. Perform. Manag. **2**(4), 392–410 (2016)

24. O'Brien, D.T.: Custodians and custodianship in urban neighborhoods: a methodology using reports of public issues received by a city's 311 hotline. Environ. Behav. **47**(3), 304–327 (2015)

25. Rivenbark, W.C., Ballard, E.C.: Using citizen surveys to influence and document culture change in local government. Pub. Perform. Manag. Rev. **35**(3), 475–484 (2012)

26. Clark, B.Y., Brudney, J.L., Jang, S.G., Davy, B.: Do advanced information technologies produce equitable government responses in coproduction: an examination of 311 systems in 15 US cities. Am. Rev. Pub. Adm. **50**(3), 315–327 (2020)

Research on Cross-cultural Participatory Design by Design Teams Based on Chinese Cultural Background

Rui Xi[1,3]([✉]), Xin-Li Wei[1], De-Chuan Wang[1], Xian-Gang Qin[1], Torkil Clemmensen[3], and Wen-Jun Hou[1,2]

[1] School of Digital Media and Design Arts,
Beijing University of Posts and Telecommunications, Beijing 100876, China
xr09113@126.com
[2] Beijing Key Laboratory of Network Systems and Network Culture,
Beijing University of Posts and Telecommunications, Beijing 100876, China
[3] Department of Digitalization, Frederiksberg, Denmark

Abstract. With the acceleration of globalization, the acculturation issue of design is becoming an emerging challenge. At the same time, as one of the several design patterns in service design, which is becoming a mainstream in design society, has been adopted by more and more designers in design practice. Based on the output of a design workshop on acculturation issue of design, we presented the process of and learnings from participatory design aiming at helping foreigners living in China to use WeChat. To that end, we described the practice, problems and achievements, lessons learned, and outlook into the future for design practice using participatory design to address the acculturation issue.

Keywords: Participatory design · Cross-cultural design · WeChat redesign

1 Introduction

With the rapid development of globalization, reflecting the multi-cultural harmony and designing for acculturation is becoming a new challenge. As a comprehensive design patterns, participatory design (i.e. co-design) contains several factors such as comprehensive service, design, users and the environment. Given its close connection with the designers and users of properties, participatory design had been known as getting "user" in the process of creation. The design practice pattern of collective innovation has been created, making it a popular design theory in the cross-cultural design process [1]. This paper is unwound from the cultural background with China-based design team to cross-cultural participatory design perspective starting with Chinese localization applications re-engineering of the micro letter as a case study to explore the characteristics and problems of the Chinese design team in the design process and propose appropriate solutions and suggestions.

© Springer Nature Switzerland AG 2020
F. F.-H. Nah and K. Siau (Eds.): HCII 2020, LNCS 12204, pp. 228–239, 2020.
https://doi.org/10.1007/978-3-030-50341-3_18

2 Background

The way East and West cultures view the world can be traced back to the two very different thinking systems of Aristotle and Confucius thousands of years ago. Eastern and Western social structures, personal consciousness and cognitive styles, and worldview systems are inextricably linked. Westerners are relatively more independent about the characteristics of things and believe that the behavior of controlling things is based on the rules of domination. The interdependence of the Oriental people, the characteristics of collectivism and the general view of the problem are consistent, that things depend on the interaction of multiple factors. There are large differences between Chinese and Western cultures, and most of the current theories on Participatory design come from Western cultural backgrounds. However, these design theories from the West, whether it can better be effective in the Chinese cultural background of the design teams?

2.1 Participatory Design

Participatory is a deeper, more personalized collaborative process, and this term should be used selectively, perhaps we should call this field "cooperative design." We need to recognize that the entire design process is a negotiation to be successful and done, to reach an agreement, compromise and meet the process. Thomas Kvan et al. [3] summarized participatory design as a closed-coupled design process and a loosely coupled design process. The main difference between the two participatory design processes is the continuous relationship between users and designers throughout the participatory process. The theory of participatory design mainly refers to that during the design process, the designer encourages and guides users to participate in the creative process and solve problems together, blurring the identity boundary between the designer and the user, and hopes that the results presented will make users more satisfied. Participatory design differs from participatory design mainly in that there will not be any benefit elements in the participatory design process, and whether the beneficiaries use products to distinguish them from people-oriented design methods [4, 5].

2.2 WeChat

The latest report from market research company App Annie shows that Facebook was the most used application by netizens in the world in 2018, and Facebook Messenger was the most downloaded application. Besides, the top five most commonly used apps by Internet users are Facebook, WhatsApp, Facebook Messenger, WeChat, and Instagram. With the rapid development of mobile media technology, Facebook, WeChat, and other social network services (SNS) have penetrated the daily lives of mobile phone users and changed their lifestyles. As a social application based on Chinese cultural background, WeChat does well accommodate the characteristics of local social networking, and it also has a significant influence on the international social stage. The "observation report" carried out an inventory of the lives of foreign users in China. The report shows that foreign users in China send 60% more messages per month than typical Chinese users and use audio and video features 42% and 13% more frequently than Chinese users, respectively. However, WeChat is still not applicable to the process of Western users.

The workshop design practice in the latter part of this article is mainly based on the designer's exploration of the use of social applications by foreigners in China. Therefore, it is necessary to choose social applications that are relatively familiar to both designers and users. According to the above data, WeChat is a relatively suitable choice.

3   WeChat Redesign Workshop

To understand the characteristics of cross-cultural participatory design among design teams with a Chinese background, this article carried out the topic of WeChat redesign. Specifically, by recording the various stages of participatory design, the Chinese design teams and foreign WeChat users participate in the design process, emotional state, and design principles.

Workshop Background. The workshop is based on two design methods, UCD and Participatory Design, with 10 Chinese design teams. The only core topic of this design workshop is to design WeChat that is suitable for foreign users to use habits, to solve or slow down the pain points of foreigners in China using WeChat. Interestingly, each group of design team members comes from different disciplinary backgrounds, from the background of science and engineering disciplines such as interaction design, digital media technology, and the other part from the background of sociology, psychology, and other humanities. Designers from different disciplines but based on the same cultural background intersect together to develop WeChat redesign issues under two sets of design models. The focus of the workshop is on design practice. At the same time as achieving specific design results, it must be rooted in theory and design reflection. The final design purpose of the workshop is to 1) introduce and compare the similarities and differences between the two design methods of UCD and Participatory Design through design practices 2) explore the characteristics of the Chinese cultural background design teams in the process of cross-cultural design. This article focuses on the introduction and elaboration of the Participatory Design teams.

Arrangement and Participants. Participants in this workshop are young designers from the first and second grades of graduate students in the School of Digital Media and Design Art, Beijing University of Posts and Telecommunications. Designers at this stage are of certain help to our research. Some designers have just entered the field of design from other majors, and they do not have a solid grasp of design theory. Combining various background factors, the workshop restructures the settings of each team member, allowing participants with a design background and non-design background participants to form a design team, and allowing five of them to participatory design with foreign users. The other five groups use UCD design methods to carry out project practice. The workshop hopes that during the participatory design process, users and designers from different cultural backgrounds at home and abroad can compare the phenomena and characteristics of the participatory design process. And compare the differences between UCD and participatory design patterns. Among them, we are a team in the participatory design practice group.

Design Tools and Technical Support. The choice of tools is a key part of participatory design. In the design process, each group of participatory design teams is required to consider and select the appropriate design tools before writing the design process, and write the reasons for the tool selection. Most design teams will design with foreign participants using flexible [6] pen and paper prototypes, and some groups will also prepare pen-based electronic products. But in the end, most design teams mainly use paper and pen as the main design tools in the design process (Fig. 1).

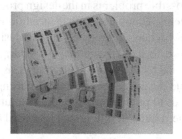

Fig. 1. Paper prototype

The cycle of the whole workshop is 5 days, and the design practice is about 4 h per day. It is divided into three major sections: requirements definition, innovative design, and design evaluation. The workshop requires the participatory design teams to conduct in-depth interviews and define requirements and users, find foreign users to develop innovative designs, make prototypes and evaluate them in three parts. The UCD teams follows the traditional design pattern. After each group completes a stage of the design task, the workshop requires each design team to present an elaboration of the task principles and share the design report.

In-Depth Interviews and User and Demand Definition. The cross-cultural redesign of WeChat is a very broad subject. To further focus on the pain points and needs of foreign users in China using WeChat, through practice, the UCD design group and the participatory design group will use two different methods to collect Persona's background materials. Most of the data sources of the UCD teams come from the research literature data as user support. Compared with the participatory design group, the participatory design teams choose a combination of literature data and user interviews to conduct research. Besides, each participatory design team students will conduct in-depth interviews with foreign users at this stage. During the first user interview, we found that in the beginning, each team would have difficulty communicating with the language, resisting the phenomenon of communicating with foreigners and feeling self-lost. During the team's interview, members of the non-designed Chinese team will choose to work on records and data in small group hours to avoid positive contact with foreign users. Students with a design background will be more willing to communicate with foreign users. At the same time, the students of the UCD design team do not choose to communicate with users. Instead, they use internal brainstorming and data analysis methods to define users and potential design requirements.

Innovative Design Practice. Through previous investigations, the workshop asked the participatory design teams to determine a design requirement, and required foreign users who matched the searched user portraits to participate in the process of innovative design. The UCD design team uses traditional design processes to develop design practices and output results, such as drawing low-fidelity design prototypes and drawing user journey maps.

Hypothesis. Before starting participatory design, the workshop requires the participatory design team to predict possible problems in the design process and propose solutions based on the predicted problems. Compared with the traditional UCD design mode, the participatory design requires higher requirements on the designer's design theory and practical experience. Therefore, to avoid the participatory design team's post-design process from appearing "misguided by the user's innovative ideas" and forgetting their own designer's responsibilities and design concepts. Before starting the participatory design practice, the design team needs to predict possible design solutions and ideas for foreign users, and propose and define related design principles based on design predictions.

Design Practice Process. In the design practice process, we found that almost all participatory design teams will adopt Thomas Kvan's [3] loosely coupled design process, and design teams that do not use closed-coupled design process. This may be due to the relative difficulty in finding foreign participants, poor language communication, and the participatory design team not paying enough attention to the proportion of foreign users participating in the design process to make suggestions. At the same time, we found that preparing paper prototypes can achieve better design results than allowing users to create freely on paper. Besides, during the communication process, some groups will have a special phenomenon. When foreign users develop a design, it may be due to privacy reasons. When drawing and creating, they do not want the designer to watch it all the way. Most foreign users prefer to be able to show it to designers after creation. After that, the designer went to discuss with the users to understand their design ideas (Fig. 2).

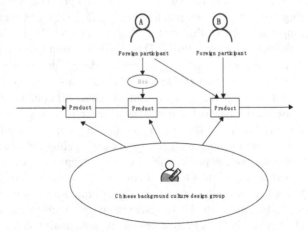

Fig. 2. Loosely coupled design process

Design Results. After developing design practices with foreign users, the design team needs to summarize and translate the design results with professional design tools. Regardless of whether it is based on the UCD design pattern or the participatory design pattern, the workshop requires each group to systematically produce interactive design prototypes based on the requirements defined earlier (Figs. 3 and 4).

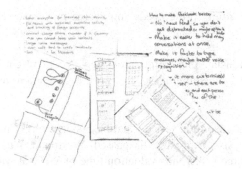

Fig. 3. Participatory design draft

Fig. 4. High fidelity prototype

Availability Assessment. Based on the design results, each design team was asked to select the appropriate usability evaluation criteria and 10 foreign users to conduct usability evaluation based on the design prototype. Through statistical related test indicators, understand the advantages and disadvantages of the design results, and finally, iterate and improve the design results based on the evaluation results.

Evaluation Criteria. During the evaluation process, the team mainly used the Nielsen Usability Test and the SUS Software Evaluation Questionnaire as the evaluation principle. The main reason for using the SUS software to evaluate the test questionnaire is because the questionnaire is simple in structure and fits the focus of design evaluation. At the same time, it has the advantages of simple and convenient assessment, which reduces the difficulty in finding suitable candidates for cross-cultural design time assessment in the time dimension. As WeChat is a localized application in China, in the process of perfecting the design, it is not only necessary to study the needs of foreign users for WeChat, but also to take into account the suggestions of Chinese users on the results of WeChat redesign. So we looked for 10 Chinese users and 10 foreign users to conduct design evaluations.

Evaluation Tasks. According to the needs and design point, we set up three tasks of sending voice:

1. Send English and translate into Chinese text by voice, then send to the other party;
2. View the voice sent by the other party, convert it to text and translate it;
3. Send a 5 s voice message;

Evaluation Results. Based on the test evaluation results of 10 Chinese users and 10 foreign users, the analysis of the steps is passed. We found that for Chinese users, completing the same three tasks, the evaluation time of WeChat was 4.6 min, and the prototype took 1.125 min, which illustrates the convenience of the design prototype for user operation from the time dimension. According to the operating steps, the first task requires 9 steps, and part of the test takes 12 steps to complete. When testing the same task on the prototype, the user's step fit is 100%, and the task can be completed in only 6 steps. The test of the second task is similar to the first task. When users use WeChat, errors occur to varying degrees, resulting in wasted steps. For the third task, WeChat and the prototype did not show much difference. According to the data of the task completion steps of foreign users, it is very difficult to complete the first task using WeChat. Two users did not complete the task. The average number of users who completed the task was 11.25, and the error operation rate reached 1/4. For the same task, using the prototype to operate, the user completion rate is 100%, the average number of operations is 4.8, and the error operation rate is 1/6. The second task cannot be completed in WeChat. WeChat was designed without considering the need for foreign users to send voice to text. There is not much difference between the two solutions to the third task. The user's completion rate is 100%. The prototype users did not misoperate. WeChat experienced 4 misoperations. In general, foreign users rate the design prototype slightly higher than Chinese users. The detailed data are as follows:

Data Analysis

Descriptive Statics. Table 1 shows the SUS scores for WeChat and design prototypes by Chinese users. The average SUS score for WeChat is 53.5, the standard deviation is 16.1322658, and the average SUS score for design prototypes is 75.75, with a standard deviation of 11.88749343. Chinese users have higher SUS ratings for design prototypes than WeChat.

Table 2 shows the SUS scores of WeChat and design prototypes by foreign users. The average SUS score of WeChat is 52, the standard deviation is 18.0843981, the average SUS score of design prototypes is 80.75, and the standard deviation is 10.55558878. Foreign users have higher SUS ratings for design prototypes than SUS ratings for WeChat.

Table 1. Descriptive statistics of SUS scores of WeChat and design prototypes by Chinese users.

Number	WeChat SUS	Prototype SUS
1	67.5	55
2	42.5	80
3	35	65
4	37.5	62.5
5	60	75
6	77.5	95
7	80	90
8	40	77.5
9	40	72.5
10	55	85
Means	53.5	75.75
SD	16.1322658	11.88749343

Based on Bangor's SUS scoring standard (Fig. 5), Chinese users consider the prototype design's Adjective ratings to be OK ~ GOOD, the Grade Scale is C, and Acceptability Ranges are Acceptable; foreign users consider the prototype design's Adjective ratings to be OK ~ GOOD, and the Grade Scale is B. Acceptability Ranges is Acceptable.

Table 2. Descriptive statistics of SUS scores of WeChat and design prototypes by foreign users.

Number	WeChat SUS	Prototype SUS
1	25	100
2	82.5	100
3	67.5	75
4	55	77.5
5	27.5	80
6	25	77.5
7	67.5	85
8	55	72.5
9	62.5	62.5
10	52.5	77.5
Means	52	80.75
SD	18.0843981	10.55558878

In general, foreign users rate the design prototype slightly higher than Chinese users.

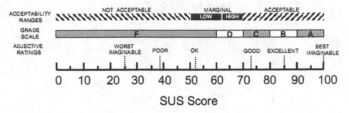

Fig. 5. SUS rating standard [7]

Inferential Statistics. The normal distribution test was performed on the SUS score data in Tables 1 and 2, and the K-S results were used to obey the normal distribution (Table 3).

Table 3. Chinese users' SUS score paired sample T test for WeChat and design prototype.

Paired Samples Statistics

		Mean	N	Std. Deviation	Std. Error Mean
Pair 1	chsuswechat	53.5000	10	17.00490	5.37742
	chsusprototype	75.7500	10	12.53052	3.96250

Paired Samples Correlations

		N	Correlation	Sig.
Pair 1	chsuswechat & chsusprototype	10	.491	.149

Paired Samples Test

		Paired Differences			95% Confidence Interval of the Difference				
		Mean	Std. Deviation	Std. Error Mean	Lower	Upper	t	df	Sig. (2–tailed)
Pair 1	chsuswechat – chsusprototype	-22.25000	15.38623	4.86555	-33.25665	-11.24335	-4.573	9	.001

The data shows that $t = -4.573$, sig $= 0.001 < 0.05$, indicating that Chinese users have significantly different SUS scores on WeChat and SUS scores on design prototypes (Table 4).

The data shows that $t = -3.866$, sig $= 0.004 < 0.05$, indicating that the SUS score of WeChat by foreign users is significantly different from the SUS score of the design prototype (Table 5).

The data shows that Sig $= 0.333 > 0.05$, indicating that there is no significant difference in the SUS scores of the design prototype between Chinese users and foreign users.

Table 4. SUS score pairing sample T test for foreign users on WeChat and design prototypes.

Paired Samples Statistics

		Mean	N	Std. Deviation	Std. Error Mean
Pair 1	ensuswechat	52.0000	10	19.99305	6.32236
	ensusprototype	80.7500	10	11.66964	3.69026

Paired Samples Correlations

		N	Correlation	Sig.
Pair 1	ensuswechat & ensusprototype	10	-.037	.919

Paired Samples Test

		Paired Differences							
					95% Confidence Interval of the Difference				
		Mean	Std. Deviation	Std. Error Mean	Lower	Upper	t	df	Sig. (2-tailed)
Pair 1	ensuswechat – ensusprototype	-28.75000	23.51861	7.43724	-45.57420	-11.92580	-3.866	9	.004

Table 5. Chinese and foreign users of SUS prototype of independent samples T-test scores.

Summary Data

	N	Mean	Std. Deviation	Std. Error Mean
Sample 1	10.000	75.750	11.888	3.759
Sample 2	10.000	80.750	10.556	3.338

Independent Samples Test

	Mean Difference	Std. Error Difference	t	df	Sig. (2-tailed)
Equal variances assumed	-5.000	5.027	-.995	18.000	.333
Equal variances not assumed	-5.000	5.027	-.995	17.752	.333

Hartley test for equal variance: F = 1.268, Sig. = 0.3571

95.0% Confidence Intervals for Difference

	Lower Limit	Upper Limit
Asymptotic (equal variance)	-14.853	4.853
Asymptotic (unequal variance)	-14.853	4.853
Exact (equal variance)	-15.562	5.562
Exact (unequal variance)	-15.572	5.572

4 Discussion and Summary

Being keenly aware of the challenges and potential of cross-cultural participatory design is an exciting and memorable experience, and the ingenuity and exchange of experience demonstrated by young designers is a return on this experience. Here, we share the experience and lessons learned through observations in the workshop and analysis after the workshop. We hope to provide some references and suggestions for designers of future Chinese cultural background to carry out the cross-cultural design.

Build Relationships. In the process of cross-cultural design exchange, the design team should think and learn to establish a trusting design atmosphere and connection with users. Interestingly, this step of establishing connections often requires Chinese designers to overcome their inner caution and psychological barriers to oral English communication. This step is often based on the results of Chinese designers seeking the first foreign friend to join the design team. If foreign users join the design team with a willing and friendly attitude, this will encourage designers to find more foreign users in the later stage and start to show positive optimism attitude. If the designer is rejected when seeking the first foreign user to join the design practice, the post-design team will exacerbate the strong resistance to finding foreign users to participate in the design and increase the frustration.

Understanding the Background Culture. We surveyed and interviewed other students in the participatory design team. During the two participatory design processes, they will consciously or unintentionally understand the national cultural background of the foreign users they invited to avoid disrespect during the design process. The user's situation and phenomenon are very important links in the cross-cultural design process.

Prepare Appropriate Design Materials. The participatory design practice process lasted a total of 2 days, during which we continued to improve the preparation of materials. On the first day, we only prepared blank paper and pens. We hope to avoid too many elements to limit users' creativity and thinking. On the second day, we added paper prototypes. After two days of comparison, we found that preparing paper prototypes was not It will limit thinking, and it can also prompt users about some WeChat interaction processes and interaction pain points. Therefore, we recommend that designers can appropriately provide some design tools with hints to help users think when they start participatory design.

The Characteristics of UCD Design Method and Participatory Design Method in Cross-cultural Design. At the end of the workshop, 10 design teams (5 UCD design teams and 5 participatory design teams) respectively wrote the design guidelines for the two design practices on the blackboard based on the 5-day design practices. We summarized it and found:

1) Throughout the design process, we must fully respect the objective differences between different user groups, consider the different opinions of users, and develop adaptive design guidelines for subsequent stages.
2) In the user research phase, we need to consider using different research methods based on cultural differences between different user groups and predict the impact of research methods on subsequent design phases. At the same time, the protection of user privacy is very important.
3) During the sketch design stage, designers need to focus on a pain point for further exploration, rather than focusing on design performance.

4) Participatory design requires inviting users to participate in the design process. Collaborators need to guide users to use the right tools to express their ideas and explore the reasons behind those ideas.
5) During the prototyping phase, designers need to have a clear definition of the problem to guide the design on the right path.
6) UCD needs further design based on data and literature. It is necessary to provide multiple versions of the design for subsequent evaluations.
7) The Participatory design needs to invite users to the design team for a culturally adaptive design. Design multiple prototypes based on user needs and present them in a simple and straightforward manner.
8) During the testing phase, we need to find users who match the character model and provide them with simple testing tasks and a suitable testing environment. Collaborators need to avoid subjective biases.

Acknowledgement. The practice of this design workshop is a very rare experience and learning opportunity. Participatory design is not a rare design pattern, but cross-cultural participatory design practice is a rare and precious topic. Thanks to Professor Torkil Clemmensen, Qin Xiangang and Hou Wenjun for their guidance and support. Thanks to the group members for their expertise, the team's design practice has been successful and the corresponding design results have been achieved. Thanks to the sharing and communication of other design teams, let us Think about and contrast the differences and characteristics between cross-cultural Participatory design and cross-cultural UCD design.

References

1. Sanders, E.B.N., Stappers, P.J.: Co-creation and the new landscapes of design. CoDesign **4**, 5–18 (2008)
2. Dou, W.: A review of research on the differences between eastern and western thinking—a review of Nisbett's "regionality of thinking: differences between eastern and western thinking and the reasons. J. Peking Univ. (Philos. Soc. Sci.) **42**(4), 131–136 (2015)
3. Kvan, T.: Participatory design: what is it? Autom. Constr. **9**, 409–415 (2000)
4. Albinsson, L., Lind, M., Forsgren, O.: Co-design: an approach to border crossing, network innovation (2019)
5. Norman, D.A., Draper, S.W.: User Centered System Design: New Perspectives on Human-Computer Interaction. L. Erlbaum Associates Inc, Hillsdale (1986)
6. Li, Y., Guan, Z., Dai, G.: Research on pen user interface development tools. J. Softw. **14**(3), 392–400 (2003)
7. Bangor, A., Kortum, P., Miller, J.: Determining what individual SUS scores mean: adding an adjective rating scale. J. Usability Stud. **4**, 114–123 (2009)

Model-Based Systems Engineering for Sharing Economy Service Systems Design Using Structure-Behavior Coalescence Process Algebra

Yu-Chen Yang[1][✉] and William S. Chao[2]

[1] National Sun Yat-Sen University, Kaohsiung, Taiwan
ycyang@mis.nsysu.edu.tw
[2] Association of Chinese Enterprise Architects, Taipei, Taiwan

Abstract. The central theme of Model-Based Systems Engineering (MBSE) is a modeling language with model consistency of systems structure and systems behavior. In this paper, we developed a Channel-Based Multi-Queue Structure-Behavior Coalescence Process Algebra (C-M-SBC-PA) as the modeling language for model singularity of the MBSE sharing economy service systems design. In C-M-SBC-PA, only a single diagram is used to specify the semantics of the design of the sharing economy service system. Overall, the model consistency will be fully guaranteed in the MBSE sharing economy service systems design when the C-M-SBC-PA method is adopted.

Keywords: Model-Based Systems Engineering · Modeling language · Sharing economy service systems design · Structure-Behavior Coalescence · Process algebra · Model singularity · Model consistency

1 Introduction

As a formal application of modeling to support system requirements, design, analysis, verification, and validation tasks beginning in the conceptual design phase and continuing throughout development and later life cycle phases, model-based systems engineering (MBSE) aims to promote systems engineering activities that have traditionally been performed using the document-based approach and result in enhanced specification and design quality, reuse of system specification and design artifacts, as well as communication between development teams (Blaha and Rumbaugh 2004; Arlow and Neustadt 2005; Weilkiens 2008; Friedenthal et al. 2014; Dori 2016).

The core theme of the MBSE is a consistent model, i.e., systems modeling language (SysML), of the system's (static) structure and (dynamic) behavior, with an emphasis on using model-based methods and tools to develop and improve the model. However, since SysML is a multi-diagram approach based on UML 2.0, there are always some inconsistencies between different diagrams in the SysML design of a system (Apvrille et al. 2004; Malgouyres and Motet 2006; Paige et al. 2007; Allaki et al. 2015; Bashir et al. 2016).

© Springer Nature Switzerland AG 2020
F. F.-H. Nah and K. Siau (Eds.): HCII 2020, LNCS 12204, pp. 240–253, 2020.
https://doi.org/10.1007/978-3-030-50341-3_19

In this paper, we developed the channel-based multi-queue structure-behavior coalescence process algebra (C-M-SBC-PA) (Qin et al. 2018; Yang et al. 2018) as the modeling language for model singularity of MBSE sharing economy service systems design. Using C-M-SBC-PA, only one single diagram is adopted to specify the semantics of the system. Therefore, the model consistency will be fully ensured in the MBSE sharing economy service systems design.

The rest of this paper is organized as follows. Section 2 deals with the related MBSE modeling studies. The (C-M-SBC-PA as a single diagram for MBSE sharing economy service systems design is detailed in Sect. 3. After describing the C-M-SBC-PA method used in this paper, we will validate the approach with a case study in Sect. 4. Conclusions of this paper are in Sect. 5.

2 Background

In the model-based systems engineering user group, people often use the Systems Modeling Language (SysML) to specify the (static) structure and (dynamic) behavior of the system. The SysML concepts include (1) an abstract syntax that defines the language concepts and is described by a metamodel, and (2) a concrete syntax, or notation, that defines how the language concepts are represented and is described by a user model (Weilkiens 2008; Friedenthal et al. 2014).

Since SysML is a multi-diagram approach based on UML 2.0, there are always some inconsistencies between different diagrams in the user model (Apvrille et al. 2004; Malgouyres and Motet 2006; Paige et al. 2007; Allaki et al. 2015; Bashir et al. 2016). There are two ways to resolve inconsistencies in the SysML design of a system. The first method is to use a metamodel. To ensure and check consistency, the metamodel defining the abstract syntax of the modeling language needs to provide a unified semantic framework for defining consistency rules to impose constraints on the structure or behavior constructs of the SysML systems specification. The Object Management Group (OMG) defines a language that represents metamodels, called Meta Object Facility (MOF) that is used to define UML, SysML and other metamodels. Various mechanisms are used in MOF, such as Object Constraint Language (OCL) (Przigoda et al. 2016), Foundational UML (fUML) (OMG 2013b), The Action Language for Foundational UML (Alf) (OMG 2013a), Process Specification Language (PSL) (ISO TC-184), and so on. However, all the mechanisms used in MOF do not provide a unified semantic framework from which each diagram in the user model will be projected as a view of the SysML metamodel.

The second method to ensure and check model consistency is to provide a single diagram for the SysML user model specification. The Object Process Methodology (OPM), conceived and developed by Professor Dov Dori, is a system modeling paradigm that unifies two things inherent in the system: objects and processes (Dori 2002). OPM is able to consider processes that are parallel to the object, depicting an excellent single diagram framework that avoids model inconsistencies by unifying all the information into the unified model and limiting the complexity through a scaling mechanism.

In this paper, we develop the channel-based multi-queue structure-behavior coalescence process algebra (C-M-SBC-PA) as the modeling language for MBSE sharing economy service systems design. In C-M-SBC-PA, only one single diagram is used to design the semantics of the system. Therefore, by using the C-M-SBC-PA method, the model consistency can be completely guaranteed in the MBSE sharing economy service systems design.

3   Method of Channel-Based Multi-queue SBC Process Algebra

3.1   Channel-Based Value-Passing Interactions

The block is the fundamental modular unit for describing systems structure in SysML (Weilkiens 2008; Friedenthal et al. 2014). It can define a type of conceptual or physical entity; a hardware, software, or data component; a person; a facility; or an entity in the natural world. A channel is a mechanism for agent communication via message passing (Qin et al. 2018; Yang et al. 2018). A message may be sent over a channel, and another agent is able to receive messages sent over a channel it has a reference to. Each channel defines a set of parameters that describes the arguments passed in with the request, or passed back out once a request has been handled. The signature for a channel is a combination of its name along with parameters as follows:

<channel name> (<parameter list>)

The parameters in the parameter list represent the inputs or outputs of the channel. Each parameter in the list is displayed with the following format:

<direction> <parameter name> : <parameter type>

Parameter direction may be in, out, or inout. We formally describe the "channel signature" as a relation $K \subseteq \Lambda \times \Theta$, where Λ is a set of "channel names" and Θ is a set of "parameter lists".

An interaction (Qin et al. 2018; Yang et al. 2018) represents an indivisible and instantaneous communication or handshake between the caller agent (either external environment's actor or block) and the callee agent (block). In the channel-based value-passing approach as shown in Fig. 1, the caller agent interacts with the callee block through the channel interaction. In the figure, getPastDueBalance(in studentId: String; out PastDueBalance: Real) is a channel signature. Figure 1 also depicts that the "getPastDueBalance" channel is **required** by the caller and is **provided** by the callee block.

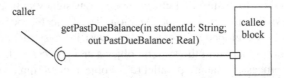

Fig. 1.   Channel-based value-passing interaction

The external environment uses a "type 1 interaction" to interact with a block. We formally describe the channel-based value-passing "type 1 interaction" as a relation

$G \subseteq B \times K \times \Gamma$, where B is a set of "external environment's sectors" and K is a set of "channel signatures", and Γ is a set of "blocks".

Two blocks use a "type 2 interaction" to interact with each other. We formally describe the channel-based value-passing "type 2 interaction" as a relation $V \subseteq \Gamma \times K \times \Gamma$, where Γ is a set of "blocks", and K is a set of "channel signatures".

We can also formally describe the channel-based value-passing "type 1 or 2 interaction" as a relation $\Delta \subseteq \Theta \times K \times \Gamma$, where Θ is a set of "external environment's actors or blocks", K is a set of "channel signatures", and Γ is a set of "blocks".

3.2 Entities of Channel-Based Multi-queue SBC Process Algebra

As shown in Table 1, we assume a relation K of channel signatures, and use $k_1, k_2...$ to range over K. Further, we let Λ be the set of channel names, and use $ch_1, ch_2...$ to range over Λ. We let Θ be the set of parameters, and use $p_1, p_2...$ to range over Θ. We let G be the relation of type 1 interactions, and use $g_1, g_2...$ to range over G. We let V be the relation of type 2 interactions, and use $v_1, v_2...$ to range over V. We let Δ be the relation of type 1 or 2 interactions, and use $a_1, a_2...$ to range over Δ. We let S be the set of state expressions, and use $s_1, s_2...$ to range over S. Further, we let X be the set of state variables, and use $X_1, X_2...$ to range over X. We let Φ be the set of state Constants, and use $A_1, A_2...$ to range over Φ. We let B be the set of actors, and use $\beta_1, \beta_2...$ to range over B. We let Γ be the set of blocks, and use $b_1, b_2...$ to range over Γ. Finally, we let Ξ be the set of actors or blocks, and use $\rho_1, \rho_2...$ to range over Ξ.

Table 1. Entities of C-M-SBC-PA

Entity set or relation	Entity name	Type of entity	Entity set or relation	Entity name	Type of entity
K	$k_1, k_2...$	channel signatures	S	s_1, s_2	state expressions
Λ	ch_1, ch_2	channel names	X	$X_1, X_2...$	state variables
Θ	$p_1, p_2...$	parameter lists	Φ	$A_1, A_2...$	state constants
G	$g_1, g_2...$	type 1 interactions	B	$\beta_1, \beta_2...$	actors
V	$v_1, v_2...$	type 2 interactions			
Δ	$a_1, a_2...$	type 1 or 2 interactions	Γ	$b_1, b_2...$	blocks
	I, J,...	indexing sets	Ξ	$\rho_1, \rho_2...$	actors or blocks

3.3 Mathematics of Channel-Based Multi-queue SBC Process Algebra

In addition to interactions, we need a means to constitute new states from old ones. The basic operators always appear in some form or others, allowing sequentialization of interactions or summation of states or parallel composition of states or recursive definition of a state or replication of a state or null state.

Summation of States: The binary operator "+", summation, combines two state expressions as alternatives. For example, the state expression s_1+s_2 can proceed non-deterministically either as the state expression s_1 or the state expression s_2; as soon as one performs its first interaction the other is discarded.

Parallel Composition of States: Parallel composition of two state expressions s_1 and s_2, usually written $s_1 \| s_2$, is the key stereotype distinguishing the process algebras from sequential models of state executions. Parallel composition permits the executions in s_1 and s_2 to proceed independently and concurrently.

Recursive Definition of a State: The operators presented so far depict only finite interaction and are therefore insufficient for full computability, which contains non-terminating (or looping) behavior. Recursion is the operator that allows finite descriptions of infinite behavior. For example, $\mathbf{fix}(X = s)$ is understood as abbreviating the recursive definition of an infinite behavior denoted by the "X" state variable.

Replication of a State: Replication is the other operator that allows finite descriptions of infinite behavior of a state. For example, replication $!s$ is understood as abbreviating the parallel composition of a countably infinite number of s state expressions.

Null State: Process algebras usually also include a null state expression, denoted as *STOP*, which has no interaction points. It is completely inactive and its unique intention is to act as the inductive anchor on top of which some interesting state expressions can be generated.

3.4 Syntax of Channel-Based Multi-queue SBC Process Algebra

The syntax of C-M-SBC-PA is defined by the following Backus-Naur Form (BNF) grammar, as shown in Fig. 2.

(1) <System> ::= <FixIFD> {" $\|$ " <FixIFD>}

(2) <FixIFD> ::= "**fix**(" <State_Variable>"="<IFD>
                        " $\bullet$ " <State_Variable> ")"

(3) <IFD> ::= <Type_1_Interaction> {" $\bullet$ " Type_1_Or_2_Interaction>}

(4) <Type_1_Or_2_Interaction> ::= <Type_1_Interaction>

                        | <Type_2_Interaction>

Fig. 2. Channel-based value-passing interaction

Rule 1 describes that parallel composition of one or more recursive interaction flow diagrams (i.e. FixIFD) defines the C-M-SBC-PA state expression of a system.

Rule 2 describes that a recursive interaction flow diagram (i.e. FixIFD) is defined by the recursion of an interaction flow diagram (*i.e.* IFD).

Rule 3 describes that an interaction flow diagram (i.e. IFD) is defined by a type_1 interaction (i.e. Type_1_Interaction) followed by zero or more type_1_or_type_2 interactions (i.e. Type_1_Or_2_Interaction).

Rule 4 describes that the type_1_or_2 interaction (i.e. Type_1_Or_2_Interaction) is either a type_1 interaction (i.e. Type_1_Interaction) or a type_2 interaction (i.e. Type_2_Interaction).

3.5 State Expression of a System in Channel-Based Multi-queue SBC Process Algebra

In C-M-SBC-PA, the state expression of a sharing economy service systems design is defined as $\bigsqcup_{i=1,m} \text{FixIFD}_i$ and the expression of FixIFD$_i$ is defined as $\textbf{fix}(X_i = \bullet_{j=1,n} a_{ij} \bullet X_i)$, where $a_{i1} = g_{i1}$ for all $i \in 1,m$. To combine them together, we summarize that in C-M-SBC-PA the MBSE sharing economy service systems design is then formally defined as "$\textbf{fix}(X_1 = g_{11} \bullet a_{12} \bullet a_{13} \bullet \ldots \bullet a_{1n} \bullet X_1)\bigsqcup$ $\textbf{fix}(X_2 = g_{21} \bullet a_{22} \bullet a_{23} \bullet \ldots \bullet a_{2n} \bullet X_2) \bigsqcup \ldots \bigsqcup \textbf{fix}(X_m = g_{m1} \bullet a_{m2} \bullet a_{m3} \bullet \ldots \bullet a_{mn} \bullet X_m)$".

3.6 Transitional Semantics of Channel-Based Multi-queue SBC Process Algebra

In giving meaning to C-M-SBC-PA, we shall use the following transition system

$$(S, \Delta, T)$$

which consists of a set S of state expressions, a set Δ of "type 1 or 2 interactions", and a relation $T \subseteq S \times \Delta \times S$, where $(s_j, a, s_k) \in T$ is denoted by $s_j \xrightarrow{a} s_k$.

The semantics for S consists in the transition rules of each relation T over $S \times \Delta \times S$. These transition rules will follow the construct of state expressions.

As shown in Fig. 3, we give the complete set of transition rules; the names Prefix, Parallel, Recursion and Constant indicate that the rules are associated respectively with Prefix, Parallel Composition and Recursion and with Constants.

The rule for Prefix can be read as follows: Under any circumstances, we always infer $a \bullet s \xrightarrow{a} s$. That is, a state expression, with an interaction prefixed to it, will use this interaction to accomplish the transition.

There are two transition rules for parallel composition. Rule Parallel$_1$ indicates that from $s_1 \xrightarrow{a} s_1$ we shall infer $s_1 \bigsqcup s_2 \xrightarrow{a} s_1 ' \bigsqcup s_2$. Rule Parallel$_2$ indicates that from $s_2 \xrightarrow{a} s_2$ we shall infer $s_1 \bigsqcup s_2 \xrightarrow{a} s_1 \bigsqcup s_2 '$.

The rule for Constants can be read as follows: the rule of Constants asserts that each Constant has the same transitions as its defining expression.

Based on the C-M-SBC-PA transitional semantics, whenever $s \xrightarrow{a_{11}} \ldots \xrightarrow{a_{mn}} s'$, we call $(a_{11} \ldots a_{mn}, s')$ a derivative of s. It is convenient to collect the derivatives of a state expression s into the C-M-SBC-PA transition graph (TG) of s. We use the C-M-SBC-PA

Prefix	$\dfrac{}{a \bullet s \xrightarrow{a} s}$
Parallel$_1$	$\dfrac{s_1 \xrightarrow{a} s_1'}{s_1 [] s_2 \xrightarrow{a} s_1' [] s_2}$
Parallel$_2$	$\dfrac{s_2 \xrightarrow{a} s_2'}{s_1 [] s_2 \xrightarrow{a} s_1 [] s_2'}$
Recursion	$\dfrac{s\{\mathbf{fix}(X{=}s)/X\} \xrightarrow{a} s'}{\mathbf{fix}(X{=}s) \xrightarrow{a} s'}$
Constant	$\dfrac{s \xrightarrow{a} s'}{A \xrightarrow{a} s'} \quad (A \stackrel{def}{=} s)$

Fig. 3. Transition rules for C-M-SBC-PA

transition graph to define the execution of the entire system, as shown in Fig. 4. In the C-M-SBC-PA transition graph of a system, the state expression is represented by a labeled circle; the edge is used to represent the "transition" between the two state expressions; the starting state expression is usually represented by an arrow with no origin pointing to the state expression.

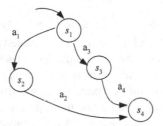

Fig. 4. Diagram of the transition graph TG_1

We can also list the relationships that represent the transition graph. Table 2 shows the relation "TGR_i" of the transition graph "TG_i".

3.7 Transitional Graph of FixIFD in Channel-Based Multi-queue SBC Process Algebra

In C-M-SBC-PA, the state expression of FixIFD$_i$ is formally defined as "$\mathbf{fix}(X_i{=}g_{i1} \bullet a_{i2} \bullet a_{i3} \bullet \ldots \bullet a_{in} \bullet X_i)$". We use the C-M-SBC-PA transition graph TG_i to define the execution of the FixIFD$_i$ state expression, as shown in Fig. 5.

We can also list the relationships that represent the transition graph of the FixIFD$_i$ state expression. Table 3 shows the relation "TGR_i" of the transition graph "TG_i".

Table 2. Relation TGR_1 of the transition graph TG_1

S_1	Δ	S_2
s_1	a_1	s_2
s_2	a_2	s_4
s_1	a_3	s_3
s_3	a_4	s_4

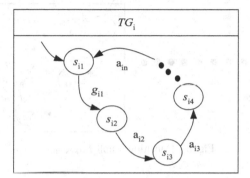

Fig. 5. Transition Graph for FixIFD

Table 3. Relation TGR_i for state expression "FixIFD$_i$"

S_1	Δ	S_1
s_{i1}	g_{i1}	s_{i2}
s_{i2}	a_{i2}	s_{i3}
s_{i3}	a_{i3}	s_{i4}
$\bullet$	$\bullet$	$\bullet$
s_{in-1}	a_{in}	s_{i1}

3.8 Transitional Graph of a System in Channel-Based Multi-queue SBC Process Algebra

In C-M-SBC-PA, the state expression of the MBSE sharing economy service systems design is formally defined as "fix(X1=g11$\bullet$a12$\bullet$a13$\bullet$...$\bullet$a1n$\bullet$X1) $\bigsqcup$ fix(X2=g21$\bullet$a22$\bullet$a23$\bullet$...$\bullet$a2n$\bullet$X2) $\bigsqcup$ ...$\bigsqcup$ fix(Xm=gm1$\bullet$am2$\bullet$am3$\bullet$...$\bullet$amn$\bullet$Xm)".

We use the C-M-SBC-PA transition graph TG_{system} to define the execution of the MBSE sharing economy service systems design, as shown in Fig. 6.

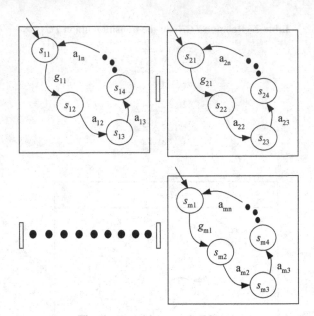

Fig. 6. Transition graph TG_{system}

We can also list the relationships that represent the transition graph of a system. Table 4 shows the relation TGR_{system} of the transition graph TG_{system}.

Table 4. Relation TGR_{system}

S_1	Δ	S_2
s_{11}	g_{11}	s_{12}
s_{12}	a_{12}	s_{13}
s_{13}	a_{13}	s_{14}
•	•	•
s_{1n-1}	a_{1n}	s_{11}

S_1	Δ	S_2
s_{21}	g_{21}	s_{22}
s_{22}	a_{22}	s_{23}
s_{23}	a_{23}	s_{24}
•	•	•
s_{2n-1}	a_{2n}	s_{21}

S_1	Δ	S_2
s_{m1}	g_{m1}	s_{m2}
s_{m2}	a_{m2}	s_{m3}
s_{m3}	a_{m3}	s_{m4}
•	•	•
s_{mn-1}	a_{mn}	s_{m1}

4   Case: Meal Delivery Sharing Economy Service System

4.1   Meal Delivery Sharing Economy Service System

Definitions for the sharing economy come from different disciplines. Examples are economics, business administration, healthcare and law Yang et al. (2018). Sharing economy is an expression referring to a form of collaborative consumption which can be defined as app-based platforms allowing consumers/borrowers to engage in monetized exchanges with providers/lenders through peer-to-peer-based services or temporary access to goods, as shown in Fig. 7.

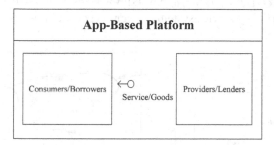

Fig. 7.   Diagram of sharing economy

Meal delivery sharing economy service system (MDSESS) connects customers with couriers who provide the meal delivery service on their own non-commercial vehicles such as UberEATS and ele.me, partners with local restaurants in selected cities around the world and allows customers to order meals and utilizes its existing network to deliver ordered meals in minutes.

Behaviors of the meal delivery sharing economy service system consist of: a) *Registering_Courier_Account* behavior, b) *Placing_an_Order* behavior, c) *Accepting_a_Delivery_Request* behavior, d) *Paying_the_Order* behavior and e) *Rating_the_Courier* behavior.

In the *Registering_Courier_Account* behavior, a platform manager shall use the *Register_Courier_Account_UI* component to input the corresponding data for this courier account registration. After that, the courier account registration data will be saved to the *MDSESS_Database* component. In the *Placing_an_Order* behavior, MDSESS displays all restaurants close to customers. Customers can see the menu and place their orders directly through the app. Once an order is placed, all related data will be saved to the *MDSESS_Database* object. In the *Accepting_a_Delivery_Request* behavior, a courier just taps the screen to accept the delivery request. Once the acceptance is confirmed, all related data will be saved to the *MDSESS_Database* object. In the *Paying_the_Order* behavior, customer uses the *Pay_the_Order_UI* object to accomplish the payment and gets a receipt report. In the *Rating_the_Courier* behavior, customers use the *Rate_the_Courier_UI* object to rate the courier.

4.2 Channel-Based Multi-queue SBC State Expression of the Meal Delivery Sharing Economy Service System

We first use the C-M-SBC-PA to design the meal delivery sharing economy service system. The channel-based multi-queue state expression of the meal delivery sharing economy service system, sMDSESS, is defined as "fix(X1=g11•v12•X1) □ fix(X2=g21•v22•g23•g24•v25•X2) □ fix(X3=g31•v32•g33•g34•v35•X3) □ fix(X4=g41•v42•g43•X4) □ fix(X5=g51•v52•X5)".

We use the C-M-SBC-PA transition graph TG_{MDSESS} defined as "$TG_1 \square TG_2 \square TG_3 \square TG_4 \square TG_5$" to represent the state expression of the meal delivery sharing economy service systems design, as shown in Fig. 8.

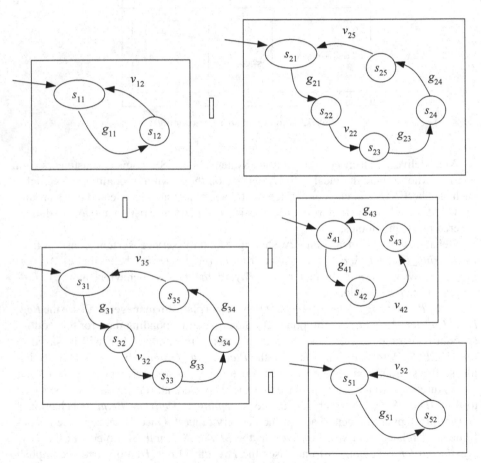

Fig. 8. Transition graph TG_{MDSESS}

We use a TG relation $TGR_{MDSESS} \subseteq S_1 \times \Xi \times \Lambda \times \Theta \times \Gamma \times S_2$ defined as "$TGR_1 \cup TGR_2 \cup TGR_3 \cup TGR_4 \cup TGR_5$" to represent the C-M-SBC-PA transition graph TG_{MDSESS} of the state expression of the MBSE meal delivery sharing economy service systems design, as shown in Table 5.

Table 5. Relation TGR_{OSS}

S_1	Ξ	Λ	Θ	Γ	S_2
			g_{31}		
s_{31}	Courier	Show_a_Delivery_Request_CALL		Accept_a_Delivery_Request_UI	s_{32}
			v_{32}		
s_{32}	Accept_a_Delivery_Request_UI	SQL_Select_a_Delivery_Request	in Courier_Number; out a_Delivery_Request_Query	MDSESS_Database	s_{33}
			v_{33}		
s_{33}	Courier	Show_a_Delivery_Request_RETURN	out a_Delivery_Request	Accept_a_Delivery_Request_UI	s_{34}
			v_{34}		
s_{34}	Courier	Accept_a_Delivery_Request	in Accept_a_Delivery_Request_Form	Accept_a_Delivery_Request_UI	s_{35}
			g_{35}		
s_{35}	Accept_a_Delivery_Request_UI	SQL_Insert_Accept_a_Delivery_Request	in Accept_a_Delivery_Request_Query	MDSESS_Database	s_{31}

S_1	Ξ	Λ	Θ	Γ	S_2
			g_{11}		
s_{11}	Platform_Manager	Register_Courier_Account	in Register_Courier_Account_Form	Register_Courier_Account_UI	s_{12}
			v_{12}		
s_{12}	Register_Courier_Account_UI	SQL_Insert_Register_Courier_Account	in Register_Courier_Account_Query	MDSESS_Database	s_{11}

S_1	Ξ	Λ	Θ	Γ	S_2
			g_{21}		
s_{21}	Customer	Show_Restaurants_and_Meals_CALL		Place_an_Order_UI	s_{22}
			v_{22}		
s_{21}	Place_an_Order_UI	Customer_GPS_Positioning	out Customer_GPS_Coordinates	Customer_GPS_P (P= AAA000 to ZZZ999)	s_{23}
			g_{23}		
s_{23}	Customer	Show_Restaurants_and_Meals_RETURN	out Restaurants_and_Meals	Place_an_Order_UI	s_{24}
			g_{24}		
s_{24}	Customer	Place_an_Order	in Place_an_Order_Form	Place_an_Order_UI	s_{25}
			v_{25}		
s_{25}	Place_an_Order_UI	SQL_Insert_Place_an_Order	in Place_an_Order_Query	MDSESS_Database	s_{21}

S_1	Ξ	Λ	Θ	Γ	S_2
			g_{41}		
s_{41}	Customer	Pay_the_Order_CALL		Pay_the_Order_UI	s_{42}
			v_{42}		
s_{42}	Pay_the_Order_UI	SQL_Insert_Pay_the_Order	in Pay_the_Order_Query	MDSESS_Database	s_{43}
			g_{43}		
s_{43}	Customer	Pay_the_Order_RETURN	out Receipt_Report	Pay_the_Order_UI	s_{41}

S_1	Ξ	Λ	Θ	Γ	S_2
			g_{51}		
s_{51}	Customer	Rate_the_Courier	in Stars	Rate_the_Courier_UI	s_{52}
			g_{52}		
s_{52}	Rate_the_Courier_UI	SQL_Insert_Rate_the_Courier	in Rate_the_Courier_Query	MDSESS_Database	s_{51}

5 Conclusions

This paper proposes the channel-based multi-queue structure-behavior coalescence process algebra (C-M-SBC-PA) as the modeling language for model singularity of the MBSE sharing economy service systems design. In C-M-SBC-PA, only one single diagram is used to specify the semantics of the design of the sharing economy service system. In general, when the C-M-SBC-PA method is used, the model consistency in the MBSE sharing economy service system design will be fully guaranteed.

Acknowledgement. The authors wish to express their thanks to the anonymous references for their valuable comments, which help clarify subtle points and triggered new ideas.

References

Allaki, D., Dahchour, M., Ennouaary, A.: A new taxonomy of inconsistencies in UML models with their detection methods for better MDE. Int. J. Comput. Sci. Appl. **12**(1), 48–65 (2015)

Apvrille, L., Courtiat, J., Lohr, C., de Saqui-Sannes, P.: TURTLE: a real-time UML profile supported by a formal validation toolkit. IEEE Trans. Softw. Eng. **30**, 473–487 (2004)

Arlow, J., Neustadt, I.: UML 2 and the Unified Process: Practical Object-Oriented Analysis and Design. Addison-Wesley, Boston (2005)

Bashir, R.S., Lee, S.P., Khan, S.U.R.: UML Models consistency management: guidelines for software quality manager. Int. J. Inf. Manage. **36**, 883–899 (2016)

Blaha, M.R., Rumbaugh, J.R.: Object-Oriented Modeling and Design with UML, 2nd edn. Pearson, London (2004)

Dori, D.: Model-Based Systems Engineering with OPM and SysML. Springer, New York (2016). https://doi.org/10.1007/978-1-4939-3295-5

Dori, D.: Object-Process Methodology: A Holistic Systems Paradigm. Springer, New York (2002). https://doi.org/10.1007/978-3-642-56209-9

Friedenthal, S., Moore, A., Steiner, R.: A Practical Guide to SysML The Systems Modeling Language, 3rd edn. Morgan Kaufmann, Burlington (2014)

ISO TC-184 (Technical Committee on Industrial Automation Systems and Integration). ISO 18629 Process Specification Languages (PSL)

Malgouyres, H., Motet, G.: A UML model consistency verification approach based on meta-modeling formalization. In: Proceedings of the 2006 ACM Symposium on Applied Computing, pp. 1804–1809 (2006)

OMG: Action Language for Foundational UML (Alf). Object Management Group, Needham, MA (2013a)

OMG: Semantics of a Foundational Subset for Executable UML Models (fUML). Object Management Group, Needham, MA (2013b)

Paige, R.F., Brooke, P.J., Ostroff, J.S.: Metamodel-based Model Conformance and Multiview Consistency Checking. ACM Trans. Softw. Eng. Methodol. **16**, 11 (2007)

Przigoda, N., Wille, R., Drechsler, R.: Analyzing inconsistencies in UML/OCL models. J. Circ. Syst. Comput. **25**(3), 1640021 (2016)

Qiu, G.-P., Sun, S.-P., Lee, Z., Chao, W.S.: A structure–behavior coalescence approach for model singularity. In: Bhatia, S.K., Tiwari, S., Mishra, K.K., Trivedi, M.C. (eds.) Advances in Computer Communication and Computational Sciences. AISC, vol. 759, pp. 343–350. Springer, Singapore (2019). https://doi.org/10.1007/978-981-13-0341-8_31

Sundararajan, A.: The Sharing Economy: The End of Employment and the Rise of Crowd-Based Capitalism. The MIT Press, Cambridge (2016)

Weilkiens, T.: Systems Engineering with SysML/UML: Modeling, Analysis, Design. Morgan Kaufmann, Burlington (2008)

Yang, Y.-C., Tsai, C.-T., Chao, W. S.: A structure-behavior coalescence systems modeling approach for service systems design. In: Proceedings of the 2018 International Conference on HCI in Business, Government, and Organizations (2018)

Forecasting the Subway Volume Using Local Linear Kernel Regression

Yu-chen Yang[1,2,3], Chao Ding[1,2,3], and Yong Jin[1,2,3(✉)]

[1] National Sun Yat-sen University, Kaohsiung City, Taiwan
`ycyang@mis.nsysu.edu.tw`
[2] The Hong Kong Polytechnic University, Hung Hom, Hong Kong
`jimmy.jin@polyu.edu.hk`
[3] University of Hong Kong, Pok Fu Lam, Hong Kong
`chao.ding@hku.hk`

Abstract. Entrusted by the Kaohsiung Rapid Transit Corporation (KRTC), this study attempts to devise a more effective methodology to forecast the passenger volume of the subway system in the city of Kaohsiung, Taiwan. We propose a local linear kernel model to incorporate different weights for each realized observations. It enables us to capture richer information and improve rate of accuracy. We compare different methodologies, for example, $ARIMA$, Best in-sample fit $ARIMA$, linear model, and their rolling versions with our proposed local linear kernel regression model by examining the in-sample and out-of-sample performances. Our results indicate that the proposed rolling local linear kernel regression model performs the best in forecasting the passenger volume in terms of smaller prediction errors in a wide range of measurements.

Keywords: Subway Volume Forecasting · Local linear kernel regression · $ARIMA$ model

1 Introduction

Kaohsiung city is the second largest city in Taiwan with a population of approximately 2.77 million. The Kaohsiung Mass Rapid Transit System (hereafter "KMRT"), the city's subway system, covers the metropolitan areas of the city and is operated by the Kaohsiung Rapid Transit Corporation (hereafter "KRTC") under the contract with the local government. KMRT consists of two lines with 36 stations covering a distance of 42.7 km. The Red Line and the Orange Line started their operation for services on March 9 and September 14,

Y. Jin—We thank the anonymous reviewers, the track associate editor, and the participants at Taiwan Summer Workshop on Information Management for helpful discussions and useful suggestions. Yong Jin also acknowledges the financial support of the PolyU Central Research Grant (Project No. G-YBZV). This work is partially supported by the Intelligent Electronic Commerce Research Center from the Featured Areas Research Center Program within the framework of the Higher Education Sprout Project by the Ministry of Education (MOE) in Taiwan.

© Springer Nature Switzerland AG 2020
F. F.-H. Nah and K. Siau (Eds.): HCII 2020, LNCS 12204, pp. 254–265, 2020.
https://doi.org/10.1007/978-3-030-50341-3_20

2008, respectively. The number of passengers that KMRT served in 2014 reached about 168,093 people per day and the accumulated volume of passengers has been over 200 million people since it is launched in early 2008.

The number of the passengers has been increasing drastically since year 2008. In order to better plan and operate the transportation systems[1], understanding and forecasting the number of passengers are extremely crucial. Prior literature has attempted to develop appropriate models for forecasting passenger traffic flows, e.g. air traffic flows (Carson et al. 2011; Fildes, Wei and Ismail 2011), the passenger numbers in trains (Nielsen et al. 2014), and the freight markets (Batchelor et al. 2007). KRTC also studies the forecasting of the subway volumes internally and publishes a report titled "The Study of Kaohsiung Subway Volume Forecasting - $ARIMA$ Approach" (hereafter "the REPORT (2014)").

Carson et al. (2011) propose an aggregating individual markets (AIM) approach to predict air travel demand, while Fildes et al. (2011) examine several popular approaches to forecast short- to medium-term air passenger traffic flow. Nielsen et al. (2014) present an innovative counting technique using the weighting systems installed in trains to predict the passenger numbers in the capital region of Denmark. Batchelor et al. (2007) investigate the performance of prevalent time series models, including $ARIMA$ models, VAR models, and $VECM$ models, in forecasting spot and freight rate. Batchelor et al. (2007) find that VECM models generate the best in-sample fit and that all models beat a random walk benchmark in out-of-sample forecasting. The REPORT (2014) applies the $ARMIA$ model to fit the time series data of the Kaohsiung subway volumes and tests the in-sample performance over the historical time series.

Due to the unsatisfactory predictive capability of the current $ARIMA$ models, the KRTC entrusts us to conduct further research on forecasting the number of passengers with smaller prediction errors. We first consider the linear models, which are able to capture the additional local economy and weather information, see Woodridge (2002), Jin et al. (2014). Fan (1992, 1993) proposes an innovative approach in the estimation of unknown regression functions using kernel weighted local linear methods[2], called the local linear kernel regression. The basic prediction problems are the same for both linear model and local linear kernel regression, however, the coefficients are estimated using the weighted realized information in local linear kernel regression, which helps to capture the nonlinearity in historical data. Li and Racine (2004) further discuss how to select the optimal bandwidths in the above mentioned kernel weighting problem using the cross-validation method. Several applications are studied using Li and Racine (2004)'smethodology, for example, Zhu (2014) shows that the local linear kernel regression can provide a better way to predict the crude oil price with much better prediction accuracy. In this paper, we will also apply the local linear kernel regression method in dealing with the subway volume data.

---

[1] For example, daily operations optimizing, strategic planning and revenue distributing among the operations and etc.

[2] For further reference, see Ruppert and Wand (1994), Fan and Gijbels (1995) and etc.

In this article, using the data provided by KRTC and the Kaohsiung City Government, we compare several different prediction methods, including $ARIMA$ models as in the REPORT (2014), linear model, local linear kernel regression and their rolling versions. Both in-sample and out-of-sample tests are conducted and the rolling local linear kernel regression demonstrates the best prediction abilities in forecasting the future subway volumes with considerably small prediction errors. We suggest that the KRTC consider our proposed model to conduct future KMRT demand predictions.

The remainder of the paper is organized as follows. The next section presents our proposed forecasting methodologies. Section 3 describes the data and pre-treatment. We run the unit root test and construct the predictive models. The comparison of different prediction models are then analyzed in Sect. 4. Finally, Sect. 5 provides discussions and conclusions.

2   The Model

2.1   The Basic Prediction Problem

Consider the basic prediction problem with the following general regression form:

$$y = g(x) + \mu$$

where x is the vector of explanatory variables, y is the response variable and μ is the noise term.

In the current application of $ARIMA$ model, only the information of the time series $\{y_i\}_{i=1}^n$ is captured. Following the REPORT (2014), we also include the local gasoline price, the local unemployment rate, the logarithm of the rainfall level, and the temperature of Kaohsiung and others as the explanatory variables, thus the vector x contains not only the lagged information of y, but also the other explanatory variables.

Linear Model. When $g(\cdot)$ is a linear function, the prediction problem is

$$y = a + x'b + \mu$$

and the parameters are simply estimated by the ordinary least squire method,

$$min_{a,b} \sum_{i=1}^n (Y_i - a - X_i'b)^2$$

where (Y_i, X_i) are sample realizations. In the linear model, the coefficients a, b are fixed, independent of the input vector x.

Local Linear Kernel Regression. Following Fan (1992, 1993), the information for each realized observation (Y_i, X_i) should not be equally weighted in estimating the coefficients of a, b for different input vector x, if considering the prediction model as a local linear function

$$y = a(x) + x'b(x) + \mu,$$

and the information is weighted by the kernel $K(\frac{X_i - x}{h})$, the parameters $a(x), b(x)$ are estimated by

$$min_{a,b} \sum_{i=1}^{n} (Y_i - a - (X_i - x)'b)^2 K(\frac{X_i - x}{h})$$

where (Y_i, X_i) are sample realizations, $K(\cdot)$ is the kernel function, h is the bandwidth.

The optimal bandwidth h can be selected using cross validation methods (Li and Racine 2004) as below:

$$CV_f(h_1, ..., h_s) = \frac{1}{n^2} \sum_{i=1}^{n} \sum_{j=1}^{n} \bar{K}_h(X_i, X_j) - \frac{2}{n(n-1)} \sum_{i=1}^{n} \sum_{j \neq i, j=1}^{n} K_h(X_i, X_j)$$

when using the integrated squared error as the loss function.

Zhu (2014) shows that the local linear kernel regression can provide a better way to predict the crude oil price with much better prediction accuracy. In this paper, we also apply the local linear kernel regression method in dealing with the subway volume data.

3   Data

3.1   Data Description and Pre-treatment

Our data is provided by Kaohsiung Rapid Transit Corporation and Kaohsiung City Government. The database includes five time series: the logarithm of the monthly subway volume, the local gasoline price, the local unemployment rate, the logarithm of the rainfall level, and the temperature of Kaohsiung[3]. The database spans from April 2008 to December 2013, including a total of 69 observations for each time series.

We impose three unit root tests on the logarithm of the monthly volume and other explanatory variables (Augmented Dickey-Fuller test, KPSS test and Philipps-Perron test). Table 1 demonstrates the three unit root test statistics and their p-values. Only the $ln(volume)$ cannot reject the existence of unit root

---

[3] We follow the REPORT (2014), which suggests the local gasoline price, the local unemployment rate, the logarithm of the rainfall level, and the temperature of Kaohsiung may affect the subway volume, and all the times series are collected from Kaohsiung City Government.

Table 1. Unit root test

	ADF test	PP test	KPSS test
ln(volume)	−5.2432	−8.2428	2.9062
	(< 0.01)	(< 0.01)	(< 0.01)
Gasoline	−4.3656	−2.8406	1.9320
	(< 0.01)	(0.2335)	(< 0.01)
Unemployment	−2.5096	−2.4148	1.5869
	(0.3681)	(0.4066)	(< 0.01)
ln(rainfall)	−3.9612	−4.3683	0.0398
	(0.0167)	(< 0.01)	(> 0.1)
Temperature	−5.0849	−3.4333	0.0432
	(< 0.01)	(0.0579)	(> 0.1)

Table 1 demonstrates the three unit root test statistics and their p-values. The three unit root tests are Augmented Dickey-Fuller test, KPSS test and Philipps-Perron test.

at 1% level, while there are insufficient evidence to argue the four explanatory variables also have the unit root[4]. Thus we take the first order differences of $ln(volume)$ and keep the other explanatory variables in the predictive model.

3.2 Predictive Models

After accounting for the unit root issues, we set up the basic predictive model as below:

$$\Delta ln(Volume)_t = \alpha + \beta_1 \Delta ln(Volume)_{t-1} + \beta_2 ln(Volume)_{t-1} + \beta_3 Gas_{t-1}$$
$$+ \beta_4 Unemployment_{t-1} + \beta_5 Ln(Rainfall)_{t-1} + \beta_6 Temperature_{t-1} + \epsilon_t$$

where $ln(Volume)_t$ is the logarithm of the subway volume at time t, Gas_{t-1} is the local gasoline price at time $t-1$, $Unemployment_{t-1}$ is the local unemployment rate at time $t-1$, $Ln(Rainfall)_{t-1}$ is the logarithm of the rainfall level at time $t-1$, $Temperature_{t-1}$ is the temperature of Kaohsiung at time $t-1$. Thus given the information at time $t-1$, we would like to forecast the difference in logarithm of the subway volume at time t, then obtain the subway volume prediction at time t.

In the next section, we would like to apply $ARIMA$, linear model and local linear kernel regression to demonstrate the predictive capability in both training and holdout samples.

---

[4] Because the unit root test results may be driven by the "Pseudo Long Memory Phenomenon" in a piecewise stationary time series as documented in Jin and Yau (2012), therefore we apply multiple unit root tests here.

4   Empirical Results

With the objective of providing a better forecasting method, we compare four different methodologies including the REPORT $ARIMA$, the best in-sample fitted $ARIMA$, the linear model and the local linear kernel model. We divide the sample into two groups: 1. we use the first 50 observations as the training sample, which is used to construct the fitted model; 2. the remaining 19 observations as the holdout sample, which is used to test performance of the constructed model.

In the REPORT (2014), the internal statisticians only apply the $ARIMA$ model and the best fitted model is $ARIMA(0,1,1)$. However, they only consider the in-sample fitting and testing. Therefore in this paper, we consider both $ARIMA(0,1,1)$ and the best in-sample fitted $ARIMA$ using the in-sample observations (50 observations). Further we also utilize the linear model and the local linear kernel model to capture additional information provided by Kaohsiung Rapid Transit Corporation and the local government.

4.1   Performance Measures

We implement several performance measures which are common in literature (e.g. Hyndman and Koehler 2006; Steyerberg et al. 2010; Zhu, 2014; Zhong et al. 2015 and etc.). Our performance measures include Mean Squared Prediction Error (MSPE), Mean Squared Prediction Percentage Error (MSPE), Mean Absolute Percentage Error (MAPE), R^2, Directional Accuracy Ratio and etc.

MEAN SQUARED PREDICTION ERROR (MSPE)
Mean Squared Prediction Error (MSPE) is a widely used performance measure (Hyndman and Koehler 2006) to test the validity of a prediction model with the following form:

$$MSPE = \frac{1}{N} \sum_{i=1}^{N} (Y_i - \hat{Y}_i)^2$$

where N is the number of observations in the training/holdout sample, Y_i is the realized observation and $\hat{Y}_i$ is the prediction value. MSPE is to measure the dispersion of the realized observations and the prediction values.

MEAN SQUARED PREDICTION PERCENTAGE ERROR (MSPPE)
Mean Squared Prediction Percentage Error (MSPPE) is a percentage version of the dispersion between the realized observations and the prediction values, with the following form:

$$MSPPE = \frac{1}{N} \sum_{i=1}^{N} (\frac{Y_i - \hat{Y}_i}{Y_i})^2.$$

MEAN ABSOLUTE PERCENTAGE ERROR (MAPE)
Stutzer (1996) and Zhong et al. (2015) argue that the MAPE is a more robust dispersion measure in testing the pricing errors. Thus we also include MAPE as an alternative dispersion measure as below:

$$MAPE = \frac{1}{N} \sum_{i=1}^{N} |\frac{Y_i - \hat{Y}_i}{Y_i}|.$$

ρ (CORRELATION)

ρ is the correlation between the prediction values and the true observations, which not only measures the level of co-movement but also measures the direction of co-movement (the sign of ρ).

R^2 (EXPLAINED VARIATION)

R^2 is a widely used performance measure for continuous outcomes in both in-sample test and out-of-sample test. Steyerberg et al. (2010) address that R^2 is an overall performance measure, with the following alternative definition:

$$R^2 = \rho^2$$

where ρ is the correlation.

DIRECTIONAL ACCURACY RATIO

Directional Accuracy Ratio is a descriptive measure, which measures the percentage accuracy in direction in the prediction values:

$$Directional\ Accuracy\ Ratio = \frac{\#(sign(Y_i) = sign(\hat{Y}_i))}{N}.$$

4.2 Empirical Results

In the REPORT (2014), only *ARIMA* model and in-sample performance are discussed. However, in a forecasting problem, testing the performance in the holdout sample is much more important than just testing in the training sample. Therefore in this section we will discuss both in-sample and out-of-sample performances of different methods. There are four basic prediction models addressed in our prediction comparisons:

1. REPORT *ARIMA*
   The REPORT *ARIMA* is the prediction model mentioned in the REPORT (2014), i.e. $ARIMA(0,1,1)$. The coefficients are estimated by the training sample.
2. Best In-sample fitted *ARIMA*
   The best in-sample fitted *ARIMA* is the prediction model with the best AIC, AICc and BIC performance in running the training sample, i.e. $ARIMA(1,1,0)$[5].
3. Linear Model
   The linear model is the model mentioned in Sect. 2.1.1.
4. Local Linear Kernel Regression
   The local linear kernel regression is the model mentioned in Sect. 2.1.2.

---

[5] $ARIMA(0,1,1)$: AIC $= -69.18$; AICc $= -68.92$; BIC $= -65.4$. $ARIMA(1,1,0)$: AIC $= -66.38$; AICc $= -66.12$; BIC $= -62.6$.

In-Sample Comparison. In-sample comparison examines the in-sample performance on the training sample after calibrating the prediction models by the training sample. We first fit the models using training data, then test their performance. Please notice that in-sample testing does not examine the predictive capability but shows how much variation (in the training sample) can be explained by the fitted models. Figure 1 shows the in-sample fitted time series ($ln(Volume)$) for four different fitting methods (REPORT $ARIMA$, Best-fit $ARIMA$, Linear Model, Local Linear Kernel Regression) and all the models provide satisfactory performance in in-sample fitting.

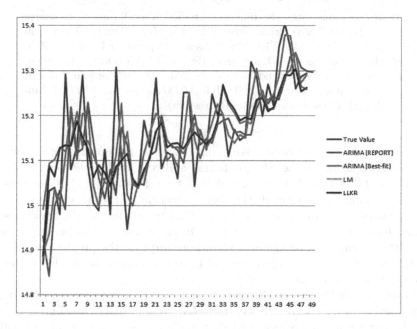

Fig. 1. In-sample fitted time series

Figure 1 shows the in-sample fitted time series ($ln(Volume)$) for four different fitting methods (REPORT $ARIMA$, Best-fit $ARIMA$, Linear Model, Local Linear Kernel Regression).

Table 2 demonstrates the different prediction performance measures (Mean Squared Prediction Error (MSPE), Mean Squared Prediction Percentage Error (MSPPE), Mean Absolute Percentage Error (MAPE), R^2 (Explained Variation), ρ (Correlation) and DAR (Directional Accuracy Ratio)) of the dependent variable $\Delta ln(Volume)$ for four different in-sample fitting methods (REPORT $ARIMA$, Best-fit $ARIMA$, Linear Model, Local Linear Kernel Regression) . Two $ARIMA$ models provide a better overall performance and a higher directional accuracy ratio. They can explain the variation by around 80%. However, the linear model and the local linear kernel regression model have much smaller mean squared errors and two percentage error measures.[6]

---

[6] We delete the two observations with the true value 0 in calculating the percentage error measures.

Table 2. In-sample performance

	ARIMA(REPORT)	ARIMA(Best-fit)	LM	LLKR
MSPE	0.013	0.014	0.009	0.007
MSPPE	21.678	14.521	4.019	2.724
MAPE	1.913	1.982	1.253	1.098
R^2	0.799	0.776	0.443	0.570
ρ	0.894	0.881	0.665	0.755
DAR	0.857	0.857	0.735	0.755

Table 2 demonstrates the different prediction performance measures (Mean Squared Prediction Error (MSPE), Mean Squared Prediction Percentage Error (MSPPE), Mean Absolute Percentage Error (MAPE), R^2 (Explained Variation), ρ (Correlation) and DAR (Directional Accuracy Ratio)) of the dependent variable $\Delta ln(Volume)$ for four different in-sample fitting methods (REPORT $ARIMA$, Best-fit $ARIMA$, Linear Model, Local Linear Kernel Regression).

Out-of-Sample Comparison. We mainly focus on the out-of-sample comparison because it demonstrates the prediction ability in a *Holdout Sample*. Notice that the $ARIMA$ models have limited long term forecasting abilities, thus we propose a rolling version for all the four prediction methods: at any time t in holdout sample, we will use all the observations from 1 to t as the training sample, and forecast the value at time $t + 1$. On one hand, we can benefit from all up-to-date information; on the other hand, we improve the prediction ability of $ARIMA$ model a lot.[7] Therefore, we will have a total of eight prediction models to compare in this section.

Figure 2 shows the in-sample fitted time series ($ln(Volume)$) for eight different prediction methods (REPORT $ARIMA$, Best-fit $ARIMA$, Linear Model, Local Linear Kernel Regression and their rolling versions). Overall, the rolling versions provide a better predictive capacity in fitting the out-of-sample time series than the non-rolling models.

Table 3 demonstrates the different prediction performance measures (Mean Squared Prediction Error (MSPE), Mean Squared Prediction Percentage Error (MSPPE), Mean Absolute Percentage Error (MAPE), R^2 (Explained Variation), ρ (Correlation) and DAR (Directional Accuracy Ratio)) of the dependent variable $\Delta ln(Volume)$ for eight different prediction methods (REPORT $ARIMA$, Best-fit $ARIMA$, Linear Model, Local Linear Kernel Regression and their rolling versions). For non-rolling versions, two $ARIMA$ models have smaller MSPE, MSPPE and MAPE. However, their prediction points have almost zero variation explanatory power in either R^2 or Directional Accuracy Ratio; this is mainly

---

[7] For example, the $ARIMA(0, 1, 1)$ has very weak prediction ability, because according to the formula, $Y_t = Y_{t-1} + \rho\epsilon_{t-1} + \epsilon_t$, we cannot forecast $t + 2$ value with any variations. Similarly in our results, the non-rolling version predicted values are constant for $t + 1$ to $t + 19$.

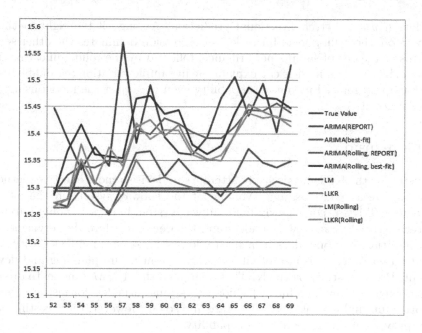

Fig. 2. Out-of-sample fitted time series

Table 3. Out-of-sample performance

	ARIMA(RE)	ARIMA(Bf)	LM	LLKR	ARIMA(R, RE)	ARIMA(R, Bf)	LM(R)	LLKR(R)
MSPE	0.011	0.011	0.016	0.022	0.014	0.016	0.009	0.009
MSPPE	1.000	0.999	11.710	27.893	2.209	25.082	1.895	1.498
MAPE	1.000	1.000	2.168	2.993	1.303	2.358	1.151	0.999
R^2	NA	0.108	0.523	0.557	0.539	0.176	0.421	0.416
ρ	NA	0.329	0.723	0.746	−0.734	−0.420	0.649	0.645
DAR	0.000	0.222	0.500	0.500	0.222	0.389	0.556	0.556

Table 3 demonstrates the different prediction performance measures (Mean Squared Prediction Error (MSPE), Mean Squared Prediction Percentage Error (MSPPE), Mean Absolute Percentage Error (MAPE), R^2 (Explained Variation), ρ (Correlation) and DAR (Directional Accuracy Ratio)) of the dependent variable $\Delta ln(Volume)$ for eight different prediction methods (REPORT $ARIMA$ (marked with RE), Best-fit $ARIMA$ (marked with Bf), Linear Model, Local Linear Kernel Regression and their rolling versions (marked with R)).

because $ARIMA$ model has no long term prediction power thus there is no variation in the prediction values when using the $ARIMA$ model. Among all the four methods, local linear kernel regression provides the highest R^2 and considerably small MSPE. Linear model provides slightly weaker, but still satisfactory performance in predicting the subway volume in the holdout sample.

The rolling methods provide better prediction performances for all four methods than the non-rolling versions. Compared with the $ARIMA$ models, our two proposed methodologies demonstrate lower in prediction error measures (MSPE, MSPPE and MAPE), higher variation explanation measure R^2, larger positive correlation ρ and better directional prediction. Among all the eight methods comparison, the rolling local linear kernel regression dominates the other seven in terms of the out-of-sample performance, followed by the rolling linear model. Though the $ARIMA$ models can explain the in-sample variation reasonably well, they have very limited predictive capability even we adjust the model using the rolling method.

5   Conclusion

Entrusted by the KRTC, this study attempts to devise a more effective methodology to forecast the passenger volume of the subway system in the city of Kaohsiung, Taiwan. For a newly-built subway system in a metropolitan area, it is utterly crucial to accurately understand the demand before the service is put into operation. Not only does it facilitate flow of passenger, public security, and operation efficiency, it is also of vital importance in future planning and development. Previous study by the KRTC has applied the $ARIMA$ model to predict the passenger volume in a linear fashion by various variables, for instance, gasoline price, unemployment rate, temperate and so on. However, there is still room for improvement on the predictive capability.

In this study, we propose a local linear kernel model to incorporate different weights for each realized observations. It enables us to capture richer information and improve rate of accuracy. To this end, we compare different methodologies, for example, $ARIMA$, Best in-sample fit $ARIMA$, linear model, and their rolling versions with our proposed local linear kernel regression model by testing the in-sample and out-of-sample performances. Our results indicate that the proposed rolling local linear kernel regression model performs the best in forecasting the passenger volume in terms of smaller prediction errors in a wide range of measurements. Because of the adjusted weights through the kernel function, the predictive capability of the rolling local linear kernel regression model outperforms all the other tested models. In conclusion, we suggest that the KRTC adopt the proposed model for future demand predictions.

References

Batchelor, R., Alizadeh, A., Visvikis, I.: Forecasting spot and forward prices in the international freight market. Int. J. Forecast. **23**(1), 101–114 (2007)

Carson, R.T., Cenesizoglu, T., Parker, R.: Forecasting (aggregate) demand for US commercial air travel. Int. J. Forecast. **27**(3), 923–941 (2011)

Fan, J.: Design-adaptive nonparametric regression. J. Am. Stat. Assoc. **87**(420), 998–1004 (1992)

• Fan, J.: Local linear regression smoothers and their minimax efficiencies. Ann. Stat. **21**, 196–216 (1993)

Fan, J., Gijbels, I.: Data-driven bandwidth selection in local polynomial fitting: variable bandwidth and spatial adaptation. J. Roy. Stat. Soc. Ser. B (Methodol.) **57**, 371–394 (1995)

Fildes, R., Wei, Y., Ismail, S.: Evaluating the forecasting performance of econometric models of air passenger traffic flows using multiple error measures. Int. J. Forecast. **27**(3), 902–922 (2011)

Hyndman, R.J., Koehler, A.B.: Another look at measures of forecast accuracy. Int. J. Forecast. **22**(4), 679–688 (2006)

Jin, Y., Nimalendran M., Ray, S.: Volatility and Directional Information-Based Trading in Options. Working paper (2014)

Jin, Y., Yau C.Y.: A new Sequential Change Point Detection Test in Time Series. Working paper (2012)

Kaohsiung Rapid Transit Corporate Report: The Study of Kaohsiung Subway Volume Forecasting - *ARIMA* Approach (2014)

Li, Q., Racine, J.: Cross-validated local linear nonparametric regression. Stat. Sinica **14**(2), 485–512 (2004)

Nielsen, B.F., Frølich, L., Nielsen, O.A., Filges, D.: Estimating passenger numbers in trains using existing weighing capabilities. Transportmetrica A Transp. Sci. **10**(6), 502–517 (2014)

Ruppert, D., Wand, M.P.: Multivariate locally weighted least squares regression. Ann. Stat. **22**, 1346–1370 (1994)

Steyerberg, E.W., et al.: Assessing the performance of prediction models: a framework for some traditional and novel measures. Epidemiology (Cambridge, Mass.) **21**(1), 128 (2010)

Woodridge, J.M.: Econometric Analysis of Cross Section and Panel Data. MIT Press, Cambridge (2002)

Zhong, X., Jin, Y., Cao, J., Zheng, W:. On the Empirical Likelihood Option Pricing. Working Paper (2015)

Zhu Y.: Crude Oil Price Prediction. Working Paper (2014)

Predicting Music Emotion
by Using Convolutional Neural Network

Pei-Tse Yang[1], Shih-Ming Kuang[1], Chia-Chun Wu[2], and Jia-Lien Hsu[1(✉)]

[1] Department of Computer Science and Information Engineering,
Fu Jen Catholic University, New Taipei City, Taiwan, R.O.C.
alien@csie.fju.edu.tw
[2] Graduate Institute of Applied Science and Engineering, Fu Jen Catholic University,
New Taipei City, Taiwan, R.O.C.

Abstract. Explosive growing and ubiquitous accessing of digital music encourage the need for the content analysis of music objects. Music emotion, as a significant component of affective content, convoy high-level semantics of music objects. Provided with proper features, music emotion recognition could be formulated as a regression problem or a training/classification process, in which the emotions are represented as vectors in the dimensional space or categorical tags, respectively. In this paper, we would like to propose a machine learning-based approach to predict dimensional emotion of music objects without a sophisticated feature extraction process. Meanwhile, the exponential frequency resolution of Constant-Q Transform mirrors the human auditory system. First, we apply the Constant-Q Transform on music objects to derive the spectrogram, which is the corresponding visual representation of audio signals. Then, we make use of the convolutional neural network, which is commonly and successfully applied to analyze the visual image, on spectrogram for predicting music emotion. Experimental results show that our approach is promising and effective. By using the ten-fold cross-validation, our approach achieves the Top-3 accuracy as high as 82.24% in the valence dimension and 81.80% in the arousal dimension.

Keywords: Music emotion recognition · Convolutional neural network

1 Introduction

Music Emotion Recognition (MER) is an interesting and promising research issue field of Music Information Retrieval (MIR), and has received attention nowadays. Although some theories and models were presented in the society of MIR, some issues remain unsolved. For example, it is still challenging to properly describe *expressed* emotions of music objects. Meanwhile, *perceived* emotions could be subjective and vary considerably from individual to individual. Thus, researchers attempt to investigate MER from different aspects. For instance,

This research was supported by the Ministry of Science and Technology under Contract No. 108-2221-E-030-013-MY2 and 106-2221-E-030-019-MY2.

© Springer Nature Switzerland AG 2020
F. F.-H. Nah and K. Siau (Eds.): HCII 2020, LNCS 12204, pp. 266–275, 2020.
https://doi.org/10.1007/978-3-030-50341-3_21

in [7], the authors exploit music genres to predict essential emotions. In [2], the authors collect physiological data by using the IoT devices to construct classification model. In addition, Hsu et al. make use of EEG signals to explore emotion, and consider the individual differences to construct personalized model for predicting perceived emotions [6].

Generally, there are two different kinds of emotion models: the *discrete emotion model* and the *dimensional emotion model* [5]. In the discrete model, emotions are divided into some discrete states and represented as tags, for instance, happiness, anger, and sadness. In the dimensional model, the emotion space is used to demonstrate the concept of emotions in which emotions are represented as vectors in the n-dimensional space. Based on the dimensional emotion model, Thayer proposes the two dimensions of emotional coordinate: *valence* axis and *arousal* axis [17], in which valence represents the way one judges a situation from positive to negative and arousal represents the degree of excitement.

Table 1. Accuracy and approach of music emotion classification in MIREX from 2014 to 2018.

Year/Code	Feature + Approach	$acc(\%)$
2014/PP1 [14]	MFCC + two-level SVM	66.63
2015/LK2	*	66.17
2016/LS1 [11]	FFT & MFCC + CNN	63.30
2017/PLNPH1 [15]	pre-train encoder + SVM	69.83
2018/WB1 [1]	STFT + CNN	61.17

* The report is missing; the hyperlink of the report is not valid.

In the MIR society, several approaches have been proposed for emotion classification tasks. Table 1 summarizes the regular event of Music Information Retrieval Evaluation eXchange (MIREX) [4] from 2014 to 2018. The SVM-based approaches have been widely used in the beginning [9]. Along with the progress of the machine learning technique, researchers started to apply neural networks to emotion classification tasks [3]. Meanwhile, the method used for extracting features from acoustic content is also crucial to prediction accuracy. According to [10,13], the Constant-Q Transform (CQT) preserves the most acoustic features and achieves good performance whether in music genre classification or music emotion recognition. As a result, using CQT as a feature extraction method and applying CNN to construct prediction models would be able to achieve a prospective and reasonable performance.

In this paper, we would like to present our approach to predict music emotion by using CNN. The input of the problem is an audio clip of music object; and the output is a two-dimensional emotion vector in the valence and arousal dimensions. We make use of various feature extraction and feature transformation methods to convert audio clips into spectrograms. Then, we apply CNN on the corresponding spectrograms to construct our model for classification.

The rest of this paper is organized as follows. First, in Sect. 2, we provide a detailed description of the proposed approach, including feature extraction and system architecture. In Sect. 3, we present the experimental results and performance evaluation. Finally, we conclude this paper in Sect. 4.

2   Approach

In this section, we briefly introduce the feature extraction, the sliding window, and the quantification applied in our approach. Then we will present our system architecture and describe our approach.

2.1   Feature Extraction

To apply CNN, we have to fit the input requirement of CNN, which is a fix dimensional matrix, while music excerpts given for music emotion recognition are usually sequential signals. Thus, we convert the music excerpts into spectrograms that contain features of the original acoustic content.

According to [8], researchers make use of Fourier Transform to extract the music features. While processing the music excerpts, Short-Time Fourier Transform (STFT), which is a Fourier-related transform, is designed for determining the sinusoidal frequency and phase content of local sections of a signal as it changes over time [18]. However, STFT fails to address high and low frequencies. Constant Q Transform (CQT) provides a varying time-frequency resolution and it outperforms STFT when processing high and low frequencies. CQT is calculated into the log frequency domain rather than the linear frequency domain, such as STFT, and its window length changes in the wake of frequency. Therefore, low and high frequencies result in high spectral resolution and high temporal resolution, respectively. In addition, we select the Mel-frequency Cepstral Coefficient (MFCC) as one of our feature extraction method, which is commonly used in processing sound signals. MFCC not only can be used as features in speech recognition but also have an increased usage in music information retrieval applications, for instance, genre classification and audio similarity measures [12].

In our experiments, we perform STFT, CQT, and MFCC to convert music excerpts into spectrograms. To further observe the relation between high and low frequencies and music emotion recognition prediction, we additionally implement pitch Chroma [8], which converts the input spectrogram into a 12 semitone represented spectrogram.

2.2   Sliding Window

The dataset, we used in this project, provides valence and arousal coordinates for each 0.5 s. Intuitively, we apply a sliding window of 0.5 s to audio clips and compose with its corresponding coordinates as training and testing pairs.

However, adequate continuity (a period of time span) of music stimulus is also crucial to sustain emotion. The 0.5-s interval may not provide enough information both from audio clips and V-A coordinates. Thus, in our experiments, we apply various width of sliding windows to determine the most suitable period. We average the relative V-A coordinates in each slice and regard it as its ground truth. In addition, since music is a sequence structure, each signal is high-related to the previous and following one, we also apply sliding windows with or without 50% overlapping in each sliding window size, respectively.

2.3 Quantification

The results of emotion recognition tasks are numerical data which are vectors in the dimensional space, containing valence and arousal dimensions. However, we apply CNN to deal with the classification task of music objects in this paper. Thus, we quantize each dimension into 21 categories. To be more specific, the valence and arousal dimensions in our dataset are values between -1 to 1, inclusively, we round them to the nearest tenth and regard each tenth value as a label. Quantizing the vectors not only make it effective to predict dimensional emotion of music objects, but also provide a more clear and unsophisticated evaluation process, for instance, confusion matrix and Fuzzy-3 accuracy. We show an example of the distribution of the valence dimension and the arousal dimension after performing quantification in Fig. 1. We also show some examples of labels with its corresponding spectrogram in Fig. 2.

2.4 System Architecture

Referring to Fig. 3, our system consists of two stages: model construction and the evaluating phase. In model construction, we first apply a sliding window on the music excerpts into equal length slices and convert them into spectrograms. Then, we validate the performance using ten-fold cross-validation. In the evaluating phase, we will report Top-1 accuracy, Top-3 accuracy, and Fuzzy-3 accuracy, which will be described in more details in Sect. 3.4.

Our training procedure follows standard CNN training methods. The model consists of three layers and the input size is $64 \times 64 \times 3$. For the first two layers in the network, they interleave two-dimensional convolutional layers with filter size 3×3, a max pooling layer and a dropout layer and using ReLU as activation function. The last layer first converts the $3D$ feature maps to a $1D$ feature vectors and output a one-hot vector by two Dense layers to predict 21 categories. We show the output shape and the parameters of each layer in Table 2. We train 100 epochs for all experiments and the optimization process is based on Adam optimizer with learning rate 5e$-$5.

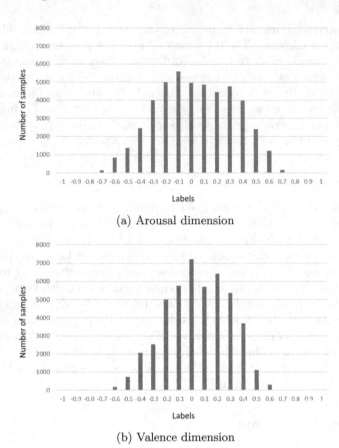

(a) Arousal dimension

(b) Valence dimension

Fig. 1. The distribution of arousal and valence dimension.

3   Experiments

3.1   Dataset

We use EmoMusic [16] as our dataset which contains a thousand songs from Free Music Archive (FMA). Each song is a 45 s excerpt. In every 45 s excerpt, the first 15 s does not provide valence and arousal coordinates, the collector indicates that the impact of music on emotions is diminutive in the beginning stage. The following 30 s provides V-A coordinates for each 0.5 s and the value is between −1 to 1, inclusively.

3.2   Music Continuity to Emotions

In order to investigate the most suitable music period for the emotion classification, we apply different width of sliding windows to the song excerpts with or without 50% overlapping excerpts, respectively. To be more specific,

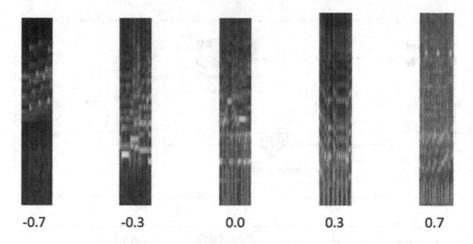

| -0.7 | -0.3 | 0.0 | 0.3 | 0.7 |

Fig. 2. Examples of labels with its corresponding spectrogram.

each overlapping slice includes the last 50% of the previous slice and the first 50% slice length of the next song excerpt. Then, we convert the slices to its CQT-spectrogram. The results are reported in Table 3.

According to Table 3, the window size of 5 s with 50% overlapping is the best both in valence dimension and arousal dimension, 56.66% and 64.61% respectively. The results of 5 s slice outperform the results of 0.5 s slice and 10 s, and all of the results of the slice with 50% overlapping have a better performance than without overlapping. Thus, music continuity indeed has a significant impact on the prediction of emotional coordinates, but a surfeit or paucity of acoustic features may not be able to classify the emotions.

3.3 Feature Extraction to Emotions

Due to various kinds of feature extraction methods that can preserve acoustic features, using different methods directly affect the prediction of V-A values. Therefore, we performed five different feature extraction methods to convert the slice, including STFT, CQT, MFCC, Chroma STFT, and Chroma CQT. The slice length is base on the results in Sect. 3.2, which is 5 s with 50% overlapping and each slice were labeled by the same approach in Sect. 3.2. The results are reported by categorizing Chroma and non-Chroma in Table 4.

For non-Chroma, using CQT-spectrogram as input reach the highest performance and the main difference among them is that only CQT achieves a high spectral resolution at low frequencies and high temporal resolution at high frequencies. For Chroma, the performance dropped significantly due to loosing the high and low frequencies features after performing Chroma. Therefore, high and low frequencies feature is an important cause to affect one's emotions.

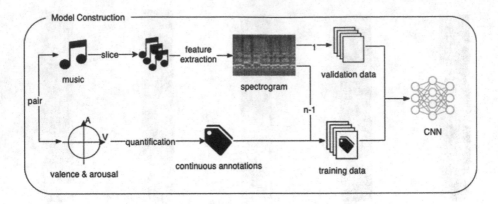

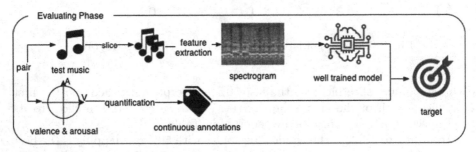

Fig. 3. An illustration of system architecture.

Table 2. The parameters of our CNN model.

Layer	Output	#P
Convolution2D	$62 \times 62 \times 32$	896
Convolution2D	$60 \times 60 \times 32$	9, 248
MaxPooling2D	$30 \times 30 \times 32$	0
Dropout	$30 \times 30 \times 32$	0
Convolution2D	$28 \times 28 \times 64$	18, 496
Convolution2D	$26 \times 26 \times 64$	36, 928
MaxPooling2D	$13 \times 13 \times 64$	0
Dropout	$13 \times 13 \times 64$	0
Flatten	10, 816	0
Dense	64	692, 288
ReLU	64	0
Dropout	64	0
Dense	21	1, 365
Sigmoid	21	0
Total		759, 221

3.4   Evaluation

The experiments in Sect. 3.2 and Sect. 3.3 report the Top-1 accuracy. However, it is quite ambiguous to classify two or more neighboring coordinates in V-A space, so using Fuzzy-3 accuracy as evaluation would more convincible and tenable in our work. Fuzzy-3 accuracy considers the labels that the error is plus and minus 1 unit as correct prediction and thus it will be able to meet the ambiguous boundaries between emotions. We showed an example of defining targets for the mentioned evaluation methods in Fig. 4. We assumed that the predictions of undepicted labels are not greater than predictions that had shown. We noted that label 0 is the target of top-1 since it has the highest score among all predictions. For top-3, we select the top three highest scores, label 0, label -0.1 and label -0.9, as the targets. Lastly, label -0.1, label 0 (ground truth) and label 0.1 are the targets that meet the definition of Fuzzy-3 accuracy. Therefore, in this example, all the mentioned evaluation methods will be count as a positive prediction.

Table 3. The performance vs. window sizes

Window size	$acc_{valence}(\%)$	$acc_{arousal}(\%)$
0.5 s (baseline)	23.66	27.43
1 s	20.41	27.97
1 s w/ OL	25.13	39.83
3 s	28.72	37.64
3 s w/ OL	35.71	47.46
5 s	35.42	55.47
5 s w/ OL	**56.66**	**64.61**
7.5 s	23.22	25.69
7.5 s w/ OL	36.75	28.98
10 s	37.16	29.88
10 s w/ OL	44.88	35.82

Note: OL represents 50% overlapping.

Table 4. The performance vs. feature extraction methods

Features	$acc_{valence}$ (%)	$acc_{arousal}$ (%)
STFT (baseline)	52.49	61.52
CQT	**56.66**	**64.61**
MFCC	42.50	47.69
Chroma STFT	29.16	45.38
Chroma CQT	38.33	49.21

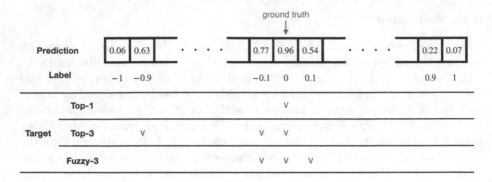

Fig. 4. An illustration of matching criteria for evaluation methods.

Table 5. The overall performance evaluation

Evaluate approach	$acc_{valence}(\%)$	$acc_{arousal}(\%)$
Top-1 accuracy	56.66	64.61
Top-3 accuracy	82.24	81.80
Fuzzy-3 accuracy	80.51	80.83

Our approach achieves the Fuzzy-3 accuracy 80.51% in the valence dimension and 80.83% in the arousal dimension. However, the Top-3 accuracy is as high as 82.24% and 81.80% in the valence dimension and arousal dimension, respectively.

Comparing to similar approaches showed in Table 1, the output of their classification task is categorized into 5 categories while in our work, we make a prediction based on 21 categories. Although the performance is similar, our work is more advanced and our approach is more integrated (cf. Table 1 and Table 5).

4   Conclusion

In this paper, we propose a machine learning-based approach to predict dimensional emotion of music objects. In our approach, we apply various feature extraction and transformation methods to convert music objects into spectrograms, which will be served as inputs of CNN for emotion prediction. We also perform experiments to further investigate factors and parameters of our approach. According to our comprehensive performance study, the CQT-based transformation with overlapping five-second sliding window achieves the Top-3 accuracy of more than 80%. The experiment results show that our approach is simple and effective.

References

1. Bian, W.: Convolutional neural networks for music mood classification tasks. In: The 14th Music Information Retrieval Evaluation eXchange, MIREX (2018)

2. Byun, S., Lee, S.: Emotion recognition using tone and tempo based on voice for IoT. Trans. Korean Inst. Electr. Eng. **65**, 116–121 (2016)
3. Delbouys, R., Hennequin, R., Piccoli, F., Royo-Letelier, J., Moussallam, M.: Music mood detection based on audio and lyrics with deep neural net. In: Proceedings of the 19th International Society for Music Information Retrieval Conference, ISMIR, September 2018
4. Downie, J., West, K., Ehmann, A., Vincent, E.: The 2005 music information retrieval evaluation exchange (MIREX 2005): preliminary overview. In: Proceedings of the 6th International Society for Music Information Retrieval Conference, ISMIR, pp. 320–323, September 2005
5. Eerola, T., Vuoskoski, J.K.: A comparison of the discrete and dimensional models of emotion in music. Psychol. Music **39**, 18–49 (2011)
6. Hsu, J.-L., Zhen, Y.-L., Lin, T.-C., Chiu, Y.-S.: Affective content analysis of music emotion through EEG. Multimedia Syst. **24**(2), 195–210 (2017). https://doi.org/10.1007/s00530-017-0542-0
7. Koutras, A.: Song emotion recognition using music genre information. In: Karpov, A., Potapova, R., Mporas, I. (eds.) SPECOM 2017. LNCS (LNAI), vol. 10458, pp. 669–679. Springer, Cham (2017). https://doi.org/10.1007/978-3-319-66429-3_67
8. Lerch, A.: An Introduction to Audio Content Analysis: Applications in Signal Processing and Music Informatics. Wiley-IEEE Press, Hoboken (2012)
9. Li, T., Ogihara, M.: Detecting emotion in music. In: Proceedings of the 4th International Society for Music Information Retrieval Conference, ISMIR, March 2003
10. Lidy, T.: CQT-based convolutional neural networks for audio scene classification and domestic audio tagging. In: Proceedings of the Detection and Classification of Acoustic Scenes and Events 2016 Workshop, DCASE, Hungary, Hungarian, pp. 1032–1048. Tampere University of Technology, Department of Signal Processing, September 2016
11. Lidy, T., Schindler, A.: Parallel convolutional neural networks for music genre and mood classification. In: The 12th Music Information Retrieval Evaluation eXchange, MIREX (2016)
12. Müller, M.: Information Retrieval for Music and Motion, 1st edn. Springer, Heidelberg (2007)
13. Oramas, S., Nieto, O., Barbieri, F., Serra, X.: Multi-label music genre classification from audio, text, and images using deep features. In: Proceedings of the 18th International Society for Music Information Retrieval Conference, ISMIR, October 2017
14. Panda, R., Rocha, B., Paiva, R.P.: Mirex 2014: Mood classification tasks submission. In: The 10th Music Information Retrieval Evaluation eXchange, MIREX (2014)
15. Park, J., Lee, J., Nam, J., Ha, J.W.: Representation learning using artist labels for audio classification tasks. In: The 13th Music Information Retrieval Evaluation eXchange, MIREX (2017)
16. Soleymani, M., Caro, M., Schmidt, E., Sha, C., Yang, Y.: 1000 songs for emotional analysis of music. In: Proceedings of the 2nd ACM International Workshop on Crowdsourcing for Multimedia, New York, NY, USA, pp. 1–6. ACM, October 2013
17. Thayer, R.: The Biopsychology of Mood and Arousal. Oxford University Press, New York (1990)
18. Wikipedia contributors: Short-time fourier transform – Wikipedia, the free encyclopedia (2019). https://en.wikipedia.org/w/index.php?title=Short-time_Fourier_transform&oldid=916238882. Accessed 17 Oct 2019

Social Media, Digital Commerce and Marketing

The Challenges to Leverage User Generated Contents in B2B Marketing

Ajit Ashok Aras[1] and Xin Xu[2([⊠])]

[1] Sharp Singapore Electronics Corporation, Device Business, Singapore, Singapore
ajitaras@gmail.com
[2] Department of Management and Marketing, Hong Kong Polytechnic University,
Kowloon, Hong Kong
xin.xu@polyu.edu.hk

Abstract. This study explores the emerging phenomenon of User Generated Content (UGC) in Business to Business (B2B) digital marketing. It offers deep insights into the challenges in UGC generation in B2B context which can help develop frameworks, to leverage UGC for marketing outcomes. Exploratory field research approach was adopted to examine the state of UGC and other similar practises in the B2B industry. Semi-structured interviews were conducted with key B2B practitioners in Asia. Interview data was analyzed through thematic analysis to understand the challenges and possibilities for UGC in B2B, through the words and meanings attached to them by B2B practitioners. Iterations between data analysis and reference to relevant literature, was done to guide theory development and subsequent data collection. Based on this understanding a UGC Leverage Framework was developed, which is grounded in practice and relevant theories. This study has established a basic theoretical framework about the challenges for UGC generation in B2B industry. As this is the first research study to explore UGC in B2B contexts, it's findings fill a gap in current literature and offer suggestions for further research. The outcome of this study gives B2B marketing practitioners and researchers, a sound understanding of the challenges involved. Thus helping them find ways to leverage UGC to effectively approach potential customers, at a time when traditional ways are losing effectiveness over the technology empowered B2B buyers.

Keywords: User Generated Contents · B2B marketing

1 Introduction

Internet and Social Media Networks have enabled customers to take control of their own buying journey – whereas marketing is losing control of the customers' buying journey (and hence the selling process). Even B2B buyers complete more than 60% of their buying journey before contacting suppliers' representative (Dixon and Adamson 2011). Customers don't want to be interrupted by marketing messages. Modern technology development in "ad-blocking" enable customers to realize this wish. This development poses significant challenge for marketers in reaching potential leads and attracting new

F. F.-H. Nah and K. Siau (Eds.): HCII 2020, LNCS 12204, pp. 279–297, 2020.
https://doi.org/10.1007/978-3-030-50341-3_22

customers. B2B marketing too is shifting from interruptive outbound to inbound marketing. Personalized Content marketing through educative and consultative content seems a possible good approach to reach potential leads. But low entry barriers and popularity of content marketing mean that, there is huge amount of "content clutter" that marketers must cut through, in order to reach potential leads. Further new technologies like VPN (Virtual Private Network) pose a big hurdle in identifying the content viewer and thus in personalizing content. Besides customers are generally skeptical about marketing generated content (MGC). User Generated Content (UGC) offers a brand-new avenue for marketers to overcome these challenges. These challenges are faced by B2C marketers as well as B2B marketers. Addressing these challenges, however, could be quite different in B2B as compared to B2C due to the inherent differences between the two streams of marketing.

1.1 Research Objectives

B2B marketing need new digital marketing tools to overcome the challenges in reaching the tech-savvy potential customers. The outcomes of previous B2C studies show a strong possibility that UGC leverage can help B2B marketers in overcoming these challenges and reach their goals. However, the usage of UGC in B2B is minimal. This paradox calls for a research in this topic. Most academic research in marketing has been geared toward B2C rather than B2B issues. B2B field suffers from limited number of studies (Wiersema 2013). There is no academic study focusing on User Generated Content (UGC) in the B2B context. This empirical research shall be the first one to explore the state of UGC in B2B. It shall study the reasons of low UGC leverage in B2B, focusing on the challenges that the users (current customers) and marketers face in UGC generation and leverage. Then we shall review the traditional B2B marketing practices, that are closest to UGC. These research objectives shall be met by conducting an interpretive empirical research through interviews with B2B marketers and iterating those findings with established theory.

1.2 Research Questions

- What is the state of UGC in B2B?
- What are the challenges if any, in UGC specific to a B2B setting?
- How can B2B marketers encourage the creation of UGC that can maximize B2B marketing outcomes?

2 Literature Review

As Holliman and Rowley (2014) found, content marketing gives sales organizations the power to tell a compelling story of their brand and the responsibility to avoid use of explicit selling language. An effective inbound marketing approach must be based on a solid understanding of customers' requirements and how content can be leveraged to address those requirements. Further as pointed out by Kock and Rantala (2017), B2B buyers whether digital-savvy or old-school types expect customer centric contents, based on actual customer experience. Digital channels enable customers to express positive and negative experiences (Kietzmann et al. 2011) with a much wider audience in a much shorter time compared to traditional Word of Mouth (WOM). User Generated Content (UGC) can be viewed as an overview of how customers make use of Social Network Sites, to share their experiences and views (Kaplan and Haenlein 2010). The Organisation for Economic Cooperation and Development mandates that UGC must meet three basic requirements, OECD (2007). First, it needs to be published either on a publicly accessible website or on a social networking site accessible to a selected group of people. Second, it needs to show a certain amount of creative effort and finally, it needs to have been created outside of professional routines and practices (Kaplan and Haenlein 2010; Smith et al. 2012).

While a customer progresses through the stages of purchasing journey and graduates to purchase stage, B2B purchasing managers tend to form strong bonds with those suppliers who satisfy both the firm's organizational needs and the purchasing manager's personal needs (Tellefsen 2002; Holliman and Rowley 2014). In the post-purchase stage, such satisfied customers can be encouraged to generate UGC about their experiences with the product usage or benefits. Such UGC can then be curated and channelized by sales company in an online community to create an area for providing more in-depth information to potential customers in a peer-to-peer setting (Straker et al. 2015).

2.1 Effectiveness of UGC on Purchase Intention

Several B2C studies have concluded the effectiveness of UGC on consumer purchase behavior, and are relevant to form a theoretical background of this study. While there are contradictory findings on whether the valence or volume of UGC affects purchase intentions more, UGC itself has a clear influence on purchase intentions. Chari et al. (2016) suggest the usage of UGC as the new form of "customer testimonials." Their study points out that ad-scepticism fuels trust towards brand related UGC (UGBR). Marketers can thus leverage UGC especially while targeting sceptics. An in depth understanding of UGC impact on B2B marketing goals is essential. Owusu et al. (2016) studied various features of UGC, in terms of their relative effectiveness in influencing web purchase intentions. They found that relevance, credibility and up-to-date-ness are the key features of UGC that positively influence purchase intentions.

2.2 Differences Between B2B and B2C Marketing

While research requirements exist in B2B field, academic research in marketing has been mostly geared towards B2C rather than B2B issues. B2B field suffers from limited number of case studies (Wiersema 2013). Most studies mentioned above are conducted in B2C settings, hence their outcomes can't be applied as-it-is to B2B marketing practice, given the differences between B2C and B2B business environments. The differences between the B2B and B2C markets are a result of unique decision-making processes and type of ingredient like products transacted in B2B (Brown et al. 2012; Swani et al. 2017). B2B products and services tend to be more technical and utilitarian in nature. Also, B2B buying decisions generally have more at stake in terms of performance and economic risks. Hence B2B buyers follow more elaborate and formal decision-making process which is much longer than in case of B2C. To address such requirements, both buyers' and sellers' value and pursue long-term and collaborative relationships, unlike in case of B2C (Homburg et al. 2010; Zablah et al. 2010; Swani et al. 2017). These long-term relationships should create a fertile ground for generation of UGC.

Moore et al. (2013) point out differences between B2B and B2C marketers with regards to their utilization of social media technologies. B2B salespeople utilize professional networking sites (i.e., LinkedIn) whereas B2C salespeople utilize social networking sites (i.e., Facebook). Iankova et al. (2018) point out that B2B organizations value SMM less than B2C for Relational Oriented activities. Swani et al. (2017) compared the popularity of social media content across B2B and B2C markets by analyzing Facebook message likes and comments. Their finding suggests that B2B viewers are particularly drawn to corporate brand names as compared to product brand names (Brown et al. 2012; Swani et al. 2017). Swani et al. (2017) further found that in case of messages that use functional appeals, B2B had a higher number of likes than B2C social media messages. Messages containing links and cues for information search are more popular among B2B viewers as compared to B2C viewers. B2B customers tend to respond and share such messages that contain informational cues (Mudambi 2002; Swani et al. 2017). Swani et al. (2017) attribute the lower comment rate among B2B viewers to the B2B context, which is highly involved, requires substantial cognitive resources, and has higher perceived risks than the B2C context. Notably however they found that, in case of messages containing information search cues or links, B2B viewers gave a higher number of comments than B2C.

2.3 Literature Review Summary and Gaps

The outcomes of previous B2C studies highlighting benefits of UGC and the characteristics of UGC which affect purchase intentions, suggest that there is good potential to leverage UGC in a B2B context. Swani et al. (2014, 2017) findings are significant inputs for B2B marketers aiming for higher viewership and engagement through content marketing. Since UGC is a specialization in marketing content, some of these findings should apply to UGC marketing. There is however some gap in these studies in terms of the SMM platforms that they were conducted on. These studies were conducted on social networking sites Facebook (Swani et al. 2014) and Twitter (Swani et al. 2017) while B2B marketing commonly utilize professional networking sites such as LinkedIn and SlideShare, as per the findings of Moore et al. (2013). The differences in B2B social media viewers' response to marketing content as compared to B2C viewers, therefore point to the need for a more focused study on benefits of UGC and ways to leverage it in the B2B context. As of now, there are no study focused on UGC in the B2B context. This is clearly a gap in the current literature, which this study targets to fill in. This study will be the first one to conduct such empirical research to leverage UGC in a B2B setting. The outcome of this study will therefore give B2B marketers the critical knowledge needed to leverage UGC, as a brand-new effective way to attract and convert new leads, at a crucial time when traditional ways are losing effectiveness.

3   Research Method

3.1   Overview of Research Method

We adopted an inductive and interpretive, theory building research approach in this study, to identify and emphasize key points from the actual experience of practitioners (Rowlands 2005). Semi-structured face-to-face interviews helped to tap the field experience, knowledge and vision of the practitioners who are proficient in B2B marketing. Data analysis started with deriving first order themes from the interview contents. Further interviews were guided by the initial interview data analysis. The emerging theoretical outcomes are reiterated with existing literature in related fields like Social Media Marketing and B2B marketing. This is to ensure that the emerging theory is firmly grounded in practice and supporting theories in related fields.

3.2   Data Collection

Following Nag and Gioia (2012) and Braun and Clarke (2013), interviews were conducted with B2B and B2B2C Marketing Practitioners, in order to get insights from the "ground zero" of B2B industry. Efforts were made to recruit interviewees from companies at various stages of digital and social media marketing, in order to seek "maximum variation", to make sure to catch general trends as well as any contrasting cases. Recruitment of subsequent new interview participants was done in parallel to data collections. This is to verify or contradict the emerging data codes and themes with upcoming information from fresh informants. Participants were from B2B industry in general. This helped the research by getting much broader perspective of the B2B industry and at the same time helped to identify the UGC related trends and challenges or pain points that are common across the industry. All the interviewees were at a mid/advanced level of Marketing expertise and hands-on experience in the digital, social and content marketing activities of their companies, so that the study benefits from their ability to relate to UGC with B2B buyers. The list of B2B Practitioner who participated in the interview, is in Appendix A.

3.3   Interview Questionnaire

Interview questionnaire was designed to catch the challenges in UGC leverage in B2B and to capture practitioners' vision about feasibility of UGC leverage rather than sticking only to actual usage. Format of interview has been semi-structured interview protocol with open ended questions to encourage the interviewees to share their experiences as well as their perspectives and even their novel ideas without being restricted by researcher's perspective. Probing techniques such as "Laddering" were deployed (Saaka et al. 2004) to gain deeper insights. Flexibility was exercised to achieve depth of questions in UGC and to catch the feasibility of effectiveness of UGC or traditional practices like UGC. The interview questionnaire flowed through initial background questions about the interviewee's experience in B2B marketing, to questions about general Digital marketing strategies to specific questions about exposure to UGC and it's leverage. Then there were some deep-dive questions on UGC which were asked only to seasoned marketers who had a fair exposure of UGC leverage.

3.4 Data Preparation and Analysis

Interviews were recorded with permission from informants so that key points of informants' statements can then be picked up from the recordings for further analysis and coding can be applied with informant's own words. The interview recordings were transcribed into verbatim text – for further analysis and coding.

Thematic Analysis method was employed for Data Analysis, as this was the best match based on the size of data available – 12 interviews, (Braun and Clarke 2013). The findings from preceding interviews were leveraged to align and finetune the approach and questionnaire for the next interviews. While the end goal was to derive mutually orthogonal categories – each interview was coded to pick up distinct patterns or codes. Codes were picked up from interview verbatim transcript, employing language used by informants. A classification of the distinct codes was done to consolidate the codes into higher level categories. By rearranging those, we could derive following distinct categories...

a.   Effectiveness UGC over MGC.
b.   Definition and the characteristics of UGC.
c.   Earning and finding UGC.
d.   Challenges in UGC generation and leverage.

   I.   Buyer side
   II.   Marketer side

e.   Current practices in traditional domain for UGC or similar content.

   I.   Working around the challenges of generating UGC

After more than 10 interviews were done the linkages between first order categories emerged. These were analysed and iterated to derive second-order themes at an abstract level. These second-order themes are assembled into orthogonal categories towards building a theoretical framework, through qualitative thematic analysis and theory building techniques, with iterations to current knowledge from related fields. The theoretical framework thus evolved throws light on the challenges faced by buyers and marketers in creation and leverage of UGC.

3.5 Validation

As this research was done ground up through the experiences and ideas of B2B practitioners – we engaged a few of the participants to validate this resulting theory model. The goal was to confirm that the analysis and the abstract level models developed, retain the inputs and ideas of the practitioner and stay true to those inputs. Review discussions were held with select participants who are relatively senior in the field and more experienced in Digital Marketing. The discussions started with showing the theoretical model of Challenges in UGC creation in B2B to the practitioner participants and getting their views on the correctness of these models, in terms of the inputs that were received during the interviews. 3 such validation discussions were held. We received confirmatory responses from all these discussions.

4 Identified Themes and Findings

This study found that the concept and usage of UGC is not well implemented yet in the B2B industry. B2B marketers believe that UGC shall be better accepted and effective than MGC, even in the B2B context. But the leverage of UGC in it's pure form is almost non-existent. We first look at B2B practitioners' interpretation of UGC and UGC effectiveness. Then we will look at the challenges on the buyer side and the marketer side that inhibit the generation and the leverage of UGC. Understanding these challenges can help us develop a framework to work around them and identify the steps to be taken to encourage the creation and the leverage of UGC.

4.1 Definition and the Characteristics of UGC

Firstly, we explored the definition and characteristics of UGC in the views of B2B practitioners. The definition of UGC varied a fair bit among the practitioners. In the simplest sense UGC is considered as sharing with the world through some creative efforts, real user feedback about a product or service that this user has experienced or used. This is quite in line with the definition of UGC in the extant literature, (Kaplan and Haenlein 2010; Smith et al. 2012; OECD 2007). As UGC is generated by the freewill of users, there is little or no control that the marketers can exercise over UGC, particularly it's valence. In this sense UGC is like PR (Public Relations) in the marketing mix, it's earned media and not paid or owned media.

As for the desired characteristics of UGC, Genuineness tops the list. This is no surprise given that UGC's main merit lies in UGC's perceived credibility and trustworthiness, versus that of MGC. Genuineness in UGC is crucial for it to be perceived as a content that is voluntarily generated by user and not as marketing generated content packaged as UGC. The next important characteristic of UGC is being "spreadable". Being spreadable is important for UGC because it's the very essential requirement for it to reach the intended audience – the potential customers, in as large number as possible. Combining the above 2 themes, we would interpret that the UGC should be widely spreadable and at the same time, should be perceived as genuine.

Other top desired characteristics that emerged commonly during the interviews are being beneficial to customers and bearing relevance to customer needs. Relevance can also be time dependent, in terms of stage of customers' buying journey.

4.2 Effectiveness of UGC Over MGC in B2B

All the B2B practitioners that we interviewed during this study, agree that UGC does affect purchase decisions, though their opinions about the level and type of effectiveness vary. Customer eWOM (UGC) has a causal impact on consumer purchasing behaviour, (Chevalier and Mayzlin 2006). B2B buying process involves high value decision making.

As such, B2B buyers do thorough due diligence and do seek feedback and peer reviews to enable them to take 'informed' buying decisions. Right from the initial interviews, the data reflected marketers' belief about the positive influence of UGC on B2B purchase decisions and hence the resulting significant benefit to B2B marketing outcomes.

The significance of UGC increases as more and more initial buying research is conducted before the first contact with a sales company. In this stage of initial research, a positive review about a company or it's product or service in form of UGC is particularly effective to swing the potential buyer in favour of such company whose products or services are positively reviewed, in that UGC. UGC delivers it's value for the potential buyer and therefore for the marketing firm in several ways. Firstly, UGC penetrates through the buyer scepticism which is main hurdle for MGC (Cheong and Morrison 2008). In this sense UGC lowers the 'guard' and invokes 'trust' which helps it to grab attention and make an impact. UGC generally is delivered in simple language of the users in contrast MGC which tends to be jargon heavy and complex in the pursuit of proving a point. The authenticity and trustworthiness as a content, that UGC enjoys derives from this fact, that it is the user's voice.

4.3 Earning UGC

B2B Marketers believe that a user would advocate for a product or service that the he has used, if he is absolutely delighted with it. The product or service should be par excellence to provoke an user to advocate for it. B2B marketers understand this point very well. From this angle UGC starts to look like a simple magical tool that can influence potential buyers to positively consider a company's products or services as long as the company serves it's current customers exceptionally well. In that case UGC should be abundant in B2B, as several companies serve their customers well.

4.4 Looking for UGC – Reality Strikes

Though customer delight shall translate to UGC in theory, it seldom happens so simply in reality, especially in case of B2B industry. Reflected in the comments of P8…

> "… Actually, I'm struggling when I've naturally got UGC… actually never will the content generate on its own."

This situation of lack of natural UGC generation in the B2B business context is in stark contrast to the abundance of UGC in B2C context. UGC is appreciated by the B2B marketing practitioners as a potent tool. There is also a broad level familiarity with the concept of UGC. But as a matter of fact, the generation and leverage of UGC is very low in the B2B context. This is the fact that makes this study very interesting and essential for the B2B theory and practise. The focus of this research is thus on gaining a deep understanding of challenges in the generation of UGC in B2B context, any of which came from the very nature of B2B business. A detailed understanding of these challenges would help to work around those challenges towards the generation and leverage of UGC in B2B.

5   Challenges in the Generation and Leverage of UGC

This study relies on the multilevel framework of Technology Acceptance and Use (Venkatesh et al. 2016) to the extent of arranging the motivations, hurdles and usage value of generating UGC (Fig. 1). User means any B2B customer who has experienced a product or service and therefore can be a potential creator of UGC contents. 'Marketer' represents any individual marketer or a team or organization who want to encourage creation of UGC and leverage UGC for marketing outcomes. The purple boxes (Perceived ease of use, Perceived usefulness and UGC intention) in the diagram are the key elements that lead to UGC creation. During this study we realised that each of these elements are influenced by a dyadic pair of Users' side and Marketers' side factors. This is one of the key differences in B2B UGC as compared to B2C UGC where the factors affecting UGC creation are mostly user related, namely to express personal identity, have social interactions with other consumers or brands, obtain or disseminate information, or simply be entertained (Malthouse et al. 2016). These dyadic pairs of Users' and marketers' side factors can be grouped into Organizational factors, Operational factors and Outcome related factors. Environmental factors have an overall influence on the conversion of UGC intention into actual UGC.

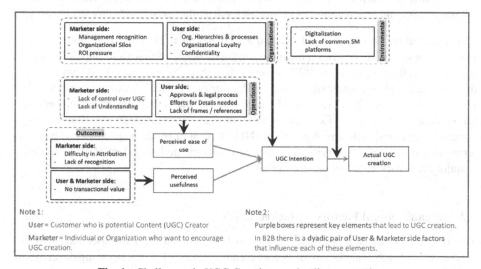

Fig. 1. Challenges in UGC Creation – a dyadic perspective

5.1   Organizational Factors

Organizational factors affect the intention to generate UGC on the user side and the intention to encourage UGC on the marketer side. Organizational factors are one of the dominating factors that affects UGC intention and is elaborated in the next paragraphs.

5.2   Organizational Factors – User Side

Organizational Hierarchies and Processes. Organizational hierarchies play a major role in the generation of UGC or the lack of it. UGC creation is to a great extent a spontaneous action as is seen in case of B2C UGC generation. In B2B however the buying decision and the evaluation of a product or a service are group activities. As such there are processes for each stakeholder to follow towards sharing his viewpoints generally internally first and then to the respective vendor, through "proper channel", a pre-assigned feedback or escalation path which is far cry from open social media. Besides such extreme cases itself are less common because most of the B2B products and services are agreed upon to specifications usually detailing each aspect of performance. In B2B environments buyers are highly involved, rational and hence demonstrate high levels of cognition as compared to B2C, (Gilliland and Johnston 1997). As such when a product delivers good results it is expected to do so, depriving it of a 'wow' moment which might trigger a spontaneous UGC.

Organizational Loyalty/Conflict of Interest. UGC in it's basic sense means endorsing other company's (usually a vendor's) product or service, in open media. This can create a potential conflict of interest, which may lead to major hesitations in generating such UGC. While generating UGC, any B2B user could be overwhelmed by the concerns of whether his organization approves of him endorsing other company's product or service.

Confidentiality. In B2C context, when a user mentions in his UGC that 'the restaurant was awesome' – it still carries a meaning for the audience of that UGC and reflects positively about the restaurant. In B2B however such short "praise" type UGC won't work, due to much higher complexity of the product or the service. A much elaborate UGC would be necessary. Elaborations which could very likely conflict with the confidentiality clauses in the non-disclosure agreement. B2B business deals are almost always covered by a Non-disclosure Agreement (NDA). A lot of product specifics and buy-sell terms might be considered critical enough to be maintained confidential. This becomes a major roadblock to the generation of UGC.

5.3   Organizational Factors – Marketer Side

The organizational factors create hurdles to UGC not only on the user side. On the marketers' side too organizational factors create a roadblock to encouraging the creation of UGC, though in different ways – as elaborated in the next sections.

Management Buy-In. On the marketers' side management buy-in is a major factor that sets the emphasis and direction of UGC leverage. Unfortunately, in most B2B companies there is lack of management buy-in as of now. There are various factors leading to this situation. One of the factors is the limited understanding about the benefits of UGC from a marketing perspective. Another factor is attribution. Attribution of UGC efforts to business goals is not easy with currently available technologies. The lack of management buy-in translates to lack of recognition of UGC related efforts by the marketing and sales teams. This in turn discourages the marketing and sales teams from putting in efforts in UGC creation.

Organizational Silos. Encouraging users to generate UGC is a team activity on the parts of Marketing organization. Content creation is the forte of Marketing and marcom teams – so they need to be involved to ensure that the UGC generated is of value. However, marketing can't be completing UGC activity by themselves. Reason is UGC involves a user (customer) and generally the sales or technical support teams in a sales organization have the closest relationships with the customer. This relationship is important to coordinate the generation of UGC and seek appropriate approvals to leverage that UGC. But often sales teams are not recognized or incentivized for their efforts in content creation. So, in order to ensure generation of UGC, organizations need to break down organizational silos and work as a team to ensure the success. Most organizations are not designed for this. Such joint responsibilities risk creating confusion among various teams of the selling organization and becomes a hurdle to UGC generation.

ROI Pressure. In today's time of tight budgets Marketing teams usually have a high pressure to show ROI on their content investment. UGC as a content generation activity is not well understood and well attributed. As such Marketing teams would have tough time justifying their investment in UGC related efforts and to secure a buy-in for this new content creation avenue. As a result, the tendency is to stay with time tested or previously successful content generation strategies. This dark cloud has a silver lining as well though. Generally, the content creation costs related to UGC are much lower than conventional contents. As such it is worth taking the risks and trying it out.

5.4 Operational Factors

Operational factors focus on the actions and processes that the Users as well as Marketing and Sales teams have to undertake to generate or encourage generation of UGC in B2B. These factors mainly affect the perceived ease of generating UGC on the user side and the perceived ease encouraging UGC on the marketers' side. These are elaborated in the next paragraphs.

5.5 Operational Factors – User Side

Approvals and Legal Process. As we discussed above, B2B organizations are often hierarchical and require approvals on part of the user for publishing or generating UGC. Legal approval processes can be lengthy and cumbersome especially in global organizations where several factors such as branding messages, international regulations, confidentiality or such, need to be considered and cleared before a content can be released to public. This time and efforts consumed in the process, significantly reduce the ease of UGC creation on the user side. It also deters marketers from aiming for those case studies or to encourage users to create UGC.

The Devil in the Detail. As we discussed in the previous sections UGC in B2B context is meaningful only when certain specifics about the user, the product or service and it's particular benefits are mentioned. Consumers consider credibility of the source of UGC when evaluating UGC, (Owusu et al. 2016). This creates a burden on the user and significantly reduces the perception of ease in generation of UGC. Besides these specifics could very likely conflict with the confidentiality clauses in the non-disclosure agreement. The added burden of seeking legal or other approvals can add to the difficulty of the user who wants to generate UGC. This requirement of details, raises the bar for B2B UGC. This reduces the perceived ease of generating UGC in B2B.

Lack of Frames or Platforms. B2C industry can rely and leverage on popular plat-forms like Facebook, Instagram and so on where UGC can be generated and shared. The scene in B2B however is very different. B2B marketers can utilize professional networking sites like LinkedIn (Moore et al. 2013) but the penetration is limited. There is no single credible platform that has deep penetration across B2B practitioners. B2B users therefore can't count on a single place where UGC about various brands' offerings resides. By definition, UGC needs to be published either on a publicly accessible web-site or on a social networking site accessible to a selected group of people (Kaplan and Haenlein 2010; Smith et al. 2012). While several B2B suppliers support peer reviews on their websites, there are no established websites or platforms where a potential user can compare reviews about offerings from several vendors supplying similar product or service, all at one place. This lack of common platform is a double whammy for UGC in B2B. The potential users don't have a common platform to compare reviews as men-tioned above. Besides such lack of platforms and hence frames or formats significantly reduces the ease of UGC generation.

5.6   Operational Factors – Marketers' Side

Lack of Control Over UGC. Control over generated content, rather the lack of control is one major concern for the marketers, in encouraging and leveraging UGC. Tradition-ally marketers and marketing companies have been used to content which they have full control upon. UGC however is very different in this aspect. UGC gains it's strength from the fact that it is independent of marketers' influence. Organic (unpaid) brand related UGC is more effective than sponsored (paid) UGC, (Kim and Lee 2017). UGC is the sharing of users' experience in their own words and might sometimes be in a way that marketers won't like it to be told. Marketers have difficulty to come to terms with this fact.

The tight rope between control and spread of content in Social Media is fundamental issue that marketers and marketing organizations need to come to terms with (Felix et al. 2017). As Social Media Marketing is just establishing among B2B practitioners there is discomfort with the lack of control over content. This creates hesitations among B2B marketers towards actively leveraging UGC in their marketing activities.

Lack of Understanding. There is very little understanding among B2B marketers about the benefits of UGC and the ways to leverage it. In fact, some of the marketers we interviewed had not considered UGC leverage in their marketing goals, until they were triggered by this study. The lack of understanding severely hampers the marketers' ability to leverage UGC. It negatively affects the ease of UGC leverage among B2B mar-keters. A better understanding of the challenges in UGC and ideas to overcome them, could be very beneficial to B2B marketers to further the cause of UGC leverage. This study focused on the challenges and ways of UGC leverage in B2B context should help this cause.

5.7 Outcome Related Factors – Users' and Marketers' Side

No Transactional Value. UGC related activities in B2B can't be transactional. Small rewards like a coffee voucher, that might work well in B2C setting won't make a mark in a B2B setting where the buying decision impact much larger values. This is in line with the findings of Kim and Lee (2017) that marketers should encourage customer peer-to-peer communications in natural ways rather than using monitory ways. On the other hand, bigger rewards can't be offered either because it might create compliance issues or even legal issues. This lack of transactional value affects both the user and the marketers. The users who wants to generate UGC thus doesn't see any transactional value in it. From the marketers' side as well, this becomes a roadblock in their attempt to motivate the users to generate UGC. Though such lack of transactional value comes out as a roadblock in the initial phase, the same can make UGC more authentic and hence trustworthy in the B2B context. Besides the non-transactional values such as association or network can be leveraged in B2B UGC.

5.8 Outcome Related Factors – Marketers' Side

Difficulty in Attribution. As with any content and more so for UGC, marketers have a challenge of attribution of the contents to business goals. One of the main challenges in attribution comes from the lack of understanding and hence acknowledgment of the influence of UGC. Marketers find it challenging to attribute certain piece of UGC to specific marketing outcomes. This difficulty has an impact when marketers are attempting to secure budgets from management for UGC efforts.

Lack of Recognition. UGC generation efforts on the sales company side needs breaking down of silos and teamwork across the organization. Often UGC generation needs active involvement and follow up by customer facing Sales teams or Customer service teams. The output of this efforts is content which is UGC (User Generated Contents). Contents is the forte of marketing and marcom teams. Content generation is not part of Sales KPI, be it UGC or otherwise. This is a hurdle where the teams who are in the best position to encourage UGC, thanks to their relationships with the customer, are not recognized for their efforts in UGC generation.

5.9 Environmental Factors

Digitalization – or the Lack of it. Digitalization influences across the spectrum from the initiation to the execution of UGC. Digitalization influences the culture. The culture of creating and sharing contents over social media, depends to a great extent on digitalization in the industry. Most B2B industries except for IT, lack significant Digitalization.

Digitalization influences the extent to which a user can exercise his intention to create and share UGC in the open social media. There is a factor of digital resources available to the individual as well as the overall penetration of digital social media among the industry where the user's audience would be. Digitalization also influences the amount of efforts that the marketers take towards UGC. Lower levels of digitalization translate to lower recognition of UGC and similar digital marketing efforts and therefore lower emphasis on it. B2B companies are thus losing out on leveraging the potent tactic of UGC marketing, as a result of their poor understanding of the digital concepts. There is a silver lining to this however, that digitalization is catching up in B2B industry as well.

Lack of Common Platforms. The influence of lack of frames or platforms as part of operational factors on the perceived ease of UGC generation was discussed in earlier sections. Further, the lack of commonly established and recognized social media platforms in B2B also affects the amount of UGC generation intention that can translate to actual UGC. As mentioned before in this report unlike B2C, B2B industry lacks commonly recognized social media platforms. As such when a user wants to create and share UGC he would tend to share in a one to one conversation or in closed media among a certain group for example. Such UGC exists in B2B but unfortunately it can't be fully leveraged since today's technology lacks the tools to scan such closed segments of internet. Such word-of-mouth is difficult to track and leverage widely, because it is part of private conversation and hence can't be shared in open internet or social media.

5.10 Exploring Traditional Domain for UGC or Similar Content

While UGC in it's pure form is rare in B2B industry, for the reasons discussed above – we explored the practitioners' experiences for activities similar to UGC in the digital and traditional domain. The interview data shows that, UGC in a little broader definition exists in B2B industry, albeit it's not always recognized and referred to as UGC. This study thus becomes the first attempt to tie the loose ends and consolidate and formalize the understanding on this topic. Customer success stories and customer testimonials are considered a potent weapon in B2B marketing. Leading customers' testimonials are used in online or offline peer-to-peer communication to educate and motivate lagging customers to adopt that product or service.

Such customer testimonials are considered as 'demonstrable value records' that can convince potential users to consider the product or service positively. Marketing companies thus can use UGC as a form of "customer testimonial" to tackle brand scepticism, (Chari et al. 2016). B2B marketing firms take the initiative of conducting assisted trials of new products or services for their lead customers, with the aim of generating valuable field outcomes data, that can be leveraged in marketing messages with the consent of the lead customer. Such data can then be presented to potential audience as a discussion or a joint statement or a press release.

In B2B2C type of markets where the product is sold by the B2B customer to the end consumer pretty much as-it-is; it's common to approach end customers, generally with the free sample of the product in exchange for a review. The end customer is required to try the product first-hand and then share his experience on record. End customer is free to share either positive or negative review as per his discretion. Such reviews are then compiled into a use case paper or a video to be shared with potential audience. These case studies videos are then used as a tool to educate other end users about the features of the product, as well as motivate the B2B customers, the distributors or finished product makers, to consider the product positively.

Another common form of content sharing encouraged is peer-to-peer sharing. This is in line with the finding of Smith et al. (2012), that marketers should provide a space where conversation can occur, not just customer to brands but also customer to customer. Such sharing sessions are generally closed-door sessions – which helps manage sensitivities related to confidentiality involved. Typically, a company would invite one of the key members from a satisfied customer and request him to share his experience to a limited audience who can potentially use the same product or service. There are also one-to-one conversations encouraged where the potential customer can talk directly to the current customer – even without the presence of the marketing company's representatives. Such facility to have a direct conversation with actual user, gives potential users not only the ease of understanding the product but also a confidence boost that the supplier has 'nothing to hide'.

Analyst generated contents is another strong stream of content often leveraged in B2B marketing. Such content traditionally is generated by analyst websites or forums. In the modern form of it the content is generated by Key-opinion-leaders (KOLs). Such content is usually a comparative analysis of similar products or services, that highlight advantages and disadvantages or assign ranking to products within a category. Marketers often quote such advantages or high rankings in their marketing pitch.

As can be seen above in this section – it is common to leverage contents which are generated with users' help or contents that are generated by third-party analysts. The contents generated by B2B users (UGC) have to be generally coerced or initiated by the marketers – though the outcome shall still be user's story. As P11 put it...

"That's the best-case scenario that you or your brand is so loved that people want to promote your services... But mostly in B2B, it's at a stage where you have to coerce or ask politely for someone to become an ambassador of yours."

The good part is that, such Semi-UGC can be still effective, particularly in B2B. As P12 aptly put it...

"I think in our industry we have a chance. Because I agree, you know, if you have such thing, right, Semi-UGC for a restaurant, this is bullshit, you don't believe it. But in B2B whenever you add up like some facts and figures, right, " <quote> this is a project we delivered you know, it was like 10 months - but we delivered in 5 months thanks to Supplier A, because they did this and that... <inquote> " whenever you add-up facts & figures which we can do quite easily in B2B. That it is going beyond the, person's appetite it is more becoming like a fact. Then you know even if it is like driven by marketing people, they think that marketing is just, you know, I mean creating the concept and the content but the content inside is real authentic. This is our advantage"

6 Discussion and Implications

B2B customers journeys are transforming rapidly (Dixon and Adamson 2011) and hence B2B marketers need new effective ways to reach new potential customers. Studies in B2B marketing are very few (Wiersema 2013). UGC based content marketing could be a effective new way for B2B marketers to reach new potential customers. But there is no study focusing on UGC in B2B context. B2B practitioners too, tend to neglect the potential of UGC in achieving B2B marketing goals (Holliman and Rowley 2014). Researchers can thus significantly contribute to advancing the state of the art in B2B UGC. This study makes the first important step to empirically explore the current status and the reasons of under-leverage of UGC in B2B, through the views of B2B practitioners themselves. Based on the findings we propose the first model which details the challenges to UGC generation in B2B. We used the Technology Acceptance and Use model to tabulate the various challenges faced by B2B practitioner in UGC generation. 'Ease of Use', 'Usefulness' and 'UGC intention' are the key elements leading to UGC creation. We identified various factors that influence the elements which lead to UGC generation. These factors can be grouped as Environmental, Organizational, Operational and Outcome related. We found that the Organizational, Operational and Outcome related factors influence the elements in dyadic pairs. The pairs are made up of Marketers' side and Users' side factors. These dyadic pairs of factors influencing the elements, imply that in a B2B context, UGC generation can't be just left to customers. B2B marketers need to take an active role in UGC generation. This study is thus the first to highlight marketers' side role and challenges in UGC generation. A better understanding of challenges to UGC generation in B2B would contribute significantly to business-to-business marketing literature. The model developed by this study enables B2B marketers to understand in-depth, the challenges they would need to overcome to enable UGC generation. Practitioners can use the in-depth understanding from this model, to work around those challenges and leverage UGC in achieving B2B marketing goals.

Here we would like to share and relate a recent example of B2B UGC here. This is in public domain, on YouTube. The link to this video is https://youtu.be/cDtuNhsA-Lk (accessed 20th Aug 2019). In this example the customer is University of New South Wales (UNSW). UNSW is a business. The supplier of the product, in this case MS Teams software, is Microsoft. MS Teams is a software that is designed to be used by businesses to facilitate their team communications. This is thus a B2B business case. Microsoft is leveraging this video to reach out potential business customer for it's product – MS Teams, through YouTube. Thus, this is a clear example of B2B Marketing UGC. We must declare that we didn't have access to Microsoft or UNSW to assess the facts. But it is obvious looking at the video that, Microsoft has helped UNSW in developing this video. The video talks about UNSW's journey into providing an engaging learning experience to its students. Microsoft stays low profile until almost the end of the video. There is also no one from Microsoft featured in this video. Microsoft gets a mention at the very end of the video as the 'enabler' of UNSW in this journey. Microsoft gets valuable potent content for it's (MS Teams') marketing effort. At the same time UNSW benefits from branding and image building as a tech savvy university dedicated to offering an engaging learning experience. Above all this YouTube video still serves as a convincing content, as it embeds all the factual details about the project. The video is thus an example of the ways to overcome the challenges identified by this model and leverage UGC in B2B marketing.

7 Limitations and Suggestions for Future Research

We hope that the B2B UGC challenges model developed here, can guide further much needed research in this subject. Due to limited availability of participants in any single industry sector - this study recruited informants across the B2B industry and couldn't focus on a particular sector. A future study can zoom-in on each sector or a group of sectors classified by the level of Digitalization in those sectors, to understand the influence of each dimension. This study is a beginning in understanding of UGC leverage in B2B. Since this was one of the first study in this area, a qualitative approach was adopted. This approach helped in identifying the challenges involved in UGC creation. Future studies can build on these findings to develop a framework to work around these challenges to leverage UGC in B2B marketing.

This study investigated UGC utility, challenges and leverage through the views of mostly B2B marketers. Future studies can investigate the factors through the views of B2B buyers. That might reveal new dimensions beyond the findings of this study. The nature and structure of organizations are changing. The boundaries of today's networked organizations are blurring in line with the collaborative relationships evolving between producer buyers and suppliers, both offline and online media creation. Future studies can research the conducive conditions that this change creates for UGC.

Appendix A: Table 1: Interview Participants' Information

Sr. No.	Interviewee's Role	Company	Industry	Company scale	Business model B2B / B2C / B2B2C	Questionnaire (Original / Revised)
1	Regional Marketing Lead - AP	Semiconductor Technology Company	Semiconductor	Multinational	B2B	Original
2	Head of Digital Communications - AP & MEA	Large Logistics Company	Logistics	Multinationa;	B2B & B2B2C	Original
3	Global Vice President - B2B	Multinational Consumer Goods Company	Consumer Goods	Multinational	B2B2C	Original
4	Founder & CEO	Corporate Consultancy - Transformation	Corporate Consultancy	SG Based	B2B	Revised
5	Founder & CEO	Marketing Solutions Technology Company	IT Enabled Services	SG Based	B2B	Revised
6	Ex. Regional Marketing Manager - Asia	Oil & Gas Company	Energy	Multinational	B2B	Original
7	Director Marketing - AP	Automotive Components Company	Automotive Batteries	Multinational	B2B & B2B2C	Revised
8	Head of Marketing - AP	Top ITES Company	IT Enabled Services	Multinational	B2B	Revised
9	Senior Account Manager Enterprise	HR related Enterprise Software Company	IT Enabled Services	Medium-size International	B2B	Revised
10	Director of Marketing	Computer data storage company	Semiconductor	Multinational	B2B & B2B2C	Revised
11	Managing Director	B2B Marketing Consultancy	Consultancy	SG Based	B2B	Revised
12	Chief Marketing Officer - Malaysia	Building Materials Manufacturer	Infrastructure	Multinational	B2B & B2B2C	Revised

Legend :   AP = Asia Pacific,   MEA = Middle East & Africa.

References

Braun, V., Clarke, V.: Successful Qualitative Research: A Practical Guide for Beginners. Sage, Thousand Oaks (2013)

Brown, J.J., Reingen, P.H.: Social ties and word-of-mouth referral behavior. J. Consum. Res. **14**(3), 350–362 (1987)

Brown, B.P., Zablah, A.R., Bellenger, D.N., Donthu, N.: What factors influence buying center brand sensitivity? Ind. Mark. Manage. **41**(3), 508–520 (2012)

Chari, S., Christodoulides, G., Presi, C., Wenhold, J., Casaletto, J.P.: Consumer trust in user-generated brand recommendations on facebook. Psychol. Market. **33**(12), 1071–1081 (2016)

Cheong, H.J., Morrison, M.A.: Consumers' reliance on product information and recommendations found in UGC. J. Interact. Advert. **8**(2), 38–49 (2008)

Chevalier, J.A., Mayzlin, D.: The effect of word of mouth on sales: online book reviews. J. Mark. Res. **43**(3), 345–354 (2006)

Christodoulides, G.: Branding in the post-internet era. Mark. Theory **9**(1), 141–144 (2009)

Dixon, M., Adamson, B.: The Challenger Sale: Taking Control of the Customer Conversation. Penguin (2011)

Felix, R., Rauschnabel, P.A., Hinsch, C.: Elements of strategic social media marketing: a holistic framework. J. Bus. Res. **70**, 118–126 (2017)

Gilliland, D.I., Johnston, W.J.: Toward a model of business-to-business marketing communications effects. Ind. Mark. Manage. **26**(1), 15–29 (1997)

Goh, K.Y., Heng, C.S., Lin, Z.: Social media brand community and consumer behavior: quantifying the relative impact of user-and marketer-generated content. Inf. Syst. Res. **24**(1), 88–107 (2013)

Grewal, R., Lilien, G.L.: Business-to-business marketing: Looking back, looking forward. In: Lilien, G.L., Grewal, R. (eds.) Handbook of business to business marketing, pp. 1–14. Edward Elgar Press (2012)

Halligan, B., Shah, D.: Inbound Marketing, Hoboken (2010)

Hennig-Thurau, T., Gwinner, K.P., Walsh, G., Gremler, D.D.: Electronic word-of-mouth via consumer-opinion platforms: what motivates consumers to articulate themselves on the internet? J. Interact. Mark. **18**(1), 38–52 (2004)

Holliman, G., Rowley, J.: Business to business digital content marketing: marketers' perceptions of best practice. J. Res. Interact. Mark. **8**(4), 269–293 (2014)

Homburg, C., Klarmann, M., Schmitt, J.: Brand awareness in business markets: When is it related to firm performance? Int. J. Res. Mark. **27**(3), 201–212 (2010)

Iankova, S., Davies, I., Archer-Brown, C., Marder, B., Yau, A.: A comparison of social media marketing between B2B, B2C and mixed business models. Industrial Marketing Management (2018)

Järvinen, J., Karjaluoto, H.: The use of Web analytics for digital marketing performance measurement. Ind. Mark. Manage. **50**, 117–127 (2015)

Jeong, H.J., Koo, D.M.: Combined effects of valence and attributes of e-WOM on consumer judgment for message and product: The moderating effect of brand community type. Internet Res. **25**(1), 2–29 (2015)

Kaplan, A.M., Haenlein, M.: Users of the world, unite! The challenges and opportunities of Social Media. Bus. Horiz. **53**(1), 59–68 (2010)

Kietzmann, J.H., Hermkens, K., McCarthy, I.P., Silvestre, B.S.: Social media? Get serious! Understanding the functional building blocks of social media. Bus. Horiz. **54**(3), 241–251 (2011)

Kim, M., Lee, M.: Brand-related user-generated content on social media: the roles of source and sponsorship. Internet Res. **27**(5), 1085–1103 (2017)

Kock, H., Rantala, T.: Innovating the use of digital channels in B2B sales with customers. In: ISPIM Innovation Symposium, p. 1. The International Society for Professional Innovation Management (ISPIM), June 2017

Li, F., Pieńkowski, D., van Moorsel, A., Smith, C.: A holistic framework for trust in online transactions. Int. J. Manag. Rev. **14**(1), 85–103 (2012)

Liu, Y.: Word of mouth for movies: its dynamics and impact on box office revenue. J. Mark. **70**(3), 74–89 (2006)

Lusch, R.F., Vargo, S.L.: Service-dominant logic—a guiding framework for inbound marketing. Mark. Rev. St. Gallen **26**(6), 6–10 (2009)

Malthouse, E.C., Calder, B.J., Kim, S.J., Vandenbosch, M.: Evidence that user-generated content that produces engagement increases purchase behaviours. J. Mark. Manag. **32**(5–6), 427–444 (2016)

Moore, J.N., Hopkins, C.D., Raymond, M.A.: Utilization of relationship-oriented social media in the selling process: a comparison of consumer (B2C) and industrial (B2B) salespeople. J. Internet Commer. **12**(1), 48–75 (2013)

Mudambi, S.: Branding importance in business-to-business markets: three buyer clusters. Ind. Mark. Manage. **31**(6), 525–533 (2002)

Nag, R., Gioia, D.A.: From common to uncommon knowledge: Foundations of firm-specific use of knowledge as a resource. Acad. Manag. J. **55**(2), 421–457 (2012)

OECD. Participative web and user-created content: Web 2.0, wikis, and social networking. Paris: Organisation for Economic Co-operation and Development (2007)

Owusu, R.A., Mutshinda, C.M., Antai, I., Dadzie, K.Q., Winston, E.M.: Which UGC features drive web purchase intent? A spike-and-slab Bayesian variable selection approach. Internet Res. **26**(1), 22–37 (2016)

Ramos, L., Young, G.O.: The social technographics of business buyers. Forrester research, Cambridge, 20 February (2009)

Rowlands, B.H.: Grounded in practice: Using interpretive research to build theory. Electron. J. Bus. Res. Methodol. **3**(1), 81–92 (2005)

Saaka, A., Sidon, C., and Blake, B.F.: Laddering. A "how to do it" manual–With a note of caution. Research reports in consumer behavior: How to series. Ohio: Cleveland State University (2004)

Smith, A.N., Fischer, E., Yongjian, C.: How does brand-related user-generated content differ across YouTube, Facebook, and Twitter? J. Interact. Mark. **26**(2), 102–113 (2012)

Straker, K., Wrigley, C., Rosemann, M.: Typologies and touchpoints: designing multi-channel digital strategies. J. Res. Interact. Mark. **9**(2), 110–128 (2015)

Swani, K., Brown, B.P., Milne, G.R.: Should tweets differ for B2B and B2C? An analysis of Fortune 500 companies' Twitter communications. Ind. Mark. Manage. **43**(5), 873–881 (2014)

Swani, K., Milne, G.R., Brown, B.P., Assaf, A.G., Donthu, N.: What messages to post? Evaluating the popularity of social media communications in business versus consumer markets. Ind. Mark. Manage. **62**, 77–87 (2017)

Tellefsen, T.: Commitment in business-to-business relationships: the role of organizational and personal needs. Ind. Mark. Manage. **31**(8), 645–652 (2002)

Trusov, M., Bucklin, R.E., Pauwels, K.: Effects of word-of-mouth versus traditional marketing: findings from an internet social networking site. J. Mark. **73**(5), 90–102 (2009)

Wiersema, F.: The B2B agenda: the current state of B2B marketing and a look ahead. Ind. Mark. Manage. **4**(42), 470–488 (2013)

You, Y., Vadakkepatt, G.G., Joshi, A.M.: A meta-analysis of electronic word-of-mouth elasticity. J. Mark. **79**(2), 19–39 (2015)

Zablah, A.R., Brown, B.P., Donthu, N.: The relative importance of brands in modified rebuy purchase situations. Int. J. Res. Mark. **27**(3), 248–260 (2010)

Venkatesh, V., Thong, J.Y., Xu, X.: Unified theory of acceptance and use of technology: a synthesis and the road ahead. J. Assoc. Inf. Syst. **17**(5), 328–376 (2016)

Investigating Linguistic Indicators of Generative Content in Enterprise Social Media

Elisavet Averkiadi[1]([✉]), Wietske Van Osch[1,2], and Yuyang Liang[1]

[1] Michigan State University, East Lansing, USA
{averkiad,liangyuy}@msu.edu
[2] HEC Montreal, Montreal, Canada
wietske.van-osch@hec.ca

Abstract. Teamwork is at the heart of most organizations today. Given increased pressures for organizations to be flexible, and adaptable, teams are organizing in novel ways, using novel technologies to be increasingly agile. One of these technologies that are increasingly used by distributed teams is Enterprise Social Media (ESM): web-based applications utilized by organizations for enabling communication and collaboration between distributed employees. ESM feature unique affordances that facilitate collaboration, including interactions that are generative: group conversations that entail the creation of innovative concepts and resolutions. These types of interactions are an important attraction for companies deciding to implement ESM. There is a unique opportunity offered for researchers in the field of HCI to study such generative interactions, as all contributions to an ESM platform are made visible, and therefore are available for analysis. Our goal in this preliminary study is to understand the nature of group generative interactions through their linguistic indicators. In this study, we utilize data from an ESM platform used by a multinational organization. Using a 1% sub sample of all logged group interactions, we apply machine-learning to classify text as generative or non-generative and extract the linguistic antecedents for the classified generative content. Our results show a promising method for investigating the linguistic indicators of generative content and provide a proof of concept for investigating group interactions in unobtrusive ways. Additionally, our results would also be able to provide an analytics tool for managers to measure the extent to which text-based tools, such as ESM, effectively nudge employees towards generative behaviors.

Keywords: Enterprise Social Media · Generative interactions · Text classification · Virtual teams · Team collaboration · Corporate innovation

1 Introduction

ESM are web-based applications that offer users various features to enable them to effectively communicate with each other, network, organize, leverage information available on the platform, and collaborate. ESM have a set of affordances [11] that promote collaborations to occur. By extension, it therefore seems to have the potential to foster

© Springer Nature Switzerland AG 2020
F. F.-H. Nah and K. Siau (Eds.): HCII 2020, LNCS 12204, pp. 298–306, 2020.
https://doi.org/10.1007/978-3-030-50341-3_23

group generative collaborations - group exchanges that involve the creation of innovative ideas and solutions. One of these unique affordances of ESM, namely visibility, allows all contributions to the platform to become visible to anyone who has access to the system. Not only has this affordance been shown to enhance collaboration, and thus possibly generative collaborations, but also offers a unique opportunity to study such group behaviors. Given the visibility of text-based interactions between users and within groups, server-side data from ESM can be used for research purposes, thus eliminating the bias of self-reporting methods and allowing researchers to explore important antecedents to behaviors in unobtrusive ways. This gives us an opportunity to improve the existing theoretical understanding of the nature of group interactions that occur on ESM platforms, yet also to improve such interactions on ESM, and other similar collaboration tools.

Our objective in this preliminary study is to understand the nature of group generative interactions through their linguistic indicators. There is copious server-side data to be leveraged from ESM, in particular the text-based asynchronous, and synchronous, messages that are exchanged within groups, specifically as this information pertains to the antecedents of effective creative collaboration. To conduct this research, we used an ~1% subsample of all group interactions from data provided by an ESM platform used by a multinational organization, and applied machine-learning models to classify the text data as generative or non-generative interactions and extracted the linguistic antecedents for the classified generative content.

2 Theoretical Background

2.1 Generativity and Group Generative Interactions

Generativity was first conceptualized in 1950, in work on the stages of psychosocial development, by psychoanalyst Erikson (1950) [6]. It has since been leveraged repeatedly in the social science and humanities disciplines. These disciplines have utilized this concept to refer to the creative progress and social change; a meta review of the major theories of generativity are presented by Van Osch (2012) [17] and Van Osch and Avital (2010) [16]. Generative interactions in virtual teams are a process of creating new knowledge, reconceptualizing a problem and/or a solution. In essence, generativity is defined as creating, originating, or producing [2, 21]. Generative interactions have further consequences, such as revealing tensions among users that were otherwise unknown, cross-boundary differences are highlighted, new perspectives are shared, and various other forms of creativity stimulants are exposed to an online team [3, 9]. By focusing on these interactions among employees, we could investigate a critical stimulant for innovations in organizations [16].

Generative interactions are conversations that aim to generate novel concepts, ideas, or solutions [16]. Rather than a single type of interaction, Tsoukas (2009) [15] inferred from creative cognition research [5] three distinct forms of conceptual change, which have received a great amount of attention. These typologies of generative interactions can help us understand the different ways in which novel concepts emerge in the context of generative interactions. One form of generativity, expansion, involves recycling and expanding the use of an existing concept from its core use, in order to match a new situation. Reframing, a second form of generativity, is a type of generative collaboration that frequently involves creatively deconstructing an existing concept and reconstructing it to fit a new situation. The third type, combination, involves combining two or more already existing concepts in new ways.

Generativity can thus stem from combining existing concepts in new ways [22], expanding the use of an existing concept from its core use to match a new situation (i.e., expansion), or by creatively deconstructing an existing concept and reconstructing it to fit a new situation (i.e., reframing) [16]. Reframing is a much more disruptive form of generativity, as it often challenges the status quo [16]. We operationalize these three types of conceptual change to identify generativity in text data.

2.2 ESM and Generative Interactions

Research thus far has accumulated evidence that ESM are an appropriate tool to facilitate information exchanges within teams, and thus, by extension may facilitate group generative interactions [12, 18, 20]. ESM platforms enable an information contribution process that results in an eco-system for supporting the generation of innovative concepts [4, 10]. However, it is not clear how, why, when, and to what extent these benefits occur. The scarcity of evidence provides the impetus for this investigation with the aim of finding ways to identify occurrences of generative interactions as a first step toward enabling improved such interactions in ESM.

Users of ESM platforms are able to communicate with other users through synchronous and asynchronous communication. Given increased pressures for organizations to be flexible and adaptable, teams need to organize in increasingly agile ways, using technologies such as ESM to facilitate more flexible communications and collaborations. ESM, as an integrated social media platform for internal communications [13], allows both synchronous and asynchronous communication (e.g., posts and threads). However, despite the mode of communication selected within the ESM, all communications are text-based thereby allowing team members to curate and edit messages between each other. These messages also persist – they are there to refer back to at a later time, and accessible to all team members. Within these text-based messages between employees, there is copious information that could be analyzed to understand the nature of these interactions, what makes them effective, and identifying the antecedents of successful creative interactions.

Generative interactions are a critical antecedent for innovation to occur [2]. They are an important component of group collaborations, as a company's ability to innovate is closely linked to their chances to survive and thrive [1, 7, 8, 14]. ESM have a lucrative impact on companies and the economy worldwide. Four out of five companies use ESM, and an estimated $100 billion is invested on ESM worldwide [19]. Companies investing in implementing ESM as their collaboration tool are particularly interested in generative interactions. All types of generative interactions (i.e. expansion, reframing, and combining) result in some form of new knowledge, which overtime, could become competitive value for an organization [8]. Breakthrough solutions are more likely to occur through generative interactions; they increase the likelihood of innovation [15].

3   Method and Results

3.1   Data

The data used for this study is provided by a multinational organization that researches and consults in the domain of human-computer interactions. Additionally, the organization builds technology and develops office space solutions for a variety of client domains: corporate offices, healthcare, educational institutions, and government institutions. The organization has over 80 locations around the world, and more than 11,00 employees across these locations. The organization launched an ESM tool with the objective of enabling connections, communication, and collaboration, among employees, in an effective way across its locations around the world. The ESM platform had accumulated 10,000 users over the course of five years. Of these 10,000 users, 91% (9,000 users) of its users are members of teams, who actively participate in group discussions.

Using data from this ESM, with permission from the multinational organization, offers a relevant object of study: its employees are distributed across locations and time zones, the users have been utilizing the platform for five years, and the data includes active employee teams. These criteria make the data relevant for our exploration of the linguistic indicators of group generative interactions. The data included 20,000 threads, of which 219 (~1%) were used for our exploratory study.

3.2   Method

Data Preparation. Before implementing a machine-learning classifier, the data was prepared by labelling text from the group threads with a code for the presence or absence of generative activity. Given the small sub-sampled used in this study, the three types of generative activity aforementioned were collapsed into one category. The coding scheme used for labelling the data can be seen in Table 1.

Table 1. Code scheme for labelling.

Type	Code	Description
Generative activity	1	Presence of any of the three typologies of generativity (expansion, reframing, combination)
Non-generative activity	0	Absence of any of the three typologies of generativity (expansion, reframing, combination)

We trained human coders to identify the text that contained elements of one of the three types of generative activity (reframing, expanding, combining), with the use of a coding manual that included definitions and examples of each.

Subsequently, the text was lemmatized – a method of reducing a word to its base form. We also extracted features from the text using the 'bag of words' method, which represents the text as a numerical description of its occurrence in the data (the number of times it appears). TF-IDF was also implemented at this stage, in order to vectorize the text.

Model Implementation. In order to identify the linguistic indicators of generative inter-actions, we used a machine-learning approach. We implemented several machine learn-ing models, including Random Forest, AdaBoost (Adaptive Boosting), Naïve Bayes (Multinomial), Support-Vector Machine (SVM), and Logistic Regression, to find the one that was best suited for classifying the data as generative or non-generative. Using performance measures such as f-1 score, accuracy, and Area Under the Curve, we were able to compare the models implemented and identify the best performing one. Once we identified the best performing model, we were able to use it to extract the top 20 important words for distinguishing generative activity.

3.3 Results

The results of the models we implemented can be seen in Table 2. Due to the contrast in performance, we can conclude that Random Forest was the best performing model with a 76% accuracy score, a score of 80% for AUC, and 83% for the f − 1 score. These are satisfactory results for a ~1% sub-sample. Adaptive Boosting (AdaBoost) was the second-best performing model, with 71% accuracy, but lower AUC and f − 1 scores. The worst performing model was Naïve Bayes with 44% accuracy, 59% AUC score, and 53% f − 1 score.

Table 2. Model performance: f-1 score.

Model	AUC	Accuracy	f − 1
Random forest	0.80	0.76	0.83
Adaptive boosting	0.70	0.71	0.81
Naïve Bayes	0.59	0.44	0.53
SVM	0.67	0.69	0.78
Logistic regression	0.72	0.66	0.72

Table 3. Model performance: all measures.

Model	f − 1	
	0	1
Random forest	0.90	0.67
Adaptive boosting	0.88	0.67
Naïve Bayes	0.55	0.49
SVM	0.83	0.64
Logistic regression	0.76	0.61

Table 4. Top 20 important features.

Term	Score
Like	0.0601
Work	0.0403
People	0.0313
Way	0.0268
One	0.0254
New	0.0214
Value	0.0194
Product	0.0183
Business	0.0181
Take	0.0179
Time	0.0172
Hi	0.0171
Place	0.0167
Today	0.0162
Different	0.0158
Need	0.0158
Feel	0.0144
Right	0.0144
Leader	0.0144
Project	0.0143

In more detail, the f − 1 score (seen in Table 3) for the two categories displays the performance of the models at correctly classifying either one. At a more granular level, Random Forest still seems to be the best performing model as it was correct 90% of the time at classifying the instances of non-generative text and correct 67% of the time at classifying generative content. In contrast, the Naïve Bayes model was correct 49% of the time at classifying non-generative content and correct 55% of the time at correctly classifying generative content. Due to the results above, we used the Random Forest model to produce the top 20 important features in the data, which are the linguistic indicators that help us identify instances of generative interactions. These terms are significant for the machine-learning model; they aid with distinguishing the generative and non-generative activity indicators in the text data (Fig. 1, Tables 4 and 5).

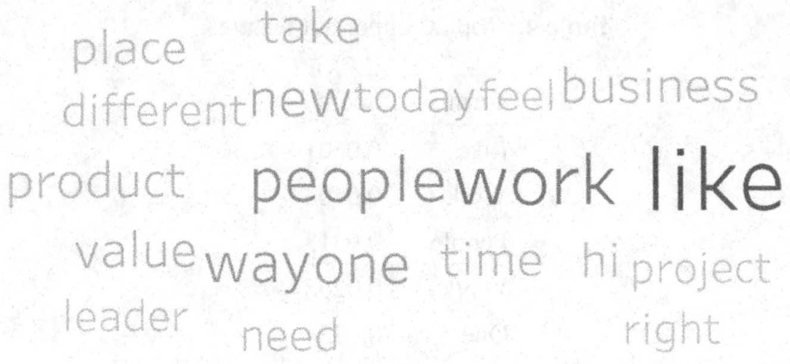

place take
different new today feel business

product people work like

value wayone time hi project

leader need right

Fig. 1. Word cloud with top 20 important terms.

Table 5. Sample generative and non-generative interactions.

Type	%	Sample
Generative activity	28%	"Two factors which I feel either hinder or help engagement, are 'autonomy' which Rob & Bob mentioned, and 'change' or 'impact'. There is a management concept of 'leading' with a light touch', people want to understand the limits, the outside boundaries of the work they are asked to do"
Non-generative activity	72%	"The [*organization name*] interns had the opportunity to participate in Chicago yesterday. It was great to see the [*organization name*] show so full and have such an exciting buzz around it"

4   Discussion

Terms such as 'work', 'business', 'product', 'project', and others, are essential linguistic indicators of generative interactions. These indicators are important in distinguishing team exchanges that involve generativity from those that do not. Our findings showed that 28% of the interactions in the data were generative, while 72% were non-generative content, indicating that indeed ESM is a source of generative interactions.

Though our preliminary study used a small portion of the data corpus available, thereby allowing us to only differentiate generative versus non-generative interactions, it shows promise of using machine learning to reliably discern not only when team exchanges in ESM are generative in nature—and thus identify potential root-causes of breakthrough innovations—but also possibly in distinguishing between the different types of generative interactions, namely combination, expansion, and reframing.

Being able to identify the linguistic indicators of distinct types of generative interactions would allow us to not only theorize the nature of generative interactions occurring through ESM, but also develop theoretical models of the precursors that result in distinct types of ESM-based generative interactions. For instance, the ways in which groups interact with each other and with the ESM in the context of these interactions might be different when groups are engaged in combination, expansion, or reframing. Such insights are theoretically important to obtain holistic understandings of the boundary conditions for different types of generative interactions as well as practically important to provide managers guidance for eliciting different types of generative interactions in an attempt to encourage productive uses of ESM. Hereto, more data will have to be labelled, and further experimentation with machine learning algorithms will be needed to produce an accurate classifier for multiple categories of generative interactions.

Acknowledgement. This material is based upon work supported by the National Science Foundation under Grant No. 1749018. Any opinions, findings, and conclusions or recommendations ex- pressed in this material are those of the author(s) and do not necessarily reflect the views of the National Science Foundation.

References

1. Abernathy, W.J., Clark, K.B.: Innovation: mapping the winds of creative destruction. Res. Policy **14**(1), 3–22 (1985)
2. Avital, M., Te'eni, D.: From generative fit to generative capacity: exploring an emerging dimension of information systems design and task performance. Inf. Syst. J. **19**(4), 345–367 (2009)
3. Burke, M., Marlow, C., Lento, T.: Feed me: motivating newcomer contribution in social network sites. In: CHI 2009: Proceedings of the 27th International Conference on Human Factors in Computing Systems, pp. 945–954 (2009)
4. Beck, R., Pahlke, I., Seebach, C.: Knowledge exchange and symbolic action in social media-enabled electronic networks of practice: a multilevel perspective on knowledge seekers and contributors. MIS Q. **38**(4), 1245–1270 (2014)
5. Dunbar, K.: How scientists think: On-line creativity and conceptual change in science. In: Ward, T.N., Smith, S.M., Vaid, J. (eds.) Creative Thought. American Psychological Association, Washington, DC 461–494 (1997)
6. Erikson, E.H.: Childhood and Society. W.W. Norton and Company, New York (1950)
7. Hambrick, D.C.: Some tests of the effectiveness and functional attributes of Miles and Snow's strategic types. Acad. Manag. J. **26**(1), 5–26 (1983)
8. Henderson, R.M., Clark, K.B.: Architectural innovation: the reconfiguration of existing product technologies and the failure of established firms. Adm. Sci. Q. **35**(1), 9–30 (1990)
9. Harvey, S.: Creative synthesis: exploring the process of extraordinary group creativity. Acad. Manag. Rev. **39**(3), 324–343 (2014)
10. Kane, G.C.: The evolutionary implications of social media for organizational knowledge management. Inf. Organ. **27**(1), 37–46 (2017)
11. Leonardi, P.M., Huysman, M., Steinfield, C.: Enterprise social media: definition, history, and prospects for the study of social technologies in organizations. J. Comput. Mediated Commun. **19**(1), 1–19 (2013)
12. Leonardi, P.M.: Social media, knowledge sharing, and innovation: toward a theory of communication visibility. Inf. Syst. Res. **25**(4), 796–816 (2014)
13. Leonardi, P.M., Vaast, E.: Social media and their affordances for organizing: a review and agenda for future research. Acad. Manag. Ann. **11**(1), 150–188 (2017)
14. Lieberman, M.B., Montgomery, D.B.: First- mover advantages. Strateg. Manag. J. **9**(1), 41–58 (1988)
15. Tsoukas, H.: A dialogical approach to the creation of new knowledge in organizations. Organ. Sci. **20**(6), 941–957 (2009)

16. Van Osch, W., Avital, M.: Generative Collectives. In: ICIS 2010 Proceedings (2010). http://aisel.aisnet.org/icis2010_submissions/175
17. Van Osch, W.: Generative Collectives. Ipskamp Publishers, Netherlands (2012)
18. Van Osch, W., Steinfield, C.W.: Boundary spanning through enterprise social software: an external stakeholder perspective. In: Proceedings of the International Conference on Information Systems (ICIS), Milan, Italy (2013)
19. Van Osch, W.: The business side of social media. Int. Innov. **195**, 27–29 (2015)
20. Van Osch, W., Steinfield, C.W.: Strategic visibility in enterprise social media: implications for network formation and boundary spanning. J. Manag. Inf. Syst. **35**(2), 647–682 (2018)
21. Webster, M.: Generativity. In: Merriam-Webster Online Dictionary (2009)
22. Wisniewski, E.J.: When concepts combine. Psychon. Bull. Rev. **4**(2), 167–183 (1997)

Usability Studies of E-Commerce Checkout Process: A Perspective from Thailand

Patcharee Butnampetch[1] ⓘ, Panja Sasithonwan[1] ⓘ, Butsakorn Teeranan[1] ⓘ,
and Thippaya Chintakovid[2(✉)] ⓘ

[1] Department of Information Technology, Faculty of Information Technology and Digital Innovation, King Mongkut's University of Technology North Bangkok, Bangkok 10800, Thailand
[2] Information Landscape Research Unit and Department of Library Science, Faculty of Arts, Chulalongkorn University, Bangkok 10330, Thailand
thippaya.c@chula.ac.th

Abstract. Shopping cart abandonment is one of major problems that can affect conversion rate for e-commerce. A complex or ambiguous checkout process can result in customers discarding their purchase transactions. This research examined Thai online buyers' experience with a checkout process of e-commerce websites and m-commerce applications. Usability studies were conducted with three different sample groups. They were asked to use two different types of e-commerce platforms to purchase either retail or technology-based products. A working age group with general knowledge about technology tested retail m-commerce applications. Another working age group who was tech-savvy tried out e-commerce websites selling technology products. The elderly group performed a test on retail m-commerce applications. Similar usability issues were found among the three user groups. A violation of visibility principle was a major factor causing unsuccessful task completion in the usability tests.

Keywords: Usability test · Checkout procedure · Visibility principle

1 Introduction

1.1 Motivation

Business values of e-commerce in Thailand have steadily increased owing to growing interest of the business sector and changing lifestyles of Thai people. According to [1], business-to-customer (B2C) e-commerce values in Thailand were 703,290.4 million baht in 2016 and 759,002.8 million baht in 2017. In 2018, the value of B2C e-commerce was estimated to be 865,414.9 million baht. Considering the growth of B2C e-commerce market in Thailand, there is no doubt that business competition among B2C e-commerce vendors would be high.

To attract and retain its customers, any e-commerce website or e-commerce mobile application (m-commerce) must be perceived by customers that it requires minimal effort to successfully purchase products. Designing a good user experience for Thai

F. F.-H. Nah and K. Siau (Eds.): HCII 2020, LNCS 12204, pp. 307–321, 2020.
https://doi.org/10.1007/978-3-030-50341-3_24

e-commerce or m-commerce, thus, has been a challenging issue faced by e-commerce firms.

Customers interact with websites or mobile applications through a series of activities, ranging from searching for products, product browsing, comparing different choices, adding to cart, placing an order, checking out, and so on. One of major problems that can affect conversion rate for e-commerce is shopping cart abandonment. Baymard Institute [2] compiled statistics on e-commerce shopping cart abandonment from forty-one studies and calculated an average cart abandonment rate. Based on these studies, the average cart abandonment rate was 69.57%.

Various reasons can be attributed to the abandonment of e-commerce shopping cart. A long or complex checkout process is one of the top three reasons why customers abandon their shopping carts [2]. Design of the checkout procedure could largely be a culprit for the troubles faced by the customers during the checkout process. An impact of poor design on e-commerce user experience is likely to be different among different groups of customers. Different levels of technology experience and prior knowledge about e-commerce may differently affect how customers perceive and interact with e-commerce mobile applications and websites.

The objective of this research was to examine checkout experiences of online buyers in Thailand. The study focused on checkout processes of two e-commerce platforms: m-commerce applications and e-commerce websites. Three studies were conducted with three different groups of users who had experience in online shopping for less than or equal to six months. The first user group was customers who were in the working age, which will be referred later as Study 1 (Working Age Group). The second user group was fifty years old and more, which will be referred to as Study 2 (Elderly Group). The third user group was customers who were in the working age and interested in technology, which will be referred to as Study 3 (Tech-Savvy Group). Results from these studies were used to propose design guidelines for a checkout process of Thai e-commerce mobile applications and websites.

1.2 Related Works

Prior research has investigated reasons why customers abandon their shopping carts. Reasons for shopping cart abandonment can be largely grouped into two factors: factors related to design of websites or applications and factors related to other non-design issues such as personal concerns, shop's policy, other technical issues, and etc.

Non-design problems include customers' concerns such as feeling unsafe to give credit information [3]. Inability to ship on a desired date [3], and unsatisfactory return policy [3] are also contributing factors to cart abandonment. Technical errors of websites or applications [3] can also affect customers' shopping experience.

For factors related to designs, designs of websites and applications inflicting negative shopping experience could be problems of visual design, interaction design, and so on. Examples of the visual design problems are small font size, too vivid colors, and too complex graphical elements [4, 5]. Regarding the interaction design, forcing customers to register before they can place items in the shopping cart [3] causes friction during the shopping process. Complex arrangement of web pages [3] which leads to confusion, is another example of poor interaction design. Problems with a design of checkout process have been listed as one of the top three reasons of shopping cart abandonment [2]. The checkout process that is too long or too complex can also cause users confusion and urge them to leave websites or applications.

2   Methodology

A method of usability testing was used as a data collection technique. Each study recruited different sample groups, as described in Sect. 2.1. Each sample group was asked to perform five tasks. Description of each task is provided in Sect. 2.2. Test data of Study 1 (Working Age Group) and Study 3 (Tech-Savvy Group) were collected between October, 2018 and January, 2019. For Study 2 (Elderly Group), the data were collected from December, 2018 to January, 2019.

2.1   Participants

All of the studies recruited male and female participants who had experience in shopping online no more than 6 months. In Study 1 (Working Age Group) and Study 3 (Tech-Savvy Group), participants were between 20–45 years old. A key difference between the participants in Study 1 and Study 3 was that the participants in Study 1 had general experience with technology whereas the participants in Study 3 were more keen about technology. For Study 2 (Elderly Group), participants were fifty years old and more. We considered this group as the elderly both in terms of their age and their low level experience with technology. Number of participants was 32 in Study 1, 31 in Study 2 and 30 in Study 3. All three studies employed a purposive sampling method. Each individual participant took part in only one study. Therefore, this research recruited ninety-three participants.

2.2   Tasks and Measurement of Successful Task Completion

For all studies, the same set of tasks were assigned to the participants. The tasks included adding to cart, adding a shipping address, selecting a shipping method, choosing a payment method, and placing an order. A list of products was given to the participants in order to save browsing time. To reduce an effect of familiarity, each participant was assigned to use an m-commerce application or e-commerce website that he/she had never used it before.

For Study 1 (Working Age Group) and Study 2 (Elderly Group), top five retail m-commerce applications in Thailand were selected based on the rank dated February, 2018 available on https://ipricethailand.com [6]. https://ipricethailand.com was a website providing a rank of online shops in Thailand. The rank was calculated based on average rate of site visits in each quarter, a rank of applications on mobile phones, number of followers on social media, and number of employees. Each participant was assigned to test only one retail m-commerce application that they had never used before the test. We attempted to achieve an equal number of participants testing each application. A mobile phone running on the same operating system with the participant's own mobile phone was provided for carrying out the tasks.

For Study 3 (Tech-Savvy Group), top four e-commerce websites selling technology products were chosen according to the rank dated February, 2018 available on https://ipricethailand.com [6]. Each participant was provided a computer laptop to carry out the tasks. Each one of them was asked to test only one e-commerce website. We tried to assign an equal number of participants to try out each website.

Table 1 shows number of participants testing each application/website in Study 1, Study 2, and Study 3.

Table 1. Number of participants testing each application/website

Study 1 (Working Age Group)	Study 2 (Elderly Group)	Study 3 (Tech-Savvy Group)
Application A (5 participants)	Application A (6 participants)	Website A (8 participants)
Application B (8 participants)	Application B (6 participants)	Website B (8 participants)
Application C (5 participants)	Application C (6 participants)	Website C (7 participants)
Application D (6 participants)	Application D (6 participants)	Website D (7 participants)
Application E (8 participants)	Application E (7 participants)	

During the test, time to complete the tasks and errors while conducting the tasks were recorded. We also kept track of successful and unsuccessful task completion. Measurements of successful task completion were specified as shown in Table 2.

Table 2. Measurements of successful task completion

Tasks	Measurements of success
Adding to cart	Participants selected a product, added to cart, and pressed a button to confirm the product selection
Adding a shipping address	Participants filled in their own address and pressed a button to specify this address as a shipping address
Selecting a shipping method	Participants selected a shipping method with the lowest cost and pressed a button to confirm the chosen shipping method
Choosing a payment method	Participants selected a payment method, filled in relevant information, and pressed a button to confirm the chosen payment method
Placing an order	Participants pressed a button to confirm the order

2.3   Test Materials and Test Procedure

All studies were conducted at either participants' home, workplace or coffee shops and followed the same test procedure. Steps of the procedure are described below.

1. Participants were asked to read and sign an informed consent form before they began the test.
2. Researchers had an informal conversation with participants to make them feel relaxed.
3. Participants completed questions asking about their demographic details and online shopping experience. Details included gender, age, educational level, occupation, frequency of online shopping, and previously used retail e-commerce websites or m-commerce applications (for Study 1 and Study 2) and e-commerce websites selling technology products (for Study 3). For the question asking about e-commerce websites or m-commerce applications that the participants had purchased products, each participant could choose multiple answers.
4. Participants performed all five tasks in a sequential order, i.e. adding to cart, adding a shipping address, selecting a shipping method, choosing a payment method, and placing an order. They were asked to think aloud during the test. The researchers observed participants' behavior and took note on the data collection form.
5. Participants were also asked to evaluate satisfaction of each activity and fill out a usability questionnaire related to the checkout process. However, in this paper, only results regarding task completion and usability issues will be explained in the Results and Discussion section.
6. At the end of the test, debriefing session was conducted to discuss any further feedback the participants might have.

3 Results and Discussion

Data about participants' demographics and online shopping experience are described in Sect. 3.1. Results on task completion, usability issues and discussion, and design guidelines based on the research findings are presented in Sect. 3.2.

3.1 Participants' Demographics and Online Shopping Experience

Participants' demographics and online shopping experience of all participants are shown in Table 3 to Table 8 below.

Study 1 (Working Age Group). As shown in Table 3, most of the participants were female. The age range with the highest number of participants was 31–35 years old, followed by 36–40 years old. Most participants held a bachelor's degree. Thirteen participants worked in a public sector whereas nineteen of them worked in a private sector.

For online shopping experience of participants in Study 1, most participants did not frequently purchase products online. Twenty participants had made a purchase once or twice a month. Lazada.co.th and shopee.co.th were previously visited by most of the participants. Twenty-seven out of thirty-two participants had purchased via lazada.co.th. In the same vein, twenty participants had visited shopee.co.th. See Table 4 for more details.

Table 3. Demographic details of the working age group

Demographic details		Number of participants (percentage)
Gender	Male	8 (25.00)
	Female	24 (75.00)
Age (years old)	20–25	2 (6.25)
	26–30	4 (12.50)
	31–35	14 (43.75)
	36–40	8 (25.00)
	41–45	4 (12.50)
Education	High school/Vocational certificate	3 (9.38)
	Diploma	5 (15.62)
	Bachelor's degree	21 (65.62)
	Master's degree	3 (9.38)
Occupation	Civil officers	13 (40.63)
	Employees of private companies	19 (59.37)

Table 4. Online shopping experience of the working age group

Online shopping experience		Number of participants (percentage)
Online shopping frequency	Once a month	10 (31.25)
	Twice a month	10 (31.25)
	Three times a month	5 (15.60)
	Four times a month	3 (9.40)
	More than four times a month	4 (12.50)
Previously used	Lazada	27 (84.40)
e-commerce sites or	Shopee	20 (62.50)
m-commerce	Central Online	2 (6.25)
Applications	ShopAt24	7 (21.90)
(multiple answers)	JD Central	2 (6.25)
	Others	3 (9.40)

Study 2 (Elderly Group). Similar to Study 1, female participants took part in this study more than male participants. Out of thirty-one participants, twenty-three of them were between 50–55 years old. A bachelor's degree was the educational level with the highest number of participants, which was sixteen, followed by a master's degree held by ten participants. Approximately 71% of the participants were civil officers. Refer to Table 5 for further details of the elderly group's demographics.

Table 5. Demographic details of the elderly group

Demographic details		Number of participants (percentage)
Gender	Male	9 (29.03)
	Female	22 (70.97)
Age (years old)	50–55	23 (74.19)
	56–60	5 (16.13)
	61–65	3 (9.68)
Education	High school/Vocational certificate	3 (9.68)
	Diploma	1 (3.23)
	Bachelor's degree	16 (51.61)
	Master's degree	10 (32.26)
	Doctoral degree	1 (3.23)
Occupation	Civil officers	22 (70.97)
	State enterprise officers	2 (6.45)
	Retirees	3 (9.68)
	Business owners	1 (3.23)
	Freelancers	3 (9.68)

Table 6 displays details about online shopping experience of the elderly group. Twenty-three elders made an online purchase once or twice a month, indicating infrequent online shopping. The highest number of the elderly had visited lazada.co.th. Shopee.co.th ranked second for the website/application that the participants had bought products from.

Table 6. Online shopping experience of the elderly group

Online shopping experience		Number of participants (percentage)
Online shopping frequency	Once a month	15 (48.39)
	Twice a month	8 (25.81)
	Three times a month	2 (6.45)
	Four times a month	2 (6.45)
	More than four times a month	4 (12.90)
Previously used	Lazada	28 (90.32)
e-commerce sites or	Shopee	12 (38.71)
m-commerce	Central Online	1 (3.23)
Applications	ShopAt24	2 (6.45)
(multiple answers)	Others	11 (35.48)

Study 3 (Tech-Savvy Group). Unlike Study 1 and Study 2, Table 7 shows that twenty-two male participants, which was more than female participants, took part in the study. The participants fell into the age range of 31–35 and 36–40 years old more than other age ranges. All of the participants graduated with a bachelor's degree or higher. In addition, two-thirds of the participants were civil officers.

Table 7. Demographic details of the tech-savvy group

Demographic details		Number of participants (percentage)
Gender	Male	22 (73.00)
	Female	8 (27.00)
Age (years old)	20–25	1 (3.33)
	26–30	7 (23.33)
	31–35	11 (36.67)
	36–40	10 (33.33)
	41–45	1 (3.33)
Education	High school/Vocational Certificate	0 (0.00)
	Diploma	0 (0.00)
	Bachelor's degree	22 (73.33)
	Master's degree	8 (26.67)
Occupation	Civil officers	20 (66.67)
	Employees of private companies	10 (33.33)

Table 8. Online shopping experience of the tech-savvy group

Online shopping experience		Number of participants (percentage)
Online shopping frequency	Once a month	6 (20.00)
	Twice a month	16 (53.33)
	Three times a month	5 (16.67)
	Four times a month	2 (6.67)
	More than four times a month	1 (3.33)
Previously used e-commerce sites (multiple answers)	Advice	17 (56.67)
	JIB	13 (43.33)
	Banana	13 (43.33)
	IT City	3 (10.00)

As shown in Table 8, more than half of the participants purchased products online twice a month. For the previously visited e-commerce websites selling technology products in Thailand, seventeen participants had visited advice.co.th whereas thirteen participants had purchased technology products from jib.co.th (JIB) and bnn.in.th (Banana), respectively.

3.2 Task Completion and Usability Issues

This section presents number of successful task completion and time to successfully complete a task in seconds for each study. Usability issues found in each study help explain why some participants were not able to successfully perform the tasks and why it took so long to successfully complete some tasks.

Study 1 (Working Age Group). Number of successful task completion by the working age group is shown in Table 9. Some tasks of some applications were not successfully completed by all participants.

Table 9. Number of successful task completion by the working age group

Tasks	Application A (5 participants)	Application B (8 participants)	Application C (5 participants)	Application D (6 participants)	Application E (8 participants)
Adding to cart	5	8	4	6	8
Adding a shipping address	5	8	5	4	7
Selecting a shipping method	4	6	2	5	5
Choosing a payment method	5	7	5	6	7
Placing an order	5	8	5	6	8

For the task 'adding to cart,' a participant using Application C did not finish the task because the language of a button was different from the setting. The different language confused the participant, thus making the participant keep finding the right button to press.

For the task 'adding a shipping address,' a few participants using Application D and Application E were not able to complete the task. Application D required the participants to fill out information that the participants were unsure about. Since the participants were not confident about their information, they refrained from entering the data. The application detected these missing information and kept alerting the participants. The participants still did not enter any information, so this problem led to the participants' inability to proceed further. For Application E, the participant was unsuccessful to finish the task due to an inability to locate a button to add a shipping address.

For the task 'selecting a shipping method,' there were unsuccessful cases in all applications. A reason was that those participants did not directly select a shipping method. They relied on the default shipping method set by the applications.

For the task 'choosing a payment method,' a participant using Application B was unsuccessful because he/she did not notice the button whereas a participant using Application E was not familiar with the term used on the button.

Table 10 shows time to complete a task in seconds for this group. For some applications, it took longer than others to successfully complete some tasks.

Table 10. Time to successfully complete a task by the working age group (seconds)

Tasks	Application A	Application B	Application C	Application D	Application E
	Median (Min, Max)	Median (Min, Max)	Median (Min, Max)	Median (Min, Max)	Median (Min, Max)
Adding to cart	15 (9, 74)	18 (7, 30)	21 (16, 25)	19 (8, 30)	42 (5, 141)
Adding a shipping address	115 (60, 144)	131 (117, 240)	60 (30, 99)	107 (80, 193)	162 (130, 200)
Selecting a shipping method	21 (5, 43)	14 (11, 174)	14 (7, 20)	12 (1, 48)	20 (4, 175)
Choosing a payment method	42 (7, 63)	7 (4, 145)	7 (5, 84)	6 (1, 17)	6 (1, 60)
Placing an order	1 (1, 1)	1 (1, 5)	1 (1, 1)	1 (1, 1)	1 (1, 1)

For Application A, the task 'selecting a shipping method' and the task 'choosing a payment method' had the highest median of time to complete the tasks, compared to other applications. Options for shipping methods were not displayed clearly, causing the participants to look for the options longer that it should be. Similarly, the participants took some time to locate a payment method that was familiar to them.

The time to complete the task 'adding a shipping address' in Application B showed a median that is second to the highest median of Application E. Many reasons leading to this time delay were a difficulty in locating the 'add a shipping address' button, too many choices for provinces, unsystematic sorting of province options, and unnecessary words shown on the screen.

In Application D, for the task 'adding a shipping address', a median time of successful task completion listed as third rank after Application E and Application B. Since the application required the participants to manually type all relevant information and insistently requested for information that the participants were not sure about, it took the participants quite a long time to complete the tasks.

For Application E, the task 'adding a shipping address' took the longest time to complete. Several reasons were as follow. It was unclear where the button was, so the participants could not find it. Wording on a button was difficult to understand. The participants could not find desired options. For the 'adding to cart,' the median time of Application E was the highest because the participants read product details before making their decision.

Study 2 (Elderly Group). Table 11 displays number of elder participants who successfully completed the tasks for each application. For the elderly group, the main reason for unsuccessful completion of the task 'adding a shipping address,' 'selecting a shipping method,' and 'choosing a payment method' was because all three steps were shown on the same screen of Application A, Application B, and Application E. Each of the step was not obviously seen as a separate step. Therefore, the unsuccessful participants mistakenly skipped the tasks. For the task 'adding to cart,' a participant testing Application A could not complete the task because the participant was unable to locate the shopping cart. The words used on a button to confirm the selection of products were also ambiguous.

Table 11. Number of successful task completion by the elderly group

Tasks	Application A (6 participants)	Application B (6 participants)	Application C (6 participants)	Application D (6 participants)	Application E (7 participants)
Adding to cart	5	6	6	6	7
Adding a shipping address	4	6	6	6	6
Selecting a shipping method	5	5	6	6	4
Choosing a payment method	6	6	5	6	7
Placing an order	6	6	6	6	7

Table 12 shows time to successfully complete a task by two dimensions, i.e. tasks by applications. Compared to other applications, the medians of time to complete a task by using Application A were found to be highest in several tasks.

Table 12. Time to successfully complete a task by the elderly group (seconds)

Tasks	Application A	Application B	Application C	Application D	Application E
	Median (Min, Max)	Median (Min, Max)	Median (Min, Max)	Median (Min, Max)	Median (Min, Max)
Adding to cart	86 (64, 239)	65 (30, 154)	65 (8, 330)	83 (19, 191)	67 (20, 213)
Adding a shipping address	252 (128, 270)	155 (125, 215)	135 (66, 297)	210 (130, 416)	176 (105, 234)
Selecting a shipping method	30 (19, 43)	29 (20, 40)	18 (8, 21)	16 (6, 133)	20 (7, 32)
Choosing a payment method	52 (24, 99)	34 (12, 91)	17 (9, 121)	42 (11, 146)	48 (11, 94)
Placing an order	19 (10, 35)	18 (6, 30)	14 (5, 17)	20 (10, 27)	8 (7, 59)

Application A had the highest mean of time to complete the task 'adding to cart' due to several issues. The problems were mostly related to the button for confirming the product selection in two aspects, i.e. a language of the words used on the button and a location of the button. The meaning of the words used on the button were unclear and written in English. In addition, the button was located beyond the boundary of the screen. The participants had to scroll down to see and press the button.

The median of time to complete the task 'adding a shipping address' was also found to be the highest with Application A. The participants had to spend some time to search for shipping address form because an access to the shipping address form was shown in conjunction with other tasks.

For the task 'selecting a shipping method,' the median of time to complete the task was highest for the participants testing Application A. An ambiguous symbol confused the participants when they were trying to fill out information.

Similarly, for the task 'choosing a payment method,' the highest median of time to complete the task was found with the participants using Application A. The problem was that this task was designed and displayed on the same page with other shopping activities. This design approach caused the participants to spend some time looking for a section of an interface that they could choose a payment method.

For Application D, the median of time to complete the task 'placing an order' was found to be the highest because a confirmation button was shown below a boundary of a screen. The participants had to scroll down in order to see and press the confirmation button.

Study 3 (Tech-Savvy Group). As shown in Table 13, for some tasks of some applications, there were a small number of participants who were unsuccessful in completing the tasks. A participant testing Website A unsuccessfully added a shipping address because the button was placed near other irrelevant buttons. One of the reasons a participant failed to complete the task because Website B asked for citizen ID in order to add a shipping address.

Table 13. Number of successful task completion by the tech-savvy group

Tasks	Website A (8 participants)	Website B (8 participants)	Website C (7 participants)	Website D (7 participants)
Adding to cart	8	8	7	7
Adding a shipping address	7	6	7	7
Selecting a shipping method	8	8	4	6
Choosing a payment method	8	8	7	7
Placing an order	8	7	7	7

For the task 'selecting a shipping method,' a few participants failed to complete the task on Website C because the participants could not understand what information the website was requesting. On Website D, information about shipping method was unclear, making the participants hesitant to perform the task.

Time to successfully complete a task in seconds by the tech-savvy group is shown in Table 14. Considering the medians, Website B showed the poorest performance. Due to a poor navigational design, the task 'adding to cart' of Website B had the highest median of time to complete the task.

For the task 'adding a shipping address,' too much information requested by Website B was a culprit of the highest median of time to complete the task.

For the task 'selecting a shipping method,' the median of time to complete the task on Website B was highest because the participants spent some time to select options and read details about shipping.

For the task 'choosing a payment method,' tab colors and words on the tab confused the participants, causing a time delay when performing the task.

The results of task completion and the found usability issues revealed that the principle of visibility could have a high impact on users' experience and comprehension while interacting with m-commerce applications and e-commerce websites. The visibility and

Table 14. Time to successfully complete a task by the tech-savvy group (seconds)

Tasks	Website A	Website B	Website C	Website D
	Median (Min, Max)	Median (Min, Max)	Median (Min, Max)	Median (Min, Max)
Adding to cart	28.5 (15, 83)	30 (19, 138)	23 (12, 36)	10 (3, 50)
Adding a shipping address	85 (31, 180)	188.5 (129, 226)	137 (115, 360)	80 (30, 122)
Selecting a shipping method	13 (5, 198)	68 (1, 130)	7.5 (1, 22)	16 (1, 80)
Choosing a payment method	7 (3, 19)	39.5 (8, 110)	14 (3, 48)	10 (2, 60)
Placing an order	1 (1, 3)	3 (1, 27)	1 (1, 2)	1 (1, 3)

comprehensibility of action buttons, action links, arrangement of buttons, arrangement of sections of each step, words and languages used on the button are important issues to take into consideration when designing a checkout process.

In order to reduce a chance of purchase abandonment, general guidelines for a design of checkout process are proposed below.

1. Each step of a checkout process must be clearly marked. For example, if these activities, i.e. adding a shipping address, selecting a shipping method, and choosing a payment method, are supposedly designed on the same screen, a section of one activity should be easily noticeable and distinguishable from other activities.
2. Language used on action buttons or links must be comprehensible by users.
3. Position of action buttons or links must be easily noticeable by users. If possible, the action buttons and links should be displayed on the current screen at all time.
4. Instructions and rationale for requesting information within any form must be clear and make sense to users.

4   Conclusion

This research had a goal to examine online buyers' experience with a checkout process of m-commerce applications or e-commerce websites in Thailand. Three usability studies were conducted. Study 1 involved a sample group of thirty-two buyers who were between 20–45 years old and had experience in shopping via e-commerce mobile applications. Five m-commerce applications tested in the first study were m-commerce selling a wide variety of products, such as apparels, housewares, electronics, and etc. Results found interesting usability problems which were ambiguous design of options, no explanation regarding required information, using confusing language and etc.

Study 2 investigated m-commerce shopping experiences of the Thai elderly. Like the first study, the scope of the m-commerce applications included the applications selling various kinds of products. The usability of popular m-commerce applications was tested by a sample group of thirty-one elderly users. The old users were fifty years and older and had experiences in shopping via m-commerce applications. A main usability problem was that users did not know where they were in the application because the application did not have status information or any text indicating the step the users were in. This problem caused usage mistakes, thereby making buyers not prefer to buy products via applications. If steps of the applications can be clearly designed, it would be easier for the elderly to use the applications.

Lastly, study 3 examined behaviors of thirty buyers who were between 20–45 years old and had experiences in shopping with e-commerce websites selling technology-based products. Results found that the design of e-commerce websites was difficult to use due to several reasons, for example, the meaning of words did not match with users' expectations; colors used in the navigation bar were not easily distinguishable from the background; users were forced to enter personal data; payment forms did not follow an international standard, and so on.

Based on the research's findings, results of task completion and found usability issues were similar across all sample groups. A violation of the principle of visibility was a major root of almost all usability problems found in the tests.

Acknowledgements. This research was partly supported by Ahancer Co., Ltd., a user experience (UX)/user interface (UI) design agency based in Bangkok, Thailand.

References

1. Value of e-Commerce Survey in Thailand 2018. https://www.etda.or.th/publishing-detail/value-of-e-commerce-survey-in-thailand-2018.html. Accessed 31 Jan 2020
2. Cart Abandonment Rate Statistics. https://baymard.com/lists/cart-abandonment-rate. Accessed 31 Jan 2020
3. Appleseed, J., Holst, C., Grønne, T., Scott, E., Smith, L., Vind, C.: E-commerce checkout usability: exploring the customer's checkout experience. Baymard Institute, Copenhagen (2017)
4. Castilla, D., et al.: Effect of web navigation style in elderly users. Comput. Hum. Behav. **55**(B), 909–920 (2016)
5. Lim, W., Ting, D.: E-shopping: An analysis of the uses and gratifications theory. Modern Appl. Sci. **6**(5), 48 (2012)
6. E-commerce war in Thailand. https://ipricethailand.com/insights/mapofecommerce/. Accessed 21 Feb 2018

Effects of Avatar Cuteness on Users' Perceptions of System Errors in Anthropomorphic Interfaces

Yue Cheng[1](✉), Lingyun Qiu[1], and Jun Pang[2]

[1] Guanghua School of Management, Peking University, Beijing 100871, China
yuecheng@pku.edu.cn, qiu@gsm.pku.edu.cn
[2] School of Business, Renmin University of China, Beijing 100872, China
pangjun@rmbs.ruc.edu.cn

Abstract. Anthropomorphic design has been widely used in human-computer interactions. Anchored on the baby schema (Kindchenschema) theory, we propose that integrating cuteness elements in an anthropomorphic system can significantly alleviate the users' negative perceptions of system errors. The results of a laboratory experiment reveal that avatar cuteness can significantly reduce users' perceived severity of software errors taking place during human-computer interactions. This study not only explores the factor of avatar age in anthropomorphic interface design, but it also introduces the concept of cuteness into HCI research. Practical implications of these findings for human-computer interface design are discussed.

Keywords: Anthropomorphic system · Avatar · Age · Cuteness · Kindchenschema · Software error

1 Introduction

Anthropomorphic design refers to the endowments of human-like characteristics, motivations, intentions, or emotions in information systems [1]. Along with the wide application of anthropomorphic systems, researchers have examined the effects of anthropomorphic interface of information systems on user experiences in various contexts, including e-commerce [2, 3], decision support systems [4], and online education [5]. Most research finds that anthropomorphic designs have positive impacts on users' perceptions. For example, it can increase users' trust and use intention towards the systems [2, 6]. Meanwhile, researchers have also found that the effects of anthropomorphic interface are highly contingent upon the concrete design of various avatar features, such as gender [7], ethnicity [8], appearance [9], facial expressions [10], and representations [11]. However, little research so far has investigated whether or not the age of an avatar may influence users' perceptions of an anthropomorphic system.

Based on the baby schema (Kindchenschema) theory [12], we propose that avatar age is also an important design element that can affect users' perceptions. When the avatar is a child, it might induce different reactions as compared to the scenario when the avatar is an adult. Because people unconsciously interact with anthropomorphic

© Springer Nature Switzerland AG 2020
F. F.-H. Nah and K. Siau (Eds.): HCII 2020, LNCS 12204, pp. 322–330, 2020.
https://doi.org/10.1007/978-3-030-50341-3_25

systems in the way they interact with humans [13], and they usually evaluate children and adults with different criteria. Specifically, users may feel a stronger perception of *cuteness* when interacting with an embodied avatar with child-like appearances and behavioral characteristics [14]. Social psychology studies have revealed that cuteness perceptions can trigger care-taking behaviors and promote social engagement [15]. Marketing researchers have also found that cute product designs can not only help consumers form a warm impression of a brand but also build up brand attachments [16]. However, the factor of cuteness has received relatively little attention in HCI research.

In addition, the usage scenarios also matter in evaluating anthropomorphic designs. In this paper, we focus on the scenario when errors occur in human-computer interaction. Various system errors are almost inevitable in system use, which often lead to negative user experience [17]. However, there is little research on how to improve user experience through the design of error messages or prompts for correction [18]. Service marketing literature has suggested that appropriate interaction design can effectively alleviate users' negative feelings when service failure occurs [19]. Therefore, we chose to explore the effects of avatar cuteness in this particular scenario of system error. In summary, this paper attempts to answer the following research question: can avatar cuteness in anthropomorphic systems decrease users' negative perceptions when an error occurs?

2 Theoretical Foundation and Hypotheses Development

2.1 Anthropomorphic Design in Information System

Originated from the interaction design between humans and robots, studies of anthropomorphic designs date back to the 1970s [20]. An information system can be anthropomorphized through various methods [21], such as representing the system with an avatar, demonstrating the personality of the system by texts and voice, and establishing attachments between users and the system by expressing emotions [22].

Previous studies have shown that anthropomorphic interface design generates positive user reactions because they enable users to interact with the system in the same way they interact with human beings [23], which can stimulate more social interactions between a user and the system [24]. Previous research have suggested that anthropomorphic interface can increase users' trust in the system [6]. Users find interacting with anthropomorphic systems more joyful [25] and they feel more immersed in virtual environments [26] and become more willing to use such systems [2]. Users' learning abilities are also improved when interacting with systems with avatars [27].

Users' perceptions of anthropomorphic systems are heavily influenced by the appearance and behavioral characteristics of the avatars used. For example, users prefer a system whose avatar shares similar demographic characteristics with their own, including gender [7] and ethnicity [8]. Besides, they would infer the system performance based on avatar appearance. For example, a system is perceived as more powerful when the avatar being dressed more professionally [9].

This being said, the age of an avatar, which is another important demographic characteristic, has received relatively less attention compared with other demographic factors. Among the few papers examining the effect of avatars' age, Baylor and Plant (2005) found that middle-aged avatars were more likely to stimulate girls' interests in mathematics and science than younger avatars. Rosenberg-Kima et al. (2008) found that interacting with young cool avatars can improve female learners' self-efficacy than old cool avatars.

2.2 Cuteness[1]

In this paper, we propose that a key difference between a "child" avatar and an "adult" avatar is the perception of baby schema and cuteness. Proposed by Lorenz (1943), the baby schema (Kindchenschema) theory summarizes a series of physical characteristics of infants, including large round eyes, round and protruding cheeks, protruding foreheads, round faces, big heads, and thick extremities [31]. People would perceive a higher level of cuteness when an object scores higher on baby schema [14].

Researchers have found that most people show strong love in cute infants [32] because the cuteness of infants is a primary elicitor of caregiving behaviors from adults [12]. Mammalian infants-particularly human infants-are incapable of taking care of themselves, cuteness evolved as an adaptive mechanism for attracting nurturing behaviors from adults, thereby increasing their survival chance [32, 33]. The ability to recognize and differentiate cute entities from non-cute ones reflects an innate human motive to nurture and care for the offspring. Given the evolutionary role of cuteness, people's responses to cute entities are biologically hardwired [34]. People's preferences for cute entities are not limited to living things. Non-living objects with cute designs can also trigger cuteness perception. For example, Mickey Mouse, with its supernormal large head and big round eyes, is adored by the audience [35]. Products with cute features, such as rounded appearance and soft materials [36], small size [37], and soft colors [38], are very popular among consumers.

People's responses to cuteness are both affective and inferential. In terms of affect, cuteness could generate sensory pleasure [34, 39] as well as complex emotions, including tenderness [15] and empathy [40, 41]. These emotions would elicit prosocial behaviors [23]. In terms of inferential responses, cute entities are associated with physical weakness and vulnerability [42], warmth [30], honesty [43], as well as youth and vitality [44]. These inferences can motivate people's nurturing and caring-giving behaviors [32], and foster them to pay more attention to cute entities [45].

2.3 Hypotheses Development

When using an anthropomorphic system, users will perceive a higher level of cuteness if the avatar looks and behaves like a young child rather than an adult [14]. As discussed above, we expect that this cuteness perception can lead to a prosocial mindset of caretaking and helping. When an error occurs, this mindset will make the user become more helpful and more willing to resolve the problem. When a user would like to solve the problem rather than criticize the system, he or she is likely to perceive the error as less severe.

---

[1] Nenkov and Scott (2014) propose two distinctive dimensions of cuteness, namely baby schema cuteness and whimsical cuteness, which is characterized by "capricious humor and playful disposition". In this paper, cuteness refers to the baby schema cuteness only.

Besides, a user may apply different schemes when evaluating avatars of different age. In general, people tend to believe that mistakes made by children are not as fatal as those made by adults due to their lack of capabilities. As a result, the same mistake made by a child is more forgivable and less severe than that by an adult. Therefore, we posit:

H1: Avatar cuteness decreases users' perceived severity of a system error.

Prior research has shown that cuteness elicits warmth, kindness, and attractiveness perceptions [30, 32, 42], and triggers prosocial behaviors and social engagements [32]. Feelings like warmth and kindness are associated with perceived social closeness [46]. Berry (1991) found that people with warm faces have higher social closeness scores than those with faces that are judged as less warm. In the same vein, a cute avatar will make the system be perceived as socially closer to the users as it triggers higher warmth perception than a less cute avatar. Therefore, we posit:

H2: Avatar cuteness increases the users' perceived social closeness with the system.

3 Methods

3.1 Experiment Stimuli

A single factor (cuteness: low vs. high) between-subject laboratory experiment was conducted to test these hypotheses. We developed a mock-up system that claimed to evaluate a subject's word processing capability by asking the subject to count the frequency of certain keywords from several pre-stored textual snippets. Subjects were asked to interact with the system and complete the evaluation task as fast as they can. Based on their performance, the top 25% of the subjects could get additional cash rewards. The system was designed with an intentional error so that the subject had to redo one-round of counting.

Avatar cuteness was manipulated by varying the look of the avatar and the font of the instructions which represented the conversation. As shown in Table 1, subjects in the low cuteness group saw a male adult avatar and the on-screen texts were presented in a formal Chinese font[2], while those in the high cuteness group saw a baby boy avatar and the on-screen texts were presented in a childish style Chinese font[3]. A pretest was first conducted to ensure that the two designs can effectively manipulate subjects' perception of cuteness. Thirty-seven subjects were recruited for the pretest. They were asked to browse the user interface of the two groups one by one (with the presentation order counterbalanced) and then assess the two avatars' age, cuteness, and physical attractiveness respectively. The results showed that the perceived age of the baby boy was significantly younger than the male adult avatar ($M_{adult} = 27.38$ vs. $M_{child} = 8.51$, $p < 0.001$), and the avatar of baby boy was perceived as significantly cuter than the adult avatar ($M_{adult} = 4.51$ vs. $M_{child} = 5.70$, $p < 0.001$). Meanwhile, there was no significant difference in perceived attractiveness between the two avatars ($M_{adult} = 4.59$ vs. $M_{child} = 4.95$, $p > 0.237$). These results showed that our manipulation of avatar cuteness is effective.

---

[2] The font selected is "SimSun", which is similar to the "Times New Roman" font in English.

[3] The font selected is "HanYiQingKong", which is similar to the "Comic Sans" font in English.

Table 1. Stimuli design

	Adult	Child
Avtar		
Font	关键词　三农　　：12次已保存 关键词　农民　　：8次已保存 关键词　农业　　：21次已保存 关键词　现代化　：9次已保存 关键词　改革　　：　次保存失败	关键词　三农　　：12次已保存 关键词　农民　　：8次已保存 关键词　农业　　：21次已保存 关键词　现代化　：9次已保存 关键词　改革　　：　次保存失败

3.2 Measures

Measures for perceived severity is adapted from Pronk et al. (2010). Subjects respond to two questions, "How serious do you think the system error is?" and "How serious do you think the consequences of this mistake are?" on 7-point scales. Measures for social closeness is adapted from Ward and Broniarczyk (2011). Subjects rated "How close do you think the relationship between you and the system is, comparing the system to a person?" on a 7-point scale. Subjects' gender and age were measured as control variables.

3.3 Procedures

The experiments were conducted in a behavioral lab. All experiment instructions, stimuli, and questionnaires are stored and presented through a self-administrated online survey system. A total of 77 undergraduate students were recruited to participate in the experiment in exchange for a cash reward. The average age is 21.8 years, and 54.54% of them were female.

Upon arrival, the subjects were randomly assigned to one experimental condition and were asked to finish two word-counting tasks. In each task, the subject was asked to count the frequency of the five specific keywords. The task could only finish when all five answers were correct. In the second task, the system would intentionally display a "save failure", so the subjects had to finish an additional count in order to complete the task. After completing the two tasks, subjects were required to complete a questionnaire containing the measures for all variables. Upon the completion of the questionnaire, subjects are debriefed, thanked, and dismissed.

4 Results

Table 2 summarizes the group means and the standard deviations of perceived error severity and social closeness. The Cronbach alpha for perceived error severity is 0.947.

Table 2. Descriptive Statistics of Dependent Variables

	N	Perceived error severity		Perceived social closeness	
		Means	Std.	Means	Std.
Low avatar cuteness	38	4.737	1.234	3.105	1.158
High avatar cuteness	39	3.910	1.662	3.026	1.112
Total	77	4.318	1.515	3.065	1.128

We then performed a one-way ANOVA to test the effects of avatar cuteness on perceived error severity and social closeness. Participants in the high cuteness group perceived the error as significantly less severe ($M_{low} = 4.74$ vs. $M_{high} = 3.91$, $p < 0.017$), thus H1 is supported. However, there is no significant between-group difference in terms of perceived social closeness ($M_{low} = 3.11$ vs. $M_{high} = 3.03$, $p > 0.758$). Therefore, H2 is not supported.

5 Discussion

5.1 Summary of Findings

The results of our experiment suggest that avatar cuteness can significantly decrease users' perception of error severity as expected. Nevertheless, it fails to lead to higher perceived social closeness. There could be two possible explanations. First, social closeness can be effectively activated as long as the interaction partner is anthropomorphic [49]. Second, the perception of social closeness can be shaped by interacting with the system for an extended period of time, which was not the case in our experiment.

5.2 Theoretical Contributions and Practical Implications

The present research makes three theoretical contributions. First, our research addresses the research gap of avatar age. Specifically, we found that people interacting with a child avatar tends to perceive the error as less severe when a service failure takes place. This finding extends our understanding of people's responses to anthropomorphic design in human-computer interaction.

Secondly, we introduce the concept of cuteness into the field of human-computer interaction, and employ it to explain the effect of avatar age. In recent years, with the growth of a new generation of young consumers, the word "Moe" (a Japanese word for cuteness) has attracted much attention, especially in the East Asian countries [50].

However, most of early studies on cuteness have been conducted by scholars in the fields of social psychology, marketing, and journalism. This study not only introduces cuteness in the HCI field, but also examines its applicability in the design of anthropomorphic systems.

Third, we take system error as a research scenario and broaden the boundaries of HCI research. Error handling is a very typical application scenario of HCI; however, there is little research focusing on this particular scenario. These research took the perspectives of system builders such as programmers rather than ordinary users [19]. Some studies have explored the role of error message design in improving user experience. For example, Linderman and Fried (2004) proposed several design principles. Seckler et al. (2012) focused on the layout of error messages. Our research is aimed at end users. We examine the role played by the avatar cuteness in the specific scenario of system errors. By transplanting theories of service failure and recovery in service marketing, we enrich the scope of IS research.

The research also has important implications for practitioners. Our results show that system designers can consider adding cuteness design elements in interactions when software errors are likely to occur. It could alleviate users' negative perceptions of the error and thus reducing dissatisfaction. The appearance and interaction style of the avatar both work effectively in cuteness design.

5.3 Limitation and Future Research

This research has some limitations. First, we manipulated cuteness by varying avatar age and fonts. Future research can examine other forms of cuteness manipulation such as language style and avatar voice. Second, we created one particular system error in the experiment. Subsequent research can use other experimental tasks and error scenarios to verify our findings. Third, we adopted a lab experiment in this study, and all participants were university students. Future studies can use field experiments or natural experiments so as to improve the external validity.

References

1. Epley, N., Waytz, A., Cacioppo, J.T.: On seeing human: a three-factor theory of anthropomorphism. Psychol. Rev. **114**(4), 864–886 (2007)
2. Qiu, L., Benbasat, I.: Evaluating anthropomorphic product recommendation agents: a social relationship perspective to designing information systems. J. Manag. Inf. Syst. **25**(4), 145–182 (2009)
3. Wang, W., Qiu, L., Kim, D., Benbasat, I.: Effects of rational and social appeals of online recommendation agents on cognition- and affect-based trust. Decis. Support Syst. **86**, 48–60 (2016)
4. Li, M., Jiang, Z., Fan, Z., Hou, J.: Expert or Peer? Understanding the implications of virtual advisor identity on emergency rescuer empowerment in mobile psychological self-help services. Inf. Manag. **54**(7), 866–886 (2017)
5. Kanda, T., Sato, R., Saiwaki, N., Ishiguro, H.: A two-month field trial in an elementary school for long-term human-robot interaction. IEEE Trans. Rob. **23**(5), 962–971 (2007)
6. Waytz, A., Heafner, J., Epley, N.: The mind in the machine: anthropomorphism increases trust in an autonomous vehicle. J. Exp. Soc. Psychol. **52**, 113–117 (2014)

7. van den Hende, E.A., Mugge, R.: Investigating gender-schema congruity effects on consumers' evaluation of anthropomorphized products. Psychol. Mark. **31**(4), 264–277 (2014)
8. Qiu, L., Benbasat, I.: A study of demographic embodiments of product recommendation agents in electronic commerce. Int. J. Hum Comput Stud. **68**(10), 669–688 (2010)
9. Liew, T.W., Tan, S.: Exploring the effects of specialist versus generalist embodied virtual agents in a multi-product category online store. Telematics Inform. **35**(1), 122–135 (2018)
10. Bartneck, C., Reichenbach, J.: Subtle emotional expressions of synthetic characters. Int. J. Hum Comput Stud. **62**(2), 179–192 (2005)
11. McBreen, H.M., Jack, M.A.: Evaluating humanoid synthetic agents in E-Retail applications. IEEE Trans. Syst. Man Cybern. Part A Syst. Hum. **31**(5), 394–405 (2001)
12. Lorenz, K.: Die Angeborenen Formen Möglicher Erfahrung. Zeitschrift für Tierpsychologie **5**(2), 235–409 (1943)
13. Reeves, B., Nass, C.I.: The Media Equation: How People Treat Computers, Television, and New Media Like Real People and Places. Cambridge University Press, New York (1996)
14. Alley, T.R.: Head shape and the perception of cuteness. Dev. Psychol. **17**(5), 650–654 (1981)
15. Sherman, G.D., Haidt, J.: Cuteness and disgust: the humanizing and dehumanizing effects of emotion. Emot. Rev. **3**(3), 245–251 (2011)
16. Jia, H.M., Park, C.W., Pol, G.: Cuteness, Nurturance, and Implications for Visual Product Design in The Psychology of Design: Creating Consumer Appeal, pp. 168–179. Routledge, New York (2016)
17. Lewis, C., Norman, D.A.: Designing for Error in Readings in Human–Computer Interaction, pp. 686–697. Morgan Kaufmann, Massachusetts (1995)
18. Shneiderman, B.: Designing computer system messages. Commun. ACM **25**(9), 610–611 (1982)
19. Kukka, H., Goncalves, J., Heikkinen, T., Suua, O. P., Ojala, T.: Touch Ok to continue: error messages and affective response on interactive public displays. In: Proceedings of the 4th International Symposium on Pervasive Displays, pp. 99–105. ACM, Saarbruecken (2015)
20. Vukobratovic, M.: How to control artificial anthropomorphic systems. IEEE Trans. Syst. Man Cybern. **5**, 497–507 (1973)
21. Fong, T., Nourbakhsh, I., Dautenhahn, K.: A survey of socially interactive robots. Robot. Auton. Syst. **42**(3–4), 143–166 (2003)
22. Fink, J.: Anthropomorphism and human likeness in the design of robots and human-robot interaction. In: Ge, S.S., Khatib, O., Cabibihan, J.-J., Simmons, R., Williams, M.-A. (eds.) ICSR 2012. LNCS (LNAI), vol. 7621, pp. 199–208. Springer, Heidelberg (2012). https://doi.org/10.1007/978-3-642-34103-8_20
23. Wang, T., Anirban, M.: How Consumers Respond to Cute Products in The Psychology of Design: Creating Consumer Appeal, pp. 149–167. Routledge, New York (2015)
24. Duffy, B. R.: Anthropomorphism and Robotics. In: The Society for the Study of Artificial Intelligence and the Simulation of Behaviour (2002)
25. Li, B.J., Lwin, M.O.: Player see, player do: testing an exergame motivation model based on the influence of the self avatar. Comput. Hum. Behav. **59**, 350–357 (2016)
26. Gerhard, M., Moore, D., Hobbs, D.: Embodiment and copresence in collaborative interfaces. Int. J. Hum Comput Stud. **61**(4), 453–480 (2004)
27. Moreale, E., Watt, S.: An agent-based approach to mailing list knowledge management. In: van Elst, L., Dignum, V., Abecker, A. (eds.) AMKM 2003. LNCS (LNAI), vol. 2926, pp. 118–129. Springer, Heidelberg (2004). https://doi.org/10.1007/978-3-540-24612-1_8
28. Baylor, A.L., Plant, E.A.: Pedagogical agents as social models for engineering: the influence of agent appearance on female choice. In: Artificial Intelligence in Education: Supporting Learning Through Intelligent and Socially Informed Technology, pp. 65–72. IOS Press (2005)
29. Rosenberg-Kima, R.B., Baylor, A.L., Plant, E.A., Doerr, C.E.: Interface agents as social models for female students: the effects of agent visual presence and appearance on female students' attitudes and beliefs. Comput. Hum. Behav. **24**(6), 2741–2756 (2008)

30. Nenkov, G.Y., Scott, M.L.: "So Cute I Could Eat It Up": priming effects of cute products on indulgent consumption. J. Consum. Res. **41**(2), 326–341 (2014)
31. Hildebrandt, K.A., Fitzgerald, H.E.: Facial feature determinants of perceived infant attractiveness. Infant Behav. Dev. **2**, 329–339 (1979)
32. Glocker, M.L., Langleben, D.D., Ruparel, K., Loughead, J.W., Gur, R.C., Sachser, N.: Baby schema in infant faces induces cuteness perception and motivation for caretaking in adults. Ethology **115**(3), 257–263 (2009)
33. Darwin, C., Prodger, P.: The Expression of the Emotions in Man and Animals. Oxford University Press, USA (1998)
34. Berridge, K.C., Kringelbach, M.L.: Affective neuroscience of pleasure: reward in humans and animals. Psychopharmacology **199**(3), 457–480 (2008)
35. Gould, S.J.: Mickey mouse meets konrad lorenz. Nat. History **88**(5), 30–36 (1979)
36. Marcus, A.: the cult of cute: the challenge of user experience design. Interactions **9**(6), 29–34 (2002)
37. McVeigh, B.J.: How hello kitty commodifies the cute, cool and camp: 'Consumutopia' versus 'Control' in Japan. J. Mater. Cult. **5**(2), 225–245 (2000)
38. Masubuchi, S.: Kawaii Shōkōgun (Cute Syndrome). Nihon Hōsō Shuppan Kyōkai, Tokyo (1994)
39. Hildebrandt, K.A., Fitzgerald, H.E.: Adults' responses to infants varying in perceived cuteness. Behav. Proc. **3**(2), 159–172 (1978)
40. Griskevicius, V., Shiota, M.N., Neufeld, S.L.: Influence of different positive emotions on persuasion processing: a functional evolutionary approach. Emotion **10**(2), 190–206 (2010)
41. Shiota, M.N., Keltner, D., John, O.P.: Positive emotion dispositions differentially associated with big five personality and attachment style. J. Positive Psychol. **1**(2), 61–71 (2006)
42. Berry, D.S., McArthur, L.Z.: Some components and consequences of a babyface. J. Pers. Soc. Psychol. **48**(2), 312–323 (1985)
43. Gorn, G.J., Jiang, Y., Johar, G.V.: Babyfaces, trait inferences, and company evaluations in a public relations crisis. J. Consum. Res. **35**(1), 36–49 (2008)
44. Hellen, K., Sääksjärvi, M.: Development of a scale measuring childlike anthropomorphism in products. J. Mark. Manag. **29**(1–2), 141–157 (2013)
45. Maier Jr., R.A., Holmes, D.L., Slaymaker, F., Reich, J.N.: The perceived attractiveness of preterm infants. Infant Behav. Dev. **7**(4), 403–414 (1984)
46. Berry, D.S.: Accuracy in social perception: contributions of facial and vocal information. J. Pers. Soc. Psychol. **61**(2), 298 (1991)
47. Pronk, T.M., Karremans, J.C., Overbeek, G., Vermulst, A.A., Wigboldus, D.: What it takes to forgive: when and why executive functioning facilitates forgiveness. J. Pers. Soc. Psychol. **98**(1), 119–131 (2010)
48. Ward, M.K., Broniarczyk, S.M.: It's Not Me, It's You: how gift giving creates giver identity threat as a function of social closeness. J. Consum. Res. **38**(1), 164–181 (2011)
49. Eyssel, F., De Ruiter, L., Kuchenbrandt, D., Bobinger, S., Hegel, F.: 'If You Sound Like Me, You Must Be More Human': on the interplay of robot and user features on human-robot acceptance and anthropomorphism. In: 2012 7th ACM/IEEE International Conference on Human-Robot Interaction (HRI), pp. 125–126. IEEE (2012)
50. Dale, J.P.: Cute studies: an emerging field. East Asian J. Popular Cult. **2**(1), 5–13 (2016)
51. Linderman, M., Fried, J.: Defensive Design for the Web: How to Improve Error Messages, Help, Forms, and Other Crisis Points. New Riders Publishing, California (2004)
52. Seckler, M., Tuch, A.N., Opwis, K., Bargas-Avila, J.A.: User-friendly locations of error messages in web forms: put them on the right side of the erroneous input field. Interact. Comput. **24**(3), 107–118 (2012)

Human Computer Interaction Aspects of Enterprise Social Networks: An Empirical Validation of Adoption Model in a Developing Country

Ghada Refaat El Said(✉) (iD)

Future University in Egypt (FUE), 90th Street, Fifth Settlement, New Cairo, Egypt
ghadarefaat_04@hotmail.com, ghada.refaat@fue.edu.eg

Abstract. This paper suggests an adoption model for Enterprise Social Networks (ESN) based on Human Computer Interaction aspects in a developing country, Egypt. The study starts with an exploratory phase, where semi-structured interviews were conducted with ten of ESN users, from different operation levels, and in two organizations. Thematic analysis of interviews data suggested personal cognitive dimension of ESN adoption, such as: Perceived Value, Privacy, Power Distance Cultural Dimension, Management Support, Interactivity, and Usability. In light of these interview results, an adoption model was built.

The model was validated using a survey administered with a convenient sample of 82 permanent employees from different backgrounds and in various managerial levels, in the same two organizations operating in Egypt.

The statistical analysis of the model suggests that Interactivity, Perceived Value, Management Support, and Usability were found to have substantial influences on ESN Adoption. The suggested integrated model helps for better understanding of ESN from the users' perception. This paper contributes with implications for ESN's researchers, developers, and managers. This research presents a plausible, integrated framework for investigating the target phenomenon, especially for un-explored cultures.

Keywords: Enterprise Social Networks · ESNs · Human Computer Interaction · ESNs adoption model · IT in developing countries

1 Introduction

Enterprise Social Networks have been receiving growing attention within academia and business in recent years. Enterprises have been looking at social networks as a knowledge management and communication tool to improve collaboration and innovation among employees. Enterprise Social Networks (ESN) have the potential to change the landscape of workplaces by allowing members of an organization to share, communicate, and develop ideas unconstrained by geographical, temporal, or organizational hierarchy.

To date, and in most cases, ESN did not fulfill the organizations' expectations due to lack of attention to human aspects during implementation [1]. Recently, human factors

© Springer Nature Switzerland AG 2020
F. F.-H. Nah and K. Siau (Eds.): HCII 2020, LNCS 12204, pp. 331–338, 2020.
https://doi.org/10.1007/978-3-030-50341-3_26

were suggested to be one of the main prerequisites for a successful implementation of Enterprise Social Networks. Hence, a growing body of literature begins to investigate users' perception towards ESN [2].

This paper investigates Human Computer Interaction aspects of Enterprise Social Networks; most specifically, the paper looks at antecedents of adoption for ESN. The paper aims to contribute to research by suggesting and validating ESN adoption model in a developing country, Egypt, where the use of social network is widespread.

The paper begins by giving some background on past literature on human aspects of Enterprise Social Network (ESN) and the case of social networks penetration in Arab countries in general and in Egypt in specific. This is followed by a description of the research methodology, where an exploratory semi-structured interviews were conducted with a sample of ESN users to generate mature hypotheses, based on which an adoption model was suggested.

This was followed by a comprehensive reporting of data analysis and results presentation. Finally the findings and their implications are discussed, and limitations of the current work are cited with suggestions of possible relevant future work.

2 Literature Review

2.1 Enterprise Social Networks (ESN) and HCI

Enterprise social networks have the potentials to improve company internal communication, collaboration and innovation processes [3]. ESN connect employees unbounded with hierarchical, time, and location barriers, and hence improve knowledge transfer within the company [4].

Little previous work investigated prerequisites for the successful adoption of an ESN from the Human Computer Interaction aspects. One of these studies recommended that it is essential that employees have the basic knowledge needed to use the new tool; it is vital to clarify which functions offer what kind of benefits, limitation of the tool, and what kind of content is useful to share [1]. According to the study, employees should be able to decide when a traditional telephone call or face-to-face meeting might be a better choice. Length, frequency and visibility of information shared via the ESN need to be also identified [1].

Other previous work, on the same research strand, analyzed motives for employees to use ESN in an early-adoption stage and how users' behavior can be classified in a post-acceptance stage of ESN implementation [5]. The study also looked at how users' perception of privacy and trust affect the intention to use an ESN and the intention to share knowledge on ESN.

2.2 Social Network Penetration in Arab Countries

Social Network has grown worldwide to become an essential part of Internet use, it became a vital component of any firm's strategy to expand their reach and improve their services. In the Arab countries, the number of social media users has increased since 2013, where Egypt did a tremendous boost. While in 2013 most of Arab nations used the internet mainly to check email, this changed in 2018 as a total of 97% of internet Arab users used Social Networks to communicate and receive news update, with 83% of them do so daily [6].

Egypt is reported to have the largest population of Internet users in the Middle East and North Africa region [6]. In 2017, the total number of Egyptian Face book active users reached 35 million (22 million male users and 12 million female users). In 2018, face book was used by 83% Egyptian Internet users, Whats-App was used by 77%, and Instagram and Snap-chat were used by 51%. It was also reported that the average time Egyptians spent online per week reached 26.2 h [6].

Still, Egypt has not yet adopted the full developmental opportunities of the Internet in business, such as Enterprise Social Network (ESN) platforms, as have other countries in the region. The adoption of new IT innovations in Egypt is usually seen as a real challenge; Hence, Egypt's approach to ESN adoption can offer important lessons for other developing countries.

This Study focus on Human Computer Interaction factors affecting adoption of ESN in Egypt, representing a developing country under-represented and under-researched in IT adoption research, but where the potential benefits are high.

3   Research Methodology

3.1   Research Procedures

This research follows an inductive approach, where investigation is done without trying to fit the data into a pre-existing model. First: investigational semi-structured interviews were conducted with a small representative sample of ESN users, to generate plausible research hypotheses, and accordingly suggest hypothetical research model. Second: the suggested model was validated using a survey conducted over a larger sample.

Interview sessions were conducted with 10 ESN employees of two different organizations. Each session was 20–30 min long, and was recorded using a portable recorder. Data collection was completed by saturation; this is when a feeling of closure is obtained with repeated answers. Participants were interviewed around their general experience with the enterprise social network tools in their work place, expressing their interest, challenges, and drive to utilise these tools.

The interviews began by asking about the contribution of ESN tools to the organization's knowledge sharing and communication. This was followed by broad questions aiming to find out what the ESN tools are being used for, what motivate participants to use these tools, and what problems, if any, participants experienced while using the tools. During the interview sessions, participants were asked to point out what they like/dislike in ESN tools they are using in their organization, and suggest ways to improve it.

All sessions were conducted in Arabic, the mother tongue of all of the interviewees, as well as the interviewer, the author of this research, who transcript the data in English language. Data collected in interviews were analysed using Thematic Analysis technique [7]. Thematic analysis goes beyond counting expressions and moves on to identifying patterns, *themes*, across data sets describing the phenomenon under investigation [8]. Themes suggest a set of constructs that participants had consistently emphasized as antecedents of ESN adoption in their work place. As some of these constructs, are supported by previous relevant ESN literature, this provided a good justification to pursue further investigation, hence formulating the research hypothetical model illustrated in the following section.

The model was validated using a survey administered with a larger sample of 82 participants from the same organizations. All the items used in the survey have been drawn from the literature, sharing a similar context to the current one, where they were quoted to be reliable and valid to measure constructs of the phenomenon that they intend to represent. The survey was designed in English, where none of the items were modified by changing the wording of the question.

3.2 Research Sample

Convenience sampling technique was conducted as participation in the study was voluntary. The sample size depended on the number of volunteers who were willing to participate in the study. The sample includes staff with different background, education, and managerial levels, such as: administration staff, engineers, marketing coordinators, and public relations from two entrepreneur organizations working in the areas of construction and insurance services.

All participants self reported at least an intermediate level of technology familiarity, working with their organization for at least 3 months. Males represent 65% of the sample and females represent 35% of the overall sample. The investigational semi-structured interview included 10 participants, while 82 participants filled and returned back the survey.

4 Data Analysis and Discussion

4.1 Thematic Analysis

Through systematic thematic analysis of the interviews scripts, ideas were organized into general conceptual themes. The themes capture a set of factors that the interviewees had consistently emphasized as having influence on their perception of usage of ESNs. Thematic analysis of the interviews resulted in six main themes that reveal factors affecting users' decision to use or not use the ESN tools in their work place, as following:

Theme 1: Interactivity & Theme 2: Usability
Interactivity was mentioned by all interviewees as an issue concerning the ESN use in their work place. While all participants expressed the necessity for ESN to be highly dynamic and engaging interactive activities, such as chat rooms and meetings online. The main concern for interviewees was the poor participation opportunities they are allowed to have. Interviewees suggested some ideas to increase interactivity with their colleagues, such as shared drop box and online forums. One interviewee cited (an engineer): *"Online interactive meetings on ESN would save lots of useless F2F meeting times.... this would keep me more focused ...online voting, discussion, message board, and a chat room.. Something like a break room for informal discussion with colleagues before the meeting..."*. Many of the interviewees who are not using ESN expressed that

after their registration, they found that the content is overwhelming, within which it was not easy to find topics of interest from a quick scan. Other expressed that the tool was not usable, not easy to learn, and not obvious.

Theme 3: Power Distance & Theme 4: Management Support
Majority of the participants expressed that the ESN would facilitate communication with supervisor, such communication is weak in work place. Other participants expressed that the ESN gives opportunity to participate in decision making. One interviewee (a secretary) cited: *"Most of the time we are unwilling to participate in decisions … we just follow passively unless we are encouraged by our supervisor"*. Another interviewee (an HR manager): *"We encourage our employee to use the ESN in place… they are encouraged to contribute with content and share knowledge"*. Egypt is classified as high power distance culture [9]. In organization with a high power distance culture, communication takes place vertical downwards, with no or little horizontal communication, and a large communication gap exists between managers and employees [10].

Theme 5: Perceived Value & Theme 6: Privacy
During interviews, participants envisaged ESN would provide value to them throughout mobility, rapidity, and timing. Value is expressed by participants as the degree of convenience that allows employee to communicate on business issues via mobiles in different place and times, unbounded with working hours and office place. Rapidity in sharing news, taking votes, reaching consensus on deadline, commenting on shared documents, all were expressed as value added by ESN tools. On the other hand, some of participants expressed that such use of ESN would violate their privacy and would take priority over their private life outside work.

Based on the results of thematic analysis, an ESN adoption model was hypothesized in terms of six independent variables and one dependent variable, as illustrate in Fig. 1. The model hypothesizes that Perceived Value, Privacy, Power Distance, Management Support, Interactivity, and Usability, have significant effect on ESN adoption.

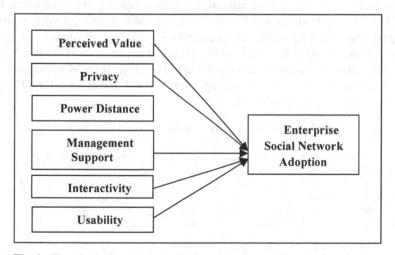

Fig. 1. Hypothetical research model for enterprise social networks adoption.

4.2 Model Validation

The model was validated according to the following sequence: first, validity and relia-bility of the research items and constructs were assessed. Second, multiple discriminant function analysis was conducted for model testing.

Item reliability was checked by calculating item loading as well as the correlation between each item and its corresponding construct. All items were found with adequate reliability with items' loading and item-construct correlation are at least 0.60.

Constructs' reliability was checked and was found adequate as all constructs had composite reliability scores above 0.8, average variance extracted scores exceeding 0.5, and Cronbach's Alpha scores were all higher than 0.6. Additionally, all items were found to have much higher loading in their assigned constructs than in the other constructs, this suggests the discriminant validity of all of the used items.

Correlation coefficients between each construct and its associated items were calcu-lated using Pearson Correlation Coefficient. A significant correlation was found between all constructs and all their associate items. A reliability check was done for the overall model using Cronbach alpha which was found higher than 0.80 except for the construct: Power Distance. Accordingly this constructs was dropped from the research model. Meanwhile, all the remaining constructs had composite reliability above 0.8, AVE above 0.5, and Cronbach's Alpha higher than 0.6. This suggests that remaining constructs, after dropping Power Distance, had adequate reliability.

Multiple discriminant function analysis (MDFA) technique was used to assess the research model. MDFA is appropriate when the independent variables are interval and the dependent variables are categorical [11], which was the case in the current research. In the current study, participants select between three levels of ESN adoption (1: Adoption: using an interactive ESN tool at work place with exchange of data; 2: Non-adopters: not using the ESN; 3: using the existing ESN to retrieve data with no contribution from the user).

MDFA analysis showed a statistically significant function indicating that the model is satisfactorily significant in differentiating between adopters and non-adopters. Based on the Discriminant loadings and F-value, listed in Table 1, the following constructs are suggested to have a significant effect on the ESN adoption: Perceived Value, Man-agement Support, Interactivity, and Usability. While the relationship between Adoption and Privacy construct was not found significant. Therefore, it could be suggested that these four factors (Perceived Value, Management Support, Interactivity, and Usability) significantly affect the initial adoption of ESN.

Table 1. Discriminant analysis of the ESN adoption model.

Construct	Discriminant loading	F-value	P-level	Coefficient	Adopter mean	Adopter SD	Non-adopter mean	Non-adopter SD
Perceived value	0.643	62	0.000	0.682	2.68	0.71	3.56	1.05
Privacy	0.266	30	0.000	0.222	2.10	0.87	3.28	0.82
Management support	0.634	63	0.000	0.667	3.10	1.35	2.66	0.47
Interactivity	0.934	84	0.000	0.934	3.05	0.86	3.85	0.46
Usability	0.845	74	0.000	0.823	2.24	0.77	3.86	0.89

5 Conclusion and Limitations

This study establishes a framework to investigate Human Computer Interaction-based adoption model. The study focuses on Enterprise Social Networks (ESN) adoption in a developing country. A small sample of representative users in two organizations in Egypt participated in interviews around their general preferences and perception of using ESN in their work place. Thematic analysis of interviews data suggested the hypothetical research model for ESN adoption. The suggested model was empirically tested and results highlight some of factors affecting ESN implementation. The model was found to be valid to discriminate ESN adopters from non-adopters.

According to the research findings, the adoption of ESN innovations, which can be considered a relatively new to some developing countries, depends on some major human computer interaction aspects, such as: Perceive value added from using the tool; Management support, Ease of use and obviousness of the design, Degree of interactivity with the tool. In most of developing countries cases, serious challenges in these four factors are faced: poor management, poor user engagement in design, or poor utilization of technology, resulting in poor adoption of IT innovations.

Interactive nature of social networks and the familiarity and ease of use of such tools were found to be especially important as positively and significantly affect ESN Adoption. A number of interface design guidelines can be suggested to increase degree of interactivity within the enterprise context, such as integration with other enterprise tools, enterprise knowledge management for example, as well as ESN hypermedia discovery-based navigation.

Perceived value was mainly expressed as the ESN ability to share knowledge and being fit with business tasks. Recommendations can be given for ESN designers, where user involvement in analysis and design phase of systems is crucial. By considering users' understanding of the business process and task characteristics, this would more likely result in successful ESN implementation and ensure that the resulting system would fit the task need.

Managers should build a culture of knowledge sharing, praise individual's contributions to the organization knowledge and provide appropriate feedback to users' engagement in knowledge sharing.

The research, by providing an understanding of the users' perception of Enterprise Social Networks, contributes to building an adoption model of ESN within organizations, especially in a context similar to the research context, which is developing country. The study highlights human-based prerequisites for a successful ESN adoption.

The current study does not focus on the description and analysis of best-practice approaches for already adopted ESN, this could be considered as future work of the current research. Future work would further extend the ESN adoption model, suggested by this research, to examine usage and impact on individual's and organization performance.

One of the main limitations of this research is that two different ESN tools adopted in two different organizations were included, differences in human computer interaction aspects and functions usability were not considered. Such differences might cause diverse users' perception.

References

1. Schuh, G., Schwartz, M.: Prerequisites for the Successful Launch of Enterprise Social Networks. In: Lödding, H., Riedel, R., Thoben, K.-D., von Cieminski, G., Kiritsis, D. (eds.) APMS 2017. IAICT, vol. 513, pp. 239–246. Springer, Cham (2017). https://doi.org/10.1007/978-3-319-66923-6_28
2. Chin, Y., Evans, N., Choo, K.: Exploring factors influencing the use of enterprise social networks in multinational professional service firms. J. Organ. Comput. Electron. Commer. **2**(5), 99–110 (2016). https://doi.org/10.1080/10919392.2015.1058118
3. Iriberri, A., Leroy, G.: A life-cycle perspective on online community success. ACM Comput. Surv. **41**(2), 1–29 (2009). https://doi.org/10.1145/1459352.1459356
4. Wenger, E., McDermott, R., Snyder, W.M.: Cultivating Communities of Practice: A Guide to Managing Knowledge. Harvard Business School Press, Boston (2002)
5. Wehner, B., Ritter, C., Leist, S.: Enterprise social networks: A literature review and research agenda. Comput. Netw. **114**, 125–142 (2017). https://doi.org/10.1016/j.comnet.2016.09.001
6. Crowd Analyzer, Social Media Users in Egypt: Face book Insights and Usage in Egypt (2018). https://www.digitalmarketingcommunity.com/indicators/facebook-insights-usage-in-egypt-2018. Accessed 29 Jan 2019
7. Bernard, H.R., Ryan, G.W.: Analyzing Qualitative Data. Sage, Thousand Oaks (2012)
8. Guest, G.: Applied Thematic Analysis. Sage, Thousand Oaks (2012)
9. Hofstede, G.: Cultures Consequences: Comparing Values Behaviours Institutions and Organisations across Nations. SAGE Publishing, Thousand Oaks (2001)
10. Khatri, N.: Consequences of power distance orientation in organisations. Vis. J. Bus. Perspect. **13**(1), 1–9 (2009). https://doi.org/10.1177/097226290901300101
11. Hair, F., Anderson, E., Tatham, L., Black, C.: Multivariate Data Analysis with Readings, 4th edn. Prentice Hall, Englewood Cliffs (1995)

Virtual Reality Online Shopping (VROS) Platform

Yu-Chun Huang(✉) and Shu-Yun Liu

Graduate Institute of Design Science, Tatung University, 40, Sec. 3, Zhongshan N. Rd.,
Taipei, Taiwan
ych@gm.ttu.edu.tw

Abstract. Since 1980, with the advent of the personal computer (PC), and the development of the Internet, the first "online shopping" appeared in the world. However, many limitations still exist in current online shopping. For instance, experience, environment, interface, or the screen size are entirely different from physical shopping stores. Here, we implemented a system prototype—Virtual Reality Online Shopping (VROS) Platform, which brought the physical shopping experience into the VR world by incorporating VR hardware—Samsung HMD Odyssey+ as the platform base. The VROS was created by the core concept of "home-hub", which included five different spaces: living room, kitchen, farm, home library and walk-in closets. Different spaces represented as the entrance of shopping categories were connected to the different online shopping stores. The users were able to organize the shopping goods (no matter the user had or still on the wishlist) in the VROS home. To evaluate the VROS, we recruited two subjects to do the two-step experiments by using protocol analysis. The VROS is current an off-line system but is able to apply to real online shopping stores in next version, such as Amazon and eBay.

Keywords: Online shopping · Virtual reality

1 Introduction

The development of the personal computer (PC) and the Internet introduced the new behavior of "online shopping" since 1980. The first online shopping behavior—TV shopping, transformed the traditional shopping in 1984 [1]. Traditional shopping allows people to physically interact with the products through a multitude of senses: sight (ophthalmoception), hearing (audioception), taste (gustaoception), smell (olfacoception or olfacception), and touch (tactioception) before making decisions. In contrast, during online shopping, people are restricted by visual (monitor) and auditory (speaker) inputs and can only use the "browser to search keywords" or use the "classification" to find the products of interest. Nevertheless, internet endows the power of easy and quick browsing/comparing the items/stores across the world, which is not achievable in the physical world.

© Springer Nature Switzerland AG 2020
F. F.-H. Nah and K. Siau (Eds.): HCII 2020, LNCS 12204, pp. 339–353, 2020.
https://doi.org/10.1007/978-3-030-50341-3_27

However, there are many limitations in current 2D online shopping— the shopping experience, shopping environment, interface, or even the restricted screen size. The challenge of this research lies in how to create a more natural and intuitive shopping environment by using the benefits of physical shopping and 2D online shopping.

VR devices have recently become more popular, less expensive and widely integrated into multiple fields [2–5]. Thus, VR could potentially be used as an alternative bridge to connect the physical and online shopping stores. Since this is an ongoing project and we have previously discussed the preliminary scenario of the VR online shopping [6], we will implement a system prototype—"VROS" by using Samsung HMD Odyssey+ as the VR hardware and Unity as the platform base. To evaluate the possibility of VROS, we used protocol analysis to test the system by two-stage experiments.

2   Methodology and Steps

To create a more natural and more intuitive shopping experience, we combined both the significance of "online shopping" and "physical store shopping" into the virtual reality online shopping (VROS) system by using VR hardware. Through the VROS system, we expected the users can smoothly, safely, appropriately, and easily shop at the VR, and even better than the physical experience. The methodology and steps are as follow.

2.1   The First Step: System Concept

The concept of the VROS was established by the results of the online shopping preferences from the view of "environment", "product" and "experience" [6].

2.2   The Second Step: Implementation

In order to implement the VROS prototype, the step included three stage:

3D modeling. We built the 3D model as the VROS environment based on the result of the first step.
System framework. We discussed the system framework, system installation including the selection of hardware and Unity platform establishment.
Manipulation. We discussed the manipulation in VROS.

2.3   The Third Step: Scenario Demonstration and Evaluation

In order to create an adequate VR online shopping environment, we used the scenario demonstration and two-stage experiments to evaluate the VROS system as described below:

Experiment S1. Shopping experiments in "traditional 2D online shopping environment".
Experiment S2. Shopping experiments in "VROS environment".

3 System Concept

The VROS concept was followed by the previous study of 2D online shopping experience [6]. The VROS system consists of three main structures: shopping environment, shopping product and shopping experience (see Table 1).

On the other side, shopping happens in our daily life. All the shopping goods we purchased physically and virtually exist in our living environment. "Home" is the most fundamental space for human beings. Therefore, we used "home-hub" as the core concept of the VROS. All the shopping activities would start from the virtual home-hub, which could teleport to the worldwide e-shops. Through VROS, whether the "items are already purchased" or the "items are on the wish-list", the users can easily arrange them into the home-like environment. There are five characters as below.

Table 1. Comparison between physical shopping, 2D online shopping and VROS.

		Physical shopping	2D online shopping	VROS
Environment	Space	3D panorama	2D webpage	3D panorama
	Category	Physical aisle	2D words or icon	3D space
	Viewport	3D panorama	2D	3D panorama
Product	display	Physical products	2D photos or video	3D products
	Information	Narrow displayed onto physical product	2D words	2D interface floated next to the product
	Review	2D review and video	n/a	2D interface floated next to the product
	Shopping list	Physical cart	2D in shopping cart	On 3D wall
	Wishlist	n/a	2D in shopping cart	3D products
Experience	Social	Collaboration shopping with real people	n/a	Social network based collaboration shopping
	Control	Hand	Mouse	Hand gesture with 3D controller

3.1 Home-Hub

The VROS was an entrance of online shopping home spot. The layout can be customized by the users. In home-hub, there are four teleports in four different space (kitchen, living room, home library and walk-in closets), which were represented as different entrances of shopping categories (Fig. 1). For instance, the kitchen can be teleported to grocery, such as real farm or "Coop"; the living room can be teleported to the entertainment, electronics or home furniture, such as IKEA; the home library can be connected to "Amazon"; and walk-in closets on 2nd floor can be teleported to fashion shop, such as Uniqlo or Macys.

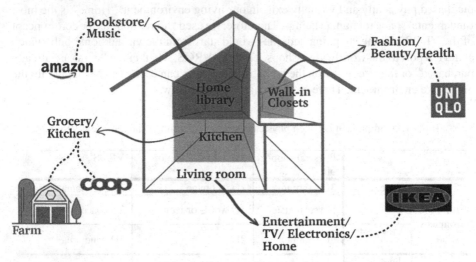

Fig. 1. Concept of home-hub.

3.2 Hand Gesture Control

In the VR environment, the user is able to use the hand gesture to naturally interact with the virtual products to enhance the ability of physical shopping experience, such as grabbing or touching a product, 3D panorama appreciating the products or putting the products into the bag (see Fig. 2).

3.3 Product Display and Wish-List

In the VROS home-hub, the product display would be the same as in the physical shop. The products on the wishlist were shown in grayscale (see Fig. 6-H round neck sweatshirt), but can be arranged in VROS home. When the user picked up the product (such as Fig. 6-C wooden rocking horse) the product would turn back to the original (wooden color).

3.4 Floating Interface (Information and Shopping List)

When the user stopped by or got close to the products, the floating interface emerged with the product information and rating. In order to quickly check the shopping bag items, the shopping bag lists were shown on the wall of the living room.

Fig. 2. Hand gesture in VROS (grab, hold, flip, throw and drop).

3.5 Collaboration Shopping

Shopping is usually a very personal behavior. However, according to the previous study [6], most people might share shopping lists with specific people (such as family, colleagues or friends). In the VROS, users could customize a specific person as a collaborative shopping friend. When your collaborative shopping friend was online, the grayscale person would turn into color. At the same time, the user can invite him/her to join the shopping.

4 System Implementation

4.1 3D Modeling

In order to implement a "home-hub" based VROS prototype, first, we created a 3D model of VROS shopping environment. The VROS was composed of five main spaces: living room, kitchen, home library, walk-in closet, and farm. Different spaces contained specific products. And each space will be redirected to the related online shopping stores (see Table 2).

Since the VROS was performed on the Unity engine, it is difficult to build a complicated model. Hence, the 3D model (including scene, space, and elements) was established in Rhino. The final model would export as .3Ds file and import to the Unity.

4.2 System Framework

In this research, we used Unity 2018.3.9 as our virtual space environment and "Samsung HMD Odyssey+" as our hardware, which included one headset and two motion controllers. To implement the VROS, the system framework was introduced as shown below (Fig. 3). The user was able to control the VR world by wearing headset (Samsung HMD Odyssey+) and holding the pair of motion controllers. The headset was embedded with a head tracker, which monitored the user's head location. And the user holding the motion controllers are able to input the signal of user's actions (such as moving or

Table 2. 3D modeling and elements.

Space		Elements	Control	Connecting e-shop
Living		Sofa		IKEA
		Tea table		IKEA
		Wooden horse	V	Amazon
		Heineken	V	Coop, Wholefood
		human	V	Collaboration shopping
		speakers		Pchome
		plants		Amazon
Kitchen		Refrigerator	V	農場
		Counter		IKEA
		High chair		IKEA
		Appliance		Home depot
		Philippe Starck juice maker		Google shopping store
		Apple		Wholefood
Home library		Book 1	V	Amazon
		Book 2	V	Amazon
		Chair		IKEA
		Tea table		IKEA
Walk-in closet		Clothes	V	Muji、Uniqlo
		Dress	V	Muji、Uniqlo
		Kate bag	V	Yahoo, mytheresa

(continued)

Table 2. (*continued*)

Farm		Chicken farm	V	Coop, Wholefood
		Dairy farming	V	Coop, Wholefood
		Sheep farm	V	Coop, Wholefood

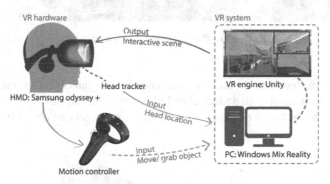

Fig. 3. System framework.

grabbing objects) to the computer. Meanwhile, the user would get the feedback from the interactive scene (projecting by VR engine: Unity) in real time through the VR system. To install the VROS system, there are three parts as below.

1. Setup headset: since the Samsung HMD Odyssey+ was compatible with Windows Mixed Reality, in Unity, there are only two steps to finish setup. First, change the environment to Universal Windows Platform and choose "XR Settings/Virtual Reality supported". Second, import "Windows Mixed Reality Toolkit" to assets from Unity.
2. Import 3D model: we build a 3D model (4.1) in Rhino and import 3ds file to Unity.
3. Combination of headset, controllers and Unity: in Unity, we create a camera as the view of VR headset. To display the virtual controller in VR, we imported "motion controller" from assets, which the users could be more immersive in VR environment when seeing the handed controllers.

4.3 Manipulation

Move and Teleport. In order to experience physical, simple and quick shopping (like 2D online shopping), the VROS used the point to point quick moving to other spaces instead of walking in the VR environment. The user can naturally move forward/backward by thumbing up/down the motion controller. Compared to traditional VR environment, to teleport to a specific product, the user can easily point the "blue spot" near the product by using the motion controller instead of using the keyboard: A, S, D, or W (see Fig. 4).

Fig. 4. Point to point navigating.

Interaction with Product. In order to simulate grabbing an object in reality, the user can intuitively pick up or grab a product by holding the side button (Fig. 5). The product will drop off if the button is released. Also the user can transfer an object from one hand to the other.

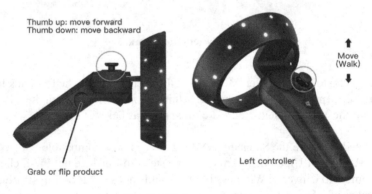

Fig. 5. Motion controller.

Product Display and Scale. In physical shopping, the products would be placed onto the shelves or showroom. However, in 2D online shopping, the user can only imagine the real products by watching the small pictures at the restricted 2D screen (e.g. magnifying larger or smaller the pictures of the product). As to Table 3, shopping in both "physical store" or "VROS", the user can naturally and easily experience the original scale of the products, even trying on the clothes in VROS. In the future version, to increase the shopping efficiency, we will add the feature: "changing style", "color" or "size" into the functions.

Table 3. Evaluation experiments.

	Environment	Scale	Zoom in/out	Fitting	Change style
Physical store shopping		Original scale	n/a	Yes	Yes
2D online shopping		Smaller scale to fit the webpage	Magnifying larger or smaller	no	yes
VROS		Original scale	n/a	Yes (fitting in VR environment)	Not yet (will put the feature on it)

5   Scenario Demonstration and Evaluation

5.1   Scenario Demonstration

Jane wanted to do some shopping. She put on the headset and calibrated the relation of headset and controllers. And then she started the VROS system and went into the home-hub. The initial spot started at the living room (Fig. 6-A). First, she saw the wooden rocking horse in grayscale that she would like to buy for her daughter, was on the floor (Fig. 6-C). The wooden horse turned to color when she picked it up and put it into the shopping bag. Meanwhile, she found her father—"John" just came online and turned into color from grayscale. John asked Jane to prepare Heineken beers for his visit tonight. Jane then put Heineken beers into shopping bag (Fig. 6-B). Interested in a newly released book, she used motion controllers to move to the second floor. When she picked up the book from the bookshelves, the information of the books—"How Architecture works" appeared next to the virtual book (Fig. 6-D, E, F). Since she liked it a lot, she naturally put it into the shopping bag. Then she went to the walk-in closets. She found a beautiful round neck sweatshirt (Fig. 6-G). The sweatshirt turned to pink from grayscale when she took it out from the closet, and the details (material, price and rate) of the shirt appeared next to it (Fig. 6-H, I). To prepare dinner, Jane realized she need to get some fresh food at the grocery. She went downstairs to the kitchen and checked the memo from the refrigerator (Fig. 6-J, K). At the same time, she was teleported to the "farm", her favorite grocery shop (Fig. 6-L, M, N). She finally bought brown eggs, lamb ribs and a bottle of milk. And she went back to home and check the shopping bag from the wall of living room (Fig. 6-O).

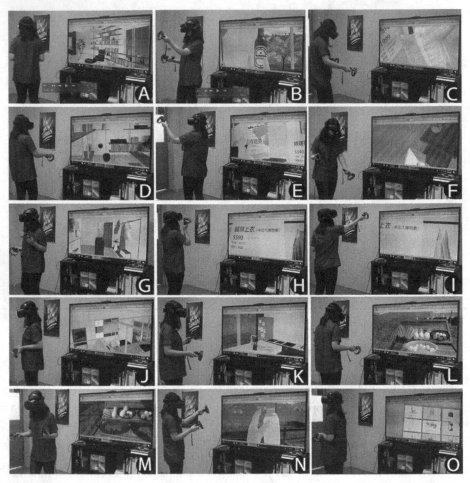

Fig. 6. System demonstration: A) Jane started the VROS and enter the home-hub; B) She picked up a bottle of Heineken from the table; C) She saw the wooden rocking horse and she put it into the wishlist; D) She went to bookshelves on second floor; E) She picked up a book "How Architecture works" from the bookshelf; F) She picked up the book and put it into shopping bag; G) She went to the walk-in closet; H) She found a round neck sweatshirt; I) It turned to original color "pink", when she hold the cloth; J, K) She went downstairs to the kitchen, she found the reminder from the refrigerator; L, M, N) She went to the farm to buy eggs, lamb ribs and milk; O) She went back to the home-hub to check the shopping bag from the wall.

5.2 Evaluation

In order to evaluate and compare the differences between the VROS prototype and the 2D online shopping, we created evaluation experiments to test the system. We recruited two subjects (S1 and S2, between 25 and 40 years of age), who prefer going online shopping (including worldwide e-shops) than physical stores. To test the VROS, each subject was individually requested to do two-stage experiments: Part 1. Shop in 2D online shopping stores; Part 2. Shop in the VROS (see Table 4). In each experiment, the subject was assigned to shop the same 9 items: Heineken beer, eggs, milk, lamb rib, books, clothes, Kate bag and wooden horse. The goal of the experiments is to evaluate the differences when the users shop the same goods in different platforms. As to the experiments, we used "audio/video retrospection" and "coding system", as part of protocol analysis [7, 8], which transformed verbal and video into protocol and reveal thinking process to verify the possibility of the VROS.

Table 4. Evaluation experiments

Experiments		Subject 1 (S1)	Subject 2 (S2)
Part 1. 2D online shopping	Assigned to buy 9 items: Heineken, egg, milk, lamb rib, books, clothes, Kate bag and wooden horse	Exp 1-1 S1 used his way to buy 9 assigned products (e.g. google search engine or specific website)	Exp 2-1 S2 used his way to buy 9 assigned products (e.g. google search engine or specific website)
Part 2. VROS shopping	Assigned to buy 9 items: Heineken, egg, milk, lamb rib, books, clothes, Kate bag and wooden horse	Exp 1-2 S1 tried to buy 9 assigned products in VROS	Exp 2-2 S2 tried to buy 9 assigned products in VROS

During the two stage experiments (see Table 4), the subjects were requested to think aloud and recorded by video and audio recorders. The audio/video retrospection would be transferred into text, split into segments and then marked by defined coding scheme (see Table 5).

The results of two-stage experiments showed that S1 spent approximately similar amount of time shopping in both the VROS (Exp S1-1) (see Fig. 7) and the 2D online shops (Exp S1-2) (see Fig. 8), even though this was his/her first time using the VROS platform. S2 spent only 2 min longer in the VROS. It seems that, in the VROS, both S1 and S2 can easily and simply finished the tasks without any doubts. Although in the current version of VROS, every product has only one option and the subject can simply buy the goods without spending time to make the decision. However, in 2D online shopping, to find the specific products, the coding scheme (Exp S1-2) (see Fig. 7) showed that S1 kept using "GS", "ES", "W", "R" and "B" to make the decision.

Compared to the coding scheme in Exp S1-1 (VROS) and Exp S1-2 (2D online shopping), the products in home-hub based VROS has been "categorized" and adequately

Table 5. Coding scheme

Category	Coding	Clarification
Environment	●	N: Navigate in VROS
	●	B: Browse in webpage
Search	●	GS: Google search
	●	ES: Search from specific e-commerce
	●	W: Keyword search
	●	SC: Search by category
Comparison	●	P-Z: Compare price
	●	P-I: Compare info
	●	P-R: Compare review
Interaction	●	C-T: Click to view photo
	●	V-T: virtually touch
	●	D-A: Drop to shopping bag
	●	A: Checking shopping bag
Assistant	●	K: Ask for the help
Move	●	R: Scroll up/ down
	●	M: Virtually move
Purchase	●	FO: Finalize order

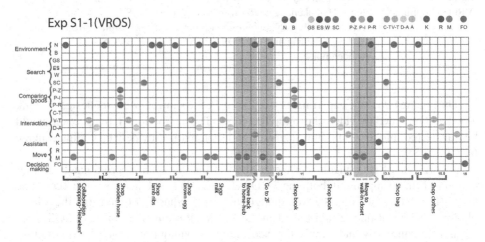

Fig. 7. Exp S1-1(VROS) coding scheme

placed in related home-hub "space". For instance, grocery can be found in refrigerator connected to the farm or supermarket. The coding scheme "M and N in VROS" is approximately equal to "GS, ES and R in 2D online shopping". The results indicated the

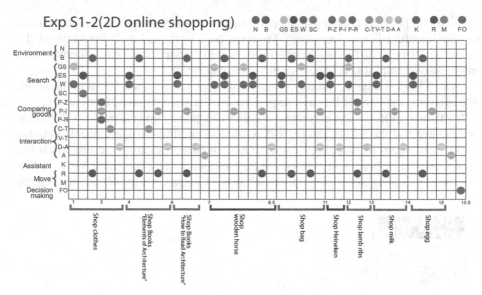

Fig. 8. Exp S1-2 (2D online shopping) coding scheme

home-hub (space classification), in which users could panorama viewing the products, augmented the shopping experience in virtual space rather than repeatedly searching on the multiple webpages (see coding scheme: ES and GS) in the restricted 2D screen.

The results of Exp S2-2 are similar, S2 spent most of time checking the products over and over across multiple website while buying the Kate bag. He/she was debating between the "official website" and "second-hand shop (like eBay)". Further VROS features will be improved by adding the similar or different condition products in the same space.

6 Conclusion

The objective of the research is to explore a new vision of online shopping platform by using the VR technology (Virtual-Reality Online shopping system/VROS). VROS incorporates the concept of "home-hub", which could be not only a product storage or showroom but also a "teleport" connecting to different online shopping stores, such as Amazon, Uniqlo or Coop…etc. Either products you wish to buy or you already have could be rearranged into the home-hub. Five different spaces (living room, kitchen, home library, walk-in closet and farm) are created in the VROS. The users can shop intuitively and naturally from specific home-hub space (such as the walk-in closet) classification and teleport to the related online shopping stores. It breaks the limitation of using keywords or text classifications to find the products.

By using protocol analysis, the results show the possibility of VROS in different views. The users can easily, quickly and adaptively shop in VROS without training. Although the VROS is an earlier system prototype and has not gone online yet, the VROS poses a new experience of online shopping. The feedbacks from the subjects implied that products arranged in the personal virtual space would encourage the users to think carefully before purchasing. From the point of the sellers, it would be good if the advertisement can be ubiquitous embedded into every personal virtual home, which might also be helpful to enhance product sales volume.

The VROS is a system prototype and needs continuous improvement in the future. When buying daily goods, the subjects preferred to use the traditional 2D online shopping rather than the VROS. This is because that they can quickly find the products they need. We believe that the VROS can be widely used in the future if more people get used to this new means of shopping behavior. One other feedback from the subjects is that "point to point teleport" sometimes is not easy to control. In the future, the VROS will be improved by adding the moving option of "walk." Compared to the 2D online shopping

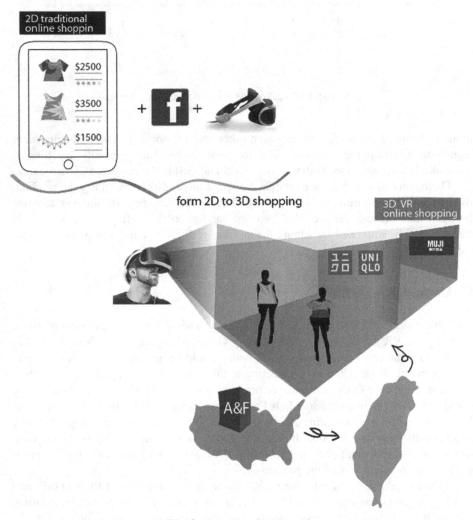

Fig. 9. Concept of VR world

stores, the users have multiple option to find the goods before making a decision. Hence the future VROS will include similar or different condition products or even the different e-commerce options.

In the future study, the VROS can approach "VROS world" by connecting to the social network (e.g. Facebook). By extending the 2D online shopping stores to the 3D online shopping stores, every user will be represented as avatar and hold a customized house and experience physical shopping atmosphere without being restricted into a physical space, and can quickly switch among the places to shop around the world (see Fig. 9).

References

1. Kasana, M.J., Chaudhary, M.N.: A comparative study of eBay and Amazon in online shopping. Int. Res. J. Commer. Arts Sci. 5(2), 263–275 (2014)
2. Sutherland, I.E.: A head-mounted three dimensional display. In: Proceedings of the Fall Joint Computer Conference, Part I, 9–11 December 1968, pp. 757–764 (1968)
3. Dawood, N., Benghi, C., Lorenzen, T., Pencreach, Y.: Integration of urban development and 5D planning. In: Proceedings of the 9th International Conference on Construction Applications of Virtual Reality, Sydney, Australia, pp. 217–228 (2009)
4. Vorländer, M.: Auralization: Fundamentals of Acoustics, Modelling, Simulation, Algorithms and Acoustic Virtual Reality. Springer, Heidelberg (2007). https://doi.org/10.1007/978-3-540-48830-9
5. Huang, Y.-C., Han, S.R.: An immersive virtual reality museum via second life. In: Stephanidis, C. (ed.) HCI 2014. CCIS, vol. 434, pp. 579–584. Springer, Cham (2014). https://doi.org/10.1007/978-3-319-07857-1_102
6. Huang, Y.-C., Hu, S.-Y., Wang, S.-T., Huang, S.C.-C.: Exploration of virtual reality-based online shopping platform. In: Stephanidis, C. (ed.) HCII 2019. CCIS, vol. 1034, pp. 81–88. Springer, Cham (2019). https://doi.org/10.1007/978-3-030-23525-3_11
7. Newell, A., Simon, H.A.: Human Problem Solving. Prentice-Hall, Englewood Cliffs (1972)
8. van Someren, M.W., Barnard, Y.F., Sandberg, C.: The Think Aloud Method: A Practical Guide to Modelling Cognitive Processes. Academic Press, London (1994)

Captivating Product Experiences: How Virtual Reality Creates Flow and Thereby Optimize Product Presentations

Kai Israel[1], Lea Buchweitz[1], Dieter K. Tscheulin[2], Christopher Zerres[1(✉)], and Oliver Korn[1]

[1] Offenburg University, Badstrasse 24, 77652 Offenburg, Germany
`christopher.zerres@hs-offenburg.de`
[2] University of Freiburg, Platz der Alten Synagoge, 79085 Freiburg, Germany

Abstract. Well-designed and informative product presentations can support consumers in making purchase decisions. There are plenty of facts and details about a product of interest. However, also emotions are an important aspect for the purchase decision. The unique visualization opportunities of virtual reality (VR) can give users of VR applications the feeling of being there (*telepresence*). The applications can intensely engage them in a *flow* experience, comprising the four dimensions of *enjoyment, curiosity, focused attention* and *control*. In this work, we claim that VR product presentations can create subjective product experiences for consumers and motivate them to reuse this innovative type of product presentation in the future, by immersing them in a virtual world and causing them to interact with it. To verify the conceptual model a study was conducted with 551 participants who explored a VR hotel application. The results indicate that VR product presentations evoke positive emotions among consumers. The virtual experience made potential customers focus their *attention* on the virtual world and aroused their *curiosity* about getting more information about the product in an enjoyable way. In contrast to the theoretical assumption, *control* did not influence the users' *behavioral intentions* to reuse VR product presentation. We conclude that VR product presentations create a feeling of *telepresence*, which leads to a *flow* experience that contributes to the *behavioral intention* of users to reuse VR product presentations in the future.

Keywords: Flow theory · Virtual reality · Telepresence · Product presentation · Product experience

1 Introduction

Retailers want to sell their products. They invest much time and effort in presenting a product in an appealing way that attracts potential customers and arouses their interest. As soon as a potential customer is interested in a product, retailers need to provide detailed information about it in order to facilitate a positive purchase decision.

However, when it comes to high-priced products and services, consumers may not decide only on appealing product presentations and dry facts [1]. Often, emotional

© Springer Nature Switzerland AG 2020
F. F.-H. Nah and K. Siau (Eds.): HCII 2020, LNCS 12204, pp. 354–368, 2020.
https://doi.org/10.1007/978-3-030-50341-3_28

aspects have a major influence on the purchase decision. [1]. However, creating an emotional experience when presenting products can be a challenge for retailers.

We assume that product presentations using virtual reality (VR) can create an emotional product experience that can lead to increased readiness for the regular use of product presentations in VR. The unique visualization opportunities of VR applications can give potential customers the feeling of being in a different place [2]. The consumers are immersed in the virtual world and are engaged in exploring it. The free exploration entertains the potential customers and arouses their *curiosity* [1]. As a result of the immersion and engagement, customers experience an intrinsically enjoyable and optimal state [3–5], which can positively affect their *behavioral intentions*, such as *purchase decisions* or *frequency of use* [4, 6].

For example, a couple plan to visit the Maldives for their honeymoon. They want to have an unforgettable holiday and probably plan to spend a large amount of money. They want to be sure that, for example, the hotel will fulfill their expectations. The travel agency can show the couple many images of the hotel and share plenty of information about the rooms and the facilities. However, the couple will still struggle to imagine how it really feels to be in the hotel. We suggest that it would be beneficial if the travel agency could provide the couple with a virtual hotel presentation to promote a subjective product experience. The couple would feel they were actually in the hotel and could engage with the virtual world by exploring the hotel resort. The couple would be curious to explore everything and would feel entertained by this innovative way of product presentation. They may enter a state of focused attention and enjoyment and decide to book the hotel because they have been able to judge from a personal experience that the hotel will meet their expectations.

In this paper, we claim that VR product presentations can support customers in emotionally engaging with a virtual product experience by immersing them in a virtual world and causing them to interact with it. We further claim that this intensive engagement will increase their readiness to reuse VR product presentation applications in the future.

2 Related Work and Hypotheses Development

The feeling of being there is often described in literature as *telepresence*. *Telepresence* occurs when consumers engage with and directly react to a virtual environment created by a medium [4, 7–9]. In line with other researchers, we assume that due to its unique visualization opportunities, VR technology can provide a high degree of *telepresence* [1, 10, 11].

The immersion in the virtual world attracts the consumers' full attention and causing them to interact with it. This state of deep engagement and focus is widely known as the *flow* experience. Csikszentmihalyi [12] describes *flow* as an intrinsically optimal state that results in intense focus, time distortion, loss of self-consciousness and increased motivation [3–5]. Numerous scientific indications support the theoretical assumption that *telepresence* can trigger such a *flow* experience. For example, several researchers report that *telepresence* positively affects *enjoyment*, *curiosity*, *focused attention* and *control* in social media or online games [1, 4, 10, 13]. All these aspects are reported regularly to be part of the theoretical construct of *flow* [3–5].

Enjoyment is an inherent part of the flow construct, since flow itself is described as pleasant, interesting, exciting and fun [4]. In VR, interesting and exciting virtual worlds can be created that offer users an entertaining new (product) experience [1]. On the one hand, this extraordinary human-computer interaction is perceived as enjoyable by the users [14]. On the other hand, the novel and exciting stimuli of the virtual environment, such as the 360° panoramic images or interactive menus [4, 15], can arouse users' *curiosity* [4]. Moon and Kim describe *curiosity* as a combination of inquisitiveness and technical competence while engaged in an activity [16]. Users can escape into a virtual world and freely explore it on their own. In this context, previous research has shown that telepresence is an important predictor that increases user *curiosity* [1].

To reach a flow state, the users' *attention* needs to focus deeply on the action performed [4]. The more a user is absorbed by and immersed into an activity, the greater their concentration is [17]. For VR, head-mounted displays are often used, which completely enclose the user's field of view. Therefore, the users are visually isolated from the physical world, which facilitates *focused attention,* directed entirely at the virtual world.

Flow is also characterized by *control* [18]. *Control* refers to the users' ability to successfully navigate through the virtual environment, without being frustrated [19] and to understand how the virtual world responds to inputs [20]. As suggested by Wang et al. [21] responsive interactive elements can create a feeling of control. In VR worlds, for example, users can explore the environment around them by simply turning their heads and they can navigate via gaze interaction. We therefore expect that these intuitive interaction functions could convey a sense of *control* to users.

In accordance with the mentioned studies, the following hypotheses are examined in the context of VR product presentations:

H_1: *The feeling of telepresence created by a VR product presentation has a positive influence on the user's perceived enjoyment of such an application.*

H_2: *The feeling of telepresence created by a VR product presentation has a positive influence on the curiosity aroused in the user through such an application.*

H_3: *The feeling of telepresence created by a VR product presentation has a positive influence on the user's perceived control of such an application.*

H_4: *The feeling of telepresence created by a VR product presentation has a positive influence on the user's focused attention.*

Previous research studies have shown the positive effects of *flow* on the *behavioral intentions* of consumers, such as *purchase decisions* or *frequency of use* [4, 6]. For example, Pelet et al. have shown that social media users experience a state of *flow* during usage, which results in a *behavioral intention* to *frequently reuse* social media [4]. In another work, Liu investigated the relation between the state of *flow* users experience while playing online games and their *intention to replay* the game [13]. The results reveal that a *flow* experience is an important predictor of the *users' replay intention* [13]. There is also evidence in tourism research that *flow* facilitates *behavioral intentions*: Ali has studied the relationship between the *quality of a hotel website* and the consumers' *purchase intentions* [6]. The results show that the *quality of a hotel website* (e.g. usability, functionality) affects users' *perceived flow*, which has a positive effect on their *satisfaction* and on their *intention to purchase* [6].

We assume that this positive effect between a *flow* state and the users' *behavioral intentions* also applies for product presentations in VR. Based on the previous findings the hypotheses to be tested are as follows (Fig. 1):

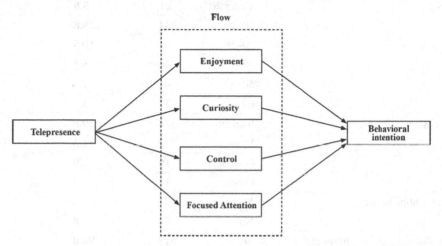

Fig. 1. Conceptual research framework.

H_5: *The user's perceived enjoyment created by a VR product presentation has a positive influence on the behavioral intention to reuse such an application.*
H_6: *The curiosity aroused in the user through a VR product presentation has a positive influence on the behavioral intention to reuse such an application.*
H_7: *The user's perceived control mediated by a VR product presentation has a positive influence on the behavioral intention to reuse such an application.*
H_8: *The user's focused attention created by a VR product presentation has a positive influence on the behavioral intention to reuse such an application.*

3   Study

3.1   Study Participants

A total of 569 people took part in the study, including 334 students from a German university and 235 non-students from companies and organizations. Eighteen questionnaires had to be excluded due to missing values, thus 551 study participants reached the final sample for data evaluation.

The gender distribution was 45.2% female and 54.8% male (Table 1). The majority of respondents (58.8%) were aged between 20 and 29 at the time of the survey. Approximately one-third of the study participants stated that they were older than 29 years. Almost all respondents owned a smartphone (98.2%) and had heard the term "virtual

Table 1. Characteristics of respondents (n = 551).

Characteristics		Frequency	Percentage (%)
Gender	Female	249	45.2
	Male	302	54.8
Age	Under 20	21	3.8
	20–29	324	58.8
	30–39	91	16.5
	40–49	46	8.3
	50–59	41	7.4
	60+	28	5.1
Profession	Student	328	59.5
	Employee	189	34.3
	Pensioner	16	2.9
	Others	18	3.3
Smartphone owner	Yes	541	98.2
	No	10	1.8
Familiar with term "virtual reality"	Yes	518	94.0
	No	33	6.0
Virtual reality used	Yes	273	49.6
	No	278	50.4

reality" at least once before the survey (94.0%). VR systems were already used by half of the respondents (49.6%) before the survey.

The data were analyzed using the PLS-SEM method, which is often used in the context of new technologies and is well established in behavioral research [22, 23]. The SmartPLS 3.2.6 software was used to calculate the structural equation model [24].

3.2 Task: VR Product Presentation

Since VR systems represent a rather new way of communication, it could not be assumed at the beginning of the study that the participants already had experience with this new technology and are therefore not able to assess the technology. For this reason, a VR application was created using 43 professional 360-degree panoramic images of a hotel (Fig. 2).

The tour was displayed on the Samsung Galaxy S7 smartphone in combination with the corresponding Gear VR headset. Within the application, the participant could visually fix predefined points in the room in order to change the viewpoint. Study participants were also able to access other areas of the hotel, like the lobby, by using an additional menu.

Fig. 2. Screenshot from VR product presentation.

3.3 Operationalization

The multi-item scales for the operationalization of all constructs have been adapted from previous research and transferred to the present research. The individual items were measured using a seven-point Likert-scale, ranging from "strongly disagree" (1) to "strongly agree" (7). In order to operationalize *perceived enjoyment* (five items), the scale devised by Childers et al. was used [25]. The construct of *curiosity* was based on three items by Agarwal and Karahanna [5]. The scale of Ghani and Deshpande [20] was used to operationalize the constructs *focused attention* (four items) and *control* (three items). The operationalization of *telepresence* (three items) was based on the scale by Klein [26]. Four items were used to measure *behavioral intention* based on the work by Venkatesh [27] and Lee and Lehto [28].

3.4 Design of the Study

The study was conducted between November 2016 and February 2017 under laboratory conditions. The experiment was divided into four phases (Fig. 3). The first phase served to introduce the study. The participants watched a video explaining VR systems and the further steps of the study. Subsequently, the participants were asked to fill out a questionnaire that contained questions regarding sociodemographic characteristics, past experiences with VR systems, and personal travel habits (Phase 2). At the beginning of the third phase, the participants were introduced to the VR system. After the participants put on the VR headset and adjusted it to their personal needs, an audio file was played presenting the study scenario. In the scenario, the study participants had to imagine being in the final stage of planning a holiday trip, and they had an opportunity to get a first impression of the preferred hotel by using a VR system. The maximum duration of the virtual hotel tour was limited to ten minutes. After the end of the tour, the study the participants were asked to evaluate the VR experience in a second questionnaire (Table 2).

Phase 1. Introductory video.   **Phase 2.** First questionnaire.

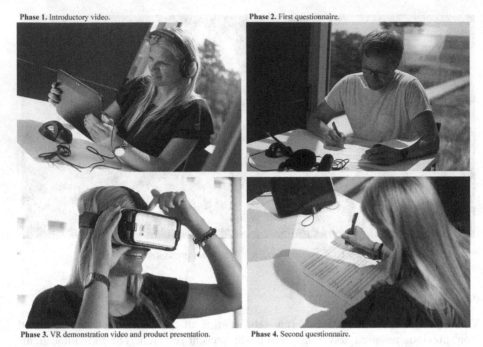

Phase 3. VR demonstration video and product presentation.   **Phase 4.** Second questionnaire.

Fig. 3. Design of the study.

4 Results

4.1 Assessment of the Measurement Model

The assessment of the measurement model is based on internal consistency, convergence and discriminant validity [23]. The Cronbach's alpha coefficient (α) and the factor reliability (ρc) were used to evaluate the internal consistency of the measurement model [22]. Since each construct of the measurement model met the minimum requirements of both criteria, internal consistency can be confirmed.

In order to evaluate the convergence validity, outer loadings, indicator reliability and the average variance extracted are analyzed. For this purpose, it was first verified whether the individual indicators had a high outer loading on the assigned construct. In this context, a significant outer loading above 0.7 is regarded as an acceptable value [23]. This minimum requirement was met by all indicators (Table 2). Furthermore, the indicator reliability was determined by the squared factor loadings, whose required limit value of 0.5 was exceeded by all factor loadings with a value of 0.708 [23]. The mean value of all squared factor loadings assigned to a construct represents the average variance extracted (AVE). This should also exceed the limit value of 0.5, which is fulfilled by all constructs [22]. Thus, the convergence validity is proven.

Table 2. Validity and reliability of the constructs.

Construct and items	Loading	α	ρA	ρc	AVE
Criteria	>0.7	>0.7	>0.7	>0.7	>0.5
Behavioral intention (BI)		0.886	0.895	0.922	0.749
Assuming I had virtual reality glasses, then I would ...					
Use them to virtually observe a hotel facility	0.903				
Use them to get information about the hotel	0.766				
Use them to get an impression of the hotel	0.917				
Recommend them to others who want to get an Impression of the hotel	0.866				
Control (CTRL)		0.723	0.795	0.830	0.620
During the virtual tour ...					
I had the feeling of having control over the virtual simulation	0.835				
I knew what I had to do to use the virtual simulation correctly	0.781				
I clearly knew what to do in the virtual simulation	0.743				
Curiosity (CURI)		0.858	0.866	0.914	0.781
The virtual tour ...					
Excites my curiosity	0.914				
Arouses my imagination	0.802				
Makes me curious	0.930				
Enjoyment (ENJ)		0.899	0.906	0.926	0.715
Using the virtual reality application ...					
Is fun	0.865				
Is enjoyable	0.899				
Is pleasant	0.911				
Is entertaining	0.754				
Is exciting	0.789				
Focused Attention (FOCA)		0.876	0.891	0.915	0.729
During the virtual tour ...					
I was deeply engrossed in the virtual simulation	0.872				
I was intensely absorbed by the virtual simulation	0.882				
My attention was focused on the virtual simulation	0.867				
I fully concentrated on the virtual simulation	0.790				

(continued)

Table 2. (*continued*)

Construct and items	Loading	α	ρA	ρc	AVE
Telepresence (TELE)		0.820	0.836	0.893	0.737
While I was using the virtual reality application, I felt as if I were in another world	0.773				
Through the virtual simulation I had the feeling of really experiencing the situation	0.887				
When I navigated through the virtual world, I felt I was in a different place	0.909				

Table 3. Squared-inter-correlations between constructs (AVE shown in bold on diagonal) and HTMT.85 criterion (gray).

	BI	CTRL	CURI	ENJ	FOCA	TELE
BI	**0.865**	0.207	0.666	0.622	0.570	0.504
CTRL	0.038	**0.787**	0.278	0.377	0.268	0.229
CURI	0.344	0.055	**0.884**	0.790	0.660	0.583
ENJ	0.314	0.096	0.486	**0.846**	0.621	0.579
FOCA	0.261	0.053	0.333	0.312	**0.854**	0.742
TELE	0.186	0.037	0.239	0.249	0.407	**0.858**

The determination of discriminant validity is based on the Fornell-Larcker criterion. To fulfill this criterion, the AVE of a latent variable must be greater than the squared correlation with the other latent variable [29]. Table 3 shows that the Fornell-Larcker criterion was met by all constructs. The heterotrait monotrait ratio of correlations (HTMT) was additionally used to check discriminant validity. As shown in Table 3, the conservative limit of 0.85 was not exceeded and discriminant validity was confirmed [30].

4.2 Assessment of the Structural Model

For evaluating the structural model, the coefficients of determination (R^2), predictive relevance (Q^2), standardized root mean square residual (SRMR) and the strength and significance of the path coefficients were examined.

The significance of the path coefficients was determined by the interpretation of Cohen [31]. The model had a high explanatory quality, since the value of the declared variance was above the threshold for almost all endogenous variables.

The cross-validated redundancy approach (Stone-Geisser criterion) was used to determine the forecast relevance of the structural model. It is characterized by the systematic replacement of the data points of the original data set by estimation parameters [32–34]. To calculate the predictive relevance, the blindfolding procedure was chosen,

Table 4. Results of hypothesis testing.

	Relationships	Path coefficient	CI (Bias Corrected)	t-Value	p-Value	Supported
H1	TELE → ENJ	0.499***	[0.422, 0.567]	13.518	0.000	Yes
H2	TELE → CURI	0.489***	[0.402, 0.565]	11.875	0.000	Yes
H3	TELE → CTRL	0.194***	[0.099, 0.280]	4.164	0.000	Yes
H4	TELE → FOCA	0.638***	[0.580, 0.690]	22.893	0.000	Yes
H5	ENJ → BI	0.231**	[0.098, 0.371]	3.348	0.001	Yes
H6	CURI → BI	0.306***	[0.166, 0.436]	4.384	0.000	Yes
H7	CTRL → BI	0.003	[−0.075, 0.082]	0.075	0.941	No
H8	FOCA → BI	0.204***	[0.104, 0.317]	3.797	0.000	Yes

Note: *** p < 0.001, ** p < 0.01.

which confirms the predictive relevance ($Q^2 > 0$) for all endogenous variables. Thus, the Stone-Geisser criterion was fulfilled and the predictive capability of the structural model was proven. With a value of 0.057, the SRMR was below the recommended threshold value of 0.08, so that a high quality of adjustment can be observed for the overall model [22, 23].

In order to verify the research hypotheses, an analysis of the path coefficients was carried out. The strength of the path coefficients was determined using the PLS algorithm, whereas the significance of the path coefficients was determined using the bootstrapping method (5,000 subsamples). As illustrated in Table 4, seven of the eight proposed relationships were highly significant. Based on the theoretical assumption, the extraordinary feeling of *telepresence* has a positive influence on the occurrence of a *flow* experience. Besides *focused attention* (β = 0.638***), *telepresence* also has a significant influence on *perceived enjoyment* (β = 0.499***), *curiosity* (β = 0.489***) and *control* (β = 0.194***). In addition, our results provide empirical evidence that the *flow* dimensions *enjoyment* (β = 0.231**), *curiosity* (β = 0.306***) and *focused attention* (β = 0.204***) positively influence the users' *behavioral intention* to use a VR system in the future. Only the assumed relationship between *control* (β = 0.003) and the users' *behavioral intention* to use a VR system in the future could not be confirmed (Fig. 4).

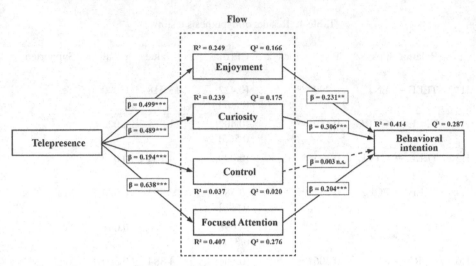

Fig. 4. PLS results of the structural model.

5 Discussion and Recommendations

This study presents a conceptual research framework that investigates the relationships between the extraordinary feeling of being there, called *telepresence*, and its impact on the occurrence of a *flow* experience in the context of VR hotel presentations. Furthermore, the study discovers what effects this *flow* state has on consumers' *behavioral intention* to use a VR system for product presentations in the future. The validation of the postulated relationships was conducted based on a study with 551 participants.

As our study confirms, the extraordinary feeling of being there creates a *flow* experience for the potential customer, which significantly influences the users' *behavioral intention* to use a VR system in the future. In accordance with Pelet et al. [4], we empirically prove that *telepresence* has positive effects on the *flow* dimensions *enjoyment*, *control*, *curiosity* and *focused attention*. The strength of the identified relationships is also approximately consistent with the findings of Pelet et al. [4], which the researchers were able to demonstrate in relation to social media use. As our results show, the feeling of *telepresence* in VR hotel presentations has a significant influence on the *focused attention* ($\beta = 0.638***$), *enjoyment* ($\beta = 0.499***$), *curiosity* ($\beta = 0.489***$) and *control* ($\beta = 0.194***$). Especially due to the system-inherent visual isolation of the user from the real world, the feeling of *telepresence* generates a high degree of *focused attention*. In virtual worlds, potential customers can thus concentrate almost entirely on the visualized product information. In addition, the results show that this novel form of product presentation is perceived as enjoyable and arouses the users' *curiosity* about the product. Simultaneously, *telepresence* enhances the sense of *control* for the user.

In contrast to previous research [4, 6], we investigated the impact of the *flow* experience on users' *behavioral intention* to use a VR system for product presentation in the future. In this context, our results demonstrate that the *flow* experience determines the *behavioral intention* of the users primarily through the aroused *curiosity* ($\beta = 0.306***$) and *enjoyment* ($\beta = 0.231**$). Retailers who want or need to appeal to their customers on an emotional level can therefore derive particular benefit from VR product visualization in the future.

Contrary to the hypothesis, we could not find empirical evidence for the relationship between *control* and users' *behavioral intention* to reuse a VR system. Although the perceived *control* of the VR hotel presentation was considered by the study participants to be high (MV = 6.42, SD = 0.88), this high level of control did not influence users' *behavioral intention* to use a VR system in the future. A possible explanation for this result is that the participants considered the use of the VR hotel presentation to be inherently easy [35, 36]. The usability of the VR hotel presentation could not have been an obstacle for the users, since the interaction with such the application occurred in a natural, intuitive way. Therefore, this inherent system characteristic could be a reason why study participants did not attribute any significant influence to the flow dimension control when assessing future intentions of use. This could be a further advantage for retailers, as this novel form of product presentation is considered by potential customers to be highly controllable, and technical hurdles in human-computer interaction could be reduced.

6 Conclusion

Giving potential customers the computer-mediated feeling of being in a different place is a powerful marketing tool that could change the traditional way of presenting products and services [1, 2, 10]. In this respect, it is crucial for retailers to develop an understanding of the factors that can significantly influence consumers' be*havioral intention* to use a VR system in the future.

The results of the study reveal that the extraordinary feeling of *telepresence* conveyed by VR systems has a positive influence on the *flow* dimensions of *enjoyment*, *curiosity*, *control* and *focused attention*. Based on these findings, we conclude that the results support the positive effects of a VR hotel presentation on the *flow* experience. This new type of product presentation is an interesting experience for the users, in which they like to linger, and therefore they want to reuse it in the future.

The results of the study provide several basic recommendations for the development of a successful VR product presentation. When creating VR applications, developers should pay special attention to the two influencing factors of *curiosity* and *enjoyment*. Since these two factors are crucial for consumers' *behavioral intention* to use a VR system in the future, VR applications should arouse *curiosity* (e.g. various points of interest, interactive menus) and be enjoyable (e.g. pleasant ambiance, colorful panoramic images). Although our results do not confirm that the sense of *control* has an influence on the intention to reuse a VR system, the intuitive handling (e.g. gaze interaction) of VR applications should be maintained. Otherwise, the inherent sense of *control* could possibly be negated, which would have a negative impact on users' *behavioral intention* to reuse a VR system.

If these recommendations are carefully considered, the VR product presentation for marketing purposes can be valuable for both retailers and consumers. While consumers experience a new and exciting product experience, retailers could improve their customer relationships through VR product presentations and thus increase revenue [1].

366   K. Israel et al.

6.1 Limitations and Future Research

A limitation of the study is the large proportion of participants under 30 years of age. By distributing the study participants more diversely among the different age groups, future studies could identify age-specific characteristics that could contribute to a more general understanding of the occurrence of the *flow* experience and users' *behavioral intention* to reuse a VR system in the future.

Although our study has a large sample size, the cultural background of the study participants is homogenously distributed. Replication of the study with participants having a different cultural background could therefore lead to different research results. Both the occurrence of the *flow* experience and users' *behavioral intention* to reuse a VR system in the future could be influenced by cultural differences such as technology affinity. Further studies should therefore address this limitation and investigate these cultural differences.

Furthermore, the present study could not determine any evidence of a significant relationship between the *flow* dimension *control* and users' *behavioral intention* to reuse a VR system. Nevertheless, it would be interesting to investigate whether the sense of *control*, mediated through *telepresence*, is perceived by users as an inherent system characteristic. In particular, future studies could examine how factors such as navigation, controller handling, or the positioning of control elements (e.g. buttons) in virtual space influence the user's sense of *control*. Based on these findings, the usability of VR applications could be further improved in the future.

References

1. Israel, K., Zerres, C., Tscheulin, D.K.: Presenting hotels in virtual reality: does it influence the booking intention? J. Hosp. Tour. Technol. **10**(3), 443–463 (2019). https://doi.org/10.1108/JHTT-03-2018-0020
2. Guttentag, D.A.: Virtual reality: applications and implications for tourism. Tour. Manage. **31**(5), 637–651 (2010). https://doi.org/10.1016/j.tourman.2009.07.003
3. Koufaris, M.: Applying the technology acceptance model and flow theory to online consumer behavior. Inf. Syst. Res. **13**(2), 205–223 (2002). https://doi.org/10.1287/isre.13.2.205.83
4. Pelet, J.-É., Ettis, S., Cowart, K.: Optimal experience of flow enhanced by telepresence: evidence from social media use. Inf. Manag. **54**(1), 115–128 (2017). https://doi.org/10.1016/j.im.2016.05.001
5. Agarwal, R., Karahanna, E.: Time flies when you're having fun: cognitive absorption and beliefs about information technology usage. MIS Q. **24**(4), 665–694 (2000). https://doi.org/10.2307/3250951
6. Ali, F.: Hotel website quality, perceived flow, customer satisfaction and purchase intention. J. Hosp. Tour. Technol. **7**(2), 213–228 (2016). https://doi.org/10.1108/JHTT-02-2016-0010
7. Steuer, J.: Defining virtual reality: dimensions determining telepresence. J. Commun. **42**(4), 73–93 (1992). https://doi.org/10.1111/j.1460-2466.1992.tb00812.x
8. Heeter, C.: Being there: the subjective experience of presence. Presence Teleop. Virt. Environ. **1**(2), 262–271 (1992). https://doi.org/10.1162/pres.1992.1.2.262
9. Kim, T., Biocca, F.: Telepresence via television: two dimensions of telepresence may have different connections to memory and persuasion. J. Comput.-Mediat. Commun. **3**(2) (1997). https://doi.org/10.1111/j.1083-6101.1997.tb00073.x

10. Tussyadiah, I.P., Wang, D., Jung, T.H., tom Dieck, M.C.: Virtual reality, presence, and attitude change: empirical evidence from tourism. Tour. Manage. **66**, 140–154 (2018). https://doi.org/10.1016/j.tourman.2017.12.003

11. Israel, K., Tscheulin, D.K., Zerres, C.: Virtual reality in the hotel industry: assessing the acceptance of immersive hotel presentation. Eur. J. Tour. Res. **21**, 5–22 (2019)

12. Csikszentmihalyi, M.: Beyond Boredom and Anxiety. The Experience of Play in Work and Games. Jossey-Bass, San Francisco (1975)

13. Liu, C.-C.: A model for exploring players flow experience in online games. Inf. Technol. People **30**(1), 139–162 (2017). https://doi.org/10.1108/ITP-06-2015-0139

14. Song, K., Fiore, A.M., Park, J.: Telepresence and fantasy in online apparel shopping experience. J. Fash. Mark. Manage. **11**(4), 553–570 (2007). https://doi.org/10.1108/13612020710824607

15. Huang, M.-H.: Designing website attributes to induce experiential encounters. Comput. Hum. Behav. **19**(4), 425–442 (2003). https://doi.org/10.1016/S0747-5632(02)00080-8

16. Moon, J.-W., Kim, Y.-G.: Extending the TAM for a World-Wide-Web context. Inf. Manag. **38**(4), 217–230 (2001). https://doi.org/10.1016/S0378-7206(00)00061-6

17. Csikszentmihalyi, M.: Flow: The Psychology of Optimal Experience. Harper and Row, New York (1990)

18. Engeser, S., Rheinberg, F.: Flow, performance and moderators of challenge-skill balance. Motiv. Emot. **32**(3), 158–172 (2008). https://doi.org/10.1007/s11031-008-9102-4

19. Novak, T.P., Hoffman, D.L., Yung, Y.-F.: Measuring the customer experience in online environments: a structural modeling approach. Mark. Sci. **19**(1), 22–42 (2000). https://doi.org/10.1287/mksc.19.1.22.15184

20. Ghani, J.A., Deshpande, S.P.: Task characteristics and the experience of optimal flow in human-computer interaction. J. Psychol. **128**(4), 381–391 (1994). https://doi.org/10.1080/00223980.1994.9712742

21. Wang, L.C., Baker, J., Wagner, J.A., Wakefield, K.: Can a retail web site be social? J. Mark. **71**(3), 143–157 (2007). https://doi.org/10.1509/jmkg.71.3.143

22. Henseler, J., Hubona, G., Ray, P.A.: Using PLS path modeling in new technology research: updated guidelines. Ind. Manage. Data Syst. **116**(1), 2–20 (2016). https://doi.org/10.1108/IMDS-09-2015 0382

23. Hair, J.F., Hult, T.M., Ringle, C.M., Sarstedt, M.: A Primer on Partial Least Squares Structural Equation Modeling (PLS-SEM). SAGE Publications, Thousand Oaks (2017)

24. Ringle, C.M., Wende, S., Becker, J.-M.: Smartpls 3. Bönningstedt: SmartPLS. http://www.smartpls.com

25. Childers, T.L., Carr, C.L., Peck, J., Carson, S.: Hedonic and utilitarian motivations for online retail shopping behavior. J. Retail. **77**(4), 511–535 (2001). https://doi.org/10.1016/S0022-4359(01)00056-2

26. Klein, L.R.: Creating virtual product experiences: the role of telepresence. J. Interact. Mark. **17**(1), 41–55 (2003). https://doi.org/10.1002/dir.10046

27. Venkatesh, V.: Determinants of perceived ease of use: integrating control, intrinsic motivation, and emotion into the technology acceptance model. Inf. Syst. Res. **11**, 342–365 (2000)

28. Lee, D.Y., Lehto, M.R.: User acceptance of YouTube for procedural learning: an extension of the technology acceptance model. Comput. Educ. **61**, 193–208 (2013). https://doi.org/10.1016/j.compedu.2012.10.001

29. Fornell, C., Larcker, D.F.: Evaluating structural equation models with unobservable variables and measurement error. J. Mark. Res. **18**(1), 39 (1981). https://doi.org/10.2307/3151312

30. Henseler, J., Ringle, C.M., Sarstedt, M.: A new criterion for assessing discriminant validity in variance-based structural equation modeling. J. Acad. Mark. Sci. **43**(1), 115–135 (2015). https://doi.org/10.1007/s11747-014-0403-8

31. Cohen, J.: Statistical Power Analysis for the Behavioral Sciences. Lawrence Erlbaum Associates Publishers, Hillsdale (1988)

32. Stone, M.: Cross-validatory choice and assessment of statistical predictions. J. Roy. Stat. Soc. Ser. B (Methodol.) **36**, 111–147 (1974)

33. Geisser, S.: A predictive approach to the random effect model. Biometrika **61**(1), 101 (1974). https://doi.org/10.2307/2334290

34. Chin, W.W.: The partial least squares approach for structural equation modeling. In: Marcoulides, G.A. (ed.) Modern Methods for Business Research, pp. 295–336. Lawrence Erlbaum Associates Publishers, Mahwah (1998)

35. Liu, Y., Li, H., Carlsson, C.: Factors driving the adoption of m-learning: An empirical study. Comput. Educ. **55**(3), 1211–1219 (2010). https://doi.org/10.1016/j.compedu.2010.05.018

36. Subramanian, G.H.: A replication of perceived usefulness and perceived ease of use measurement. Decis. Sci. **25**(5–6), 863–874 (1994). https://doi.org/10.1111/j.1540-5915.1994.tb01873

How to Attract More Viewers in Live Streams? A Functional Evaluation of Streamers' Strategies for Attraction of Viewers

Xiaoyun Jia[1] , Ruili Wang[1](✉) , James H. Liu[1] , and Tian Xie[2]

[1] Massey University, Auckland 0745, New Zealand
Ruili.wang@massey.ac.nz
[2] Wuhan University, Wuhan 430072, China

Abstract. Live streaming is becoming popular and has attracted large numbers of online viewers. It becomes a social commerce venue where streamers can gain commercial benefits from building the relationship with viewers. Before building relationship with more viewers, how to attract more viewers is the essential foundation in the live streaming industry. This article explores and evaluates what strategies and techniques streamers use to attract more viewers through data source triangulation and methodological triangulation. In details, data were collected from streamers' self-reports, viewers' self-reports and online actual behavior; interviews, focus groups and online observation were applied, based on the characteristics of data. Through multiple triangulation, we identified three strategies and techniques for attracting viewers: (i) to increase streamer-viewer interactions, (ii) to create synergy with other streamers, and (iii) to conduct self-promotion. Findings were indicated by the popular streamers and verified by both focus groups and online observations. Our paper contributes to understanding streamer-viewer interactions in computer mediated communication. Live streaming platforms also benefit from this study in terms of platform design and marketing.

Keywords: Human-computer interactions · Human online behavior · Live streaming · Persuasive strategies · Attraction of viewers · Multiple triangulation · Online platform design · Online platform marketing

1 Introduction

Social commerce as a new version of e-commerce which makes use of relationships and interactions in social networks for business benefits [1], has evolved quickly and become popular since its emergence [2]. With the advancement of technology, the social commerce venues evolve from blogs, social networking sites and social shopping websites, to live streaming which has been widely accepted as a new place for social interactions [3]. Live stream-watching has become more and more popular globally. As a form of new media, live streaming allows instant communication during the live streams. In a live stream, the streamer not only gives performances but also interacts with viewers.

© Springer Nature Switzerland AG 2020
F. F.-H. Nah and K. Siau (Eds.): HCII 2020, LNCS 12204, pp. 369–383, 2020.
https://doi.org/10.1007/978-3-030-50341-3_29

This makes their shows different from the traditional ones. We define such performances with live interactions as the *"interactive performances"*.

Platforms such as Twitch, Facebook Live, YouTube Live and Periscope have attracted large audiences online. For example, Twitch, as the leading live streaming platform in the US, has over 15 million viewers each day [4]. However, the largest live streaming market is in China. The Chinese live streaming industry has been booming since 2016. There were 398 million live streaming users in 2017 [5]. The number of users increased by 28.4% compared to the year before [5]. The expected scale of users was projected to reach 507 million in 2019 [5].

Practically, attracting more viewers is the first step to be a success in the live streaming industry. With more viewers, streamers can become popular and their channels can become hot. Also, streamers are more likely to receive more income with more viewers in their channels [6]. As a result, streamers strive to attract viewers.

However, no research has focused specifically on streamers' strategies and techniques on viewers' attraction in live streaming. To investigate this question, we used novel multiple triangulation and explored this from three different perspectives. We firstly investigated it from the streamer's perspective to identify their strategies and techniques to attract viewers. We interviewed 10 popular streamers who had more than 100,000 followers in each of their own channels at the time of their interviews. Also, we conducted 3 focus group interviews to verify these identified strategies and techniques from viewers' perspectives. In addition, 305 hours of online observations were conducted to validate whether these strategies and techniques could be observed online.

2   Background

Limited research has been conducted on how to attract more viewers in live streaming so far. However, we identified some characteristics of viewers' attraction in live streaming from previous research. Game-play tournaments were found to attract more users (both streamers and viewers) than no tournaments in Twitch [7]. Also, celebrities were thought to attract more viewers than non-celebrities [8].

We also reviewed the strategies and techniques of viewers' attraction in the related fields. To attract viewers through web sites, it was necessary to value interactivity, immersion and connectivity and make a balance of them [9]. As to the design of the web pages, the pages with a main large picture, pictures of celebrities, few words, and a search bar could more easily attract young viewers [10]. In blogs, bloggers attracted more viewers by linking others' blogs to their pages since this improved the quality of their blogs and made their blogs become destination sites [11]. Technically, a mobile content recommender system (M-CRS) was also proposed to attract viewers. In this system, personalized content recommendations would be generated after recording and analyzing readers' browsing habits and histories [12].

The relationships between people's personality traits and strategies were explored in the game field [13]. Findings showed conscientious people were more easily motivated by strategies such as goal setting, simulation, self-monitoring, and feedback; while those who were more open to experience tended to be demotivated by strategies such as rewards, competition, comparison, and cooperation [13].

3 Research Methods

3.1 Triangulation and Triangulation Model

Data source triangulation and methodological triangulation are used in this study. Using more than one triangulation in a single study is multiple triangulation. In detail, we investigate streamers' strategies and techniques in viewers' attraction from three perspectives: streamers' perspective—to investigate streamers' strategies and techniques in viewers' attraction, viewers' perspective—to verify streamers' behavior and explore why viewers gift, and actual online behavior—to validate streamers' behavior in practice. Triangulating different perspectives can supplement information and provide a comprehensive understanding of the phenomenon, increase the validity of the study, and make the results more convincing [14].

Methods are applied according to the characteristics of each data source. Streamers' strategies and techniques can be obtained through one-on-one interviews since one-on-one interviews are flexible, and help collect detailed and in-depth information [15, 16]. Viewers' opinions on streamers' behavior and their motivations for gifting can be gathered through focus group interviews since focus group interviews allow discussion, and suit for relatively larger participants [17]. The actual behavior information can be collected through online observation. Triangulating these three methods helps to take advantage of the pros of each method. Our multiple triangulation model is shown in Fig. 1.

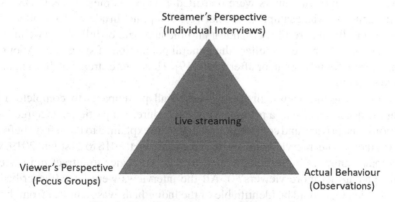

Fig. 1. Triangulating between 3 perspectives

3.2 Sampling, Procedures and Data Analysis

3.2.1 Individual Interviews

Sampling
10 popular streamers with enormous followers (all over 130,000) at the time of interviews were chosen as participants, 5 males and 5 females. They all confirmed that each of their streams had over 5,000 viewers in the last 3 months, which far reaches the massive

Table 1. Details of streamers

Coded No.	Gender	Contents	Age	No. of followers
S1	M	Talk show	20	Over 650,000
S2	F	Instrument playing	27	Over 500,000
S3	M	Singing	49	Over 510,000
S4	F	Dancing	22	Over 520,000
S5	M	Game-play	28	Over 250,000
S6	M	Appearance/physical attractiveness	27	Over 180,000
S7	F	Instrument playing and instrument selling	22	Over 130,000
S8	F	Eating	25	Over 240,000
S9	F	Anime culture	21	Over 270,000
S10	M	Outdoor activities	32	Over 320,000

standard for streams in live streaming [3]. The average age of the participants was 27.6. The details of the interviewed streamers are shown in Table 1.

Procedures
Criterion-based and purposive sampling strategies [18] were used when selecting and recruiting participants. Streamers were recruited 4 ways: online forums (BBS), social networking apps, snowball sampling and network sampling. In addition to content-based criterion such as the nature of their shows and the numbers of followers, we also took into consideration their ages to reflect the general population of streamers. About 70% of streamers were found born in or after 1990 [19]. Thus, more streamers born in or after 1990 were selected.

To conduct our interviews, firstly, we asked all participants to complete a brief demographic questionnaire as a pre-interview procedure. All participants agreed to the terms of consents, privacy and confidentiality that were explained to them fully before the interviews started. The interviews took place from 28th Oct, 2018 to 21st Jan, 2019, when the participants answered questions related to their strategies to attract more viewers ("How do you attract more viewers?"). All the interviews were later transcribed into text. Information that could be identifiable of the individuals was removed from the text. The interviews and original transcripts were in Chinese. We employed the Brislin model [20, 21] to ensure the accuracy of the translation.

3.2.2 Focus Group Interviews

Participants
23 people who, in the last 6 months, had experience with watching a wide range of streams were selected to be the participants. They were put into 3 separate focus groups with 7, 8 and 8 participants in each group, respectively. Demographic breakdowns were as follows: ages were from 18 to 32 with the average age of 21.2 years old.

All participants self-identified as Chinese. Focus groups members include students and workers/professionals. Details of three groups are shown in Table 2.

Table 2. Details of focus groups

Group No.	No. of participants	Coded No.	Average age	Gender
G1	8	A1–A8	21.4	2 female, 6 male
G2	8	A9–A16	18.5	1 female, 7 male
G3	7	A17–A23	18.9	2 female, 5 male

Procedures
The recruitment was done via advertisements posted on university internal bulletin boards, online forums (BBS) and social networking sites. All participants confirmed that they participated in the study voluntarily. Similar to procedures described in Sect. 3.1, we asked them to complete a brief demographic questionnaire first. Then they were asked to discuss and answer the key question: "how do you choose a streamer/channel?" These interviews were audio-recorded and lasted on average 1 hour. Terms of consent, privacy and confidentiality were fully explained in the pre-interview instructions. Information pertaining to individual's identity was then removed from the study. The transcripts were acquired and translated in the same procedure as explained in Sect. 3.1.

3.2.3 Observations

Participants
167 channels/streamers (89 female, 78 male) from 6 live streaming platforms were selected randomly as participants. There were 113 talent-show streamers (65 female, 48 male) and 54 game-play streamers (24 female, 30 male) from 6 popular Chinese live streaming platforms. The content of the selected streamers spanned from game-play, singing, dancing, instrumental music, food eating to talk shows, outdoor activities, anime culture, etc.

Procedures
Our observations were conducted with different durations ranging from10 minutes to 3 hours according to the length of each stream. The total observation time was 305 hours. Notes were taken during online observations.

3.2.4 Data Analysis

After immersing in the data and fully understanding the information, investigators analyzed and captured the essence of the information from both individual interviews and focus group interviews, then clustered the transcripts according to different themes using thematic analysis [22].

4 Strategies and Techniques for Attracting Viewers

Based on our multiple triangulation, we induced three convergent strategies for viewers' attraction. The three convergent strategies and techniques are (i) to increase streamer-viewer interactions; (ii) to create synergy with other streamers; and (iii) to conduct self-promotion. The divergent strategy and technique is: to work closely with the guilds and platforms.

4.1 Strategy 1: To Increase Streamer-Viewer Interactions

From the Streamers' Perspective
Promoting interactions between streamers and their viewers was deemed as a useful strategy. Streamers noticed several advantages in promoting streamer-viewer interactions: (i) active interactions between the viewers and the streamer *"made the content of the shows more exciting and attractive since the shows also added elements of the viewers' ideas"* (S4). (ii) Interactions with streamers also increased viewers' sense of participation. (iii) More interactions, more online text communication from the viewer's side. This helped to make the channel appear "hot" on the live streaming platform. The hotness of the channel was articulated as being associated with the size of the audience, the texts from the viewers, and digital gifts being sent to the streamer. Normally, the hotter the channel, the more likely the channel would be highly ranked and given a prominent place in the front page of the entire platform, which in turn, attracted even more viewers to visit the channel, since channels on the front page were easier for prospective viewers to see and visit. Also, *"the more online texts in the channel, the better the atmosphere in the channel, the more alive the stream was, and the more likely a new viewer was to stay in the channel"* (S2). The basic technique for maintaining streamer-viewer interactions was to *"have a fixed streaming schedule so that viewers would turn up when his/her favored streamer was on"* (S7).

Furthermore, according to streamers, *"the streamer-viewer interactions should not only be promoted during the real-time streams, but also outside streaming hours"* (S7). Streamers noticed the importance of *"turning up often to show their viewers that they were still there"* (S7). For example, posting some status, photos, captions, information either in their streaming page or other social media websites where they had connections with their fans and viewers.

From the Viewers' Perspective
According to the focus group members, effective interactions between streamers and their viewers were an essential reason for them to watch a stream and follow a streamer. They admitted that *"more good interactions and attention from streamers attracted them to attach more to the streamers"* (A22). Besides, apart from the interactions between streamers and viewers, focus group members expressed that they also expected good interactions between themselves and other viewers.

Focus group members mentioned that they also *"enjoyed the interactions with the streamers they like outside streaming hours"* (A1). They perceived that more streamer-viewer interactions would promote more engagement. Besides, they *"preferred streamers who can stream on a fixed schedule*" (A14) so that they knew when to expect the streams. For viewers, they felt that "*watching streams was a kind of companion*" (A21).

From the Actual Online Behavior

In our observation, all the streamers we observed were seen to give feedback or responses to viewers during their streams. Most of them were also observed to initiate a topic and encourage their viewers to text, reply, and interact. Online interactions were not limited to online verbal and written communications; other interactions included creating online activities such as raffles or quizzes with prizes.

Streamer-viewer interactions were found to account for a large proportion of time in a stream. According to our observation, the average interaction and communication time between the talent show streamers and their viewers was well over 50% of the whole streaming time. For the game-play streamers, the situation was a little different. Among all the 54 game-play streamers, the average interaction and communication time was all less than 30%.

138 out of 167 streamers mentioned in their channels/pages or declared during the streams that they had a fixed streaming schedule. All of the streamers except the ones from the YY platform were found to post photos, captions, information, or status in streamer pages (YY does not support this function at the time of observation) to maintain interactions and communications with their viewers outside streaming hours as well.

4.2 Strategy 2: To Create Synergy with Other Streamers

From the Streamers' Perspective

Most streamers believed that they could attract more viewers by creating synergy with other streamers. Two techniques were commonly used to create the synergy: recommendation and PK (player kill)/VS (versus). Streamers believed that they could elicit the flow of viewers between two channels by using these two techniques.

Recommendation: One streamer recommended their "friends" or team members (other streamers) to their viewers. Streamers said they often helped each other through this way.

PK (player kill)/VS (versus): PK or VS is a form of cooperation or competition with other streamers. Streamer A could video call Streamer B who was also streaming online; B could decide whether to answer the call or not. If B responded it, then A and B would connect with each other and both of them would show on the viewers' screens side by side. After seeing both streamers and their performances, the viewers in Streamer A's channel were likely to visit Streamer B's channel and vice versa. In this way, streamers could "channel" viewers from each other's channels. Figure 2 shows that two streamers are in the PK mode. Viewers could easily visit the other streamer in the PK/VS mode by just clicking a button.

From the Viewers' Perspective

Focus group members acknowledged that they "*would go to visit or even follow other streamers if these streamers were recommended by the streamer they like*" (A18).

Fig. 2. It shows that it is easy for the viewers to visit the other streamer's channel by clicking the button highlighted in red. (Color figure online)

In addition, they admitted that in the PK/VS mode they *"would visit and also follow the other streamers if they found the other streamer was attractive"* (A3).

From the Actual Online Behavior
According to our observations, 128 out of 167 streamers were observed to use this strategy, and both techniques (recommendations and PK/VS) were used by streamers. Besides oral recommendation in the streams, some streamers were also found to recommend their friends or team members by listing them at the bottom of their channels. The viewers could easily enter other streamers channels by clicking their icons as shown in Fig. 3. However, not all the platforms had this function. Figure 4 shows that some streamers were working as a team. It seems streamers who were familiar with each other tended to cooperate often in the PK/VS modes. According to our observation, PK/VS was widely used in talent show streamers, while game-play streamers did not use it as much as talent show streamers.

4.3 Strategy 3: To Conduct Self-promotion

From the Streamers' Perspective
From our interviews, self-promotion was the third most effective strategy to attract viewers. Streamers believed that, with fame and popularity, they could easily attract more viewers. Therefore, streamers tried many ways to create their fame and awareness. Streamers mentioned two techniques for self-promotion categorized by content.

Performance-related self-promotion: Streamers posted their video clips of their best performances to their personal pages on the platforms and/or on third-party platforms as a kind of advertisement. For example, *"the video clips with the streamers' names or streaming IDs were posted to popular third-party platforms or social media such as Weibo and Tik Tok"* (S4 & S5). When viewers were interested in the streamers' performances, they may go to the streamers' channels to watch more live performances/streams.

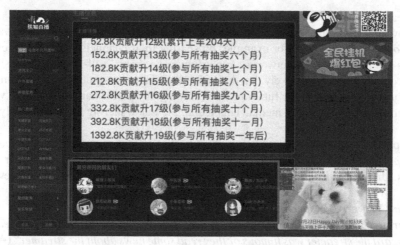

Fig. 3. One streamer listed his "friends" at the bottom of his page. (Highlighted in red). (Color figure online)

Fig. 4. Streamers were in the same team (Xiaozhou Team) (highlighted in red). All the streamers had over 500,000 followers/fans except the first one. (Color figure online)

Performance-unrelated self-promotion: Some streamers also promoted themselves by creating news or developing content or skills in other fields unrelated to their live streaming performances. When a person was famous or popular in one area, he/she would easily create fame in other areas as well. For example, a talk show presenter "*released a single as a singer in KuGou*" (S1) to help him attract more fans/viewers who liked his singing to his talk show channel.

Streamers also reported some other self-promotion techniques:

Snow ball technique: Streamers *"encouraged viewers to recommend them (streamers) to other viewers"* (S8), for example, by sharing their channels or performances to viewers' family, friends, or networks. According to streamers' self-reports, when someone liked a streamer, it was likely that their friends and family would like the streamer as well. Some platforms had the functions of recording any performances as a short video and sharing it through social media. This technique made sharing more efficiently and easily.

Proper self-presentation approach: streamers disclosed the importance of *"choosing the proper and attractive hashtags, captions, profile pictures, etc."* (S4 & S7) for their streams. Unique, vivid, and novel self-presentation was deemed to attract more viewers.

From the Viewers' Perspective

Focus group members confirmed that they would like to *"search for a particular streamer if they heard the streamer was famous or they read some news about the streamer"* (A17). They also admitted that they tended to *"choose to watch the shows which are "HOT" (or recommended) in the live streaming platforms"* (A6 & A11). Also, focus group members said they *"would like to watch a stream and follow a streamer recommended by other people, especially their family or friends"* (A2).

Focus group members also disclosed that they *"would like to choose the streamers with attractive hashtags, captions, profile pictures, or self-presentation"* (A16 & A20) when they wanted to search a new streamer/channel.

From the Actual Online Behavior

Both performance-related and performance-unrelated techniques for self-promotion were observed. In all the 167 streamers observed, 144 of them were found to use at least one technique mentioned above. Figure 5 and Fig. 6 are the screenshots of performance-related and performance-unrelated self-promotion, respectively. It seems that streamers from different platforms used different techniques for self-promotion, which were determined by the functions of different platforms. Streamers from Douyu and Xiongmao tended to post their videos with good performances in their personal pages or at the bottom of their channels. However, streamers from Kwai liked posting other unrelated short videos, normally comedy videos. Also, some streamers were found to link their IDs of other media (e.g., Weibo) to their live streaming channels.

The snowball technique was also observed by investigators. Streamers were observed to encourage viewers to share their channel links in viewers' social media. With regards to the proper self-presentation technique, streamers were seen to use hashtags, profile pictures, captions, etc. However, investigators could not define, to what extent, they were proper and attractive.

4.4   Strategy 4: To work closely with the guilds and platforms

Most streamers disclosed that they joined the guilds, and their guilds could channel some viewers to them with the help of platforms. Therefore, it was essential to work closely

Fig. 5. Performance-related self-promotion. The game-play streamer posted some of his game-playing clips with good performance at the bottom of his channel (highlighted in red). (Color figure online)

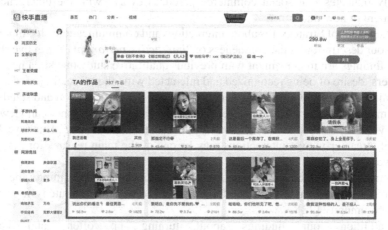

Fig. 6. Performance-unrelated self-promotion. The talk show streamer mentioned her songs in her personal page and posted some comedy episodes in her channel (highlighted in red). (Color figure online)

with guilds and platforms. Streamers mentioned there were several ways that their guilds and platforms could help:

- Initial entry: When a viewer entered a platform, he/she would be assigned to a channel automatically. Streamers or their guilds paid the platform to get more random viewers. Viewers admitted that they might stay or even follow the streamers if they found streamers attractive after they were assigned to a channel. In our observation, we found we would be assigned to a channel by the platform. However, we could not know whether the platform assigned us to that channel randomly or deliberately.
- Recommendation system & hot streamer list: Viewers received recommendations continuously and automatically during their stream-watching. Also, there was a hot streamer list which kept updating on the platform. Some streamers would pay their platforms to get recommended or to be listed on the hot streamer list, so that more viewers may visit their channels. Focus group members confirmed that they were likely to visit streamers recommended by the platforms, or check the hot streamer list and visit them. However, in our observation, we could not know whether the streamers paid for their recommendations.

The two techniques mentioned above were brought up by streamers, partially verified by viewers, but could not be validated by online observation.

5 Discussion

Our study indicates that social commerce practices evolve with the emergence and development of new platforms.

The key point of Strategy 1 is about interactions and communications. Its importance supports our description of the uniqueness of "*interactive performances*" in live streaming. Our findings are in agreement with previous qualitative study that streamers noted the viewers' desire of being recognized and interacted with, therefore, they made efforts to recognize viewers and offered viewers opportunities to participate in and stand out in the streams in Twitch [3]. This consistence reflects that no matter American viewers or Chinese viewers, they all value the "social" side of stream-watching. This reveals that pursuit of streamer-viewer interactions may be one of the main reasons for viewers to watch live streams.

Our findings also indicate the importance of having a fixed streaming time, which is well consistent with previous study that keeping a consistent schedule is important in building community [23].

In addition, our findings about turning up often, and keeping connected/communication with viewers support previous studies on online phatic culture which was popular in blogging and social networking like Facebook. As a new form of online communication, it aims to "maintain connections or audiences, to let one's network know that one is still 'there'", rather than to express information or focus on content [24]. Our findings demonstrate the existence and the use of phatic communications in the live streaming realm.

Furthermore, our findings that streamers spent time on communication and interactions are consistent with the previous study that chatting (streamer-viewer interactions) accounts for the largest proportion of streaming activities [8]. We firstly note the differences in time spent on interactions between talent show streamers and game-play streamers. Game-play streamers need to concentrate to win the game, and that is probably why their interactions are less than talent show streamers'.

In Strategy 2, no previous research has explored whether recommendations and PK (or versus) can attract more viewers. However, the reciprocal streamers who gifted each other were found to appear more often on the popular streamers list [25], which in return, might make streamers more easily accessed by viewers on live streaming platforms. As observed in our study, streamers who are familiar with each other tend to compete in the PK/VS mode, which can be regarded as a reciprocal relationship as well. Differences in genres in using PK/VS are found as well. Reasons might be the same as we talked above that game-play streamers need to focus on their games.

In Strategy 3, streamers are found to try different means to promote themselves, which is in agreement with the previous finding that streamers using other social media platforms for promotion [26]. It reveals the importance of reaching and using a variety of means. This supports the previous research that platforms should provide tools for streamers' self-promotion [26, 27].

In the online media culture, self-promotion is concomitant with self-presentation or self-expression. Our findings that streamers make use of profile pictures, selfies and captions to attract more viewers, is consistent with previous studies that profile pictures, captions and selfies all serve as tools for self-presentation, strategic communication and performative utterances [28, 29]. Therefore, the importance of self-presentation or self-expression is highlighted. The proper, unique and attractive self-presentation or self-expression should be used.

In addition, our findings show that some viewers are motivated to search for and watch some streamers' streams because of their curiosity. In the live streaming field, curiosity was only found to be influential on viewers' gifting behavior [30]. Our study extends previous research and finds out that curiosity may be one of the motivators of stream-watching.

In Strategy 4, streamers cooperating with platforms and their guilds to make use of more resources, in fact, is a way of promotion as well. It is considered as less fundamental than the first three strategies as Strategy 4 could not be verified by all the three data sources of triangulation.

6 Implications and Limitations

This study provides innovative methods in HCI. It integrates multi-methods (including individual interviews, focus group and actual behavior observation) in one study and explores a phenomenon from three different standpoints, which helps us comprehensively understand the phenomenon. In addition, our study expands the scope of the research objects. Multiple categories in live streaming are included rather than a single category. Our results provide a comprehensive description of viewer attraction in the live streaming realm.

In terms of practical implications, both platforms and streamers benefit from our study. For platforms and the live streaming industry, our research is beneficial for knowledge of marketing and platform design. Platforms may add more functions which can promote streamer-viewer interactions, strengthen the cooperation among streamers, and provide more ways/means for streamers' self-promotion. Streamers/practitioners may attract more viewers by adopting the strategies and techniques reported here. They may also develop their own strategies and techniques based on our findings. Furthermore, other fields related to pervasion may also benefit from our study.

This study is not without limitations. Firstly, the psychological aspect of the attraction of viewers in relation to the effectiveness of such strategies and techniques needs further investigation, e.g. why viewers watch streams? Why and under what circumstance a particular strategy is more effective than the others? Secondly, it will be interesting to investigate whether cultural differences exist in the strategies and techniques for viewers' attraction.

Acknowledgement. We would like to thank the following people for their assistances: Mr. Qiuwu Jia, Ms. Chunyu Sun, Ms. Bin Li, Mr. Allan Bingqi Huang, Mr. Junzhao Li, Mr. Xin Chen, Ms. Shuang Zuo, Mr. Lei Wu, Mr. Yonghui Long, Mr. Zhiming Zhang, and Mr. Weikun Zhou. We also thank the editors and anonymous reviewers for their excellent comments and suggestions.

References

1. Liang, T.P., Ho, Y.T., Li, Y.W., Turban, E.: What drives social commerce: the role of social support and relationship quality. Int. J. Electron. Commer. **16**(2), 69–90 (2011)
2. Curty, R.G., Zhang, P.: Social commerce: looking back and forward. Proc. Am. Soc. Inf. Sci. Technol. **48**(1), 1–10 (2011)
3. Hamilton, W.A., Garretson, O., Kerne, A.: Streaming on twitch: fostering participatory communities of play within live mixed media. In: Proceedings of the 32nd Annual ACM Conference on Human Factors in Computing Systems, pp. 1315–1324. ACM. Toronto Canada (2014)
4. Twitch. https://twitchadvertising.tv/audience/. Accessed June 2019
5. iiMedia. http://www.iimedia.cn/62340.html. Accessed June 2019
6. Zhu, Z., Yang, Z., Dai, Y.: Understanding the gift-sending interaction on live-streaming video websites. In: Meiselwitz, G. (ed.) SCSM 2017. LNCS, vol. 10282, pp. 274–285. Springer, Cham (2017). https://doi.org/10.1007/978-3-319-58559-8_23
7. Kaytoue, M., Silva, A., Cerf, L., Meira, W., Jr., Raïssi, C.: Watch me playing, I am a professional: a first study on video game live streaming. In: Proceedings of the 21st International Conference on World Wide Web, pp. 1181–1188. ACM, New York (2012)
8. Tang, J.C., Venolia, G., Inkpen, K.M.: Meerkat and periscope: I stream, you stream, apps stream for live streams. In: Proceedings of the 2016 CHI Conference on Human Factors in Computing Systems, California, USA, pp. 4770–4780. ACM (2016)
9. Bhatt, G.: Bringing virtual reality for commercial Web sites. Int. J. Hum. Comput. Stud. **60**(1), 1–15 (2004)
10. Djamasbi, S., Siegel, M., Tullis, T.: Generation Y, web design, and eye tracking. Int. J. Hum. Comput. Stud. **68**(5), 307–323 (2010)
11. Mayzlin, D., Yoganarasimhan, H.: Link to success: How blogs build an audience by promoting rivals. Manage. Sci. **58**(9), 1651–1668 (2012)
12. Chiu, P.H., Kao, G.Y.M., Lo, C.C.: Personalized blog content recommender system for mobile phone users. Int. J. Hum. Comput. Stud. **68**(8), 496–507 (2010)

13. Orji, R., Nacke, L.E., Di Marco, C.: Towards personality-driven persuasive health games and gamified systems. In: Proceedings of the 2017 CHI Conference on Human Factors in Computing Systems, Denver, USA, pp. 1015–1027. ACM (2017)
14. Carter, N., Bryant-Lukosius, D., Blythe, J., Neville, A.: The use of triangulation in qualitative research. In: Oncology nursing Forum, pp. 545–547 (2014)
15. Kazmer, M.M., Xie, B.: Qualitative interviewing in Internet studies: Playing with the media, playing with the method. Inf. Community Soc. 11(2), 257–278 (2008)
16. Rubin, H.J., Rubin, I.S.: Qualitative Interviewing: The Art of Hearing Data. Sage, London (2011)
17. Bohnsack, R.: Group discussion and focus groups. Companion Qual. Res. 210, 221 (2004)
18. Mason, J.: Qualitative Researching. Sage, London (2011)
19. Xinhuanet. http://www.xinhuanet.com/english/2019-09/11/c_138384107.htm. Accessed Aug 2019
20. Brislin, R.W.: Back-translation for cross-cultural research. J. Cross Cult. Psychol. 1(3), 185–216 (1970)
21. Lee, C.C., Li, D., Arai, S., Puntillo, K.: Ensuring cross-cultural equivalence in translation of research consents and clinical documents: a systematic process for translating English to Chinese. J. Transcult. Nurs. 20(1), 77–82 (2009)
22. Braun, V., Clarke, V.: Using thematic analysis in psychology. Qual. Res. Psychol. 3(2), 77–101 (2006)
23. Pellicone, A.J., Ahn, J.: The Game of performing play: understanding streaming as cultural production. In: Proceedings of the 2017 CHI Conference on Human Factors in Computing Systems, Denver, USA, pp. 4863–4874. ACM (2017)
24. Miller, V.: New media, networking and phatic culture. Convergence 14(4), 387–400 (2008)
25. Tu, W., Yan, C., Yan, Y., Ding, X., Sun, L.: Who is earning? Understanding and modeling the virtual gifts behavior of users in live streaming economy. In: 2018 IEEE Conference on Multimedia Information Processing and Retrieval (MIPR), Florida, USA, pp. 118–123. IEEE (2018)
26. Kietzmann, J.H., Hermkens, K., McCarthy, I.P., Silvestre, B.S.: Social media? Get serious! Understanding the functional building blocks of social media. Bus. Horiz. 54(3), 241–251 (2011)
27. Tafesse, W., Wien, A.: Implementing social media marketing strategically: an empirical assessment. J. Mark. Manage. 34(9–10), 732–749 (2018)
28. Jerslev, A., Mortensen, M.: What is the self in the celebrity selfie? Celebrification, phatic communication and performativity. Celebr. Stud. 7(2), 249–263 (2016)
29. Tifferet, S., Vilnai-Yavetz, I.: Self-presentation in LinkedIn portraits: common features, gender, and occupational differences. Comput. Hum. Behav. 80, 33–48 (2018)
30. Li, B., Hou, F., Guan, Z., Chong, A.Y.L.: What drives people to purchase virtual gifts in live streaming? The mediating role of flow 2018. In: 22nd Pacific Asia Conference on Information Systems (PACIS), n.p. Association for Information Systems, Yokohama, Japan (2018)

Identification of Key Factors Affecting Logistics Service Quality of Cross-border E-commerce

Peng Jiang[1], Hang Jiang[2(✉)], Yi-Chung Hu[3], Chongen Liang[1], and Shiyuan Wang[1]

[1] School of Business, Shandong University, Weihai, China
[2] School of Business Administration, Jimei University, Xiamen, China
hangjiang@jmu.edu.cn
[3] Department of Business Administration, Chung Yuan Christian University, Taoyuan, Taiwan

Abstract. As cross-border e-commerce has broad market space and rapid development momentum, more and more manufacturing enterprises begin to explore the application of cross-border e-commerce, especially small and medium-sized enterprises. Therefore, it is crucial to identify the logistics factors that affect cross-border e-commerce logistics service quality, which is important to promote the development of the industry. In this paper, a hybrid multiple criteria decision making method, combining fuzzy theory and DANP model is proposed. According to the results of empirical study, scale of enterprise assets, number of employees, financial standing, emphasis on logistics business and convenience are identified as the key criteria affecting logistics service quality of cross-border e-commerce.

Keywords: Key factors · Logistics service quality of cross-border e-commerce · MCDM · Fuzzy theory · DANP

1 Introduction

With the implementation of the "Belt and Road" initiative and the continuous introduction of relevant supporting policies, more and more traditional enterprises have begun to involve in cross-border business. As a new way of transaction, cross-border e-commerce, relying on the popularity and advantages of the Internet, can break through the constraints of time and space and provide a more open multilateral market, which has become an important engine to promote the development of China's foreign trade industry. According to the latest customs data, the total import and export trade of our country reached 30.50 trillion yuan in 2018 with an increase of 9.6%. At the same time, according to the China Electronic Commerce Development Report 2018, the development of "Belt and Road" has promoted the gradual opening of the policy of cross-border e-commerce in the countries, the popularization of Internet and the further improvement of supporting facilities such as payment methods and logistics, all of which have to some extent promoted the rapid development of cross-border e-commerce in China. As the report stated, the total amount of e-commerce transactions is 31.63 trillion yuan in 2018 with an increase of 8.5%, which can be recognized that the scale of cross-border e-commerce transactions has grown dramatically. The development of cross-border e-commerce pushes forward

© Springer Nature Switzerland AG 2020
F. F.-H. Nah and K. Siau (Eds.): HCII 2020, LNCS 12204, pp. 384–396, 2020.
https://doi.org/10.1007/978-3-030-50341-3_30

the development of cross-border logistics. Of the many related issues, the cross-border e-commerce logistics service quality is an area of enormous interest for both academics and practitioners.

With the rapid development of cross-border e-commerce, the demands of consumers on the timeliness, experience, cost and other aspects of cross-border logistics services are increasing. However, at this stage, China's logistics infrastructure construction is relatively weak, and supporting services are not perfect. More specifically, cross-border e-commerce transactions need to go through many links such as warehousing, distribution, customs clearance, and commodity inspection, resulting in high operating costs [1]. In addition, because of the multi-level demand for logistics services from cross-border e-commerce, such as the cross-border e-commerce of many enterprises to the consumer model (B2C), its own small batch, high-frequency logistics demand characteristics increase the burden of logistics enterprises' operating costs. Moreover, most of the enterprises engaged in cross-border e-commerce logistics in China are mainly engaged in a certain business or a special line, and the service resources are seriously divided, so it is difficult to form a comprehensive logistics service system, and it is unable to effectively gather the business flow, information flow, capital flow and physical logistics [2]. Therefore, considering the rapid development of cross-border e-commerce and the increasing demand of consumers for cross-border e-commerce logistics, it is crucial to establish an evaluation system to clarify the interaction between cross-border e-commerce and modern logistics, and to identify the logistics factors that affect cross-border e-commerce logistics service quality (LSQ), which is also important to promote the development of the industry.

Identifying the key factors affecting logistics service quality (LSQ) of cross-border E-commerce is a typical Multiple Criteria Decision Making (MCDM) problem. MCDM methods are often used to deal with problems characterized by several non-commensurable and conflicting (competing) criteria, where there may be no solution that satisfies all criteria simultaneously [3]. Based on reviewing the previous studies, more and more MCDM methods are wildly applied to different research issues, such as the analytical hierarchy process (AHP), the analytical network process (ANP) [4], and the decision-making trial and evaluation laboratory (DEMATEL) [5]. However, the methods used in previous researches have some limitations. First, the AHP method requires that the aspects and criteria should be independent of each other, whereas these assumptions cannot be realized in reality [6]. Second, ANP can accommodate interdependence and feedback among criteria and alternatives. But a serious problem is that because of the limitations in human cognition and shortcomings in the typically used one-to-nine scale, the consistent pairwise comparisons are not easy to achieve, especially for a matrix with high order [7]. Moreover, traditional Likert scales have been the major way in evaluating performance through questionnaires [8]. However, this scale cannot deal with the cognitive uncertainty among the linguistic values such as 'disagree', 'fair', and 'disagree'. Relative to the Likert scale, uncertain and imprecise data can be represented by fuzzy numbers in many practical circumstances [9]. Song [10] and Xu [11] applied the fuzzy comprehensive evaluation method and fuzzy-AHP, respectively, to the issues related to the cross-border e-commerce logistics. Based on the literature review, therefore, a novel hybrid MCDM technique, named fuzzy-DANP, is proposed in this paper, solving two problems at the same time: comparison and cognitive uncertainty.

The remainder of this paper is organized as follows. Section 2 reviews the related literature on logistics service quality of cross-border E-commerce and establishes the prototype decision structure, and Sect. 3 introduces the proposed Fuzzy-DANP model. Section 4 applies the proposed method to identify key factors affecting logistics service quality of cross-border E-commerce using the fuzzy semantic questionnaire assigned the fuzzy numbers to different natural representations, such as "fair" and "agree". Section 5 discusses the various outcomes, and provides the conclusions of this study.

2   Literature Review

Because cross-border e-commerce involves different subjects, there are many factors might affect the LSQ of cross-border e-commerce. Therefore, it is essential to establish a reasonable index system to evaluate the LSQ of cross-border e-commerce by considering multiple factors. The comprehensive index is useful to identify the key factors affecting the LSQ of cross-border e-commerce, and make decision to improve the service quality. According to the previous studies, the factors affecting the LSQ of cross-border e-commerce logistics can be cataloged into three dimensions, namely, enterprise characteristics, service experience, logistics cost.

2.1   Enterprise Characteristics

The dimension of enterprise characteristics mainly considers the influence of internal factors on LSQ. Jia [12] stated that the strength of the enterprise determines the fixed assets and current assets of the enterprise, and the employees reflect the size of the enterprise, which have a positive impact on the LSQ. The financial standing mainly refers to the liquidity, indirectly reflects the volume of orders [13]. The more enterprises attach importance to logistics, the better the LSQ [12]. In summary, the enterprises with large scale and a certain amount of funds and orders would pay a great attention to the importance of logistics and provide a better customer experience.

2.2   Service Experience

Service experience is an important component of measuring LSQ, and it is the consumer's cognition of service quality. To measure LSQ, several authors began with a viewpoint of physical logistics operations, for example variables of timeliness, availability and condition [14]. Mentzer, Flint [15] introduced a model with nine variables: information quality, ordering procedure, ordering release quantity, timeliness, order accuracy, order quality, order condition, order discrepancy handling and personnel contact quality. Grant [16] investigated LSQ in UK food processing, including core variables like availability, time (order cycle time and delivery time), but also included variables examining customer service experience and satisfaction as outputs for a structural path model based on an actual service experience; e.g. general assessment of supplier quality, feelings towards suppliers, and future purchase intentions from that supplier.

Grant also extended notions of LSQ and satisfaction towards customer loyalty which has been an ongoing discussion in the out-sourcing and relationship literature [17, 18]. This is critical in researching service quality as the firm's goal is to enhance performance to retain current customers and attract new ones and suggests a notion of developing long-term relationships as opposed to transactional activities [19].

2.3 Logistics Cost

Different logistics models could cause different costs. The total cost of logistics is also an important aspect of logistics service quality. Zhao [20] concentrated on the cost and aging of cross-border e-commerce logistics, and provided the fourth party logistics alliance to solve this difficulty. Both Dou and Wu [21], Guo [22] stated in their studies that the high cost of cross-border e-commerce logistics, long transportation cycle, and many links have a negative impact on the LSQ.

According to the literature review, the research framework is summarized in Table 1.

Table 1. The formal research framework

Goal	Dimensions	Criteria
Identification of key factors affecting logistics service quality of cross-border e-commerce	Enterprise characteristics	Scale of enterprise assets (Emphasis on hardware) (A1)
		Number of employees (A2)
		Financial standing (Liquidity, product turnover) (A3)
		Emphasis on logistics business (A4)
	Service experience	Service attitude (A5)
		Convenience (Receiving, returning, etc.) (A6)
		Timeliness (Order processing, delivery time) (A7)
		Safety (Cargo damage, security of user information, etc.) (A8)
		Accuracy (Misdistribution) (A9)
		After-sale service (A10)
	Logistics cost	Transport cost (A11)
		Warehousing cost (A12)
		Management cost (A13)
		Stock holding cost (A14)

3 Methodology

In this paper, the proposed Fuzzy MCDM model consists of the triangular fuzzy numbers and the DANP method. The characteristics of the triangular fuzzy number for dealing with the cognitive uncertainty are described in Subsect. 3.1. Subsect. 3.2 demonstrates how to obtain the relevant weights of each criterion by using the Fuzzy DANP model.

3.1 Triangular Fuzzy Numbers

In the real world, many decisions involve imprecision since goals, constraints, and possible actions are not known precisely [23]. When making decisions in a fuzzy environment, the result of decision-making is highly affected by subjective judgments that are vague and imprecise. The sources of imprecision include namely unquantifiable information, incomplete information, non-obtainable information, and partial ignorance. Fuzzy set theory [24] was first introduced as a mathematical way to represent and handle vagueness in decision-making.

Questionnaire survey is one of the most common ways to obtain data in management decision-making. Undoubtedly, the 5-point Likert scale is commonly used. However, the traditional 5-point Likert scale assumes that the differences between the successive categories are equal [25] and cannot deal with the cognitive uncertainty. For instance, the ratings of 1, 2, 3, 4 and 5 may be set to "strongly disagree", "disagree", "fair", "agree" and "strongly agree", respectively. In other words, "fair" is transformed to the same scale point for each respondent, although each respondent has her or his subjective thinking for different natural representations. However, the cognitive uncertainty among these natural representations of preference should be taken into account. In other words, it is reasonable for each respondent to subjectively express her or his own measurements for different natural representations.

A linguistic variable is a variable with linguistic words or sentences in a natural language [26]. In Fuzzy DANP procedure, in order to generate fuzzy pairwise comparison matrix, a fuzzy scale with five different degrees of influence is needed. The degree of influence with five linguistic terms, (no influence, very low influence, low influence, high influence, very high influence), can be treated as a linguistic variable defined in the closed interval [0, 1]. Each linguistic value can be represented by the triangular fuzzy number, which is a fuzzy set in the universe of discourse that is both convex and normal [26]. As depicted in Fig. 1, instead of assigning a scale point to a linguistic value, "low influence" and "high influence" can be represented as triangular fuzzy numbers (a, b, c) and (b, c, 1) ($0 < a < b < c < 1$), respectively. Each respondent can be asked to assign a triangular fuzzy number to each of the above linguistic values in the questionnaire.

3.2 Fuzzy DANP

Ouyang, Shieh [3] and Tzeng and Huang [27] proposed a novel DANP consisting of DEMETEL and ANP by taking the total influence matrix generated by DEMATEL as the unweighted supermatrix of ANP directly, avoiding the troublesome pairwise comparisons for ANP.

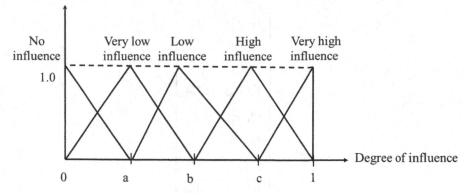

Fig. 1. Triangular fuzzy numbers for fuzzy pairwise comparison matrix

To determine the Fuzzy DEMATEL total influence matrix, T, the fuzzy direct influence matrix, Z, is first constructed using the fuzzy degree of effect between each pair of elements taken from respondent questionnaires. Suppose zij = (zlij, zcij, zuij) be the fuzzy assessment that the degree to which factor i have impact on factor j, specified as a linguistic value, (no influence, very low influence, low influence, high influence, very high influence),

$$Z = \begin{bmatrix} \left(z_{11}^{l}, z_{11}^{c}, z_{11}^{u}\right) & \left(z_{12}^{l}, z_{12}^{c}, z_{12}^{u}\right) & \cdots & \left(z_{1n}^{l}, z_{1n}^{c}, z_{1n}^{u}\right) \\ \left(z_{21}^{l}, z_{21}^{c}, z_{21}^{u}\right) & \left(z_{22}^{l}, z_{22}^{c}, z_{22}^{u}\right) & \cdots & \left(z_{2n}^{l}, z_{2n}^{c}, z_{2n}^{u}\right) \\ \vdots & \vdots & \ddots & \vdots \\ \left(z_{n1}^{l}, z_{n1}^{c}, z_{n1}^{u}\right) & \left(z_{n2}^{l}, z_{n2}^{c}, z_{n2}^{u}\right) & \cdots & \left(z_{nn}^{l}, z_{nn}^{c}, z_{nn}^{u}\right) \end{bmatrix} \tag{1}$$

where n is the number of factors. All diagonal elements are zero. **Z** is then normalized to produce the normalized fuzzy direct influence matrices,

$$\mathbf{X} = \lambda \mathbf{Z} \tag{2}$$

where

$$\lambda = \frac{1}{\max\limits_{i,j}\left\{ \max \sum\limits_{i=1}^{n} z_{ij}, \max \sum\limits_{j=1}^{n} z_{ij} \right\}} \tag{3}$$

Then

$$X^{l} = \begin{bmatrix} x_{11}^{l} & x_{12}^{l} & \cdots & x_{1n}^{l} \\ x_{21}^{l} & x_{22}^{l} & \cdots & x_{2n}^{l} \\ \vdots & \vdots & \ddots & \vdots \\ x_{n1}^{l} & x_{n2}^{l} & \cdots & x_{nn}^{l} \end{bmatrix} \tag{4}$$

$$X^c = \begin{bmatrix} x_{11}^c & x_{12}^c & \cdots & x_{1n}^c \\ x_{21}^c & x_{22}^c & \cdots & x_{2n}^c \\ \vdots & \vdots & \ddots & \vdots \\ x_{n1}^c & x_{n2}^c & \cdots & x_{nn}^c \end{bmatrix} \tag{5}$$

$$X^u = \begin{bmatrix} x_{11}^u & x_{12}^u & \cdots & x_{1n}^u \\ x_{21}^u & x_{22}^u & \cdots & x_{2n}^u \\ \vdots & \vdots & \ddots & \vdots \\ x_{n1}^u & x_{n2}^u & \cdots & x_{nn}^u \end{bmatrix} \tag{6}$$

Then the fuzzy total influence matrices, T^l, T^c and T^u, are generated by $X(I - X)^{-1}$.

$$T^l = \begin{bmatrix} t_{11}^l & t_{12}^l & \cdots & t_{1n}^l \\ t_{21}^l & t_{22}^l & \cdots & t_{2n}^l \\ \vdots & \vdots & \ddots & \vdots \\ t_{n1}^l & t_{n2}^l & \cdots & t_{nn}^l \end{bmatrix} \tag{7}$$

$$T^c = \begin{bmatrix} t_{11}^c & t_{12}^c & \cdots & t_{1n}^c \\ t_{21}^c & t_{22}^c & \cdots & t_{2n}^c \\ \vdots & \vdots & \ddots & \vdots \\ t_{n1}^c & t_{n2}^c & \cdots & t_{nn}^c \end{bmatrix} \tag{8}$$

$$T^u = \begin{bmatrix} t_{11}^u & t_{12}^u & \cdots & t_{1n}^u \\ t_{21}^u & t_{22}^u & \cdots & t_{2n}^u \\ \vdots & \vdots & \ddots & \vdots \\ t_{n1}^u & t_{n2}^u & \cdots & t_{nn}^u \end{bmatrix} \tag{9}$$

According to the Reference [3], the total influence matrix of DEMATEL can be treated as an unweighted supermatrix for ANP. Therefore, a crisp total influence matrix should be generated. In practice, defuzzification converts a fuzzy number into a crisp real number. Defuzzification is to locate the best non-fuzzy performance (BNP) value. The widely used center-of-area (COA) [28] is employed to generate BNP value, BNP_o:

$$BNP_o = \frac{(o_u - o_l) + (o_c - o_l)}{3} + o_l, \tag{10}$$

where (o_l, o_c, o_u) denote the performance values of the objective. Then the crisp total influence matrix is generated,

$$T = \begin{bmatrix} \frac{t_{11}^l + t_{11}^c + t_{11}^u}{3} & \frac{t_{12}^l + t_{12}^c + t_{12}^u}{3} & \cdots & \frac{t_{1n}^l + t_{1n}^c + t_{1n}^u}{3} \\ \frac{t_{21}^l + t_{21}^c + t_{21}^u}{3} & \frac{t_{22}^l + t_{22}^c + t_{22}^u}{3} & \cdots & \frac{t_{2n}^l + t_{2n}^c + t_{2n}^u}{3} \\ \vdots & \vdots & \ddots & \vdots \\ \frac{t_{n1}^l + t_{n1}^c + t_{n1}^u}{3} & \frac{t_{n2}^l + t_{n2}^c + t_{n2}^u}{3} & \cdots & \frac{t_{nn}^l + t_{nn}^c + t_{nn}^u}{3} \end{bmatrix} \tag{11}$$

A weighted matrix, **W**, can be obtained by normalizing **T**, and the global weight of each factor is obtained by multiplying **W** by itself several times until a limiting supermatrix, $\mathbf{W}^*$, is derived.

Causes and effect can be derived from **T** [29]. For **T**, each row was summed to obtain the value denoted by d, and each column of the total influence matrix was summed to obtain the value denoted by r. Then $d + r$ is the prominence, and shows the relative importance of the corresponding factor, where larger prominence implies greater importance; and $d - r$ is the relation, where a positive relation means the corresponding factor tends to affect other elements actively, referred to as a *cause*, and a negative relation means the corresponding factor tends to be affected by other elements, referred to as an *effect*.

4   Empirical Study

There were 80 consumers of cross-border e-commerce are invited to join this study. Of the 80 questionnaires distributed to the respondents, 56 were returned to the researchers, and 53 of these were valid. In the first questionnaire, each respondent is asked to assign a triangular fuzzy number to each of the linguistic values with a, b, and c. Then, according to the data collected from questionnaires, calculate the arithmetic mean of a, b, and c, respectively. The linguistic variables are show in Table 2.

Table 2. The linguistic variables with triangular fuzzy numbers

Linguistic	Crisp number	Triangular fuzzy numbers
No influence	0	(0, 0, 0.19)
Very low influence	1	(0, 0.19, 0.47)
Low influence	2	(0.19, 0.47, 0.72)
High influence	3	(0.47, 0.72, 1)
Very high influence	4	(0.72, 1, 1)

In the second questionnaire, each respondent is asked to give a crisp value to generate the initial direct influence matrix. And then, using the triangular fuzzy numbers shown in Table 2 to replace the crisp value to generate the fuzzy initial direct influence matrix. Using the DEMATEL method, through Eqs. (1)-(11), the crisp total influence matrix is shown in Table 3, and the prominence and relation of each criterion is summarized in Table 4.

Table 3. The crisp total influence matrix

T	A1	A2	A3	A4	A5	A6	A7	A8	A9	A10	A11	A12	A13	A14	D
A1	0.095	0.156	0.141	0.162	0.226	0.165	0.192	0.175	0.178	0.248	0.174	0.189	0.214	0.153	2.470
A2	0.152	0.102	0.141	0.167	0.227	0.169	0.199	0.177	0.186	0.257	0.174	0.198	0.220	0.163	2.533
A3	0.158	0.151	0.095	0.169	0.233	0.174	0.197	0.183	0.187	0.259	0.179	0.204	0.210	0.170	2.570
A4	0.148	0.148	0.111	0.099	0.224	0.164	0.185	0.163	0.172	0.244	0.169	0.193	0.209	0.157	2.386
A5	0.078	0.087	0.071	0.094	0.082	0.092	0.098	0.086	0.099	0.156	0.091	0.100	0.116	0.090	1.341
A6	0.143	0.147	0.144	0.153	0.220	0.105	0.187	0.161	0.169	0.245	0.165	0.188	0.203	0.159	2.389
A7	0.098	0.100	0.096	0.111	0.166	0.122	0.089	0.131	0.130	0.198	0.119	0.138	0.159	0.119	1.777
A8	0.129	0.129	0.129	0.142	0.197	0.144	0.167	0.097	0.159	0.220	0.153	0.172	0.186	0.146	2.171
A9	0.105	0.117	0.105	0.121	0.191	0.138	0.158	0.134	0.093	0.206	0.136	0.165	0.180	0.134	1.983
A10	0.055	0.064	0.052	0.053	0.091	0.064	0.070	0.065	0.067	0.064	0.056	0.066	0.077	0.061	0.907
A11	0.120	0.126	0.120	0.127	0.194	0.142	0.156	0.132	0.152	0.219	0.094	0.172	0.186	0.142	2.081
A12	0.097	0.100	0.096	0.100	0.150	0.105	0.122	0.104	0.108	0.186	0.114	0.084	0.145	0.108	1.621
A13	0.085	0.094	0.093	0.091	0.142	0.096	0.120	0.100	0.106	0.187	0.110	0.130	0.088	0.107	1.550
A14	0.132	0.144	0.134	0.145	0.198	0.146	0.167	0.152	0.154	0.230	0.150	0.181	0.188	0.097	2.219
r	1.596	1.665	1.531	1.737	2.541	1.825	2.108	1.859	1.960	2.919	1.884	2.181	2.382	1.807	

Table 4. The prominence and relation of each criterion

Criteria	d	r	d + r	RANK	d − r
A1	2.470	1.596	4.066	5	0.874
A2	2.533	1.665	4.198	2	0.868
A3	2.570	1.531	4.101	4	1.038
A4	2.386	1.737	4.123	3	0.649
A5	1.341	2.541	3.882	12	−1.200
A6	2.389	1.825	4.215	1	0.564
A7	1.777	2.108	3.885	11	−0.331
A8	2.171	1.859	4.030	6	0.312
A9	1.983	1.960	3.943	9	0.023
A10	0.907	2.919	3.826	13	−2.013
A11	2.081	1.884	3.965	8	0.197
A12	1.621	2.181	3.802	14	−0.560
A13	1.550	2.382	3.932	10	−0.832
A14	2.219	1.807	4.026	7	0.412

Table 5 shows the weighted supermatrix, which is obtained by normalizing the total influence matrix, and Table 6 shows the limiting supermatrix derived from the weighted supermatrix. Table 7 shows the overall rankings for factors, which are arranged in ascending order of the Borda score of each factor.

Table 5. The weighted supermatrix

	A1	A2	A3	A4	A5	A6	A7	A8	A9	A10	A11	A12	A13	A14
A1	0.060	0.094	0.092	0.093	0.089	0.090	0.091	0.094	0.091	0.085	0.092	0.087	0.090	0.084
A2	0.095	0.061	0.092	0.096	0.089	0.093	0.094	0.095	0.095	0.088	0.092	0.091	0.092	0.090
A3	0.099	0.090	0.062	0.097	0.092	0.095	0.094	0.098	0.096	0.089	0.095	0.094	0.088	0.094
A4	0.093	0.089	0.073	0.057	0.088	0.090	0.088	0.088	0.088	0.083	0.090	0.088	0.088	0.087
A5	0.049	0.052	0.046	0.054	0.032	0.050	0.046	0.046	0.050	0.054	0.049	0.046	0.049	0.050
A6	0.090	0.089	0.094	0.088	0.087	0.058	0.089	0.086	0.086	0.084	0.088	0.086	0.085	0.088
A7	0.061	0.060	0.063	0.064	0.065	0.067	0.042	0.070	0.066	0.068	0.063	0.063	0.067	0.066
A8	0.081	0.077	0.084	0.082	0.077	0.079	0.079	0.052	0.081	0.075	0.081	0.079	0.078	0.081
A9	0.066	0.070	0.069	0.070	0.075	0.075	0.075	0.072	0.047	0.071	0.072	0.076	0.076	0.074
A10	0.035	0.038	0.034	0.031	0.036	0.035	0.033	0.035	0.034	0.022	0.030	0.030	0.032	0.034
A11	0.075	0.076	0.078	0.073	0.076	0.078	0.074	0.071	0.078	0.075	0.050	0.079	0.078	0.078
A12	0.061	0.060	0.063	0.058	0.059	0.058	0.058	0.056	0.055	0.064	0.060	0.039	0.061	0.060
A13	0.053	0.056	0.061	0.053	0.056	0.053	0.057	0.054	0.054	0.064	0.058	0.060	0.037	0.059
A14	0.083	0.086	0.088	0.084	0.078	0.080	0.079	0.082	0.079	0.079	0.080	0.083	0.079	0.054

Table 6. The limiting supermatrix

	A1	A2	A3	A4	A5	A6	A7	A8	A9	A10	A11	A12	A13	A14
A1	0.088	0.088	0.088	0.088	0.088	0.088	0.088	0.088	0.088	0.088	0.088	0.088	0.088	0.088
A2	0.090	0.090	0.090	0.090	0.090	0.090	0.090	0.090	0.090	0.090	0.090	0.090	0.090	0.090
A3	0.091	0.091	0.091	0.091	0.091	0.091	0.091	0.091	0.091	0.091	0.091	0.091	0.091	0.091
A4	0.085	0.085	0.084	0.084	0.085	0.085	0.085	0.085	0.085	0.084	0.085	0.085	0.084	0.085
A5	0.049	0.049	0.049	0.049	0.048	0.049	0.049	0.049	0.049	0.049	0.049	0.049	0.049	0.049
A6	0.085	0.085	0.085	0.085	0.085	0.085	0.085	0.085	0.085	0.085	0.085	0.085	0.085	0.085
A7	0.063	0.063	0.063	0.063	0.063	0.063	0.063	0.063	0.063	0.063	0.063	0.063	0.063	0.063
A8	0.078	0.078	0.078	0.078	0.078	0.078	0.078	0.078	0.078	0.078	0.078	0.078	0.078	0.078
A9	0.070	0.070	0.070	0.070	0.070	0.070	0.070	0.070	0.070	0.070	0.070	0.070	0.070	0.070
A10	0.033	0.033	0.033	0.033	0.033	0.033	0.033	0.033	0.033	0.033	0.033	0.033	0.033	0.033
A11	0.074	0.074	0.074	0.074	0.074	0.074	0.074	0.074	0.074	0.074	0.074	0.074	0.074	0.074
A12	0.058	0.058	0.058	0.058	0.058	0.058	0.058	0.058	0.058	0.058	0.058	0.058	0.058	0.058
A13	0.055	0.055	0.055	0.055	0.055	0.055	0.055	0.055	0.055	0.055	0.055	0.055	0.055	0.055
A14	0.080	0.080	0.080	0.080	0.080	0.080	0.080	0.080	0.080	0.080	0.080	0.080	0.080	0.080

As presented in Table 7, the criteria were ranked as A2 > A3 = A6 > A1 = A4 > A8 = A14 > A11 > A9 > A7 > A13 > A12 = A5 > A10, according to the overall ranking obtained using the Borda score. After discussing the results with experts, the key criteria affecting logistics service quality of cross-border e-commerce were identified: Scale of enterprise assets (A1), Number of employees (A2), Financial standing (A3), Emphasis on logistics business (A4) and Convenience (A6). According to the crisp total influence matrix in Table 4, a causal diagram is shown in Fig. 2.

Table 7. The overall ranking for the factors

Criteria	DEMATEL	DANP	Borda score	Overall rankings
A1	5	3	8	4
A2	2	2	4	1
A3	4	1	5	2
A4	3	5	8	4
A5	12	13	25	12
A6	1	4	5	2
A7	11	10	21	10
A8	6	7	13	6
A9	9	9	18	9
A10	13	14	27	14
A11	8	8	16	8
A12	14	11	25	12
A13	10	12	22	11
A14	7	6	13	6

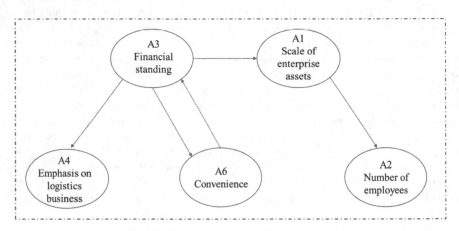

Fig. 2. The causal diagram for key factors

5   Discussion and Conclusions

As cross-border e-commerce has broad market space and rapid development momentum, more and more manufacturing enterprises begin to explore the application of cross-border e-commerce, especially small and medium-sized enterprises. According to the statistical data of China Electronic Commerce Research Center, more than 300,000 Chinese foreign trade enterprises have launched their cross-border e-commerce business in the past few years. As a new way of transaction, cross-border e-commerce, relying on the popularity and advantages of the Internet, can break through the constraints of time and space and provide a more open multilateral market, which has become an important engine to promote the development of China's foreign trade industry. Therefore, small and medium-sized enterprises should strive to improve the logistics service capacity to promote the growth of cross-border e-commerce business. They should start from the following two aspects:

First, the financial situation of an enterprise, especially the liquidity of assets and the turnover rate of products, represents the comprehensive operation ability of an enterprise. The better the financial status of an enterprise is, the stronger its operation ability is. According to Fig. 1, financial standing is identified as the headstream, since the improvement of financial standing will lead other key factors' improvement. An enterprise with good working capital will pay more attention to logistics. A typical performance is that enterprises will provide customers with very convenient logistics services. The stronger the ability of liquidity capital management and the larger the scale of liquidity capital, the better the ability to improve the quality of logistics service. Therefore, enterprises should spare no effort to improve the scale of liquidity capital.

Second, the scale of enterprise assets represents the image of the enterprise. Enterprise entity assets often determine the business scale of the enterprise, so the scale of enterprise determines the number of employees directly. As we all know, logistics industry is not only a labor-intensive industry, but also a technology intensive industry. Strong logistics network needs a large number of employees to support. At the meanwhile, sufficient service personnel is the most basic requirement of high-quality logistics services.

References

1. Zhong, Z.: The problems and countermeasures of cross-border e-commerce logistics model in China. J. Com. Econ. **5**, 107–109 (2018)
2. Xue, X.F., et al.: The research on the impact of cross-border e-commerce logistics service capacity on customer calue. J. Com. Econ. **6**, 79–81 (2017)
3. Ouyang, Y.-P., Shieh, H.-M., Tzeng, G.-H.: A VIKOR technique based on DEMATEL and ANP for information security risk control assessment. Inf. Sci. **232**, 482–500 (2013)
4. Saaty, T.: The Analytic Hierarchy Process. McGraw-Hill, New York (1980)
5. Jiang, P., et al.: Using a novel grey DANP model to identify interaction between manufacturing and logistics industries in China. Sustainability **10**, 3456 (2018)
6. Hu, Y.-C., Tsai, J.-F.: Backpropagation multi-layer perceptron for incomplete pairwise comparison matrices in analytic hierarchy process. Appl. Math. Comput. **180**(1), 53–62 (2006)
7. Xu, Z., Wei, C.: Consistency improving method in the analytic hierarchy process. Eur. J. Oper. Res. **116**(2), 443–449 (1999)
8. Jiang, P., et al.: Green supplier selection for sustainable development of the automotive industry using grey decision-making. Sustain. Dev. **26**, 890–903 (2018)
9. Hwang, C., Hong, D.H., Seok, K.H.: Support vector interval regression machine for crisp input and output data. Fuzzy Sets Syst. **157**, 1114–1125 (2006)
10. Song, L.: Research on the construction and strategy of cross-border e-commerce logistics model based on fuzzy comprehensive evaluation method. Sci. Technol. Dev. **15**(8), 890–897 (2019)

11. Xu, X.L.: International competitiveness improvement of cross-border e-commerce logistics based on fuzzy-AHP. J. Com. Econ. **20**, 93–95 (2018)
12. Jia, Y.X.: Research on cross border e-commerce logistics model based on game theory and fuzzy comprehensive evaluation. Zhejiang Gongshang University: Hang Zhou (2017)
13. Liu, X.Q., You, M., Yang, F.Y.: Review on cross-border logistics. J. Com. Econ. **9**, 145–148 (2019)
14. Emerson, C.J., Grimm, C.M.: Logistics and marketing components of customer service: an empirical test of the Mentzer, Gomes and Krapfel model. Int. J. Phys. Distrib. Logist. Manag. **26**(8), 29–42 (1996)
15. Mentzer, J.T., Flint, D.J., Hult, T.M.: Logistics service quality as a segment-customized process. J. Mark. **65**, 82–104 (2001)
16. Grant, D.B.: UK and US management styles in logistics different strokes for different folks. Int. J. Logist. Res. Appl. **7**(3), 181–197 (2004)
17. Juntunen, J., Juga, J., Grant, D.B.: Short-run versus long-run trade-offs in outsourcing relationships: impacts on loyalty and switching propensity. Strateg. Outsourcing Int. J. **3**(3), 211–225 (2010)
18. Juga, J., Juntunen, J., Grant, D.B.: Service quality and its relation to satisfaction and loyalty in logistics outsourcing relationships. Manag. Serv. Qual. **20**(6), 496–510 (2010)
19. Grant, D.B.: The transaction-relationship dichotomy in logistics and supply chain management. Supply Chain Forum Int. J. **6**(2), 38–48 (2005)
20. Zhao, G.H.: A new approach to solving the difficult logistics of cross-border e-commerce: forth party logistics. China Econ. Trade Herald **9Z**, 16–20 (2014)
21. Dou, C.C., Wu, H.F.: Research on the problems and countermeasures of cross-border electricity supplier logistics. Storage Transp. Preserv. Commod. **9**, 155–156 (2015)
22. Guo, Y.F.: The analysis of Chinese cross-border electricity supplier logistics' difficulties and suggestions. Storage Transp. Preserv. Commod. **9**, 153–154 (2015)
23. Zadeh, L.A.: The concept of a linguistic variable and its application to approximate reasoning. Inf. Sci. **8**(3), 199–249 (1975)
24. Zadeh, L.A.: Fuzzy sets. Inf. Sci. **8**(3), 338–353 (1965)
25. Sharma, S.: Applied Multivariate Techniques. Wiley, Singapore (1996)
26. Tseng, M.L.: A causal and effect decision-making model of service quality expectation using grey-fuzzy DEMATEL approach. Expert Syst. Appl. **36**(4), 7738–7748 (2009)
27. Tzeng, G.-H., Huang, J.-J.: Multiple Attribute Decision Making: Methods and Applications. CRC Press, Boca Raton (2011)
28. Kuncheva, L.I.: Fuzzy Classifier Design. Physica-Verlag, Heidelberg (2000)
29. Lin, C.-L., Hsieh, M.-S., Tzeng, G.-H.: Evaluating vehicle telematics system by using a novel MCDM techniques with dependence and feedback. Expert Syst. Appl. **37**, 6723–6736 (2010)

Effects of Online Reviews on Consumer Evaluation of Products: How Are They Different Among Search, Experience and Credence Products?

Weiling Ke[1]([⊠]) and Xiaorong Aileen Guo[2]

[1] Southern University of Science and Technology, Shenzhen, China
kewl@sustech.edu.cn
[2] Interlake High School, Seattle, WA 98004, USA
neelia2012@gmail.com

Abstract. Motivated by the lack of research on how online reviews affect consumers' evaluation of credence products, we conduct this research. This research in progress explores how emotions embedded in peer-generated online reviews affect consumers' evaluation and attitude toward different types of products (i.e., search, experience and credence products). Drawing upon information processing theory, construal level theory and literature on online reviews, we propose that the effects of emotions (i.e., valence and arousal) on consumers' trust toward the related products are moderated by product type. In particular, credence products have higher strengthening effects, compared to search products and experience products. In addition, we argue that psychological distance aroused by the review context weakens the moderating effects of product type. Our research findings have the potential to enrich our understanding of how online reviews affect consumers' evaluation of different types of products, especially credence products.

Keywords: Online reviews · Credence product · Emotion · Construal level

1 Introduction

The past ten years have seen researchers devote a lot of attention to the study of online product reviews. These studies mainly investigate the following issues: the influence of product reviews on firm sales (Gu et al. 2012; Zhu and Zhang 2010), effects of online product reviews on the formulation of consumers' purchasing decisions (Liu and Kara-hanna 2017; Cheung et al. 2012), drivers for consumers' generation of online product reviews (Dellarocas et al. 2010; Huang et al. 2017), and characteristics of effective online product reviews (Huang et al. 2013, 2018). There is consistent support for the notion that online review systems play an important role in guiding customers' evaluation of the related products and purchasing decisions. More importantly, these studies provide great insights into how to manage online product reviews to better facilitate customers' purchase behaviors which eventually would result in firm sales (e.g., Ludwig et al. 2013; Yin et al. 2014, 2017).

© Springer Nature Switzerland AG 2020
F. F.-H. Nah and K. Siau (Eds.): HCII 2020, LNCS 12204, pp. 397–404, 2020.
https://doi.org/10.1007/978-3-030-50341-3_31

A careful literature review reveals that there exists a severe limitation. The extant literature has primarily focused on examining online reviews' effects on consumers of experience and search products, while ignoring those on customers of credence goods. In general, consumers make their purchasing decisions based on price and quality information. Search, experience and credence goods are different in terms of their pre-buying and post-buying costs of quality detection (Andersen and Philipsen 1998). Specifically, search products' characteristics feature low pre-buying costs of quality detection. Consumers can learn about the products' quality by comparing and inspecting their attributes before buying. Experience goods feature high pre-buying and low post-buying costs of quality detection. Consumers learn this type of products' attributes after buying and consuming and apply such information to further consumption. Credence goods are characterized as high pre-buying and high post-buying costs. The utility of credence goods, such as daily vitamin supplements, legal services and spiritual guidance, cannot be exactly determined even after consumption. Hence, consumers of credence products, compared to those of search and experience products, suffer more severe information asymmetry and their purchase decisions involve much higher risk (Nelson 1970; Darby and Karni 1973).

However, we have little understanding of whether online reviews have similar effects on customers' purchasing credence goods and how they affect individuals' purchase decision making. Consequently, there is little guidance for the management regarding how to better manage online review systems to facilitate the sales of credence goods. Such shortfall in the literature is poignant, given that credence goods markets are of great economic importance. For example, healthcare spending accounts for 17.7% of GDP in the US in 2018 (Center of Medicare and Medicaid Services 2018). Its share of GDP has been growing for decades and is likely to continue to grow in developed countries (Chernew et al. 2012). Therefore, it is imperative to investigate how online reviews influence consumers' credence product purchase differently from search and experience goods.

To address this shortfall in the literature, this study intends to explore how uncertainty involved in search, experience and credence products affect the effectiveness of online reviews' influence on customers' evaluation of the related product. To this end, we draw upon information processing theory (Slovic and Västfjäll 2010; Tversky and Kahneman 1974), construal level theory (Trope and Liberman 2003, 2010) and online review literature to develop our research model. Specifically, following the notion that decision making under risk involves more experiential evaluation than analytic deliberation (Loewenstein et al. 2001), we contend that emotions embedded in online reviews have greater influence on consumers' trust toward credence products than experience and search products. In addition, recognizing that the context of review system may affect consumers' representations of purchase decisions, we propose that product type's moderating effects are further moderated by psychological distance.

The rest of this paper is organized as follow. First, we will provide a literature review on online reviews, decision making under risk, and construal level theory, and present our research hypotheses. Second, we describe how we plan to collect data to test research model. We conclude this paper by brief discussion of the current research's theoretical contributions and managerial implications.

2 Theoretical Background and Research Hypotheses

2.1 Online Reviews

Online reviews refer to peer-generated evaluations that are posted on company or third party web sites (Mudambi and Schuff 2010). There exist many studies on how content of online reviews affects consumers' perceived helpfulness of the reviews and evaluation of the related product (e.g., Ludwig et al. 2013; Schindler and Bickart 2012; Yin et al. 2014, 2017). In particular, emotion expressed by reviewers is identified as a critical factor affecting the efficacy of reviews, such as review helpfulness and diagnostics. For example, Schindler and Bickart (2012) investigate how strong emotion affects perceived review helpfulness. Ludwig et al. (2013) examine how valence of online reviews affect the percentage of consumers purchasing products. A consensus of this stream of research is that emotion embedded in online reviews can substantially influence how consumers process the reviews (Kuan et al. 2015), which eventually affect their evaluation and attitude toward the related product (Kronrod and Danziger 2013; Rocklage and Fazio 2020).

For the purpose of the current research, we conceptualize emotion of online reviews as having two dimensions, namely valence and arousal (Niedenthal 2008). Arousal refers to energy level of activation that is operationalized primarily through added exclamation points and capitalization (Rocklage and Fazio 2020). Valence refers to the extent to which an online review is positive (Yin et al. 2014). The significant effects of emotion valence have gained support from previous studies (e.g., Ludwig et al. 2013; Kronrod and Danziger 2013; Yin et al. 2014). Similarly, emotion arousal embedded in online reviews has significant influences on consumers' judgments and decision making (Rocklage and Fazio 2020; Schindler and Bickart 2012; Yin et al. 2017).

2.2 Decision Making Under Risk

Decision making under risk and uncertainty is the most active research area that provides insights into how people make judgements and decisions (Loewenstein et al. 2001). For example, expected utility theory suggests that people make decisions under risk by assessing the severity and likelihood of possible outcomes of different options and then conducting an expectation-based calculus to come up with a decision. While expected utility theory has been a strong normative benchmark, psychological and behavior economic theories have challenged it by emphasizing that feelings triggered by the decision situations can significantly affect judgements and decision making (Isen and Geva 1987; Nygren et al. 1996). Consequently, there is a convergence of theoretical perspectives supporting the notion that decision making under risk and uncertainty is driven by both cognitive and affective factors (Loewenstein et al. 2001). Accordingly, dual information processing theory posits that decision making under risk and uncertainty involves dual information processing, i.e., analytic and experiential evaluation (Loewenstein et al. 2001). Analytic evaluation involves analytical, deliberative and rational thinking, while experiential processing is conducted in an intuitive, automatic, and natural manner (Slovic and Västfjäll 2010; Tversky and Kahneman 1974). Many previous studies show that affective reactions to stimuli are often more rapid and basic than cognitive evaluations (e.g., Zajonc 1984; LeDoux 1996). Also, affect such as emotions often conflict with cognitive evaluations (Loewenstein et al. 2001). In particular, when uncertainty level is high, people perceive the risk as feelings and affect experienced at the moment of decision making becomes the primary driver in judgements (Loewenstien et al. 2001).

In this current research, we follow the notion mentioned above and focus on how emotions embedded in online reviews affect consumers' judgment and decision making. The rationale for choosing to focus on effects of emotions embedded in online reviews is that there exists strong evidence from previous empirical investigations that exposing individuals to affective cues can lead to affective evaluations and judgments (Lau-Gesk and Meyers-Levy 2009; Lench et al. 2011). In other words, by reading online reviews with emotions, consumers will sense the reviewer's emotions and affect becomes a critical factor driving their evaluation and decision making (Lench et al. 2011). Indeed, Chevalier and Mayzlin (2006) find that favorable reviews help to increase product sales, whereas negative ratings has negative impact on product sales. In the view that we have many previous studies lending support for the significant effects of emotions on consumers' processing of online reviews and evaluation of the related products (e.g., Ludwig et al. 2013; Yin et al. 2014, 2017), we build upon this baseline relationship and develop our research model. In particular, we focus on the effects of emotions' valence and arousal and examine how they affect consumers' trust toward different types of products.

Based on the uncertainty involved, products can be categorized into search, experience and credence products (Andersen and Philipsen 1998). Search products are characterized by their low pre-buying costs of quality detection. That is, the buyer can learn by comparing and inspecting the goods' attributes before purchase. Some examples of search products are furniture, cameras and computers. Experience products have the characteristics feature of high pre-buying costs of quality detection. That is, the buyer learns the product's attributes after his or her purchase and consumption of the product. Hence, the post-buying costs of quality detection are low for experience products and the experience gained from consumption can be used for further purchase of the product. Examples for experience products are music records and movies, wine, and hotel service. Credence products have both high pre-buying costs and post-buying costs of quality detection. The quality of credence product cannot be exactly determined even after consumption. Examples of credence products are health services, daily supplements and spiritual guidance. Due to the costs of quality detection, consumers' judgments and decision making on these three types of products involve different levels of risk and uncertainty, with highest uncertainty for credence products, followed by experience products and then search products.

Hence, other than being influenced by economic factors, credence product purchase decisions are driven by consumers' trusting belief and positive affect toward the product. This implies that online reviews influencing evaluation of search and experience products may not have similar effects for consumers of credence goods. In other words, the innate differences between search, experience and credence products have significant implications for effectiveness of online reviews. However, the extant literature on how online reviews affect consumers' evaluation of reviews and the related products has neglected the effects of uncertainty in information processing. This negligence could be the possible cause for the mixed findings of previous studies on how different types of emotions embedded in online reviews affect consumers' judgments and decision making.

Applying the above-mentioned notion that risk and uncertainty lead individuals to rely on affect as information for their judgments and decision making, we expect that product types would moderate how emotions embedded in online reviews affect consumers' evaluation of the related products. Specifically, credence products, with the characteristics feature of the highest level of information asymmetry among the three types of products, would allow emotions in the reviews to exert the greatest effects on consumers' evaluation of the products. In contrast, search products, with the lowest level of uncertainty involved in both pre-purchase and post-purchase, would make emotions embedded in online reviews to have the least influences on consumers' evaluations of the products. Accordingly, we hypothesize the following.

Hypothesis 1. Product type moderates the effects of emotion valence on consumers' trust toward the product.

Hypothesis 1a. Credence product, compared to experience product, has greater moderating effects on the relationship between emotion valence and consumers' trust toward the product.

Hypothesis 1b. Experience product, compared to search product, has greater moderating effects on the relationship between emotion valence and consumers' trust toward the product.

Hypothesis 2. Product type moderates the effects of emotion arousal on consumers' trust toward the product.

Hypothesis 2a. Credence product, compared to experience product, has greater moderating effects on the relationship between emotion arousal and consumers' trust toward the product.

Hypothesis 2b. Experience product, compared to search product, has greater moderating effects on the relationship between emotion arousal and consumers' trust toward the product.

2.3 Construal Level Theory

Construal level theory (CLT) suggests that psychological distance of a target (i.e., an event, object or individual) influences an individual's mental representations, evaluation, affect and downstream behaviors (Trope and Liberman 2003, 2010). Psychological distance is a subjective experience in which the target is close to or far away from the self, here, and now (Liberman and Trope 1998). There are four different ways in which the target is away from the individual, namely in time, space, social distance, and hypotheticality, which constitute four distance dimensions (i.e., temporal, spatial, social and hypothetical) (Trope and Liberman 2010). When an event takes place here, in the present, is happening to the individual and/or with certainty, the individual will sense a low psychological distance from the target and mentally represent the event at a low construal level. In contrast, when the event takes place in a distant location, later in time, to others and/or with ambiguity, the individual will sense a high psychological distance from the target and have a mental representation of the event at a high construal level (Fujita et al. 2006; Trope and Liberman 2003).

It is well established that perceived psychological distance affects people's decision making under risk and uncertainty (Sagristano et al. 2002; Trope and Liberman 2010). Specifically, psychological distance, which is directly related to construal level, affects decision making under risk and uncertainty by changing the weighs placed on the inputs going into the evaluation (Sagristano et al. 2002). In particular, when evaluating a target object or event, psychological distance, with high construal level, would make people place more weight on desirability features and less weight on feasibility features. Given that uncertainty is about the odds of possible outcomes, it can be regarded as a feasibility feature of the target. Therefore, psychological distance would attenuate the effects of uncertainty. In addition, psychological distance leading to abstract thinking makes individuals to be more positive about the happening of positive outcomes. Therefore, psychological distance reduces perceived risk involved in decision making under uncertainty (Smith and Trope 2006).

We apply this logic to the current research context by proposing weakening effects of psychological distance on the moderating effects of product type. In the online review context, there are many cues that can affect consumers' psychological distance (Huang et al. 2013). For example, the demographic information of reviewers can affect psychological distance sensed by the consumers reading the reviews (Liang et al. 2013; Trope and Liberman 2003). When a reviewer's geographic location, social status, age and even name are close to that of the consumer, the consumer will sense a low level of psychological distance. In contrast, when a reviewer's demographics are very different from that of the consumer, the consumer will sense a high level of psychological distance. In addition, psychological distance in one dimension can affect psychological distance in another dimension (Trope and Liberman 2003, 2010). As such, we focus on investigating the effects of psychological distance that is aroused by the reviewer's demographics relative to that of the consumer. In particular, we are interested in the effects of special distance. The farther the reviewer's geographic location is away from that of the consumer, the higher psychological distance the consumer will sense. With the high level of psychological distance, the consumer would have more optimistic view about the happening of positive outcomes. Also, the consumer would focus more on desirability features than feasibility characteristics of the options, thereby reducing the effects of uncertainty. Hence, we expect psychological distance aroused in the online review context to attenuate the moderating effects of uncertainty caused by different types of products. Accordingly, we hypothesize as follow.

Hypothesis 3. Psychological distance weakens the moderating effects of product type on the relationship between emotion valence and consumers' trust toward the product.
Hypothesis 4. Psychological distance weakens the moderating effects of product type on the relationship between emotion arousal and consumers' trust toward the product.

3   Research Method and Potential Contributions

To test our research model, we will conduct experiments with subjects recruited through Amazon Mechanical Turk. This research has the potential to provide a nuanced understanding of how emotions embedded in online reviews affect consumers' evaluation of different types of products. In addition, by considering the effects of psychological distance aroused by the review context, the current research would extend our understanding of online reviews. It provides a systemic analysis of how emotions affect consumers' judgments and decision making from a perspective that includes the stimuli (i.e., online reviews), the objects (i.e., related products) and the context (i.e., through psychological distance). Given the lack of research on how online reviews affect consumers' evaluation of credence products and the increasingly large market growth of credence goods, such understanding is critical and would provide practitioners with the requisite guidance for the design of online review systems for these three types of products, thereby enriching our understanding of effective reviews that best guide consumers in evaluating different products, especially credence products.

References

Andersen, E.S., Philipsen, K.: The evolution of credence goods in customer markets: exchanging "pigs in pokes". Paper presented at the DRUID Winter Seminar, Middelfart (1998)

Centers for Medicare and Medicaid Services: National Health Expenditure Data (2018). https://www.cms.gov/Research-Statistics-Data-and-Systems/Statistics-Trends-and-Reports/NationalHealthExpendData/NationalHealthAccountsHistorical

Chernew, M.E., Newhouse, J.P.: Health care spending growth. In: Handbook of Health Economics, vol. 2, pp. 1–43 (2012)

Cheung, C.M.Y., Sia, C.L., Kuan, K.K.Y.: Is this review believable? A study of factors affecting the credibility of online consumer reviews from an ELM perspective. J. Assoc. Inf. Syst. 13(8), 618–635 (2012)

Chevalier, J.A., Mayzlin, D.: The effect of word of mouth on sales: online book reviews. J. Mark. Res. 43(3), 345–354 (2006)

Darby, M.R., Karni, E.: Free competition and the optimal amount of fraud. J. Law Econ. 16(1), 67–88 (1973)

Dellarocas, C., Gao, G.D., Narayan, R.: Are consumers more likely to contribute online reviews for hit or niche products? J. Manag. Inf. Syst. 27(2), 127–157 (2010)

Fujita, K., Trope, Y., Liberman, N., Levin-Sagi, M.: Construal levels and self-control. J. Pers. Soc. Psychol. 90(3), 351 (2006)

Gu, B., Park, J., Konana, P.: The impact of external word-of-mouth sources on retailer sales of high-involvement products. Inf. Syst. Res. 23(1), 182–196 (2012)

Huang, L.Q., Tan, C.H., Ke, W.L., Wei, K.K.: Comprehension and assessment of product reviews: a review-product congruity proposition. J. Manag. Inf. Syst. 30(3), 311–343 (2013)

Huang, L.Q., Tan, C.H., Ke, W.L., Wei, K.K.: Helpfulness of online review content: the moderating effects of temporal and social cues. J. Assoc. Inf. Syst. 19(6), 503–522 (2018)

Huang, N., Hong, Y.L., Burtch, G.: Social network integration and user content generation: evidence from natural experiments. MIS Q. 41(4), 1035–+ (2017)

Isen, A.M., Geva, N.: The influence of positive affect on acceptable level of risk: the person with a large canoe has a large worry. Organ. Behav. Hum. Decis. Process. 39, 145–154 (1987)

Kronrod, A., Danziger, S.: Wii will rock you! the use and effect of figurative language in consumer reviews of hedonic and utilitarian consumption. J. Consum. Res. 40(4), 726–739 (2013)

Kuan, K.K.Y., Hui, K.L., Prasarnphanich, P., Lai, H.Y.: What makes a review voted? an empirical investigation of review voting in online review systems. J. Assoc. Inf. Syst. 16(1), 48–71 (2015)

Lau-Gesk, L., Meyers-Levy, J.: Emotional persuasion: when the valence versus the resource demands of emotions influence consumers' attitudes. J. Consum. Res. 36(4), 585–599 (2009)

LeDoux, J.: Emotional networks and motor control: a fearful view. Emot. Motor Syst. **107**, 437–446 (1996)

Lench, H.C., Flores, S.A., Bench, S.W.: Discrete emotions predict changes in cognition, judgment, experience, behavior, and physiology: a meta-analysis of experimental emotion elicitations. Psychol. Bull. **137**(5), 834–855 (2011)

Liang, S.W.-J., Ekinci, Y., Occhiocupo, N., Whyatt, G.: Antecedents of travellers' electronic word-of-mouth communication. J. Mark. Manage. **29**(5–6), 584–606 (2013)

Liberman, N., Trope, Y.: The role of feasibility and desirability considerations in near and distant future decisions: a test of temporal construal theory. J. Pers. Soc. Psychol. **75**(1), 5–18 (1998)

Liu, Q.Q.B., Karahanna, E.: The dark side of reviews: the swaying effects of online product reviews on attribute preference construction. MIS Q. **41**(2), 427−+ (2017)

Loewenstein, G.F., Weber, E.U., Hsee, C.K., Welch, N.: Risk as feelings. Psychol. Bull. **127**(2), 267–286 (2001)

Ludwig, S., de Ruyter, K., Friedman, M., Bruggen, E.C., Wetzels, M., Pfann, G.: More than words: the influence of affective content and linguistic style matches in online reviews on conversion rates. J. Mark. **77**(1), 87–103 (2013)

Mudambi, S.M., Schuff, D.: What makes a helpful online review? a study of customer reviews on amazon. Com. Mis Q. **34**(1), 185–200 (2010)

Nelson, P.: Information and consumer behavior. J. Polit. Econ. **78**(2), 311–329 (1970)

Niedenthal, P.M.: Emotion concepts. In: Handbook of Emotions, vol. 3, pp. 587–600 (2008)

Nygren, T.E., Isen, A.M., Taylor, P.J., Dulin, J.: The influence of positive affect on the decision rule in risk situations: focus on outcome (and especially avoidance of loss) rather than probability. Organ. Behav. Hum. Decis. Process. **66**(1), 59–72 (1996)

Rocklage, M.D., Fazio, R.H.: The enhancing versus backfiring effects of positive emotion in consumer reviews. J. Mark. Res. **57**(2), 332–352 (2020)

Sagristano, M.D., Trope, Y., Liberman, N.: Time-dependent gambling: odds now, money later. J. Exp. Psychol.: Gen. **131**(3), 364 (2002)

Schindler, R.M., Bickart, B.: Perceived helpfulness of online consumer reviews: the role of message content and style. J. Consum. Behav. **11**(3), 234–243 (2012)

Slovic, P., Västfjäll, D.: Affect, moral intuition, and risk. Psychol. Inq. **21**(4), 387–398 (2010)

Smith, P.K., Trope, Y.: You focus on the forest when you're in charge of the trees: power priming and abstract information processing. J. Pers. Soc. Psychol. **90**(4), 578 (2006)

Trope, Y., Liberman, N.: Temporal construal. Psychol. Rev. **110**(3), 403 (2003)

Trope, Y., Liberman, N.: Construal-level theory of psychological distance. Psychol. Rev. **117**(2), 440 (2010)

Tversky, A., Kahneman, D.: Judgment under uncertainty - heuristics and biases. Science **185**(4157), 1124–1131 (1974)

Yin, D.Z., Bond, S.D., Zhang, H.: Anxious or angry? Effects of discrete emotions on the perceived helpfulness of online reviews. MIS Q. **38**(2), 539–560 (2014)

Yin, D.Z., Bond, S.D., Zhang, H.: Keep your cool or let it out: nonlinear effects of expressed arousal on perceptions of consumer reviews. J. Mark. Res. **54**(3), 447–463 (2017)

Zajonc, R.B.: On the primacy of affect. Am. Psychol. **39**(2), 117–123 (1984)

Zhu, F., Zhang, X.Q.: Impact of online consumer reviews on sales: the moderating role of product and consumer characteristics. J. Mark. **74**(2), 133–148 (2010)

The Evolution of Marketing in the Context of Voice Commerce: A Managerial Perspective

Alex Mari[1]([✉]), Andreina Mandelli[2], and René Algesheimer[1]

[1] Chair for Marketing and Market Research, University of Zurich, Zurich, Switzerland
{alex.mari,rene.algesheimer}@business.uzh.ch
[2] Department of Marketing, SDA Bocconi School of Management, Milan, Italy
andreina.mandelli@sdabocconi.it

Abstract. The world is confronted with the rise of voice assistants, increasingly used for shopping activities. This paper examines managers' perceptions of the evolution of voice assistants and their potential effects on the marketing practice. Shopping-related voice assistants are likely to radically change the way consumers search and purchase products with severe impact on brands. However, the behavior of these AI-enabled machines represents a "black box" for brand owners. The study of the managers' interpretation of a voice-enabled marketplace is critical as it may influence future marketing choices. The authors use an inductive theory construction process to study the phenomenon of voice commerce through the eyes of AI experts and voice-aware managers. A mixed-method approach paced three distinct data collection phases. First, systematic machine behavior observations (Amazon Alexa) unfolded the unique characteristics of voice shopping. Second, in-depth interviews with 30 executives drew the current brand owner's challenges and opportunities in the context of voice commerce. Third, an expert survey with international managers (N = 62) revealed the expected impact of voice assistants on the shopping process. Findings show that managers consider voice assistants a disruptive technology assuming a central relational role in the consumer market. However, they often divergence in opinions across industry, function, and seniority level. Besides, managers' familiarity with voice commerce is correlated to a higher optimism towards voice technologies (opportunity for brands) but also a greater sense of urgency (short-term focus) with implications for marketing strategy. This article offers support to brand owners explaining how voice assistants work and examining their effects on consumption. The authors discuss empirical results while providing managerial guidelines to create resilient and sustainable brands in the era of voice commerce.

Keywords: Voice assistant · Voice commerce · Marketing · Machine behavior

1 Introduction

Artificial intelligence (AI) turns objects into machines that exhibit aspects of human intelligence [1]. The application of a combination of AI techniques to objects, such as automatic speech recognition (ASR) and natural language understanding (NLU), is

© Springer Nature Switzerland AG 2020
F. F.-H. Nah and K. Siau (Eds.): HCII 2020, LNCS 12204, pp. 405–425, 2020.
https://doi.org/10.1007/978-3-030-50341-3_32

exhibiting profound effects on the practice of marketing [2, 3]. AI-powered smartphones, smart homes, and smart speakers connect the various nodes of consumers' lives into one ubiquitous experience while providing new forms of knowledge, entertainment, and shopping [4]. These modern machines are expected to collect relevant information about consumers, learn from such data, and identify consumption patterns, all to predict future individual behaviors [5, 6]. Through such a process, smart objects are able to personalize and contextualize experiences with the potential to alter both consumer [e.g., 7, 8] and managerial behavior [e.g., 9, 10].

The subset of AI-enabled machines with the fastest adoption rate, even above smartphones and tablets [11], are the so-called "voice assistants". The term voice assistant (VA) refers to conversational agents that perform tasks with or for an individual—whether of functional or social nature—and own the ability to self-improve their understanding of the interlocutor and context [12]. VAs, also called smart speaker assistants [13] or intelligent personal assistants [14], can take various forms of in-home devices such as Bluetooth speakers (e.g., Amazon Echo) and built-in software agents for smartphones and computers (e.g., Apple Siri). All the major tech companies are commercializing in-place voice platforms, with a dominance of the U.S. (Amazon Echo, Apple HomePod, Google Home) and China-based manufacturers (Alibaba Tmall Genie, Xiaomi Xiao AI, and Baidu Xiaodu). As of today, over 200 million in-home voice devices are installed globally, with mainland China registering a record year-on-year penetration growth of 166% in 2019 [15].

Although the world is confronted with the rise of AI-powered VAs, increasingly used for their shopping capabilities, the algorithms underlying the intelligence of VAs represent a "black box" difficult, if not impossible, to decode [16, 17]. These agents will incrementally influence consumer behaviors as they become better at learning consumer preferences and habits. In doing so, VAs may assume a central relational role in the consumer market and progressively mediate market interactions, with a severe impact on brand owners.

The ecosystem in which the firm operates has a profound impact on how the firm can make (and react to) changes [18]. From a network-based perspective [19], changes in the ecosystem structure (e.g., the introduction of a new node like Amazon Alexa) may cause further modification in terms of relationship establishment and technology development. Managers' interpretations of the marketplace and sense-making of the exchange mechanisms related to activities, resources, and actors [20] are "theories-in-use," posited to influence and guide companies' marketing choices [21]. This research seeks to examine managers' perceptions regarding the evolution of shopping-related VAs and their potential impacts on the marketing practice. In particular, this article aims to offer support to brand owners explaining how VAs work and examining their effects on consumption.

2   Theoretical Background

2.1   The Rise of Voice Marketing and Voice Commerce

Although the most popular VA functions are simple commands like playing music, providing weather information, and setting up alarms [22], an increasing number of users are seeking more sophisticated experiences through the interaction with third-party (branded) apps.

From a marketing perspective, VAs represent a new direct-to-consumer touchpoint for brands [23] that incentivizes novel forms of interaction between consumers and brands [24]. Over 100,000 voice applications are available on the Alexa Skills Store, and 10,000 official apps' "actions" can be downloaded for Google Home. These applications are used to perform a variety of tasks, such as hailing an Uber ride (utility), guiding the tasting of Talisker whiskey (entertainment), obtaining stain removal tips from Tide (informational), learning all about Mars from Nasa (educational). As the adoption of VAs grows, it is strategic for brands to develop a strong voice presence that fulfills the needs of sophisticated consumers as well as those with disabilities [25].

From a commercial standpoint, voice applications may represent a new revenue stream for premium services such as interactive stories or exclusive features. In-app (or in-skill) purchasing allows users to shop products in a seamless fashion using payment options associated with their account. For instance, with Domino's skill, customers can build a new pizza order, repurchase the most recent one, or track each stage of the delivery process. In this dynamic context, the number of consumers who have completed at least one purchase through a smart speaker is rising fast. However, the penetration of voice commerce varies widely among product categories. For instance, 21% of U.S. VA owners purchase entertainment such as music or movies, 8% household items, and 7% electronic devices [26].

The act of placing orders online using VAs goes under the names of "voice commerce," "voice shopping," or "v-commerce". This phenomenon is not limited to the transactional phase of the purchasing process but concerns all the commerce capabilities that allow users to search for a product, listen to reviews, add items to a shopping list, track the order, access customer service, and so on. As such, it has the potential to substantially alter all the stages of the consumer journey, from search to (automated) repurchase [e.g., 27, 28].

2.2 Unique Characteristics of AI-Enabled Voice Assistants

A key driver for the VA's rapid diffusion is the promise of fast, repeatable, and low-cost decision-making combined with an increased level of accuracy, achieved through network effects and feedback loops. Unique from other machines, VAs can naturally converse with users, contextually elaborate requests, and expand their knowledge while learning from mistakes.

VAs are built to mimic natural human-to-human interactions. As such, they react to interlocutors when their name is called and assume a persona ("I") to refer to themselves. Similar to interpersonal relationships, VAs "memorize" relevant facts during the conversation to give a sense of continuity to the following interactions. The ability of VAs to display emotions through voice [4] and a sense of "spontaneity" using casual language or jokes makes them pleasant conversational partners [14].

VAs become context-aware when the interactions with humans, and other machines, are personalized to the current context. Providing adaptive and context-specific responses requires them to collect and process contextual clues such as the identity of the user, location of the device, time, and purchasing history [1]. Context-awareness is a constituting factor of VAs, allowing them to precisely learn personal consumer's preferences and automate routines [29].

Increasingly, AI-powered assistants display self-learning abilities that make them different from the initial programming of their developers [30, 31]. Unsupervised AI systems, which operate without manual human annotation, allow VAs to detect unsatisfactory interactions or failures of understanding and automatically recover from these errors. For instance, if a user systematically misspells the name of a song, the system "learns" to address the issue and deploys corrections shortly after. While learning from mistakes, VAs expand their knowledge and reduce friction during interactions [32]. Automatically applying adjustments to a large number of queries using self-learning techniques allows VAs to develop at a faster pace. As such, a significant leap in VAs' capabilities may be expected [10].

The diffusion of context-aware and self-learning conversational assistants may lead to a transformation of how shoppers search for product information and make purchase decisions.

2.3   The Agency Role of Voice Assistants

In today's digital age, an increasing number of choices involve the use of AI-enabled agents. These agents assume different forms, from chatbot to newsfeed, and achieve economies of scale and scope for product-related searches as they self-improve the more they are used. Even search engines, the heart of web applications, have become increasingly personalized in their delivery of results, to the extent that they can also be considered recommendation agents [33]. VAs assume the role of an agent during the shopping process and beyond [34]. In fact, VAs can be conceptualized as interaction decision aid tools that generate personalized suggestions with an attempt to match products to consumers' expressed preferences or implicit behaviors [36]. These algorithms are indispensable in online shopping environments where a potentially extensive set of alternatives are available. Research has shown that agents help consumers by reducing consumers' information overload and search complexity [34, 35]. As a result, they have the potential to improve the quality of consumer decisions [34, 37–39], which also increases consumer satisfaction and loyalty [40]. Corporate managers also positively embrace algorithms that lower search, transaction, and decision-making costs for consumers [41].

The relationship between VAs and their users can be described as an agency relationship. Characterized by *information asymmetry*, such a relationship requires the consumer to trust the ability of a VA to perform the requested tasks while taking its users' interests into account [39]. However, given their central role in a complex ecosystem, a *goal incongruence* between the user and the VA provider might be expected [42]. As such, VAs need to be envisioned as a multi-stakeholder agent, where the strategic goals of the retailer, merchant, advertiser, and VA itself need to coexist [33].

In this context, VAs are expected to match consumer preferences more closely than if they had chosen independently [43]. That is thanks to their ability to collect data systematically and silently over time [44].

2.4 Literature on Voice Assistants

The voice touchpoint is rapidly becoming a focal point in research because of its swift adoption and disruptive potential in buying dynamics. Recent studies have produced insights on the functional characteristics of VAs [13, 51, 52], their adoption and social roles [14, 53, 54]; attitude towards technology [55–57], and applications for marketing [43, 58]. However, these investigations have not led to a deeper understanding of the consequences for consumers and brand owners as a result. At the same time, studies on consumer technologies for shopping, such as personal computers, smartphones, and tablets, seem insufficient to understand the unique nature of this new channel and shopping method. In contrast to other consumer touchpoints, VAs are, in fact, designed to process one request at a time and on a turn-by-turn basis to decrease the speech recognition error rate coming from a possible voice overlap. This style of interaction represents a radical difference compared to communicatively richer devices like computers or smartphones, which present multiple pieces of information on a screen concurrently. Although exemplary research on consumer behavior and media possess insights that are likely transferable to VAs, the peculiarities of this technology require new theories that are not yet fully developed [58].

Despite the significance of the phenomenon to our daily lives and the society at large, the study of VAs as a new shopping medium remains substantially unexplored. Munz and Morwitz [27] conducted six experiments demonstrating that information presented by voice is usually more difficult to process than when presented visually. Choice difficulty produces a lack of differentiation between auditory choice options that leads, according to the authors, to greater acceptance of the assistant's recommendations, but also to a higher likelihood of deferring choice compared to options presented visually.

Sun [28] and her co-authors from academia and Alibaba Inc. used a natural experiment to explore the effect of voice shopping on consumer search and purchasing behavior. According to the researchers, the usage of Alibaba Genie leads consumers to purchase more quantity and spend more. In terms of search behavior, after adopting the VA, on average, consumers searched more categories, and products within the same category.

A conceptual paper by Labecki, Klaus, and Zaichkowsky [59] concludes that voice commerce presents both challenges and opportunities for brand owners. On the one hand, e-commerce has paved the way for voice shopping, bringing consumers to overcome the initial diffidence of buying without directly seeing, touching, or smelling an object. On the other hand, voice technologies further limit the users' senses, asking consumers to make shopping decisions without browsing photos, videos, or any other visual content.

VAs are "always on" devices that can process (or even automate) orders with a simple command and without providing additional information such as credit cards or address details. However, the uniqueness of VA technologies brings up a new set of interaction rules modeled after the active (and proactive) nature of these smart devices that companies need to learn how to master [60]. To the author's knowledge, there is no empirical academic work exploring the effect of voice commerce from a managerial perspective.

3   Methodology

Using a "theories-in-use" (TIU) approach [61], this research seeks to examine managers' perceptions regarding the evolution of shopping-related VAs and their potential effects on the marketing practice. To study these fast-changing market dynamics within the context of voice commerce, we employed an inductive theory construction process based on a mixed-method approach (machine observations, in-depth interviews, and expert surveys). Theories-in-use research is a natural approach for creating theories best suited for addressing broad and profound questions still unexplored [70]. Data were collected and analyzed with the objective of identifying a novel "grounded theory" [62].

This research begins with the observation of a "real-world marketing-relevant phenomena and then identify constructs and relationships that can explain them" [63, p. 3]. Such phenomenon-construct mapping process was built on three district phases.

First, the authors observed Amazon Alexa's choice architecture (U.S. version) to explore the machine behavior in the context of voice commerce. Data were systematically collected during over 100 direct interactions with Alexa and 40 video reviews on social media to determine the common machine behavior in the shopping mode (*see* Sect. 4.1).

Second, the authors conducted a total of 30 semi-structured in-depth interviews (Dec'18) with corporate executives, consultants, and researchers selected for both their proven knowledge about AI technology and their diverse background (marketing and business, data science, IT). The TIU approach sees study participants as "theory holders" and "active partners" with whom researchers co-create new theory constructs [70]. One-to-one participants' conversations with expert participants did not employ theoretical perspectives in order to facilitate the emergence of insights. Conversations were audio-taped, and transcriptions analyzed adopting an inductive line-by-line coding approach using NVivo v12 for Mac. Following a constant comparative data analysis [62], codes were grouped into themes and then re-evaluated to ensure that they reflect data extracts. The emerging conceptual nodes were related to the dual agency and market mediator roles of VAs as well as the main consequences of the diffusion of shopping-related VAs for brands (*see* Table 1).

Third, a multi-industry expert survey with Swiss and European managers (N = 62) was conducted to collect managers' present and future-oriented perspectives on how VAs' diffusion may alter the path to purchase process and in-market dynamic. Expert respondents were recruited for their expertise in e-commerce through a database made available by NetComm Suisse (the largest eCommerce association in Switzerland) and participated on a voluntary basis. Building on the previous research phase (qualitative study), recommendation agents' literature and the VA studies, the authors analyzed the managers' anticipated consequence that using VAs has on their: 1) customer base; 2) marketing and branding strategies; 3) future action plan. In each questionnaire's session, the focus of the study "in-home voice assistants like Amazon Echo, Google Home, and Apple HomePod" was repeated to avoid confusion with other VAs types.

The survey composed of a total of 53 randomized questions (5-point Likert scale) was divided into five sessions: i) anticipated effects on consumers; ii) anticipated effects on brands; iii) anticipated reactions from brands; iv) personal attitude; v) personal information. A link to the Qualtrics survey was shared via email with the managers, and data were analyzed using SPSS Statistics v26 for Mac. This research draws a comprehensive overview of the challenges and opportunities arising with the diffusion of VAs from the eyes of voice commerce-aware managers (*see* Sect. 4.2).

4 Findings

4.1 Choice Architecture on Voice Assistant

Voice assistants' retailers, such as Amazon or Alibaba, function as "choice architects" that organize the general context in which people make decisions while voice shopping [47]. In the context of voice commerce, a distinction can be made between VAs designed to find the best-suited products (product brokering) and vendor (merchant brokering) [45]. A popular example of a product brokering recommendation agent is Amazon Alexa, whereas Google Home is a retailer-neutral provider that, at the current state, suggests a selection of merchants. For the purpose of this article, the authors focus on the former type.

Generally speaking, Alexa proposes two distinct interaction flows based on whether users: a) buy in a new product category or b) repurchase in the same category. At the same time, the voice commerce retailer fulfills three main search objectives: 1) broad match; 2) exact match; 3) automated match (Fig. 1).

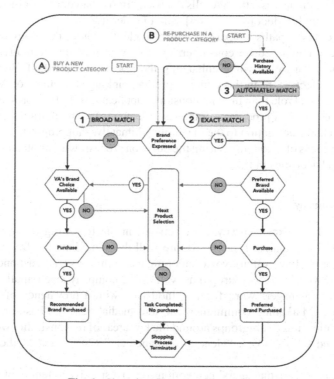

Fig. 1. Shopping flow on Amazon Alexa

First, during a "broad match," a user asks Alexa to recommend items for a generic product category, such as "batteries" or "toilet paper". Being the first time the consumer purchases in the searched category using an Alexa device connected to an Amazon.com account, the VA interprets the individual's request for products and makes recommendations accordingly. Alexa suggests the selected "top search result" in the form of a *default option*. A default is the choice option that individuals adopt unless they actively choose an alternative [46, 71]. This suggestion, similar to a pre-checked box on the Internet [48], is designed such that only a single item is presented to a consumer at a time. The sequential presentation (versus simultaneous) of additional items continues only if the consumer answers "No" to the assistant's question, "Do you want to order this?". The purchasing process ends when a user agrees to buy the item or quits the operation.

Second, whenever a user expresses a clear brand preference, for instance, "Duracell batteries" or "Colgate toothpaste," Alexa performs a search for the "exact match". In case the mentioned brand is not available, the VA will sequentially recommend new items until the user makes a definitive decision.

Lastly, whenever a user buys on Alexa, the information about the bought item is stored in the system. This information is retrieved in the following purchases within the same product category, whether the user had previously expressed a brand preference (exact match) or not (broad match). When the purchase history is available, Alexa performs an "automated match" that allows the user to complete the transaction or seek alternative products swiftly. In this case, the VA tells the user, "Based on your order history, I found one matching item [product information]. Shall I order it?"

In all three search paths, Alexa presents a single item at a time, sequentially. Consequently, the VA may reduce consumers' visibility of product alternatives [49] and increase brand polarization while enhancing the risk of the so-called filter bubble or echo chamber effects [50]. In this context, product ranking algorithms on VAs assume an even more critical role than in other consumer applications. In fact, providing visibility on the lowest level of product alternatives (one option) is an additional step towards the complete choice delegation to the machine. Ultimately, shopping-related VAs might drive to a user's loss of autonomy during the decision process, with implications for their assessment and decisions [44].

4.2 Expert Survey

Key findings of the expert survey are discussed in the following paragraphs. Study respondents (28% Female; $M\ age = 40$) are well distributed among frequency of VA usage (never or rarely vs. often), voice shopping usage (never vs. at least once), country of residence (Switzerland vs. Europe) as well as the company size (small vs. medium or large). These managers work for 10+ industries with a prevalence of "Consumer goods" (26%), "Marketing, communication, and media" (24%), "Fashion and retail" (21%). In addition, three sub-groups around the key areas of responsibility were formed: "Marketing and sales" (43%), "General management" (24%), and "Other function" (33%).

The authors analyze managers' perceptions on a) disruptive potential of voice assistants for marketing; b) possible threats for brand owners; c) customer-centricity of VAs;

d) effect of VAs on the shopping process; e) short- and long-term relevance of voice commerce.

4.3 The Disruptive Potential of Voice Assistants for Marketing

A review of the current studies on AI-powered VAs led to the definition of seven propositions representing, in the authors' view, the potential driver of a disruptive market change. Exploratory factor analysis shows the presence of two distinct factors influencing the perception of managers towards the potential disruption of voice commerce for marketing. Concerning factor one "market mediation" (4 items, 45% variance, loading from .675 to .865), a total of 87% of managers agree that VAs will become "powerful marketing, sales, and distribution channel" ($M = 4.19, SD = 0.74, P < .001$) [43]. Roughly 80% of respondents see VAs as "technology increasingly able to influence consumer's choices" ($M = 4.02, SD = 0.89, P < .001$) [58]. Three-fourths of the study participants believe that VAs will become a "new middleman between brands and consumers" ($M = 3.90, SD = 1.04, P < .001$) [23], and around two-thirds (67%) expect a "severe impact on consumer brands" ($M = 3.81, SD = 1.07, P < .001$) [24]. While functioning as a "salesperson," VAs are redefining relationships among consumers and brands. Managers might be concerned by the rapid adoption of VAs as the bargaining power is shifting in favor of VA manufacturers [12, 23, 69]. This fear is primarily expressed towards Amazon, accounting for nearly 45% of the total U.S. retail e-commerce [26].

In factor two, named "customer experience" (3 items, 20% variance, from .662 to .836), 58% agree VAs will "remove traction from customer experience" ($M = 3.53, SD = 1.02, P < .001$) [72, 73]. Not surprisingly, those managers that often use VAs (vs. never or rarely) believe with a higher degree that VAs will "win consumer's trust better than other technologies" ($P = .015$) [43]. Overall, the study participants seem undecided about the VAs' promise to "make the user smarter by adding a layer of intelligence".

4.4 Possible Threats to Brand Owners

The outcome of the second phase of this research (in-depth interviews) is summarized in six propositions that reflect the primary concern of AI-aware experts connected to the diffusion of voice commerce (Table 1).

Search algorithms represent the gatekeeper for modern companies. Compared to display enabled smart devices, the optimization of voice search results on VAs present structural challenges due to the nature of consumer interactions, and information framing. As such, nearly two-thirds (65%) of managers believe that brands will "have reduced visibility on voice assistants compared to other touchpoints" ($M = 3.65, SD = 1.11, P < .001$). Participants' viewpoints appear to be different among functions and seniority levels. Respondents in the "Marketing and sales" function believe to a greater extent than "General management" that brands will have reduced visibility on VAs ($P = .074$). At the same time, "C-level" is less concerned than "Mid-management" on the same topic ($P = .069$).

Table 1. Experts' view on possible threats for brand owners.

Propositions	Exemplary quote
Reduced brand visibility	*"During a product search, by the time you get to the third item, you have forgotten what the first was and what the price of the second one was. You're done beyond the third results."* Dr. A. K. Pradeep, CEO at MachineVantage
Rising private label strength	*"If I ask Alexa to send me twenty AA batteries, I will probably get Amazon's branded batteries. However, if I explicitly ask for Duracell, I receive my preferred brand, provided it is available on the platform. Thus, companies have to invest in branding even more than they did before so that consumers asked for a product by the name."* Jim Sterne, Emeritus Director of the Digital Analytics Association (DAA)
Increasing cost of impression (advertising)	*"Voice commerce brings up a "real estate" problem. While I can display several ads on the same Google Search results page, I don't have the same ad space on smart speakers. Thus, I expect the cost of voice ads to be more than two times higher than regular search ads. Am I able to justify this cost increase?"* Maurizio Miggiano, Head of Digital at Generali
Reduced access to consumer data	*"Amazon observes every consumer's step and uses this information to customize campaigns. My problem is not necessarily to pay Alexa or similar platforms to reach my consumers but that I do not have individual-level data needed to develop the relationship with consumers further."* Lorenzo Farronato - VP Marketing Communications at Swarovski
Universality of the impact across categories	*"It doesn't matter whether you are selling gold jewelry or a Rolls-Royce. Alexa does commoditize entire product categories, all the way from diamonds to detergents. Your brand has become a commodity fighting for air space."* Dr. A. K. Pradeep, CEO at MachineVantage
Ongoing performance assessment of past purchase	*"When consumers will ask Alexa to repurchase a preferred brand of whiskey, for instance, the voice assistant will answer, "I have discovered a new brand of whiskey which is proven to be healthier, cheaper and appreciated by other users. Would you like to try it?". In this context, brands will constantly need to justify their leadership position in the consumer's shopping cart."* Cosimo Accoto, Research Affiliate at MIT

Managers are aware that Amazon's biased placement on VAs of its private labels might challenge national brands. A total of 71% of respondents "somewhat agree" or "strongly agree" that Alexa will "disproportionally place its private labels while penalizing other consumer brands" ($M = 3.76, SD = 1.00, P < .001$). With Amazon's private label portfolio growing to 135 brands and 330 exclusive brands, an increasing number of product categories may be gradually affected by private labels. Those participants that have never purchased on VAs (vs. at least once) think, to a greater extent, that Alexa will disproportionally place its private label compared to other consumer brands ($P = .061$). In this context, search advertising in the form of voice assumes a paramount role in the marketing practice. Compared to web browser navigation, where search engines can display ten results per page and up to five advertisements, VAs can only suggest a few results with limited space for sponsored messages. This scarcity of space might increase competition among advertisers with a consequent rise in advertising costs. Among respondents, 61% agree that "advertising cost on voice assistants would be higher than web-based advertising because of the limited space available for sponsored messages (paid recommendations)" ($M = 3.65$, $SD = 1.21$, $P < .001$).

Furthermore, voice assistant retailers might function as a gatekeeper of consumer information while improving their power position in the market. While "General management" has a moderate view on this topic, "Marketing and sales" managers think that VA manufacturers will not have access to relevant consumer information ($P = .042$). In case VA manufacturers decide not to share consumer data and insights with brand owners, there might be a higher likelihood of cross-category "commoditization" [64]. Quoting the conversation with one expert, "Alexa does commoditize entire product categories, all the way from diamonds to detergents". A total of 44% of managers "somewhat disagree" or "strongly disagree" with the statement that "low involvement product categories will be the only affected by the voice assistant's diffusion" ($M = 2.68$, $SD = 1.18$, $P = .036$). It is possible to observe a substantial divergence of opinion among functions and seniority levels. While "General management" believes that voice commerce will only affect low involvement product categories, "Marketing and sales" ($P = .034$) and "Other functions" ($P = .054$) do not believe the disruption is only limited to these categories. Also, "C-level" does not consider this effect "universal" across categories differently from "Mid-management" ($P = .052$).

Moreover, three-fourths of respondents believe those VAs will "ongoingly re evaluate the consumer's product choice and suggest better alternatives" ($M = 3.85$, $SD = 0.94$, $P < .001$). In a context in which brands are required to continually justify their positions, competition might increase.

4.5 Customer-Centricity of Voice Assistants

This section of the questionnaire deals with the manager's perceptions about the level of customer-centricity demonstrated by VAs. Questions are formed around three key concepts in human-computer interaction: trusting belief [65, 66], perceived personalization [67], and intention to adopt as a delegated agent [67].

In terms of competence, 53% of study participants trust that VAs possess a "good knowledge of products" ($M = 3.34$, $SD = 1.17$, $P = .026$). Differently from "Marketing and sales" ($P = .091$) and "Other functions" ($P < .001$), "General management" does not believe that VAs show a good understanding of the products.

On average, respondents do not believe that VAs put the "customer's interest first" ($M = 2.73$; $SD = 1.23$, $P = .084$). This sentiment is stronger in managers that "never or rarely" use a VA ($P = .038$), "never" purchase on VAs ($P = .031$), and work for "large organizations" with more than 10,000 employees ($P = .014$). Remarkably, over 85% of the respondents "somewhat agree" or "strongly agree" that VAs "want to understand customer's needs and preferences" ($M = 4.24, SD = .918, P < .001$), showing a trustworthy belief of benevolence, i.e., the agent cares about the user and acts in the user's interest.

Furthermore, when evaluating the integrity of VAs, nearly two-thirds (65%) declared they "somewhat disagree" or "strongly disagree" with the statement that VAs "provide unbiased product recommendations" ($M = 2.21, SD = 1.20, P < .001$). In particular, respondents who have never purchased through a VA (vs. purchased at least once) believe that VAs provide unfair recommendations to a higher extent ($P = .032$).

Overall, managers do not believe VAs to be of integrity, i.e., to adhere to a set of principles that the user finds acceptable ($M = 2.66, SD = 1.11, P = .020$), with "Consumer goods" managers showing a more significant skepticism towards VAs than managers working for "Marketing, communication, media" ($P < .001$), "Fashion and retailer" ($P = .009$), and "Pharma and health" ($P = .070$) companies.

In terms of perceived personalization, that is, the extent to which VAs understand and represent a user's personal opinion, 63% of managers agree that VAs "provide tailored advice to customers" ($M = 3.68, SD = 1.00, P < .001$). The assistive nature of the interaction with VAs implies a delegation of responsibility, at least in the absence of explicit requests by the user (exact match). In this respect, 55% of respondents agree that consumers will "delegate to VAs the repurchase of as many products as they can in an automated way" ($M = 3.42, SD = 1.15, P = .006$). In essence, managers seem to have realized that the ultimate goal of voice commerce is the automation of the buying experience.

4.6 Effect of Voice Assistants on the Shopping Process

The hypotheses presented by Häubl and Trifts [34] in their seminal research on the effect of interactive decision aids in an online shopping environment, were adapted to capture the managers' opinion on the effect of VAs on shopping behavior. In particular, managers shared their opinion on three measures: the amount of search for product information, consideration set size, and decision quality.

According to 77% of respondents, the use of VAs for shopping "reduces the number of products for which detailed information is obtained" ($M = 3.90, SD = 0.95, P < .001$). In line with the literature [68], 81% of managers see a risk in the "reduction of the number of alternatives seriously considered by the user" (consideration set size) ($M = 3.98, SD = 0.91, P < .001$). Shall this expectation become real in practice, brand owners might assist in a higher tendency of users to select the recommended *default option*.

In terms of decision quality, roughly two-thirds of participants (68%) believe that voice commerce will "reduce the user's probability of switching to another brand, after making the initial purchase decision" ($M = 3.56, SD = 1.05, P < .001$). In other words, there is an assumption that VAs may introduce *lock-in mechanisms* that will reduce the user's variety seeking, with potential visibility issues for challenging brands. In the same direction, two-thirds of respondents believe that voice commerce leads to a "reduction in consumers' product choice autonomy" ($M = 3.63, SD = 1.04, P < .001$).

Overall, managers working for "Consumer goods" companies are particularly doubtful about the ability of VAs to improve consumers' decision-making. They do not believe that VAs will lead to a "higher degree of confidence in the shopping decisions," differently from "Consultant" ($P = .038$) and "Fashion and retailer" ($P = .045$) managers.

4.7 Short- and Long-Term Relevance of Voice Commerce

While assessing managers' overall perceptions in terms of VA-related challenges and opportunities, nearly three-fourths of the respondents (74%) believe that voice commerce represents a "great opportunity for their brand" ($M = 3.87$, $SD = 0.97$, $P < .001$). At the same time, 77% consider it a significant challenge ($M = 3.97$, $SD = 0.75$, $P < .001$). This dual mindset captures the current state-of-mind of the companies that see voice commerce as a revolution in marketing and brand management, but also a phenomenon with potentially detrimental consequences.

In terms of phenomenon relevance, roughly 70% of managers believe that voice commerce is important for their industry ($M = 3.82$, $SD = 0.98$, $P < .001$) and the future of their company ($M = 3.92$, $SD = 0.93$, $P < .001$). Regardless of industry and function, respondents with a high frequency of VA usage (vs. never or rarely) see the practice of shopping using in-home VAs more strategic in both the short-term (1 to 3 years) to win shares and long-term (3 to 5 years) for the future of their company.

Overall, managers operating in Switzerland find this technological trend less critical for their country compared to European managers ($P = .066$). At the same time, European managers believe to a greater extent than the Swiss that voice commerce is "important to win shares in the short-term" ($P = .053$).

Figure 2 shows the activities that managers expect their customers to conduct using VAs. Almost three-fourths of respondents, coming from both B2B and B2C organizations, believe that customers will "Reorder products," followed by "Track orders of products" (71%), "Research products" (68%), and "Buy products" (66%). Although nearly 50% of the managers expect to carry out all the listed activities, unsurprisingly most of the B2B organizations give less weight to activities such as "Automate the repurchase of products (e.g., subscriptions)" (53%), "Buy services related to products" (48%), and "Retrieve deals, sales, and promotions" (47%).

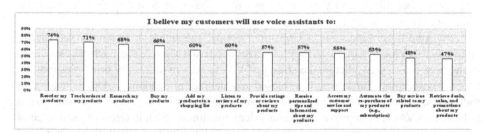

Fig. 2. How managers expect their customers to use VAs.

Based on their current understanding of the challenges and opportunities that voice commerce brings up, managers believe that the best way for their company to react is to: "Employ a voice optimization strategy to improve search ranking results" (40%), "Build a voice presence to develop voice-related experiences" (39%), "Invest in advertising on voice assistant platform - paid recommendations" (35%). While listing their company's top 3 priorities (Fig. 3), respondents generally attributed a lower importance to branding-related activities, with "Create a voice identity" ranking highest (31%), followed by "Build relevant branded apps (skills or actions)" (27%), and "Invest in branding activities to increase consumer's brand recall" (27%).

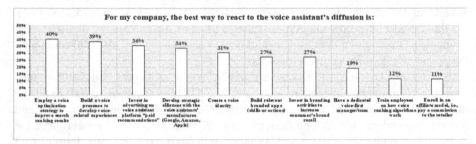

Fig. 3. Managers' anticipated best way to react to the VA's diffusion.

5 Discussion

The main goal of this paper was to investigate how managers perceive the evolution of voice assistants and their potential effects on marketing practice. There is no doubt that managers look at VAs as a disruptive technology able to radically change the ecosystem in which their company operates. In the managers' view, VAs may assume a central relational role in the consumer market and progressively mediate market interactions, with a severe impact on brand owners. VAs represent not only new powerful marketing, sales, and distribution channel but also a middleman between brands and consumers, which will increasingly influence consumers' choice. However, this research found that managers often diverge in their opinions on the basis of four key factors: industry, function, seniority level, and familiarity with voice commerce.

Among different industries, "Consumer goods" managers show a remarked skepticism towards VAs. In particular, they have a reduced trust towards the machine, especially in the area of integrity, that is, the ability of VAs to adhere to a set of principles that the user finds acceptable and provide unbiased product recommendations. Opposite to other industries, in particular, "Fashion and retailer," managers working for CPG firms do not believe that VAs will improve consumer's decision quality both in terms of the degree of confidence in the shopping decisions and overall decision-making abilities. Opinions' divergence between these two industries might be driven by the historical dependence of consumer goods companies from intermediaries (retailers) functioning as the gatekeeper of their distribution. Fashion managers appear significantly less concerned about potentially unfair VA's manufacturer practices and the influence that the VA might exercise on consumer's decision making. This might be due to the importance of a multi-sensory experience during the selection process. Besides, automated purchases through product subscription seem less relevant for the fashion industry than others because only a few selected items have the potential to be automatically reordered (e.g., underwear or sneakers). In that context, also given the acceleration of digital practices, the fashion industry might look at the evolution of VAs more from a voice marketing perspective than from a transactional standpoint [75, 76].

Participants' perception significantly differs between "Marketing and sales" managers and those in "General management". Marketers appear to feel threatened by the uncertain effect that VAs may have on their brands. Their higher exposure to the practicalities of new consumer touchpoints and applications compared to general managers might be reflected in the belief that brands will have reduced visibility on VAs and limited access to relevant consumer information. Opposite to general managers, marketers believe to a greater extent that voice commerce will affect several product categories and not only low involvement ones. Such divergent perspective comes mostly from a disagreement on the current VAs' competence. Marketers believe that VAs have a good understanding of products, while general managers appear hesitant about such capabilities. In the context of voice commerce, these two groups of managers have a different sense of urgency that might turn in a strategic misalignment.

In terms of seniority level, a similar dynamic can be noticed between "C-level" executives and "Mid-management". Senior executives are less worried about the impact of VAs on their brands. For instance, they do not consider Amazon's biased placement of its private labels a potential challenge to national brands. Additionally, they do not believe that VAs will affects product categories other than low involvements ones.

A key factor influencing the opinion of the study participants is the familiarity with voice commerce, i.e., those who have purchased at least once using a voice assistant. Voice commerce users consider AI-enabled VAs a strategic touchpoint with the potential to drive market share growth in the short-term (1 to 3 years). Extant research posits that companies tend to overestimate the benefit of AI in the short-term but underestimated it in the long-term [5]. However, non-voice commerce users seem to minimize the short-term impact of voice shopping while predicting its long-term effect.

Figure 4 shows a conceptual framework underlining the relevance of being a voice commerce user in the formation of beliefs, attitudes, intentions, and behaviors towards this phenomenon. Building on the theory of reasoned action (TRA) [74], the authors show that manager's usage of voice commerce is correlated with their a) trust towards VAs (beliefs), b) perception of VA's personalization and consumer's intention to delegate the buying process to the VA (attitude), c) view of VA as a disruptive technology, d) view of the importance of voice commerce for their industry and the opportunity for their brand (intention). Direct experience with a shopping-enabled VAs also contributes to i) dual short- and long-term strategic focus, as well as, ii) more articulated planning to act (and react) to change (behavior). In particular, voice commerce users expect their companies to structure an action plan according to a mix of strategic (e.g., build a voice presence), tactical (e.g., buy voice search ads), organizational actions (e.g., run organization-wide training on voice).

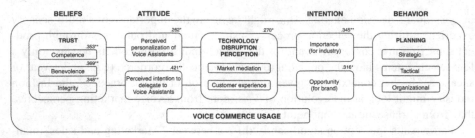

Fig. 4. Conceptual framework. Correlation between "voice commerce usage" and any variable in the model (2 tailed). P-value reported as P < .05 (*), P < .01 (**), P < .001 (***).

6   Conclusions

This study was motivated by the swift adoption of shopping-related voice assistants and their potential effect on the marketing practice. We aimed to improve the understanding of managers' perceptions regarding VAs and their link to future marketing choices. In the absence of extant academic research, we used an inductive theory construction process based on a theories-in-use approach. Beginning with the observation of a real-world marketing-relevant phenomenon, we employed a phenomenon-construct mapping process following a mixed-method approach. We studied the phenomenon of voice commerce through the eyes of AI experts and voice-aware managers in three district data collection phases. First, systematic machine behavior observations unfolded the unique characteristics of voice shopping. Second, in-depth interviews with executives drew the current brand owner's challenges and opportunities in the context of voice commerce. Third, an expert survey with international managers revealed the expected impact of voice assistants on the shopping process.

We conclude that managers have a shared understanding of voice commerce's challenges and opportunities for their brands. A dual mindset sees voice commerce as a revolution in marketing and brand management, but also a phenomenon with potentially detrimental consequences. Our findings show that often managers diverge in their opinions on the basis of four key factors: industry, function, seniority level, and familiarity with voice commerce.

This study sheds light on the manager's perspective on this relevant topic and provides further structure and guidance to brand owners. However, this research is not without limitations. The quality of collected data was preferred to quantity turning in a reduced sample size (N = 62). Future cross-industry studies on multiple functions and seniority levels should better represent the managers' population with an adequate sample size. Researchers and marketers urge to further explore this emerging stream of research to anticipate the effects of voice commerce on both consumers and brands as a result.

7   Managerial Implications

Managers' interpretations and individual sense-making of the marketplace are posited to influence and guide companies' marketing choices. Within the context of voice shopping, brand owners need to carefully monitor its evolution to understand the effects on their consumers' behavior better while preparing to (re)act. The results of this research offer support to brand owners for developing resilient and sustainable brands in the context of voice commerce. In particular, this article explains how VAs work and examining their effects on consumption.

In order to successfully face a potential market disruption coming from the diffusion of VAs, managers should employ a series of sequential actions to spread the awareness of voice technologies across their organizations.

First, managers are called to understand the unique VA's characteristics, together with its agency and market mediation role. As such, brand owners need to explore how the VA's choice architecture can influence the path to purchase process. In particular, they need to anticipate their consumer's reaction to the machine behavior when searching for products according to a broad, exact, and automated match. Understanding the potential effects of *default* or *lock-in mechanisms* on the customer base is deemed fundamental. However, this exploratory task is made more difficult by the continuous evolution of VAs and their choice architecture.

Second, brand owners need to explore opportunities and challenges emerging from the dissemination of VAs. As consumers' relationships with VAs shift from limited influence to steadfast dependency, brands need to understand how to redesign their value chain [24]. The objective of their brand should be to gain (or protect) a "top of mind" position while building strong relationships with consumers. When consumers are able to express their brand preferences and have a strong attachment to the brand, they become less conditioned by the machine behavior. This brand building (or strengthening) process does not happen on the voice touchpoint in isolation but requires a brand activation across channels. Paradoxically, companies are called to further invest in traditional branding activities that drive brand awareness and recall before they can benefit from the fast growth of voice commerce [23].

Third, managers should understand the divergent views across the organization about the evolution of VAs for marketing. Creating a voice-first strategy that includes a mix of strategic, tactical, and organizational actions requires managers to reach an internal alignment on the strategic relevance of VAs. This study shows the importance of gaining direct experience with the voice shopping process. Not only voice commerce users have a more optimistic view of VAs, in terms of beliefs, attitudes, and intentions, but they also have a higher sense of urgency (behavior). Since a short-term focus might help brand owners to react faster to the market changes, companies need to foster the usage of voice shopping across the organization. Such a direct experience might help the organization to acquire maturity and examine how to leverage voice marketing and voice commerce to grow its brand(s) sustainably.

In light of these firm's exogenous changes, researchers are called to further study the interplay between consumers and brands in response to "machine behaviors" [31].

Acknowledgments. We thank NetComm Suisse and e-Business Institute for their support in collecting the survey data and Nicolas Bonvin for his assistance in analyzing the data.

References

1. Huang, M.H., Rust, R.T.: Artificial intelligence in service. J. Serv. Res. **21**(2), 155–172 (2018)
2. Hoffman, D.L., Novak, T.P.: Consumer and object experience in the internet of things: an assemblage theory approach. J. Consum. Res. **44**(6), 1178–1204 (2018)
3. Davenport, T., Guha, A., Grewal, D., Bressgott, T.: How artificial intelligence will change the future of marketing. J. Acad. Mark. Sci. **48**(1), 24–42 (2020)
4. Schmitt, B.: From atoms to bits and back: a research curation on digital technology and agenda for future research. J. Consum. Res. **46**(4), 825–832 (2019)
5. Shankar, V.: How artificial intelligence (AI) is reshaping retailing. J. Retail. **94**(4), 6–11 (2018)
6. Kaplan, A., Haenlein, M.: Siri, Siri, in my hand: who's the fairest in the land? On the interpretations, illustrations, and implications of artificial intelligence. Bus. Horiz. **62**(1), 15–25 (2019)
7. Giebelhausen, M., Robinson, S.G., Sirianni, N.J., Brady, M.K.: Touch versus tech: when technology functions as a barrier or a benefit to service encounters. J. Mark. **78**(4), 113–124 (2014)
8. Holzwarth, M., Janiszewski, C., Neumann, M.M.: The influence of avatars on online consumer shopping behavior. J. Mark. **70**(4), 19–36 (2006)
9. Davenport, T.H.: The AI Advantage: How to Put the Artificial Intelligence Revolution to Work. MIT Press, Cambridge (2018)
10. Arnold, T.J., Grewal, D., Motyka, S., Kim, N., Sharma, A., Srivastava, R.: Store manager-store performance relationship: a research note. J. Retail. **95**(2), 144–155 (2019)
11. Newman, N.: The Future of Voice and the Implications for News. Report by Reuters Institute and University and Oxford, UK (2018)
12. Mari, A.: Voice commerce: understanding shopping-related voice assistants and their effect on brands. In: IMMAA Annual Conference. Northwestern University in Qatar, Doha (2019)
13. Bentley, F., Luvogt, C., Silverman, M., Wirasinghe, R., White, B., Lottridge, D.: Understanding the long-term use of smart speaker assistants. Proc. ACM Interact. Mob. Wearable Ubiquitous Technol. **2**(3), 1–24 (2018)
14. Han, S., Yang, H.: Understanding adoption of intelligent personal assistants. Ind. Manag. Data Syst. **118**(3), 618–636 (2018)
15. Kinsella, B.: Smart Speaker Installed Base to Surpass 200 Million in 2019, Grow to 500 Million in 2023 (Voicebot.ai). https://voicebot.ai/2019/04/15/smart-speaker-installed-base-to-surpass-200-million-in-2019-grow-to-500-million-in-2023-canalys/. Accessed 15 Apr 2019
16. Voosen, P.: The AI detectives. Science **357**(6346), 22 (2017)
17. Rai, A.: Explainable AI: from black box to glass box. J. Acad. Mark. Sci. **48**(1), 137–141 (2020)
18. Håkansson, H., Snehota, I.: No business is an island: the network concept of business strategy. Scand. J. Manag. **22**(3), 256–270 (2006)
19. Snehota, I., Hakansson, H.: Developing Relationships in Business Networks, vol. 11. Routledge, London (1995)
20. Henneberg, S.C., Naudé, P., Mouzas, S.: Sense-making and management in business networks—some observations, considerations, and a research agenda. Ind. Mark. Manag. **39**(3), 355–360 (2010)
21. Ford, D., Mouzas, S.: Networking under uncertainty: concepts and research agenda. Ind. Mark. Manag. **39**(6), 956–962 (2010)
22. Sciuto, A., Saini, A., Forlizzi, J., Hong, J.I.: Hey Alexa, what's up?" A mixed-methods studies of in-home conversational agent usage. In: Proceedings of the 2018 Designing Interactive Systems Conference, pp. 857–868 (2018)

23. Sterne, J.: Artificial Intelligence for Marketing: Practical Applications. Wiley, Hoboken (2017)
24. Mandelli, A.: Intelligenza artificiale e marketing: Agenti invisibili, esperienza, valore e business. EGEA spa (2018)
25. Simms, K.: How voice assistants could change the way we shop. Harv. Bus. Rev. https://hbr.org/2019/05/how-voice-assistants-could-change-the-way-we-shop. Accessed 30 Jan 2020
26. eMarketer: Which Select Activities Have US Smart Speaker Owners Done on Their Smart Speakers. https://www.emarketer.com/chart/230338/which-select-activities-have-us-smart-speaker-owners-done-on-their-smart-speakers-of-respondents-by-demographic-aug-2019. Accessed 28 June 2019
27. Munz, K., Morwitz, V.: Not-so easy listening: roots and repercussions of auditory choice difficulty in voice commerce (2019). SSRN 3462714
28. Sun, C., Shi, Z.J., Liu, X., Ghose, A., Li, X., Xiong, F.: The Effect of Voice AI on Consumer Purchase and Search Behavior (2019). SSRN. https://ssrn.com/abstract=3480877
29. Knote, R., Janson, A., Eigenbrod, L., Söllner, M.: The what and how of smart personal assistants: principles and application domains for IS research. In: Multikonferenz Wirtschaftsinformatik (MKWI). Lüneburg, Germany (2018)
30. Grewal, D., Hulland, J., Kopalle, P.K., Karahanna, E.: The future of technology and marketing: a multidisciplinary perspective. J. Acad. Mark. Sci. 48(4), 1–8 (2020)
31. Rahwan, I., Cebrian, M., Obradovich, N., Bongard, J., Bonnefon, J.F., Breazeal, C., Crandall, J.W., et al.: Machine behaviour. Nature 568(7753), 477–486 (2019)
32. Sarikaya, R.: The technology behind personal digital assistants: an overview of the system architecture and key components. IEEE Signal Process. Mag. 34(1), 67–81 (2017)
33. Abdollahpouri, H., et al.: Beyond personalization: research directions in multistakeholder recommendation. arXiv preprint arXiv:1905.01986 (2019)
34. Häubl, G., Trifts, V.: Consumer decision making in online shopping environments: the effects of interactive decision aids. Mark. Sci. 19(1), 4–21 (2000)
35. Li, S.S., Karahanna, E.: Online recommendation systems in a B2C E-commerce context: a review and future directions. J. Assoc. Inf. Syst. 16(2), 72 (2015)
36. Shen, A.: Recommendations as personalized marketing: insights from customer experiences. J. Serv. Mark. 28(5), 414–427 (2014)
37. Diehl, K., Kornish, L.J., Lynch Jr., J.G.: Smart agents: When lower search costs for quality information increase price sensitivity. J. Consum. Res. 30(1), 56–71 (2003)
38. Benbasat, I., Wang, W.: Trust in and adoption of online recommendation agents. J. Assoc. Inf. Syst. 6(3), 72–101 (2005)
39. Xiao, B., Benbasat, I.: E-commerce product recommendation agents: use, characteristics, and impact. MIS Q. 31(1), 137–209 (2007)
40. Liang, T.P., Chen, H.Y., Turban, E.: Effect of personalization on the perceived usefulness of online customer services: a dual-core theory. In: Proceedings of the 11th International Conference on Electronic Commerce, pp. 279–288, August 2009
41. Wathieu, L., Brenner, L., Carmon, Z., Chattopadhyay, A., Wertenbroch, K., Drolet, A., Gourville, J., et al.: Consumer control and empowerment: a primer. Mark. Lett. 13(3), 297–305 (2002)
42. Bhattacherjee, A.: Individual trust in online firms: scale development and initial test. J. Manag. Inf. Syst. 19(1), 211–241 (2002)
43. Dawar, N., Bendle, N.: Marketing in the age of Alexa. Harv. Bus. Rev. 96(3), 80–86 (2018)
44. André, Q., Carmon, Z., Wertenbroch, K., Crum, A., Frank, D., Goldstein, W., Yang, H.: Consumer choice and autonomy in the age of artificial intelligence and big data. Cust. Needs Solut. 5(1–2), 28–37 (2018)
45. Guttman, R.H., Moukas, A.G., Maes, P.: Agent-mediated electronic commerce: a survey. Knowl. Eng. Rev. 13(2), 147–159 (1998)

46. Thaler, R.S., Sunstein, C.: Nudge: Improving Decisions About Health, Wealth and Happiness. Yale University Press, New Haven (2009)
47. Thaler, R.H., Sunstein, C.R., Balz, J.P.: Choice architecture. Behav. Found. Public Policy, **i-18**, 428–439 (2013)
48. Johnson, E.J., Shu, S.B., Dellaert, B.G., Fox, C., Goldstein, D.G., Häubl, G., Larrick, R.P., et al.: Beyond nudges: tools of a choice architecture. Mark. Lett. **23**(2), 487–504 (2012)
49. Pariser, E.: The Filter Bubble: How the New Personalized Web is Changing What We Read and How We Think. Penguin, London (2011)
50. Colleoni, E., Rozza, A., Arvidsson, A.: Echo chamber or public sphere? Predicting political orientation and measuring political homophily in Twitter using big data. J. Commun. **64**(2), 317–332 (2014)
51. Gollnhofer, J.F., Schüller, S.: Sensing the vocal age: managing voice touchpoints on Alexa. Mark. Rev. St. Gallen **35**(4), 22–29 (2018)
52. Hoy, M.B.: Alexa, Siri, Cortana, and more: an introduction to voice assistants. Med. Ref. Serv. Q. **37**(1), 81–88 (2018)
53. Purington, A., Taft, J.G., Sannon, S., Bazarova, N.N., Taylor, S.H.: "Alexa is my new BFF" social roles, user satisfaction, and personification of the Amazon Echo. In: Proceedings of the 2017 CHI Conference Extended Abstracts on Human Factors in Computing Systems, pp. 2853–2859 (2017)
54. Schweitzer, F., Belk, R., Jordan, W., Ortner, M.: Servant, friend or master? The relationships users build with voice-controlled smart devices. J. Mark. Manag. **35**(7–8), 693–715 (2019)
55. Moriuchi, E.: Okay, Google!: An empirical study on voice assistants on consumer engagement and loyalty. Psychol. Mark. **36**(5), 489–501 (2019)
56. Ahmadian, M., Lee, O.K.D.: AI-based voice assistant systems: evaluating from the interaction and trust perspectives (2017)
57. Luo, X., Tong, S., Fang, Z., Qu, Z.: Frontiers: machines vs. humans: the impact of artificial intelligence chatbot disclosure on customer purchases. Mark. Sci. **38**(6), 937–947 (2019)
58. Kumar, V., Dixit, A., Javalgi, R.R.G., Dass, M.: Research framework, strategies, and applications of intelligent agent technologies (IATs) in marketing. J. Acad. Mark. Sci. **44**(1), 24–45 (2016)
59. Labecki, A., Klaus, P., Zaichkowsky, J.L.: How bots have taken over brand choice decisions. In: Arai, K., Bhatia, R., Kapoor, S. (eds.) FTC 2018. AISC, vol. 881, pp. 976–989. Springer, Cham (2019). https://doi.org/10.1007/978-3-030-02683-7_72
60. Rijsdijk, S.A., Hultink, E.J.: How today's consumers perceive tomorrow's smart products. J. Prod. Innov. Manag. **26**(1), 24–42 (2009)
61. Argyris, C., Schon, D.: Theory in Practice: Increasing Professional Effectiveness. Jossey-Bass, Oxford (1974)
62. Glaser, B.G., Strauss, A.L.: Discovery of Grounded Theory: Strategies for Qualitative Research. Routledge, Abingdon (2017)
63. MacInnis, D.J., Morwitz, V.G., Botti, S., Hoffman, D.L., Kozinets, R.V., Lehmann, D.R., Lynch Jr., J.G., Pechmann, C.: Creating boundary-breaking, marketing-relevant consumer research. J. Mark. **32**(1), 93–105 (2019)
64. Pradeep, A.K., Appel, A., Sthanunathan, S.: AI for Marketing and Product Innovation: Powerful New Tools for Predicting Trends, Connecting with Customers, and Closing Sales. Wiley, Hoboken (2018)
65. McKnight, D.H., Choudhury, V., Kacmar, C.: Developing and validating trust measures for e-commerce: an integrative typology. Inf. Syst. Res. **13**(3), 334–359 (2002)
66. Wang, W., Benbasat, I.: Recommendation agents for electronic commerce: effects of explanation facilities on trusting beliefs. J. Manag. Inf. Syst. **23**(4), 217–246 (2007)
67. Komiak, S.Y., Benbasat, I.: The effects of personalization and familiarity on trust and adoption of recommendation agents. MIS Q. **30**(4), 941–960 (2006)

68. Häubl, G., Murray, K.B.: Double agents: assessing the role of electronic product recommendation systems. Sloan Manag. Rev. **47**(3), 8–12 (2006)
69. Mari, A.: The Rise of machine learning in marketing: goal, process, and benefit of AI-driven marketing. Research Report on ResearchGate (2019)
70. Zeithaml, V.A., Jaworski, B.J., Kohli, A.K., Tuli, K.R., Ulaga, W., Zaltman, G.: A theories-in-use approach to building marketing theory. J. Mark. **84**(1), 32–51 (2020)
71. Brown, C.L., Krishna, A.: The skeptical shopper: a metacognitive account for the effects of default options on choice. J. Consum. Res. **31**(3), 529–539 (2004)
72. Kemp, D.: Using smart speakers to engage with your customers. Har. Bus. Rev. https://hbr.org/2019/05/using-smart-speakers-to-engage-with-your-customers. Accessed 30 Jan 2020
73. Daugherty, P.R., Wilson, H.J.: Human + Machine: Reimagining Work in the Age of AI. Harvard Business Press, Brighton (2018)
74. Fishbein, M., Ajzen, I.: Beliefs, Attitude, Intention, and Behavior: An Introduction to Theory and Research. Addison-Wesley, Reading (1975)
75. Kalbaska, N., Cantoni, L.: Digital fashion competences: market practices and needs. In: Rinaldi, R., Bandinelli, R. (eds.) IT4Fashion 2017. LNEE, vol. 525, pp. 125–135. Springer, Cham (2019). https://doi.org/10.1007/978-3-319-98038-6_10
76. Kalbaska N, Sádaba T, Cantoni L.: Fashion communication: between tradition and digital transformation. Stud. Commun. Sci. **2**, 269–285 (2018)

User Experience Testing vs. Marketing Experts – Can Empirical Research Beat Practical Knowledge in Dialog Marketing?

Christina Miclau[1]([⊠]), Barbara Woerz[2], Laura Heiland[2], Dennis Hess[2], Beatrice Weber[1], Alice Emmler[1], Hans-Peter Saar[1], Jonas Belke[1], Niklas Hose[1], Oxana Ernst[1], and Andrea Mueller[1]

[1] Offenburg University of Applied Sciences, Badstrasse 24, 77652 Offenburg, Germany
`christina.miclau@hs-offenburg.de`
[2] Burda Direct GmbH, Hubert-Burda-Platz 2, 77652 Offenburg, Germany

Abstract. To reach customers by dialog marketing campaigns is more and more difficult. This is a common problem of companies and marketing agencies worldwide: information overload, multi-channel-communication and a confusing variety of offers make it hard to gain the attention of the target group. The contribution of this paper is four-fold: we provide an overview of the current state of print dialog marketing activities and trends (I). Based on this corpus we identify the main key performance indicators of dialog marketing customer interaction (II). A qualitative user experience study identifies the customer wishes and needs, focusing on lottery offers for senior citizens (III). Finally, we evaluate the success of two different dialog marketing campaigns with 20,000 clients and compare the key performance indicators of the original hands-on experience-based print mailings with user experience tested and optimized mailings (IV).

Keywords: User experience tests · Key performance indicators · Dialog marketing · Print mailing · Lottery gambling · Senior citizens

1 Introduction

Finding a successful way to sell offers to customers is a challenge for communication experts since the beginning of marketing: What is the right product or service and the right marketing mix? How can we gain attention of the target group? Will customers read and understand our messages and react as expected?

Inviting people to play a game with a marketing campaign appears to be easy, but to make them invest money is another dimension, because the player might probably not win and the stake is irrecoverably lost. Additionally, there are competitors in the market of lottery, which conduct criminal activities so the reputation of this branch is notoriety. Trust, good reputation and reliability appear as the main success factors that lottery providers should address in their communication with the target group.

Especially for older generations from 65 years and up, classic media, like letters, TV and radio are very important and reliable sources of information. To gain the attention

© Springer Nature Switzerland AG 2020
F. F.-H. Nah and K. Siau (Eds.): HCII 2020, LNCS 12204, pp. 426–444, 2020.
https://doi.org/10.1007/978-3-030-50341-3_33

of this aged target group it is important to fulfill their expectations and needs. However, many dialog marketing campaigns fail – just because they do not address the needs and emotions of their target group. If marketing experts would know about the inner feelings and wishes of the customers, there would probably be a higher chance of success.

Until now, most marketing experts rely on their hands-on experience and create marketing campaigns for their customers based on their own meanings and beliefs. Customer Experience Tracking is an innovative method to investigate the interaction of users with classic and internet-based dialog marketing instruments, focused on learning about their emotions while the interaction takes place [1]. The method offers a scientific approach to identify customers' emotions, wishes and irritations by interacting with the marketing campaign medium, like a website or a print mailing. This way we evaluate the statements, eye movements and facial expression of the user while the interaction with the marketing campaign runs to gain deeper insights into the customer's mind [2].

2 Related Work

2.1 Dialog Marketing Evolution

The standardized evaluation of key performance indicators allows us to assess, which mailing performed better with the target group of elderly persons. Thus, research can reveal, if user experience tested mailings can gain more attention, interest and action than hands-on expert developed ones [3].

Dialog marketing is one of the oldest options of advertising: In the 1950s, the emphasis was on direct sales, in the 1960s on direct print mailing and ten years later on telephone marketing. In the following 30 years, databases, IT-supported production, sales concepts and IT-supported integration of all parameters became increasingly relevant. From the 2010s onwards, the range of customer demands changed towards participation and co-determination, which is inspired by social media applications [4].

Digitalization in particular is constantly creating new opportunities to address customers. This allow more flexibility in customer contact. At the same time, it increases the complexity of the decision-making process regarding the choice of media. The decision makers often use the instruments and media of communication, which have already had a positive influence on advertising campaigns in the past. Above all, interactive media has an advantage over traditional media, as feedback can be used to measure the impact of advertising more effectively [5].

Dialog marketing focuses and aims at a long-term relationship and interaction with the customers [4]. A company action is followed by a reaction of the person addressed, whereupon the company reacts, the target person reacts again etc. The customer should not be treated as an anonymous person and a relationship should be established through interactive marketing with measurable contacts [4, 6].

The prerequisite for dialogue marketing is that the target group must be identifiable. Without this, no direct customer contact can take place. As soon as the company knows about its target group and its needs, etc., for example new customers can be addressed via mailings. Dialog marketing serves to establish a relationship with the customer. If the purchase is not a one-time purchase, but followed up by other purchases, a customer relationship can be established and purchases are made based on customer loyalty

[4]. Dialog marketing should convey information and individuality, leading to a direct response and build trust in the relationship. Furthermore, it is the image of a brand among customers and prospects [4].

The primary objectives of dialogue marketing are customer acquisition, reacquisition, loyalty, service improvement, product and service sales, branding as well as brand management. Just as important is the increase of turnover [6]. For this case study, the key performance indicators "sales increase", "customer retention with cross- and up-selling" and "customer recovery" are particularly relevant.

2.2 Information Overload and Personalization

In recent years, the offer of virtual advertising space on the internet has grown sharply: Online surfers react to the advertising overkill by installing advertising blockers and subscribing to newsletters. This stimulus satiation can be avoided by using real time marketing: Advertising is only sent to selected recipients, with content adapted to their needs and in the right quantity. Particularly real-time printing extends the push possibilities [7]. Communication via print media has the advantage of legally low shipping thresholds. In addition, the print medium serves as a reminder service for the receiving person [8] and simultaneously appeals to several senses [9]. The intensity of contact when opening a printed letter is much higher than in an online newsletter [10]. Nowadays, a postal mailing stands out more in the mailbox than an e-mail in overflowing electronic mailboxes [7].

Through the print channel, which has a high development potential, the response and ultimately the number of sales can be increased. Another advantage is the perception in the print sector. This is because it is often perceived better than online advertising messages. A disadvantage is that the personalization of print products is used less often in the mail order business. However, dynamic generation of print pages can be done easily with good technology. Both, the results of recommendation engines on the purchasing behavior of online users and the customer data stored on membership cards during offline shopping can serve as a database for individualized and personalized print products.

2.3 Brand Experience and Trust

Brand experience is the process of building strong and positive impressions that can be communicated to customers [11]. Schmitt defines brand as a rich source of affective, sensory as well as cognitive associations resulting in memorable and rewarding experiences with the brand [12]. Palmer substantiates the significance of brands by indicating the contribution of both interpersonal and brand relationships to consumer's product experience [13].

Brands can potentially fulfill various tasks for consumers such as added emotional value to functional products, symbolize quality and reduce buyer's risk. The relative concept of added value enables customers to make a purchase based on superiority over competing brands [14] and can be judged by customers in many ways. Gentile, Spiller and Noci [15] found evidence that value is linked to the desire for positive experiences. Additional value can give customers confidence in the choices they make.

Accordingly, emotions play a central role in this context as intuitive connection that is only developed to a few brands out of many that consumers interact with.

Most of the extra benefits considered over and beyond the basic product or service, can be allocated to one of the four headings [14]:

- Confirmation of attributes - brand personality conveys functional claims;
- Satisfying aspirations - additional offer of status, recognition and esteem;
- Shared experiences - joint vision of shared associations and experiences;
- Joining causes - social contribution perceived when purchasing a brand because of the association with charitable concerns.

The expression of brand personality should therefore always be aligned with the company objectives [16]. The brand personality itself can be considered as the DNA of brands [17], the unique identity and the underlying values reflecting the big picture [18]. The differential advantage therefore lies in the intangible assets of today's businesses [14]. The term brand image describes the picture perceived by the target group, formed through various contacts with a brand [18]. Enhancing brand strengths can therefore be considered as part of management challenges [19].

Consumers rather expect psychological and emotional satisfaction, resulting in the fact that the quality of the consumption experience plays an increasingly important role in the decision process and the brand loyalty [20]. The term experience has particularly become popular in the context of product and service design since the end the twentieth century. User experience as human-centered design approach [21] is a critical issue in almost every business sector [22], as it is becoming an economical factor.

Changing consumer lifestyle regarding diversified and personalized needs requires a design based on research – aiming to improve the interaction and increase the efficiency. User study and research obtains to provide a better understanding of user's thinking and behavior and thus to meet their needs and improve the user experience [20]. Preferences, the cognitive mode and way of thinking between ordinary users and professional designers is very different and consumers are becoming increasingly eager to participate in the design process to optimize their own experiences. Consequently, these experiences can only be evaluated from the user perspective [20].

The user experience concept involves all parts within the interaction process [23], the user itself and the product or service, hence all should be included in the evaluation process [20]. The product or service is adapted to the actual use – the usability – with the goal of minimizing negative side effects such as mismatches between actual functionalities and desired ones. Products and services should easily be understood by consumers to ensure a higher satisfaction level [24].

Usability measurements should contain three components [25]:

- Effectiveness, user's ability to complete tasks and quality of outcomes,
- Efficiency (level of resource consumed in task-performing) and
- Satisfaction.

Tests should be repeated continuously [25]. The result of studying user behavior is a high level of usability and a product or service that meets consumer's usage habits and needs [21]. The better the user experience is, the more likely it encourages to build a sense of identity with the brand, which represents a concept of sustainable business development [25].

3 Key Performance Indicators of Consumer Interaction

The advertising effect of direct marketing activities improves with the frequency of their repetition. Dialog marketing is characterized by learning effects. As a result, dialog marketing activities become more efficient. There are two ways to improve direct marketing activities through testing: The first is to use test campaigns to contact a small proportion of the total target group in advance of an actual campaign. Based on the reactions, the communication tools can be improved and sent to the remaining target group. The second possibility is to carry out A/B tests. The A/B test is a test method and can be used to evaluate two versions of a mailing, the original version is tested against a slightly modified version. The two mailing versions are sent out and the reactions of both are compared [10].

The evaluation and performance measurement of direct marketing activities usually takes place after a campaign. Success monitoring shows whether the objectives pursued have been achieved and examines reasons for failure. Key performance indicators help decision makers to derive the information they need from a process as a basis for improvements [28]. The difficulty is to choose appropriate key performance indicators. This depends on the environment in which they are used [29]. Key performance indicators are used in processes of all kinds, including direct marketing. Knowing how to select the right key performance indicators is also linked to understanding what is important for improving a direct marketing activity [30, 31].

A special attribute of direct marketing is the aimed release of direct and measurable response activities of the target group. Direct response marketing explicitly prompts recipients to respond, e.g. through inbound calls, orders, coupons, visits to landing pages. These reactions of a recipient lead to direct communication between the recipient and the company, which can be systematically recorded and analyzed. This 1:1 relationship between sender and recipient makes direct marketing a marketing instrument that can best be controlled using key figures.

The reactions of the recipients are measured by the response rate. It is one of the most frequently used indicators in direct marketing success monitoring [31]. Further key performance indicators and methods most frequently used in practice to measure success of direct marketing campaigns are the determination of reach, cost ratios and profitability analyses. They provide information on the success of the activities carried out.

The reach indicates the number of addresses actually contacted. It is easy to determine for direct media. The advantage of direct media is that they usually give the sender feedback if a message has not been received, e.g. non-existent e-mail address, full mailbox or in the case of direct mailings a delivery error [31]. The recipients actually reached must be taken in proportion to the total number of recipients.

– Reach = Number of mailings delivered/Total number of quantity dispatched

Another related parameter is the response rate. It relates the number of responses to the number of people actually addressed [32, 33]. The response rate can be differentiated by characteristics in which the target group differs, e.g. response rate of older and younger customers [31].

– Response rate = Number of responses/Number of mailings delivered

However, the respond of the recipients can be different in direct marketing. In this case study one of the two mailings asks the target group for a call. That's why we additionally want to address key performance indicators used in call center operations: In this area, the service level is a common key figure for measuring service quality. The service level can be determined by dividing the number of calls whose time in the queue is shorter than a specified acceptable waiting time by the total number of calls [34]. For example, a service level of 80% in a call center means that eight out of every ten phone calls were answered by the call center agents before 20 s, the agreed time limit.

The key performance indicators mentioned so far are parameters that are among the classic in direct marketing and easy to determine. Reach and response rate provide information about the number of recipients addressed. They do not provide an overview of the costs and profitability of a direct marketing campaign.

To check profitability, it is necessary to determine the costs. Both the costs per contact and the costs per response can provide this information. From the costs per response, the costs per interest and the costs per order can be derived, considering the type of response. These cost key figures enable to evaluate different direct marketing channels and target groups [31, 35].

– Cost per contact = Total cost of the campaign/Number of contacts made
– Cost per interest = Total cost of the campaign/Number of interested persons
– Cost per order = Total cost of the campaign/Number of orders

In addition to the costs, the return generated by the campaign must also be taken into account in order to assess the economic viability of the action. In terms of the return achieved the key performance indicator return per mailing measures the performance of a campaign. This key figure is determined by relating the return generated by a direct marketing campaign with the number of all direct mailings delivered [10].

Return per mailing = Total return of the direct marketing campaign/Number of mailings delivered

The fractional arithmetic shows: the key performance indicator return per mailing decreases as the number of mailings delivered increases. The break-even point analysis determines the number of items delivered from which the costs of a campaign are covered. Before a direct marketing campaign is implemented, a break-even analysis can show whether the achievement of a calculated break-even quantity is realistic. It expresses, whether the campaign is successful or not [35].

To determine the quantity-related break-even of a direct marketing campaign, the total costs of the campaign are divided by the unit profit per direct mailing. The unit profit is the difference between the sales prices and the unit costs [31].

– Break even point = Total cost of the campaign/Unit profit per mailing

As soon as a direct marketing campaign is initiated, the first customer reactions are achieved. The response curve usually reaches its peak three to four days after the mailing, after which the reactions to the mailing tend to decrease [36]. Thus, meaningful key figures can be determined shortly after the start of a direct marketing campaign.

The key figures are based on measurable reactions of the recipients, but not the emotional and cognitive effects of a mailing. They can certainly be positive and precede the response. For a complete measurement of success, it is therefore advisable to conduct additional surveys and observations to measure the cognitive and emotional effects of mailings on target groups [31].

4   Qualitative User Experience Study

4.1   Target Group Description

This case study has been initiated as cooperation between the Offenburg University and BurdaDirect, which is part of one of the biggest publishing houses in Germany Hubert Burda Media. The aim is to optimize two different types of mailings – PIN Code and direct sales in the Customer Experience Tracking Laboratory of Offenburg University.

The insights of the user experience testing have been incorporated into a new version of each mailing. All mailings were sent out to 20,000 target group addresses in Germany to check, whether the established or optimized version achieves better responses. The success of the user experience testing is highly dependent on whether the selected test persons fit the target group of the mailing campaign. Therefore, it is important to know and understand the characteristics and composition of the given target group. For this purpose, the cooperating company provided statistical data on the place of residence, gender and age of customers, see Fig. 1.

All of the addressed persons had already participated their free of charge lottery gambling. Most participants come from North Rhine Westphalia (17.1%), Bavaria (16.8%) and Baden-Wuerttemberg (15.5%). Furthermore, it turns out that more than half of the participants are female in an age between 61 and 80 years. It can therefore be considered, that a large part of the current customers is born in the 1940s at the end of World War II. At this time about 40% of the total national housing stock in Germany was destroyed and the populace often had no access to food, electricity, water and gas [37]. Based on that background it is highly probable that the average person in the target group grew up in times of poverty, lack of resources and has a different perspective on lotteries and the worth of prizes than younger generations. An elderly target group like this brings up special requirements regarding the design and the organization of the user experience testing. The questionnaire should be kept short and focused, using an adequate vocabulary to ensure the test person has no difficulties in following the procedure [38].

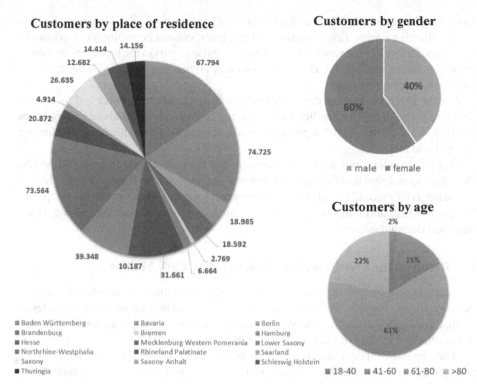

Customers by place of residence

14.414 14.156
12.682
26.635
4.914
20.872
67.794
74.725
73.564
18.985
18.592
39.348 2.769
10.187 6.664
31.661

- Baden Württemberg
- Brandenburg
- Hesse
- Northrhine-Westphalia
- Saxony
- Thuringia
- Bavaria
- Bremen
- Mecklenburg Western Pomerania
- Rhineland Palatinate
- Saxony-Anhalt
- Berlin
- Hamburg
- Lower Saxony
- Saarland
- Schleswig Holstein

Customers by gender

40%
60%

■ male ■ female

Customers by age

2%
22% 15%
61%

■ 18-40 ■ 41-60 ■ 61-80 ■ >80

Fig. 1. Statistical data of customers participating the company's lottery by place of residence, gender and age.

4.2 Design of the Empirical Study

Qualitative interviews were conducted implementing the advantages of getting as much information out of the interviews as possible. In comparison to quantitative research, that refers to counts and measures of things, the quality of the answers are essential [39]. The personal 1:1 interviews took place in the Customer Experience Tracking Lab of Offenburg University and lasted between 20 and 45 min. Throughout the flexible interview situation, it was possible to interact spontaneously with the test persons and ask again to provide additional information. Supporting instruments in the lab were the mobile eye tracker, which records the eye movement and further cameras for recording voice, gestures and facial expressions [1].

First, the PIN code concept was tested secondly the direct sales concept. Data were collected by means of a standardized survey, meaning that every interview is based on the same questionnaire with the same interviewer. Therefore, it is possible to compare answers and it contributes to the completeness [40]. Eleven test persons, mainly out of the main target group – female persons at an age of 61 years and older – were invited to the interview.

The design of the survey questionnaire was based on the analysis of the established and already evaluated mailings of Burda Direct. The questions were arranged in two sections: the first part related to the layout, design and content of the letter and the second part related to demographic variables. The first section worked with open questions to the following topics: first impression of the letter, comprehensibility, completeness, reliability, factors of motivation to read the letter and take part in the lottery, expectations about the further procedure, chance of winning, layout and design. There were also concept specific questions.

For the PIN code mailing concept questions about the phone number and the scratch pad were prepared and for the direct sales mailing concept questions about the prices and ordering ticket. In the second section, respondents were asked to indicate the following: age, job and residence.

Before the interviews started the scenario has been described to each test person: They should imagine that they are at home and find the letter in their postbox. The task was to act as they would usually do. Very important for the testing was that the test person thought out loud and told the interviewer as much as possible about their thoughts and emotions during the interview.

4.3   Results of the User Experience Testing 1: PIN Code Mailing

The user experience testing was followed by the evaluation of the findings and the redesign of the concepts. As the analysis of the eye tracking did not maintain relevant results, the focus was on the interviews. The two mailing concepts showed differences and similarities in the critical elements that must be improved.

The original PIN code mailing is a one-pager, which briefly describes the offer and prompts the recipient to call by phone. The call is free of charge and call center agents provide further information about the offer, which may lead to an order for a competition subscription.

The main critical points only concerning the PIN code concept are the arrangement of the letter, the word PIN code and the unclear explanation of the procedure of the lottery. The most noticeable change of the letter is the creation of a visualization, which shows the course of the competition. Five out of six test persons had difficulties to understand the process of the lottery. Thanks to pictographs and short notes the visualization is easy to understand, gives an overview about the procedure and the letter a more creative design.

The word PIN code is transformed into access key and personal key. Half of the test persons said, that the word PIN code is only used for smartphones or banking operations and did not fit to the topic of a lottery. Furthermore, the scratch pad gets a new function, layout and placement. It is now covering the possible profit instead of the PIN code customer number. The test persons criticized the use and sense of the field. It was perceived as annoying, unappealing and pointless. In combination with the name PIN code it reminded more of a letter from a bank, as already mentioned. Now the scratch pad is integrated into the text and thus is placed in the center of the letter. In the original version the field could be found in the lower right corner with a conspicuous border. By covering the profit amount tension is built up and entices the reader to become active. With the new structure of the scratch pad and the visualization of the further process the letter becomes more structured.

The test persons did not understand the profit division into installments and asked if also a one-off payment is possible. Therefore, short simple sentences were created, showing the possibilities, how the profit can be received. In agreement with the company a profit distribution in installments but also as a one-time payment is possible.

Furthermore, the call procedure was explained more in detail. This was necessary because the test persons were afraid of talking to a robot, being on hold for a long time, having to give more personal details or being persuaded to buy a magazine subscription. In the visualization it is pointed out, that they will talk to a competent employee. This is supposed to build up trust and to take away their fear of being ripped off. Test persons also criticized the hotline number because it is a typical lottery number in Germany and does not have a serious effect. In arrangement with the company this problem could not be solved and the number had to stay the same. The only thing to build up trust was to point out that the call is for free. Finally, the signature was replaced because it was not in the alignment. This contributed to a better layout.

There are some more points of criticism that could not be fixed: The signature was described as copied and impersonal. It was difficult to find a new useful signature as this were the only indications. To create a fitting signature more details concerning this topic need to be carried out. In order to deal with the complaints about the impersonal design, the idea of creating the whole letter in hand writing was discussed. Due to the lack of time and resources, this idea was not implemented. Finally, the test persons asked for more networking elements. Because of the fact, that the company could not create a specific mail address, it was not possible to insert this new element.

4.4 Results of the User Experience Testing 2: Direct Sales Mailing

The also already established and optimized direct sales mailing consists of two pages. The first page, a letter, describes the lottery subscription offer in detail. On the second page, the recipient receives a visual overview of the lottery subscription elements – participation in several raffles, bonus points, chance to win additional 100,000 € and a 20 € cash gift upon registration. In addition, there is an order card on the bottom of the page and a free returning letter, which can be used by stating the account number and tearing of the card.

Based on the findings of the user experience testing, various changes have been applied to the Direct sales mailing. Four adjustments concerning the layout: The test persons complained about the reading comfort. Therefore, page margins on both sides were increased and the font sizes have been standardized. This improved the reading flow and made it appear more professional. Secondly, the text was significantly shortened. The number of repetitions was reduced, and the text was written more strikingly, as all test persons criticized an over-saturation of information. Thirdly, formulations that were bold were deleted, as it was assessed nonprofessionally.

The test persons had problems to find contract conditions, because the original mailing did not refer to it at all. Therefore, the first page of the new mailing contains a reference to the small print, containing the conditions of participation and cancellation. The mailing now appears more trustworthy.

The text of the mailing was simplified. The number of superlatives and redundancies were reduced and the wording is now generally more objective. Almost half of the respondents linked the "euphoric" written text with a dubious offer. For this reason, the phrase "Exclusively for you", has been removed.

Most of the adjustments in the direct sales mailing were realized in terms of content: A customer satisfaction seal of approval was placed directly on the top of the first page in order to counteract the concerns expressed by the test persons about the credibility of the offer. The new mailing mentions the lottery subscription already at the end of the first paragraph. In the original letter, the test persons became aware of this at a much later stage. One third of the test persons did not become aware of this at all or only upon notice from the head of testing.

A reference to the monthly subscription costs was made regarding the monetary gift granted at the time of conclusion of the contract. It is explicitly stated that the gift of money gives back half of the monthly costs of participation. Two thirds of the test persons did not find the money present per se convincing.

The material awards listed in the mailing are marked with a number of loyalty points required to receive them. Customers can now easily calculate how many months they would need to play in order to earn loyalty points for a certain award. Exactly this uncertainty – as a result of the lack of information in the established mailing – was criticized by almost all test persons. The new mailing shows a non-cash bonus from each the low, medium and high point segment. This is intended to provide customers with a transparent overview. Half of the test persons expressed the wish to see higher-value rewards when selecting the material awards. The order of the possible winning elements on the second page changed so that the most attractive one is on top and the least interesting at the bottom. All of the test persons had the opinion that the 20 € money gift is not particularly interesting.

The conditions of participation and cancellation were supplemented with additional information on automatic renewal of the subscription and cancellation options. All test persons criticized the lack of information on these important topics. The company's brand, on the other hand, was considered positively and trustworthily. Important information such as the cancellation option is now described clearly in the new mailing among the listed benefits. This leads to a more serious mailing, which is much more in line with the customer's idea of the brand and the company.

In the user experience testing, the test persons expressed further suggestions, which were not implemented in the new mailing for various reasons. An interesting recommendation was the option of a trial month with prepayment. This would remove the subscription character and allow the customer full cost control. A further suggestion was the placement of a concrete contact person with e-mail address and telephone number in the letter, since some test persons expressed the discomfort with calling a computer voice. The additional profit as pension was noticed very late in the original mailing, although half of the test persons classified it as very interesting. The suggestion was made to put the additional profit as pension more forward.

4.5 General Optimization Challenges

Besides the various mailing specific changes, there were also numerous adaptions affected both mailings equally. The most comprehensive adjustments were made regarding formulations: The wording in both mailings has been changed generally to an unpretentious addressing with less superlatives and no repetitions.

The text was kept as long as necessary to include all relevant information but also as short and direct as possible to enable a quick and easy understanding. These adjustments were made since many test persons noted the text would be over exaggerated and partly confusing. For instance, in both mailings the wording was adjusted from "for you personally" to "selected customers" since test persons rated it as overdone, knowing the mailing is also sent to many other customers.

The text layout in both mailings was modified to facilitate the reading flow and visual overview: wider side margins to better fit the text into the field of view and unified font type and size. Especially the small printed terms on the backside of the mailings have been enlarged and separated in shorter, thinner text blocks, since test persons had issues to read these sections.

One of the key adjustments regarding the layout was to replace the words raffle service from the address field of the letter by a large printed company logo. All the tested persons noted that the tendering company has a trustworthy and good image, but they would have instantly thrown the unopened mailing away reading the words raffle service knowing it is a lottery mailing.

Overall, the goal was to optimize the combination of wording and layout while using the strong and positive image of the company to create an impression of a serious, high-quality lottery offering. This was important since all test persons remarked they were negatively surprised by the way the lottery mailings as it did not match the good brand image of the case study company.

5 Findings

5.1 Analysis of Findings

The optimized PIN code and direct sales mailings (5,000 each) were printed and dispatched on the November 19th 2019 coincident with the established mailings of the case study company. The success of the PIN code mailing was measured by the total number of net inbound calls – number of total calls adjusted by the number of recalls, whereas the success of the direct sales mailing was measured by the number of returned order forms. The measurement was performed for about one month until 11th of December 2019 see Table 1.

Considering PIN code mailing response ratios about 37.1% respectively 41.4% were achieved. For this type of lottery, the hosting company defines response ratios over 30% as extraordinary good. Therefore, the established as well as the optimized PIN code mailing campaign can be classified as very successful.

Furthermore, it shows that despite the already high response ratio of the original mailing the user experience optimized PIN code mailing achieved a percentage response increase of +4.28%, considered as the best result ever. Therefore, the changes made to the PIN code mailing based on the findings in the user experience testing can be considered successful.

The direct sales mailing campaign shows different results. The original mailing achieved a response ratio of 0.48%, which the hosting company defines as acceptable for this type of lottery. The user experience optimized mailing however achieved a

Table 1. Results of both mailing campaigns

	PIN code		Direct sales	
	Established mailing	Optimized mailing	Established mailing	Optimized mailing
Number of dispatched mailings	5,000	5,000	5,000	5,000
Number of responses/returned order forms (total)	1,855	2,069	24	10
Response ratio (%)	37.10%	41.38%	0.48%	0.20%
Delta	**+4.28%**		**−0.28%**	

response ratio of 0.20%, which the company classifies as poor. Therefore, the changes made to the direct sales mailing based on the findings in the user experience testing must be considered as not performance-enhancing.

This raises the question, why the user experience optimization produces excellent results in one case and poor results in the other one. As an explanation approach, why the optimized PIN code mailing performed better than the established mailing, two factors can be considered: The first and probably most influential factor is that the new layout is cleaned up and reduced to its most relevant parts. The focus of the new mailing is to give a better guidance on what to do and where to call. This facilitates the participation process and results in more incoming calls. A second but less verifiable factor may be that the new mailing was only adjusted in some sections, but not changed fundamentally. So the customer notices the new and better design but also recognizes the basic structure of the old mailing to which she or he is accustomed. This combination of new layout and known structures may be a key factor to achieve a higher participation while maintaining the initial degree of trust.

While the good result of the PIN code mailing can be explained relatively easy, it is much more complicated to find out which reasons led to the poor result of the direct sales mailing. In total two possible reasons are identified: The first and most likely reason is that the given data basis of the target group wasn't detailed enough. It only showed overall target group information concerning average age, gender and place of residence of the currently free participating customers without including the type of lottery they played. For this reason, a mainly female target group was assumed for both mailings. During the evaluation of the mailing campaign, it turned out that the direct sales lottery is mostly played by male customers. Therefore, incorrect test persons with a main share of women were assumed for the direct sales mailing. The second factor is related to the assumptions that were made regarding the success of the PIN code mailing: While the PIN code mailing still has many connections to the old design the direct sales mailing was changed fundamentally. It is conceivable that too many changes were made, which resulted in customers refusing the participation due to uncertainty.

5.2 Analysis of Mailing Lists and Responders

As explained the old and new concepts were dispatched with the intention to generate comparative values. In order to prove the same starting point, the target groups are analyzed individually and the results are shown in Table 2.

Table 2. Demographic facts about the mailing target groups

		Gender in %		Age in years					
		Male	Female	No answer	<80	61–80	41–60	18–40	Average
PIN code	Established concept	46	54	535	720	3,080	570	95	71
	Optimized concept	45	55	530	796	2,941	618	115	71
Direct sales	Established concept	47	53	535	740	2,995	619	111	71
	Optimized concept	46	54	546	807	2,987	555	105	71

The group of persons, which received the old concept of the PIN code mailing consists of 46% male and 54% female customers. The group with the optimized concept consists of 45% male and 55% female customers. The average age was 71 years. Thus, the structures of the target groups are almost identical. The direct sales concept shows the same results. 47% of the group, which received the established concept, are male customers and 53% female customers. The optimized concept was sent to a group with 46% male and 54% female customers. Again, both groups have an average age of 71 years as it was the case with the PIN code concept. These figures also show the similarities of the target groups. The figures prove that all concepts had the same basis in terms of target group structure.

After receiving the results of the testing and comparing the numbers it was necessary to take a look at the replies. A service level of 100% could not be achieved. Therefore, information on gender, age and place of residence could only be obtained in about half of the calls, see Table 3.

The old concept achieved 1,855 net calls. 47% of the calls contain further information, showing that 49% are female and 51% male callers. The average age is 71 years. The new concept achieved 2,069 net calls. 49% could be analyzed more in detail: 51% of the callers were female and 49% male. The average age is also 71 years. As we can see, the structure is very similar, leading to the conclusion that both concepts appeal the same target group. Also conspicuous is the similar distribution of the caller's residence. Most of the calls from both concepts came from North-Rhine-Westphalia (established concept: 19%; optimized concept: 18%), Baden-Wuerttemberg (established concept: 19%; optimized concept: 17%) and Bavaria (established concept: 17%; optimized concept: 17%). These states are followed by Lower Saxony (established concept: 8%; optimized concept:

Table 3. Demographic facts about the mailing target group

		Gender in %		Average age in years	Top-3-residences
		Male	Female		
PIN code	Established concept	51	49	71	North-Rhine-Westphalia, Baden-Wuerttemberg, Bavaria
	Optimized concept	49	5	71	North-Rhine-Westphalia, Baden-Wuerttemberg, Bavaria
Direct sales	Established concept	55	45	69	Baden-Wuerttemberg, Bavaria, Lower-Saxony
	Optimized concept	29	71	70	Bavaria

10%) Hessen (established concept: 7%; optimized concept: 8%) and Saxony (established concept: 6%; optimized concept: 5%). This distribution goes along with the population of all persons contacted.

34 persons responded, with the intention of ordering a subscription. Since in some cases the information provided was incorrect, e.g. wrong IBAN, there were only 29 orders in total. 22 orders were from recipients, who had received the established mailing version. Whereas seven orders were placed by recipients who received the optimized concept.

The average age of the orders is 69 years. 55% of the customers are male and 45% female. With 27% of the responses, most of the orders came from Baden-Wuerttemberg. 23% of the customers each come from Bavaria and Lower Saxony, 18% from North-Rhine-Westphalia, and 5% each from Saxony-Anhalt and Hessen. This is also equivalent to the target group structure. The optimized direct sales concept generated seven orders with 29% male and 71% female orders. The average age is 70 years.

Every response came from another state and only Bavaria contained two orders. The outstanding difference between the responders of the old and new concept may also be an indicator for the not performance-enhancing user experience testing. As the optimized concept based on female opinions although the direct sales lottery was mainly played by male customer in the past, as they rather react to that kind of mailing.

6   Final Evaluation and Recommendations

The central dialogue marketing objectives of the project are sales increase, customer retention with cross- and upselling as well as customer recovery. In order to achieve these goals, the determination of the key performance indicators cost per order, response rate and service level are classified as suitable. These key performance indicators are in use by the case study company, reflecting the positive or negative reaction to small adaptions in the mailings.

Additionally, the marketing experts annually report their learnings and regularly send out different versions of mailings. A/B tests are applied in order to compare different approaches and target groups, e.g. differentiation between male and female. Currently, the evaluation is solely quantitative based on target values.

It is suggested to add the indicators "return per mailing" and "break even per campaign", to obtain an even more informative evaluation. Return per mailing enables to determine whether a direct mailing campaign is successful overall or not. The break even per campaign expresses the percentage of the total number of mailings that must achieve a positive response in order to reach the break-even point [10]. Key performance indicators do not cover any emotional and cognitive effect of mailings. Therefore, additional surveys and observations have to be conducted in order to better understand the target group.

Before launching new products or modifying mailings, companies should reflect them in the course of a user experience testing. The knowledge gained from the testing – the customer's point of view – should then be implemented within the optimization process. This ensures that the product appeals to the target group and customers are addressed correctly. Furthermore, companies should especially take the phases before- and after-use more into account when designing products [41]. The phase before-use is about the customer's expectations – in this case when receiving a mailing. In the phase after-use, the focus is on processing the experienced use. The authors see the danger here that the consistently negative reception of the mailing by the test persons could stick to the brand.

Even though the response rate for direct sales mailing has dropped, the project team is convinced that the following recommendations are generally more in line with the brand and therefore promise long-term success. During the user experience testing, all test persons remarked that the dubious marketing of the product did not match the good brand image of the company. It is advised to use the image to make the mailings more transparent and reliable. With reference to the interrelationships between brand image, identity and positioning [43], the authors believe that the established direct sales mailing poses a threat to the brand image. This can influence brand positioning and identity in a way that is not intended.

We recommend to design mailings, adopted according to the user experience and to control the success with the existing key performance indicators. Lull criticizes a lack of resources and time in terms of research methods in many companies and admonishes researchers of initial assumptions from numbers [42].

Additionally, a few critical aspects concerning user experience testing have to be considered: user feedback can be interpreted in many ways, users can be uncertain about the task, the environment and other conditions such as the interviewer can influence the results and the user knows he or she is performing a test. The concept of needs is abstract and therefore it is complex to gasp and users can find it difficult to verbalize their needs [22].

7 Limitations and Future Work

Being aware of these critical aspects, user studies can help companies to understand their customers better. Taking preferences, behavior and way of thinking into account when designing products, the customer satisfaction can, in turn, be increased. It then might even be possible to market personalized rewards in the future by using the existing customer data, as male and female preferences differ.

Print media within dialog marketing context might be regarded as outdated or even needless in today's business activities. But, especially the typical mailing target group of golden agers is considered as rewarding. Furthermore, it can contribute to a unique selling position, as it appeals to many senses and it bypasses the online information overload.

The current evaluation process of the marketing experts is comprehensive, but only focused on numerical factor. To remain competitive, customer preferences need to be taken in account within profound user studies as their feedback is indispensable for creating user-friendly products. Additionally, the expertise and experience of an expert can be considered as key success factor in creating suitable products.

As in our case the optimization of the PIN code concept was a big success whereas the realization of the optimized direct sales concept did not work as expected even though in both cases wishes and improvement suggestions of the test persons were considered. To conclude, we want to point out that it can be challenging to find out the actual preferences of customers and to combine them with expert's knowledge, but a competitive advantage can be reached on the long-term perspective.

References

1. Mueller, A., Gast. O.: Customer Experience Tracking – Online-Kunden conversion-wirksame Erlebnisse bieten durch gezieltes Emotionsmanagement. In: Keuper, F. et al. (eds.) Daten-Management und Daten-Services – Next Level, Berlin, pp. 313–343 (2014)
2. Mueller, A., Stopfkuchen, M.: E-Joy – markenerlebnisse messbar machen. In: Keuper, F., Schomann, M. (eds.) Entrepreneurship heute – Unternehmerisches Denken angesichts der Herausforderungen einer vernetzten Wirtschaft, Berlin, pp. 201–238 (2015)
3. Buttkus, M., Eberenz, R.: Performance Management in Retail and the Consumer Goods Industry: Best Practices and Case Studies. Springer, Cham (2019). https://doi.org/10.1007/978-3-030-12730-5
4. Holland, H.: Dialogmarketing: Offline- und Online-Marketing, Mobile- und Social Media-Marketing. Vahlen Franz GmbH, Munich (2016)
5. Deutscher Dialogmarketing Verband e.V.: Dialogmarketing Perspektiven 2018/2019: Tagungsband 13. wissenschaftlicher interdisziplinaerer Kongress fuer Dialogmarketing. Springer, Wiesbaden (2019). https://doi.org/10.1007/978-3-658-25583-1
6. Krafft, M., Hesse, J., Hoefling, J., Peters, K., Rinas, D.: International Direct Marketing: Principles, Best Practices, Marketing Facts. Springer, Heidelberg (2007). https://doi.org/10.1007/978-3-540-39632-1
7. Gerhard Maertterer: Branchentrends im Dialogmarketing: Real-Time-Printing: Von Zuckerberg zu Gutenberg (2016). https://www.ddv.de//fileadmin/user_upload/pdf/Branchentrends/Eversfrank_Gruppe_Realtime_Printing_GerhardMaertterer.pdf
8. Verlegh, P., Voorveld, H., Eisend, M.: Advances in Advertising Research (Vol. VI): The Digital, the Classic, the Subtle, and the Alternative. Springer, Wiesbaden (2016). https://doi.org/10.1007/978-3-658-10558-7
9. Weht, J.: Vorzuege der Print-Personalisierung im Omnichannel-Handel. https://prudsys.de/die-vorzuege-der-print-personalisierung-im-omnichannel-handel/

10. Spandl, T., Ploetz, W.: Direktmarketing mit Printmedien. Springer, Wiesbaden (2018). https://doi.org/10.1007/978-3-658-21464-7
11. Tynan, C., McKechnie, S.: Experience marketing: a review and reassessment. J. Mark. Manag. **25**(5–6), 501–517 (2009)
12. Schmitt, B.: Experiential Marketing. J. Mark. Manag. **15**(1–3), 53–67 (1999)
13. Palmer, A.: Customer experience management: a critical review of an emerging idea. J. Serv. Mark. **24**(3), 196–208 (2010)
14. Baker, M.J, Hart, S.J.: The Marketing Book. Oxford, Boston (2008)
15. Gentile, C., Spiller, N., Noci, G.: How to sustain the customer experience: an overview of experience components that co-create value with the customer. Eur. Manag. J. **25**(5), 395–410 (2007)
16. Straker, K., Wrigley, C., Rosemann, M.: Typologies and touchpoints: designing multi-channel digital strategies. J. Res. Interact. Mark. **9**(2), 10–128 (2015)
17. Smith, K., Hanover, D.: Experiential Marketing: Secrets, Strategies, and Success Stories from the World's Greatest Brands. Wiley, Hoboken (2016)
18. Esch, F. R.: Concepts and frameworks of brand management: brand identity: the guiding star for successful brands. In: Schmitt, B.H., Rogers, D.L. (eds.) Handbook on brand and experience management, Cheltenham, U.K, Northampton, pp. 58–76 (2008)
19. Meyer, A., Brudler, B., Bluemelhuber, C.: Managerial concepts: every-body's darling? The target groups of a brand. In: Schmitt, B.H., Rogers, D.L. (eds.) Handbook on Brand and Experience Management, Cheltenham, U.K., Northampton, pp. 99–112 (2008)
20. Ahram, T., Falcao, C.: Advances in usability and user experience: Proceedings of the AHFE 2019 International Conferences on Usability and User Experience, and Human Factors and Assistive Technology, July 24–28, 2019, Washington D.C. Springer, New York (2020). https://doi.org/10.1007/978-3-030-19135-1
21. International Organization for Standardization: ISO 9241-210:2010: Ergonomics of human-system interaction: Part 210: Human-centred design for interactive systems (2010)
22. Marcus, A., Wang, W.: Design, User Experience, and Usability: Users, Contexts and Case Studies: HCI International Proceedings, Part III. Springer, Cham (2018). https://doi.org/10.1007/978-3-319-91806-8
23. Park, J., Han, S.H., Kim, H.K., Cho, Y., Park, W.: Developing elements of user experience for mobile phones and services: survey, interview, and observation approaches. In: Human Factors and Ergonomics in Manufacturing and Service Industries, New Jersey, vol. 23, pp. 279–293 (2013)
24. Lin, C.J., Cheng, L.Y.: Product attributes and user experience design: how to convey product information through user-centered service. J. Intell. Manuf. **28**, 1743–1754 (2017). https://doi.org/10.1007/s10845-015-1095-8
25. International Organization for Standardization: ISO 9241-11:2018: Ergonomics of human-system interaction - Part 11: Usability: Definitions and concepts (2018)
26. Gitman, L.J., McDaniel, C.D.: The Future of Business: The Essentials. Australia (2009)
27. Jiao, J., Zhang, Y., Helander, M.: A Kansei mining system for affective design. In: Expert Systems with Applications, Amsterdam, vol. 30, pp. 658–673 (2006)
28. Franceschini, F., Galetto, M., Maisano, D.: Management by Measurement: Designing Key Indicators and Performance Measurement Systems. Springer, Heidelberg (2007). https://doi.org/10.1007/978-3-540-73212-9
29. Parmenter, D.: Key Performance Indicators: Developing, Implementing, and Using Winning Key Performance Indicators. Wiley, Hoboken (2019)
30. Fitz-Gibbon, C.T.: Performance indicators. Clevedon Multilingual Matters (1990)
31. Zerres, C.: Handbuch Marketing-Controlling. Springer, Heidelberg (2017). https://doi.org/10.1007/978-3-662-50406-2

444   C. Miclau et al.

32. Stone, B., Jacobs, R.: Successful Direct Marketing Methods: Interactive, Database, and Customer-Based Marketing for Digital Age. McGraw-Hill, New York (2008)
33. Davis, J.A.: Measuring Marketing: 110+ Key Metrics Every Marketer Needs. Wiley, Hoboken (2013)
34. Li, J., Liu, Y., Tsung, F., Huo, J., Su, Q.: Statistical monitoring of service levels and staffing adjustments for call centers. Qual. Reliab. Eng. Int. **32**, 2813–2821 (2016)
35. Spiller, L.D., Baier, M.: Contemporary Direct and Interactive Marketing, Chicago (2012)
36. Winkelmann, P.: Marketing und Vertrieb: Fundamente fuer die Marktorientierte Unternehmensfuehrung. Munich (2010)
37. Akbulut-Yuksel, M., Khamis, M., Yuksel, M.: For better or for worse: the long-term effects of postwar mobilization on family formation. In: Applied Economics, London, vol. 48, pp. 2771–2784 (2016)
38. Rebelo, F., Soares, M.: Advances in Ergonomics in Design. Proceedings of the AHFE 2016 International Conference on Ergonomics in Design. Springer, Heidelberg (2016). https://doi.org/10.1007/978-3-319-41983-1
39. Berg, B., Lune, H.: Qualitative Research Methods for the Social Sciences, New York (2017)
40. Boehler, H.: Marktforschung, Stuttgart (2004)
41. Geis, T., Johner, C.: Usability Engineering als Erfolgsfaktor: Effizient IEC 62366- und FDA-konform dokumentieren. Beuth Verlag, Wien (2015)
42. Lull, D.: Discussions in User Experience: Healthcare for User Frustration. Berkeley (2017)
43. Esch, F.R.: Corporate Brand Management: Marken als Anker strategischer Fuehrung von Unternehmen. Springer, Wiesbaden (2014). https://doi.org/10.1007/978-3-8349-3862-6
44. Regier, S., Schunk, H., Koenecke, T.: Marken und Medien: Fuehrung von Medienmarken und Markenfuehrung mit neuen und klassischen Medien. Springer, Wiesbaden (2016). https://doi.org/10.1007/978-3-658-06934-6

Effectiveness of Banner Ads: An Eye Tracking and Facial Expression Analysis

Thanh-An Nguyen, Constantinos K. Coursaris[⊠], Pierre-Majorique Léger,
Sylvain Sénécal, and Mark Fredette

HEC Montréal, Montréal H3T 2A7, Canada
constantinos.coursaris@hec.ca

Abstract. The present paper explores how attention and emotions influence the effectiveness of banner ads. Participants performed a goal-oriented search on a website which had banner ads displaying indulgent food products (i.e., chocolate). Eye movements and facial expressions were recorded. Attention was measured by total fixation duration. Emotional valence was automatically inferred from facial expressions using facial analysis software. Results show that attention and emotional valence are positively associated with ad recognition and that emotions influence purchase intention differently depending on the degree of attention. Emotional valence is positively associated with purchase intention when attention is low, but negatively related when attention is high. The findings highlight the importance in defining marketing goals when designing online banner ads. Additional implications for both theory and practice are discussed.

Keywords: Eye tracking · Automatic facial analysis · Banner ads · Emotions · Total fixation duration

1 Introduction

Banner advertisements (ads) have been one of the most popular forms of online marketing. Surveys reported that banner ads revenue has been growing during the past years and will continue growing in the coming years [1]. Nonetheless, the effectiveness of banner ads is an ongoing debate. On the one hand, it is argued that banner ads have little effect, because consumers intentionally avoid viewing ads. This phenomenon is known as banner blindness [2]. Eye-tracking studies reveal that most banner ads are rarely directly attended to, but instead are processed at a pre-attentive level [3]. Banner ads may also increase users' perceived workload, cause distraction, and are detrimental to primary task performance [3]. On the other hand, there is evidence showing that exposure to banner ads enhances brand awareness [2], attitudes towards brands [4], and repeat purchases [5].

The effectiveness of banner ads is usually measured in relation to attitudes, ad recognition, ad recall, click-through rates, and purchase intention. Prior research found that viewers' attention is among the factors that determine the effectiveness of banner ads. For instance, levels of attention paid to an ad influences brand awareness. The longer

© Springer Nature Switzerland AG 2020
F. F.-H. Nah and K. Siau (Eds.): HCII 2020, LNCS 12204, pp. 445–455, 2020.
https://doi.org/10.1007/978-3-030-50341-3_34

viewers pay attention to banner ads, the better they remember and recognize the ads later [4]. Attention to online ads is also positively associated with recall and purchase intention [6]. Using eye-tracking technology, earlier studies have reported that even at a minimal level of attention (i.e., to the extent that viewers may not realize having seen the banner ads), viewers' attitudes toward the exposed ads were still affected [4, 7]. This is because at low attention, information could be unconsciously learnt, which could subsequently change viewers' preferences and attitudes [8]. In addition to the informational appeal of banner ads, emotional responses are also important in boosting advertising effectiveness [9]. Research suggests that emotional ads (i.e., ads that intentionally induce emotions) increase click-through rates [10] and enhance brand favorability [11]. In traditional media such as television, brand awareness is successfully built on emotional rather than rational appeals [12], as viewer engagement begins with "a conscious or more likely unconscious, emotional response" [13]. Also, emotional ads are more effective for certain product categories more so than others; e.g. emotional ads work better for hedonic than for utilitarian products and for products with low rather than high involvement [14].

Given the importance of attention and emotion in driving the effectiveness of online advertising this study investigates how these two factors (i.e., emotion and attention) influence the effectiveness of hedonic/indulgent food banner ads in an adult population. Hedonic or indulgent foods are defined as products that are attractive due to their tastiness yet cognitively unfavorable due to their high caloric content and/or low nutritional quality. Results in this study show that the longer web users paid attention to a product ad, the more likely they recognized the product later and that the impact of emotion on purchase intention varies at different levels of attention. In particular, at low attention, happy consumers were more likely to buy hedonic foods than less happy individuals. At higher attention levels, the opposite was observed.

There are several motivations for undertaking this study. First, very few food studies investigating the effects of food advertising have been undertaken with an adult population and the findings have been inconsistent [15]. Second, the potential interaction between emotion and attention and its consequent effect on the effectiveness of food banner ads have not been yet investigated. Third, most studies use upstream brand outcomes including attitude, recall, and recognition, or click-through rates as metrics of banner ad effectiveness [2]. However, as recall and click-through rates may not reflect ad effectiveness in low attention situations [2, 4], this study considers the outcomes of brand recognition and purchase intention in measuring ad effectiveness. Fourth, rather than relying on self-reported measures, this study assesses attention and emotions objectively using eye tracking and automatic facial expression detection technologies, a mixed-methods approach that has been underutilized in the context of online advertising.

2 Literature Review and Theoretical Foundation

2.1 The Customer Journey

Any advertisement is a "complex piece of communication", and for it to be effective, the audience's attention is required [16]. Visual attention is a multilevel selection process where some sensory information is processed deeper than others [17, 18]. This biological mechanism is essential to offset the limitation of human brain in simultaneously processing all the visual information received through the eyes [17]. Visual attention can be measured by visual fixation, a condition where the eyes remain relatively stationary over an object, mainly for optimal visual processing [19]. Eye fixation is obtained from an eye-tracker, which is a device that records where viewers look, how long they look, and other eye-related parameters such as blinking and pupil diameter [20]. Different measures have been used to quantify attention in online advertising such as percentage of clicks [6], number of fixations [3, 4, 21], total dwell time [21], and total fixation duration [4, 7]. Using different measures of attention may lead to different results as these metrics may reflect different aspects of attention. For instance, [4] found that the number of fixations was not significantly related to recognition but th e total fixation duration was. Total fixation duration (total time the eyes remain fixated) is usually adopted as a proxy for cognitive effort and the extent of cognitive processing of information [22]. Although eye tracking technology has been predominantly employed in recent years to explore the relation between attention and food choice/preference, a clear link has not yet been established. Earlier studies have reported on a non-significant difference in attention between savory and non-savory foods [23], while attention was shown to be automatically directed to tasty foods [24]. In an attempt to better attribute attention and food preferences, a model predicting food choice based on several eye-tracking parameters has previously been proposed [25]. Product categories used in the model ranged from healthy items (e.g., apple, salad) to beverages (e.g., soft drink, beer); hedonic snacks, however, were not included in the categories. The findings support the assumption that food decisions, especially decisions related to hedonic/indulgent items, could be a complex process [26] due to the "affectively attractive but cognitively unfavorable" [27] nature of the products.

Several perspectives have been put argued to explain the influence of emotions on food choice and food consumption, including: affect transfer; affective evaluation; affect regulation; and self-regulation. Affect transfer states that in the low thinking condition, objects associated with positive valence induce positive attitude and vice versa [28]. This psychological effect is often observed in food advertising targeting children [29]. When individuals are engaged in more effortful thinking, two mechanisms describe the influence of affect on food choice: affective evaluation and affect regulation [30]. Affective evaluation, or emotion congruence as a broader term, states that a person's attitude or judgement is influenced in a direction which is congruent with his or her emotional state [28, 30]. Individuals who experience positive emotions form more positive attitude toward a stimuli and are more ready to engage in activities than those who are in negative emotional state [31]. Another model of explaining the effect of emotions under thinking conditions is *affect regulation*. This model posits that people in a pleasant state avoid actions that potentially destroy their state while people with negative affect tend to engage in actions that can instantly uplift their mood. If emotion changing cues in the environment are salient, affect regulation is likely to occur [32]. Among product categories, hedonic foods such as snacks high in sugar demonstrate a particularly prominent emotion changing property [30]. Last but not least, *self-regulation* explains food intake behaviors by assuming that self-control over eating functions on limited resources [31] which could be depleted by other cognitive processes. Negative emotions are believed to diminish such resources while positive emotions aid in their replenishment [33].

Given the multitude of theoretical perspectives put forth attempting to explain the effects of emotion on advertised audiences, the lack of sufficient empirical research in this area, and the mixed findings on the effects of food advertisements on adults, a priori hypotheses cannot be put forth. Instead, the following propositions regarding the effects of banner ads on web users are presented to guide this study.

P1. Emotional valence is positively associated with brand recognition
P2. Attention is positively associated with brand recognition
P3. Attention is positively associated with purchase intention
P4. The effect of attention on the relationship between emotional valence and purchase intention will be negative.

3 Methodology

3.1 Research Design

A lab experiment was conducted at a large Canadian university to gather data on web users' visual attention, emotional response, and purchase intention following exposure to banner ads. Anonymous data collection was completed in one week. Participants received a 20$CAN Amazon gift card for taking part in the study. A mixed-methods approach yielded data collected by means of eye-tracking technology, facial expression emotion detection software, and a short online survey upon completion of the experiment. PROC GLIMMIX in SAS Statistical Software (SAS Institute Inc., Cary, North Carolina) was used in the data analysis, i.e. to test the effect of emotional valence, total visual fixation duration, and their interaction on brand recognition and purchase intention. The study was approved by the Ethics Committee of the authors' institution.

3.2 Participants

A convenience sample of 48 adults, screened for normal or corrected-to-normal vision was recruited for this study. A single source bias test was conducted, where data were randomly rearranged (i.e., paired) so that each participant provided responses to only the independent variable or the dependent one [34]. The test results showed that brand attitude correlates with purchase intention for the full sample (n = 828; b = 0.6647) to a highly similar level as when using the paired sample (n = 414; b = 0.6382). Thus, only a minimal difference between the correlations of the two data sets exists (d = 0.0265), hence single source bias is not a threat in this study. Of the 48 participants recruited, 19 had incomplete fixation and valence data. Hence, the data analysis was performed on responses from 29 participants.

3.3 Procedure

Prior to the experiment, participants reviewed and signed an informed consent form, and were briefed about the experimental task. Next, participants were seated in front of a computer. A nine-point calibration test was performed to assure the accuracy of gaze tracking. Thereafter, participants were asked to go to a Walmart microsite and search for recipes that have Oreo products as ingredients. The purpose was to mimic the natural browsing process, where Internet users are usually occupied with their primary tasks. The microsite has a large rotating banner (i.e., a banner that automatically runs ads on a loop) on the header and a vertical banner on the left. The banners display snack products from different brands (see Fig. 1). Sixteen distinct banner ads were used, with each ad corresponding to a different brand (Oreo being one of the 16 advertised brands). The advertised products are mainly chocolate and cookies. Therefore, participants naturally encountered up to 16 brands while performing their primary task. After finding the recipe, participants were directed to a short online survey. The survey asked participants to self-report their attitude towards the brand, their purchase intention from the brand, as well as a brand recognition test.

Fig. 1. The microsite used in the experiment   **Fig. 2.** Automatic facial expression analysis

3.4 Apparatus and Measures

Noldus Observer XT (Noldus, Wageningen, Netherlands) and CubeHX (Montréal, Canada) [35] was used to performed the synchronization between attention (eye-tracking) and emotions (facial expression analysis) data, which are described below.

Levels of attention were measured by a Tobii X60 eye-tracking device (Tobii Technology, Sweden). The device uses near-infrared light to illuminate participants' eyes, causing a reflection pattern on the corneas and pupils. The device's sensors capture images of the eyes and the reflection patterns, which are then processed by advanced image-processing algorithms [20]. To determine the level of attention, an area of interest (AOI) was created for each naturally encountered product image displayed in each ad during the task, and the total fixation duration on each AOI was measured.

Participants' emotions were extracted using FaceReader 6 (Noldus, Netherlands). FaceReader is an automatic facial expression analysis software. It analyzes facial expressions by: identifying the face region in a video image; creating a 3D-model of the face; classifying the model using an artificial neural network that was trained with nearly 2000 manually annotated images [36]. For any facial expression, FaceReader outputs intensity values of six basic emotions (i.e., sadness, surprise, disgust, anger, fear and happiness) and a neutral state. The outputs are logged with timestamps, allowing them to be synchronized with events [37] (see Fig. 2). Events occur when eyes fixate on an AOI, and intensity values are averaged over the fixation period.

Emotional valence (the negative/positive or unpleasant/pleasant dimension of emotion) is then calculated as the intensity of happiness divided by the sum of the intensity values of sadness, disgust, surprise, anger and fear.

After participants completed their experimental task, to test for brand recognition, a list of snack products (see Fig. 3) was presented on screen and subjects chose items that they remembered seeing on the microsite. Recognition is coded as 1 (one) for correctly recognized products and 0 (zero) for products incorrectly recognized or for products that were fixated but not recognized.

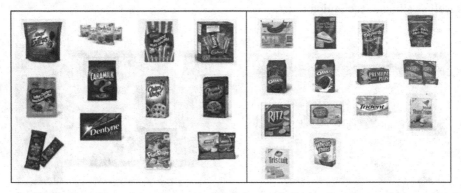

Fig. 3. Brands' products presented to participants during the brand recognition test

Purchase Intention

A list of brands whose products appeared in banner ads was presented to participants, who were then asked if they had intention to buy any of them. Purchase intention was measured using a 2-item, 7-point semantic differential scale: "very improbable vs. very probable" and "possible vs. impossible" [38].

4 Results

4.1 Recognition

Results reveal that participants' ability to recognize brands subsequently to an initial impression of the brand in a banner ad is positively affected by their emotional valence ($\beta = 2.437$, $p < 0.05$). As participants feel more positive when looking at a product in banner ads, they are more likely to recognize the product later. Results also show that the more attention paid to an online product ad, the higher the recognition probability ($\beta = 0.565$, $p < 0.05$). Thus, propositions 1 and 2 are supported (Table 1).

Table 1. Regression results: emotional valence and attention on recognition

Variables	Estimate	Standard error	t value	p
Intercept	−1.002	0.419	−2.39	0.0314
Emotional valence	2.437	1.125	2.17	0.0334
Attention	0.565	0.246	2.30	0.0244
Emotional valence × Attention	−0.795	0.524	−1.52	0.1334

4.2 Purchase Intention

Results demonstrated that attention (see Fig. 4) is positively related with purchase intention ($\beta = 0.758$, $p < 0.001$); hence, participants' intent to buy increases as they pay more attention to the online banner ads. Furthermore, the effect of attention on the relationship between emotional valence and purchase intention was significant at one-tailed ($p = 0.035$). In particular, for fixations less than 1.41 s (based on $1.41 = 1.009/0.717$), purchase intention is positively affected by emotion, whereby consumers are more likely to make a purchase when they experience a positive emotion (i.e. happiness). In contrast, when the visual fixation on the products is greater (fixation duration ≥ 1.41 s), consumers' likelihood to buy the advertised brand's product tends to decrease as emotional valence increases. The plot in Fig. 5 illustrates this interaction effect for total fixation durations of 200 ms and of 5 s. Thus, propositions 3 and 4 are supported (Table 2).

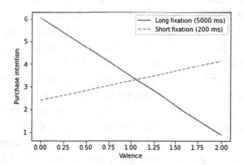

Fig. 4. Heatmap of user visual attention

Fig. 5. Valence and purchase intention, by attention

Table 2. Regression results: emotional valence and attention on purchase intention

Variables	Estimate	Standard error	t value	p
Intercept	2.247	0.345	6.51	<0.0001
Emotional valence	1.009	0.624	1.62	0.1101
Attention	0.758	0.205	3.70	0.0004
Emotional valence × Attention	−0.717	0.388	−1.85	0.0685

5   Discussion and Concluding Comments

This study examined the effects of attention and emotional valence and attention paid to banner ads on the user's ability to subsequently recognize advertised brands' products and their intention to purchase them. Forty-eight participants searched for a recipe on a designated website. Using eye tracking technology and automatic facial expression analysis to infer emotional valence, results from this study confirm the positive relation between attention and brand recognition. Also, an interaction effect of attention and emotions on brand recognition was not found. This means the impact of emotions on brand recognition is not dependent on attentional levels and vice versa. This result suggests the impact of emotions on brand recognition, and, more broadly, brand awareness, even at low levels of attention. In addition, at low level of attention, the intention to purchase indulgent snack food increases as positive valence increases. Simply put, consumers who experienced happiness during viewing of the banner ads expressed a greater intention to buy the advertised product. At higher levels of attention, the opposite was observed. When consumers feel positive but spend a longer time processing a banner ad, their likelihood to buy decreases. This may be attributed to the availability and utilization of cognitive resources during the processing of the advertisement, making the web user more skeptical and critical of the advertisement's message, thereby lowering their willingness to purchase the advertised product.

This study also demonstrates how affect influences purchase intention of indulgent food varies at different levels of attention to banner ads. If visual attention is assumed to be "the amount of conscious thinking going on" ([12], p. 67), its effect could be interpreted in the context of low and high thinking conditions. In the low thinking/low attention situations, consumers' intentions of purchase are in accord with their valence. Underlying mechanisms could be deduced from the affect primacy theory [39] or the implicit misattribution model [40]. The former states that affective responses are first reactions before any cognitive activities. Thus, without further cognitive activities take place, responses are likely to be in accord with the affect experienced. The implicit misattribution model assumes the automatic attribution of one's emotional state to the target objects. For example, without thoughtful evaluation, consumers in a happy state may engage in a purchase decision because they unconsciously link sources of their positivity to the product. On the other hand, for higher thinking/higher attention situations, emotional valence is negatively associated with the purchase intention of hedonic foods. This could be explained from the theoretical lens of affect regulation (i.e., people tend to behave in a direction that improves their negative mood or maintains their positive mood) or the self-regulation hypothesis (i.e., consumption of hedonic food is the result of self-control failure due to negative emotions), although the latter is less likely to account for the behaviors in the context of food choice [30]. While self-regulation fails to explain the phenomenon in this context, it is plausible that varied mechanisms might be triggered for different food types.

For practitioners, the study highlights the importance of setting marketing goals when designing banner ads. An ad campaign for the purpose of creating brand awareness should be different from one created to elicit purchase intention. Also, as shown, varied metrics for measuring advertising effectiveness can yield different results. Thus, choosing the right measures to evaluate the impact of digital ads is critical.

This exploratory study paves the way for a broader research program in relation to disentangling the factors impacting the effectiveness of banner ads. Future research could involve a between-subject research design where the groups are exposed to distinct manipulations of the creative execution (i.e., the banner ad design) or test for 'environmental' factors ranging from the effect of webpage content congruency with banner ad content to the effect of purchase decision involvement on the current understanding as emergent from the results of this study. Additionally, qualitative data could have be collected so as to enrich the understanding of the mechanism explaining the effectiveness of banner ads. Lastly, other quantitative data collection methods may be utilized, including eye-fixation related potential [41], so as to delve deeper in the neurophysiological bases of the studied phenomena.

References

1. eMarketer. Display Ad Spending, by Format. https://forecasts-na1.emarketer.com/584b26021 403070290f93a58/5851918a0626310a2c1869ec. Accessed 28 June 2018
2. Drèze, X., Hussherr, F.-X.: Internet advertising: is anybody watching? J. Interact. Mark. 17(4), 8–23 (2003)
3. Burke, M., et al.: High-cost banner blindness: ads increase perceived workload, hinder visual search, and are forgotten. ACM Trans. Comput. Hum. Interact. 12(4), 423–445 (2005)
4. Lee, J., Ahn, J.-H.: Attention to banner ads and their effectiveness: an eye-tracking approach. Int. J. Electron. Commer. 17(1), 119–137 (2012)
5. Manchanda, P., et al.: The effect of banner advertising on internet purchasing. J. Mark. Res. 43(1), 98–108 (2006)
6. Goodrich, K.: Anarchy of effects? Exploring attention to online advertising and multiple outcomes. Psychol. Mark. 28(4), 417–440 (2011)
7. Hervet, G., et al.: Is banner blindness genuine? Eye tracking internet text advertising. Appl. Cogn. Psychol. 25(5), 708–716 (2010)
8. Acar, A.: Testing the effects of incidental advertising exposure in online gaming environment. J. Interact. Advert. 8(1), 45–56 (2007)
9. Poels, K., Dewitte, S.: How to capture the heart? Reviewing 20 years of emotion measurement in advertising. J. Advert. Res. 46(1), 18 (2006)
10. Lothia, R., Donthu, N., Hershberger, E.K.: The impact of content and design elements on banner advertising click-through rates. J. Advert. Res. 43(4), 410 (2003)
11. Heath, R., Brandt, D., Nairn, A.: Brand relationships: strengthened by emotion, weakened by attention. J. Advert. Res. 46(4), 410 (2006)
12. Heath, R.: Emotional engagement: how television builds big brands at low attention. J. Advert. Res. 49(1), 62 (2009)
13. Plummer, J., Zaltman, G., Mast, F.: Engagement: definitions and anatomy. ARF-Advertising Research Foundation (2006)
14. Geuens, M., De Pelsmacker, P., Faseur, T.: Emotional advertising: revisiting the role of product category. J. Bus. Res. 64(4), 418–426 (2011)
15. Boyland, E.J., et al.: Advertising as a cue to consume: a systematic review and meta-analysis of the effects of acute exposure to unhealthy food and nonalcoholic beverage advertising on intake in children and adults 1, 2. Am. J. Clin. Nutr. 103(2), 519–533 (2016)
16. Rossiter, J.R., Bellman, S.: Marketing Communications: Theory and Applications. Prentice-Hall, Upper Saddle River (2005)
17. Kastner, S., Pinsk, M.A.: Visual attention as a multilevel selection process. Cogn. Affect. Behav. Neurosci. 4(4), 483–500 (2004). https://doi.org/10.3758/CABN.4.4.483

18. Lallement, J.: The effects of time pressure on information processing. Rech. Appl. En Mark. (Engl. Ed.) **25**, 45–69 (2010)
19. Skavenski, A.A., et al.: Quality of retinal image stabilization during small natural and artificial body rotations in man. Vis. Res. **19**(6), 675–683 (1979)
20. Djamasbi, S.: Eye tracking and web experience. AIS Trans. Hum. Comput. Interact. **6**(2), 37–54 (2014)
21. Resnick, M., Albert, W.: The impact of advertising location and user task on the emergence of banner ad blindness: an eye-tracking study. Int. J. Hum. Comput. Interact. **30**(3), 206–219 (2014)
22. Helmert, J.R., et al.: Have an eye on the buckled cucumber: an eye tracking study on visually suboptimal foods. Food Qual. Prefer. **60**, 40–47 (2017)
23. Hummel, G., et al.: The influence of the arrangement of different food images on participants' attention: an experimental eye-tracking study. Food Qual. Prefer. **62**, 111–119 (2017)
24. Motoki, K., et al.: Tastiness but not healthfulness captures automatic visual attention: preliminary evidence from an eye-tracking study. Food Qual. Prefer. **64**, 148–153 (2018)
25. Gere, A., et al.: Visual attention accompanying food decision process: an alternative approach to choose the best models. Food Qual. Prefer. **51**, 1–7 (2016)
26. Wang, E., Cakmak, Y.O., Peng, M.: Eating with eyes – comparing eye movements and food choices between overweight and lean individuals in a real-life buffet setting. Appetite **125**, 152–159 (2018)
27. Shiv, B., Fedorikhin, A.: Heart and mind in conflict: the interplay of affect and cognition in consumer decision making. J. Consum. Res. **26**(3), 278–292 (1999)
28. Petty, R.E., Briñol, P.: Emotion and persuasion: cognitive and meta-cognitive processes impact attitudes. Cogn. Emot. **29**(1), 1–26 (2015)
29. Hebden, L., King, L., Kelly, B.: Art of persuasion: an analysis of techniques used to market foods to children. J. Paediatr. Child Health **47**(11), 776–782 (2011)
30. Garg, N., Wansink, B., Inman, J.J.: The influence of incidental affect on consumers' food intake. J. Mark. **71**(1), 194–206 (2007)
31. Macht, M.: How emotions affect eating: a five-way model. Appetite **50**(1), 1–11 (2008)
32. Andrade, E.: Behavioral consequences of affect: combining evaluative and regulatory mechanisms. J. Consum. Res. **32**(3), 355–362 (2005)
33. Muraven, M., Baumeister, R.F.: Self-regulation and depletion of limited resources: does self-control resemble a muscle? Psychol. Bull. **126**, 247–259 (2000)
34. Ostroff, C., Kinicki, A.J., Clark, M.A.: Substantive and operational issues of response bias across levels of analysis: an example of climate-satisfaction relationships. J. Appl. Psychol. **87**(2), 355 (2002)
35. Léger, P.-M., Courtemanche, F., Fredette, M., Sénécal, S.: A cloud-based lab management and analytics software for triangulated human-centered research. In: Davis, F.D., Riedl, R., vom Brocke, J., Léger, P.-M., Randolph, A.B. (eds.) Information Systems and Neuroscience. LNISO, vol. 29, pp. 93–99. Springer, Cham (2019). https://doi.org/10.1007/978-3-030-01087-4_11
36. Noldus. FaceReader Methodology. https://www.noldus.com/documentation/facereader-methodology. Accessed 28 June 2018
37. Riedl, R., Léger, P.-M.: Tools in NeuroIS research: an overview. In: Riedl, R., Léger, P.-M. (eds.) Fundamentals of NeuroIS. SNPBE, pp. 47–72. Springer, Heidelberg (2016). https://doi.org/10.1007/978-3-662-45091-8_3
38. Lee, W.-N., Yun, T., Lee, B.-K.: The role of involvement in country-of-origin effects on product evaluation. J. Int. Consum. Mark. **17**, 51–72 (2005)
39. Zajonc, R.B.: Feeling and thinking: preferences need no inferences. Am. Psychol. **35**(2), 151–175 (1980)

40. Jones, C.R., Fazio, R.H., Olson, M.A.: Implicit misattribution as a mechanism underlying evaluative conditioning. J. Pers. Soc. Psychol. **96**(5), 933–948 (2009)
41. Léger, P.M., et al.: Precision is in the eye of the beholder: application of eye fixation-related potentials to information systems research. J. Assoc. Inf. Syst. **15**(10) (2014)

An Exploration of Personalization in Digital Communication. Insights in Fashion

Tekila Harley Nobile[✉] and Nadzeya Kalbaska

USI - Università della Svizzera italiana, Lugano, Switzerland
{tekila.harley.nobile,nadzeya.kalbaska}@usi.ch

Abstract. Developing effective personalization has become a priority for many firms. Online personalization is considered a key trend for the future of retailing. Despite the vast research and interest in online personalization by academics and practitioners, its understanding remains fragmented and there is not a comprehensive and updated definition, which is able to capture its complexity. Hence, this research aims to provide an analysis of the definitions of online personalization in order to identify elements in common and sources of discrepancies of the concept. The five key elements that are identified are offerings, knowledge, channels, purpose and contextual factors. Moreover, critical issues that hinder the development of a clear understanding of the topic are discussed, such as the overlap with the concepts of customization and perceived personalization. Subsequently, following a similar procedure, a review of the state of the art of personalization studies specific to fashion in the online context is conducted. The study also identifies directions for further research.

Keywords: Personalization · Customization · Digital fashion · Fashion communication · E-commerce

1 Introduction

The retail environment is constantly evolving due to technological advances and innovative business models. New technologies are modifying the way in which retailers connect with consumers, who increasingly search for products and information online [1, 2]. An e-tailer can offer a wider range of products compared to traditional retailers [3]. As a result, consumers are exposed to many products and a variety of information. However, such overload of choice, both in terms of products and services paired with the related information, can be extremely overwhelming for consumers' decision-making process [3, 4]. Hence, firms are increasingly looking at online personalization, the focus of this study, to overcome the issue of consumers' decision making and to reach a competitive advantage through differentiation [5]. On the one hand, personalization can enable retailers to reach the desired consumer, and on the other, it can support consumers in making informed decisions, in the most efficient and effective way. The relevancy of online personalization is supported both by academics and practitioners and it is considered an important trend for the future. It attracts interest from many academic fields

© Springer Nature Switzerland AG 2020
F. F.-H. Nah and K. Siau (Eds.): HCII 2020, LNCS 12204, pp. 456–473, 2020.
https://doi.org/10.1007/978-3-030-50341-3_35

such as computer science, social science and cognitive sciences [5, 6]. Personalization is also widely adopted by firms as part of their online strategies and it is important to understand the concept to support firms in the allocation of their marketing budgets [5]. Yu and Cude [7] suggest that the importance of personalization is such to impact the definition of advertising, which is attributed from the American Marketing Association the characteristic of non-personal. Hence, personalization is so important that it yields the need for re-examining elements of other notions [7].

The concept of personalization is not new, it dates back to any trade relationship [5, 8], which involves establishing a relationship between two parties, and it has been applied for centuries, predating the internet [9].

In early research, personalization was usually associated and studied with concepts of segmentation and targeting or utilized in the contexts of mass customization and one-to-one marketing [10]. The concept of one-to-one marketing, introduced as a response to the challenge of competing in a global market, is part of customer relationship management practices [10, 11]. Such solution involves customizing a product offering to fit customers' needs. In specific, it requires two steps: establishing a one-to-one relationship and mass customization. The interaction with each customer enables to learn about this customer and others. These steps allow customizing the product, which is considered as a firm's biggest competitive advantage. Nonetheless, the successful accomplishment of such steps requires high investment in information technology to both store and analyze the data [11].

The expected benefits of one-to-one marketing and relationship management drove the interest in personalization and it is in the mid-1960s that IT started to being used in direct marketing to personalize services. Personalization is applied both offline and online, yet nowadays it generally happens on the internet [12–14]. Therefore, this paper will focus on personalization online.

The advancements in information and communication technology enabled to take online personalization to the next level [5, 7, 14]. Moreover, the availability and proliferation of big data, which firms have access to, supported the implementation of various personalization strategies. Hence, personalization in online contexts has been extensively researched to identify its benefits. For example, in social sciences, it has been studied in order to understand whether it provides positive marketing outcomes. Such expectations are supported by the following well-established theories. According to Festinger's (1954) cognitive dissonance theory, individuals are more likely to embrace information that is attitude-consistent and prefer information that aligns with their perspective [15]. Consistent with Petty and Cacioppo's (1986) elaboration likelihood model, messages that are relevant to consumers should increase their motivation to process the information [18]. Moreover, other work from psychology, such as theories on persuasion and influence principles, has been adopted to support personalization studies [16].

Even though personalization is expected to provide many benefits, there is research that shows contrasting results, not supporting this assumption [4, 17]. The effective application of big data for personalization represents a challenge and some individuals respond negatively to it [10, 12, 18–22]. For example, Yu and Cude [7] show that the most typical response to online personalized advertisement, such as emails, is that of deleting it without even opening it.

When referring to personalization, scholars address a wide range of different yet related topics. Moreover, there is not a commonly accepted terminology and definition of personalization [4, 17]. Shanahan et al. [21] suggest that in order to overcome the inconsistent results it is necessary to better understand personalization. Hence, the main aim of this study is to analyze how online personalization is defined by the academic literature to detect points in common and discrepancies. Then, an analysis of personalization in digital fashion is conducted.

2 Methodology

The identification of the definitions involved three steps. The first step was conducted to identify definitions of personalization online, whereas the second and third steps aimed at detecting studies of online personalization specific to fashion. Firstly, through a review of the literature, definitions of personalization adopted in studies focused on the online context were analyzed. From this analysis, the key features that were found to be shared by multiple definitions and the sources of inconsistencies were examined in greater detail. This enabled to extract five elements of personalization from the definitions.

Secondly, a systematic literature review on online personalization in fashion was conducted. To identify the papers relevant to online personalization in fashion the Scopus database was utilized. The keywords "web personalization fashion" OR "online personalization fashion" were inserted in the search of the article title, abstract and keywords. Both the terms "web" and "online" were inserted due to the lack of consistent terminology found in the literature. No restrictions were applied in order to gain a broad view of the existing research in the field of fashion. The search gave 60 results. However, many of the results were not relevant for the study or utilized the term "fashion" as an adjective and did not focus on the fashion industry such as in the studies of Wu et al. [24] and Raufi et al. [20], hence not considered pertinent for the fashion personalization analysis. Seven studies were considered significant for the fashion section of the paper. Lastly, an advanced search on Scopus was conducted. The keyword "personalization" was utilized to find relevant research by restricting it to the following journals, chosen based on their rankings: "Journal of Fashion Marketing and Management", "Journal of Global Fashion Marketing", "Fashion Theory - Journal of Dress Body and Culture", "International Journal of Fashion Design", "Fashion and Textiles", "Fashion Practice". The search gave six results, five were considered relevant for analysis as one of them did not contain personalization as a keyword. Of these five, one was already identified in the second step.

3 Online Personalization: Definitions

The interdisciplinarity of personalization research results in fragmented knowledge regarding its conceptualization, as there is not a generally accepted definition of the concept. Arguably, despite the extensive research in personalization, the lack of common terminology still represents one of the obstacles to fully understand the concept and all its facets [8]. Various meanings have been attributed to personalization, providing a range of different definitions. Personalization does not exist alone but as a component of an overall marketing strategy. Hence, depending on the focus of the study, different definitions are provided [9]. Moreover, some scholars do not define personalization in their study, as they assume its clarity [4, 17, 24].

During the analysis, the first issue identified was that the terms "personalization", "online personalization" or "web-personalization" were often utilized interchangeably. Recently, personalization is mostly referred to as an internet-related concept. Such use of terms creates confusion within the literature of personalization and it is challenging to contextualize personalization research in online contexts [25].

A major source of confusion identified is the overlap of personalization with other concepts. The basic idea of personalization that emerges from the definitions, on which most scholars agree upon, is that of individualization, which is achieved by considering individuals' specific preferences and is utilized as a synonym of personalization. Personalization usually starts with the elicitation of individuals' preferences and continues with a message individualized according to the specifics elicited [26, 27]. Therefore, personalization is generally considered as an umbrella term for preference matching and tailoring, as it deals with the adaptations done exclusively for individual users. It involves creating a match between a message and a recipient [5, 22, 24, 25, 28–31]. Another concept adopted to define personalization is that of persuasion. Being exposed to a match that reflects one's interest, it is expected that the consumer will process the information with more attention and as a result the match should be more persuasive [25, 26]. Walrave et al. [13] in their study recognize personalization as the creation of persuasive messages.

In defining personalization, multiple scholars highlight the process nature of the concept. According to Raufi et al. [20] "Web personalization is considered a process that consists of building models of individual user goals, preferences, and knowledge, as well as using such models throughout each interaction with users to adapt the proffered content to their preferences" (p. 2379). According to Tran [10] the element that the various definitions have in common is that of considering personalization as a process. Huang and Rust [30] and Murthi and Sarkar [32] consider it as the process of utilizing consumers' information to provide the offering. The latter summarize the process of personalization in three stages, namely learning, matching and evaluation. The first stage involves learning about consumers and their preferences through data collection, the matching phase consists of matching the offerings to consumers based on the preferences learnt, and the final stage implicates the evaluation of the first two stages.

Salonen and Karjaluoto [25] highlight a different aspect of the process in the definition by suggesting that personalization is a company-driven process, to differentiate it from customization as a consumer-driven process.

However, such distinction is not accepted by all the scholars and there is a major controversy in differentiating the concepts. Moreover, a stream of research differentiates between actual and perceived personalization, arguing that they are distinct constructs. Various interpretations of customization and perceived personalization are analyzed.

3.1 Customization

A major controversy in defining personalization derives from its overlap with the concept of customization.

A stream of research utilizes the same terminology interchangeably for both personalization and customization. For example, Desai [6] defines personalization as "the process of providing customized information, presentation and structure of the website based on the need of the user" (p. 51). Moreover, Zhang and Wedel [33] identify three levels of customization, mass, segment and individual. The individual level is considered as the one that is personalized to each individual.

Others consider customization a sub-concept of personalization. According to Montgomery and Smith [9] personalization is a more refined concept than customization. Srinivasan et al. [3] refer to customization as "the ability of an e-retailer to tailor products, services, and the transactional environment to individual customers" with the advantage of reducing the time spent searching for what customers want (p. 42). It is referred to as a service that better meets individual customer needs and intensifies competition [34]. Ansari and Mela [18] differentiate between on-site and external customization. On-site, the customization of the webpage content can be performed by the company or by the consumer himself; whereas the external customization approach aims to attract a consumer to a website through other communication methods, whose content is relevant to the individual, such as emails, banners, affiliate sites. Arguably, from such definitions no critical difference is found from those of personalization analyzed, suggesting that personalization and customization are considered overlapping concepts with no characterizing features.

Another stream of research considers them two different concepts [18]. Also in this case, there is a lack of terminology specific to customization. The use of terminology to refer to customization online or offline is not always clearly defined. For example, Ansari and Mela [18] refer to it as e-customization, yet the term customization is also used in online settings [3].

Those who differentiate personalization from customization do so depending on who starts the process. Personalization is considered as a process automated by the marketer, whereas customization as demanded directly by the consumer. According to Schilke et al. [36] the concept of personalization should not be confused with customization and the difference is determined by who is in control of the content. Customization refers to the appearance features, for example, colors, text fonts and display of information. Following such distinction, personalization can be considered as a system-firm initiated process and customization as another form of personalization which is consumer-driven [5, 6, 9, 37]. Yet, also such distinction is not uniformly accepted by the scholars. For example, in Srinivasan et al. [3], customization online is defined as a process starting from the e-tailer. Hence, distinguishing the concepts based on the initiator of the process could be misleading, especially online, where there is a constant interaction between the user and the firm. Therefore, also for customization no definition is without consistency issues.

3.2 Actual and Perceived Personalization

Another concept that emerges from recent definitions is that of perception [14, 26, 38, 39]. Xiao and Benbasat [39] adopt the term of "perceived personalization" and define it as the extent to which an individual believes that a personalization system actually understands his/her preferences. Lee and Park [14] suggest that the personalization of online services is formed by the perception of the combination of the features offered by the store to a consumer during their experience online.

A message produced by a personalization system may be perceived as not personalized; whereas a generic one may be interpreted as personalized [38, 39]. Actual personalization occurs when the sender of the personalized message intentionally modifies a generic one to fit the preferences based on the individuals' data; whereas perceived personalization depends on how the individual believes it fits his/her preferences. Perceived personalization makes it difficult to understand what consumers actually consider as personalization. This is because consumers do not always know what their preferences are or they do not have any preference at all. As a result, they form their preferences depending on situational cases, which makes it challenging to measure actual preferences, causing errors in the personalization process [21, 26]. According to Li [26] actual and perceived personalization represent different constructs; where the firm is in control of actual personalization, whereas the consumer of the perceived one.

4 Personalization Elements

This section analyses the features of personalization extracted from the definitions. Various features were identified and grouped under five broad elements, namely offerings, knowledge, channels, purpose and contextual factors. Additionally, each of these elements can be of various types, generating different definitions.

Wu et al. [24] define web personalization as "the adjustment and modification of all aspects of a website that are displayed to a user in order to match that user's needs and wants", suggesting that the definition is broad-based and that it focuses on the adaptation performed for each individual (p. 2). Arguably, it is a rather narrow definition as it presents only one possible channel through which personalization can be offered online and there are many other channels through which it can be delivered. Lee and Park [14] identify three aspects of online service personalization: offer, recognition and personal advice. Offer is represented by the personalized options provided to the consumer, recognition refers to individuals' personal information and personal advice to the various types of suggestions. The elements identified are discussed in greater detail in the next sections to identify the sources of commonalities and discrepancies.

4.1 Offerings

Broadly, offerings in the definitions can refer to any of the marketing elements [22, 27]. The offerings identified in the definitions are of various types, including products [22, 40], services [22, 30], and content [5, 12, 14, 27, 41, 42]. According to Senecal and Nantel [43] products can be differentiated depending on their qualities, which can be of two types: experience qualities, which cannot be determined prior to purchase or search qualities, which can be identified before purchase. The content delivered can be in the form of communication messages, information about products or services, advertising messages and online content information searches. Moreover, each of these offerings can be personalized at different granularity levels.

The strategy of personalizing messages with personally identifiable information, such as greeting a consumer by its name, is widely used by firms and has been extensively studied by scholars. A name is considered to be an important aspect of oneself and it has the potential of activating self-reference. By increasing the relevancy of the content, it is argued that it leads to information processing [7, 26, 31, 44]. Information such as the name is considered "non-informative" content, this information is not related to the product. However, it is difficult to argue that any kind of information is "non-informative". For example, adding a name could be interpreted as a source of quality and thus provide indirect information. Wattal et al. [45] explore how different types of information in personalized emails impact consumer behavior. Indeed, consumers responded negatively to personal information, such as the use of the name. Whereas, they reacted positively to product-based personalization. Hence, the study shows that consumers do not always respond positively to personalized messages and that their responses depend on familiarity and the type of information personalized, suggesting a difference between informative and "non-informative" content. In contrast, according to Sahni et al. [46] adding the recipient name in the subject line provides positive outcomes, such as increased opening rates of emails, a reduction in un-subscriptions from the email campaign and an increase in sales. Two important factors that impact the type of offerings suggested to consumers have been identified: justification, which justifies the fit between the message and the personal information adopted, and the perceived utility present in the offer. In the absence of justification of the offering, individuals experienced higher reactance and lower click-through rate, yet responses to the message did not vary with an explicit justification from the firm. Hence, to avoid negative responses, it is suggested that firms should highlight the utility of the offering [42].

4.2 Knowledge

From the definitions [7, 10, 30, 32, 40, 42, 44, 47, 48] it clearly emerges that to provide the personalized offerings, information from the consumer is necessary. The knowledge can be retrieved from various sources. It can be based on consumer identity information, consumers' current behaviour, consumers' past behaviour and location [19]. Online users are often required to insert their personal information such as name, address, gender, age. This information is stored to create a user profile. Tam and Ho [49] refer to it as "personalized web content associated with the self or past episodic experience of the user" (p. 870). Moreover, when consumers interact online, data files in the form of cookies are stored, which enable the server to retrieve the information in the subsequent visits [24]. Personalization based on consumers' past purchases is referred to as behaviour-based personalization [40].

4.3 Channels

In the definitions considered, the channels identified were: websites [22, 29], social media, such as Facebook and emails [10]. Yu and Cude [7] in their definition suggest that personalized offerings can be delivered through various distribution media.

Selecting not only the right channel for personalization but also the most adequate mixture of channels is extremely important for personalization effectiveness. According to Shephard et al. [50] the platforms that are adopted to convey promotional media are key in influencing purchase behavior. Furthermore, the literature shows a gradual move of the interest of personalization on various types of channels and not just on traditional channels such as emails and websites.

Shanahan et al. [21] examine participants' ability to recognize personalization on social media compared to other forms such as emails, telemarketing and text messages. The study shows that personalization might be much more effective on social media compared to other channels and suggests that this result could be due to the interactive feature of social media and its intrinsic personal nature. Similarly, it is proposed that through the use of conversational agents such as chatbots, firms will be able to better engage consumers through the use of personalized information [51]. Additionally, the characteristics of the channel on which the personalized offering is presented are also important. For example, Bleir and Eisenbeiss [52] show that personalization increases advertising effectiveness only on motive congruent websites, where the motive of the advertising and the website match.

4.4 Purpose

The purpose of personalization is clearly stated in the definitions. Personalization is a customer-oriented strategy which aims to meet customer needs and preferences [5, 12, 25, 29]. In the definition of Aguirre et al. [12] the purpose is broadly described as "to maximize immediate and future business opportunities" (p. 35). A stream of literature on personalization researches the effects of personalization, in order to understand whether the purpose of personalization can be reached effectively and efficiently.

4.5 Contextual Factors

A few recent definitions have been found that take into consideration contextual factors, which are those factors that are not totally under the control of the firm. The only factor explicitly mentioned in the definitions is that of time. Aguirre et al. [12] highlight in their definition the importance of time in delivering the right content to the right person. Similarly, Salonen and Karjaluoto [25] in their definition emphasize the importance of delivering the options at the right time. Providing the right messages at the right time and in the right way has proven to be challenging as contextual factors impact its effectiveness.

The issue of time is attracting attention in personalization. Time in web-personalization represents a context for interaction. The timing element is extremely important, yet it presents many issues as consumers' preferences are not stable and therefore it demands an understanding of consumers' immediate context [25]. Salonen and Karjaluoto [25] contribute to the advancement of the understudied area of temporal dynamics. To provide a better understanding of contextual effects, they incorporate motives within personalization by adopting the fundamental motives framework. Motivation is an important driver of preferences, hence accurate timing in personalization is difficult to achieve without a motivation match as web-personalization is about matching preferences. Moreover, the effectiveness of personalization has been found to diminish as time passes. Bleir and Eisenbeiss [52] confirm that personalized banner advertising loses effectiveness as time passes since the last visit.

Research is addressing the importance of contextual factors for personalization, such as consumers' characteristics, personal disposition, privacy concerns and emotions as they represent a challenge for firms because they cannot be controlled and make it difficult to capture behavioral responses to influence attempts [5, 13, 25]. However, the integration of contextual factors in personalization studies is relatively recent [25], which explains the lack of their integration in the definitions. Consistent with the principle of equifinality [53], it is suggested that no single configuration of factors such as time, privacy, trust, personal disposition and emotions can fully explain personalization as alternative configurations of these are likely to occur. Hence, the integration of these factors in personalization studies is essential.

5   Application of Personalization Elements to Recommendation Systems

In order to show the complexity of personalization as a construct formed by various elements, the example of recommendations is utilized, as they are widely used by practitioners and they are also extensively researched by scholars. Recommendations are information sources that can be personal or impersonal [54]. The recommendation itself does not assume that it is personalized. Hence, recommender systems for personalization are introduced. Subsequently, the elements previously identified of offerings, knowledge, channels, purpose and contextual factors are adopted to discuss personalized recommender systems.

Recommender systems are defined by Nguyen and Ricci [55] as "information search tools that alleviate information overload by suggesting items that are likely to suit users' needs and preferences" (p. 6). Consumers tend to "satisfice" meaning that they make a purchase when they discover a product that meets their basic criteria, even though a more in-depth search would result in a better offering, as their engagement in a broader search could be overwhelming. Recommendation agents represent a solution to such problem [57]. Recommendation agents' effectiveness depends on the extent to which they learn about individuals and their decision rules [34]. According to Ricci et al. [56], in their basic form, personalized recommendations are suggested as ranked lists of items. To do so, recommender systems try to predict the offering for the customer through data collected explicitly or in an inferential way. The data used by recommender systems refers to a user, items, or a transaction, determined by the relation between the user and the various items. Moreover, three categories of information that can be used for recommendations are identified: individual knowledge about the user, social knowledge from the community of the user and content knowledge about the items recommended.

Various types of offerings can be recommended, such as products, services and information, which support consumers' search, selection and reduce uncertainty. According to Zhang et al. [58] online product recommendations are produced by the system from consumers' past purchases and preferences or from the experience of other consumers with the product.

According to Senecal and Nantel [43] the possibility to provide recommendations is among the best ways to personalize the relationship for an online retailer. They research the influence of online product recommendations on consumer product choices by taking into consideration the type of product and the type of website. Different types of websites are considered: the sellers and third parties websites. Results show that online recommendations influence consumers' online product choices. Moreover, influence is higher for products with experience qualities; while the type of website does not influence consumers' choice to follow a product recommendation and does not affect perceived trustworthiness, as consumers pay more attention to the recommendation rather than the website on which the offer is presented. In contrast, Schreiner et al. [5], whose research focuses on the ideal design of personalized product recommendations in advertisements in different channels such as package inserts, email advertising and banner advertising, found that the channel is the most important attribute in personalization.

In recommender systems, contextual information is defined as additional information that directly impacts the relevancy of the recommendations. Context-aware recommendations take into consideration elements such as individuals' social setting and mood, the weather and the time [5, 35].

Zhang et al. [58] focus on online product recommendations in social shopping communities, which have the potential of providing real-time personalized recommendations. A model is developed to show not only how enabling factors (self-reference and vividness) but also how inhibitors (deceptiveness and information overload) of online product recommendations influence consumers' decision process and customer loyalty. Schreiner et al. [5] empirical results show that product recommendations in advertisements are generally not accepted, due to the quality of the recommendations and privacy. Hence, the knowledge from the algorithm is only one of the factors that should be considered in order to provide appropriate product recommendations.

Recently, perception is being used to study recommendations' effectiveness. Whang and Im [48] focus on how the personalization of a recommender system is perceived by individuals and investigate its effects. The results indicate that individuals, when they perceive the recommendations to be personalized, have higher trusting beliefs and intentions. The interesting finding is that individuals responded positively to the claim of personalization, meaning that the claim itself affects consumers' belief, not only the actual recommendation.

6 Online Personalization in Fashion: Introduction

Fashion represents a vehicle for self-expression. Individuals utilize fashion to express their self-identity and find their individuality [59]. Therefore, it is assumed that personalization is extremely relevant in the fashion domain. Fashion is experiencing a major digital transformation, which is affecting all its facets, from design to marketing, sales and communication [59]. Online channels for fashion purchases are becoming increasingly popular among consumers, hence the growing importance of e-commerce in fashion. However, the possibility of e-retailing to provide mass-information and a wide range of products at any type of customer seems in contrast to consumers' desire for uniqueness. Moreover, it is argued that it can be much easier to ignore suggestions from a computer compared to a persuasive sales assistant in a store [60, 61]. However, the possibility to interact with individuals globally represents a big potential of online shopping environments for providing personalized offerings [17, 23, 62]. According to Jain et al. [63] retailers need to communicate to consumers through all the channels in real-time and utilize the lifestyle data available to provide personalized communication. Additionally, fashion represents an important field for research related to computer vision and studies are advancing the field by focusing on image retrieval, fashion parsing and fashion recommendation [64]. Hence, it is necessary to gain a better understanding of personalization in fashion online contexts.

6.1 Online Personalization in Fashion: Definitions

Similarly to the previous section, the definitions identified in the papers that discuss personalization are examined in order to understand the state-of-the-art of personalization in the fashion field.

Limited definitions of personalization specific to the fashion field were found, mainly because the studies adopted general definitions. Moreover, in some studies, it is not clear to what they refer to as personalization. The major issue of controversy in the studies is the lack of differentiation between personalization and customization.

Koch and Benlian [65] refer to personalization as "the endowment of a promotional campaign with personal references such as greetings" (p. 38). In the study, personalization is considered as one of the marketing mix elements for the customer web experience. Trivedi and Trivedi [66], who study the moderating role of personalization in fashion apps, generally refer to it as a variable that describes the level to which a product or service can be tailored for the consumer. Yet, it is not explained what personalization represents in fashion apps. Whereas, Jain et al. [63] adopt the concept of hyper-personalization: it "works as a tool to marketer to provide the personalized information about the customers", and it involves three main areas: social listening, data analysis and content (p. 3). However, from such definitions, no apparent distinction between personalization and hyper-personalization can be identified and they seem to be considered as overlapping.

Lewis and Loker' [2] study, which explores employees' perspectives on retail in-store technologies including customization and personalization, does not provide a definition of personalization. However, a difference between the concepts emerges: customization seems to be connected to products, whereas personalization to services. This assumption is derived from the findings, which suggest that employees recognized the importance of satisfying consumers' individual needs through product customization or personalization of services through social media.

The overlap of personalization with customization discussed in the first section of the paper is also evident in the fashion studies [23, 66]. Wu et al. [23] define personalization as "the customization of a product to the needs of one consumer" (p. 73). Yet, throughout the study, they adopt the term mass-customization, considered as the co-design of an individualized product between a user and an apparel company to fit consumers' preferences.

Arguably, the overlap of the concepts derives from the multiple elements they have in common, as they both share the basic concept of individualizing an offering to match the preferences of a consumer and they contribute to the idea of uniqueness. In fact, the terms seem to be used as synonyms. Wu et al. [23] state that mass-customized products are truly unique when they are highly personalized. Yet, the difference between the terms is not clear and could be used interchangeably.

Similarly, an overlap between the concepts is found in the study of Kwon et al. [67], which analyses the perception of fashion website attributes, including customization. Kwon et al. [67] define customization as "the ability of an e-tailer to tailor products, services, and the transactional environment to individual customers" (p. 531). The findings of the study demonstrate the importance of customization and in the conclusions it is suggested that fashion e-tailers should focus on personalization in order to satisfy consumers. However, within the study, a distinction between customization and personalization is not clearly identified, hence it could be implied that they are utilized interchangeably.

6.2 Personalization Elements in Digital Fashion

Limited research is found to address the various elements of personalization specific to fashion. According to Jain et al. [63] hyper-personalization enables to provide specialized products, services and information through the use of big data. In terms of services, Tao and Xu [17] identify the subscription service offered by some retailers as a curation service that can satisfy consumers' need for personalization. It is suggested that fashion subscription services, in contrast to other subscription services, are perceived as personalized boxes rather than actual subscriptions. This is because the study shows that consumers appreciate the personal styling feature offered by such services. Hence, personalization is seen as a form of curation, such as hand-picked products for each individual online. The big data derived from consumers' past purchases on different channels provides retailers detailed information about consumers' online search pattern, purchase history, transaction's amount, advertisement clicks and email subscriptions. Such information has a crucial role in providing recommendations to consumers [63]. Contextual factors specific to online personalization in fashion are yet to be addressed, with the exception of Kwon et al. [67], who confirm that demographic variables, such as gender, influence consumers' perception of fashion websites attributes including customization.

6.3 Recommendations in Fashion Studies

The research specific to recommendations in fashion is fragmented. Consumers are exposed to a wide choice in online shopping environments. Despite having easy access to a vast amount of information, the alternatives can cause choice overload. To overcome this issue, electronic decision aids in the form of recommendations are widely adopted by fashion retailers. To assist the customer, the recommendation can be made available directly by the online vendor or by a third party [62, 64]. Moreover, research is advancing in creating outfit recommendations, which involve the recommendation of sets of items. In particular, according to Chen et al. [64] there are two requirements for fashion outfit generation, namely compatibility and personalization. Compatibility represents how the items go together, personalization refers to the match between users' preferences and the recommendations. Limited research on the various types of channels that are utilized by fashion retailers for personalization is found, with the exception of the study by Trivedi and Trivedi [66] on fashion apps. Whereas, Jain et al. [63] highlight the purpose of creating unique online customer experiences.

7 Discussion

Personalization is omnipresent in online contexts. Many firms, supported by technological advancements and access to big data, embraced the trend of personalization assuming it would provide many benefits. Nonetheless, research does not fully support the apparently obvious effectiveness of personalization over standardization. Hence, despite being a widely researched topic in different fields, it continues to attract the interest of scholars, who aim to gain a deeper understanding of the concept and all its facets.

Research highlights that even though personalization appears to be a basic concept, it is difficult to apply, suggesting that firms should be cautious when implementing personalization practices. Hence, in this study, it is suggested that a systematic understanding of personalization is necessary in order to overcome its limitations.

The study shows that there is no definition that captures all the facets of online personalization. The definitions broadly describe it as matching offerings to consumers' needs and preferences, based on the assumption that consumers not only have stable preferences but they also know what they desire.

Additionally, the study shows that in the definitions there is an overlap of personalization with customization, which are utilized as synonyms. Furthermore, the relatively recent interest in perceived rather than actual personalization [10, 21, 26] represents another source of inconsistency. Arguably, the absence of common terminology might be a cause of the lack of a comprehensive definition beyond basic assumptions.

This study utilized various definitions to gain a first understanding of the aspects that form personalization and grouped them under the broad five elements of offerings, knowledge, channels, purpose and contextual factors. Through the exemplification of recommender systems, it is suggested that the combination of all these elements form personalization. Moreover, personalization can be offered at different levels. Although it is assumed that a medium level of personalization should be most effective, an optimal level is not found [13]. Hence, personalization is not just about finding the best match to consumers' preferences, it is a complex construct. Only few definitions analyzed in the study expand it by, for example, including the timing aspect of personalization. Therefore, it is argued that an updated definition that captures most facets of personalization is necessary, especially for online settings, as firms do not have full control over all the elements.

The study shows a lack of research on personalization specific to fashion. In the field of fashion, the relevance of online personalization is connected to consumers' long-established need of individualization, the need to affirm their personal identity and differentiate themselves. Yet, it remains an understudied research area, with no clear definition. Some studies research personalization as one of the variables, such as a moderating variable of satisfaction in fashion apps [66] or as one of the advantages of subscription retailing [17]. However, the aim of the studies is not that of a deep understanding of the personalization process in the digital fashion field, evident from the lack of research on the elements.

8 Future Research Aim

The next step of the research aims to develop a comprehensive definition of personalization and identify specific terminology to the field of digital fashion communication to overcome existing inconsistencies. Arguably, an understanding of the concepts of personalization and customization and their characteristics is particularly important in fashion, as they are widely applied by fashion brands.

It is suggested that it is difficult to differentiate the concepts of personalization and customization because they are part of an iterative process and a constant transition between the two is possible. Therefore, differentiating the concepts depending on whether it is firm- or customer-driven could be limiting. A customer could proactively provide personal information and preferences. For example, when subscribing to a newsletter of a fashion brand, the individual can insert his/her personal details and state his/her preferences regarding the content to receive and at which frequency. As a result, the brand could send a newsletter customized to such information and the consumer will be fully aware of what he/she will receive. Instead, by tracking users' behavior, such as opening rates or click-through rates, the brand could personalize the offering and the consumer will not be able to fully predict the end result. Hence, from such suggestion, the predictability from a consumer perspective could be key in differentiating the concepts, as an individual would be able to mostly predict customization but not personalization because the process of personalization involves greater elaboration of data and higher creativity from the firm.

In order to verify such assumption and overcome the contradictions above-discussed, the authors will adopt the Delphi method to identify specific terminology related to the concept. Moreover, future studies could focus on analyzing the five elements specific to digital fashion to reach a comprehensive definition. Arguably, it will enable to establish stable foundations for further and conclusive research on the process of personalization in digital fashion.

References

1. Fiore, A.M.: The digital consumer: valuable partner for product development and production. Cloth. Text. Res. J. **26**, 177–190 (2008). https://doi.org/10.1177/0887302X07306848
2. Lewis, T.L., Loker, S.: Trying on the future: exploring apparel retail employees' perspectives on advanced in-store technologies. Fash. Pract. **9**(1), 95–119 (2017). https://doi.org/10.1080/17569370.2016.1262456
3. Srinivasan, S.S., Anderson, R., Ponnavolu, K.: Customer loyalty in e-commerce: an exploration of its antecedents and consequences. J. Retail. **78**(1), 41–50 (2002). https://doi.org/10.1016/S0022-4359(01)00065-3
4. Grewal, D., Roggeveen, A.L., Nordfält, J.: The future of retailing. J. Retail. **93**, 1–6 (2017). https://doi.org/10.1016/j.jretai.2016.12.008
5. Schreiner, T., Rese, A., Baier, D.: Multichannel personalization: identifying consumer preferences for product recommendations in advertisements across different media channels. J. Retail. Consum. Serv. **48**, 87–99 (2019). https://doi.org/10.1016/j.jretconser.2019.02.010
6. Desai, D.: A Study of personalization effect on users' satisfaction with e-commerce websites. J. Manag. Res. **6**(2), 51–62 (2016)

7. Yu, J., Cude, B.: 'Hello, Mrs. Sarah Jones! We recommend this product! Consumers' perceptions about personalized advertising: comparisons across advertisements delivered via three different types of media. Int. J. Consum. Stud. **33**, 503–514 (2009). https://doi.org/10.1111/j.1470-6431.2009.00784.x
8. Vesanen, J.: What is personalization? A conceptual framework. Eur. J. Mark. **41**(5/6), 409–418 (2007). https://doi.org/10.1108/03090560710737534
9. Montgomery, A.L., Smith, M.D.: Prospects for personalization on the internet. J. Interact. Mark. **23**(2), 130–137 (2009). https://doi.org/10.1016/j.intmar.2009.02.001
10. Tran, T.P.: Personalized ads on Facebook: an effective marketing tool for online marketers. J. Retail. Consum. Serv. **39**, 230–242 (2017). https://doi.org/10.1016/j.jretconser.2017.06.010
11. Pitta, D.A.: Marketing one-to-one and its dependence on knowledge discovery in databases. J. Consum. Mark. **15**(5), 468–480 (1998). https://doi.org/10.1108/EUM0000000004535
12. Aguirre, E., Mahr, D., Grewal, D., de Ruyter, K., Wetzels, M.: Unraveling the personalization paradox: the effect of information collection and trust-building strategies on online advertisement effectiveness. J. Retail. **91**(1), 34–49 (2015). https://doi.org/10.1016/j.jretai.2014.09.005
13. Walrave, M., Poels, K., Antheunis, M.L., Van den Broeck, E., van Noort, G.: Like or dislike? Adolescents' responses to personalized social network site advertising. J. Mark. Commun. **24**(6), 599–616 (2016). https://doi.org/10.1080/13527266.2016.1182938
14. Lee, E.J., Park, J.K.: Online service personalization for apparel shopping. J. Retail. Consum. Serv. **16**(2), 83–91 (2009). https://doi.org/10.1016/j.jretconser.2008.10.003
15. Beam, M.A.: Automating the news: how personalized news recommender system design choices impact news reception. Commun. Res. **41**, 1019–1041 (2014). https://doi.org/10.1177/0093650213497979
16. Kaptein, M., Markopoulos, P., de Ruyter, B., Aarts, E.: Personalizing persuasive technologies: explicit and implicit personalization using persuasion profiles. Int. J. Hum Comput Stud. **77**, 38–51 (2015). https://doi.org/10.1016/j.ijhcs.2015.01.004
17. Tao, Q., Xu, Y.: Fashion subscription retailing: an exploratory study of consumer perceptions. J. Fash. Mark. Manag. **22**(4), 494–508 (2018). https://doi.org/10.1108/JFMM-11-2017-0123
18. Ansari, A., Mela, C.F.: E-customization. J. Mark. Res. **40**, 131–145 (2003)
19. Liu-Thompkins, Y.: A decade of online advertising research: what we learned and what we need to know. J. Advert. **48**(1), 1–13 (2019). https://doi.org/10.1080/00913367.2018.1556138
20. Raufi, B., Ismaili, F., Ajdari, J., Zenuni, X.: Web personalization issues in big data and semantic web: challenges and opportunities. Turk. J. Electr. Eng. Comput. Sci. **27**, 2379–2394 (2019). https://doi.org/10.3906/elk181225
21. Shanahan, T., Tran, T.P., Taylor, E.C.: Getting to know you: social media personalization as a means of enhancing brand loyalty and perceived quality. J. Retail Consum. Serv. **47**, 57–65 (2019). https://doi.org/10.1016/j.jretconser.2018.10.007
22. Wedel, M., Kannan, P.K.: Marketing analytics for data-rich environments. J. Mark. **80**(6), 97–121 (2016). https://doi.org/10.1509/jm.15.0413
23. Wu, J., Kang, J-Y.M., Damminga, C., Kim, H.Y., Johnson, K.K.P.: MC 2.0: testing an apparel co-design experience model. J. Fash. Mark. Manag. **19**(1), 69–86 (2015). https://doi.org/10.1108/JFMM-07-2013-0092
24. Wu., D., Im, I., Tremaine, M., Instone, K., Turoff, M.: A framework for classifying personalization scheme used on e-commerce Websites. In: 36th Annual Hawaii International Conference on System Sciences, 2003. Proceedings of the IEEE, Big Island, HI, USA (2003)
25. Salonen, V., Karjaluoto, H.: About time: a motivation-based complementary framework for temporal dynamics in Web personalization. J. Syst. Inf. Technol. **21**(2), 236–254 (2019). https://doi.org/10.1108/JSIT-06-2017-0042

26. Li, C.: When does web-based personalization really work? The distinction between actual personalization and perceived personalization. Comput. Hum. Behav. **54**, 25–33 (2016). https://doi.org/10.1016/j.chb.2015.07.049
27. Oberoi, P., Patel, C., Haon, C.: Technology sourcing for website personalization and social media marketing: a study of e-retailing industry. J. Bus. Res. **80**, 10–23 (2017). https://doi.org/10.1016/j.jbusres.2017.06.005
28. Chung, T.S., Wedel, M., Rust, R.T.: Adaptive personalization using social networks. J. Acad. Mark. Sci. **44**(1), 66–87 (2016). https://doi.org/10.1007/s11747-015-0441-x
29. Da Silva, R.V., Alwi, S.F.S.: Online brand attributes and online corporate brand images. Eur. J. Mark. **42**, 1039–1058 (2008). https://doi.org/10.1108/03090560810891136
30. Huang, M.H., Rust, R.T.: Technology-driven service strategy. J. Acad. Mark. Sci. **45**(6), 906–924 (2017). https://doi.org/10.1007/s11747-017-0545-6
31. Li, C., Liu, J.: A name alone is not enough: A reexamination of web-based personalization effect. Comput. Hum. Behav. **72**, 132–139 (2017). https://doi.org/10.1016/j.chb.2017.02.039
32. Murthi, B.P.S., Sarkar, S.: The role of the management sciences in research on personalization. Manag. Sci. **49**(10), 1344–1362 (2003)
33. Zhang, J., Wedel, M.: The effectiveness of customized promotions in online and offline stores. J. Mark. Res. **46**, 190–206 (2009). https://doi.org/10.1509/jmkr.46.2.190
34. Chung, T.S., Rust, R.T., Wedel, M.: My mobile music: an adaptive personalization system for digital audio players. Mark. Sci. **28**(1), 52–68 (2009). https://doi.org/10.1287/mksc.1080.0371
35. Srivastava, A., Bala, P.K., Kumar, B.: New perspectives on gray sheep behavior in E-commerce recommendations. J. Retail. Consum. Serv. (2019). https://doi.org/10.1016/j.jretconser.2019.02.018
36. Schilke, S.W., Bleimann, U., Furnell, S.M., Phippen, A.D.: Multi-dimensional-personalisation for location and interest-based recommendation. Internet Res. **14**(5), 379–385 (2004). https://doi.org/10.1108/10662240410566980
37. Wind, J., Rangaswamy, A.: Customerization: the next revolution in mass customization. J. Interact. Mark. **15**(1), 13–32 (2001)
38. Komiak, S.Y., Benbasat, I.: The effects of personalization and familiarity on trust and adoption of recommendation agents. MIS Q. **30**(4), 941–960 (2006). https://doi.org/10.2307/25148760
39. Xiao, B., Benbasat, I.: An empirical examination of the influence of biased personalized product recommendations on consumers' decision making outcomes. Decis. Support Syst. **110**, 46–57 (2018). https://doi.org/10.1016/j.dss.2018.03.005
40. Zhang, J.: The perils of behavior-based personalization. Mark. Sci. **30**(1), 170–186 (2011). https://doi.org/10.1287/mksc.1100.0607
41. Kalaignanam, K., Kushwaha, T., Rajavi, K.: How does web personalization create value for online retailers? Lower cash flow volatility or enhanced cash flows. J. Retail. **94**(3), 265–279 (2018). https://doi.org/10.1016/j.jretai.2018.05.001
42. White, T.B., Zahay, D.L., Thorbjørnsen, H., Shavitt, S.: Getting too personal: reactance to highly personalized email solicitations. Mark. Lett. **19**(1), 39–50 (2008). https://doi.org/10.1007/s11002-007-9027-9
43. Senecal, S., Nantel, J.: The influence of online product recommendations on consumers' online choices. J. Retail. **80**(2), 159–169 (2004). https://doi.org/10.1016/j.jretai.2004.04.001
44. Dijkstra, A.: The psychology of tailoring-ingredients in computer-tailored persuasion. Soc. Pers. Psychol. Compass **2**(2), 765–784 (2008). https://doi.org/10.1111/j.1751-9004.2008.00081.x
45. Wattal, S., Telang, R., Mukhopadhyay, T., Boatwright, P.: What's in a "name"? Impact of use of customer information in e-mail advertisements. Inf. Syst. Res. **23**(3), 679–697 (2012). https://doi.org/10.1287/isre.1110.0384

46. Sahni, N.S., Wheeler, S.C., Chintagunta, P.: Personalization in email marketing: the role of noninformative advertising content. Mark. Sci. **37**(2), 236–258 (2018). https://doi.org/10.1287/mksc.2017.1066
47. Serino, C.M., Furner, C.P., Smatt, C.: Making it personal: how personalization affects trust over time. In: Proceedings of the 38th Annual Hawaii International Conference on System Sciences, Big Island, HI, USA. IEEE (2005)
48. Whang, C., Im, H.: Does recommendation matter for trusting beliefs and trusting intentions? Focused on different types of recommender system and sponsored recommendation. Int. J. Retail. Distrib. Manag. **46**(10), 944–958 (2018). https://doi.org/10.1108/IJRDM-06-2017-0122
49. Tam, K.Y., Ho, S.Y.: Understanding the impact of web personalization on user information processing and decision outcomes. MIS Q. **30**(4), 865–890 (2006). https://doi.org/10.2307/25148757
50. Shephard, A., Pookulangara, S., Kinley, T.R., Josiam, B.M.: Media influence, fashion, and shopping: a gender perspective. J. Fash. Mark. Manag. **20**(1), 4–18 (2016). https://doi.org/10.1108/JFMM-09-2014-0068
51. Thomaz, F., Salge, C., Karahanna, E., Hulland, J.: Learning from the dark web: leveraging conversational agents in the era of hyper-privacy to enhance marketing. J. Acad. Mark. Sci. **48**(1), 43–63 (2019). https://doi.org/10.1007/s11747-019-00704-3
52. Bleier, A., Eisenbeiss, M.: The importance of trust for personalized online advertising. J. Retail. **91**(3), 390–409 (2015). https://doi.org/10.1016/j.jretai.2015.04.001
53. Pappas, I.O.: User experience in personalized online shopping: a fuzzy-set analysis. Eur. J. Mark. **52**(7/8), 1679–1703 (2018). https://doi.org/10.1108/EJM-10-2017-0707
54. Ricci, F.: Travel Recommender Systems (2002). http://www.inf.unibz.it/~ricci/papers/RicciIEEEIntSys.pdf
55. Nguyen, T.N., Ricci, F.: A chat-based group recommender system for tourism. Inf. Technol. Tour. **18**, 5–28 (2018). https://doi.org/10.1007/s40558-017-0099-y
56. Ricci, F., Rokach, L., Shapira, B., Kantor, P.B.: Recommender Systems Handbook. Springer, Boston (2011). https://doi.org/10.1007/978-0-387-85820-3
57. Murray, K.B., Häubl, G.: Personalization without interrogation: towards more effective interactions between consumers and feature-based recommendation agents. J. Interact. Mark. **23**(2), 138–146 (2009). https://doi.org/10.1016/j.intmar.2009.02.009
58. Zhang, H., Zhao, L., Gupta, S.: The role of online product recommendations on customer decision making and loyalty in social shopping communities. Int. J. Inf. Manag. **38**(1), 150–166 (2018). https://doi.org/10.1016/j.ijinfomgt.2017.07.006
59. Kalbaska, N., Sádaba, T., Cantoni, L.: Editorial: fashion communication: between tradition and digital transformation. Stud. Commun. Sci. **18**(2), 269–285 (2019). https://doi.org/10.24434/j.scoms.2018.02.005
60. Guercini, S., Bernal, P.M., Prentice, C.: New marketing in fashion e-commerce. J. Glob. Fash. Mark. **9**(1), 1–8 (2018). https://doi.org/10.1080/20932685.2018.1407018
61. Bernal, P.M., Guercini, S., Sádaba, T.: The role of e-commerce in the internationalization of Spanish luxury fashion multi-brand retailers. J. Glob. Fash. Mark. **9**(1), 59–72 (2018). https://doi.org/10.1080/20932685.2017.1399080
62. Häubl, G., Murray, K.B.: Recommending or persuading?: the impact of a shopping agent's algorithm on user behavior. In: Proceedings of the 3rd ACM conference on Electronic Commerce - EC 2001, Tampa, Florida, USA, pp. 163–170. ACM Press (2001)
63. Jain, G., Rakesh, S., Nabi, K.M., Chaturvedi, K.R.: Hyper-personalization – fashion sustainability through digital clienteling. Res. J. Text. Appar. **22**, 320–334 (2018). https://doi.org/10.1108/RJTA-02-2018-0017
64. Chen, W., et al.: POG: personalized outfit generation for fashion recommendation at Alibaba iFashion. In: KDD, Anchorage (2019). https://doi.org/10.1145/3292500.3330652

65. Koch, O.F., Benlian, A.: Promotional tactics for online viral marketing campaigns: how scarcity and personalization affect seed stage referrals. J. Interact. Mark. **32**, 37–52 (2015). https://doi.org/10.1016/j.intmar.2015.09.005
66. Trivedi, J.P., Trivedi, H.: Investigating the factors that make a fashion app successful: the moderating role of personalization. J. Internet Commer. **17**(2), 170–187 (2018). https://doi.org/10.1080/15332861.2018.1433908
67. Kwon, H., Joshi, P., Jackson, V.: The effect of consumer demographic characteristics on the perception of fashion web site attributes in Korea. J. Fash. Mark. Manag. **11**(4), 529–538 (2007). https://doi.org/10.1108/13612020710824580

Localization and Cultural Adaptation on the Web: An Explorative Study in the Fashion Domain

Alice Noris[1]([⊠]), Patricia SanMiguel[2], and Lorenzo Cantoni[1]

[1] USI – Università della Svizzera italiana, Lugano, Switzerland
{Alice.noris,lorenzo.cantoni}@usi.ch
[2] ISEM Fashion Business School, University of Navarra, Pamplona, Spain
pasanmiguel@unav.es

Abstract. The use of the internet and of the (mass) media have in some way technically simplified the internationalization processes of companies, reducing the time needed in order to exchange data and information and facilitating the resolution of operational issues. Within this environment, fashion plays a relevant role; in fact, a considerable part of website and e-commerce offers come from this sector. When facing new markets, fashion companies cannot only provide unique and captivating products, but they also need to offer an opportune and personalized communication, able to cross all the cultural and linguistic boundaries that might occur. In order to face this issue a well-designed localization strategy is required. According to Mele et al. [1] localization can be defined as a "cultural translation" and when applied to online contents it consists in the adaptation of different elements such as texts, images, videos, but also units of measure, sizes or calendars. The paper aims, in this sense, to address the lack of literature concerning localization practices in the online fashion environment, providing a first framework on the depiction of the different cultural values on different fashion websites. The present study is an exploratory benchmarking of the field, realized through a comparative research, based on previous studies related to the depiction of Hofstede's [2] and Hall's [3] cultural values provided by Singh et al. and Yalcin et al. [4, 5].

Keywords: Cultural adaptation · Digital fashion · Fashion companies · Localization · Websites

1 Introduction

The scholar Marshall McLuhan in the early 1960s proposed the neologism "global village", today synonymous with globalization, to emphasize that through the diffusion of media technologies the world has taken on the typical traits of a village [6]. This term represents the status of modern men and women moving from "local", consisting in a dimension close to them, to "global", embracing the whole world. According to Magu,

---

The original version of this chapter was revised: The affiliation of the second author was corrected. The correction to this chapter is available at https://doi.org/10.1007/978-3-030-50341-3_43

the world we live in is characterized by hastening, boosting interconnections, which help people to interact with all four corners of the world crossing political and geographical boundaries [7].

Globalization has been accelerated by the birth of the most powerful mean of (mass) communication: internet. Its widespread adoption has simplified the transmission of data and information and has accelerated both general and industry-specific globalization aspects [8].

If much has been done from a technological point of view with the implementation of increasingly innovative devices and software, allowing people to overcome spatial barriers, not all the knots have been untied, neither cultural nor language barriers have been broken down. In this sense, Human Computer Interaction (HCI) studies are constantly needed in order to face the gap between the development of new technologies and their adaptation to different cultures.

In this direction while there is a consensus on the value of the localization and the cultural adaptation on the web for the sales and the marketing sector [9], or in the touristic field [10], this topic is instead under-researched when referring to the localization and cultural adaptation of online contents of fashion companies.

Localization as represented by LISA can be defined as "the process of modifying products or services to account for differences in distinct markets" (p. 13) [11].

According to Pym "localization means adapting features to suit a particular 'locale', which is in turn understood as a market segment defined by criteria including language, currency, and perhaps educational level or income bracket, depending on the nature of the communication" (p. 3) [12].

Some elements localized include date and time formats, units of measure and sizes, color conventions, iconic and legal conventions, currency, address and name formats, contents, sound and video files, connection speed, calendars and also historical, cultural and religious aspects which are shared in a given country [13, 14].

As stated by Singh et al. [4] although the importance recognized to localization by marketers, there is still a lack of competences and expertise in order to adapt online contents to the different consumers.

Furthermore, by now, the topic of localization has been addressed in the fashion field only in relation with the offline retail environment [15], or the cultural differences within the management of textile and clothing companies [16], not taking yet into account the pervasiveness and the relevance of localization/standardization issue in the online and e-commerce area.

This study aims, therefore, to explore for the first time, whether and how cultural differences affect the adaptation of web contents in fashion websites, in order to fill this research gap and to detect whether fashion companies adapt contents when addressing different online markets.

For this purpose, a benchmarking exploratory study, derived from previous studies of Singh et al. and Yalcin et al. [4, 5] and based on Hofstede's [2] four cultural dimensions and Hall's context dimension [3], has been proposed.

As a result, a new framework, which contributes to enrich cultural studies has been performed, extending the research to the digital fashion domain. The analysis has been carried out through a test on three fashion websites: Boohoo, H&M, and Uniqlo (the reasons that led us to choose these fashion brands will be explained within the research design section).

The research is organized as follows: the first section is dedicated to the literature review, in order to propose a theoretical framework. The second and the third sections have been dedicated to the research design and to the methodology, proposing different hypotheses. The fourth and the fifth section describe the results and conclude the paper.

2 Literature Review

Over the centuries, the word fashion has evolved: the term moved from the Latin word factio from facere (do, make) to the Old French word facon and to the well-known Middle English word fashion, which means shape, appearance.

Skov and Melchior [17] consider fashion as a word with two different meanings – clothing and something which is popular, trendy and usually fugacious.

Based on the studies of Craik [18], Lennon et al. [19] define fashion as "the way we wear our clothes, adorn our bodies, and train our bodies to move to highlight the relationships between bodies and their sociocultural context" (p. 170).

Many scholars, that approach this topic, in fact, are more often interested to the cultural and historical development of the concept, rather than on the global phenomenon of dress [17].

Fashion has in fact, a significative relationship with culture: the different perspectives in which we divide the English word culture (which derives from the Latin verb *colere* "to care", "to look after") such as cultivating natural/physical land, taking care of other human beings and entering in connection with God [10], can also be applied to the world of fashion; to produce clothes and cosmetics we use natural materials or we create new artificial ones; we dress according to our style, deeply influenced by our cultural background; we use ad-hoc clothes and cosmetics to communicate during major events of human life – weddings, religious ceremonies, holidays, etc. [20].

According to Hofstede, the way people dress has a symbolic value and it should be considered as one of the outer layer of each culture, since together with words, gestures, pictures or objects it carries a particular meaning, which is only recognizable by those who share the same culture [2].

Following this perspective, fashion could also be considered as a matter of communication: the way we dress ourselves is something that goes beyond functional needs. Wearing clothes helps people to communicate who they are and/or who they would like to be; thanks to fashion and the way we dress, we have the possibility to enter in relationship with other persons and communities [20], sharing (or not) particular meanings of the different cultures.

Given the variety of theories concerning cultural models proposed in the literature [21], we have chosen to keep in consideration Hofstede's model [2] in order to analyze and categorize fashion websites, because, although we are aware of the shortcomings of this research [21], the model has already been successfully validated in different research areas such as in business by Singh et al. and Yalcin et al. [4, 5], in psychology by Triandis [22], in marketing by Soares et al. [23] and in tourism by Tigre Moura et al. [24, 25] and by Mele et al. [1, 10].

Hofstede in 1980, after conducting, together with other researchers, two surveys, the first between 1967–69, and the second between 1971–73, with workers of IBM subsidiaries in 72 different countries, published his landmark study *Culture's Consequences: International Differences in Work Related Values,* performing the largest survey concerning work values and obtaining 116,000 individual answers and covering more than 30 different topics. With this research and the following updated versions, the scholar contributed to define the concept of culture also with indexes and with a big amount of data.

The 1980's model proposed by Hofstede is considered a multiple dimension model, in which culture is depicted in four bipolar dimensions: Individualism versus Collectivism, Uncertainty Avoidance, Power Distance and Masculinity versus Femininity. Later in 2010, in the third edition of *Cultures and Organizations, Software of the Mind* [2] together with Minkov, Hofstede extended his work including a fifth and a sixth dimension: the Long Term versus Short Term Orientation and the Indulgence versus Restraint dimensions. Following to Singh et al. and Yalcin et al. studies [4, 5] in the present paper we will take into consideration only the first four bipolar dimensions.

In order to define our theoretical framework, our research as proposed by Singh et al. and Yalcin et al. [4, 5] has also taken into account the studies of Edward Hall et al. [3, 26, 27], who differentiated cultures basing them on a bipolar dimension indicated with the terms Low- versus High-context.

According to Capece et al. [28] national cultures and country specific values still play a significant role in affecting online consumer behavior within e-commerce platforms, therefore their importance is widely recognized by marketers in terms of marketing and communication strategies [5].

If we consider data elaborated by Marketing Charts in 2018 [29], which show that fashion is expected to reach $765 billion sales by the year 2022, significantly affecting the e-commerce performances and influencing both domestic and international companies, it becomes clear why a particular attention should be paid to localization strategies and cultural adaptation, when firms decide to internationalize. Fashion items are considered a valuable category within e-commerce environment and despite the still evident relevance of retail-stores, online platforms have seen a significative flourishing, allowing companies to expand internationally their business and offering them the chance to increase their perspectives of growth [30].

According to Singh et al., the adaptation of digital contents to local cultures is becoming progressively relevant. The uniqueness of the web as a marketing channel due to its lack of access barriers, further increments the value of understanding of which website's contents should be adapted and which not [31].

In such an international and intercultural context, where digital communication has become ubiquitous, it is therefore crucial also for fashion companies to understand how to communicate products and cultural values, in order to succeed in the digital environment, when interfacing their own market or a new one.

3   Research Design

After detecting and analyzing the main contributions regarding web cultural adaptation based on the studies offered by Singh et al. and Yalcin et al. [4, 5], and on the researches proposed by Tigre Moura et al. [24, 25] and Mele et al. [1, 10] concerning the localization in the touristic field, which presents some similarities with the fashion domain, we opted to apply Yalcin et al. model [5], based on Singh et al. model [4] in order to pursue a first exploratory analysis on the depiction of cultural values in fashion companies' websites.

The study has been performed on websites because Web pages and e-commerce are considered the showcase on the world of a brand, and they are "owned media" fully controlled by the companies, while social-media are in most cases standardized and fashion brands often present a single international account for each social media, not considering neither technical localization practices nor the adaptation of cultural contents.

To realize the present research, the first four Hofstede's cultural dimensions [2] and Hall's dimension [3] have been taken into consideration: Individualism versus Collectivism, Uncertainty Avoidance, Power Distance, Masculinity versus Femininity and Low- versus High-context cultures.

The research analyzes the representation of cultural values proposed by three international fast fashion companies: Boohoo, H&M, Uniqlo.

These three fast fashion companies have been chosen in order to test the model because after a first preliminary review of fashion companies, they appeared to be the companies that localize the most, at least in terms of the most evident elements such as sizes, currencies, languages, media contents, etc. Another reason that lead us to consider these three companies is that these brands offer different Web pages per each country, which has been analyzed in the present paper.

Furthermore, according to SimilarWeb analysis platform [32] in 2019 H&M performed as the fashion company the highest web traffic; while Uniqlo, according to reports by Kantar Group and Modaes [33], is considered among the brands, that have mostly grown in 2019; Boohoo was chosen for convenience for the study, and because it is a brand, that according to its annual report performed in 2019 a global revenue of 856,9 million, up to 48%, clearly showing its grown [34].

The analysis of the cultural adaptation of the three companies has been carried out for the Web pages dedicated to three different countries: Australia, Italy and Russian Federation. These countries were chosen for mainly two reasons: the first one is related to their representativeness in terms of culture and language; the second one is related to their geographical distance, which allows us to better understand, whether and how companies work in terms of localization. Furthermore, the geographical positions in terms of Southern/ Northern hemisphere helped us to understand whether these brands consider or not the seasons of the countries when they put on the e-commerce their collections or whether they have a standardized strategy.

Based on the above-presented literature review we formulated the following five hypotheses.

Considering the first cultural value proposed by Hofstede [2, 35], while Australia is perceived as a relatively high Individualist culture, because people tend to take care of themselves and their close family members and the Russian Federation is considered a collectivist country, because people tend to belong to groups, composed by family, friends and not seldom the neighborhood, where human relationships are crucial, Italy place itself in between; Italy is considered an Individualist and "I" centered culture, with a collectivist influence coming from the southern area of the country.

Based on this we formulated our first hypothesis:

- Hypothesis 1: The Boohoo, H&M, Uniqlo Web pages of the Australian website show a higher level of individualism, than the Italian edition and the one related to the Russian Federation, which display instead, a higher level of collectivism.

The second dimension, which is taken into account in our research is the Uncertainty Avoidance: it refers to what extent a society is willing to accept the unpredictability of the future. In a country where there is a high level of Uncertainty Avoidance aversion, such as Russia, people might feel much more threatened and anxious by ambiguous situations, which occur during life. Also, Italy shows a pretty high score if we refer to this dimension, Australia instead, is placed in an intermediate position. Therefore, we formulated the second hypothesis as follows:

- Hypothesis 2: The Boohoo, H&M and Uniqlo Web pages of the Australian edition show a lower score of Uncertainty Avoidance if compared with the Italian and the Russian website.

The third dimension proposed is the one referred to the Power Distance, which has been individuated by analyzing to what extent people are keen on accepting inequalities in the distribution of power within any kind of institutions. Among the three nations taken into account Australia presents the lowest level of power distance, hierarchies are established for convenience and communications are usually perceived as informal and inclusive; the Russian Federation instead, presents the highest level of Power Distance, in the country the status symbol plays a significant role in people's everyday life. Italy places itself in between, since it is a nation where the Power Distance is generally well accepted in the Southern part and disliked in the Northern area. Consequently, our third hypothesis is the following:

- Hypothesis 3: The Boohoo, H&M and Uniqlo Web pages of the Russian and Italian editions display a higher degree of Power Distance, if compared with the Australian case.

The fourth Hofstede's dimension to be considered is the Masculinity versus Femininity dimension. A high score on this dimension means being a masculine society, oriented to competition and success. A feminine society is driven instead, by the importance of the quality of life and modesty. In this direction, Russia is the most feminine society among the three; Italy and Australia are rather considered masculine countries, because of their high predisposition in showing the success achieved and in expressing the importance of being a winner within the community. Based on this, we formulated our hypothesis:

- Hypothesis 4: The Boohoo, H&M, Uniqlo Web pages of the Russian websites present a lower score in the masculinity dimension preferring the femininity values, if compared with the Australian and Italian editions of the websites, which demonstrate a higher score of masculinity.

The fifth dimension, which has been taken into consideration is derived from Hall's studies [3], which describes cultures as High or Low Context.

High-context communities tend to communicate in an indirect manner, they tend to combine verbal communication with nonverbal elements such as the body language. On the contrary, Low-context countries prefer to directly communicate information using clear verbal contents. Usunier and Roulin [36], which performed their research on the influence of High- and Low-context communication of business-to-business websites, proposed a classification of countries according to levels of Low versus High-context communication styles, where Australia was displayed as a Low-Medium context country and Italy and the Russian Federation respectively as Medium and Medium-High context nations. According to this, we formed the following hypothesis for the fashion domain:

• Hypothesis 5: The Boohoo, H&M and Uniqlo Web pages of the Australian websites show more elements related to a Low-context oriented nation, while the Italian Web pages place in-between and the Russian websites present more aspects which are attributed to High-context cultures.

In the end, the preliminary review that we performed in order to select the above-mentioned fast fashion companies, led us also to consider in our study the following research question: in which measure some elements that are often considered as part of a more technical localization in fashion websites such as sizes, calendars, currencies and pictures (in our case models) [13] are displayed in Boohoo, H&M, Uniqlo country related Web page?

4 Methodology

The study has been performed through a preliminary benchmark based on researches elaborated by Yalcin et al. [5], and based on Singh et al. previous studies [4], who proposed a model (See Table 1), whose aim is to depict cultural values online. In order to make the research appropriate for fashion websites we have slightly adapted Yalcin's framework [5] indicating in italics each modification.

Singh et al.'s method [4] first and that of Yalcin et al. [5] later are based on Hofstede and Hall's studies [2, 3] and have been applied to multinationals' websites and later adapted in other fields such as tourism [1, 25], in order to depict cultural values within the online tourism environment. Singh et al. [4, 31, 37], Yalcin et al. [5], Tigre Moura et al. [24, 25] and Mele et al. [1], in order to validate their methods of evaluation of cultural values performed in their studies a content analysis, which led them to significative results in their area of interest.

In the fashion marketing and communication field as well, the content analysis has been fruitfully performed by Touchette et al. [38] in order to examine features of branded entertainment in apparel brands' or by Morris and Nichols [39] to evaluate the role of magazine advertisements in countries such as France and United States.

Table 1. Application of Yalcin et al. Model [5] based on Singh et al. studies [4]

Design - dimension	Category	Operationalization in fashion
Collectivism	Community relations	Presence or absence of community policy, giving back to community, social responsibility policy, *sustainability*
	Club Chat rooms	Presence or absence of members club, product-based clubs, chat with company people, chat with interest groups, message boards, discussion groups, *reviews* and live talks
	Newsletter	Online subscriptions, magazines, and newsletters
	Family theme	Pictures of family, pictures of teams of employees, mention of employee teams and emphasis on team and collective work responsibility in vision statement or elsewhere on the web site, and emphasis on customers as a family
	Reference, symbols and pictures of national identity	Flags, pictures of historic monuments, *anniversaries*, pictures reflecting uniqueness of the country, country specific symbols in the form of icons, and "indexes
	Loyalty programs	Frequent miles programs, customer loyalty programs, and company credit cards for specific country, special membership programs
	Link to local websites	Links to country locations, related country specific companies, and other local web sites from a particular country
Individualism	Good privacy statement	Privacy policy and how personal information will be protected or used

(continued)

Table 1. (*continued*)

Design - dimension	Category	Operationalization in fashion
	Independence theme	Images and themes depicting self-reliance, self-recognition, and achievement
	Brand or product uniqueness	Unique selling points of the product/brand and product/brand differentiation features
	Personalization	Features like gift recommendations, individual acknowledgements or greeting, and Web page personalization
Uncertainty avoidance	Customer service	FAQs, customer service option, customer contact or customer service e-mails, *chat bots*
	Guided navigation	Site maps, well-displayed links, links in the form of pictures or buttons, forward, backward up and down navigation buttons
	Tradition theme	Emphasis on history and ties of a particular company with a nation, emphasis on respect, veneration of elderly and the culture, phrases like 'most respected company', 'keeping the tradition alive', 'for generations', 'company legacy'
	Local stores and *services*	Mention of contact information for local offices, dealers, and shops
	Local terminology	Like use of country specific metaphors, names of festivals, puns, and a general local touch in the vocabulary of the Web page not just mere translation
	Toll free numbers	To call at any time around the clock
	Free trails or downloads	Free stuff, free downloads, free screen savers, free product trails, free coupons to try the products or services, free memberships, free service information or free app

(*continued*)

Table 1. (*continued*)

Design - dimension	Category	Operationalization in fashion
	Testimonials	Testimonials from customers, trust-enhancing features like reliability seals, seals of trust, and ethical business practices from third parties
Power distance	Company hierarchy information	Information about the ranks of company personnel, information about organizational chart, and information about country managers
	Pictures of CEO's and *Celebs*	Pictures of executives, important people in the industry, celebrities or *influencers*
	Quality assurance and awards	Mention of awards won, mention of quality assurance information and quality certification by international and local agencies
	Pride of ownership appeal	Web sites depict satisfied customers, fashion statement for the use of product, and the use of reference groups to portray pride
	Proper titles	Titles of the important people in the company, titles of the people in the contact information, and titles of people on the organizational charts
	Vision statement	The vision for the company as stated by the CEO or top management
Masculinity/Femininity	Quizzes and games	Games, quizzes, fun stuff to do on the web site, tips and tricks, recipes, and other fun information
	Realism theme	Less fantasy and imagery on the web site, to-the-point information
	Product effectiveness	Durability information, quality information, product attribute information, and product robustness information

(*continued*)

Table 1. (*continued*)

Design - dimension	Category	Operationalization in fashion
	Clear gender roles	Separate pages for men and women, depiction of women in nurturance roles, depiction of women in positions of telephone operators, models, wives, and mothers; depiction of men as macho, strong, and in positions of power
Low context	Rank or prestige of the company	Features like company rank in the industry, listing in Forbes or Fortune, and numbers showing the growth and importance of the company
	Hardsell approach	Discounts, promotions, coupons, and emphasis on product advantages using explicit comparison
	Explicit Comparisons	Comparison of the company to others
	Use of superlatives	Use of superlative words and sentences: like 'We are the number one', 'The top company', 'The leader', and 'World's largest'
	Terms and conditions *of use* and purchase	Product return policy, warranty and other conditions
High context	Politeness and indirectness	Greetings from the company, images and pictures reflecting politeness, flowery language, use of indirect expressions like 'perhaps', 'probably' and 'somewhat'. Overall humbleness in company philosophy and corporate information
	Softsell approach	Use of affective and subjective impressions of intangible aspects of a product or service, and more entertainment theme to promote the product

(*continued*)

Table 1. (*continued*)

Design - dimension	Category	Operationalization in fashion
	Esthetics	Attention to esthetic details, liberal use of colors, high bold colors, emphasis on images and context, and use of love and harmony appeal

In our research the benchmark sample is composed by three fast fashion brands H&M, Uniqlo and Boohoo, which have been compared considering three different country specific website versions: Australia, Italy and Russian Federation.

Table 2 shows the results of our research, also considering the above-mentioned research question and they have been organized as follows: the chosen countries have been abbreviated using "Ita" for Italy, "Ru" for the Russian Federation and "Au" for Australia and the phrase "Represented on the Website" has been abbreviated with the terms "Represent. On the Website".

To perform this exploratory study, we classified each category proposed by Yalcin et al. [5], and that composes our design dimension, with a "+" when the category is present and a "—" when it is not present (Table 2).

The process of analysis has taken place from the 14.01.2020 until the 23.01.2020, considering an average of 10–15 Web pages for each website version.

For the present research elements that are shown on the international websites of the chosen company through a direct and specific link and reference on the country specific website have been considered as present elements in our Results section and they have been indicated with an "*" in Table 2.

5   Results and Discussion

As a result of our research question we can outline in our study that the three analyzed companies Boohoo, H&M and Uniqlo tend to perform the online localization of the above-mentioned technical elements (calendars/ seasonality, currencies, models and sizes).

Considering seasonality as first aspect, we can affirm that this issue has been considered and, in most cases, the contents have been adapted by the three brands.

H&M, in each country Homepage, makes reference to the seasonality of the products or the services: on the Russian Web page are indicated mid-season must have, on the Australian one is indicated the return to school after the summer vacation and in the Italian one the next spring season. Uniqlo, as well, refers to seasonality in all the three considered countries respectively mentioning the next spring-summer season for Italy and respectively the autumn and summer sales for the Russian Federation and for Australia.

Boohoo clearly refers to summer or winter collections within the trend sections in the Russian and Australian Web pages, but not in the Italian one.

Concerning currencies, the analysis shows that it is possible to make a purchase on each company e-commerce using the currencies of the three considered countries, apart from H&M Australia, where customers do not have at their disposal an ad-hoc e-commerce section.

As highlighted for currency section, also in case of localization of models H&M, Uniqlo and Boohoo in particular, tend to change some images and people within them, depending on the three chosen countries.

The last category, which has been taken into account from a more technical point of view is the size: concerning this element, Boohoo is the company that pays more attention, adapting each size to the local units of measure. Uniqlo and H&M instead, provide tables where potential customers can compare the local sizes of the three countries with the one, which have been taken into consideration by the two companies as standard version.

Results related to application of Yalcin et al. model [5] show a different situation in terms of cultural adaptation.

First of all, it must be noted that in many cases, elements such as "Community Relations, Family Theme, Company Hierarchy Information, Pictures of CEO's and *Celebs*, Quality Assurance and Awards, Proper Titles, Vision Statements, Rank or Prestige of the Company and the Use of Explicit Comparisons" haven't been translated from a linguistic point of view by the three companies; the three brands tend to differentiate their Web pages in terms of presence or absence of specific links indicating these specific categories, directly redirecting the user from the country specific website to the international one, or simply remaining on the country-related Web Page but avoiding in this sense the linguistic translation and a more in-depth and detailed cultural adaptation.

Entering in detail in the results related to the aspects of cultural adaptation we can affirm that the hypotheses we proposed in our Research Design, according to Yalcin et al. previous studies [5], cannot all have been confirmed.

The chosen companies performed different results in terms of cultural adaptation and from this first exploratory analysis it appears evident that not all the country-specific values are taken into account when companies address localization.

Presenting each brand and its results (see Table 2), we can assert that from this first pilot study that even though Boohoo performs a high level of technical localization, it is the brand that displays the lowest level of cultural adaptation. Although the brand offers an e-commerce section per each considered country and at a first sight the Web pages looks different according to each country, the categories proposed by Yalcin et al. [5] are equally displayed within Australia, Italy and Russian Federation Web pages without any significative result. The only value which displays different results within the three countries is the Uncertainty Avoidance: Boohoo Australia shows a higher level of this value if compared with Italy and Russian Federation not confirming our second hypothesis.

H&M instead, presents a more complex framework from the cultural adaptation point of view (Table 2): in the H&M case study the hypotheses 1, 2, 3 have been confirmed. The Russian and the Italian H&M Web pages, performed the same results: if compared with the Australian Web page, a higher level of Collectivism, Uncertainty Avoidance and Power Distance is shown.

Concerning instead, our fourth and fifth hypotheses the Australian Web page could not have been taken into account in this preliminary study, because even though H&M presents an ad-hoc website for the country, it does not offer an e-commerce platform so we could not evaluate the categories Product Effectiveness and Hard/Soft Sell Approach respectively related to Masculinity/Femininity and Low/High Context values. In the case of the representation of Masculinity/Femininity values in the Russian and Italian Web pages, H&M displayed the same results not confirming our hypothesis.

In the fifth hypothesis Russia is instead, depicted as a lower context country than Italy, not confirming our assumption.

Results performed by Uniqlo (Table 2) are similar to H&M in the case of our first hypothesis related to Collectivism/Individualism: Russian Federation presented the highest score of Collectivism followed by the Italian Web page.

In the case of our second hypothesis related to Uncertainty Avoidance it must be noted that even though for the Russian H&M Web page the hypothesis was confirmed, for the Australian and Italian Web Pages results have been inverted, therefore partially confirming the overall hypothesis.

Hypotheses 3 and 4 are not confirmed: as per Boohoo the three compared countries obtained the same results in terms of Power Distance and Masculinity/Femininity values.

Finally, the fifth hypothesis shows also for Uniqlo that Russia is represented as the lowest-context country among the three not confirming our last hypothesis.

In conclusion, through this exploratory research we can affirm that as for the study proposed by Yalcin et al. [5] also in our case the hypothesis related to Masculinity/Femininity could not have been confirmed, and out of the remaining 4 hypotheses the two related to Collectivism/Individualism and to Uncertainty Avoidance have been confirmed by H&M and Uniqlo and the one related to Power Distance has been confirmed only by H&M.

6   Conclusions, Limitations, and Further Work

The objective of this paper was to propose a first preliminary step in order to check whether fashion brands perform localization activities based on country-related Web pages.

Even though, according to Singh et al. [4] researching on cultural contents on websites could be considered a valid method in order to help managers to avoid cultural misunderstanding and communication crisis, when interfacing with new markets, and designing country-specific websites, this paper underlined that in fashion there is still a gap when considering the adaptation of cultural values online.

Despite the importance recognized to the localization, the dilemma whether localizing or not, is still open, and there is also an open debate within companies on whether and how to address this issue [5].

This exploratory study is a first attempt to add to the existing literature related to online localization a framework for the fashion environment, contributing to widen the studies on online cultural depiction and localization. Additionally, the research represents a first step in order to understand whether fashion companies keep in consideration the different aspects of cultures, with whom they are interfacing or whether they tend to represent elements related to the culture of the country of origin of the brand.

In this direction, further studies are needed in order to determine whether Yalcin et al. method [5] can be applied to the fashion environment without significative changes related to the peculiarity of the field or whether we need to develop a new methodology able to detect marketing concerns, which might affect the results on the depiction of cultural values in the online fashion world.

In order to further develop this area of study also the limitations of the present research must be taken into consideration: the first one is related to the fact that the present research only considers three case studies so more extensive researches are needed, not only taking into consideration fast fashion companies, but also considering luxury brands, accessories brands and e-commerce platforms such as Asos, Yoox or Zalando, which gained through the years a key role in terms of fashion revenues. Moreover, this paper does not take into account the point of view and the direct experience of marketing and communication managers, who work within these companies, so further studies are needed also to understand how localization and cultural adaptation of values are perceived by marketers and whether they consider it a key aspect of their brand strategy.

In the end, this paper addressed two significative open questions: are fashion companies in the online environment taking into account localization and cultural adaptation strategies? Do they consider localization as a mere technical aspect, purposely avoiding cultural adaptation in favor of a more globalized strategy?

Considering our first study and the chosen samples we can assert that in the three brands a technical localization is displayed, but only a few values related to cultural adaptation are represented, further studies are therefore needed in order to widen our number of samples and to address this issue in a more detailed manner.

This first analysis shows that fashion is a very complex environment and even though it presents many similarities with other fields such as tourism [1, 10, 24, 25], it presents many peculiarities that make necessary further researches.

Annex

Table 2. Results

Technical localization									
Represent. on website	Companies								
	Boohoo_It	Bohoo_ru	Bohoo_au	Uniqlo_ita	Uniqlo_Ru	Uniqlo_Au	H&M_Ita	H&M_Ru	H&M_Au
Calendars and seasonality	–	+	+	+	+	+	+	+	+
Currency	+	+	+	+	+	+	+	+	/
Models	+	+	+	+	+	+	+	+	+
Sizes	+	+	+	+	+	+	+	+	+

(*continued*)

Table 2. (*continued*)

Collectivism

Represent. on website	Companies								
	Boohoo_It	Bohoo_ru	Bohoo_au	Uniqlo_ita	Uniqlo_Ru	Uniqlo_Au	H&M_Ita	H&M_Ru	H&M_Au
Community relations	+	+	+	+	+	+*	+*	+*	+*
Clubs or chat rooms	–	–	–	+	+	+	+	+	–
Newsletter	+	+	+	+	+	+	+	+	+
Family theme	+*	+*	+*	+*	+*	–	+	+	+
Reference, Symbols and pictures of national identity	–	–	–	–	–	–	–	–	–
Loyalty programs	+	+	+	–	+	–	+	+	–
Link to local websites	–	–	–	–	–	–	–	–	–

Individualism

	Boohoo_It	Bohoo_ru	Bohoo_au	Uniqlo_ita	Uniqlo_Ru	Uniqlo_Au	H&M_Ita	H&M_Ru	H&M_Au
Good privacy statement	+	+	+	+	+	+	+	+	+
Independence theme	+	+	+	+	+	+	–	–	+
Brand or Product uniqueness	+	+	+	+	+	+	–	–	–
Personalization	+	+	+	+	+	+	+	+	–

Uncertainty avoidance

	Boohoo_It	Bohoo_ru	Bohoo_au	Uniqlo_ita	Uniqlo_Ru	Uniqlo_Au	H&M_Ita	H&M_Ru	H&M_Au
Customer service	+	+	+	+	+	+	+	+	+
Guided navigation	+	+	+	+	+	+	+	+	+
Tradition theme	–	–	–	–	+	–	–	–	–
Local stores and *services*	–	–	+*	+	+	+	+	+	+
Local terminology	–	+	+	+	+	+	–	–	–
Toll-free numbers	–	–	–	–	+	–	+	+	+
Free trials or downloads	–	–	+	–	+	+	+	+	–
Testimonials	–	–	–	–	–	–	–	–	–

(*continued*)

Table 2. (*continued*)

Power distance

	Boohoo_It	Bohoo_ru	Bohoo_au	Uniqlo_ita	Uniqlo_Ru	Uniqlo_Au	H&M_Ita	H&M_Ru	H&M_Au
Company hierarchy information	+*	+*	+*	+	+	+	+*	+*	+*
Pictures of CEOs and *Celebs*	+*	+*	+*	+	+	+	+*	+*	+
Quality assurance and awards	+*	+*	+*	–	–	–	–	–	–
Pride of ownership appeal	–	–	–	–	–	–	+	+	–
Proper titles	+*	+*	+*	+	+	+	+	+	+*
Vision statement	+*	+*	+*	+*	+*	+*	+*	+*	+*

Masculinity

	Boohoo_It	Bohoo_ru	Bohoo_au	Uniqlo_ita	Uniqlo_Ru	Uniqlo_Au	H&M_Ita	H&M_Ru	H&M_Au
Quizzes and games	+	+	+	–	–	–	–	–	–
Realism theme	–	–	–	+	+	+	–	–	–
Product effectiveness	+	+	+	+	+	+	–	–	/
Clear gender roles	–	–	–	–	–	–	–	–	–

Low context

	Boohoo_It	Bohoo_ru	Bohoo_au	Uniqlo_ita	Uniqlo_Ru	Uniqlo_Au	H&M_Ita	H&M_Ru	H&M_Au
Rank or prestige of the company	–	–	–	+*	+*	+*	–	–	–
Hardsell approach	+	+	+	+	+	+	–	+	/
Explicit comparisons	–	–	–	+*	+*	+*	–	–	–
Use of superlatives	+	+	+	–	+	–	–	+	–
Terms and condition *of use* and purchase	+	+	+	+	+	+	+	+	+

High context

	Boohoo_It	Bohoo_ru	Bohoo_au	Uniqlo_ita	Uniqlo_Ru	Uniqlo_Au	H&M_Ita	H&M_Ru	H&M_Au
Politeness and indirectness	–	–	–	–	–	–	+	–	+
Softsell approach	–	–	–	–	–	–	+	–	/
Esthetics	+	+	+	+	+	+	+	+	–

References

1. Mele, E., De Ascaniis, S., Cantoni, L.: Localization of three european national tourism offices' websites. an exploratory analysis. In: Inversini, A., Schegg, R. (eds.) Information and Communication Technologies in Tourism 2016, pp. 295–307. Springer, Cham (2016). https://doi.org/10.1007/978-3-319-28231-2_22
2. Hofstede, G., Hofstede, G.J., Minkov, M.: Cultures and Organizations: Software of the Mind; Intercultural Cooperation and Its Importance for Survival. McGraw-Hill, New York (2010)
3. Hall, E.T.: Beyond Culture. Anchor Books, New York (1976)
4. Singh, N., Zhao, H., Hu, X.: Cultural adaptation on the web: a study of American companies' domestic and Chinese websites. JGIM. **11**, 63–80 (2003). https://doi.org/10.4018/978-1-59140-468-2.ch012
5. Yalcin, S., Singh, N., Dwivedi, Y.K., Apil, A.R., Sayfullin, S.: Culture and localization on the web: evidence from multinationals in Russia and Turkey. J. Electron. Commer. Res. **12**, 22 (2011)
6. McLuhan, M.: Understanding MEDIA: The Extensions of Man. McGraw-Hill, New York (1964)
7. Magu, S.: Reconceptualizing cultural globalization: connecting the "cultural global" and the "cultural local". Soc. Sci. **4**, 630–645 (2015). https://doi.org/10.3390/socsci4030630
8. Yip, G.S., Biscarri, J.G., Monti, J.A.: The role of the internationalization process in the performance of newly internationalizing firms. J. Int. Mark. **8**, 10–35 (2000). https://doi.org/10.1509/jimk.8.3.10.19635
9. Singh, N., Zhao, H., Hu, X.: Cultural adaptation on the web. In: Advanced Topics in Global Information Management (2005). https://doi.org/10.4018/9781591404682.ch012.ch000
10. Mele, E., De Ascaniis, S., Cantoni, L.: Localization of national tourism organizations' websites: how are world heritage sites portrayed online by European destinations for different markets? Presented at the Heritage, Tourism and Hospitality International Conference 2015, Amsterdam (2015)
11. Fry, D., Lommel, A.: The Localization Industry Primer. LISA, Switzerland (2003)
12. Pym, A.: Website Localizations. Oxford University Press, Oxford (2012). https://doi.org/10.1093/oxfordhb/9780199239306.013.0028
13. Esselink, B.: A Practical Guide to Localization. John Benjamins Pub. Co., Amsterdam (2000)
14. Cantoni, L., Tardini, S.: Internet. Routledge (2006). https://doi.org/10.4324/9780203698884
15. Liu, S., Perry, P., Moore, C.: The Standardisation-Localisation Dilemma for Luxury Fashion Retailers' Internationalisation into China (2014). https://doi.org/10.13140/2.1.1506.4001
16. Angelova, R.A.: National cultural differences and the management of textile and clothing companies in Bulgaria: three examples. IOSR J. Humanit. Soc. Sci. **21**, 29–36 (2016). https://doi.org/10.9790/0837-2108042936
17. Skov, L., Melchior, M.R.: Research approaches to the study of dress and fashion (2010)
18. Craik, J.: The Face of Fashion: Cultural Studies in Fashion. Routledge, Abingdon (1994)
19. Lennon, S., Johnson, K., Noh, M., Zheng, Z., Chae, Y., Kim, Y.: In search of a common thread revisited: What content does fashion communicate? Int. J. Fash. Des. **7**, 170–178 (2014). https://doi.org/10.1080/17543266.2014.942892
20. Kalbaska, N., Sádaba, T., Cantoni, L.: Editorial: fashion communication: between tradition and digital transformation. Stud. Commun. Sci. (2019). https://doi.org/10.24434/j.scoms.2018.02.005
21. Nakata, C.: Beyond Hofstede: Culture Frameworks for Global Marketing and Management. Palgrave Macmillan, Houndmills (2009)
22. Triandis, H.C.: The many dimensions of culture. Acad. Manag. Perspect. **18**, 88–93 (2004). https://doi.org/10.5465/ame.2004.12689599

23. Soares, A.M., Farhangmehr, M., Shoham, A.: Hofstede's dimensions of culture in international marketing studies. J. Bus. Res. **60**, 277–284 (2007). https://doi.org/10.1016/j.jbusres.2006.10.018
24. Tigre Moura, F., Gnoth, J., Deans, K.R.: Localizing cultural values on tourism destination websites: the effects on users' willingness to travel and destination image. J. Travel Res. **54**, 528–542 (2015). https://doi.org/10.1177/0047287514522873
25. Tigre Moura, F., Singh, N., Chun, W.: The influence of culture in website design and users' perceptions: three systematic reviews. J. Electron. Commer. Res. **17**, 312–339 (2016)
26. Hall, E.T.: The Dance of Life: The Other Dimension of Time. Anchor Press/Doubleday, Garden City, New York (1983)
27. Hall, E.T., Hall, M.R.: Understanding Cultural Differences. Intercultural Press, Yarmouth (1990)
28. Capece, G., Calabrese, A., Di Pillo, F., Costa, R., Crisciotti, V.: The impact of national culture on e-commerce acceptance: the italian case: culture and e-commerce. Knowl. Process Manag. **20**, 102–112 (2013). https://doi.org/10.1002/kpm.1413
29. E-Commerce Grows in the Fashion Industry. https://www.marketingcharts.com/industries/retail-and-e-commerce-106623. Accessed 20 Jan 2020
30. Guercini, S., Bernal, P.M., Prentice, C.: New marketing in fashion e-commerce. J. Glob. Fash. Mark. **9**, 1–8 (2018). https://doi.org/10.1080/20932685.2018.1407018
31. Singh, N., Kumar, V., Baack, D.: Adaptation of cultural content: evidence from B2C e-commerce firms. Eur. J. Mark. **39**, 71–86 (2005). https://doi.org/10.1108/03090560510572025
32. Similar Web. https://www.similarweb.com/. Accessed 20 Jan 2019
33. Modaes.es & Kantar Group Fashion Ecommerce Report 2019 (2019)
34. Boohoo Annual Report 2019. http://www.boohooplc.com/~/media/Files/B/Boohoo/reports-and-presentations/4412-boohoo-ar-2019.pdf. Accessed 20 Jan 2019
35. Hofstede Insights. https://www.hofstede-insights.com. Accessed 23 Jan 2019
36. Usunier, J.C., Roulin, N.: The influence of high- and low-context communication styles on the design, content, and language of business-to-business web sites. J. Bus. Commun. **47**, 189–227 (2010). https://doi.org/10.1177/0021943610364526
37. Singh, N., Matsuo, H.: Measuring cultural adaptation on the Web: a content analytic study of U.S. and Japanese Web sites. J. Bus. Res. **57**, 864–872 (2004). https://doi.org/10.1016/S0148-2963(02)00482-4
38. Touchette, B., Schanski, M., Lee, S.-E.: Apparel brands' use of Facebook: an exploratory content analysis of branded entertainment. J. Fash. Mark. Manag. Int. J. **19**, 107–119 (2015). https://doi.org/10.1108/JFMM-04-2013-0051
39. Morris, P.K., Nichols, K.: Conceptualizing beauty: a content analysis of U.S. and french women's fashion magazine advertisements. Online J. Commun. Media Technol. **3**, 49 (2013)

FashionTouch in E-commerce: An Exploratory Study of Surface Haptic Interaction Experiences

Michela Ornati[1,2]([⊠]) [iD] and Lorenzo Cantoni[1] [iD]

[1] Università della Svizzera italiana, Via G. Buffi 13, 6904 Lugano, Switzerland
`michela.ornati@usi.ch`
[2] University of Applied Sciences and Arts of Southern Switzerland (SUPSI),
Via Cantonale 16e, 6928 Manno, Switzerland

Abstract. Fashion is a communicative, hands-on embodied practice. In the digital domain, however, fashion is hands-off – consumers cannot actively sense, perceive and apprehend tactile garment qualities online as they would in an offline setting. Innovations in haptic (active touch) technologies might change this situation, enriching visual and textual content with touch feedback. To date and to the authors' best knowledge, recent research into the significance of haptic information in apparel e-commerce has not involved the use of haptic technologies. This qualitative exploratory study addressed the gap by using a novel surface haptic device to explore potential consumers' reactions to the introduction of haptic feedback in a fashion e-commerce context. The study indicates that providing richer perceptual cues – tactile and visual – with interactive surface haptic effects, adds value to the fashion customer's e-commerce journey, particularly at the information-gathering stage. The finding is moderated by the perceived risk of experiencing a disconnect between the digital touch experience and the actual garment feel.

Keywords: Touch · Surface haptic technologies · Fashion e-commerce · Digital fashion communication · Online customer experience

1 Digital Fashion and Haptic Technologies

1.1 The Digital Fashion Experience

Throughout history, fashion clothing has always been a form of expression [1, 2], an embodied practice which engages the senses [3], particularly touch. We explore the tactile properties of garments with our hands, and we feel those qualities on our bodies upon wearing them [4, 5]. In the digital domain, however, the fashion experience is hands-off. Consumers cannot apprehend tactile garment qualities online, actively sensing and perceiving as they would in an offline retail setting [6].

On fashion e-commerce websites, the tactile properties of garments are suggested with both still and moving images, sounds, and texts uploaded by brands and by customers, should the review feature be available [7]. These cognitively congruent sensory cues act as surrogates for touch sensations [8].

© Springer Nature Switzerland AG 2020
F. F.-H. Nah and K. Siau (Eds.): HCII 2020, LNCS 12204, pp. 493–503, 2020.
https://doi.org/10.1007/978-3-030-50341-3_37

The role and the importance of touch in the purchasing stage of the online customer journey has been researched and its importance debated since the early days of Internet retailing [9], but it is still an unresolved design and business issue [10, 11] with direct implications for online fashion retail [12]. Advances in human-computer interaction and mulsemedia systems leading to more engaging multisensory experiences [13–15] may help address these concerns. Specifically, innovations in haptic technologies [16] – defined as computational systems and applications aiming to *artificially reproduce the sense of touch* [17, 18] – could introduce a hands-on dimension of active texture exploration[1] within the digital fashion experience [20].

Haptics-based systems include graspable, wereable, contactless, mid-air and surface solutions which enable human-computer interaction by exploiting kinesthetics and/or tactile modalities [21]. This study exploits developments in surface haptics and makes use of an innovative haptics device, described in detail below.

1.2   Researching Surface Haptics for E-commerce: *FashionTouch*

Recent research into the significance of haptic information in apparel e-commerce [22–25] has not involved the use of surface haptic technologies for active texture exploration. The objective of the study was to address this gap with a pragmatic qualitative research design focused on exploring and describing participants' responses to the introduction of dynamic haptic surface effects in the context of a simulated fashion e-commerce interaction experience.

2   *FashionTouch* Research Design and Methodology

2.1   *FashionTouch* Design Using TanvasTouch®

The research was designed using TanvasTouch (www.tanvas.co) – an innovative surface haptic device recently made available for academic research. The device requires the interaction of both hardware and proprietary software and is safe for use in an experimental setting. Two such devices were used for this research.

TanvasTouch enables precise fingertip tracking and simultaneous surface haptic rendering. It can be programmed to accurately deliver real-time variable-intensity friction and electrostatic haptic feedback within a specific area of the touchscreen. Thus, it is possible to map specific textures and effects onto an image and to feel these effects with a swipe of a finger on the touch-enabled surface.

Using TanvasTouch to deliver dynamic haptic surface effects in the context of a simulated fashion e-commerce experience required the design of a mock fashion website featuring real clothes. Five women's and three men's garments were purposefully selected based on diverse material and surface characteristics. The garments were photographed on real models. The final photoshoot selection included five different full-color images of each item, plus a detailed image of the corresponding material, akin to the zoom-in garment images available on most fashion websites.

---

[1] Active texture exploration is defined as "the ability to infer information about object texture by using one's fingertips to scan a surface" [19].

A simple website was designed, which included a home page showcasing images of the eight garments – as shown in Fig. 1 – each leading to a dedicated garment page.

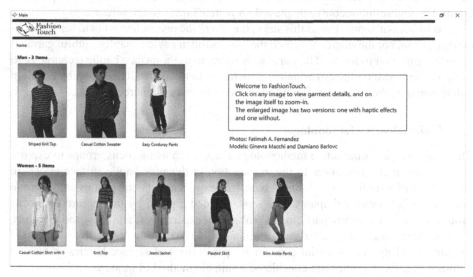

Fig. 1. *FashionTouch* mock-website home page

The garment page featured descriptive text, one main image, and four thumbnails. Clicking on the main garment image opened a zoom-in window with interactive haptic effects, shown in Fig. 2. An alternative, effect-free window was also provided.

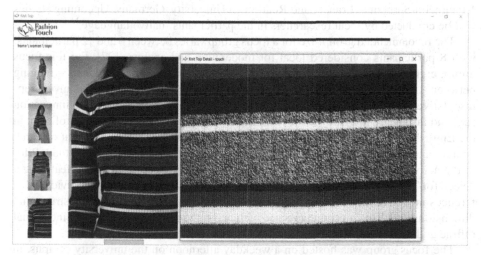

Fig. 2. The zoom-in interactive area on the *FashionTouch* application

To achieve the effects, intermediate working steps were required. Each zoom-in image was refined and contrasting textures enhanced in black and white using Photoshop.

The images were then uploaded to TanvasTouch's proprietary software environment, and surface texture characteristics matched with ad-hoc haptic feedback effects. The finished, full-color mock website – entitled *FashionTouch* – was uploaded locally on two personal computers and simultaneously displayed on paired TanvasTouch screens.

It is important to note that at this stage, the aim of the research was not to test the technology per se, nor the degree to which the TanvasTouch device enables faithful garment texture replication to touch. The purpose is rather to use a surface haptic technology to design a simulated online environment enriched with tactile feedback, thereby enabling a discussion on the relevance of haptics in the fashion e-commerce context.

2.2 *FashionTouch* Methodology

The study adopts a qualitative methodological approach using focus groups to explore and describe users' responses to the introduction of dynamic haptic surface effects in the context of a simulated fashion e-commerce experience. Focus groups are informal discussions between participants on a topic decided a priori by the researcher. Focus groups allow for exploring participants' subjective experiences, attitudes, and opinions, thereby generating data that is emic in nature [26]. As the intent of this research is to gain knowledge on potential consumers' perceptions of surface haptics in fashion e-commerce, focus groups are considered a suitable method of inquiry.

To access multiple perspectives on a specific topic, qualitative research usually relies on four to six focus groups [26]. This paper describes the findings from the first focus group of the study, which was held (in English) at USI – Università della Svizzera italiana, Switzerland, in December 2019. Additional focus groups have been planned in collaboration with the University of Applied Sciences and Arts of Southern Switzerland (SUPSI), Switzerland; ISEM Fashion Business School, Madrid, Spain; Université Paris 1 Panthéon-Sorbonne, France; and Reutlingen University, Germany. Upcoming studies will be conducted by local researchers in the participants' native language.

The recommended group size for a focus group varies between 6 and 12 participants, with 8 participants considered ideal for moderation and analysis [27]. For this focus group, eight volunteers were recruited from Master students. These students – ranging between 22 to 27 year of age, all female except one – are a homogeneous group representative of a segment of young, technology-savvy consumers attentive to innovation [28] and fashion trends. They come from international backgrounds and are proficient in the English language. Before the activity, each volunteer was informed about research content and methodology and their informed consent was collected for the study. Prior to the activity each volunteer also completed an anonymous questionnaire featuring a "Need for Touch" (NFT) 12-item scale. The scale is "designed to measure individual differences in preference for haptic (touch) information" along autotelic and instrumental dimensions [29]. The questionnaire also included some questions concerning individual offline and online shopping behavior.

The focus group was hosted on a weekday afternoon on the university campus, in a dedicated space. Food and beverages were provided. Before the focus group, each participant had the opportunity to individually interact with the touchscreen application for about ten to fifteen minutes, freely navigating between images and exploring haptic effects. After the interaction, and with the device set aside, each participant was asked to quantitatively evaluate the influence individual effects may have had on the perception of each corresponding garment. A researcher was in attendance during the entire activity.

The focus group lasted about an hour and a half. One of the researchers observed the proceedings, whilst the other moderated, following a question protocol compiled a priori. Although the focus group method emphasizes free participant exploration of a given topic, the question protocol facilitates a semi-structured group discussion steered in the direction of answering the research question [26, 27]. Thus, the discussion progressed from an exploration of participants' relationship to fashion and clothing to the elicitation of specific factors – including the availability of visual and textual information – affecting participants' self-declared attitudes and behaviors with regards to offline and online fashion shopping. Finally, the discussion focused on volunteers' perception of the *FashionTouch* experience. During the last half hour of the focus group, the moderator used the actual garments as prompts, thereby provoking a lively debate regarding surface haptics renderings and corresponding originals. In closing, volunteers shared their opinion on potential uses of surface haptic technology in the context of fashion e-commerce.

During the discussion, participants were asked to jot their ideas down on a notepad as well as to share them out loud. The entire proceedings were audio-recorded and subsequently transcribed. The data was triangulated with participants' handwritten notes and the researcher's own live observations. Individual and group-level data was analyzed using a thematic analysis method, defined as the process of "identifying, analyzing and reporting patterns in the data" [31]. The resulting document – a qualitative, low-inference description [30] of emergent themes – was discussed and reviewed by both researchers. The focus group's findings are reported in the following section.

3 First *FashionTouch* Research Findings and Limitations

3.1 *FashionTouch* Focus Group: Emergent Themes

Several themes emerged from the analysis of the focus group discussion transcript, as described below and in the participants' own words wherever possible.

Growing up by Dressing Up: Fashioning the Creative Self. Focus group participants describe their relationship with fashion and dress as intrinsically bound to their personality and way of being. Fashion is "an inspiration and part of [...] daily life," as well as a "creative outlet" for individual expression. Embodying fashion is a means to affect and control "how I want to be or feel" because clothes "are actually part of my feelings, my emotions." During childhood, dress enables a measure of independence, from "going around and deciding what to wear, what to buy" to making deliberate choices about "the way you want to present [yourself]" whether in "loud and colorful" clothing chosen as an act of rebellion, or princess-like "Disney movie" outfits with which to "walk around the house." Through dress, participants gradually discovered "new aspects" of their personality. As adults, getting dressed is both outward expression – how "to be seen for that day" – and playful fantasy – "a costume party [...] just in your head." From childhood to adulthood, dressing up is "something creative and fun." Finally, focus group participants perceive fashion as a form of art, a creative space where "a lot of things, new things [are] happening." Fashion is "innovation."

Investing vs. Wasting: Balancing the Fashion Act. Focus group participants describe their approach to fashioning a personal look or style as an ongoing strategic activity, which entails careful planning and financial discipline as well as creative vision. For one participant, building a fashion closet is a deliberate, careful form of long-term investment centered upon a coherent "style or look." Spending more now "so that I know for sure that I can wear [clothes] for the following 5 to 10 years" "is more of an investment than a waste of money" because "after a few years you have a collection of a few very good pieces and then you can use them more." Buying into fashion trends is "a waste" if "I just wear it one season and then I cannot wear it anymore," regardless of the expenditure – "if it was ten euros or 100." Other participants lament having to make compromises between "standing out" and owning "a valuable classic piece so that I have something to wear at all" because of budgetary concerns ("it's the price or the money that I am limited in"). Looking for less expensive garments in second-hand stores is one way to creatively balance the fashion act, to "find things that no one would wear now, and combine them with basic things" in order to "explore" a very personal look or style.

The Shopping Experience: From Showrooming to Webrooming. Focus group participants manage their journey between retail and e-commerce with pragmatic ease. They reluctantly admit to being frequent shoppers, as confirmed by questionnaire responses (Table 1).

Table 1. Participants' shopping frequency based on questionnaire responses

Times shopped per year	1 to 5	5 to 10	10 to 20	20 or more
N. of participants shopping in offline retail	0	4	2	2
N. of participants shopping online	2	4	2	0

Participants also described both *showrooming* and *webrooming* behaviors. Showrooming is the consumer practice of trying out the products they want in a physical store before buying them online. Webrooming is the opposite, i.e., researching products online before buying them in a physical store [32]. As a group, they tend to privilege showrooming – visiting physical venues to explore, try on and evaluate items, but shopping for them online. They shop online when stores are not accessible, or if they cannot find a product and/or size, knowing that "you can order two different sizes and send it back and it's all for free." In fact, online shopping offers "more options at once" such as greater product range, size availability, delivery options, and lower prices. However, participants also describe webrooming: "sometimes I would […] browse online first, [in] a specific store, to see if there is something interesting; and then I would go to the store" (at times with the article number) "and look for exactly *these* items." Shopping in a physical store is a fun, social activity that affords instant gratification ("having it right after paying for it") but shopping online can also be a social activity ("we just send each other messages") and "way cheaper." As mentioned before, for most participants "price is the biggest factor" affecting the choice of where to buy.

Evaluating Online Information: A Question of Trust. As a group, participants tend to go online to look for "what is new" in fashion. Consistent with their strategic approach to fashion buying, they all tend to check price and discounts, payment terms, shipping costs and service options, such as free returns. However, as individuals, they differ in terms of the kind of information they pay the most attention to. Some participants carefully check product size and length (comparing it to model height) as well as sizing guides ("I measure myself every centimeter and look at the size guide"); others don't, "because I know I can return it. So, I don't check." A few participants pay careful attention to product composition and performance ("if you get sweaty, it stinks, so it's better to choose real cotton") and product care instructions. Participants carefully examine visuals to understand "how [a product] sits on the model," but tend to consider images limited if not misleading ("I know that it will look different on me"). One participant is annoyed that she "always [has] to compromise and just trust" the visual and textual information provided by the brand. Customer reviews are either considered helpful ("the only thing I really trust") or paid-for "fake[s]." Shopping online can be a disappointing experience when "most of the things did not fit, the fabric was not how I expected [...]." Buying "things which don't necessarily change" like cosmetics, basic shoes and fashion accessories is less risky than buying fashion items such as clothing. Regardless of how much information brands may provide, garments are "still something you need to feel on your body."

3.2   *FashionTouch* Focus Group: The Interaction Experience

The Interaction Experience. The focal part of the activity is discussed in the second half of the focus group. Participants are first asked to recall and describe their interaction with the technology. Several elements emerge:

Participants put the technology to the test. "And a thing that I did is to touch the other part of the screen and then go back to the item to see the difference, to really perceive the difference of the technology and of the other part of the screen." "And then what I figured is the vibrations only come upon the contrast, because most of the items were black and grey, black and white, so only when there was the contrast of stitching, for example, then you would feel the vibrations." "I tried to touch with my entire hand but then only one finger was identified."

Participants compare the surface interaction experience with multidimensional garment manipulation, such as handling and grasping materials, rubbing fabric between the thumb and index fingers or several fingers, applying pressure to a garment and stretching it. Participants recall "pushing towards something" which is not like "grabbing [...] something between your hands – you cannot feel the thickness of the product." Stroking the surface with one finger "is not enough for touch. There must be something between two fingers, between the thumb and [...] the index finger." "When I touch something, I want to know how stretchy it is" or "to massage it. Grab it in my hand, squeeze it, take it out." Participants consider it unusual, even "weird," to explore a garment just by stroking its surface, as opposed to handling it: "I am not used to touching a thing like that."

Participants conflate garment information (visuals and text) and corresponding effects, evaluating them contextually or in comparison to real-life experience: "I could not recognize the fabric from the knowledge that I have [about] how wool feels like." "I think *we need to know* all the different feelings, *touchings* [*sic*] to then make sense out of what is what." Certain interactions are judged more effective than others in triggering "some sense of how the garment would feel like." "When I touched – I think it was the sweater for men – with the little bumps – [I] could actually […] get a sense of what it would be like to touch it." "You could actually really feel … the little jumps [in the men's corduroy pants]." "The white [stiching] lines, I could really feel them." Opinions are otherwise mixed: "the blouse was […] too hard for a [cotton] blouse," says one participant, whereas another insists that "when you stroked over the little dots you could feel the bumps, so there was a difference." When prompted with the real items, participants agree that three out of eight haptic feedback effects had a strong, even "over-amplified" correlation with the real-life feel of corresponding garments: the ribbed corduroy pants, the knit sweater and the jeans jacket with contrast stitching. Three items were judged as having no correlation, and two items as being somewhere in between.

Participants have Mixed Opinions Regarding the *FashionTouch* Experience. Several participants were "super excited to have a try" but then were "disappointed because I didn't know what to expect but then secretly in my head, I did expect *something*." Others are disappointed with the artifact itself, which is "just a screen." Some participants recall feeling frustrated and confused by the experience, and distrustful towards the technology because it is "not reliable to me, not true." Although some "would not use it because it's so misleading" others think it may be "helpful for feeling the structure" of a garment's surface. One participant observes that the technology cannot replicate "being in the store, touching something" because "to be fair" online shopping is not like going to a shop – "it's online shopping" and "not [a] substitute [for] a shopping experience."

Participants are Intrigued by the Technology. Overall, participants seem to share a positive perspective on the technology's innovative potential: "it's a great idea" which "can be improved to the point where it can be used widely" to "definitely" improve the online experience. As such, it is perceived as a technology with commercial potential, one which "could be developed" and that "a company can monetize on."

3.3 Limitations of This First *FashionTouch* Study

Study findings point to some limitations in research design, which are also opportunities for improvement and enrichment in the upcoming research steps. Firstly, focus group volunteers came from diverse international backgrounds. Although English-language proficiency is a requirement for Master studies, it is not the volunteers' native language. Thus, they may have had some difficulty in expressing certain concepts during the discussion. Secondly, the fact that the moderator was a professor may have caused participants to be reticent, at first, in expressing their opinions. Thirdly, the introduction of garments prompted a lively exchange amongst participants. This focus group section is difficult to analyze because participants spoke excitedly and simultaneously with each other. Video recording of this specific phase might have yielded more comprehensible visual as well as verbal data and might be taken into consideration for upcoming focus groups. Finally, in this study, results are derived almost exclusively from focus group data. Upcoming studies will integrate results from the questionnaires, thereby providing opportunities for triangulation.

4 *FashionTouch* Research Discussion and Conclusions

4.1 *FashionTouch*: Interpretation

Findings of the first *FashionTouch* study indicate focus group participants are interested in the sensory enrichment which surface haptic technologies might bring to the fashion e-commerce experience. They are savvy omnichannel shoppers, expressing a degree of critical weariness with regards to product information found online. Therefore, the finding is moderated by this specific customer segment's perceived risk of experiencing a disconnect – were the technology to be implemented in the future – between the digital touch feedback experience and the actual garment feel.

4.2 Practical Implications, Originality and Value

This initial exploratory study sets the groundwork for upcoming research using surface haptic technology in a fashion e-commerce context in collaboration with an international network of partner universities. The second stage of the research will capitalize on the current study's learnings, and the research design will be improved as needed. The study's initial and future insights on innovations involving surface haptic technologies in fashion digital communication will be shared to the benefit of the wider academic community. On a local level, they will also serve as stimulus for discussion and learning within the publicly funded, applied higher education communities, particularly in the context of fashion design and sartorial schools.

During the first phase of the research both the local media [33] and the fashion industry have expressed considerable interest in the practical implications of the research on touch for fashion e-commerce, confirming the originality and value of the ongoing study.

4.3 Conclusion

The *FashionTouch* research explores consumer perspectives on surface haptic technologies for fashion e-commerce by exploiting TanvasTouch, an innovative haptic technology device. The technology is still in the development stage and not yet available for widespread commercial use; when and if it will be available to consumers it might be in a radically altered or modified form. Therefore, the *FashionTouch* study makes an early-stage, original and – hopefully – a valuable contribution to the growing literature on multisensory human-computer interaction [34] and specifically, on the sense of touch in the digital fashion communication domain.

References

1. Kalbaska, N., Sádaba, T., Cantoni, L.: Editorial: Fashion communication: Between tradition and digital transformation. Studies in Commun. Sci. (2018). https://doi.org/10.24434/j.scoms. 2018.02.005
2. Geczy, A., Karaminas, V.: The End of Fashion: Clothing and Dress in the Age of Globalization. Bloomsbury, London (2019)
3. Entwistle, J.: The Fashioned Body: Fashion, Dress and Modern Social Theory. Polity Press, Cambridge (2015)
4. Field, T.: Touch. MIT Press, Cambridge (2014)
5. Lederman, S.J., Klatzky, R.L.: Haptic perception: a tutorial. Atten. Percept. Psychophys. **71**, 1439–1459 (2009)
6. Shinkle, E.: Fashion's Digital Body Seeing and Feeling in Fashion Interactives. In: Bartlett, D., Cole, S., Rocamora, A. (eds.) Fashion Media: Past and Present. Bloomsbury Academic, London (2013)
7. Huang, J., Guo, Y., Wang, C., Yan, L.: You touched it and I'm relieved! The effect of online review's tactile cues on consumer's purchase intention. J. Contemp. Mark. Sci. **2**, 155–175 (2019). https://doi.org/10.1108/JCMARS-01-2019-0005
8. Jansson-Boyd, C.V.: Perception and consumption Touch, multisensory integration and congruency. In: Jansson-Boyd, C.V., Zawisza, M.J. (eds.) Routledge International Handbook of Consumer Psychology, pp. 85–101. Routledge, Taylor & Francis Group, London (2017)
9. Citrin, A.V., Stem, D.E., Spangenberg, E.R., Clark, M.J.: Consumer need for tactile input. J. Bus. Res. **56**, 915–922 (2003). https://doi.org/10.1016/S0148-2963(01)00278-8
10. Ackerman, J.M.: Implications of haptic experience for product and environmental design. In: Batra, R., Seifert, C., Brei, D. (eds.) The psychology of design: creating consumer appeal, pp. 3–25. Routledge, New York (2016)
11. Liu, W., Batra, R., Wang, H.: Product touch and consumers' online and offline buying: the role of mental representation. J. Retail. **93**, 369–381 (2017). https://doi.org/10.1016/j.jretai. 2017.06.003
12. Manzano, R., Gavilan, D.: Autotelic and instrumental need for touch: searching for and purchasing apparel online. Int. J. Econ. Manage. Sci. **05**, 2 (2016)
13. Petit, O., Velasco, C., Spence, C.: Digital sensory marketing: integrating new technologies into multisensory online experience. J. Interact. Mark. **45**, 42–61 (2019). https://doi.org/10. 1016/j.intmar.2018.07.004
14. Covaci, A., Zou, L., Tal, I., Muntean, G.-M., Ghinea, G.: Is multimedia multisensorial? - A review of mulsemedia systems. ACM Comput. Surv. **51**, 1–35 (2018). https://doi.org/10. 1145/3233774
15. Chung, S., Kramer, T., Wong, E.M.: Do touch interface users feel more engaged? The impact of input device type on online shoppers' engagement, affect, and purchase decisions. Psychol. Mark. **35**, 795–806 (2018). https://doi.org/10.1002/mar.21135
16. Gallace, A., Spence, C.: In touch with the future: The sense of touch from cognitive neuroscience to virtual reality. Oxford University Press, Oxford (2014)
17. Bossomaier, T.R.J.: Introduction to the Senses: from Biology to Computer Science. Cambridge University Press, Cambridge (2012)
18. Culbertson, H., Schorr, S.B., Okamura, A.M.: Haptics: the present and future of artificial touch sensation. Annu. Rev. Control Robot. Auton. Syst. **1**, 385–409 (2018). https://doi.org/ 10.1146/annurev-control-060117-105043
19. O'Doherty, J.E., Shokur, S., Medina, L.E., Lebedev, M.A., Nicolelis, M.A.L.: Creating a neuroprosthesis for active tactile exploration of textures. PNAS **116**, 21821–21827 (2019). https://doi.org/10.1073/pnas.1908008116

20. Ornati, M.: Touching the cloth: haptics in fashion digital communication. In: Kalbaska, N., Sádaba, T., Cominelli, F., Cantoni, L. (eds.) Fashion Communication in the Digital Age, pp. 254–258. Springer International, Cham (2019). https://doi.org/10.1007/978-3-030-15436-3_23

21. Bayousuf, A., Al-Khalifa, H.S., Al-Salman, A.: Haptics-based systems characteristics, classification, and applications. In: Mehdi Khosrow-Pour, D.B.A., (ed.) Advanced Methodologies and Technologies in Artificial Intelligence, Computer Simulation, and Human-Computer Interaction, pp. 778–794. IGI Global, Hershey (2019)

22. Riedel, A., Mulcahy, R.F.: Does more sense make sense? An empirical test of high and low interactive retail technology. J. Serv. Mark. **33**, 331–343 (2019). https://doi.org/10.1108/JSM-12-2017-0435

23. Van Kerrebroeck, H., Willems, K., Brengman, M.: Touching the void: Exploring consumer perspectives on touch-enabling technologies in online retailing. Int. J. Retail Distrib. Manage. **45**, 892–909 (2017). https://doi.org/10.1108/IJRDM-09-2016-0156

24. Rodrigues, T., Silva, S.C., Duarte, P.: The value of textual haptic information in online clothing shopping. J. Fashion Mark. Manage. **21**, 88–102 (2017). https://doi.org/10.1108/JFMM-02-2016-0018

25. Kim, J., Forsythe, S.: Sensory enabling technology acceptance model (SE-TAM): A multiple-group structural model comparison. Psychol. Mark. **25**, 901–922 (2008). https://doi.org/10.1002/mar.20245

26. Cyr, J.: Focus Groups for the Social Science Researcher. Cambridge University Press, Cambridge (2019)

27. Barbour, R.S.: Doing focus groups. Sage, Los Angeles (2018)

28. Amed, I., Balchandani, A., Beltrami, M., Berg, A., Hedrich, S., Rölkens, F.: The State of Fashion 2019, vol. 108. McKinsey & Company, New York (2019)

29. Peck, J., Childers, T.L.: Individual differences in haptic information processing: the "Need for Touch" scale. J. Consum. Res. **30**, 430–442 (2003)

30. Sandelowski, M.: Whatever happened to qualitative description? Res. Nurs. Health **23**, 334–340 (2000)

31. Savin-Baden, M., Major, C.H.: Qualitative Research: The Essential Guide to Theory and Practice. Routledge, Milton Park (2012)

32. What is Webrooming? Definition from Techopedia. https://www.techopedia.com/definition/31036/webrooming. Access 26 Jan 2020

33. Il Quotidiano: Toccare con il Tablet (2019). https://www.rsi.ch/la1/programmi/informazione/il-quotidiano/Il-Quotidiano-12141646.html

34. Obrist, M., Gatti, E., Maggioni, E., Vi, C.T., Velasco, C.: Multisensory experiences in HCI. IEEE Multimedia **24**, 9–13 (2017). https://doi.org/10.1109/MMUL.2017.33

Cultural Appropriation in the Digital Context: A Comparative Study Between Two Fashion Cases

Teresa Sádaba[1,2]([✉]), Valeria LaFata[1,2], and Andrea Torres[1,2]

[1] ISEM Fashion Business School, Navarra University, 28027 Madrid, Spain
teresasadaba@isem.es
[2] Calle de Marquesado de Santa Marta, 3, 28027 Madrid, Spain

Abstract. The following investigation presents the definitions of cultural heritage, cultural appropriation, corporate reputation to later evaluate how could Cultural Appropriation infringement could be detrimental to a company's corporate reputation in the digital context. Two cases of cultural appropriation crisis in the fashion industry are analyzed. On the one hand, the crisis faced by Carolina Herrera due to the similarities of the firm's Resort 2020 collection and different cultural elements from communities in Mexico, and on the other hand, the crisis faced by Gucci with a blackface accusation in 2019. The paper leads us to conclude that nowadays cultural appropriation in fashion can lead to a reputational crisis because the different stakeholders of a company in the industry are evolving and demanding from them to be more aware of controversial issues, among those, the misrepresentation of a culture. Also, how digital communication arises new questions for this kind of crisis. Evaluating two of the most recent cases of cultural appropriation helps to shed light on the importance of these issues in the current world.

Keywords: Cultural appropriation · Fashion · Digital · Reputation

1 Introduction

In recent years, the fashion industry has been questioned on numerous occasions for issues regarding "cultural appropriation". Although the phenomenon is not new, social networks and online media have certainly fueled reactions of different communities towards these controversies. Nowadays, it is possible to understand the scaling and consequences of these cases in decisions such as those taken by the Mexican Government in 2020 where, after condemning actions from brands like Carolina Herrera and Louis Vuitton, it has approved the "General Law to Safeguarding the Elements of Culture and Identity of the Peoples", aimed at protecting the native culture from possible copies incurred by fashion brands.

As these controversies demonstrate, the relationship between fashion and cultural appropriation is quite complex. This complexity is given because fashion has, by

© Springer Nature Switzerland AG 2020
F. F.-H. Nah and K. Siau (Eds.): HCII 2020, LNCS 12204, pp. 504–520, 2020.
https://doi.org/10.1007/978-3-030-50341-3_38

definition, several characteristics that refer directly to the same concept of cultural appropriation; to the meaning of appropriation and to that of culture.

On one hand, fashion is also part of the cultural phenomena, some even including it in the field of the arts [1]. It is an expression of collective identities, and hence, it has been understood as a manifestation of popular culture. Cultures' history demonstrates that fashion appears in stratified civilizations where social identity is an important factor for exclusion. These socializing characteristics within fashion are clear with the configuration of groups through the dress: communicative happenings such as The Black Shirts in Italy, Blue in Spain or Gray in Cuba; of ethnic minorities; or, in a more contemporary way, the different "urban tribes": the mods, the heavies or the goths. All of them movements with a certain identity that fill the popular culture with content.

On the other hand, regarding appropriation, it is possible to find that the origin of it is usually imitation and that, precisely fashion, at its foundations, is exactly that: emulation. George Simmel explained in his *Fashion Philosophy*: "Fashion is the imitation of a given example and satisfies the demand for social adaptation; it leads the individual upon the road which all travel, it furnishes a general condition, which resolves the conduct of every individual into a mere example. At the same time, it satisfies in no less degree the need of differentiation, the tendency towards dissimilarity, the desire for change and contrast" [2, pp. 67–68]. Thus, a phenomenon can be called fashion to the extent that it is imitated and, therefore, copied by others.

But the issue with imitation is not limited to fashion as a sociological phenomenon. Years after Simmel's reflection, during the 50s, *prêt-à-porter* will be born as a way to start manufacturing fashion at a large scale to reach the masses, while getting inspiration and nurturing itself from the *haute couture*. Since then, the fashion system began to be understood as a pyramid where the cusp, represented by the luxury sector, fed the rest of the segments. By the end of the 20th century, the evolution of this model gave space to the so-called low-cost fashion, where brands were inspired by or simply copied other brands in the sector. As a consequence, nowadays is possible to find issues of "intellectual property" along the industry, where the line between copying, appropriation and inspiration is usually very thin [3].

Cultural appropriation, then, is part of this relevant debate in fashion, adding nuances of great interest. These nuances, that can be found along this article, also respond to an era of greater multicultural sensitivity and a capacity, through social networks and digital media, to provide any individual with channels to voice that sensitivity. All of this leads to question the phenomenon of cultural appropriation in fashion and its echo in the online world, with the consequent impact for brands.

This article will seek to present the relationship between cultural appropriation and fashion brands' reputation in the digital context, based on the analysis of two cases that emerged from digital landscapes and that have supposed a reputational crisis for their respective firms. It is pertinent to mention that, since the academic bibliography referencing this subject is still scarce, this research also includes non-academic texts in which the authors' points of view resulted interesting and relevant for the present paper.

After the analysis, some conclusions that place cultural appropriation and its link with fashion are listed with the aim to help the fashion sector to better understand the dimensions the issues of cultural appropriation in the digital environment have acquired.

2   Theoretical Framework on Cultural Appropriation

Cultural appropriation is a complex discussion with many nuances. It has an historical, legal, ethical, and ethnographic dimension. From the normative point of view, to define cultural appropriation is necessary to know first the origins of the term. The phrase is strongly related to that of cultural heritage, that first appeared in the terms of international law in 1907. Later on, the United Nations Educational, Scientific and Cultural Organization (UNESCO) further developed it after World War II in the wake of protecting cultural landmarks in the case of an armed conflict [4].

Nowadays, UNESCO keeps the definition developed in the 1972 Convention Concerning the Protection of the World Cultural and Natural Heritage, that defines cultural heritage as places on Earth that have an exceptional universal value because they are an irreplaceable source of life an inspiration that belongs to humanity [5]. however, the organization not only limits cultural heritage to monuments or objects, stating that lived expressions that have been inherited throughout history and that will pass on to future generations are also considered to be part of this heritage.

The two types of cultural heritage are further defined by the Intellectual Property Issues in Cultural Heritage Project: The tangible cultural heritage are all those material objects that belong to a culture while the intangible cultural heritage refers to expressions, practices and knowledge of said culture. Some examples of the latter include languages, designs, techniques, rituals, social manners, celebrations or performing arts that have been trespassed through generations becoming symbol of the culture [6].

It is from the concept of cultural heritage that cultural appropriation originates. In its most basic definition, cultural appropriation is "the act of taking or using things from a culture that is not your own, especially without showing that you understand or respect this culture" [7]. Although this definition is proper, there are deeper layers of meaning as to what cultural appropriation is.

Vézina defines cultural appropriation as "the act by a member of a dominant culture of taking a TCE [Tangible Common Equity] whose holders belong to a minority culture and repurposing it in a different context, without the authorization, acknowledgement and/or compensation of the TCE holder(s)" [8]. In this case, the element appropriated is a tangible one. However, for purposes of this paper, this definition will also embrace intangible cultural appropriation since is what is often appropriated in fashion (production techniques, words, marketing messages).

Vézina's definition introduces the roles of the dominant culture versus the minority culture. This is particularly important since one of the main characteristics that will define whether a cultural element is being appropriated or not will be the position of the culture that is victim of the appropriation [9]. As she explains, the repurpose of this element in a different context, without authorization nor compensation is also part of the cultural appropriation scheme.

This answers the question as to why not everything is cultural appropriation. While it is true that along the years humanity has exchanged cultural elements, Shand argues that appropriation of cultural heritage could be traced back to the Enlightenment ages where, due to the intellectual, political and economic dominance of Europe, all types of tangible cultural heritage items were looted from the indigenous populations and exchanged among colonials, regarding of the way they were obtained [10]. The deeper and sensitive meaning that cultural appropriation carries for those minorities whose culture is being improperly used is evident after understanding the history of those peoples.

Furthermore, cultural appropriation might not only be inappropriate because of the reasons previously stated. There are also several cases that show how cultural appropriation can be detrimental to that community in economic terms. In Guatemala, for example, a community of almost one million artisans are at risk because of the new layout of the fashion industry: fast fashion can do a garment similar in looks to that of an artisan, in a shorter period of time and at lower prices, jeopardizing the market share of said artisans when selling goods to tourists [11].

To simplify this, the Intellectual Property Issues in Cultural Heritage Project provides the definition of what they call misappropriation. Similarly defined as cultural appropriation, misappropriation can involve also a high economic harm when it "leads to profiting from the use of a cultural expression that is vital to the wellbeing and livelihood of the people who created it" [6].

2.1 International Legal Framework on Cultural Appropriation

In addressing the numerous implications associated with what is understood as 'Cultural Appropriation', it is important to approach its legal definition and to understand if there is a unanimous regulatory framework that could provide the academy with a better understanding and application of the term.

The definition of Cultural Appropriation made by the Oxford Dictionary [12] is developed under the scope of two main elements, *ownership* and *creative or artistic forms, themes, or practices*. The above-mentioned elements, due to their nature, suggest a wide and complex legal framework related to intellectual property (IP). As jurisdictions and legal systems worldwide may differ from one to another, and there is a lack of uniformity in the enforcement of legal remedies when it comes to protect intangible assets [13], the intellectual property landscape may fail to provide a common ground in Cultural Appropriation.

Most of the steps that have been taken in order to establish a common ground on the matter have been done in the legal courts [14] and by global institutions that have tried to provide a shared but not legally binding definition. For the purpose of presenting 'Cultural Appropriation' in all of its dimensions, the following Table 1 presents a brief summary on the main different legal approaches that have been made worldwide:

As shown on Table 1 most of the legal instruments that have been developed to safeguard the property of intangible assets related to cultural representations are not legally binding and do not have international enforceability. Additionally, most of the actions taken on a legal level fail to provide a wider perspective on culturally related issues such as oversimplification, racial or cultural misrepresentations, etc.

2.2 Cultural Appropriation in the Fashion Industry

'Cultural Appropriation' in the fashion industry is a more interesting issue as it can manifest itself throughout multiple practices. As Ayres argues, the line between appropriation

Table 1. Legal approaches on cultural appropriation

Legal instrument	Definition	Country/Institution	Legally binding
Arts and Crafts Act. 1990	It is illegal to offer or display for sale or sell; any art or craft product in a manner that falsely suggests it is Indian produced, an Indian product, or the product of a particular Indian tribe	USA	Yes – at a federal level in the USA territory
WIPO's Intergovernmental Committee on Intellectual Property and Genetic Resources, Traditional Knowledge and Folklore. - 2000	Traditional cultural expressions (TCEs), also called "expressions of folklore", may include music, dance, art, designs, names, signs and symbols, performances, ceremonies, architectural forms, handicrafts and narratives, or many other artistic or cultural expressions Their protection is related to the promotion of creativity, enhanced cultural diversity and the preservation of cultural heritage	World Intellectual Property	No. 66 countries have developed their own legal tools to protect TCEs with IP laws
Cultural heritage declaration. 2003	The intangible cultural heritage means the "practices, representations, expressions, knowledge, skills – as well as the instruments, objects, artefacts and cultural spaces associated therewith – that communities, groups and, in some cases, individuals recognize as part of their cultural heritage (…)" States bound by the Convention shall provide measures aimed at ensuring the viability of the intangible cultural heritage, including protection of such heritage	UNESCO	Yes. For the countries that have accepted or ratified the Convention
Declaration on the Rights of Indigenous Peoples (UNDRIP). 2007	*"Indigenous peoples have the right to maintain, control, protect and develop their cultural heritage, traditional knowledge and traditional cultural expressions, as well as the manifestation of their sciences, technologies and cultures (…). They also have the right to maintain, control, protect and develop their intellectual property over such cultural heritage, traditional knowledge, and traditional cultural expressions (…) States shall take effective measures to recognize and protect the exercise of these rights"*	United Nations	No

and inspiration in the creativity process is hard to clarify. This is why she proposes a definition of Cultural Appropriation as "an umbrella term that encapsulates different degrees of borrowing, ranging from inspiration to the theft" [15].

This is why the fashion industry has been the subject of many accusations regarding cultural appropriation. According to Shao, the issue with fashion and the use of cultural tangible or intangible symbols relies in the fact that, besides the offensive tone or the economic consequences, appropriation in fashion can also lead to stereotyping or oversimplification of a culture: when the appropriator takes an element from a different culture than its own and uses it in a way that decreases the value and the meaning for the person whose culture has been appropriated [16]. In a way, it could be said that the element is commoditized.

Singh-Kurtz also raises the question as to when cultural appropriation in fashion is considered as such. The topic is often subjective, and the confusion can present itself in entire garments, accessories, particular elements, the naming, etc. [17]. Therefore, for the purpose of better understanding of the present study, three main categories regarding cultural appropriation are proposed:

- Appropriation in design: when cultural appropriation is infringed by adding or using intangible or tangible cultural heritage elements of another culture to or for a specific piece, garment, fabric, or complement.
- Appropriation in naming: when cultural appropriation is infringed by using an intangible cultural heritage spoken element of another culture to name a brand, line, collection or garment.
- Appropriation in communications: when cultural appropriation is infringed by using intangible or tangible cultural heritage elements of another culture in the communicational strategy of a brand.

Appropriation in design is the most common case of cultural appropriation in fashion. One of the many examples is the Louis Vuitton Men's Spring 2012 collection that featured fabrics with a typical Maasai square pattern [18]. Regarding cultural appropriation in fashion and naming issues, Singh-Kurtz highlights a particular case where Kim Kardashian faced backslash after naming her body shape wear line Kimono, a word used to name a traditional Japanese garment [17]. An example for appropriation in communications is the Dior 'Sauvage' Parfum campaign that depicted a Native American dance. Despite the company working with an indigenous advocacy group, the outrage was due to an oversimplification of the Native American culture [19].

Furthermore, fashion, being a creative field, can take inspiration and examples from many cultures, therefore is necessary that firms install certain protocols to address any type of accusation of cultural appropriation that could affect the company in terms of losing high profile partners or margins and profits [20].

The following Table 2 provides a sample of cases of cultural appropriation in the fashion industry, the type of cultural issue and the area of infringement.

2.3 Fashion and Reputation in the Digital Context

In the context of digital media and social networks, anyone who feels attacked by a cultural appropriation issue has a megaphone in the social media to condemn. Companies nowadays are exposed to unprecedented scrutiny through the Internet and a 24-hour news television channels [21].

As we have pointed out in previous works: "Another change in the digital era consists of 'consumer-to-consumer' conversations, where users are empowered to express their views, and this has created a 'new equality in communication" [22].

This is why brands are, more than ever, exposed to reputation issues. Effects of the consumer's role as communicators could be positive or negative for brands' reputation.

Table 2. Cases of cultural appropriation in the fashion industry

Year	Brand	Context	Type of cultural issue	Area of infringement
2002	Dior	For the Christian Dior spring 2003 Haute Couture collection runway, the models wore the Geisha-inspired makeup and Chinese tribal costumes designed by John Galliano	Cultural Oversimplification	Communicational (Styling)
2004	Dolce & Gabbana	The Dolce & Gabbana perfume Sicily was advertised in a commercial about a Sicilian funeral, which presented an overstated stereotype of the Sicilian culture and their association to mafias	Cultural Oversimplification	Communicational
2007	Dior	Spring Haute Couture collection with Geisha inspired makeup to express inspiration from the Japanese culture	Cultural Oversimplification	Communicational (Styling)
2010	Victoria's Secret	"Wild Things" named fashion show, inspired by tribal motifs	Cultural Appropriation	Design
2012	Victoria's Secret	Karlie Kloss and Native-American Headdress	Cultural Appropriation	Communicational (Styling)
2012	Urban Outfitters	Repeated use of the term "Navajo" for marketing	Cultural Appropriation	Communicational (Naming)
2012	Louis Vuitton	Men's Kanga Collection featuring fabric with typical Maasai print	Cultural Appropriation	Design
2015	DSquared	DSquaw collection, drawing elements from indigenous Canadian tribal motifs and use of offensive term to name the collection	Cultural Appropriation/Cultural Offense	Design/Communicational
2015	KTZ	Shawan Towelling Sweatshirt design copied without authorization	Cultural Appropriation	Design

(continued)

Table 2. (*continued*)

Year	Brand	Context	Type of cultural issue	Area of infringement
2016	Moncler	In the collaboration made with art collective Friends With You, the Brand included jackets and bags baring images resembling the blackface figures seen in minstrel shows	Cultural Offense	Design
2017	Port 1961	Pieces from the clothing line's Spring 2018 collection had the quote "Every Color Matters" as an ode to the notorious "Black Lives Matter" movement that began in 2012 in response to the killing of Trayvon Martin. The brand was accused of exploiting the black culture for profit and trivializing the movement	Cultural Offense	Design
2018	Dior	Appropriation of traditional Bihor clothing from Romania in their couture collection	Cultural Appropriation	Design
2018	Dior	Featuring Jennifer Lawrence in the campaign of their cruise collection, inspired by Mexican Escaramuzas	Cultural Appropriation	Communication
2018	Gucci	Sikh turban featured in Autumn/Winter 2018	Cultural Appropriation	Design
2018	Prada	Luxury Italian fashion house Prada shut down a New York City storefront and pulled a keychain from its stock after the accessory part of their Pradamalia collection went viral for resembling blackface imagery	Cultural Offense	Design
2019	Versace Coach Givenchy	The luxury brands launched T-shirts deemed to undermine China's "One China" policy, including Hong Kong and Taiwan as separate countries	Cultural Offense	Design

(*continued*)

Table 2. (*continued*)

Year	Brand	Context	Type of cultural issue	Area of infringement
2019	Carolina Herrera	Plagiarizing and culturally appropriating designs from indigenous Mexican communities	Cultural Appropriation	Design

Positive as segmentation, direct communication from brands to consumers, engagement and loyalty can be reinforced. Negative, as crisis can arise "with just a small amount of information. It is crucial for companies and organizations to understand the role of processing information and continuing interactivity in times of crisis" [22].

With the social media, companies are facing more communication crises than ever. This is why Aula suggests that four strategies exist in regards of protocols companies should follow with social media: absence, presence, attendance and omnipresence [23]. The first three suppose from no participation whatsoever, to an active listening but no interaction to a complete participation. Omnipresence, however, is the most recommended for positive outcomes while managing online reputation because it suggests a dialogical interaction with the stakeholders [24].

Many years ago, traditional crises where characterized by different parameters, compared to those characterizing today's reputational issues. With the zenith of social media, those parameters have drastically changed through increased pace, scope and impact [25], meaning they become viral more quickly. Berger and Milkman state that anger is the most common and viral emotion online [26], Ott and Theunissen suggest its permanence is due to a "long tail"-like effect [24].

This kind of reputational crisis takes brands to consider the impact of reputation just as powerful as its financial one, in the sense that reputation generates economic benefits for the firm. To support this observation, according to Brown and Perry "financial performance counts only for 38% to 59% of the unexplained variance of reputation" [27] where "reputation could represent an intangible asset" [28].

The definition of reputation has been interpreted in many ways, considering the context and situation. Benjamin Franklin once said, "It takes many good deeds to build reputation, and only one bad one to lose". As Mr. Franklin said, reputation is a matter of being subtle on what actions are taken.

More than two decades ago, Fombrun & Van Riel took the task of developing a common definition for corporate reputation due to the inconsistencies found on the subject among the different disciplines. For an integrative view of corporate reputation, they took the following definition: a collective representation of a firm's past actions and results that describes the firm's ability to deliver valued outcomes to multiple stakeholders. It gauges a firm's relative standing both internally with employees and externally with its stakeholders, in both its competitive and institutional environments [29, 30].

In fashion, reputation is a business, an asset as long as it is good. This means that brands that have favorable reputation have more loyal customers that are more dedicated and that buy a broader range of products [31].

Barnett, Jermier & Lafferty gave an updated view on Fombrun & Van Riel's take, stating that corporate reputation is the "observers' collective judgments of a corporation based in assessments of the financial, social and environmental impacts attributed to the corporation over time" [32, p. 34].

According to these definitions, corporate reputation has three main characteristics: it is built over time, it is based on the judgment of stakeholders and is usually evaluated in terms of how the company performs on different environments, both competitive and institutional ones.

3   Comparative Study of Two Fashion Cases Related to Different Dimensions of 'Cultural Appropriation'

As proposed throughout the paper, the relationship between fashion and culture has many dimensions. The following comparative study provides examples of the types of dialogues companies can engage with communities that carry historical and ancestral traditions. These cases will provide the bases to understand that 'Cultural Appropriation' in the fashion industry can go beyond the appropriation of tangible or intangible assets and that it can lead to having an offensive tone or to the stereotyping or oversimplification of a culture.

The two following cases will be assessed from three main perspectives: the context of the crisis, the corporate brand[1], the media impact and the crisis management. The above-mentioned perspectives will provide us with the main lengths of Cultural Appropriation in a digital context.

3.1   Carolina Herrera and the Appropriation of Traditional Mexican Patterns

Crisis' Context
In June 6th, 2019, the fashion brand Carolina Herrera presented the look book of its Resort 2020 collection under the creative direction of Wes Gordon, who had been appointed for the role almost a year before. Behind the inspirations for said collections were the founder of the brand's own life, that had Venezuelan origins that later translated to New York's Upper East Side lifestyle. The resulting collection, then, was the perfect mix between the color and patterns of Latin America with the occasion dresses the clients of the brand required [33]. Some show notes mentioned the sunrises in Tulum, the dances of Buenos Aires or the colors of Cartagena as the sources of the color palettes used [34].

However, four days after the presentation of the collection, on June 10th, 2019, the Cultural Minister of Mexico, Alejandra Frausto, sent a letter to Carolina Herrera, the designer herself, and to Wes Gordon, asking them to publicly explain the arguments behind the use of elements whose origin recedes in local Mexican communities of Tenango de Doria (in Hidalgo), Tehuantepec (in Oaxaca) and Saltillo (Coahuila) [35].

According to Friedman, there were some social media comments reflecting a backlash against the brand. Towards the Venezuelan designer specifically on Twitter and

---

[1] As stated by Ind, N (1997), the corporate brand can be also defined as the "sum of values that represent the organization".

against Gordon, mostly on the Instagram post of the collection on his personal page. These comments featured several claims regarding the theft from Mexican culture [34]. Another factor for the maximization of the crisis was the publication of an Instagram post about the subject from popular account @*Diet_prada*, alleging that Carolina Herrera was not the first brand to borrow typical Mexican original designs to use in their garments [36].

It is important to stress that in no way the fashion house collaborated along the design, production or communications process with any individual from any of the communities they got their inspiration from.

Corporate Brand
See Table 3.

Table 3. Carolina herrera's corporate brand

Price	High priced products
Quality	High quality confection
Design	Classic, sober and clean-like style
Category	Luxury. Ready to wear. Fragrance division
Brand's attributes	Femininity. Elegance. Lifestyle. Cosmopolitanism. Timelessness. Sophistication
Relationship with the customers	Acquaintance-like, aspirational, informative
Communication	Direct, savvy, sophisticated, behind the scenes
Sales channels	Directly operated stores E-commerce Wholesale
Age of target consumer	Regarding their communicational target, the last five years show an implementation of a strong social media influencers-based strategy (both macro and micro influencers) to appeal to millennial audiences
Corporate brand storytelling	In the company section of the brand's webpage, a phrase by Carolina Herrera herself states: "I have a responsibility to the woman of today — to make her feel confident, modern and above all else beautiful" [xx]. The brand still has a strong relation to its founder, her vision and values for her namesake company The story it tells through images, campaigns and communications is a highly aspirational and luxurious one. The appeal of the brand also relies on the characteristics of the lifestyle it transmits. It is classic and clean, but it also looks to highlight a sensual part of the Carolina Herrera woman While having a varied portfolio that includes clothes, fragrances, glasses and jewelry, the brand has a coherent message it sends through the channels of the different categories

Crisis Management

The crisis had high impact along the major news and media outlets, such as *The BBC*, *The Guardian*, *ABC News*, *NBC News*, *CNN International*, *The New York* Times, *AP News*, *Reuters*, as well as fashion-focused media platforms like *The Business of Fashion*, *The Cut*, *The Fashion Law*, among others, that published the news across their channels.

In response to the crisis, creative director Wes Gordon stated that the collection was meant as a tribute to Mexico, rather than the intention of stealing from its culture. Later on, in an interview for *Vogue Magazine*, the designer reminisced about the controversial issue alleging that while the collection was designed with the best of intentions, sometimes intent does not matter. Furthermore, the designer recognized that he had learned a lot from that process and that "...the moral of the story is that we live in a very different world right now, and we have to respect and understand [other cultures]. That old model of taking an inspiration trip and finding things as you go is very difficult to do in 2019" [37]. On the side of the Mexican government, a law to protect this cultural heritage from being plagiarized is being resolved [38].

3.2 Gucci and the Balaclava Knit Jumper: Cultural Unawareness of a Racially Charged Design

Crisis' Context

On February 2019, Gucci went viral on Twitter when users of the social network brought attention to a Balaclava Knit Jumper part of Gucci's fall-winter 2018 ready-to-wear collection for resembling blackface imagery [39]. The product lasted on Gucci's physical and online stores for approximately one year without raising any controversy.

Blackface dates to the Nineteenth-century and started originally in the United States. It started as a form of theatrical make-up used by non-black performers to provide a caricaturist representation of black individuals. The practice gained popularity even extending across the globe to Britain. In both the United States and Britain, Blackface was most commonly used in the minstrel performance tradition [40]. Early white performers in blackface used burnt cork or shoe polish to blacken their skin and exaggerate their lips, often wearing woolly wigs, gloves, tailcoats, or ragged clothes to complete the transformation. The personification in a caricaturist way of black individuals spread stereotypes of racist images, attitudes and perceptions worldwide.

Given the history of slavery in the United States and the social and political movement of reinforcement of civil rights [41] that took place during the 21st century, Blackface became a symbol of the misrepresentation of the African-American community in entertainment and a symbol of cultural offense that shaped the perceptions and prejudices about black people in the United States [42].

Corporate Brand
See Table 4.

Table 4. Gucci's corporate brand

Price	High priced products
Quality	High-quality craftsmanship
Design	Innovative and bold design
Category	Luxury
Brand's attributes	Italian heritage. Romantic. Innovative. Progressive. Modern. Prestige. Empowered [43]
Relationship with the customers	Highly personal. High engagement with customers
Communication	Strong direct communication
Sales channels	Directly operated stores E-commerce Wholesale
Age of target consumer	62% of Gucci's eight billion in sales in 2018 came from consumers who were 35 and under (Millennials), and the brand's fastest-growing segment is consumers 24 and under (Generation Z) [44]
Corporate brand storytelling	Gucci Equilibrium: Equilibrium is Gucci's initiative aimed to *"bring positive change in order to secure a collective future"* Gucci defines itself as a brand committed in social and environmental change. Gucci's commitment focuses on three pillars: - Environmental - People: Gucci claims to encourage diversity, gender equality and active citizenship - New Models: Gucci claims that their efforts are focused on a step-change in both mindset and approach. They claim to *"constantly imagine and re-imagine what it means to make a meaningful impact"*

Crisis Management
The first tweet related to accusations of racism against Gucci was published on February 6th, 2019. Even though the Twitter user did not identify herself as a Gucci costumer, it caused reactions of Gucci adepts all over that social network. The tweet has as of this date, up to 7.6 thousand responds and 17.1 thousand likes.

External media was very much involved in the crisis. Local and international newspapers as well as Tv channels and other relevant media later replicated the news of Gucci's scandal.

The actions that Gucci took following the beginning of the crisis can be summed up, as follows:

Just one day after the allegations of racism began, on February 7th, 2019, Gucci issued on Twitter (the social network where the crisis began) a public apology stating:

"Gucci deeply apologizes for the offense caused by the wool balaclava jumper. (…) We consider diversity to be a fundamental value to be fully upheld, respected, and at the forefront of every decision we make. We are fully committed to increasing diversity throughout our organization and turning this incident into a powerful learning moment for the Gucci team and beyond." [45].

On that same day, Gucci confirmed that the item had been immediately removed from their online and physical stores. That same week, Creative Director of the brand, Alessadro Michele, sent a letter to Gucci's 18.000 employees from his personal email. The letter explained that the Balaclava jumper was a "tribute to Leigh Bowery, to his camouflage art, to his ability to challenge the bourgeois conventions and conformism, to his eccentricity as a performer, to his extraordinary vocation to masquerade meant as a hymn to freedom". He also expressed how sorry he was for evoking a racist imaginary and added "But I am aware that sometimes our actions can end up with causing unintentional effects. It is therefore necessary taking full accountability for these effects". Michele said that through his work he wanted "to give citizenship's right to the traditionally marginalized, to those who felt unrepresented, to those that history silenced or made believe they were worthless. My aim, in which personal and political are intimately interwoven, has always been to turn the pain into a chant."

One week later, on February 12, 2019, Gucci's CEO Marco Bizzari gave an interview to the newspaper WWD. On such interview, Bizzari attributed the mistake to cultural unawareness. He also admitted "The lack of knowledge of diversity and the consequent understanding are not at the level we expected, despite all the efforts we did inside the company in the last four years". Marco Bizzari also stated: "(…) our company, being a global company, is a mirror of society. The need for greater awareness and understanding is everywhere. The risk we could face is that anyone would not take this matter as serious as it is. We need to educate ourselves to make sure this does not happen again".

As informed by the Washing Post, on March 2019, Gucci announced plans for scholarships in partnership with schools across the globe, from Accra, Ghana, and Lagos, Nigeria, to Mexico City and New York [46]. The company set aside $5 million to invest in community programs in 10 North American cities, including Atlanta, Detroit, New York, Toronto and Washington. The initiatives add up to the formal policy that allows employees to spend company time volunteering in their communities. Gucci is also hiring a global director for diversity and inclusion, and it has formed an advisory council that includes model Naomi Campbell, racial justice activists, academics and a sprinkling of celebrities [47].

4   Conclusion

The comparative study of the above-mentioned cases as well as the theoretical framework presented throughout this paper, provide us with the two main aspects to identify in cases of Cultural Appropriation, (i) the offensive behavior, language, images or representation of a culture or community, which can include the oversimplification or misrepresentation of such culture and; (ii) the economic exploitation of traditional cultural expressions without giving proper recognition to the community. The former ultimately contributes to the perpetuation of historic patterns of oppression of cultures greatly affected by colonization and prevalent white western domination.

As complex as it is, the lack of legal tools that address all the dimensions of Cultural Appropriation becomes the base to a thin line between the creative world and the economical exploitation of cultural traditions. This compass of Cultural Appropriation is extremely important for the fashion industry, as the inspiration and nourishment from different cultures and realities in the creation process of the fashion houses is the key of an ever-evolving fashion industry.

Adding up to an already complex dynamic, the digital context and a globalized audience with new stakeholders and new conversations between brands and consumers, reputation crisis derived from Cultural Appropriation require a more detailed perspective and attention from fashion companies. In the digital world, Cultural Appropriation goes beyond an intrinsic relationship between the fashion brand and the affected community but rather, involves a demanding audience that expects from the brands faster call to actions and answers that please everybody.

Is it enough to implement diversity within the management structure of fashion companies or should companies go further to prevent a crisis? Unfortunately, there is no clear path when approaching the fashion creation process inspired from a cultural tradition, because with the fast paced evolution of the world, what is not seen as an offensive behavior today can be offensive tomorrow.

What seem clear now is that with the increase of social media, a more direct and transparent dialogue between fashion companies and consumers is fundamental. Fashion companies should keep a dynamic focus aligned with the corporate values and the company's strategy in order to understand the cultural dynamics engaged with a more globalized audience.

References

1. Kim, S.B.: Is fashion art? Fashion Theory **2**(1), 57–71 (1998)
2. Simmel, G.: Filosofia de la coqueteria: Filosofia de la moda; Lo masculino y lo femenino y otros ensayos, pp. 67–68 (1924)
3. Green, D.N., Kaiser, S.B.: Fashion and appropriation. Fashion Style Popul. Cult. **4**(2), 145–150 (2017)
4. Blake, J.: On defining cultural heritage. Int. Comp. Law Q. **49**(1), 61–85 (2000)
5. United Nations Educational, Scientific and Cultural Organization (UNESCO): Cultural Heritage (2017). http://www.unesco.org/new/en/santiago/culture/cultural-heritage/
6. Intellectual Property Issues in Cultural Heritage Project: Think Before You Appropriate. Things to know and questions to ask in order to avoid misappropriating Indigenous cultural heritage. Simon Fraser University, Vancouver (2015)
7. Cambridge Dictionary: Cultural Appropriation Definition (2019). https://dictionary.cambridge.org/dictionary/english/cultural-appropriation
8. Vézina, B.: Curbing Cultural Appropriation in the Fashion Industry. CIGI Papers (2019)
9. Holloway, L.N.: Cultural Appropriation and Fashion: A Line to Clarify the Line (2016)
10. Shand, P.: Scenes from the colonial catwalk: cultural appropriation, intellectual property rights, and fashion. Cult. Anal. **3**, 47–88 (2002)
11. Weinreb, S.: The Impact of Fast Fashion and Cultural Appropriation on Guatemalan Artisanship, 11 June 2019. https://www.forbes.com/sites/saraweinreb/2019/06/11/the-impact-of-fast-fashion-and-cultural-appropriation-on-guatemalan-artisanship/#2eeff68c75c9

12. Oxford Reference: Cultural Appropriation Definition (2020). https://www.oxfordreference. com/view/10.1093/oi/authority.20110803095652789
13. Scafidi, S.: Introduction: new dimensions of cultural property. Fordham Int. Law J. **31**(3), 684–689 (2008)
14. The Fashion Law: Decision in Isabel Marant, Antik Batik Battle over Mexican Design Expected This Week, 3 December 2015. https://www.thefashionlaw.com/home/decision-in-isabel-marant-antik-batik-battle-over-mexican-design-expected-this-week. Accessed January 2020
15. Ayres, J.: Inspiration or prototype? Appropriation and exploitation in the fashion industry. Fashion Style Popul. Cult. **4**(2), 151–165 (2017)
16. Shao, R.: Cultural Appropriation in Fashion Industry, 16 December 2018. https://medium. com/@shaorenchen/cultural-appropriation-in-fashion-industry-5cb625e49e21
17. Singh-Kurtz, S.: Governments are taking cultural appropriation to court, 28 August 2019. https://qz.com/quartzy/1665060/mexicos-government-is-calling-out-designers-for-rip ping-off-indigenous-designs/
18. Young, S.: Maasai people of East Africa fighting against cultural appropriation by luxury fashion labels, 7 February 2017. https://www.independent.co.uk/life-style/fashion/maasai-people-cultural-appropriation-luxury-fashion-retailers-louis-vuitton-east-africa-intellectual-a7553701.html?am
19. Lieber, C.: Dior Pulls 'Sauvage' Campaign After Facing Appropriation Backlash, 31 August 2019. https://www.businessoffashion.com/articles/news-analysis/dior-pulls-sauvage-campaign-from-instagram-after-facing-appropriation-backlash
20. Doupnik, E.: How to Fix Fashion's Cultural Appropriation Problem (2018). https://wwd.com/ fashion-news/fashion-features/fashion-cultural-appropriation-1202597241/
21. Alsop, R.J.: Corporate reputation: anything but superficial – the deep but fragile nature of corporate reputation. J. Bus. Strategy **25**(6), 21–29 (2004)
22. Sádaba, T., SanMiguel, P., Gargoles, P.: Communication crisis in fashion: from the rana plaza tragedy to the bravo tekstil factory crisis. In: Kalbaska, N., Sádaba, T., Cominelli, F., Cantoni, L. (eds.) FACTUM 2019, pp. 259–275. Springer, Cham (2019). https://doi.org/10.1007/978-3-030-15436-3_24
23. Aula, P.: Social media, reputation risk and ambient publicity management. Strategy Leadersh. **38**(6), 43–49 (2010)
24. Ott, L., Theunissen, P.: Reputations at risk: engagement during social media crises. Public Relat. Rev. **41**(1), 97–102 (2015)
25. Bridgeman, R.: Crisis communication and the net. In: Crisis communication: Practical PR Strategies for Reputation Management and Company Survival, Philadelphia, Kogan Page, pp. 169–177 (2008)
26. Berger, J., Milkman, K.L.: What makes online content viral? J. Mark. Res. **49**(2), 192–205 (2012)
27. Brown, B., Perry, S.: Removing the financial performance halo from Fortune's "most admired" companies. Acad. Manag. J. **37**(5), 1347–1359 (1994)
28. Dierickx, I., Cool, K.: Asset stock accumulation and sustainability of competitive advantage. Manag. Sci. **35**(12), 1504–1511 (1989)
29. Fombrun, C., Van Riel, C.: The reputational landscape. In: Corporate Reputation Review, pp. 5–13 (1997)
30. Fombrun, C.J., Rindova, V.: Who's tops and who decides? The social construction of corporate reputations, New York University, Stern School of Business, Working Paper, pp. 5–13 (1996)
31. Gul, R.: The relationship between reputation, customer satisfaction, trust, and loyalty. J. Public Adm. Gov. **4**(3), 368–387 (2014)
32. Barnett, M.L., Jermier, J.M., Lafferty, B.A.: Corporate reputation: the definitional landscape. Corp. Reput. Rev. **9**(1), 26–38 (2006)

33. Phelps, N.: Resort 2020 Carolina Herrera, 6 June 2019. https://www.vogue.com/fashion-shows/resort-2020/carolina-herrera

34. Friedman, V.: Homage or Theft? Carolina Herrera Called Out by Mexican Minister, 13 June 2019. https://www.nytimes.com/2019/06/13/fashion/carolina-herrera-mexico-appropriation.html

35. Beauregard, L.P.: México acusa a Carolina Herrera de apropiación cultural por su colección más reciente, 13 June 2019. https://elpais.com/elpais/2019/06/12/estilo/1560295742_2 32912.html

36. Fashion Revolution: #GiveCredit: the cultural appropriation of Otomi Embroidery (2019). https://www.fashionrevolution.org/givecredit-the-cultural-appropriation-of-otomi-embroi dery/

37. Farra, E.: Formal Is Not Elegant: Wes Gordon on Maintaining—and Modernizing—the Codes of Carolina Herrera, 3 October 2019. https://www.vogue.com/article/wes-gordon-carolina-herrera-forces-of-fashion-2019. Accessed 2020

38. Rivera, V.C.: México aprueba una ley contra plagio y la explotación de los diseños indígenas, 20 January 2020. https://enriqueortegaburgos.com/mexico-aprueba-ley-contra-plagio-y-exp lotacion-de-disenos-indigenas/. Accessed January 2020

39. Hsu, T., Paton, E.: Gucci and Adidas Apologize and Drop Products Called Racist, 7 February 2019. https://www.nytimes.com/2019/02/07/business/gucci-blackface-adidas-apologize.html. https://www.nytimes.com/2019/02/07/business/gucci-blackface-adidas-apo logize.html. Accessed 2019

40. Anderson, L.: From blackface to 'genuine negroes': nineteenth-century minstrelsy and the icon of the 'negro'. Theatre Res. Int. **21**(1), 17–23 (1996)

41. Ford, G.R.: Message on the Observance of Black History Month (1976)

42. Desmond-Harris, J.: Don't get what's wrong with blackface? Here's why it's so offensive (2014). https://web.archive.org/web/20190523182549/. https://www.vox.com/2014/10/29/7089591/why-is-blackface-offensive-halloween-costume

43. About Gucci. https://www.gucci.com/int/en/st/about-gucci

44. Arnet, G.: Gucci on track to hit 10 billion in 2020, 26 April 2019. https://www.voguebusi ness.com/companies/gucci-sales-reach-euro-10-billion

45. Ritschel, C.: 50 cent burns Gucci shirt following blackface controversy, 14 February 2019. https://www.independent.co.uk/life-style/50-cent-gucci-blackface-instagram-burn-shirt-katy-perry-boycott-a8779611.html

46. Givhan, R.: 'I was the person who made the mistake': How Gucci is trying to recover from its blackface sweater controversy, 7 May 2019. https://www.washingtonpost.com/lifest yle/style/i-was-the-person-who-made-the-mistake-how-gucci-is-trying-to-recover-from-its-blackface-sweater-controversy/2019/05/06/04eccbb6-6f7d-11e9-8be0-ca575670e91c_story.html

47. Hsu, T.: To Avoid More Racist Hoodies, Retailers Seek Diversity, 29 March 2018. https://www.nytimes.com/2018/03/29/business/fast-fashion-diversity.html?module=inline

Digital User Behavior in Fashion E-Commerce.
A Business Model Comparative Study

Patricia SanMiguel and Teresa Sádaba[(⊠)]

ISEM Fashion Business School, University of Navarra, Pamplona, Spain
{patricia.sanmiguel,teresa.sadaba}@isem.es

Abstract. This paper analyzes how consumers are interacting with brands in the new digital context. The question research is if there is any homogenization of user behavior when dealing with brands in the e-commerce or not. The paper study Digital User Behavior in Fashion e-commerce, for this purpose, user behavior of Fast Fashion (FF) and Luxury-Premium (LP) e-commerce webpages are investigated. Therefore, a group of 20 fashion brands was selected: 10 of these brands belonged to the FF category and the other 10 to the LP category. User digital behavior is analyzed using six Key Digital Behavior Variables (KDBV), all performative variables that represent how consumers interact with brands through their web pages, based on web user session analysis. Studying digital user behavior enables us to get to know fashion brand consumers and users better. As we have observed, there are increasingly few differences between the behavior of FF web site users and LP web site users.

Keywords: Digital user behavior · Fashion E-commerce · Business model · Fast fashion · Luxury Premium

1 Introduction

With the advent of digitalization, fashion is facing one of its biggest challenges as an industry. This has not only affected the organization of companies, relations with suppliers and the design process, but, above all, it has transformed the relationship with consumers, who now have an additional channel with which to gain access to fashion products: e-commerce.

In the same manner in which fashion has traditionally made contact with consumers through points of sale on highstreets and at shopping centers, e-commerce now provides a new platform, a form of access that constitutes the biggest point of sale that any brand can imagine. That is to say, through e-commerce fashion brands can achieve their ultimate potential in terms of customers.

Online commerce is a new fashion retail channel that makes new approaches possible when it comes to the relationship with consumers. In this respect, in order to enhance user experience, it is still important to develop mechanisms that simplify the purchasing and product returns process, whilst integrating social media into e-commerce in order to create a sense of expectation or new needs regarding new products, moving towards

© Springer Nature Switzerland AG 2020
F. F.-H. Nah and K. Siau (Eds.): HCII 2020, LNCS 12204, pp. 521–534, 2020.
https://doi.org/10.1007/978-3-030-50341-3_39

a more personalized shopping experience, etc. The idea has also become established that purchases should not only be designed for the computer screen, but for any mobile device that facilitates access. In short, this new channel for fashion companies requires a better understanding of consumer expectations: "Only by comprehending the factors that influence users' decision to buy fashion online will companies be able to satisfy their needs. This information will help decision-making for marketing, communication, and sales strategies, tailoring appropriate solutions for this sales channel" [1].

When we talk about consumer behavior in the field of fashion we cannot really establish any general conclusions, because the spectrum of brands is extremely extensive and, given that a luxury brand's point of sale is not the same as that of a mass market brand, then their e-commerce approaches will probably not be the same either. Understanding these differences is key when it comes to creating an effective brand strategy.

From an academic point of view, user behavior within a digital context is analyzed from a range of different perspectives [2–4]. It is true that numerous pieces of work have focused on the psychological and sociological dimensions of the online user, but there are very few studies based on big data that offer a data analysis of interest to fashion brands.

This paper seeks to address this failing and analyses how consumers are interacting with brands in the new digital context. In this respect, our paper seeks shed some light on this behavior and explore whether there are any differences amongst brands depending on their positioning and business model. To this end, we have researched user behavior in the case of fast fashion and luxury e-commerce web pages.

2   Literature Review

Fashion Business Models in an Online Context

Globalization and the emergence of new technologies have changed the way in which companies create value, modifying ways of competing on the market [5–8]. The field of fashion is not unaffected by this transformation, and business models within this industry have witnessed far-reaching changes in terms of relationships with suppliers and consumers.

In classifying fashion business models, understanding this concept as "(…) the rationale of how an organization creates, delivers, and captures value" [9], the creation of value has been segmented into models that range from luxury fashion to low-cost fashion. The fashion sector can be represented as a pyramid, ranging from a high-end/high-margin/low-volume tip to a low-end/low-margin/high-volume base (Fig. 1).

Nevertheless, this pyramid structure is highly qualifiable, because the frontiers between the different segments have progressively changed and new distinctions have emerged. For example, Kapferer and Bastien [10] point out how, in recent years, the concept of luxury has thrown up different variants such as new luxury, mass luxury, masstige, opuluxe and hyper-luxury, demonstrating that the luxury segment is not static and also undergoes variations to the extent that mass consumers may also have access to luxury goods. This change in the concept is due to the fact that "the 'luxury sector' is a macroeconomic entity comprised of heterogeneous companies and products, only a few

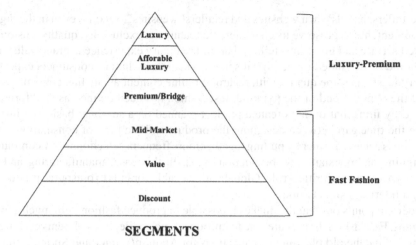

SEGMENTS

Fig. 1. Fashion sector pyramid. Source: author's own elaboration

of which follow a luxury strategy" [11]. Whatever the case may be, the very concept of luxury is somewhat hazy and "there is no scholarly consensus regarding the definition of luxury to date, but the complex nature of luxury has been discussed widely by scholars of different disciplinary origins" [12].

A recently published book explains that "luxury has existed since humans showed signs of life" and "has been reflected on for more than twenty-five centuries, from Plato to Epicure, from Luther to Mandeville and Veblen, as mentioned by Lipovestky" [13].

Scarce supply and, therefore, exclusiveness, as well as conspicuous consumption rather than consumption based on need, would appear to be characteristics typical of luxury. Being scarce and superfluous, however, luxury is linked with the human ambition to be more and have more, becoming something that forms an intrinsic and characteristic part of Man [13]. To some extent, luxury is associated with services and goods that must have a strong human content, which means that (a) to qualify as luxury, the object or part of it must be handmade, a service rendered by a human to another human; and (b) exclusive services are a sine qua non part of luxury management [10].

In an online context, the luxury segment took some time to contemplate the possibility that e-commerce might be an appropriate channel for this segment [14]. Nevertheless, and although the growth of online luxury creates transformation and risks, such as loss of exclusivity, many researchers emphasize the opportunities presented by online business development, such as the increasing purchase of luxury products by consumers in emerging and developing markets [11, 15, 16].

Nowadays, luxury brands have a massive presence on the World Wide Web. According to the latest Bain Report 2018 "Online luxury shopping continued to accelerate in 2018, growing 22% to nearly €27 billion; it now represents 10% of all luxury sales. The Americas market made up 44% of online sales, but Asia is emerging as a new growth engine for luxury online, slightly ahead of Europe. Accessories remained the top category sold online, ahead of apparel. The beauty and hard luxury (jewelry and watches) categories were both on the rise. The biggest online channels for luxury sales were e-tailers, brands' own websites and retailers' websites". Luxury, even in the digital environment, has to preserve its characteristic features of exclusivity, quality, customer-oriented service and great storytelling. Part of the luxury experience is brand value, and this should be translated to the digital sphere. That is why luxury consumers expect, at the very least, the same quality with regard to online content as off-line content.

At the opposite end of the pyramid, fast fashion has been defined as the "formulas adopted by firms that do not create a product planned on a seasonal basis, but instead reduce the time gap between designing the product and the time of consumption; this reduction is achieved either by putting together more frequent selections or by continuous redesigning and constant new production" [17]. In this case, manufacturing and the supply chain assume a critical role. Globalization enables brands to outsource production through international networks.

Guercini points out that this makes it possible to produce fashion with much shorter time gaps. Fast fashion brands are able to introduce small collections of items each week, leaving behind the old planning of collections for Autumn/Winter and Spring/Summer. This also increases the opportunities that customers have to purchase fashion throughout the year, thus modifying fashion consumer habits. Fast fashion is also defined by Sheridan et al. as "the strategies that retailers adopt in order to reflect current and emerging trends quickly and effectively in current merchandise assortments" [18]. However, this strategy is becoming increasingly prevalent in other fashion business models, even in premium models.

As Runfola and Guercini [19] have emphasized, nowadays the development of fast fashion companies is characterized by five trends: (1) innovation regarding relationships between industry and distribution in the textile and clothing pipeline is crucial; (2) the fashion industry has been undergoing a major shift in terms of manufacturing at a global level [20, 21]; (3) close communication and coordination between players within the textile and clothing pipeline have come to substitute product inventory when it comes to adapting to consumer trends [22]; (4) recent market trends towards increasing the number of seasonal collections (from two to four, or even six) have been quickly followed by a veritable explosion of collections from fast fashion businesses, even as far as the creation of weekly collections [18, 23]; (5) international expansion towards the foreign markets is considered a valuable option when it comes to sustaining business growth [24, 25].

Technology in the realm of fast fashion is allowing companies to shorten the manufacturing set-up that involves all company activities [26]. Thus, "since the birth of e-commerce, businesses have been able to make use of the Internet in reducing costs associated with purchasing, managing supplier relationships, streamlining logistics and inventory, and developing strategic advantage and successful implementation of business re-engineering" [27]. For example, Inditex has physical stores in 96 markets, but online sales in 202 markets, according to the company's Annual Report. In 2018, online sales have grown 3,200 million euros, representing a 27% growth in the last year, online sales represent 14% of sales in markets where Inditex has an integrated commercial presence (Inditex Report 2018). However, price and product differentiation are subject to a highly competitive context, where "purchasing online involves lower opportunity costs relative to offline shopping because price comparison between several online malls can be realized within a second. This aggravates price competition and leads to squeezed profits in the market" [27]. Now, companies are facing a price war in which Black Fridays, sales and promotions make the consumer more strategic in terms of their shopping [28]. Due to this price competition, consumers also present a lower degree of brand loyalty. In this sense, FF consumers are used to frequent product rotation, constant marketing campaigns and promotions to liberate stock.

Digital User Behavior

Multiple studies have focused on the use of the Internet [29, 30]. These studies have analyzed the abilities of users, their autonomy, their goals and their skills, amongst other factors. However, fewer studies have analyzed the behavior of users on web pages themselves, which is why analyses of this kind are almost non-existent in the academic literature relating to the fashion industry.

Analyses of the digital behavior of users have been carried out based on different perspectives. There are studies that analyze behavioral differences according to gender (male and female) [31] and differences between younger users and adults [29]. Others analyze the reasons that lead a user to return to a web page [32], the user's intention to visit a web site [32, 33] and the personal information that is disclosed through the users' digital footprint [34].

Studies that analyze the digital behavior of users on a web site can be based on different research methods, such as, for example, observation, interviews and Big Data. Asenjo [35] offers an in-depth study of web user behavior, and, in his research, he explains that one way of analyzing the behavior of users is via Big Data. Digital behavior can be described by three kinds of data: web structure, web content and the web user session. The first is directly linked to the structure of the web site, its connections and its surfing possibilities. The second relates to the information available, semantics, texts, videos and applications [35]. Finally, the web user session describes the click stream that each web user performs during his visit to the web site, represented by the browsing trajectories that are categorized as a session: visits, pages, time [35, 36]. This paper shall focus on this latter set of data, which make up the way of interacting with the user.

Within the fashion industry, academic research into the digital behavior of users on web pages is almost non-existent. An early study that takes into account digital user behavior when applied to the industry focuses on the behavioral differences of users from different countries [37]. Conversely, we can find a number of academic studies relating to behavior in the social media, or professional reports that analyze web behavior and have been carried out by consultants or observatories such as Brandwatch, L2 Think Tank-Gartner and Digital Fashion Brands.

3   Hypothesis and Methodology

Focusing on the differences between Luxury/Premium (LP) and Fast Fashion (FF) business models, this paper seeks to explore whether there are significant differences in consumer behavior when considering segments of brands in an online context. There is no specific literature on this matter and it could be said that fashion brands are embracing e-commerce without considering its ramifications. Therefore, the results could offer practical implications for brands. The hypotheses formulated are as follows:

H1. Different user behavior exists between the users of different fashion business models: FF and LP users

H2. Homogeneous behavior exists between FF brand consumers, on the one hand, and LP users, on the other

H3. FF brands receive more visits than LP brands as there is a greater degree of product turnover in the case of the former, and LP brands are perceived as being more exclusive

H4. The mobile phone is the digital channel preferred by FF users, given that potential consumers are younger than LP consumers

H5. A higher bounce rate for FF users is expected, given that numerous marketing campaigns associated with sales are carried out by FF brands

H6. LP visitors enjoy higher levels of quality during their web visits, given that higher-quality content is expected compared to FF users.

We started by observing the online behavior of brands, and we selected those that witnessed the highest number of visits to their website during the period April 2019 to September 2019 (six months). Then, within both categories (FF and LP), we selected the 10 brands that had the highest number of visits to their web site (e-commerce) during those six months, based on a data base of more than 300 fashion companies belonging to the observatory, digitalfashionbrands.com.

Therefore, a group of 20 fashion brands was selected: 10 of these brands belonged to the FF category and the other 10 to the LP category. The brand sample for this study includes the following brands, classified as FF or LP. All of these pages are e-commerce channels belonging to the brands themselves (Table 1).

All the data were collected through Similarwebplatform. SimilarWeb[1] is an information technology company that provides services in market intelligence, web analytics and data meaning and business intelligence for international corporations. This company provides estimated data, not absolute data.

User digital behavior [38] is analyzed using six Key Digital Behavior Variables (KDBV), all performative variables that represent how consumers interact with brands through their web pages, based on web user session analysis [35].

- Total visits: a visit consists of one individual visitor who arrives at your web site and proceeds to browse. A visit counts all visitors, no matter how many times the same visitor may have visited the site.
- Desktop traffic share: percentage of visits to the web site from a computer.
- Mobile traffic share: percentage of visits to the web site from a mobile or tablet.

---

[1] SimilarWeb provides data and insights to help businesses make better decisions, identify new opportunities and spot the latest Internet and mobile trends. This information is essential when it comes to reacting to the Internet's ever-changing environment, building high-reward and low-risk campaigns, and understanding the competitive world in which companies operate. For further information regarding similar web visits: https://www.similarweb.com/downloads/our-data-methodology.pdf.

Table 1. Brands sample

Fast fashion	Luxury/Premium
1. H&M	1. Louis Vuitton
2. Zara	2. Gucci
3. GAP	3. Chanel
4. Uniqlo	4. Coach
5. Old navy	5. Ralph Lauren
6. Mango	6. Michael Kors
7. Bershka	7. Kate Spade
8. Hollister	8. Dior
9. Abercrombie & Fitch	9. Burberry
10. Topshop	10. Hugo Boss

Source: author's own elaboration

- Visit duration: the length of time in a session. Calculation is typically the timestamp of the last activity in the session minus the timestamp of the first activity of the session.
- Pages per visit: once a visitor arrives at your web site, they will surf the web and visit a few more pages on the web site. Each individual page a visitor views is tracked as a page view.
- Bounce rate: this represents the percentage of visitors who enter the site and then leave ("bounce"), rather than continuing to view other pages within the same site.

Appendix 1 shows all of the data gathered by the tool. Having obtained the data, we carried out a descriptive statistics analysis. First, we explain the results obtained in each group and the behavior of users on the LP and FF web sites. Then we carry out a comparative analysis of LP and FF users based on a summary of the results obtained for each group.

4 Results and Discussion

Luxury-Premium

As we can observe from the data obtained from SimilarWeb (Appendix 1), Louis Vuitton was the brand that achieved the highest number of visitors within the period analyzed, generating some 65 million visitors in six months. Hugo Boss was the brand that achieved the highest volume of visitors via desktop computer (desktop traffic share of 37.28%) and Michael Kors was the brand that was most visited via mobile phone and tablet (mobile traffic share of 74.92%). The web page where users spent the most time was Gucci (visit duration of 7 min 55 s on average), also being the web site on which visitors viewed the largest number of pages (pages per visit, 9.59 on average). Finally, the web site that had the highest bounce rate was Coach, based on a figure of 49.02%. Below, consumer behavior through KDBV is presented in general terms for LP brands (Table 2):

Table 2. Luxury-premium 10 brands key digital behavior variables

Variables	Sample total	Mean	SD
Total visits	341,943,900	34,194,390	15,614,047
Desktop traffic share	314.30%	31%	3.72%
Mobile traffic share	658.50%	69%	3.73%
Visit duration	00:45:21	00:04:32	00:01:54
Pages per visit	61.47	6.147	1.93
Bounce rate	221.35%	22.14%	6.07%

Source: author's own elaboration

Table 2 shows that, amongst the LP brands and throughout the six months analyzed, the average number of visits came to 34 million, although we should highlight the standard deviation (SD) of 15 million visits, a large difference amongst the ten brands that made up the sample. Whilst Louis Vuitton generated 65 million visits during the six months analyzed, Hugo Boss achieved the lowest number of visits with a figure of 18 million.

The other variables (desktop traffic share, mobile traffic share, visit duration, pages per visit, bounce rate) present a lower SD, showing that the behavior of users is more homogeneous amongst the luxury brands analyzed. We might highlight the fact that an SD of 1.54 min for visit duration also constitutes a difference that needs to be taken account: whilst users remained an average of almost eight minutes on the Gucci web site, users on the Dior web page stayed for just three minutes.

The great difference within the sample relates to the volume of users who enter the web pages, but their behavior on the web sites is similar.

In view of these results, we can draw up a profile for digital user behavior in relation to LP brands: these users preferably browse the web sites from their mobile and stay an average of four minutes, during which time they visit some six pages on the web site.

Fast Fashion

H&M is the brand that generated the largest volume of visits to its web site, coming to 551 million during the period analyzed, followed by Zara and Gap, with 363 million and 326 million, respectively (see Appendix 2). Abercrombie & Fitch is the brand that received the largest number of visits from desktop computers (42.45%), whilst Tommy Hilfiger was the label that was most visited from mobile phones. It is interesting to note that the four brands with the highest mobile traffic share were American (Tommy Hilfiger; Old Navy; GAP; Hollister).

The web site where users stayed for the longest time was Zara (a visit duration of 7 min and 17 s on average), also being the site where users referred to the largest number of pages (pages per visit of 15.31 on average). With regard to the bounce rate, Uniqlo was the brand that presented the highest percentage (49.02%). Below, consumer behavior through KDBV is presented in general terms for FF brands (Table 3):

Table 3. Fast fashion 10 brands key digital behavior variables

Variables	Sample total	Mean	SD
Total visits	2,059,056,500	205,905,650	169,549,280
Desktop traffic share	359.60%	35.95%	5.45%
Mobile traffic share	642.03%	64.20%	5.45%
Visit duration	57.07	00:05:43	00:01:08
Pages per visit	68.05%	6.85%	3.29
Bounce rate	365.47%	36.55%	6.62%

Source: author's own elaboration

Table 3 presents a summary of the results, including the mean, as well as the standard deviation for KDBV in the case of FF brands. As we can observe, the ten brands analyzed presented more than two billion visits during the six months analyzed. Although the average for the sample comes to 205 million visits, we must pay attention to the SD, given that this comes to 169 million visits. This difference is reflected when comparing the 551 million visits generated by H&M and the 42 million achieved by Abercrombie & Fitch.

When we look at the rest of the variables, we can see that the SD is lower than that recorded for the number of visits, in which respect these variables (desktop traffic share, mobile traffic share, visit duration, pages per visit, bounce rate) present a more homogenous behavior amongst the FF brands. We might highlight the fact that, although the SD for visit duration is 1.8, when we look at the two extremes within the sample, we can see that Zara achieves a figure of 7 min and 17 s, whilst Uniqlo achieves only 3 min and 57 s (see Appendix 2).

The user behavior profile for FF brands is as follows: users preferably view web sites from their mobile phone; they spend an average of 5 min on the web site; and during this time, they visit some 7 pages on the web site.

Study of the Hypotheses
Having outlined the data obtained, we can now study our hypotheses and draw up our conclusions:

H1. The hypothesis is validated. There are differences regarding FF and LP digital user behavior. Nevertheless, these differences are becoming increasingly small. In general, we are talking about users who increasingly interact with mobile devices in both segments, who find contents of interest presented by the Top 10 brands analyzed in the LP and FF categories, and who spend between 3 and 5 min visiting the corresponding web sites.
H2. The hypothesis is not validated. There is no homogenous behavior amongst users when comparing the brands in the LP and FF groups. As we have observed, there are

significant differences regarding the data obtained in each sample. These differences can be observed in relation to all the variables analyzed: total visits, desktop traffic share, mobile traffic share, visit duration, pages per visit and bounce rate. The differences observed in the samples analyzed enable us to formulate a future hypothesis: there are significant differences regarding the digital behavior of users amongst brands within the same category.

H3. The hypothesis is validated. This is a significant difference regarding the volume of traffic generated by FF web sites and LP web sites. That is to say, a larger volume of users visits the FF brands, and they do so more frequently too: we are dealing with a difference of more than one billion visits (in the sample analyzed). This difference may occur because of three factors: the range of users addressed by FF brands is much wider than that of the LP brands; the FF brands have a greater volume of product references on the web site; and the FF brands bring out new collections and offer discounts more frequently.

H4. The hypothesis is not validated. The users who visit FF brands do not use the mobile channel more than the users who visit the LP web sites. In the samples we analyzed, the LP users employed mobile devices a little more than the FF brand visitors. The brands that brought together the largest numbers of visitors in the two samples (FF and LP) were not the brands that featured the highest percentage of visitors via mobile device. We should highlight the fact that, in order to achieve a large volume of users, brands must reach both those visitors who prefer to use a desktop and those who prefer to use a mobile device.

H5. The hypothesis is validated. The users of the FF brand web sites present a higher bounce rate than those who use LP web sites. In the sample we analyzed, the FF brands presented a bounce rate that was 144% higher than in the case of the LP brands. This is due to the higher volume of digital marketing measures implemented by the FF brands, with the users of FF web sites being more exposed to the advertising of FF brands, which, in many cases is quite intrusive, thus leading the users to reject the brands.

H6. The hypothesis is not validated. The quality of the users' experience visiting a web site is measured by the duration of the visit and the number of pages they visit on the site itself. In the case of the sample we analyzed, the quality was higher for those users who visited the FF web sites than those who visited the LP sites. The quality of the visit depends on whether the web site is attractive to consumers, both in terms of the product, the design of the web site and the quality of the contents.

5   Conclusions and Research Limitations

Studying digital user behavior enables us to get to know fashion brand consumers and users better. As we have observed, there are increasingly few differences between the behavior of FF web site users and LP web site users, but the volume of FF web site users continues to be very high. Whatever the case may be, bearing in mind the fact that the brands we analyzed are the leading brands in terms of the number of visits they received, the difference between them is striking.

This difference is coherent with regard to the business model being implemented by LP brands, who are always going to want to be more exclusive, which means they are not within reach of the majority of consumers and users. However, the fact that LP brands are achieving increasingly high numbers of visits may demonstrate that these web sites wish to reach an increasingly wide section of the public, imitating the positioning and digital marketing strategies of the FF brands. Furthermore, it is important to consider the need to work the marketing content dimension in the case of LP brands, due to the fact that they cannot base their quality of visit on product rotation in the same way as FF brands can.

In the same way as in the offline realm, where a shop must be well situated in a street with a great deal of traffic in order to establish effective sales strategies, in the online world it is essential to understand the visits that are made to a web site and their potential, in order to design a better relationship with users. To a certain extent, and bearing in mind its limitations, this paper seeks to highlight the need to acquire a greater knowledge of quantitative data and the different web variables in order to be able to implement better strategies according to the fashion business model being pursued.

The study of digital user behavior requires a more in-depth analysis, both in terms of the number of variables to be analyzed and the number of brands to be included in the sample. In spite of its limitations, this study seeks to provide a glimpse of digital user behavior within the world of fashion.

Furthermore, our study of behavior cannot be limited to a series of metrics that come from web analytics. It is important to complement these studies with more qualitative perspectives, based on methods such as in-depth interviews, focus groups and heat maps for the web sites that are analyzed.

Annex

Annex 1

	BRAND	WEB	Total visits	Traffic share desktop	Traffic share mobile	Visit duration	Pages per visit	Bounce rate
1	Louis VuittOE	louisvuitton.com	65100000	3155%	68.35%	4.55	9	38.12%
2	Gucci	gucci.com	58640000	31.34%	68.66%	7.55	9.59	42.66%
3	Chanel	chanel.com	37540000	30.20%	69.80%	3.09	6.27	40.45%
4	Coach	coach.com	31200000	27.43%	72.57%	3.24	4.52	49.02%
5	Ralph Lauren	ralphlauren.com	30333900	33.32%	66.68%	5.48	7.22	43.44%
6	Michael Kors	michaelkors.com	28520000	25.08%	74.92%	5.53	5.58	44.02%
7	Kate Spade	katespade.com	26880000	31.79%	68.21%	4.3	5.29	38.82%
8	Christian Dior	diot.com	23790000	29.77%	70.23%	2.50	3.52	53.97%

(*continued*)

(*continued*)

	BRAND	WEB	Total visits	Traffic share desktop	Traffic share mobile	Visit duration	Pages per visit	Bounce rate
9	Burberry	burberry.com	21940000	36.54%	63.36%	3.26	4.8	41.93%
10	Hugo Boss	hugaboss.com	18000000	37.28%	62.72%	3.31	5.68	46 18%

Annex 2

	BRAND	WEB	Total visits	Traffic share desktop	Traffic share mobile	Visit duration	Pages per visit	Bounce rate
1	H&M	hm.com	551900000	35.30%	64.70%	6.37	11.07	33.83%
2	Zara	zara.com	363799500	36.78%	63.22%	7.17	15.31	26.37%
3	GAP	gap.com	326400000	31.52%	68.48%	6.14	7.58	37.35%
4	Uniqlo	uniqlo.com	283000000	34.26%	65.74%	3.57	6.91	49.01%
5	Old Navy	oldnavy.gap.com	175003000	26.07%	73.93%	5.22	6.39	42.45%
6	Mango	mango.com	125100000	37.89%	62.11%	5.38	6.87	35.01%
7	Bershka	bershka.com	87190000	34.61%	65.39%	5.16	8.73	28.92%
8	Hollister	hollisterco.com	64004000	34.37%	67.18%	5.44	5.91	38.85%
9	Abercrombie & Fitch	abercrombie.com	42440000	42.45%	57.55%	6.14	6.23	37.99%
10	Topshop	topshop.com	40220000	46.27%	53.73%	4.48	8.88	35.69%

References

1. Escobar-Rodríguez, T., Bonsón-Fernández, R.: Analysing online purchase intention in Spain: fashion e-commerce. Inf. Syst. E-bus. Manag. **15**, 599–622 (2017)
2. Rios, A.E.: The impact of the digital revolution in the development of market and communication strategies for the luxury sector (fashion luxury). Cent. Eur. Bus. Rev. **5**, 17–36 (2016)
3. Goldsmith, R.E., Horowitz, D.: Measuring motivations for online opinion seeking. J. Interact. Advert. **6**, 2–14 (2006)

4. Geissinger, A., Laurell, C.: User engagement in social media–an explorative study of Swedish fashion brands. J. Fash. Mark. Manag. 177–190 (2016)
5. Boons, F., Lüdeke-Freund, F.: Business models for sustainable innovation: state-of-the-art and steps towards a research agenda. J. Clean. Prod. **45**, 9–19 (2013)
6. Wirtz, B.W., Schilke, O., Ullrich, S.: Strategic development of business models: implications of the Web 2.0 for creating value on the internet. Long Range Plann. **43**, 272–290 (2010)
7. Prieger, J.E., Heil, D.: Economic implications of e-business for organizations. In: Martínez-López, F.J. (ed.) Handbook of Strategic e-Business Management. PI, pp. 15–53. Springer, Heidelberg (2014). https://doi.org/10.1007/978-3-642-39747-9_2
8. Sandulli, F.D., Rodríguez-Duarte, A., Sánchez-Fernández, D.C.: Value creation and value capture through internet business models. In: Martínez-López, F.J. (ed.) Handbook of Strategic e-Business Management. PI, pp. 83–108. Springer, Heidelberg (2014). https://doi.org/10.1007/978-3-642-39747-9_4
9. Osterwalder, A., Pigneur, Y.: Business Model Generation: A Handbook for Visionaries, Game Changers, and Challengers. Wiley, Hoboken (2010)
10. Kapferer, J.-N., Bastien, V.: The specificity of luxury management: turning marketing upside down. J. Brand Manag. **16**, 311–322 (2009). https://doi.org/10.1057/bm.2008.51
11. Kapferer, J.-N.: The artification of luxury: from artisans to artists. Bus. Horiz. **57**, 371–380 (2014). https://doi.org/10.1016/j.bushor.2013.12.007
12. Godart, F., Seong, S.: Is Sustainable Luxury Fashion Possible. Sustainable Luxury: Managing Social and Environmental Performance in Iconic Brands. Greenleaf Publishing, Sheffield (2014)
13. Cantista, I., Sádaba, T.: Understanding luxury fashion: origins and contemporary issues. In: Cantista, I., Sádaba, T. (eds.) Understanding Luxury Fashion. PAL, pp. 3–12. Springer, Cham (2020). https://doi.org/10.1007/978-3-030-25654-8_1
14. Okonkwo, U.: Luxury Online: Styles, Systems, Strategies. Palgrave Macmillan UK, London (2010). https://doi.org/10.1057/9780230248335
15. Guercini, S., Runfola, A.: Internationalization through e-commerce. The case of multibrand luxury retailers in the fashion industry. Adv. Int. Mark. **26**, 15–31 (2015)
16. Jung, Y.J., Kim, J.: Facebook marketing for fashion apparel brands: effect of other consumers' postings and type of brand comment on brand trust and purchase intention. J. Glob. Fash. Mark. **7**, 196–210 (2016). https://doi.org/10.1080/20932685.2016.1162665
17. Guercini, S.: Relation between branding and growth of the firm in new quick fashion formulas: analysis of an Italian case. J. Fash. Mark. Manag. **5**, 69–79 (2001). https://doi.org/10.1108/EUM0000000007280
18. Sheridan, M., Moore, C., Nobbs, K.: Fast fashion requires fast marketing: the role of category management in fast fashion positioning. J. Fash. Mark. Manag. **10**, 301–315 (2006). https://doi.org/10.1108/13612020610679286
19. Runfola, A., Guercini, S.: Fast fashion companies coping with internationalization: driving the change or changing the model? J. Fash. Mark. Manag. **17**, 191, 192, 199 (2013). https://doi.org/10.1108/JFMM-10-2011-0075
20. Jones, R.: The Apparel Industry. Blackwell Publishing, Oxford (2002)
21. Gereffi, G.: International trade and industrial upgrading in the apparel commodity chain. J. Int. Econ. **48**, 37–70 (1999)
22. Milgrom, P., Roberts, J.: Communication and inventory as substitutes in organizing production. Scand. J. Econ. **90**, 275–289 (1988)
23. Doyle, S., Barnes, L., Lea-Greenwood, G., Moore, C., Morgan, L.: Supplier management in fast moving fashion retailing. J. Fash. Mark. Manag. Int. J. **10**, 272–281 (2006)
24. Choi, T.M., Chiu, C.H., To, K.M.C.: A fast fashion safety-first inventory model. Text. Res. J. **81**, 819–826 (2011)

25. Fernie, J., Alexander, N., Doherty, A.M.: International retail research: focus, methodology and conceptual development. Int. J. Retail Distrib. Manag. **38**, 928–942 (2010)
26. Arrigo, E.: Innovation and market-driven management in fast fashion companies. Symphonya Emerg. Issues Manag. **2**, 67–85 (2010)
27. Zhenxiang, W., Lijie, Z.: Case study of online retailing fast fashion industry. Int. J. e-Educ. e-Bus. e-Manag. e-Learn. **1**, 195 (2011)
28. Cachon, G.P., Swinney, R.: The value of fast fashion: quick response, enhanced design, and strategic consumer behavior. Manag. Sci. **57**, 778–795 (2011)
29. Hargittai, E., Hinnant, A.: Digital inequality: differences in young adults' use of the internet. Commun. Res. **35**, 602–621 (2008)
30. Wolny, J., Mueller, C.: Analysis of fashion consumers' motives to engage in electronic word of mouth communication through social media platforms. J. Mark. Manag. **29**, 562–583 (2013). https://doi.org/10.1080/0267257X.2013.778324
31. Dixon, L.J., et al.: Gendered space: the digital divide between male and female users in internet public access sites. J. Comput. Commun. **19**, 991–1009 (2014)
32. Castañeda, J.A., Muñoz-Leiva, F., Luque, T.: Web Acceptance Model (WAM): moderating effects of user experience. Inf. Manag. **44**, 384–396 (2007)
33. Muñoz-Leiva, F., Hernández-Méndez, J., Sánchez-Fernández, J.: Generalising user behaviour in online travel sites through the Travel 2.0 website acceptance model. Online Inf. Rev. 879–902 (2012)
34. Vervier, L., Zeissig, E.-M., Lidynia, C., Ziefle, M.: Perceptions of digital footprints and the value of privacy. In: IoTBDS, pp. 80–91 (2017)
35. Asenjo, P.E.R.: Web user behavior analysis (2011)
36. Snášel, V., Kudelka, M.: Web content mining focused on named objects. In: Tiwary, U.S., Siddiqui, T.J., Radhakrishna, M., Tiwari, M.D. (eds.) Proceedings of the First International Conference on Intelligent Human Computer Interaction, pp. 37–58. Springer, New Delhi (2009). https://doi.org/10.1007/978-81-8489-203-1_3
37. SanMiguel, P., Sadaba, T., Guercini, S.: Is online fashion a "flat world"? An analysis about brands and markets behavior. In: 2019 Global Fashion Management Conference at Paris, pp. 753–756 (2019)
38. Agichtein, E., Brill, E., Dumais, S.: Improving web search ranking by incorporating user behavior information. In: Proceedings of the 29th Annual International ACM SIGIR Conference on Research and Development in Information Retrieval, pp. 19–26 (2006)

The Effects of Cookie Notices on Perceived Privacy and Trust in E-Commerce

Jan Schiefermair and Martin Stabauer$^{(\boxtimes)}$ (iD)

Johannes Kepler University, Linz, Austria
contact@schiefermair.com, martin.stabauer@jku.at

Abstract. Website cookies have become an indispensable part of today's e-commerce due to the high benefits they provide to companies. However, to leverage their full potential, a multitude of legal framework conditions must be taken into account. A phenomenon that has emerged from this context are cookie notices which can be found on the majority of today's e-commerce websites. Such notices are primarily implemented because they are seen as a legal necessity and not due to the expectation of any inter-related benefits. However, as consumers tend to evaluate whether they intend to purchase from a specific online shop in the first few seconds of a website visit, it cannot be ruled out that this evaluation is influenced by a cookie notice. Therefore, the aim of this research is to investigate whether the most commonly found versions of cookie notices (pop-up and cookie bar) have an influence on perceived privacy and trust. The following hypotheses were subsequently tested by the means of an online experiment: in a realistically designed shopping scenario, where a simple shopping task had to be completed in a fictitious online shop, participants were each exposed to one of two cookie notice versions or no cookie notice at all. Afterwards all participants provided their responses to an online survey which allowed for the measurement of the influence on perceived privacy and e-trust. The results were differing: Despite most hypotheses were to be rejected, we arrived at a recommendation to operators of e-commerce websites to implement pop-up cookie notices.

Keywords: Cookies · Cookie notices · Privacy · Trust · E-Commerce

1 Introduction

Website cookies (henceforth referred to as cookies) are subject to highly controversial discussions in both academia and industry. Nearly no e-commerce website gets by without this technology, and their importance and usefulness for the internet is widely recognized. On the one hand, cookies are vital for the customer journey of modern e-commerce websites and are in many cases used for legitimate functions such as user identification over the duration of a shopping session, contributing to shopping cart services, and providing customers with a

© Springer Nature Switzerland AG 2020
F. F.-H. Nah and K. Siau (Eds.): HCII 2020, LNCS 12204, pp. 535–549, 2020.
https://doi.org/10.1007/978-3-030-50341-3_40

personalized, and thereby more relevant, shopping experience (see Sect. 1.1). On the other hand, they can enable an excessive collection of data and misapplication, and they can also be misused for tracking the customers and using their data for various, not always justifiable, purposes.

Over the last few years, different legal regulations have been established to govern the exorbitant usage of cookies (see Sect. 1.2). A common practice amongst website operators to deal with these regulations are so-called cookie notices which inform the users of the cookies in place and require them to consent to their usage. These notices can be found in a number of different shapes and different levels of granularity, some standardized options are discussed in Sect. 1.2. Previous literature suggests further investigations into the topic of cookie notices [1].

While there are still quite a few research gaps in this area, trust in e-commerce settings and its effects on users' purchase intentions is a well researched topic; the same is true for the relation of perceived privacy and purchase intention (for both see Sect. 1.3). Building on this foundation, it seems worthwhile to address possible correlations between the aforementioned cookie notices and both perceived privacy and trust. As consumers tend to decide on a potential purchase in the first few seconds of a website visit, it may be legitimate to presume that the presence of cookie notices and their visual appearance could make a difference [2]. This would lead to the assumption, that cookie notices are not only a legal necessity but also have a transitive influence on purchase intentions.

This research tries to partly fill the gap and answer the question *"Do cookie notices have an effect on perceived privacy and trust in e-commerce websites?"*. Consequently, we conducted an online experiment in which the participants were confronted with a simple task within the scope of a fictional online pharmacy. The website featured different versions of cookie notices. After fulfilling the task, the users had to answer questions regarding these notices, their trust towards the pharmacy and their perceived privacy. This paper is structured in five sections: the first gives an overview of the underlying terminology and the technical and legal basis; the second explains the conceptual framework and develops the hypotheses; the third section is about the experimental study conducted; and the rest of the paper elaborates on results, discussion and conclusion.

1.1 Cookies

Cookies are small fragments of information stored in a text file on the local computer. A common categorization of cookies distinguishes very roughly between a) session cookies and persistent cookies, and b) first-party and third-party cookies. The following identified use case scenarios specify this distinction in a practically applicable way, and call for different legal approaches [3]:

- *User-input cookies* keep track of the users' input over multiple pages or provide functionalities like shopping carts.
- *Authentication cookies* identify users once they have logged in without requiring them to re-enter their credentials on every page. This is done either on a session-only basis or as a persistent cookie.

- *User centric security cookies* can detect repeated failed login attempts and other security issues. To fulfill this purpose, they typically have a longer lifespan.
- *Multimedia player session cookies* are equally known as "flash cookies", named after the Adobe Flash technology, and are used to store technical data for video or audio playback.
- *Load balancing session cookies* allow for distributing the users' web requests over a pool of web servers.
- *UI customization cookies* enable users to store their preferences regarding specific services of the website like its language or the number of search results per page.
- *Social plug-in content sharing cookies* are employed when users want to share website content on a particular social network they are logged in to.
- *Social plug-in tracking cookies* are used to track users for purposes such as behavioral targeting or market research. In contrast to the previous category, these cannot be seen as strictly necessary for a service requested by the users.
- *Third party advertising cookies*, similarly with the previous category, are not deemed necessary and opposed to the "privacy by design" principle defined in the EU's General Data Protection Regulation (GDPR).
- *First party analytics cookies* help measuring audience activities and create statistics. Although these cookies are also not perceived as strictly necessary, they hardly create a privacy risk when applied correctly.

The high relevance of cookies can be observed when looking at a cookie sweep conducted by a working group of the European Commission. Only 7 out of 478 websites in the e-commerce, media, and public sectors across 8 EU member states did not make use of cookies at all. About 70% of all cookies set were third-party cookies and the e-commerce websites in the sweep employed an average of 23 cookies [4]. These high numbers are confirmed by a variety of other studies (e.g., [5,6]) as well as the exemplifying privacy notice of amazon.de which lists more than 40 third-party cookies[1].

1.2   Cookie Notices

Understandably, users can have privacy concerns when websites are (mis-)using cookies [7]. The European Union has passed regulations and directives that govern the usage of cookies and specify the requirements for users' consent. Especially relevant in this context are Directive 2002/58/EC as amended by Directive 2009/136/EC (the ePrivacy Directive), the Regulation 2016/679 (GDPR), and the upcoming ePrivacy Regulation, which will supposedly accompany the GDPR and thereby repeal the ePrivacy Directive somewhere in 2020. Regarding the complex legal situation also see [8,9].

The main requirements in this regard defined in the legal basis refer to the necessity of allowing users to prevent website operators from processing their

---

[1] https://www.amazon.de/gp/help/customer/display.html/?nodeId=GDDFZHDDG WM46YS3 (September 30, 2019).

538   J. Schiefermair and M. Stabauer

personal data in the form of cookies. One of the few exceptions are cookies that
are strictly necessary for the delivery of a service by the user (also see Sect. 1.1).
To comply with these requirements, website operators often employ so-called
cookie notices [1]. These notices inform website users of the cookies in place and
give them a choice to accept or decline the request for making use of them. The
notices can be designed in various different ways and incorporate different levels
of granularity. Two major types, namely popups and banners, are depicted in
Fig. 1 and Fig. 2, respectively. The context of these screenshots is described in
Sect. 3.

In October 2019, the Court of Justice of the European Union ruled that a
user's deselection of a pre-checked checkbox ("opt-out") is not sufficient to meet
GDPR requirements (ECJ case C-673/17). This applies to both personal and
non-personal data and also clarifies that users need to be informed about cookie
lifespan and access by third parties.

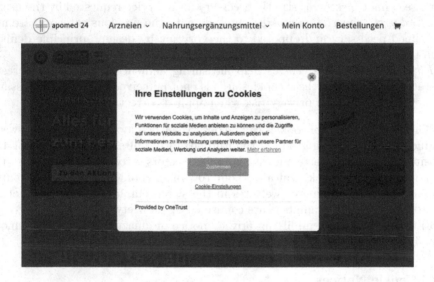

Fig. 1. Popup cookie notice

1.3   Perceived Privacy and Trust

While privacy is a heavily debated topic in both academia and industry, users'
privacy awareness and users' interest in privacy regulations seem to stagnate [10].
Nonetheless, earlier studies show that users with high expectations and demands
in privacy are less likely to buy something from online shops, which consequently
leads to the conclusion that perceived privacy has a positive effect on purchase
intention [11–13]. Information policy plays an important role, users tend to ignore
information on privacy policies when they are not presented in a suitable manner.
In an earlier study, only 0.0096% of users even opened the relevant page with

Fig. 2. Banner cookie notice

privacy information [14]. Privacy in this context is also recognized as one of the grand challenges of human-computer interaction research [15].

Likewise, trust in online settings is a widely researched topic (e.g., [16–18]) and it is closely related to trust in e-commerce contexts [19]. There is an understanding that web-based vendors need to consider a wide range of trust building measures [20]. Trust in e-commerce is generally understood as a construct with multiple dimensions: ability, benevolence, integrity and predictability [21]. The *Familiarity and Trust model* designed by Gefen [22], in which trust was measured as a unidimensional phenomenon, was later extended by Gefen and Straub [23], measuring the mentioned four dimensions of trust. Furthermore, it has been suggested to examine trusting disposition and familiarity as control variables to avoid wrong conclusions when measuring trust. Given that the stated dimensions can be found in several prominent papers dealing with trust, and the measurement model by Gefen and Straub is considered as a valid instrument for e-trust measurement, we based our research partly on this very model and introduced some adaptations to better match the specific research topic.

2 Conceptual Framework and Hypothesis Development

Building on the research presented in Sect. 1.3, we infer that cookie notices are part of an online vendor's information policy and therefore have a (positive) effect on its users' perceived privacy. Furthermore, we assume differences between the variants defined in Sect. 1.2 regarding their impact on perceived privacy. This leads to the following hypotheses:

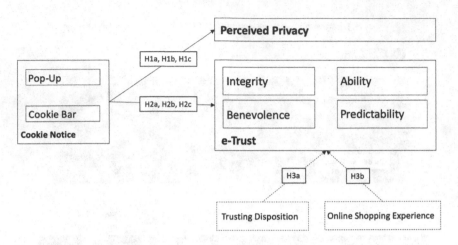

Fig. 3. Research model

Hypothesis 1a (H1a). *The presence of a cookie notice on an e-commerce website has an effect on users' perceived privacy.*

Hypothesis 1b (H1b). *The presence of a cookie notice on an e-commerce website has a* positive *effect on users' perceived privacy.*

Hypothesis 1c (H1c). *Users' perceived privacy is higher with the presence of an popup cookie notice than with a banner cookie notice.*

Moreover, we assume that the same (positive) effect of cookie notices in e-commerce settings applies to users' trust. Again, we estimate different effect sizes across the notice variants. Therefore, our second set of hypotheses reads as follows:

Hypothesis 2a (H2a). *The presence of a cookie notice on an e-commerce website has an effect on users' trust.*

Hypothesis 2b (H2b). *The presence of a cookie notice on an e-commerce website has a* positive *effect on users' trust.*

Hypothesis 2c (H2c). *Users' trust is higher with the presence of an popup cookie notice than with a banner cookie notice.*

Lastly, earlier studies have shown positive evidence that there is a positive influence of users' trusting disposition and their familiarity with the e-commerce websites as control variables both on trust and purchase intentions [23]. This is the reasoning behind our last hypotheses:

Hypothesis 3a (H3a). *Users' trusting disposition has an effect on their trust towards an e-commerce website.*

Hypothesis 3b (H3b). *Users' familiarity (reflected in their online shopping experience) has an effect on their trust towards an e-commerce website.*

Figure 3 summarizes the research model and shows the variables, the presumed relations, and the aforementioned hypotheses. As the positive effects of both perceived privacy and trust on the users' purchase intention is known, seeking proof for our new hypotheses is highly relevant for e-commerce websites considering to introduce one of the possible cookie notice variants.

3   Study Setting and Data

3.1   Online Experiment

The study was based on a between-subjects design. Participants were segmented randomly into one of three experimental groups where cookie notice was the independent variable. The first group was exposed to the webshop version with the pop-up cookie notice where interaction with the notice ("accept" or close) was necessary to continue with the task. The second group was shown a cookie bar at the bottom of the page where no interaction was necessary to complete the task although it only disappeared after a click on "accept". The third group was the control group which was not exposed to any cookie notice. Apart from the cookie notices and the sub-domains (Group 1: www.apomed24.at, Group 2: shop.apomed24.at, Group 3: de.apomed24.at) there were no differences in the experimental webshops between the three groups that could have been perceived by the participants. Design, content, and functionality were identical over all three variants.

3.2   Webshop

To examine the phenomena under conditions as closely as possible to real online shopping situations, we implemented a fully functional pharmacy online shop. The authors have chosen online pharmacies as an industry assumed to require higher levels of trust than others like online clothing stores would require. When shopping online for medical products a lot of potentially sensitive data is generated, which, in combination with personal data required to place orders (e.g., full name and shipping address), reveals information on the health status and drug usage of a particular person. Often such data is not provided deliberately by the user but is collected with the help of cookies and other tracking technologies. Illegal collection and disclosure of such data can have extensive social, existential consequences (e.g. loss of job) [24,25].

Moreover, product quality is of upmost importance in this industry, a significant share of all medical products sold online are presumed forgeries or substandard. As a consequence, the consumption of such medicine can lead from minor to heavy side effects, potentially even to the death of the consumer. It can be implied that trust is an essential success factor for online pharmacies which is the reason why we have selected this industry for our fictitious webshop "apo-med24.at" with design and content similar to well-known Austrian online pharmacies like apotheke.at or shop-apotheke.at. Additionally, common trust elements such as trust seals, ssl-certificates, and customer reviews were used in the experimental web-shop. Technically, the webshop was built on the foundation of Wordpress using the WooCommerce shop system. The different cookie notices were created using the tools "CookiePro" from OneTrust (see Fig. 1) and "GDPR Cookie Compliance" from Moove Agency (see Fig. 2).

3.3 Participants' Task

The only obvious task for participants was to select a nasal spray in the online pharmacy and to put it into the virtual shopping basket. The participants were free to decide how to achieve this goal; they could, for example, use the on-site search or browse through product categories during the decision process. Additionally, there was no limitation on the duration of this process or on the number of products the user was allowed to compare etc. The purpose was to design an online-shopping situation perceived as natural as possible, allowing users to act how they would normally do when shopping online.

3.4 Survey

In our survey, the influence of the independent variable "cookie notice" on the dependent variables "perceived privacy" and "e-trust" were measured using 5-point Likert scales stretching from "totally disagree" to "fully agree". The survey was shown to participants after fulfilling the tasks using the software *Questionpro*.

The survey consisted of 35 items in total. Several demographic data was collected such as gender, age, and highest level of education. The majority of items measured e-trust and perceived privacy. As explained in Sect. 1.3, we developed our items on e-trust based on the established model by Gefen and Straub [23]: 12 items to measure trust, and 6 items to measure the control variables. Furthermore, 6 items were adapted from [11] and aimed to measure perceived privacy. Finally, another 6 items were added to the questionnaire, providing potentially interesting and additional insights in the research area (see Sect. 4.4) while the remaining items revolved around demographics:

- Which type of cookie notice did you see on apomed24.at?
- In case you saw a cookie notice, did you agree to the usage of cookies on apomed24.at?
- In the cookie notice you saw, did you have the possibility to decline the usage of cookies?
- In general, when a website requires you to give your consent to the usage of cookies, do you agree?
- In general, what is your attitude towards being asked for consent to the usage of cookie on a website?
- Can you explain to an uninformed person what cookies are on the internet and what benefits they have?

The study involved 122 participants who completed the experiment and the survey in the period of June 2019 to July 2019 using a desktop device. Group 1 (which was shown the pop-up cookie notice) had 43 participants, Group 2 (which was shown the cookie bar) had 39 participants and the control group consisted of 40 participants. 61 participants were female and 61 were male. 71 participants were aged 20–29, 20 were aged 30–39, 17 were aged 40–49, and 14 participants were older than 50. The majority (67.2%) of participants held at least on university degree or more. Over 50% of all participants responded to shop online at least once a month and only 12.3% shop rarely online. As the IP-address of the participants was tracked during completion of the experiment, it could be ensured that all participants took part from within Austria.

4   Results

Before suitable methods of data analysis could be used to test the hypotheses, the reliability of the used measurement instrument needed to be tested. This ensures that a repetition of the used methods lead to the same results, and that items intended to measure one specific construct all measure the same dimension of it. With the exception of the construct *benevolence* all items showed a Cronbach's coefficient α above 0.7. We therefore removed one of its items which consequently lead to a value above 0.7.

When using Likert-type items measured on a Likert scale, researchers are confronted with the controversially discussed question whether parametric or non-parametric methods of analysis can be used. Generally, there is wide agreement in the literature that Likert-type items are measured on an ordinal scale, which consequently means that only non-parametric methods of data analysis can be used to analyze these items on an individual level. However, by summarizing or calculating the mean of such items measuring the same dimension, a true Likert scale can be achieved and as such data reflects interval data, the full power of parametric methods can be leveraged [26]. Figure 4 shows the results including the β coefficients, which are described in the following subsections.

4.1   Perceived Privacy

To test the hypotheses H1a, H1b, and H1c – all related to perceived privacy – we conducted an analysis of variance (ANOVA) and for post hoc analysis Scheffé's method for multiple comparisons was used. The ANOVA showed no significant differences ($\rho = 0.720$) between the three groups in regards of perceived privacy. Therefore, H1a was rejected: *The existence of a cookie notice does not significantly influence perceived privacy of an e-commerce website.*

To test H1b and H1c, Scheffé's method of multiple comparisons was used. Generally, the means of perceived privacy in the groups exposed to any cookie notice were higher in comparison to the control group. However, due to the low levels of significance ($\rho_{Pop-Up} = 0.818$ and $\rho_{CookieBar} = 0.752$) we cannot rule out

544   J. Schiefermair and M. Stabauer

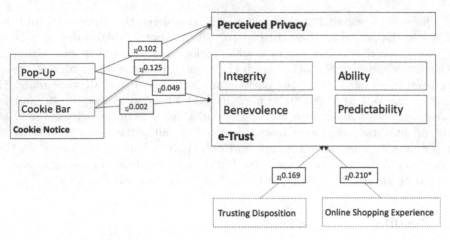

Fig. 4. Results

that these differences in the means were generated by pure coincidence. Therefore, H1b must be rejected: *The existence of a cookie notice does not positively influence perceived privacy of an e-commerce website to a significant extent.*

H1c aimed to compare the perceived privacy between the two notice variants (pop-up and cookie-bar) where we expected perceived privacy to be higher when a pop-up notice is used. Contrary to our assumption the means of perceived privacy were minimally higher in the group exposed to the cookie bar. However, the ρ-value of 0.990 did not confirm significance of this result and H1c must be rejected as well: *Perceived privacy is not significantly higher when a pop-up cookie notice is used in comparison to a cookie-bar.*

4.2 Trust

Due to missing homogeneity of variance detected for the dependent variable e-trust, the robust Welch's t-test was used instead of an ANOVA and for post hoc analysis a Games-Howell-test was conducted. The conducted Welch's t-test did not show a significant difference ($\rho = 0.919$) between the three groups and therefore H2a had to be rejected: *The existence of a cookie notice does not significantly influence e-trust for an e-commerce website.*

Similar to perceived privacy a slight difference in means could be observed using a Games-Howell test where, in particular, the means of the groups which were exposed to a cookie notice were higher compared to the control group. Since the ρ-values were relatively low ($\rho = 0.920$ and $\rho = 1.00$, respectively), these differences do not reflect a significant result. Therefore, H2b had to be rejected: *The existence of a cookie notice does not positively influence e-trust for an e-commerce website to a significant extent.*

Hypothesis H2c suggests that e-trust is higher when using a pop-up cookie notice instead of a cookie-bar. Indeed, higher values could be observed in this group. However, a ρ-value of 0.954 is not significant which leads to the rejection of H2c: *Trust towards an e-commerce website is not significantly higher when a pop-up cookie notice is used compared to the usage of a cookie bar.*

4.3   Control

To test Hypothesis H3a and H3b that are related to the control variables, the authors used a linear regression analysis. The results showed that a higher familiarity with e-commerce websites lead to a significantly higher trust in our e-commerce website ($\rho = 0.020$), although the β coefficient of 0.210 only reflects a minor positive influence. Trusting disposition, on the other hand, had no significant influence ($\rho = 0.059$) on trust. Therefore, H3a must be rejected while H3b can be accepted: *Users' trusting disposition has no significant influence on trust towards an e-commerce website. However, familiarity with e-commerce websites reflected in users' online shopping experience has a positive influence on trust towards an e-commerce website.*

4.4   Further Implications

To complement the items in the questionnaire aimed to help answer the main research questions related to perceived privacy and e-trust, the authors added additional items which could produce further valuable insights in the area of cookie notices but are not directly related to the research questions (for the questions see Sect. 3.4). At this point it has to be mentioned again, that the truth of the test persons' statements on these items was not verified in this research by methods like eye-tracking, web-analytics or similar. Therefore, the knowledge gained here is based to a large extent purely on the information provided by the test persons in the online questionnaire.

After completing the task in the experimental online shop, the participants were shown images of various cookie notices and were asked to select the notice they saw during the experiment. They could also claim not to have seen a cookie notice at all. It was noticeable that in the group with the more inconspicuous cookie bar over 30% of the test persons stated that they had not seen a cookie notice at all. In comparison, only 14% of the pop-up group could not remember seeing a cookie notice. As a result, we deviate that if website operators want to improve the perception of the cookie notice and thereby improving the chance of an opt-in, they should rather implement a pop-up cookie notice over a cookie bar.

Participants who responded to have seen a cookie notice were then asked whether or not they agreed to the use of cookies in the experimental web shop. About 60% said they agreed, about 37% disagreed and 3% could not remember. According to the test persons, around 10% more people declared consent to cookies when they were exposed to a pop-up cookie notice than the ones who saw the cookie bar. The variation between the number of given consents versus the number of rejections was also much bigger in the pop-up group than in the cookie bar group (see Fig. 5). It is therefore justifiable to assume that organizations/companies for which the collection of as many consents-to-cookies as possible is of great importance should rather implement a cookie notice in the form of a pop-up.

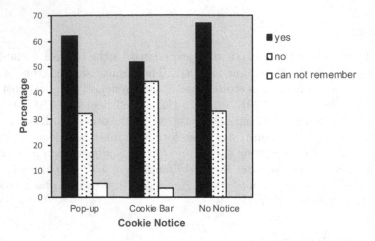

Fig. 5. Consent to cookie notice

Moreover, almost 60% of the cookie bar group stated that there was no possibility of rejection. In the pop-up group, on the other hand, only around 35% of the respondents indicated that rejection was impossible. This could be due to a missing "Decline" or "Close" button in the cookie bar, which existed in the pop-up variant. However, test persons could also have assumed that the consent mechanism for the cookie bar had been implemented in such a way that non-interaction with the notice was treated as a denial by the website provider. However, It is also possible that test persons, based on their experience with notices containing texts such as "If you continue browsing this website, you agree to the use of cookies", assumed that there was no real possibility of rejection as they had to use the web-site for the completion of the task. However, all these possible reasons for this result represent only assumptions of the authors and have not been explored in depth in this paper.

Another question added to the survey was about whether respondents normally agree to cookies when a website asks for consent or not. Over 56% said they frequently agree to the use of cookies. 18.9% always agree and about 22% rarely agree. Only 2.4% never agree to the use of cookies according to their own statements. Interesting insights were also provided by the combination of the question whether consent was given in the experiment with the question about participant's "normal" consent behavior in regards of cookies. A Chi-square test showed a significant correlation between the basic consent and the consent behavior in the experiment ($\rho = 0.000$). Test persons therefore largely behaved "normally" with regard to their consent behavior in the experiment.

It is also interesting that 4.2% of the test persons who did not give consent in the experiment stated that they always agreed to the use of cookies. The age of the test person had no significant impact on the normal behavior regarding the consent to cookies.

Almost 75% of the respondents had a neutral to very positive attitude towards being shown cookie notices by websites. This number must be seen differentiated as the groups that were shown some kind of cookie notice earlier in the experiment, evaluated this as positive to an extent of around 40%, while within the control group that was shown no cookie notice the number went down to 20%.

In order to gain an overview of the test persons' knowledge about cookies, we finally asked whether they could explain to an uninformed person what cookies are on the internet and what benefits they have. Over 70% confirmed that they could explain cookies. Another finding that could be made with the help of this question is the existence of a significant correlation between the educational level of the respondent and the ability to explain cookies. The higher the educational level of the respondents, the more likely it was that they defined cookies accurately.

5 Conclusion

This paper presented an empirical study which aimed to find out whether the presence and visual appearance of cookie notices on e-commerce websites have an effect on their users' perceived privacy and trust in the website and consequently on their purchase intention. The participants of the experiment were confronted with a highly realistic prototype of an online pharmacy and were asked to perform a simple task (select a nasal spray and put it in the basket). Without their knowledge, they were parted in groups and shown different versions of cookie notices. Later, they answered questions about their perception of the website's privacy policies and their trust in the website itself.

Our hypotheses were that cookie notices, as part of a company's information policy, had positive effects on both perceived privacy and trust, and that the effects of pop-ups were stronger than the effects of cookie bars. Most hypotheses could not be accepted, as, while the effects could be measured, they were not significant. However, the pop-up version of the cookie notice was registered twice as often by users as the bar version and also led to a greater proportion of cookie acceptance. Together with a share of 75% of users rating the notice as neutral to positive and the fact that there was no negative effect on neither perceived privacy nor trust, this leads to a recommendation to operators of e-commerce websites to implement pop-up cookie notices.

One of the limitations of this study is that the participants of the experiment were not exposed to any risks like payment or disclosure of personal data, therefore they did not experience one of the main determinants of trust, i.e. minimizing or internally justifying risk. However, in the real world cookies also play an important role in the phases before actual payment. As a future research direction, we suggest to investigate the effect of cookie notices on other important performance indicators in e-commerce like the bounce rate or conversion rate. Moreover, it will be interesting to see how future developments in the legal basis (e.g., applicability of the upcoming ePrivacy Regulation) will change behavior of both website owners and consumers. Therefore, it seems to be worthwhile to replicate this study with regard to future circumstances.

References

1. Kulyk, O., Hilt, A., Gerber, N., Volkamer, M.: "This website uses cookies": users' perceptions and reactions to the cookie disclaimer. In: Proceedings of the 3rd European Workshop on Usable Security (2018). https://doi.org/10.14722/eurousec. 2018.23012
2. Karimov, F.P., Brengman, M., Hove, L.V.: The effect of website design dimensions on initial trust: a synthesis of the empirical literature. J. Electron. Commer. Res. **12**(4), 272–301 (2011)
3. Article 29 Data Protection Working Party: Opinion on cookie consent exemption, June 2012. https://ec.europa.eu/justice/article-29/documentation/opinion-recommendation/files/2012/wp194_en.pdf
4. Article 29 Data Protection Working Party: Cookie sweep combined analysis - report, February 2015. https://ec.europa.eu/justice/article-29/documentation/opinion-recommendation/files/2015/wp229_en.pdf
5. Miyazaki, A.D.: Online privacy and the disclosure of cookie use: effects on consumer trust and anticipated patronage. J. Public Policy Mark. **27**(1), 19–33 (2008). https://doi.org/10.1509/jppm.27.1.19
6. Tappenden, A.F., Miller, J.: Cookies: a deployment study and the testing implications. ACM Trans. Web **3**(3) (2009). https://doi.org/10.1145/1541822.1541824
7. Sipior, J.C., Ward, B.T., Mendoza, R.A.: Online privacy concerns associated with cookies, flash cookies, and web beacons. J. Internet Commer. **10**(1), 1–16 (2011). https://doi.org/10.1080/15332861.2011.558454
8. Hildebrandt, M., Tielemans, L.: Data protection by design and technology neutral law. Comput. Law Secur. Rev. **29**(5), 509–521 (2013). https://doi.org/10.1016/j.clsr.2013.07.004
9. Trevisan, M., Traverso, S., Bassi, E., Mellia, M.: 4 years of EU cookie law: results and lessons learned. Proc. Privacy Enhancing Technol. **2**, 126–145 (2019). https://doi.org/10.2478/popets-2019-0023
10. Stabauer, M.: The effects of privacy awareness and content sensitivity on user engagement. In: Nah, F.F.-H., Siau, K. (eds.) HCII 2019. LNCS, vol. 11589, pp. 242–255. Springer, Cham (2019). https://doi.org/10.1007/978-3-030-22338-0_20
11. Casaló, L.V., Flavián, C., Guinalíu, M.: The role of security, privacy, usability and reputation in the development of online banking. Online Inf. Rev. **31**(5), 583–603 (2007). https://doi.org/10.1108/14684520710832315
12. Ganguly, B., Dash, S.B., Cyr, D., Head, M.: The effects of website design on purchase intention in online shopping: the mediating role of trust and the moderating role of culture. Int. J. Electron. Bus. **8**(4/5), 302–330 (2010). https://doi.org/10.1504/IJEB.2010.035289
13. Liu, C., Marchewka, J.T., Lu, J., Yu, C.S.: Beyond concern–a privacy-trust-behavioral intention model of electronic commerce. Inf. Manag. **42**(2), 289–304 (2005). https://doi.org/10.1016/j.im.2004.01.003

14. Stabauer, M.: The impact of UI on privacy awareness. In: Nah, F.F.-H., Xiao, B.S. (eds.) HCIBGO 2018. LNCS, vol. 10923, pp. 513–525. Springer, Cham (2018). https://doi.org/10.1007/978-3-319-91716-0_41

15. Stephanidis, C., et al.: Seven HCI grand challenges. Int. J. Hum.-Comput. Interact. **35**(14), 1229–1269 (2019). https://doi.org/10.1080/10447318.2019.1619259

16. Bhattacherjee, A.: Individual trust in online firms: scale development and initial test. J. Manag. Inf. Syst. **19**(1), 211–241 (2002). https://doi.org/10.1080/07421222.2002.11045715

17. Pavlou, P.A.: Consumer acceptance of electronic commerce: integrating trust and risk with the technology acceptance model. Int. J. Electron. Commer. **7**, 101–134 (2003). https://doi.org/10.1080/10864415.2003.11044275

18. Hong, I.B., Cha, H.S.: The mediating role of consumer trust in an online merchant in predicting purchase intention. Int. J. Inf. Manag. **33**(6), 927–939 (2013). https://doi.org/10.1016/j.ijinfomgt.2013.08.007

19. Lim, K.H., Sia, C.L., Lee, M.K., Benbasat, I.: Do i trust you online, and if so, will i buy? An empirical study of two trust-building strategies. J. Manag. Inf. Syst. **23**(2), 233–266 (2006). https://doi.org/10.2753/MIS0742-1222230210

20. McKnight, D.H., Choudhury, V., Kacmar, C.: The impact of initial consumer trust on intentions to transact with a web site: a trust building model. J. Strateg. Inf. Syst. **11**(3), 297–323 (2002). https://doi.org/10.1016/S0963-8687(02)00020-3

21. Mayer, R.C., Davis, J.H., Schoorman, F.D.: An integrative model of organizational trust. Acad. Manag. Rev. **20**(3), 709–734 (1995). https://doi.org/10.5465/amr.1995.9508080335

22. Gefen, D.: E-commerce: the role of familiarity and trust. Omega **28**(6), 725–737 (2000). https://doi.org/10.1016/S0305-0483(00)00021-9

23. Gefen, D., Straub, D.W.: Consumer trust in B2C e-commerce and the importance of social presence: experiments in e-products and e-services. Omega **32**(6), 407–424 (2004). https://doi.org/10.1016/j.omega.2004.01.006

24. Büttner, O.B., Schulz, S., Silberer, G.: Perceived risk and deliberation in retailer choice: an experiment on consumer behavior towards online pharmacies. In: Pechmann, C., Price, L. (eds.) Advances in Consumer Research, vol. 33, pp. 197–202. Association for Consumer Research, Duluth (2006)

25. Mackey, T.K., Nayyar, G.: Digital danger: a review of the global public health, patient safety and cybersecurity threats posed by illicit online pharmacies. Br. Med. Bull. **118**(1), 110–126 (2016). https://doi.org/10.1093/bmb/ldw016

26. Carifio, J., Perla, R.J.: Ten common misunderstandings, misconceptions, persistent myths and urban legends about likert scales and likert response formats and their antidotes. J. Soc. Sci. **3**(3), 106–116 (2007). https://doi.org/10.3844/jssp.2007.106.116

Research on Key Factors Affecting College Students' Usage Intention of Green Public Welfare Activity Platform Based on DEMATEL Method

Qi Xu[✉] and Jiong Fu

School of Design, Shanghai Jiao Tong University, Shanghai 201101, China
113059377@qq.com

Abstract. With the continuous penetration of green concepts, platforms that provide green activities and environmental information have begun to develop. Exploring the user experience to obtain key design focus of such platforms is conducive to the promotion of the environmental protection concept. This paper studies the influencing factors of the usage intention of green public welfare activity platform. Through preliminary investigation and literature summary, 10 factors affecting the willingness to use such platforms are selected. The face-to-face surveys are conducted with DEMATEL questionnaires to evaluate interactions between any two factors. The Prominence and the Relation value of factors are calculated in the DEMATEL tool and the causal diagram is drawn. The result shows that the most significant factors concerning the usage intention of green public welfare activity platforms are content availability, user friendliness, and interactive community. In order to develop these three goals, visual effect of interaction, interface aesthetics and diversification of content expressions are design points. This study provides suggestions for the design of green public welfare activity platform.

Keywords: Usage intention · DEMATEL · Environmental charity · Green design · Consumer research · Public welfare activity · Platform design

1 Introduction

With the rapid growth of the global economy and the increasingly serious environmental problems, sustainable development has become one of the main goals in China. The popularization of "Internet +" has promoted the progress of green ecological civilization in the new era. Green consumption, green life, green design are all integrated with the Internet now. Taking advantage of the Internet's convenience and high-efficiency, creating a green public welfare platform that not only reports on ecological hot issues, updates environmental protection knowledge but also promotes diversified green activities can effectively disseminate green ideas and raise green awareness. At present, the green platforms are in the development stage and how to build a platform that attracts

© Springer Nature Switzerland AG 2020
F. F.-H. Nah and K. Siau (Eds.): HCII 2020, LNCS 12204, pp. 550–561, 2020.
https://doi.org/10.1007/978-3-030-50341-3_41

users is the key. Academic research on usage intention of commercial platforms is rich, but there are not many towards green public welfare platforms. This article researches the influencing factors critical to usage intention of green public welfare platform to take tailored measures to design the platform and elevate its quality.

2   Literature Review

2.1   Green Public Welfare Activity Platform Based on Internet

The internet has promoted the transformation of the environmental protection industry. Smart environmental protection has become a trend and the green service has shown a new format [1, 2]. Environmental protection publicity with the help of new media platforms has produced considerable results. For instance, "Internet + recycling" becomes a new and efficient collecting mode as online platforms enable individuals and recycling practitioners to make appointments for onsite waste collection [3–6].

The application of Internet technology in the field of green public welfare is booming which expands the scope of public welfare and strengthens the public's enthusiasm for participating in environmental protection activities [7]. Compared with the traditional public welfare undertakings, green activities based on Internet platforms have a wider public base and social resources. The immediacy and interaction attract the public to participate in [8]. Internet-based green public welfare projects started to gain attention in recent years in China. The China Water Security Plan and Earth Hour initiated by Sina successfully advocated green events of energy conservation and low carbon. Ant Forest, another green initiative, has received a 2019 Champions of the Earth Award which is the UN's highest environmental honor. Initiated by Alipay, Ant Forest encourages users to engage in low-carbon acts and it has already turned the green good deeds of people into more than 100 million real trees.

Researches with a focus on the communication effect of green activities based on the internet indicate that professional green activity platforms integrated with internet technology are in need. In addition, dissemination and popularization are the keys [9]. Meanwhile, researches in the field of website development by nonprofit organizations provide suggestions including community through interactivity, richer information, user-friendly interface design [10, 11]. Wenham compared best practice approaches to web-marketing using the websites of UK environmental charities. It is recommended that more key customer orientation and community website features need to be developed [12].

In general, Internet-based green public welfare undertakings are in the development period in China. The related research has not yet formed a system and there are fewer studies on user experience of those platforms. Only by building an appealing platform that individuals are willing to use can we carry out environmental protection activities more effectively. Therefore, usage intention of green public welfare platform needs to be considered.

2.2 Usage Intention

The research methods of usage intention mainly include surveys, modeling, and literature research. Models such as Technology Acceptance Model (TAM), Expectation Confirmation Theory (ECT), Expectation Confirmation Model (ECM) are widely used.

Davis firstly proposed the Technology Acceptance Model (TAM) to explain and predict user acceptance of information systems or information technology [13]. The two main variables in this model are perceived usefulness and perceived ease of use. Among them, perceived usefulness reflects the degree to which individuals think the information system has improved their work efficiency; perceived ease of use reflects the degree to which individuals think the information system is easy to use [14].

The Expectation Confirmation Theory (ECT) proposed by Oliver is a basic theory for evaluating consumer satisfaction [15]. It suggests that before purchasing consumers would form initial expectations of a product or service. By comparing the initial expectations with the experience of using products or services, consumers would determine the extent to which their initial expectations are confirmed. Then satisfaction assessment is formed and in turn, affects consumers to purchase the product or service again or continuously [16].

Bhattacherjee extended the ECT model to build the Expectation Confirmation Model (ECM) of continuance [17]. ECM model mainly contains perceived usefulness, confirmation of expectation, satisfaction and continuance intention. Based on ECM, it is proved that perceived usefulness and confirmation of expectations are significant predictors of satisfaction. Continuance intention was influenced by consumer satisfaction and perceived usefulness [18]. ECM model is widely used in information systems and gains acceptance especially in explaining usage intention and user satisfaction [18, 19]. Scholars often modify and extend the model to improve its ability according to research contexts. The extensions largely considered factors like ease of use, habit, and perceived enjoyment. These contexts included e-commerce; social network sites; e-learning technologies; and various mobile-based and web-based services [20, 21]. Oghuma examined the factors that affect users' continuance intention to use mobile instant messaging and expanded the ECM to cover the context of the post-consumption stage for services [22]. Chiu conducted an online learning system as their research object and proved that satisfaction has the largest impact on the continuance intention [23]. Zou Xia researched the user satisfaction of mobile news. It confirmed that perceived aesthetics had a significant positive impact on user satisfaction [24]. Li Zhongqi included new supplementary factors when researching the influencing factors of WeChat user satisfaction, and finally formed acquired content, perceived usefulness, perceived ease of use, and aesthetics perception as four main consideration factors [25].

3 Method

3.1 DEMATEL Procedure

The DEMATEL method was developed by the Battelle Institute in the 1970s originally for studying the relationship between factors in complex systems. It has been applied to many academic fields such as solution analysis and decision making. The degree of influence between every two elements in the system is measured to quantitatively analyze the complex relationships in a situation. Matrix tool operation and mathematical theory are used to determine the causal relationship of all elements in the system [26–29].

The DEMATEL procedure generally comprises the following steps: (1) defining the influencing factors with methods such as brainstorming, expert interviews, and literature research to list and define different factors that may affect complex systems, and with a measurement scale for comparison between paired factors: score 0, 1, 2, and 3 which respectively represent "no effect", "low impact", "high impact", and "very high impact". (2) generating a direct relation matrix. (3) generating a direct/indirect relation matrix. (4) calculating the corresponding Prominence value and Relation value of each main factor. (5) drawing a causal diagram where the directions and degrees of the factors can be directly observed to extract the key influencing factors [30, 31].

3.2 Ten Main Influencing Factors

Based on the literature analysis in Sect. 2.2, this paper takes extended ECM models as references to study the influencing factors of the usage intention of the green public welfare platform. The first level dimension includes acquired content, perceived usefulness, perceived ease of use and aesthetic perception. To further extract the key factors, college students who have participated in green charities are investigated based on combined user research methods including brainstorming, observation, and in-depth interview. Besides, supplementary information to be analyzed is collected by reviewing green charity related literature and online forums. Eventually, the following ten factors are summarized and defined as the significant factors as shown in Table 1.

Table 1. Four dimensions with ten critical factors.

Dimension	Critical factors
A1 Acquired content	C1 Content availability
	C2 Interactive community
	C3 Incentive effectiveness
	C4 Service quality
A2 Perceived Usefulness (PU)	C5 Enriched degree of information
	C6 Accuracy and timeliness
	C7 Diversification of content expressions
A3 Perceived Ease of Use (PEOU)	C8 User friendliness
A4 Aesthetic perception	C9 Interface aesthetics
	C10 Visual effect of interaction

A1 Acquired Content

- C1 Content availability: the availability of green public welfare activities and related information and knowledge.
- C2 Interactive community: community interactions such as sharing, commenting, and liking by users based on platforms.
- C3 Incentives effectiveness: the effectiveness of incentives like green public welfare activities' records, points, medal walls, rewards, etc.
- C4 Service quality: the quality of services such as event review process and customer service, etc.

A2 Perceived Usefulness

- C5 Enriched degree of information: comprehensive event details and the rich types of knowledge, etc.
- C6 Accuracy and timeliness: the information being accurate and updating timely.
- C7 Diversification of content expressions: information presentation in diversified forms including text, pictures, videos, visual design, and fun design, etc.

A3 Perceived Ease of Use

- C8 User Friendliness: functions of the platform being easy and convenient to identify, understand, search and use.

A4 Aesthetic Perception

- C9 Interface Aesthetics: beautiful interface color, design style, page structure.
- C10 Visual Effect of Interaction: exquisite designs for interaction with the pages during operation including page animation, button click feedback, etc.

3.3   DEMATEL Questionnaire

Based on the 10 key influencing factors, a questionnaire is designed and one-to-one interviews were conducted. 30 college students including 15 design background professionals and 15 public welfare enthusiasts were invited as interview experts. After operating different service platforms of green public welfare activities, they were asked to rate each factor's impact on the continuous usage intention. Scores 0, 1, 2 and 3 indicate four levels of influence: 0 - no effect; 1 - low impact; 2 - high impact; and 3 - extreme height impact.

4 Results

4.1 DEMATEL Operations

Direct Relation Matrix. By processing and averaging valid data from 30 students, the standardized matrix A of the direct relation between 10 main factors is obtained as shown in Table 2.

Table 2. The elements in direct relation matrix A

	C1	C2	C3	C4	C5	C6	C7	C8	C9	C10
C1	0.00	0.11	0.06	0.12	0.14	0.12	0.10	0.14	0.09	0.09
C2	0.10	0.00	0.10	0.10	0.10	0.08	0.11	0.11	0.09	0.06
C3	0.08	0.14	0.00	0.08	0.08	0.05	0.08	0.07	0.07	0.05
C4	0.11	0.10	0.08	0.00	0.09	0.12	0.06	0.12	0.07	0.06
C5	0.13	0.10	0.10	0.11	0.00	0.09	0.12	0.08	0.06	0.07
C6	0.14	0.09	0.06	0.11	0.10	0.00	0.06	0.12	0.07	0.04
C7	0.12	0.12	0.06	0.09	0.15	0.06	0.00	0.12	0.11	0.12
C8	0.14	0.14	0.07	0.12	0.08	0.09	0.10	0.00	0.12	0.11
C9	0.14	0.14	0.09	0.12	0.06	0.06	0.10	0.16	0.00	0.12
C10	0.12	0.12	0.07	0.09	0.10	0.06	0.15	0.14	0.13	0.00

Table 3. The elements in direct/indirect relation matrix T

	C1	C2	C3	C4	C5	C6	C7	C8	C9	C10
C1	**1.02**	**1.09**	0.75	**1.00**	**1.00**	0.84	0.93	**1.11**	0.87	0.79
C2	0.97	0.87	0.69	0.87	0.85	0.71	0.83	0.96	0.77	0.67
C3	0.83	0.87	0.51	0.74	0.73	0.60	0.70	0.81	0.65	0.57
C4	0.95	0.92	0.65	0.75	0.81	0.72	0.75	0.94	0.73	0.64
C5	**1.02**	0.98	0.71	0.89	0.78	0.74	0.85	0.96	0.76	0.69
C6	0.98	0.91	0.64	0.85	0.82	0.62	0.75	0.93	0.73	0.63
C7	**1.14**	**1.12**	0.76	**0.99**	**1.02**	0.80	0.85	**1.12**	0.91	0.83
C8	**1.14**	**1.12**	0.76	**1.00**	0.95	0.82	0.93	**1.00**	0.90	0.80
C9	**1.18**	**1.16**	0.79	**1.03**	0.96	0.82	0.96	**1.17**	0.82	0.84
C10	**1.15**	**1.12**	0.77	**0.99**	0.98	0.80	**0.99**	**1.14**	0.93	0.72

Note: The elements in bold indicate factors with values above the threshold of 0.98.

Direct/Indirect Relation Matrix. Then the degrees of interactions between key factors are calculated with a DEMATEL operation tool. The λ value of 0.06013229 and the elements in the direct/indirect relation matrix T are derived. Matrix T reflects the direct and indirect relationships between the 10 main factors as shown in Table 3.

By listing all elements in the matrix T in numerical order, the quartile deviation, 0.98, of the sequence is calculated as a threshold to measure the strength of interactions between various factors. If all the values of the rows and columns corresponding to a factor in the matrix T are not above this threshold, the factor is considered to be not important and will be removed. As a result, the rows and columns of C3 and C6 are deleted here.

Prominence and Relation. According to Table 3, the Prominence value (D + R) and Relation value (D-R) of each of the ten key factors are calculated and ranked in Table 4.

Table 4. Prominence and relation values

	D + R Prominence		D − R Relation	
	Value	Ranking	Value	Ranking
C1	**19.78**	1	−0.98	8
C2	**18.37**	3	−1.97	10
C3	14.04	10	−0.02	5
C4	16.99	7	−1.26	9
C5	17.29	6	−0.52	6
C6	15.33	9	0.40	4
C7	**18.10**	4	1.00	3
C8	**19.56**	2	−0.71	7
C9	**17.80**	5	1.64	2
C10	16.80	8	2.41	1
	Mean value: 17.41			

Prominence. In the DEMATEL method, the prominence value indicates the relative weight of a factor's influence intensity in the total influence intensity of all factors. It presents the position of the factor in the system and the size of its effect: the larger the prominence value of a factor, the more important the role it plays, and the greater its influence. As shown in the data and ranking results in Table 4, the prominence value of content availability (C1), user-friendliness (C8), interactive community (C2), diversification of content expressions (C7) and interface aesthetics (C9) are larger than mean value. So, they are the key factors that influence usage intention of green public welfare platform.

Relation. The relation value refers to the degree to which a factor affects or is affected by other factors. Its absolute value indicates the intensity of the influence. A positive value indicates that the factor is a causal factor, which has a greater impact on other factors; a negative value means that the factor is a result factor, which is caused by other factors. There are 4 factors with positive relation values: C10, C9, C7, and C6. This means, in this study, visual effect of interaction, interface aesthetics, diversification of content expressions, accuracy and timeliness are 4 main causal factors. The result factors in this study are ranked according to the degree of impact, in order: interactive community (C2), service quality (C4), content availability (C1), user friendliness (C8), and enriched degree of information (C5), incentive effectiveness (C3). Among them, the value of interactive community (C2) is close to −2, which indicates that it has been greatly affected.

DEMATEL Causal Diagram
Taking D + R as the horizontal axis and D-R as the vertical axis, the following diagram is depicted in Fig. 1. A vector line shows the direction of influence from one factor to another that pointed to. According to the order of the influence value, the top 10 influence relationships are regarded as stronger influencing degree, which is indicated by solid lines.

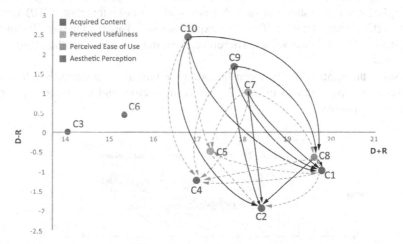

Fig. 1. The causal diagram

From the DEMATEL causal diagram, it can be seen that visual effect of interaction (C10) and the interface aesthetics (C9) strongly affect user friendliness (C8), content availability (C1), and interactive community (C2). Diversification of content expressions (C7) strongly affects content availability (C1) and interactive community (C2). User friendliness (C8) as a result factor itself also influence content availability (C1) and interactive community (C2) strongly.

4.2 Discussion

Key Factors. The top three factors with the largest Prominence values and the top three factors with the largest positive Relation values are reorganized in order as listed in Table 5.

Table 5. The top three factors in prominence and the top three factors in relation

The top three factors in prominence	The top three factors in relation
C1 Content availability	C10 Visual effect of interaction
C8 User friendliness	C9 Interface aesthetics
C2 Interactive community	C7 Diversification of content expressions

It is observed that content availability (C1), user friendliness (C8) and interactive community (C2), as the top three factors with the largest Prominence value are therefore the most significant factors critical to determining the usage intention of green public welfare platform. It also shows in Table 5 that visual effect of interaction (C10), interface aesthetics (C9), diversification of content expressions (C7) are the top three factors with the largest positive Relation values. Therefore, these three factors have the strong impact upon others.

To show the relationship between factors more intuitively, a simplified diagram of factor relationships is drawn in Fig. 2. Key result factors and key causal factors are marked with shadows.

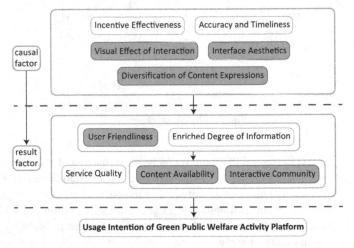

Fig. 2. The simplified relationships of factors

Suggestion. In summary, the previous analysis leads to three main suggestions on the green public welfare activity platform's design.

Improve the Content Availability. To communicate activities' information completely and clearly to users through platform design is the prior task. It has been found in research that compared with the richness of content, the ability to obtain comprehensive content information is more important for users. This implies that we should shift some focus from content creation to content availability design of green public welfare platforms. The perceptual aesthetic has been proved to be a key factor influencing content availability. Subsequent face-to-face interview indicates that interface designs like proper layouts of page content may improve content availability. The relevant information of green activities should be selected according to the degree of importance and the key information such as time, place and personnel arrangement need to be highlighted in the page design.

Improve the Community Through Interactivity. This study found that an interactive community of green public welfare platform is attractive to users. Further interviews implied that an interactive community section can provide an interactive bridge between users, enabling them to get direct and useful feedback on green activities. Moderate socialization is conducive to increasing interest in green public welfare activities and affecting participation willingness. This is consistent with cognitive design psychology. Platform interaction constructs community effects and the stickiness between users promotes the stickiness between users and the platform.

Improve the Perceived Ease of Use. According to the result, the user friendliness should be an important design criterion for green public welfare platforms. It has a direct impact on content availability and platform community while it is strongly influenced by interface aesthetics and diversification of content expressions. This implies that user interface design should aim to increase user's perceived ease of use and to further impact on content availability and platform community. As a key factor, user friendliness requests green public welfare activity platforms to be easy to understand and operate including brief sign-up links for green activities, simple steps for event feedback, highlighted search windows, etc.

5   Conclusion

In this study, factors affecting the usage intention of green public welfare activity platforms are explored and collected based on brainstorming, in-depth interview, questionnaire and literature review. A s a result, a model containing 10 main factors is obtained. Then 30 design background or public welfare enthusiasts are interviewed. Using the DEMATEL method and operation tool, the top three key factors influencing the willingness to use green public welfare platforms are extracted: content availability, user friendliness, and interactive community. They should be the key focus of platforms' designing and promoting to increase usage.

Since the green concept has become an upsurge now, this research aims at the green public welfare platforms where provide environmental information and green public welfare activities. The usage intention factor system constructed in this article lays a certain theoretical foundation for the evaluation of green public welfare platform. More importantly, the key influencing factors extracted lead to designing suggestions towards these platforms. In this way, green concepts can be promoted more effectively through green public welfare platform.

References

1. Wang, X., et al.: Research on "Internet +" promoting transformation and upgrading of environmental protection service industry—suggestions on improving green environmental protection price. Price: Theory Pract. 127–130 (2018). (in Chinese)
2. Zhang, Y., Li, N., Zhang, Y.: The research of China's urban smart environmental protection management mode. In: Bian, F., Xie, Y. (eds.) GRMSE 2014. CCIS, vol. 482, pp. 415–423. Springer, Heidelberg (2015). https://doi.org/10.1007/978-3-662-45737-5_42
3. Jian, H., et al.: Collaborative collection effort strategies based on the "Internet + recycling" business model. J. Clean. Prod. **241**, 118120 (2019)
4. Wang, J., et al.: Integrating offline logistics and online system to recycle e-bicycle battery in China. J. Clean. Prod. **247**, 119095 (2020)
5. Gu, F., et al.: Exploring "Internet + Recycling": mass balance and life cycle assessment of a waste management system associated with a mobile application. Sci. Total Environ. **649**, 172–185 (2019)
6. Zlamparet, G.I., et al.: Resource conservation approached with an appropriate collection and upgrade-remanufacturing for used electronic products. Waste Manag. **73**, 78–86 (2018)
7. Liu, Y., Lu, G.: Communication effects of environment-protection micro public welfare project: a case study of WeChat charity. Journal. Res. 102–109+151 (2017). (in Chinese)
8. Waters, R.D.: Nonprofit organizations' use of the internet: a content analysis of communication trends on the internet sites of the organizations on the philanthropy 400. Nonprofit Manag. Leadersh. **18**, 59–76 (2007)
9. Changhong, L.: Use environmental new media platform to promote environmental publicity and education. Environ. Dev. **30**, 232+234 (2018). (in Chinese)
10. Kirk, K., et al.: Website development by nonprofit organizations in an emerging market: a case study of Thai websites. Int. J. Nonprofit Volunt. Sector Mark. **21**, 195–211 (2016)
11. Lovejoy, K., Saxton, G.D.: Information, community, and action: how nonprofit organizations use social media*. J. Comput.-Mediat. Commun. **17**, 337–353 (2012)
12. Wenham, K., et al.: The marketing effectiveness of UK environmental charity websites compared to best practice. Int. J. Nonprofit Volunt. Sector Mark. **8**, 213–223 (2003)
13. Davis, F.D.: Perceived usefulness, perceived ease of use, and user acceptance of information technology. MIS Q. **13**, 319–340 (1989)
14. Chen, C.-F.: Investigating structural relationships between service quality, perceived value, satisfaction, and behavioral intentions for air passengers: evidence from Taiwan. Transp. Res. Part A: Policy Pract. **42**, 709–717 (2008)
15. Oliver, R.L.: A cognitive model of the antecedents and consequences of satisfaction decisions. J. Mark. Res. **17**, 460–469 (1980)
16. Venkatesh, V., et al.: Extending the two-stage information systems continuance model: incorporating UTAUT predictors and the role of context. Inf. Syst. J. **21**, 527–555 (2011)
17. Bhattacherjee, A.: Understanding information systems continuance: an expectation-confirmation model. MIS Q. **25**, 351–370 (2001)

18. Halilovic, S., Cicic, M.: Antecedents of information systems user behaviour-extended expectation-confirmation model. Behav. Inf. Technol. **32**, 359–370 (2013)
19. Chou, S.W., et al.: Understanding continuance intention of knowledge creation using extended expectation-confirmation theory: an empirical study of Taiwan and China online communities. Behav. Inf. Technol. **29**, 557–570 (2010)
20. Ambalov, I.A.: A meta-analysis of IT continuance: an evaluation of the expectation-confirmation model. Telematics Inform. **35**, 1561–1571 (2018)
21. Chen, S.-C., et al.: Factors influencing the continuance intention to the usage of Web 2.0: an empirical study. Comput. Hum. Behav. **28**, 933–941 (2012)
22. Oghuma, A.P., et al.: An expectation-confirmation model of continuance intention to use mobile instant messaging. Telematics Inform. **33**, 34–47 (2016)
23. Chiu, C.-M., et al.: An empirical analysis of the antecedents of web-based learning continuance. Comput. Educ. **49**, 1224–1245 (2007)
24. Zou, X., Xie, J.: The influencing factors of user satisfaction with mobile news: based on survey of students in five colleges of shanghai. Journal. Res. 77–85+149–150 (2017). (in Chinese)
25. Li, Z., Jiao, J.: Analysis of influence factors for customer satisfaction in WeChat based on DEMATEL. J. Mod. Inf. **38**, 114–119 (2018). (in Chinese)
26. Lee, Y.-C., et al.: Analysis of adopting an integrated decision making trial and evaluation laboratory on a technology acceptance model. Expert Syst. Appl. **37**, 1745–1754 (2010)
27. Li, C.W., Tzeng, G.H.: Identification of a threshold value for the DEMATEL method using the maximum mean de-entropy algorithm to find critical services provided by a semiconductor intellectual property mall. Expert Syst. Appl. **36**, 9891–9898 (2009)
28. Tsai, S.-B.: Using the DEMATEL model to explore the job satisfaction of research and development professionals in china's photovoltaic cell industry. Renew. Sustain. Energy Rev. **81**, 62–68 (2018)
29. Liu, C., Jin, Y., Zhu, X.: Extraction of key factors and its interrelationship critical to determining the satisfaction degree of user experience in taxi passenger service using DEMATEL. In: Marcus, A., Wang, W. (eds.) DUXU 2018. LNCS, vol. 10920, pp. 299–313. Springer, Cham (2018). https://doi.org/10.1007/978-3-319-91806-8_23
30. Lin, Y.T., et al.: Using DEMATEL method to explore the core competences and causal effect of the IC design service company: an empirical case study. Expert Syst. Appl. **38**, 6262–6268 (2011)
31. Lin, C.J., Wu, W.W.: A causal analytical method for group decision-making under fuzzy environment. Expert Syst. Appl. **34**, 205–213 (2008)

Success Factors in Micro-Celebrity Endorsement: The Role of Informational and Narrative Content in Product Recommendation

Wei Yang[✉] and Choon Ling Sia

Department of Information Systems, City University of Hong Kong,
Tat Chee Avenue 83, Hong Kong, Hong Kong SAR, China
wyang23-c@my.cityu.edu.hk, iscl@cityu.edu.hk

Abstract. Micro-celebrities (MCs) are people who leverage on their popularity, gained among followers, by showcasing their talent over the Internet. Given the strong influence power of micro-celebrity, micro-celebrity endorsement is becoming a valuable phenomenon. This research aims to explore the impact of informational content and narrative content, which are embedded in micro-celebrity's recommendation post, on the persuasion effectiveness. From the perspective of elaboration likelihood model (ELM) and narrative transportation theory, a research model is discussed. We propose that the informational content may positively influence persuasion effectiveness through central route, and narrative content may positively influence persuasion effectiveness through peripheral route. Moreover, follower's emotional attachment and role model-identification on the micro-celebrity may moderate the two processing. A plan for data collection and analysis is discussed. In the future, we will finish the data collection and analysis to justify the proposed hypotheses.

Keywords: Micro-celebrity endorsement (MC endorsement) · Informational content · Narrative content · Elaboration likelihood model (ELM) · Narrative transportation theory · Persuasion effectiveness

1 Introduction

Micro-celebrities (MCs) are people who leverage on their popularity, gained among followers, by showcasing their talent over the Web 2.0, and using technologies such as online communities and social networking sites (Senft 2008; Uzunoğlu and Misci Kip 2014). Famous social media bloggers, instafames, and Youtube influencers are all micro-celebrities (Abidin 2016; Marwick 2013; McQuarrie 2013). In practice, MC endorsement has become a very valuable economic phenomenon, because micro-celebrities are influential among their followers, and product endorsements are popular economic activities. There are some very classic MC endorsement cases. For instance, Wenyi is a Chinese cooking blogger with thousands of followers on Sina Weibo (the most well-known microblog in Mainland China). In 2015, Wenyi recommended a chopping board

© Springer Nature Switzerland AG 2020
F. F.-H. Nah and K. Siau (Eds.): HCII 2020, LNCS 12204, pp. 562–575, 2020.
https://doi.org/10.1007/978-3-030-50341-3_42

on Weibo, resulting in a sales of 15,000 chopping boards in a single hour, which is 1.5 times of this product's total sales in Asia in 2014 year (Huxiu 2016). Given the strong influencing power of MCs, brands are increasingly considering MC endorsement as an effective online marketing channel to reach potential consumers (Evans et al. 2017; Schouten et al. 2019; Scott 2017). In Mainland China, the number of followers has reached 588 million in 2018, with a market size for MC endorsement of RMB 10.18 billion (i research 2018).

Although there are some successful cases of MC endorsements, there are failed cases too. Ruhan (NASDAQ: RUHN), the largest MC company in Mainland China, has contracts with 113 fashion MCs. According to Ruhan's financial report, since 2017, Ruhan's earnings increase dramatically, with more than 50% of the earnings are attributed solely to their top MC. In other words, the remaining 112 MCs have not been very successful. Given the huge economic potential and challenges on MC endorsement, it is interesting and important to understand why MC endorsement is successful.

To date, the focus of many studies has been purely on the impact of MC's blog content (e.g. blog sentiment, blog volume, and sponsorship disclosure) on endorsement effectiveness, which is context free. It is, however, as MC is a human brand (Thomson et al. 2006), characteristics embedded within the MC plays an equally significant role to influence follower's product perception and purchase intention. Thus, more attention should be paid on combining the impact of MC's unique characteristics on endorsement effectiveness.

In practice, a unique characteristic of MC's product recommendation is that the MC's product recommendation always disguises itself as a non-commercial normal discoursing post by packaging it in the way of the daily life sharing or talent showcasing or both (Marwick and Boyd 2011a; Ren et al. 2012). Specifically, two different types of content, namely the narrative content and informational content are embedded in such post. Narrative content is narrative related with MC's daily life, and the focus within the MC's narrative is the episode of MC's daily life (Marwick and Boyd 2011b; Page 2012). Informational content refers to professional knowledge or detailed information on the product (Abidin and Ots 2015). When reading different types of content embedded in the recommendation, follower's different psychological accounts might be triggered. For instance, informational content is more evidence-intensive and logic-based, which may evoke the central route (Petty et al. 1983). In contrast, narrative is story in nature and not related with the product, which may evoke the peripheral routes accordingly (Green and Brock 2000). Thus, in such setting, it is important to understand how the informational content and narrative content influence the endorsement effectiveness through different psychological mechanisms.

Moreover, MC literature suggest the followers tend to generate diverse relationships with the MC, including emotional attachment and role model identification (Gannon and Prothero 2016; Khamis et al. 2017). Followers with strongly emotional attachment towards the MC may allocate more resources on the MC, thus they may read more carefully and deeply than others when facing with the narrative or informational content embedded in the recommendation (Bowlby 1979; Thomson et al. 2006). Moreover, followers, who takes the MC as a role model to learn from, are more sensitive to the informational content as it is a way to learn from the role model, and are more easily to generate imagination and empathy on the narrative as the role model is related with their ideal-selves (Lockwood and Kunda 1997; van Laer et al. 2019a). Thus, it is also interesting to consider the moderating role of follower's emotional attachment and role model identification with the MC on the two processing routes.

As MC is a broad concept and includes various types. Thus, to be more focused, we select fashion blogger, one of the largest subtypes of MC on social media, as our research subject. We propose that informational content persuades through central route, and narrative content persuades through peripheral route, which can be explained by elaboration likelihood model and narrative transportation theory (Petty et al. 1983; Green and Brock 2000). The paper is organized as the following. First, we review literature on micro-celebrity endorsement, identifying the research gaps and related theories and concepts. Then we generate the research model and develop the hypotheses. Finally, a plan for empirical test and expected outcomes are discussed. We expect the findings will contribute both theoretically and practically. By having a better understanding of MC's endorsement success, brands can apply this knowledge to select MC endorsers. Moreover, MCs can also benefit and improve their endorsement practice.

2 Theoretical Background

2.1 Literature on MC Endorsement

Academic studies have noticed on the influence power of MC and begun to shed light on the MC's endorsement phenomenon. Some research studies the impact of expert's blog content on endorsement effectiveness and finds that both expert blog's sentiment and volume may positively influence consumers' purchase decision (Luo 2017). Some studies pay attention to MC's self-owned business in broadcasting context (Chen et al. 2017). Some studies focus on different aspects of MC's sponsorship disclosure (Evans et al. 2017; Lu et al. 2014). Particularly, the sponsorship disclosure is positively influence brand attitudes and purchase intention when the product is search good or with high brand awareness (Lu et al. 2014). The disclosure language of commercial post (sponsored blog or paid Ad) will influence the follower's intention to purchase (Evans et al. 2017). To date, the focus of many studies has been purely on the impact of MC's blog content (e.g. blog sentiment, blog volume, and sponsorship disclosure) on endorsement effectiveness, which is context free. It is, however, as MC is a human brand (Thomson et al. 2006), characteristics embedded within the MC plays an equally significant role to influence follower's product perception and purchase intention. Thus, more attention should be paid on combining the impact of MC's unique characteristics on endorsement effectiveness.

2.2 The Context: Two Distinct Types of Content in the MC's Recommendation Posts

There are two distinct types of contents embedded in the MC's recommendation post: the informational content and the narrative content. On the one hand, informational content refers to information related to the products (Petty et al. 1983). Within the informational content, the product is the focus, and texts and pictures serves for better understanding on the product. For instance, if the MC recommends a dress, he/she write words and attaches close-up pictures to disclose information on the dress, such as the material quality of the dress, special designs of the dress, the occasions to wear the dress and how to match the dress with other clothes, etc… If the MC recommends cosmetics, he/she discloses the ingredients of the cosmetic, the benefits of using it and how to use it. The informational recommendation is information-intensive; thus, it could be very effective if the arguments are strong and the recipients are highly motivated for such information (see Fig. 1).

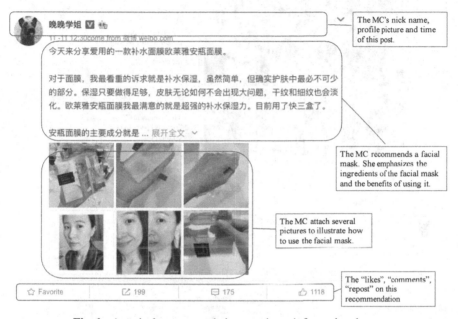

Fig. 1. A typical recommendation post in an informational way

On the other hand, narrative content refers to the MC's narrative on herself (Green and Brock 2000; Van Laer et al. 2014). Specifically, the MC just appears with the product and shares some episodes of life without mentioning too much product information. Within narrative content, the focus is the MC's narrative on the episodes of her daily life. A very typical example is the MC's post tagged with #OOTD#. In the #OOTD# post, the fashion MC shares her episodes of daily life, such as "things he/she does today", "the lunch he/she has today", or "the place he/she goes today". The MC may or may not offer several sentences to describe such episodes of life, and will attach several beautiful pictures of such episodes. In those pictures, the MC wears in beautiful clothes (the products he/she wants to recommend), the backgrounds of those pictures usually are wonderful natural sights, prosperous street views, or fine designed buildings. Moreover, the pictures are taken by professional photographer and are carefully beautified before uploading to social media (Marwick and Boyd 2011a; Senft 2008). In such cases, the

MC pretends to promote the dress-up in an unintentional and natural way, but in fact every detail is carefully prepared (see Fig. 2).

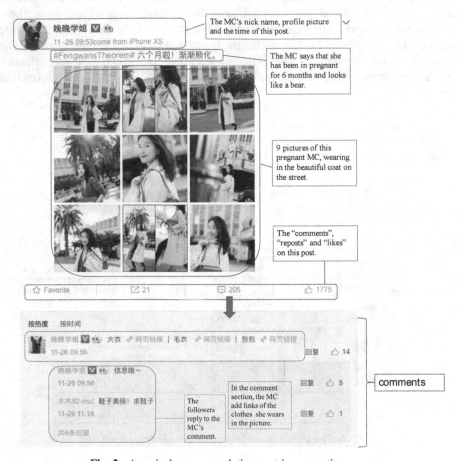

Fig. 2. A typical recommendation post in a narrative way

It is noteworthy that this two ways of recommendations are not mutually exclusive. In one recommendation post, it is possible that the MC offers product information as well as tells stories. Thus, examples in the two figure is two extreme ones to understand this two different presentation styles.

2.3 Elaboration Likelihood Model (ELM)

Elaboration likelihood model is used to explain why the persuasion effectiveness is different on different recipients, even when they are exposed to the same piece of message (Petty et al. 1983). In some cases, recipients process the information carefully, and their attitudes might be changed after considerations on the message; while in other cases, recipients glance over or even ignore the information. The difference is because that different recipients devote different amount of cognitive resources on the message due to their diverse involvement/knowledge/ability/motivation on the information (Angst and Agarwal 2009). ELM believes that when the elaboration is high, the recipient follows a central route to process the information; while when the elaboration is low, the recipient is experiencing a peripheral route. Under the central route, information is the key to influence persuasion effectiveness (Cummings and Dennis 2018). The recipient's attitude change is caused by carefully information processing. In contrast, under peripheral conditions, peripheral cues rather than information are critical for attitudes formation. Peripheral routes include source credibility, source attractiveness, message sideness, message consistency, message popularity, etc. (Cheung et al. 2012; Bhattacherjee and Sanford 2006; Liu et al. 2019).

2.4 Narrative Transportation Theory

Narrative persuasion refers to attitude change caused by narrative (e.g. stories) rather than persuasive arguments, such as movies, novels, or video games (van Laer et al. 2019a). Narrative transportation theory is a useful perspective to explain the narrative persuasion (Shen et al. 2015; van Laer et al. 2019b). It proposes that when the recipient immerses himself into the narrative, such as stories, his attitudes and intentions will be changed to reflect that story (Schlosser 2003). In other words, the story arrests the recipient into the narrative world, where the recipient (a) generating empathies with the character, (b) forming imaginations on the plots in the story, (c) forgetting the reality while consuming such narrative (Escalas 2006). Such transformational experience of the recipient is called narrative transportation. Narrative transportation persuades via realism of experience and affective responses (Green and Brock 2000). The effectiveness of narrative persuasion is due to the recipient's experiencing a like-real happened event.

Embedding narratives in ads is a prevalent phenomenon in marketing. On the one hand, some literature suggests that narrative cues, such as brand characters and visuals, are beneficial to help the consumer to generate imagination and empathy on the events happened in the narrative (Schlosser 2003). Thus, narrative transportation occurs in which the consumer will frequently interpret stories to approach brand's culture meanings, justify their identities, and inform the consumption experience (Van Laer et al. 2014; McCracken 1986). Moreover, narrative transportation can be triggered not only by purely texts, pictures can also serve as an important narrative cue to enhance imagination and empathy on the events (Phillips and McQuarrie 2010). On the other hand, regardless of the huge influence of narrative transportation on persuasion, some literature also suggests that narrative transportation might be impossible to happen if the consumer is skeptical and even resistant on the persuasion intention (Phillips and McQuarrie 2010).

2.5 Attachment Theory

Attachment theory is developed from parent-infant relationship (Malar et al. 2011). Its main proposition is when someone is in his childhood, survival is the basic need. He/she would like to seek protection from environmental threats and maintain the sense of safety. As a result, he/she would like to build emotional bonding with people who are responsive to his needs (Bowlby 1979; Loroz and Braig 2015). Attachment also exists in a person's adulthood. When an object is responsive to one's specific needs, a satisfied and committed relationship is then built (Fedorikhin et al. 2008; Thomson et al. 2006). As human beings have the tendency to maintain such intense relationship, they are mentally willing to allocate emotional, cognitive and behavioral resources towards the attachment target (Bowlby 1979).

2.6   Attainable Role-Model Perspective

Role model literature proposes that an individual compares oneself with people he aspires, and takes such aspired people as reference group to learn from (Lockwood and Kunda 1997). Such people in the reference group is role model, and the individual is called the follower. A role model, especially the one whose achievement in a specific domain is perceived as attainable by the follower, can inspires the follower's ideal self, and encourages the follower to achieve similar achievements by imitating such role model (Lockwood et al. 2002). Thus, the role model has two salient characteristics. First, the role model is perceived as obsessing some achievements in a certain domain, so the follower would like to obtain similar achievements through vicarious learning and imitation. Second, the role model's achievement in a specific domain can trigger the follower's yearning for her ideal-self. Specifically, there is a great congruency between the role model and the follower's ideal self, thus, the follower will be motivated to achieve such ideal self.

3   Theoretical Background

The research model is summarized in Fig. 3.

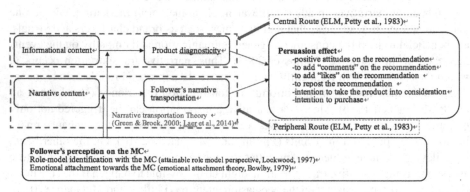

Fig. 3. The research model.

3.1   Informational Content and the Central Route

In the context of MC recommendation, product information embedding is the extent to which the recommendation post offers knowledge and descriptions related with the product. Detailed data, claims, and arguments about the product will be presented either in the texts and the pictures. For instance, the MC will introduce the components, origin, price and effect of the recommended product in the text part; at the meantime, the MC will also attach some trials or details pictures of the product as supporting information. According to ELM, if such informational content is carefully processed by recipients, a central route happens. Specifically, reading such intensive product informational embedding post, the followers can have a more comprehensive understanding on the product, if the follower use the central route to process the information (Cheung et al. 2012; Luo et al. 2015). As a result, a better understanding on the product will lead to high product diagnosticity and persuasion effectiveness.

H1: The product information embedding of the recommendation will positively influence the follower's product diagnosticity (H1a) and persuasion effectiveness (H1b).

3.2   Narrative Content, Narrative Transportation and Peripheral Route

Narrative content in the MC's recommendation refers to the extent to which the recommendation post offers narrative related with the MC herself. Similarly, as brand's narrative ads, MC also utilizes narrative when recommending products. The only difference is that in brand's ads, the narrative topic varies if it can effectively evoke consumers, while for MC's recommendation, usually the narrative content embedded in the recommendation is related to the MC herself (Phillips and McQuarrie 2010; Wang and Calder 2006). Such difference is due to the MC's unique "narrative and discourse" practice on social media. In practice, the MC spends a lot of time discoursing online (Marwick and Boyd 2011a; Marwick 2013). Particularly, MC intentionally discloses his or her everyday life by posting selfies, narrative daily life stories and so on to enhance the ordinary status (Marwick 2013). MC related narrative content is very similar as the MC's narrative based daily life sharing posts, such as interesting episodes of a pleasant journey, afternoon tea time with friends, and the MC's latest state. The MC's narrative content has two interesting characteristics. On the one hand, in such narrative recommendation, the leading role is the narrative itself, which is related with the MC. The narrative discloses daily life of the MC, which is like other normal daily life-sharing posts in the MC's social media. On the other hand, the product information in the recommendation post serves as a silent and supporting role as it only appears with the MC in the picture part and is attached as a link in the text part.

Narrative content serves as a peripheral cue to influence the follower's perception. The reason is that narrative content in the recommendation tells stories about the MC, which is not related with the product information directly. A peripheral route happens when the follower is attracted by the narrative, involves himself/herself into the MC's story, experiences a sense of being in the story (van Laer et al. 2019b). For instance, in the example of wanwan's OOTD, the MC appears with nice clothes and haircut, the postures are carefully selected, the background is elegant, and photo is taken and PSed by professional photographer. In addition, wanwan adds a paragraph to describe the pleasant weather and her thoughts in that picture. When the follower read such narrative, the follower will tend to feel entering the world described by the MC, and feels as if he/she is experiencing the same events as described by the MC (Green and Brock 2000).

Thus, according the narrative transportation theory, narrative transportation occurs and the follower will generate more positive intentions and attitudes on the narrative recommendation (i.e. the narrative message) (Escalas 2006). Based on the above arguments, we propose that,

H2: The narrative of the recommendation will positively influence the follower's narrative transportation (H2a) and the persuasion effectiveness (H2b).

3.3 Emotional Attachment

If the follower is emotional attached with the MC, he/she will allocate more resources on the MC (Bowlby 1979). Thus, when faced with a recommendation post, he/she will spend more time and cognitive resources to interpret the informational as well as the narrative content in the post. As a result, the follower will have a better understanding on information related with the product (product diagnosticity) and is more likely to immerse oneself in the story provided by the MC (narrative transportation). Based on the above arguments, we propose that,

H3: The follower's emotional attachment will positively moderate the analytical processing (H3a) and the narrative processing (H3b).

3.4 Role Model Identification

Tagged as "digital opinion leaders", "gurus", the fashion MC is perceived as possessing endowment and achievement (i.e. fashion taste) in the fashion domain (Choi and Behm-Morawitz 2017; McQuarrie 2013). The MC showcasing her fashion taste by sharing her dress-up pictures on social media and uploading tutorials on how to match a shirt with suitable skirt, shoes, and bags (Abidin and Ots 2015). From the perspective of followers, such talent showcasing in various forms is good tutorial resources for learning the MC's fashion taste. Informational content, which is offered by the MC in product recommendation post, can be considered as a specific type of resources for the follower's learning the MC's fashion taste. Thus, the follower, who identifies the MC as a role model, will have strong interest to process such informational content, as the follower consider it is a way to learn from the MC and obtain similar fashion achievement as the MC does. In a word, the follower who consider the MC as a role model to learn from, will consider the informational content as tutorials to learn and pay great attention to process such informational content in the recommendation. Based on the above arguments, we propose that:

H4a: The follower's role model identification with the MC will positively moderate the analytical processing (H4a).

According to the role-model literature, if the follower's ideal fashion self is congruent with the MC's fashion image, then the follower is more likely to take the MC as a role model to learn from (Escalas and Bettman 2017; Lockwood et al. 2002). In other words, the MC's achievement may trigger the follower's yearning of the ideal-self. As we mentioned in Sect. 2.1, narrative content in a MC's recommendation is always narrative related with the MC's life. Either in the picture or the text part, the MC appears as the limelight (Schlosser 2003). In the picture, the MC is surrounded by pleasant scenery, wearing in beautiful clothes and posing. A follower, who is taking the MC as the role model, will thinking about her ideal fashion self when facing with such pictures. As the follower's ideal self is triggered, the follower will be yearning for being as similar as the MC. Thus, when faced with the narrative picture, the follower is more likely to involve into the event happened in the picture and imagine as if he/she is wearing the same clothes standing in the same land as the fashion MC does in the pictures. Moreover, the narrative words in the text part has similar influence as the picture part. A follower with strong role-model identification with the MC tend to immerse more into the stories related with the MC, reverberate empathically to the MC in the story and feels as if he/she is experiencing the events happened on the MC. Based on the above arguments, we propose that:

H4b: The follower's role model identification with the MC will positively moderate the narrative processing.

4 Methods

To clarify the proposed hypotheses, we are going to conduct two studies. The first one is a survey based study to test hypotheses H1–H4. The second is a coding based study to test hypotheses H1b, H2b, H3, and H4.

4.1 Study 1

This study aims to test hypotheses H1–H4.

Preliminary Study. A preliminary study through interviews has been conducted first. In the preliminary study, we aim to get some practical evidence to verify our initial hypotheses and revise the original model by surprising finding from the interviews. To do so, several followers has been interviewed. Questions about the follower's attitudes on the product recommendation, their psychological feelings towards the MC, and their responses faced with narrative and informational content embedded in the recommendation will be asked. For instance, the questions are like "when you observe a recommendation post, how is your response to the narrative content in this post?", "what are your feelings towards the MC?", "do you feel emotional attached with the MC?", "will you analyze the product information provided by the MC carefully?".

The Survey. If some extra evidences are found from the interviews, we will modify the model based on the interviews. If the preliminary study validates the initial model, then we will conduct a survey to test the model.

A Pilot Study. A pilot study on 20 potential respondents will evaluate the feasibility of the survey questionnaire, and to identify any problems/need for amendments either in the questionnaire administration or instrument items. The questionnaire will be adapted based on existing instruments in prior literature, as well as self-developed scale (Moore and Benbasat 1991). Existing instruments of constructs will be adapted to the context of this research, and included in the questionnaire whenever possible.

Main Sample and Participants. The main study will empirically validate the proposed model in the context of fashion blogger endorsement, constructed based on an online survey on several chosen MC and their followers in the Greater China region (more specifically in mainland China and Hong Kong).

Specifying Research Subjects. The first step is to generate a research subject name list, including both the MCs and the corresponding followers. To do so, firstly, we have generated a list of 300 fashion bloggers on weibo, and each blogger has more than 50,000 followers. Secondly, we randomly select 100 bloggers from this original list. Thirdly, for each blogger, we randomly select 60 followers. Fourthly, we send research invitation messages to the selected 60 * 100 followers. Followers who agree with our invitation will be recruited as our participants. we expect the response rate of followers are more than 20%, thus, we can get 20 followers for each MC. By doing so, we can have 100 MCs and more than 1200 (20 * 60) followers in our research subject name list. If the response is less than 1200, then we will consider to select more MCs and corresponding followers to get at least 1200 participants.

The Online Survey Based Questionnaire. An online survey will be conducted with 2000 followers whom are in the research subject list. For the recruited participants, we will send the online questionnaire link, which is pretested in the pilot study, to all participants, and the incentive will be offered after the follower finishes the questionnaire. Moreover, the demographic information of followers will also be counted in the survey.

Measurements. The measurement will be developed based on the literature and the validity will be tested based on the pilot study.

Control Variables. Control variables such as the "congruency between the product and the MC", "follower's initial attitudes on the product", "the priority of the MC in the follower's following list" will be included.

Data Analysis. Since we want to test the mediation mechanisms in the persuasion process, the data analysis will be conducted based on the mediation analysis (MacKinnon et al. 2007).

4.2   Study 2

This study consists of a coding based analysis of product recommendation posts crawled from MC weibo to test hypotheses H1b, H2b, H3, and H4.

Sampling. We choose fashion MCs' on weibo as our research subjects. We randomly select 50 MCs from the MC pool in study 1. Their product recommendation posts within 1 months and the corresponding posts of followers who add "likes" on the recommendations will be crawled, respectively.

Operationalization of Informational Content and Narrative Content. First, we will generate criteria list for each of the two variables. Second, two PhD students in information systems will be invited as coders to independently do the coding on the posts based on the criteria. For each post, a Likert scale ranges from 1–7 will be assigned to the informational content and narrative content. If the coding results from two coders are incongruent, we will discuss the criteria and do it again. If no huge inconsistency of the two results, the final value for each observational point will be calculated as an average of the values from two coders.

Operationalization of Emotional Attachment and Role-Model Identification. First, we will generate a criteria list for emotional attachment and role-model identification. We will then generate criteria of emotional attachment and role-model identification based on the text analysis of the followers' posts and their comments on the MC's recent one month posts. Then a coding will be developed, which is similar as the procedure of coding "informational content" and "narrative content".

Persuasion Estimation. We include the positive feedback as the narrative persuasion variable measured by consumers' thumbs-up gestures on the recommendation.

Data Analysis. As this is a nested data set, which includes both the MC level data (informational content, narrative content and persuasion estimation), and the follower level data (emotional attachment & role model identification), the data will be analyzed based on the hierarchical linear model (Rai et al. 2009).

5   Expected Outcomes and Contributions

We expect the hypotheses will be supported. Thus, the important role of different content embedded in MC's product recommendation will be empirically identified. Also, the internal influencing mechanisms will be empirically explored. Further, followers' emotional attachment and role-model identification can be stressed as vital to influence such mechanism. The findings can contribute to both social commerce and endorsement literature. Firms and MCs can also utilize the findings to improve their practical performance.

References

Abidin, C.: Visibility labour: engaging with Influencers' fashion brands and #OOTD advertorial campaigns on Instagram. Media Int. Aust. **161**(1), 86–100 (2016)

Abidin, C., Ots, M.: The Influencer's dilemma: the shaping of new brand professions between credibility and commerce. In: AEJMC 2015, Annual Conference, San Fransisco, CA, 6–9 August 2015 (2015)

Angst, C.M., Agarwal, R.: Adoption of electronic health records in the presence of privacy concerns: the elaboration likelihood model and individual persuasion. MIS Q. **33**(2), 339–370 (2009)

Bhattacherjee, A., Sanford, C.: Influence processes for information technology acceptance: an elaboration likelihood model. MIS Q. **30**(4), 805–825 (2006)

Bowlby, J.: The Making & Breaking of Affectional Bonds. Tavistock, London (1979)

Chen, Z., Benbasat, I., Cenfetelli, R.: Grassroots internet celebrity live streaming" activating IT-mediated lifestyle marketing services at e-commerce websites. In: International Conference on Information (ICIS), Seoul (2017)

Cheung, C., Sia, C., Kuan, K.: Is this review believable? A study of factors affecting the credibility of online consumer reviews from an ELM perspective. J. Assoc. Inf. Syst. 13(8), 618–635 (2012)

Choi, G.Y., Behm-Morawitz, E.: Giving a new makeover to STEAM: establishing YouTube beauty gurus as digital literacy educators through messages and effects on viewers. Comput. Hum. Behav. 73, 80–91 (2017)

Cummings, J., Dennis, A.R.: Virtual first impressions matter: the effect of enterprise social networking sites on impression formation in virtual teams. MIS Q. 42(3), 697–718 (2018)

Escalas, J.E.: Self-referencing and persuasion: narrative transportation versus analytical elaboration. J. Consum. Res. 33(4), 421–429 (2006)

Escalas, J.E., Bettman, J.R.: Connecting with celebrities: how consumers appropriate celebrity meanings for a sense of belonging. J. Advert. 46(2), 297–308 (2017)

Evans, N.J., Phua, J., Lim, J., Jun, H.: Disclosing Instagram influencer advertising: the effects of disclosure language on advertising recognition, attitudes, and behavioral intent. J. Interact. Advert. 17(2), 138–149 (2017)

Fedorikhin, A., Park, C.W., Thomson, M.: Beyond fit and attitude: the effect of emotional attachment on consumer responses to brand extensions. J. Consum. Psychol. 18(4), 281–291 (2008)

Gannon, V., Prothero, A.: Beauty blogger selfies as authenticating practices. Eur. J. Mark. 50(9/10), 1858–1878 (2016)

Green, M.C., Brock, T.C.: The role of transportation in the persuasiveness of public narratives. J. Pers. Soc. Psychol. 79(5), 701–721 (2000)

Hu Xiu: (2016). https://www.huxiu.com/article/145117.html. Accessed May 2020

Khamis, S., Ang, L., Welling, R.: Self-branding, 'micro-celebrity' and the rise of social media influencers. Celebr. Stud. 8(2), 191–208 (2017)

Liu, Q., Du, Q., Hong, Y., Fan, W.: Idea Implementation and Recommendation in Open Innovation Platforms. SSRN (2019). https://ssrn.com/abstract=3480760

Lockwood, P., Jordan, C.H., Kunda, Z.: Motivation by positive or negative role models: regulatory focus determines who will best inspire us. J. Pers. Soc. Psychol. 83(4), 854–864 (2002)

Lockwood, P., Kunda, Z.: Superstars and me: predicting the impact of role models on the self. J. Pers. Soc. Psychol. 73(1), 91–103 (1997)

Loroz, P.S., Braig, B.M.: Consumer attachments to human brands: the "oprah effect". Psychol. Mark. 32(7), 751–763 (2015)

Lu, L.-C., Chang, W.-P., Chang, H.-H.: Consumer attitudes toward blogger's sponsored recommendations and purchase intention: the effect of sponsorship type, product type, and brand awareness. Comput. Hum. Behav. 34(Complete), 258–266 (2014)

Luo, C., Luo, X., Xu, Y., Warkentin, M., Sia, C.L.: Examining the moderating role of sense of membership in online review evaluations. Inf. Manag. 52(3), 305–316 (2015)

Luo, X.: Expert blogs and consumer perceptions of competing brands. Manag. Inf. Syst.: MIS Q. 41(2), 371–395 (2017)

MacKinnon, D.P., Fairchild, A.J., Fritz, M.S.: Mediation analysis. Ann. Rev. Psychol. 58, 593 (2007)

Malar, L., Krohmer, H., Hoyer, W.D., Nyffeneger, B.: Emotional brand attachment and brand personality: the relative importance of the actual and ideal self. J. Mark. 75(4), 35 (2011)

Marwick, A., Boyd, D.: To see and be seen: celebrity practice on Twitter. Convergence 17(2), 139–158 (2011a)

Marwick, A.E.: Status Update: Celebrity, Publicity, and Branding in the Social Media Age. Yale University Press, New Haven (2013)

Marwick, A.E., Boyd, D.: I tweet honestly, I tweet passionately: Twitter users, context collapse, and the imagined audience. New Media Soc. **13**(1), 114–133 (2011b)

McCracken, G.: Culture and consumption: a theoretical account of the structure and movement of the cultural meaning of consumer goods. J. Consum. Res. **13**(1), 71–84 (1986)

McQuarrie, E.: The megaphone effect taste an audience in fashion blogging. J. Consum. Res. **40**(1), 136–158 (2013)

Moore, G., Benbasat, I.: Development of an instrument to measure the perceptions of adopting an information technology innovation. Inf. Syst. Res. **2**(3), 192–222 (1991)

Page, R.: The linguistics of self-branding and micro-celebrity in Twitter: the role of hashtags. Discourse Commun. **6**(2), 181–201 (2012)

Petty, R.E., Cacioppo, J.T., Schumann, D.: Central and peripheral routes to advertising effectiveness: the moderating role of involvement. J. Consum. Res. **10**(2), 135–146 (1983)

Phillips, B.J., McQuarrie, E.F.: Narrative and persuasion in fashion advertising. J. Consum. Re. **37**(3), 368 (2010)

Rai, A., Maruping, L.M., Venkatesh, V.: Offshore information systems project success: the role of social embeddedness and cultural characteristics. MIS Q. **33**(3), 617 (2009)

Ren, Y., Harper, F.M., Drenner, S., Terveen, L., Kiesler, S., Riedl, J., Kraut, R.E.: Building member attachment in online communities: applying theories of group identity and interpersonal bonds. MIS Q. **36**(3), 841 (2012)

i research: 2018 China's Internet Celebrity Economy Development Report. http://www.iresearch china.com/content/details8_46713.html. Accessed 2018

Schlosser, A.E.: Experiencing products in the virtual world: the role of goal and imagery in influencing attitudes versus purchase intentions. J. Consum. Res. **30**(2), 184 (2003)

Schouten, A.P., Janssen, L., Verspaget, M.: Celebrity vs influencer endorsements in advertising: the role of identification, credibility, and product-endorser fit. Int. J. Advert. **39**, 1–24 (2019)

Scott, D.M.: The New Rules of Marketing and PR: How to Use Social Media, Online Video, Mobile Applications, Blogs, News Releases, and Viral Marketing to Reach Buyers Directly. Wiley, Hoboken (2017)

Senft, T.M.: Camgirls. Peter Lang Publishing, New York (2008)

Shen, F., Sheer, V.C., Li, R.: Impact of narratives on persuasion in health communication: a meta-analysis. J. Advert. **44**(2), 105–113 (2015)

Thomson, C.J., Rindflesich, A., Arsel, Z.: Emotional branding and the strategic value of the doppleganger brand image. J. Mark. **70**(1), 50 (2006)

Uzunoğlu, E., Misci Kip, S.: Brand communication through digital influencers: leveraging blogger engagement. Int. J. Inf. Manag. **34**(5), 592–602 (2014)

van Laer, T., Edson Escalas, J., Ludwig, S., van den Hende, E.A.: What happens in vegas stays on TripAdvisor? A theory and technique to understand narrativity in consumer reviews. J. Consum. Res. **46**(2), 267–285 (2019a)

van Laer, T., Feiereisen, S., Visconti, L.M.: Storytelling in the digital era: a meta-analysis of relevant moderators of the narrative transportation effect. J. Bus. Res. **96**, 135–146 (2019b)

Van Laer, T., Ruyter, K.D., Visconti, L.M., Wetzels, M.: The extended transportation-imagery model: a meta-analysis of the antecedents and consequences of consumers' narrative transportation. J. Consum. Res. **40**(5), 797 (2014)

Wang, J., Calder, B.J.: Media transportation and advertising. J. Consum. Res. **33**(2), 151–162 (2006)

Correction to: HCI in Business, Government and Organizations

Fiona Fui-Hoon Nah and Keng Siau

Correction to:
F. F.-H. Nah and K. Siau (Eds.):
HCI in Business, Government and Organizations, **LNCS 12204,**
https://doi.org/10.1007/978-3-030-50341-3

The chapter 10 was inadvertently published with an error in the name of the fourth author as Andrew McCubbins. The first name of the author was corrected.

The chapter 36 was inadvertently published with an error in the affiliation of the second author as "ISEM Fashion Business School, University of Madrid, Madrid, Spain". The name of the affiliation was corrected.

The updated version of these chapters can be found at
https://doi.org/10.1007/978-3-030-50341-3_10
https://doi.org/10.1007/978-3-030-50341-3_36

Author Index

Printed in the United States
By Bookmasters